STREE

Lanarkshire

First published in 2005 by

Philip's, a division of
Octopus Publishing Group Ltd
2-4 Heron Quays, London E14 4JP

First edition 2005
First impression 2005

ISBN-10 0-540-08833-1 (pocket)
ISBN-13 978-0-540-08833-1 (pocket)

Printed and bound in Spain
by Cayfosa-Quebecor

Contents

III **Key to map symbols**

IV **Key to map pages**

VI **Route planning**

X **Administrative and Postcode boundaries**

1 **Street maps** at 2⅔ inches to 1 mile

122 **Street maps** at 1⅓ inches to 1 mile

160 **Street maps** at 2⅔ inches to 1 mile

162 **Street map of Glasgow city centre** at 5⅓ inches to 1 mile

164 **Index** of towns and villages

166 **Index** of streets, hospitals, industrial estates, railway stations, schools, shopping centres, universities and places of interest

Digital Data

The exceptionally high-quality mapping found in this atlas is available as digital data in TIFF format, which is easily convertible to other bitmapped (raster) image formats.

The index is also available in digital form as a standard database table. It contains all the details found in the printed index together with the National Grid reference for the map square in which each entry is named.

For further information and to discuss your requirements, please contact Philip's on 020 7644 6932 or james.mann@philips-maps.co.uk

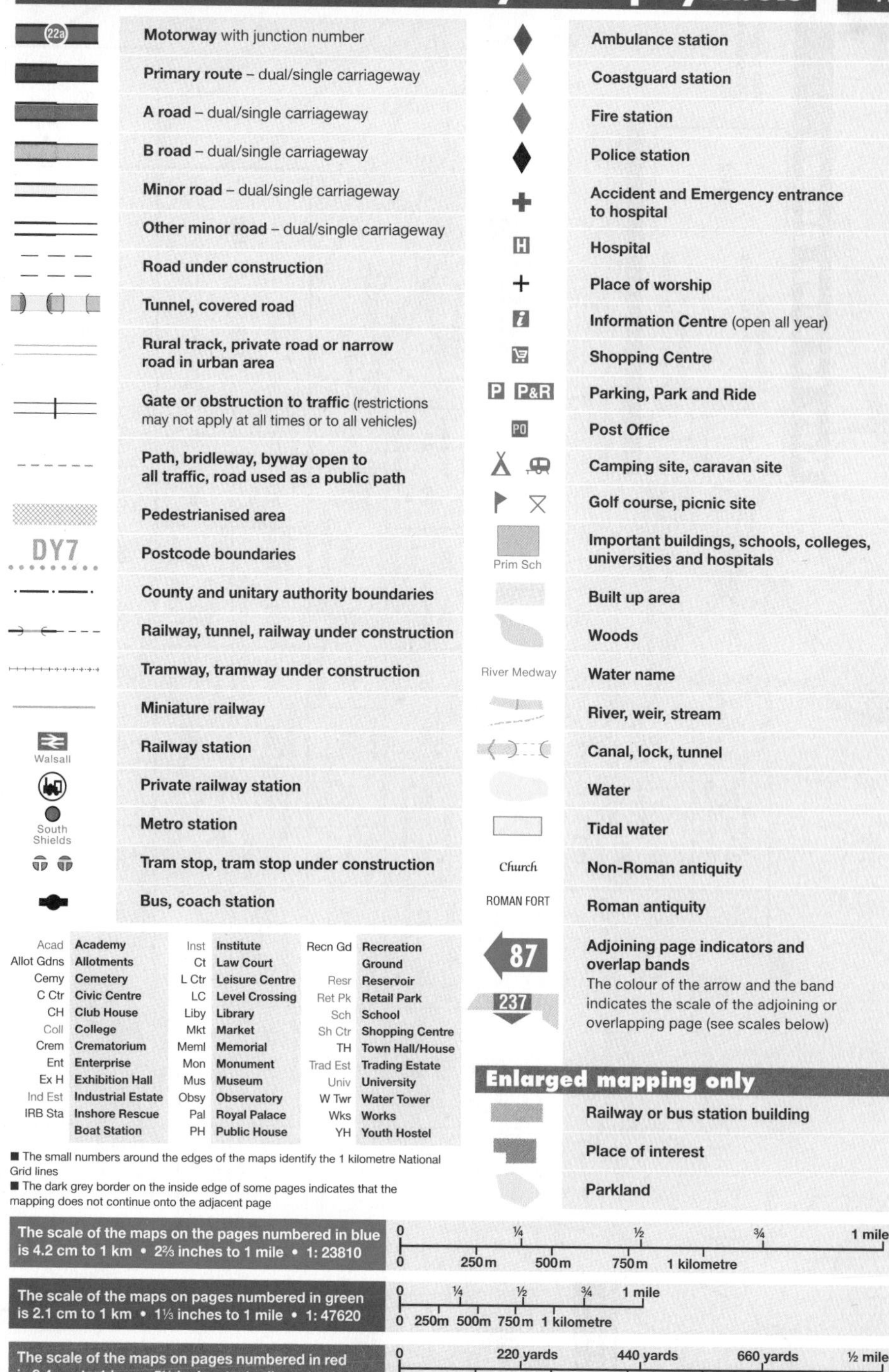

Key to map symbols
III
22a
Motorway with junction number
Primary route – dual/single carriageway
A road – dual/single carriageway
B road – dual/single carriageway
Minor road – dual/single carriageway
Other minor road – dual/single carriageway
Road under construction
Tunnel, covered road
Rural track, private road or narrow road in urban area
Gate or obstruction to traffic (restrictions may not apply at all times or to all vehicles)
Path, bridleway, byway open to all traffic, road used as a public path
Pedestrianised area
DY7
Postcode boundaries
County and unitary authority boundaries
Railway, tunnel, railway under construction
Tramway, tramway under construction
Miniature railway
Walsall
Railway station
Private railway station
South Shields
Metro station
Tram stop, tram stop under construction
Bus, coach station
Ambulance station
Coastguard station
Fire station
Police station
Accident and Emergency entrance to hospital
Hospital
Place of worship
Information Centre (open all year)
Shopping Centre
P P&R
Parking, Park and Ride
PO
Post Office
Camping site, caravan site
Golf course, picnic site
Prim Sch
Important buildings, schools, colleges, universities and hospitals
Built up area
Woods
River Medway
Water name
River, weir, stream
Canal, lock, tunnel
Water
Tidal water
Church
Non-Roman antiquity
ROMAN FORT
Roman antiquity
87
237
Adjoining page indicators and overlap bands
The colour of the arrow and the band indicates the scale of the adjoining or overlapping page (see scales below)
Acad Academy
Allot Gdns Allotments
Cemy Cemetery
C Ctr Civic Centre
CH Club House
Coll College
Crem Crematorium
Ent Enterprise
Ex H Exhibition Hall
Ind Est Industrial Estate
IRB Sta Inshore Rescue Boat Station
Inst Institute
Ct Law Court
L Ctr Leisure Centre
LC Level Crossing
Liby Library
Mkt Market
Meml Memorial
Mon Monument
Mus Museum
Obsy Observatory
Pal Royal Palace
PH Public House
Recn Gd Recreation Ground
Resr Reservoir
Ret Pk Retail Park
Sch School
Sh Ctr Shopping Centre
TH Town Hall/House
Trad Est Trading Estate
Univ University
W Twr Water Tower
Wks Works
YH Youth Hostel
Enlarged mapping only
Railway or bus station building
Place of interest
Parkland
■ The small numbers around the edges of the maps identify the 1 kilometre National Grid lines
■ The dark grey border on the inside edge of some pages indicates that the mapping does not continue onto the adjacent page
The scale of the maps on the pages numbered in blue is 4.2 cm to 1 km • 2⅔ inches to 1 mile • 1: 23810
0 ¼ ½ ¾ 1 mile
0 250 m 500 m 750 m 1 kilometre
The scale of the maps on pages numbered in green is 2.1 cm to 1 km • 1⅓ inches to 1 mile • 1: 47620
0 ¼ ½ ¾ 1 mile
0 250m 500m 750m 1 kilometre
The scale of the maps on pages numbered in red is 8.4 cm to 1 km • 5⅓ inches to 1 mile • 1: 11900
0 220 yards 440 yards 660 yards ½ mile
0 125m 250m 375m ½ kilometre

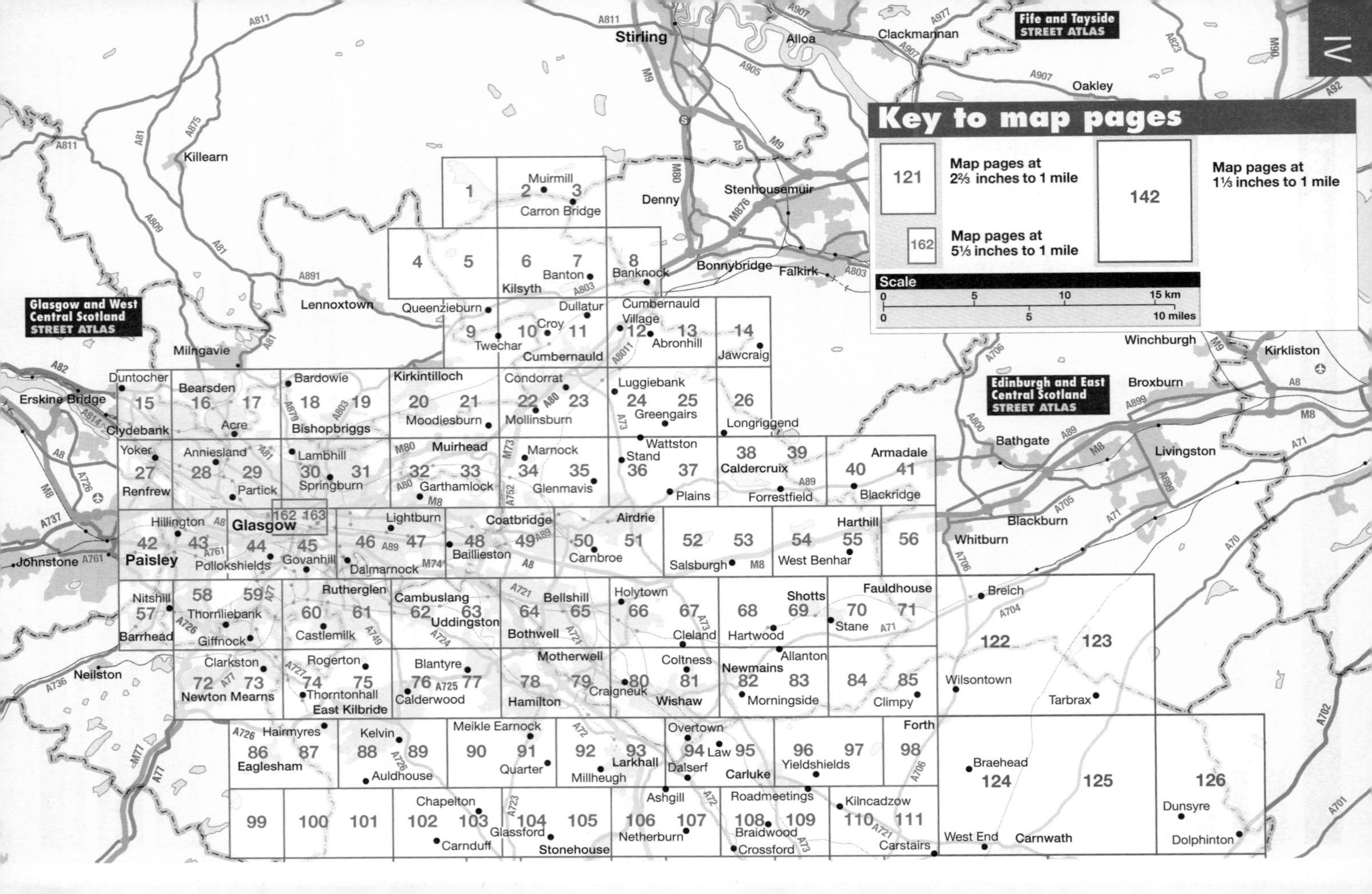
Key to map pages
121
Map pages at 2⅔ inches to 1 mile
162
Map pages at 5⅓ inches to 1 mile
142
Map pages at 1⅓ inches to 1 mile
Scale
0 5 10 15 km
0 5 10 miles
Fife and Tayside STREET ATLAS
Glasgow and West Central Scotland STREET ATLAS
Edinburgh and East Central Scotland STREET ATLAS
Stirling
Alloa
Clackmannan
Oakley
Killearn
Denny
Stenhousemuir
Bonnybridge
Falkirk
Lennoxtown
Milngavie
Winchburgh
Kirkliston
Broxburn
Bathgate
Livingston
Blackburn
Whitburn
Erskine Bridge
Johnstone
Neilston
Muirmill
Carron Bridge
Banton
Kilsyth
Banknock
Queenzieburn
Dullatur
Croy
Twechar
Cumbernauld
Cumbernauld Village
Abronhill
Jawcraig
Duntocher
Bearsden
Bardowie
Kirkintilloch
Condorrat
Luggiebank
Longriggend
Clydebank
Acre
Bishopbriggs
Moodiesburn
Mollinsburn
Greengairs
Yoker
Anniesland
Lambhill
Muirhead
Marnock
Wattston
Stand
Caldercruix
Armadale
Renfrew
Partick
Springburn
Garthamlock
Glenmavis
Plains
Forrestfield
Blackridge
Hillington
Glasgow
Lightburn
Coatbridge
Airdrie
Harthill
Paisley
Pollokshields
Govanhill
Dalmarnock
Baillieston
Carnbroe
Salsburgh
West Benhar
Nitshill
Thornliebank
Rutherglen
Cambuslang
Bellshill
Holytown
Shotts
Fauldhouse
Breich
Barrhead
Giffnock
Castlemilk
Uddingston
Bothwell
Cleland
Hartwood
Stane
Clarkston
Rogerton
Blantyre
Motherwell
Coltness
Newmains
Allanton
Wilsontown
Tarbrax
Newton Mearns
Thorntonhall
East Kilbride
Calderwood
Hamilton
Craigneuk
Wishaw
Morningside
Climpy
Hairmyres
Eaglesham
Kelvin
Auldhouse
Meikle Earnock
Quarter
Millheugh
Larkhall
Overtown
Law
Dalserf
Carluke
Yieldshields
Forth
Braehead
Dunsyre
Chapelton
Carnduff
Glassford
Stonehouse
Ashgill
Netherburn
Roadmeetings
Braidwood
Crossford
Kilncadzow
Carstairs
West End
Carnwath
Dolphinton
1 2 3 4 5 6 7 8 9 10 11 12 13 14 15 16 17 18 19 20 21 22 23 24 25 26 27 28 29 30 31 32 33 34 35 36 37 38 39 40 41 42 43 44 45 46 47 48 49 50 51 52 53 54 55 56 57 58 59 60 61 62 63 64 65 66 67 68 69 70 71 72 73 74 75 76 77 78 79 80 81 82 83 84 85 86 87 88 89 90 91 92 93 94 95 96 97 98 99 100 101 102 103 104 105 106 107 108 109 110 111 122 123 124 125 126 162 163

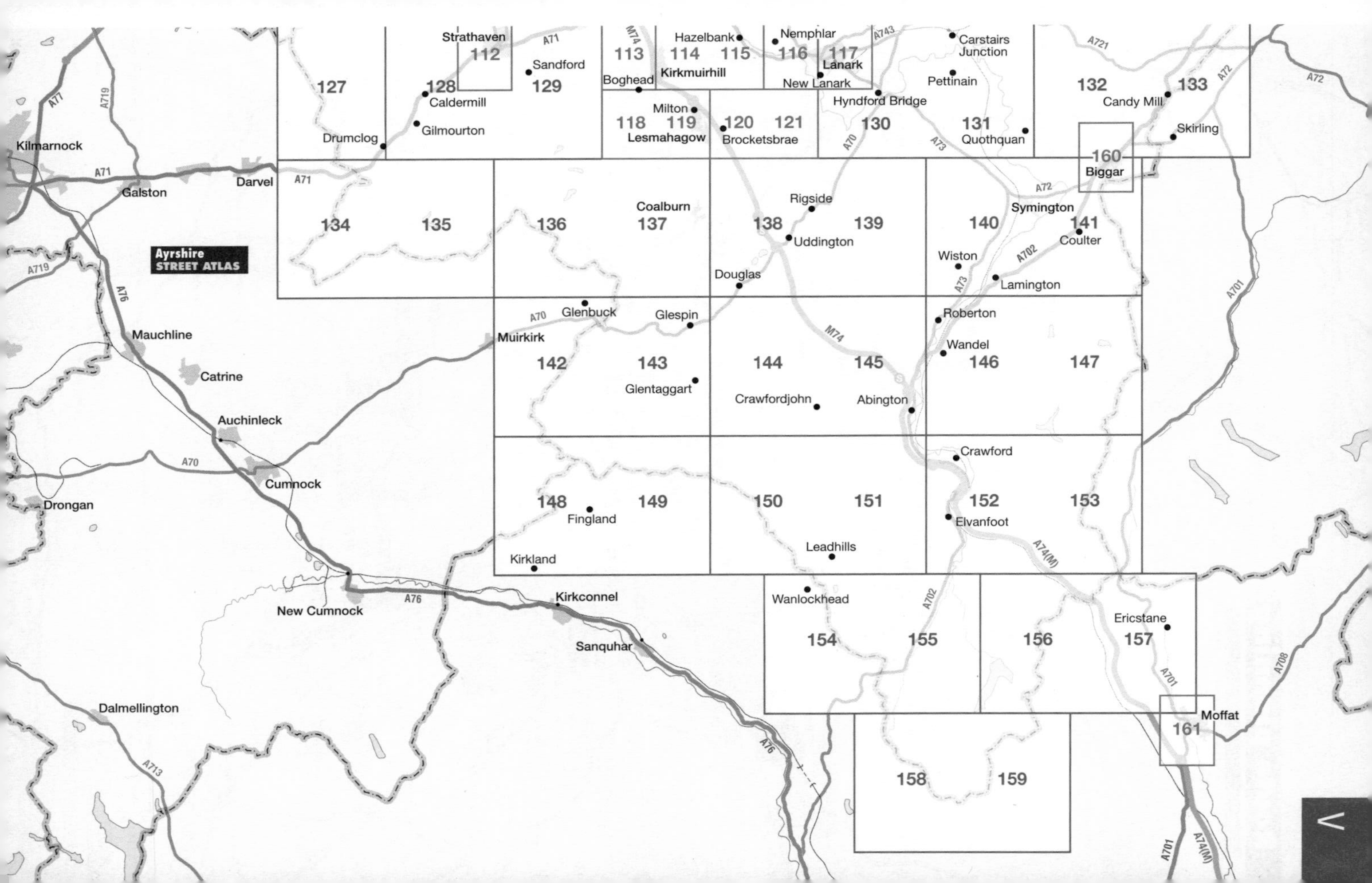
V
Ayrshire STREET ATLAS
Strathaven
112
127
128
129
Sandford
Caldermill
Gilmourton
Drumclog
113
114
115
116
117
Hazelbank
Nemphlar
Lanark
New Lanark
Boghead
Kirkmuirhill
Milton
118
119
120
121
Lesmahagow
Brocketsbrae
Carstairs Junction
Pettinain
Hyndford Bridge
130
131
Quothquan
132
133
Candy Mill
Skirling
160
Biggar
Kilmarnock
Galston
Darvel
134
135
136
137
Coalburn
138
139
Rigside
Uddington
Douglas
140
141
Symington
Coulter
Wiston
Lamington
Glenbuck
Glespin
Muirkirk
142
143
Glentaggart
144
145
Crawfordjohn
Abington
Roberton
Wandel
146
147
Mauchline
Catrine
Auchinleck
Cumnock
Drongan
Crawford
148
149
Fingland
Kirkland
150
151
Leadhills
152
153
Elvanfoot
New Cumnock
Kirkconnel
Sanquhar
Wanlockhead
154
155
156
157
Ericstane
Moffat
161
158
159
Dalmellington
A77
A719
A71
A76
A70
A713
M74
A743
A73
A721
A72
A702
A701
A74(M)
A708

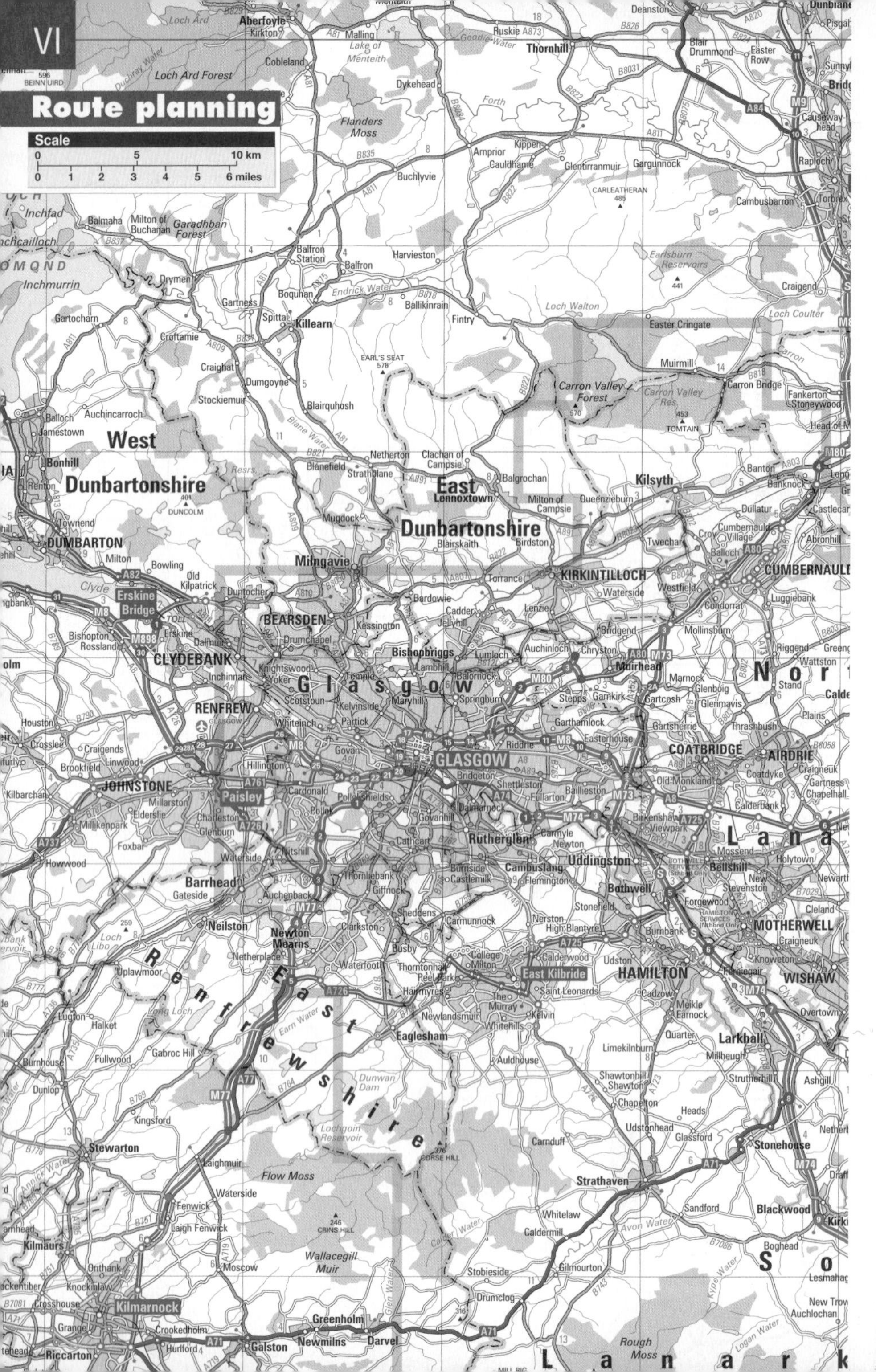
Route planning
Scale
0 5 10 km
0 1 2 3 4 5 6 miles
Loch Ard
Aberfoyle
Kirkton
Loch Ard Forest
Malling
Lake of Menteith
Cobleland
Dykehead
Flanders Moss
Ruskie
Goodie Water
Thornhill
Deanston
Blair Drummond
Easter Row
Forth
Buchlyvie
Arnprior
Kippen
Cauldhame
Gleritirranmuir
Gargunnock
Raploch
Cambusbarron
CARLEATHERAN 485
Inchfad
Balmaha
Milton of Buchanan
Garadhban Forest
Inchcailloch
Inchmurrin
Balfron Station
Balfron
Harvieston
Earlsburn Reservoirs
Craigend
Drymen
Gartness
Boquhan
Endrick Water
Ballikinrain
Fintry
Loch Walton
Loch Coulter
Gartocharn
Spittal
Killearn
Easter Cringate
Croftamie
EARL'S SEAT 578
Muirmill
Carron Bridge
Craighat
Dumgoyne
Carron Valley Forest
Carron Valley Res.
TOMTAIN 453
Fankerton
Stoneywood
Stockiemuir
Blairquhosh
Balloch
Auchincarroch
Jamestown
West Dunbartonshire
Blane Water
Bonhill
Renton
Netherton
Blanefield
Strathblane
Clachan of Campsie
Balgrochan
Kilsyth
Banton
Banknock
DUNCOLM 401
East Dunbartonshire
Lennoxtown
Milton of Campsie
Queenzieburn
Dullatur
Castlecary
Townend
DUMBARTON
Mugdock
Birdston
Twechar
Croy
Cumbernauld Village
Abronhill
Milton
Bowling
Milngavie
Blairskaith
Balloch
CUMBERNAULD
Clyde
Old Kilpatrick
Erskine Bridge
Duntocher
Torrance
KIRKINTILLOCH
Waterside
Westfield
Condorrat
Luggiebank
BEARSDEN
Bardowie
Cadder
Jellyhill
Lenzie
Kessington
Bridgend
Mollinsburn
Bishopton
Rossland
Erskine
Dalmuir
Drumchapel
Bishopbriggs
Lumloch
Auchinloch
Chryston
Muirhead
Riggend
Wattston
CLYDEBANK
Inchinnan
Knightswood
Yoker
Temple
Lambhill
Balornock
Marnock
Glenboig
Glasgow
North
Scotstoun
Kelvinside
Maryhill
Springburn
Stepps
Garnkirk
Gartcosh
Glenmavis
Stand
Caldercruix
RENFREW
Whiteinch
Partick
Garthamlock
Gartsherrie
Thrashbush
Plains
Houston
Easterhouse
Crosslee
Craigends
Linwood
Govan
Riddrie
COATBRIDGE
AIRDRIE
Brookfield
Hillington
GLASGOW
Bridgeton
Craigneuk
JOHNSTONE
Millarston
Cardonald
Shettleston
Baillieston
Old Monkland
Coatdyke
Gartness
Kilbarchan
Paisley
Pollokshields
Fullarton
Calderbank
Chapelhall
Elderslie
Pollok
Dalmarnock
Millikenpark
Charleston
Govanhill
Birkenshaw
Viewpark
Glenburn
Foxbar
Nitshill
Cathcart
Rutherglen
Carmyle
Newton
Lanark
Mossend
Bellshill
Holytown
Howwood
Waterside
Burnside
Castlemilk
Cambuslang
Flemington
Uddingston
Thornliebank
Giffnock
Barrhead
Gateside
Auchenback
Bothwell
New Stevenston
Newarthill
Forgewood
Cleland
Sheddens
Carmunnock
Nerston
High Blantyre
Stonefield
Neilston
Clarkston
Burnbank
MOTHERWELL
Newton Mearns
Busby
Loch Libo
Craigneuk
Netherplace
Waterfoot
Thorntonhall
College Milton
Calderwood
East Kilbride
Udston
HAMILTON
Knowetop
Uplawmoor
Peel Park
Ferniegair
WISHAW
Renfrewshire
East Renfrewshire
Hairmyres
The Murray
Saint Leonards
Cadzow
Long Loch
Lugton
Halket
Earn Water
Newlandsmuir
Whitehills
Kelvin
Meikle Earnock
Overtown
Eaglesham
Quarter
Larkhall
Limekilnburn
Burnhouse
Fullwood
Gabroc Hill
Millheugh
Auldhouse
Ashgill
Dunlop
Dunwan Dam
Shawtonhill
Shawton
Strutherhill
Chapelton
Kingsford
Heads
Lochgoin Reservoir
Udstonhead
Glassford
Stewarton
CORSE HILL 376
Carnduff
Stonehouse
Laighmuir
Flow Moss
Strathaven
Waterside
Fenwick
Laigh Fenwick
Sandford
Blackwood
Whitelaw
Kilmaurs
CRINS HILL 246
Caldermill
Avon Water
Boghead
Calder Water
Wallacegill Muir
Moscow
Onthank
Stobieside
Gilmourton
Knockentiber
Knockinlaw
Lesmahagow
Crosshouse
Kilmarnock
Drumclog
Kype Water
New Trows
Auchlochan
Greenholm
Glen Water
Grange
Crookedholm
Rough Moss
Logan Water
Riccarton
Hurlford
Galston
Newmilns
Darvel
Lanark

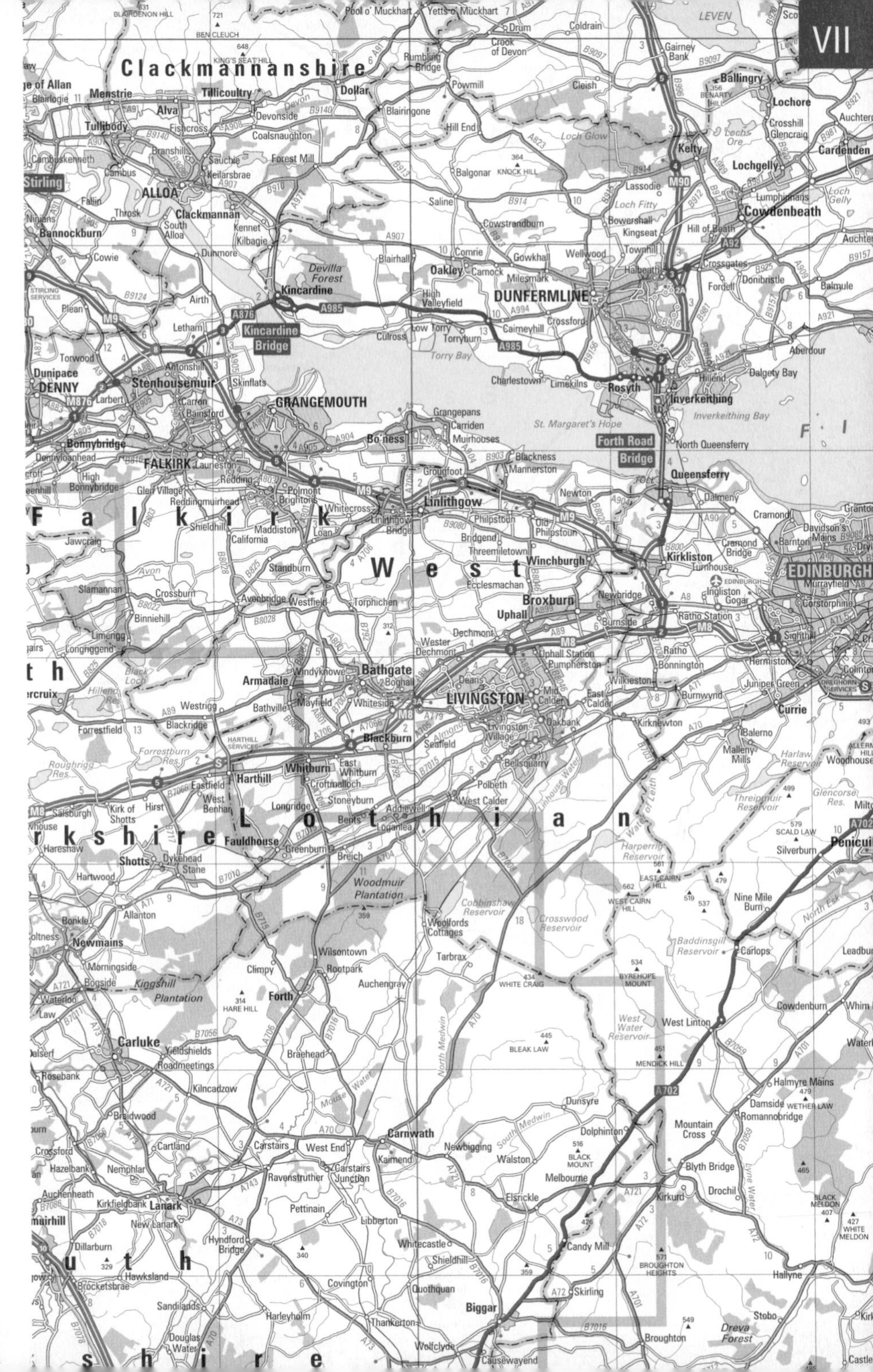
VII
Clackmannanshire
Pool o' Muckhart
Yetts o' Muckhart
Drum
Coldrain
Crook of Devon
Rumbling Bridge
Powmill
Gairney Bank
LEVEN
Ballingry
Lochore
BEN CLEUCH
KING'S SEAT HILL
BLAIRDENON HILL
Menstrie
Tillicoultry
Dollar
Blairlogie
Alva
Devonside
Blairingone
Cleish
Tullibody
Fishcross
Coalsnaughton
Hill End
Loch Glow
Crosshill
Glencraig
Lochgelly
Cardenden
Auchterderran
Cambuskenneth
Cambus
Sauchie
Forest Mill
Balgonar
KNOCK HILL
Kelty
Stirling
Keilarsbrae
ALLOA
Lassodie
Lumphinnans
Cowdenbeath
Loch Gelly
Fallin
Throsk
Clackmannan
Saline
Loch Fitty
Bannockburn
South Alloa
Kennet
Kilbagie
Cowstrandburn
Bowershall
Kingseat
Hill of Beath
Dunmore
Cowie
Comrie
Blairhall
Oakley
Carnock
Gowkhall
Wellwood
Townhill
Halbeath
Crossgates
Fordell
Donibristle
Balmule
Devilla Forest
Milesmark
STIRLING SERVICES
Airth
Kincardine
High Valleyfield
DUNFERMLINE
Plean
Cairneyhill
Crossford
Letham
Kincardine Bridge
Culross
Low Torry
Torryburn
Aberdour
Torwood
Torry Bay
Dunipace
DENNY
Antonshill
Stenhousemuir
Skinflats
Charlestown
Limekilns
Rosyth
Hillend
Dalgety Bay
Larbert
Carron
Bainsford
GRANGEMOUTH
Inverkeithing
Inverkeithing Bay
Grangepans
Carriden
St. Margaret's Hope
Bonnybridge
Bo'ness
Muirhouses
Forth Road Bridge
North Queensferry
Dennyloanhead
FALKIRK
Laurieston
Blackness
Mannerston
High Bonnybridge
Redding
Grougfoot
Queensferry
Glen Village
Polmont
Brightons
Reddingmuirhead
Newton
Dalmeny
Linlithgow
Cramond
Falkirk
Shieldhill
Maddiston
Whitecross
Linlithgow Bridge
Philpstoun
Old Philpstoun
Davidson's Mains
California
Loan
Bridgend
Threemiletown
Barnton
Cramond Bridge
Jawcraig
Kirkliston
Winchburgh
Turnhouse
EDINBURGH
Avon
Standburn
West
Ecclesmachan
Slamannan
Crossburn
Avonbridge
Westfield
Torphichen
Broxburn
Newbridge
Ingliston
Gogar
Murrayfield
Corstorphine
Binniehill
Uphall
Burnside
Ratho Station
Limerigg
Longriggend
Dechmont
Wester Dechmont
Uphall Station
Pumpherston
Ratho
Bonnington
Hermiston
Sighthill
Black Loch
Hillend Res.
Windyknowe
Bathgate
Boghall
Armadale
Deans
LIVINGSTON
Mid Calder
East Calder
Wilkieston
Burnwynd
Juniper Green
Colinton
Currie
DREGHORN SERVICES
Westrigg
Blackridge
Bathville
Mayfield
Whiteside
Forrestfield
HARTHILL SERVICES
Blackburn
Seafield
Almond
Livingston Village
Oakbank
Kirknewton
Balerno
Malleny Mills
Harlaw Reservoir
Woodhouselee
Forrestburn Res.
Roughrigg Res.
Harthill
Whitburn
East Whitburn
Bellsquarry
Linhouse Water
Eastfield
Croftmalloch
Polbeth
Kirk of Shotts
Hirst
West Benhar
Longridge
Stoneyburn
Addiewell
Loganlea
West Calder
Threipmuir Reservoir
Glencorse Res.
Salsburgh
Lothian
Bents
Water of Leith
SCALD LAW
Silverburn
Penicuik
Fauldhouse
Greenburn
Breich
Hareshaw
Harperrig Reservoir
Shotts
Dykehead
Stane
EAST CAIRN HILL
Hartwood
Woodmuir Plantation
WEST CAIRN HILL
Nine Mile Burn
Allanton
Cobbinshaw Reservoir
Crosswood Reservoir
North Esk
Bonkle
Woolfords Cottages
Baddinsgill Reservoir
Newmains
Wilsontown
Carlops
Leadburn
Morningside
Climpy
Rootpark
Tarbrax
BYREHOPE MOUNT
Bogside
Kingshill Plantation
Auchengray
WHITE CRAIG
Waterloo
HARE HILL
Forth
Law
West Water Reservoir
West Linton
Cowdenburn
Carluke
Yieldshields
Roadmeetings
BLEAK LAW
MENDICK HILL
North Medwin
Rosebank
Braehead
Halmyre Mains
WETHER LAW
Kilncadzow
Mouse Water
Dunsyre
Damside
Romannobridge
Braidwood
South Medwin
Dolphinton
Mountain Cross
Carstairs
West End
Carnwath
Newbigging
Cartland
Walston
BLACK MOUNT
Crossford
Kaimend
Hazelbank
Nemphlar
Ravenstruther
Carstairs Junction
Melbourne
Blyth Bridge
Auchenheath
Elsrickle
Kirkurd
Drochil
Lyne Water
Kirkfieldbank
Lanark
Pettinain
BLACK MELDON
WHITE MELDON
New Lanark
Libberton
Candy Mill
Dillarburn
Hyndford Bridge
Whitecastle
BROUGHTON HEIGHTS
Hawksland
Shieldhill
Hallyne
Brocketsbrae
Covington
Quothquan
Skirling
Sandilands
Harleyholm
Biggar
Stobo
Thankerton
Dreva Forest
Douglas Water
Wolfclyde
Broughton
Causewayend
Castlecraig
shire

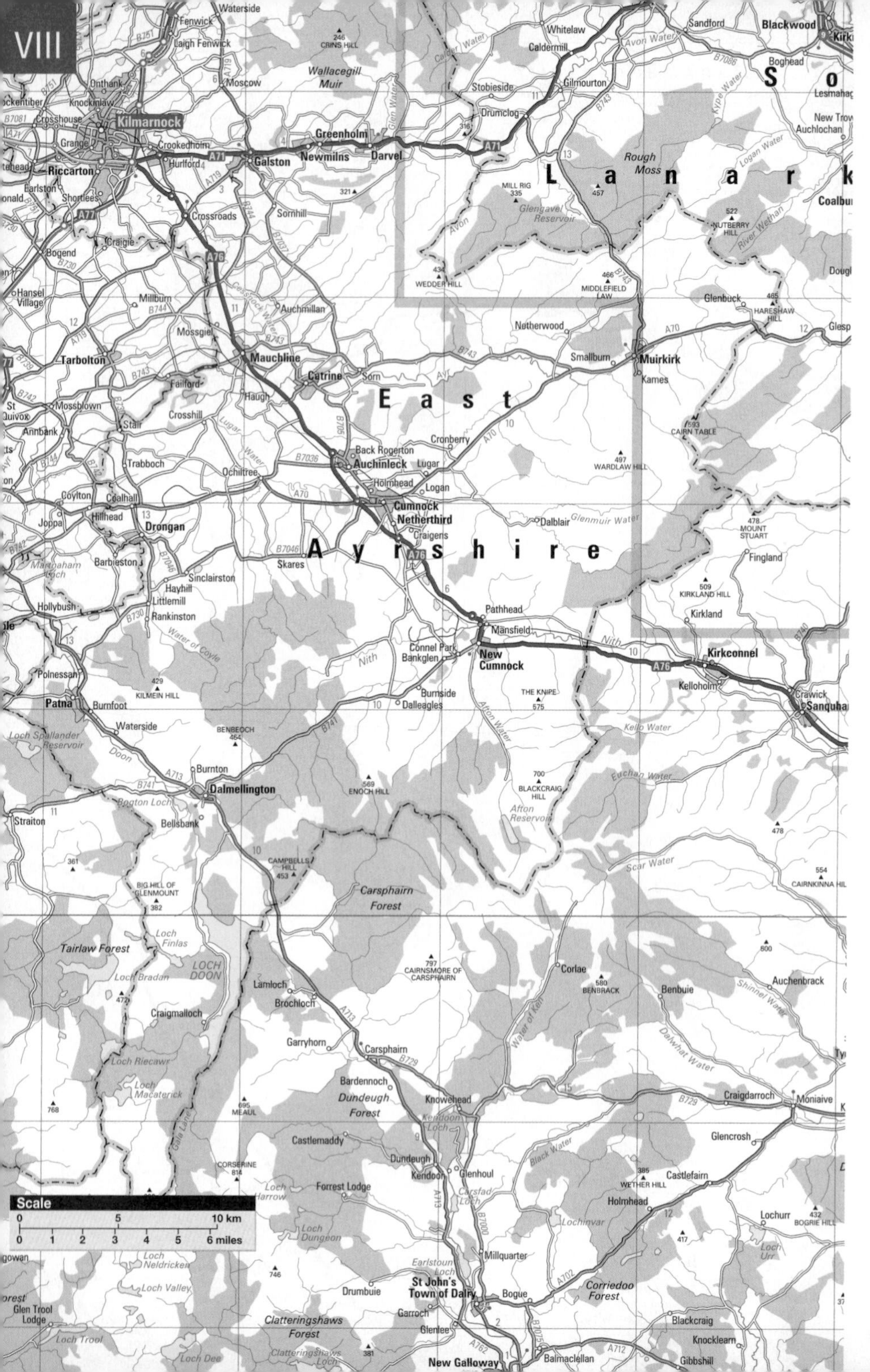

Waterside
Fenwick
Laigh Fenwick
246
CRINS HILL
Moscow
Wallacegill
Muir
Onthank
Knockmlaw
Crosshouse
Kilmarnock
Grange
Crookedholm
Riccarton
Hurlford
Galston
Greenholm
Newmilns
Darvel
Earlston
Shortlees
Crossroads
Sornhill
Craigie
Bogend
Hansel
Village
Millburn
Auchmillan
Mossgiel
Tarbolton
Mauchline
Catrine
Sorn
Failford
Haugh
Mossblown
St
Quivox
Annbank
Stair
Crosshill
Trabboch
Ochiltree
Back Rogerton
Auchinleck
Lugar
Holmhead
Logan
Cronberry
Coylton
Coalhall
Hillhead
Drongan
Joppa
Cumnock
Netherthird
Craigens
Barbieston
Skares
Sinclairston
Hayhill
Littlemill
Rankinston
Hollybush
Polnessan
Patna
Burnfoot
Waterside
Water of Coyle
429
KILMEIN HILL
BENBEOCH
464
Loch Spallander
Reservoir
Doon
Burnton
Dalmellington
Bogton Loch
Bellsbank
Straiton
361
BIG HILL OF
GLENMOUNT
382
CAMPBELLS
HILL
453
Loch
Finlas
Tairlaw Forest
LOCH
DOON
Loch Bradan
472
Craigmalloch
Lamloch
Brochloch
Garryhorn
Carsphairn
Loch Riecawr
Loch
Macaterick
768
695
MEAUL
Bardennoch
Dundeugh
Forest
Knowehead
Kendoon
Loch
Castlemaddy
Dundeugh
Kendoon
Glenhoul
CORSERINE
814
Loch
Harrow
Forrest Lodge
Carsfad
Loch
Loch
Dungeon
Loch
Neldricken
Loch Valley
746
Earlstoun
Loch
Drumbuie
St John's
Town of Dalry
Glen Trool
Lodge
Loch Trool
Clatteringshaws
Forest
Clatteringshaws
Loch
Loch Dee
381
Garroch
Glenlee
New Galloway
Balmaclellan
Bogue
Whitelaw
Caldermill
Calder Water
Avon Water
Sandford
Blackwood
Boghead
Stobieside
Gilmourton
Drumclog
316
321
MILL RIG
335
Glengavel
Reservoir
Avon
434
WEDDER HILL
Rough
Moss
457
L a n a r k
S o
Lesmahag
New Trow
Auchlochan
Logan Water
Kype Water
Coalbu
522
NUTBERRY
HILL
River Wethan
466
MIDDLEFIELD
LAW
Glenbuck
465
HARESHAW
HILL
Netherwood
Smallburn
Muirkirk
Kames
Douglas
Glesp
East
593
CAIRN TABLE
497
WARDLAW HILL
Ayr
Lugar Water
Dalblair
Glenmuir Water
478
MOUNT
STUART
Fingland
Ayrshire
509
KIRKLAND HILL
Kirkland
Pathhead
Mansfield
Nith
Connel Park
Bankglen
New
Cumnock
Kirkconnel
Kelloholm
Crawick
Sanquhar
Burnside
Dalleagles
THE KNIPE
575
Afton Water
Kello Water
569
ENOCH HILL
700
BLACKCRAIG
HILL
Afton
Reservoir
Euchan Water
478
Scar Water
554
CAIRNKINNA HILL
Carsphairn
Forest
797
CAIRNSMORE OF
CARSPHAIRN
Corlae
580
BENBRACK
Benbuie
800
Auchenbrack
Shinnel Water
Water of Ken
Dalwhat Water
Craigdarroch
Moniaive
Glencrosh
Black Water
385
WETHER HILL
Castlefairn
Holmhead
Lochinvar
Lochurr
432
BOGRIE HILL
417
Loch
Urr
Corriedoo
Forest
Blackcraig
Knocklearn
Gibbshill
Scale
0 5 10 km
0 1 2 3 4 5 6 miles

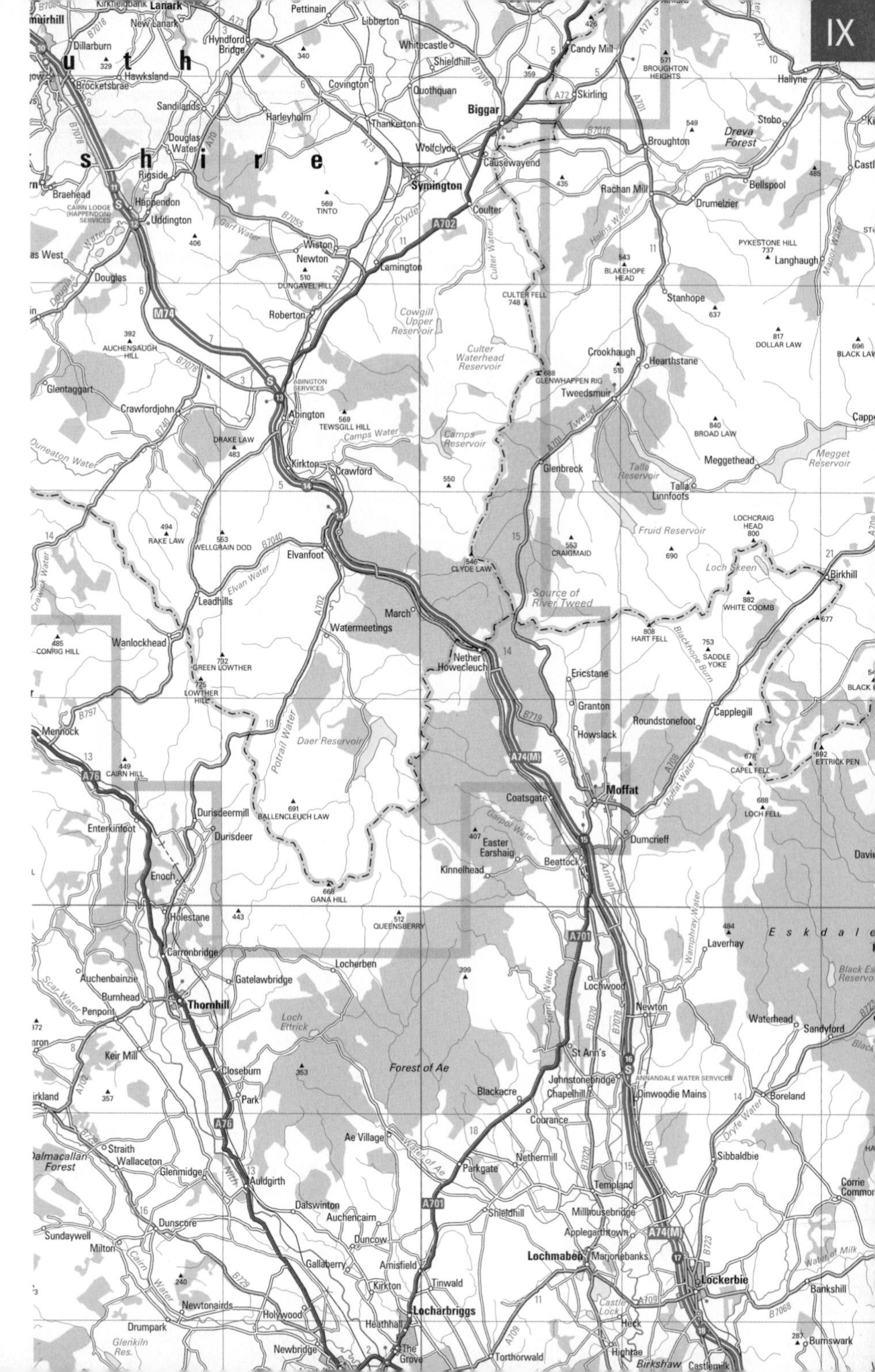
Lanark
New Lanark
Kirkfieldbank
Pettinain
Libberton
Candy Mill
Hyndford Bridge
Dillarburn
Whitecastle
Shieldhill
571 BROUGHTON HEIGHTS
Hallyne
Hawksland
Brocketsbrae
Covington
Quothquan
Skirling
Sandilands
Harleyholm
Thankerton
Biggar
Broughton
Dreva Forest
Stobo
Douglas Water
Wolfclyde
Causewayend
Castl
Rigside
s h i r e
Symington
Rachan Mill
Bellspool
Braehead
CAIRN LODGE (HAPPENDON) SERVICES
Happendon
569 TINTO
Coulter
Drumelzier
Uddington
Garf Water
Wiston
Newton
510 DUNGAVEL HILL
Lamington
Clyde
543 BLAKEHOPE HEAD
PYKESTONE HILL 737
Langhaugh
Manor Water
Douglas
Culter Water
Holms Water
Stanhope
CULTER FELL 748
Roberton
Cowgill Upper Reservoir
392 AUCHENSAUGH HILL
817 DOLLAR LAW
696 BLACK LAW
Culter Waterhead Reservoir
Crookhaugh
Hearthstane
Glentaggart
ABINGTON SERVICES
688 GLENWHAPPEN RIG
Tweedsmuir
Crawfordjohn
Abington
569 TEWSGILL HILL
840 BROAD LAW
Camps Water
Camps Reservoir
DRAKE LAW 483
Tweed
Duneaton Water
Meggethead
Megget Reservoir
Kirkton
Crawford
550
Glenbreck
Talla Reservoir
Talla Linnfoots
494 RAKE LAW
553 WELLGRAIN DOD
Elvanfoot
546 CLYDE LAW
553 CRAIGMAID
Fruid Reservoir
LOCHCRAIG HEAD 800
690
Crawick Water
Elvan Water
Loch Skeen
Birkhill
Leadhills
Source of River Tweed
882 WHITE COOMB
March
Watermeetings
485 CONRIG HILL
Wanlockhead
808 HART FELL
753 SADDLE YOKE
677
Blackhope Burn
732 GREEN LOWTHER
Nether Howecleuch
Ericstane
725 LOWTHER HILL
Granton
BLACK
Roundstonefoot
Capplegill
Potrail Water
Daer Reservoir
Howslack
Mennock
449 CAIRN HILL
Moffat Water
678 CAPEL FELL
692 ETTRICK PEN
Moffat
Coatsgate
Durisdeermill
691 BALLENCLEUCH LAW
688 LOCH FELL
Enterkinfoot
Durisdeer
Garpol Water
407 Easter Earshaig
Dumcrieff
Davi
Enoch
Kinnelhead
Beattock
Annan
668 GANA HILL
Holestane
443
512 QUEENSBERRY
Wamphray Water
484 Laverhay
E s k d a l e
Carronbridge
Locherben
399
Auchenbainzie
Gatelawbridge
Black Esk Reservoir
Scar Water
Burnhead
Thornhill
Kinnel Water
Lochwood
Penpont
Loch Ettrick
Newton
Waterhead
Sandyford
372
Keir Mill
St Ann's
353
Forest of Ae
ANNANDALE WATER SERVICES
Johnstonebridge
Closeburn
Blackacre
Chapelhill
Dinwoodie Mains
Boreland
357
Park
Courance
Dryfe Water
Ae Village
Water of Ae
Straith
Wallaceton
Dalmacallan Forest
Nethermill
Sibbaldbie
Glenmidge
Nith
Parkgate
Auldgirth
Templand
Corrie Common
Dalswinton
Dunscore
Auchencairn
Shieldhill
Millhousebridge
Sundaywell
Duncow
Applegarthtown
Milton
Cairn Water
Lochmaben
Marjoriebanks
Water of Milk
Gallaberry
Amisfield
Lockerbie
240
Kirkton
Tinwald
Bankshill
Newtonairds
Castle Loch
Holywood
Locharbriggs
Heck
Drumpark
Heathhall
287 Burnswark
Glenkiln Res.
Newbridge
The Grove
Torthorwald
Hightae
Birkshaw
Castlemilk
M74
A74(M)
A73
A70
A72
A701
A702
A76
A702
A708
A709
B7078
B7055
B7016
B712
B740
B797
B7040
B719
B729
B7020
B7076
B723
B7068

Major administrative and Postcode boundaries
County and unitary authority boundaries
Postcode boundaries
Area covered by this atlas
Scale
0 5 10 15 km
0 5 10 miles
Stirling
Falkirk
East Dunbartonshire
Renfrewshire
City of Glasgow
North Lanarkshire
West Lothian
East Renfrewshire
East Ayrshire
South Lanarkshire
Scottish Borders
Dumfries and Galloway
NS
NT
NX
NY
Clydebank
Kirkintilloch
Bishopbriggs
Milton
Govanhill
Stepps
Kilsyth
Banknock
Cumbernauld
Caldercruix
Airdrie
Coatbridge
Armadale
Harthill
Shotts
Fauldhouse
Cleland
Motherwell
Wishaw
Hamilton
East Kilbride
Eaglesham
Larkhall
Carluke
Forth
Stonehouse
Strathaven
Kirkmuirhill
Lanark
Carnwath
Biggar
Symington
Coulter
Coalburn
Douglas
Abington
Crawford
Leadhills
Wanlockhead
Moffat
Glasgow
Ibrox

2

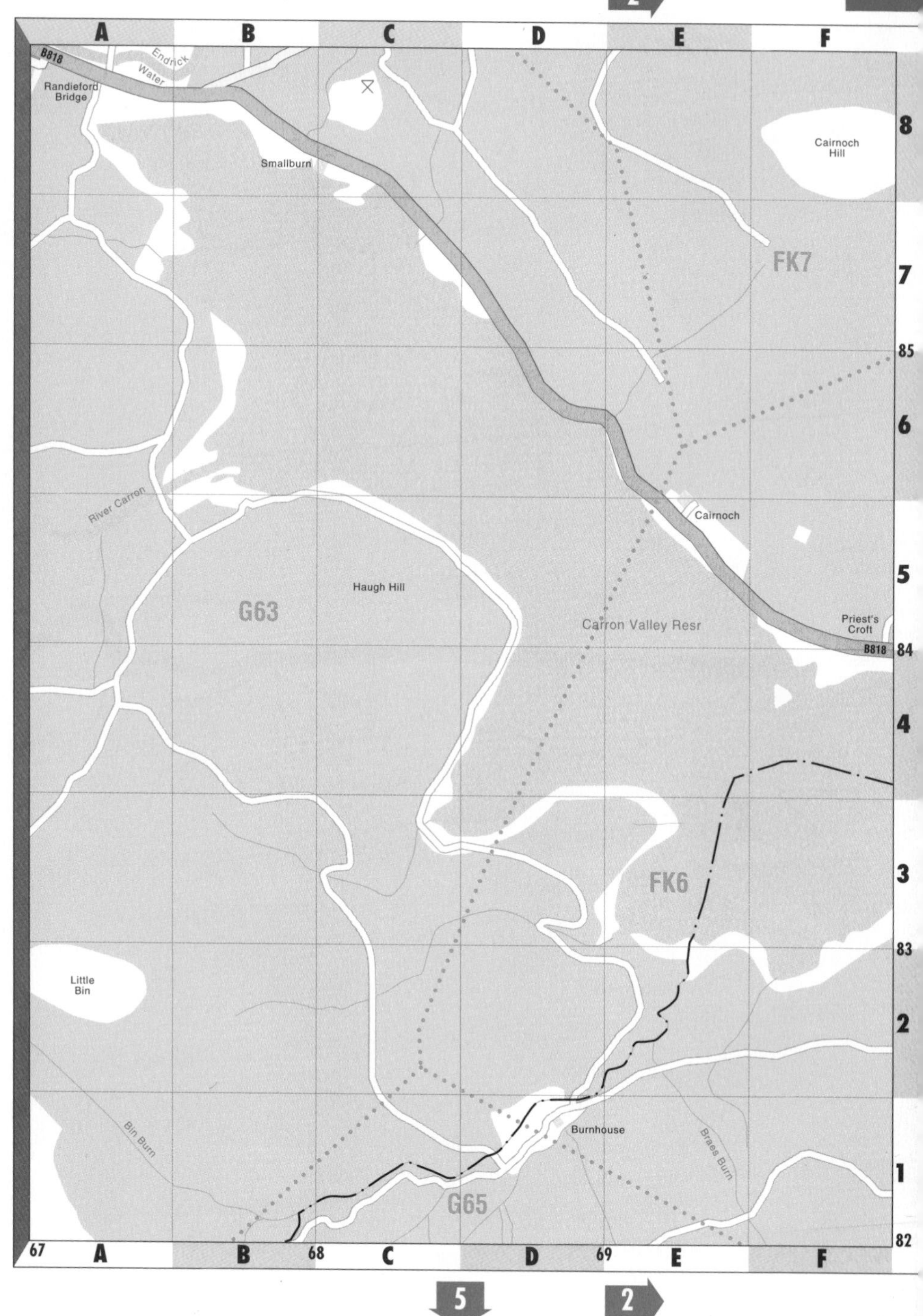
A
B
C
D
E
F
B818
Endrick Water
Randieford Bridge
Smallburn
Cairnoch Hill
8
FK7
7
85
6
River Carron
Cairnoch
Haugh Hill
G63
5
Carron Valley Resr
Priest's Croft
B818
84
4
FK6
3
83
Little Bin
2
Bin Burn
Burnhouse
Braes Burn
1
G65
82
67
68
69

5
2

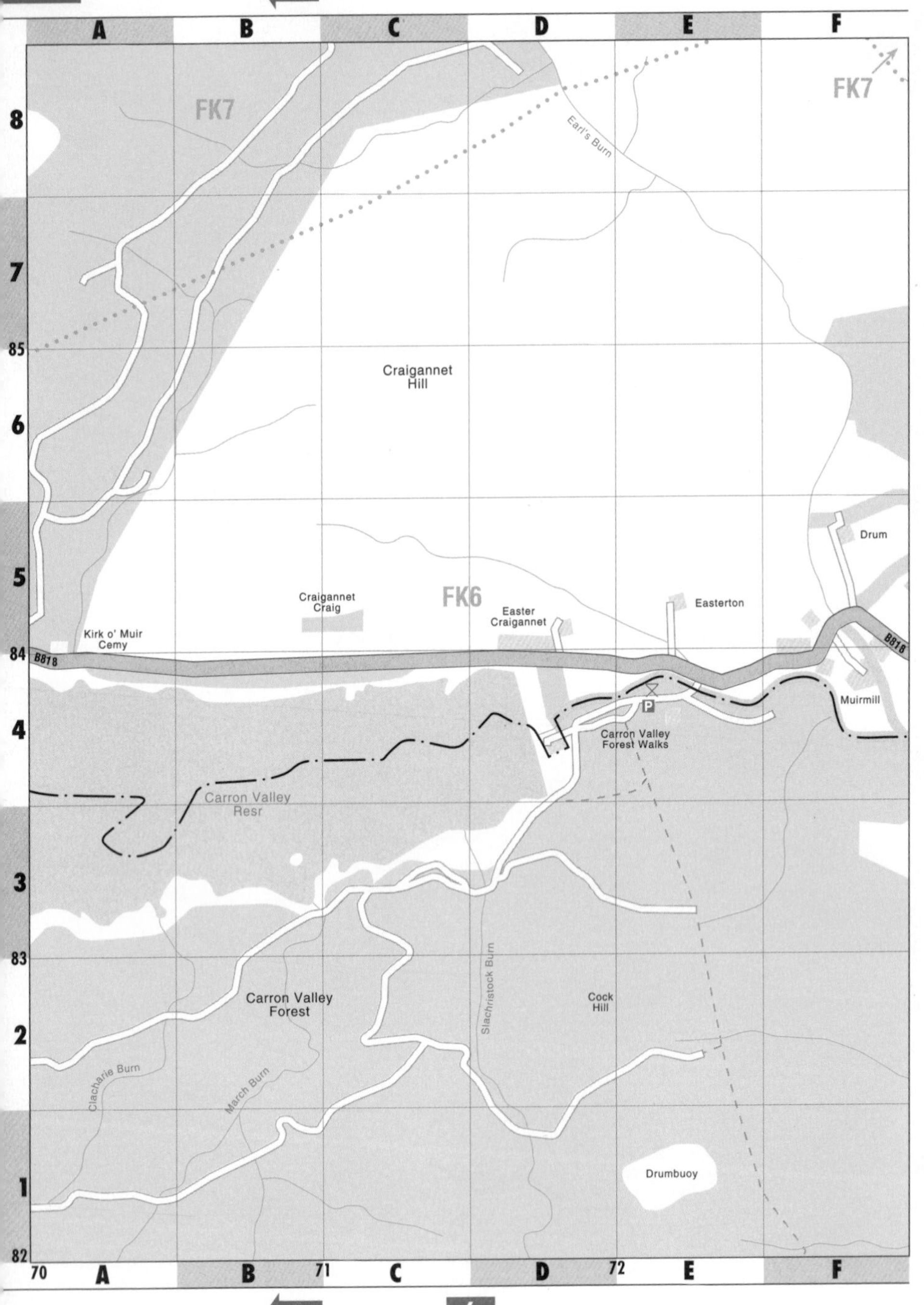
1
A
B
C
D
E
F
8
7
85
6
5
84
4
3
83
2
1
82
70
71
72
FK7
FK7
Earl's Burn
Craigannet
Hill
Drum
FK6
Craigannet
Craig
Easter
Craigannet
Easterton
Kirk o' Muir
Cemy
B818
B818
Muirmill
Carron Valley
Forest Walks
Carron Valley
Resr
Slachristock Burn
Carron Valley
Forest
Cock
Hill
Clacharie Burn
March Burn
Drumbuoy
1
6

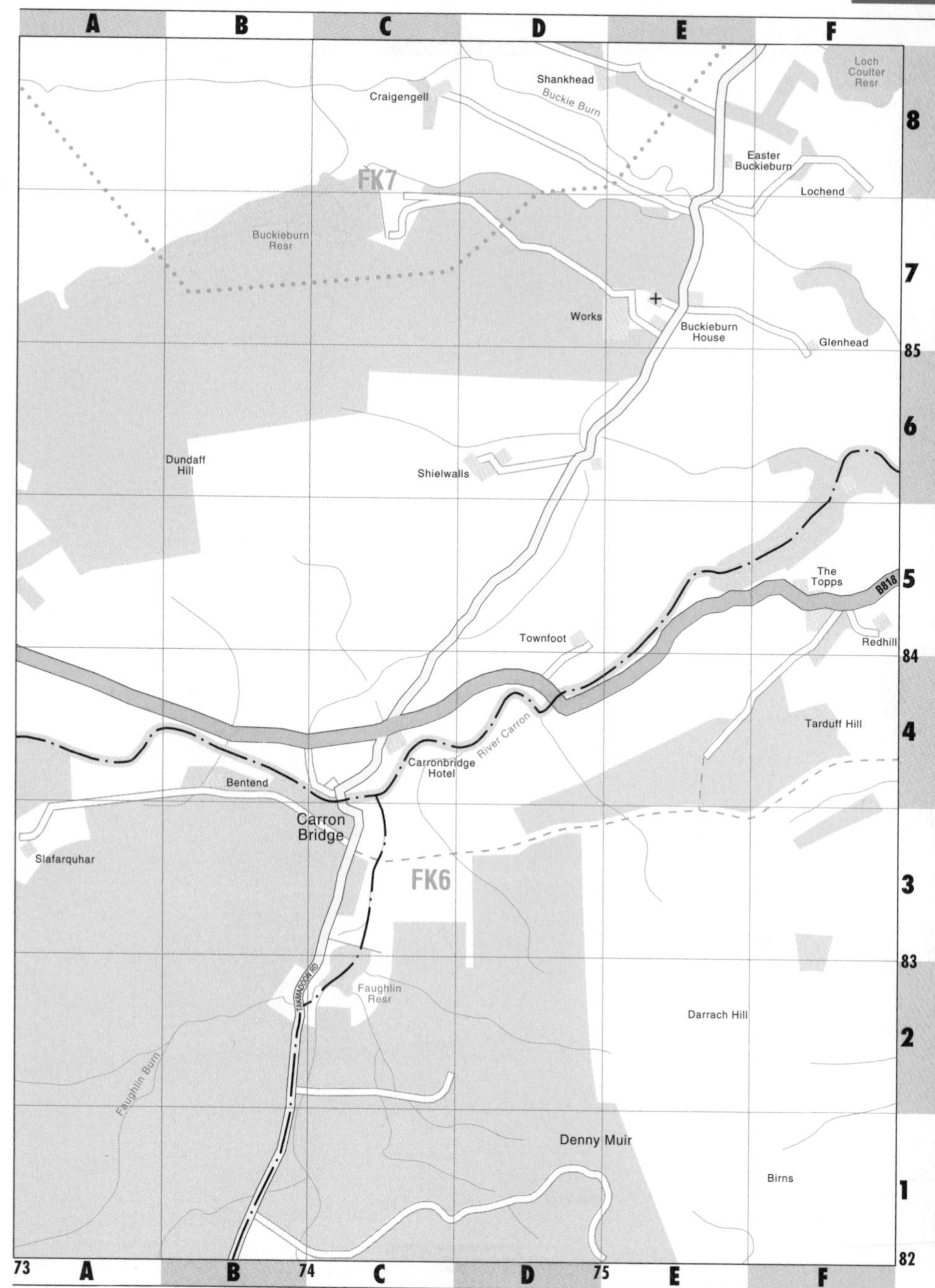
A
B
C
D
E
F
Loch
Coulter
Resr
Shankhead
Craigengell
Buckie Burn
8
Easter
Buckieburn
FK7
Lochend
Buckieburn
Resr
7
Works
Buckieburn
House
Glenhead
85
6
Dundaff
Hill
Shielwalls
The
Topps
5
B818
Townfoot
Redhill
84
Tarduff Hill
4
River Carron
Carronbridge
Hotel
Bentend
Carron
Bridge
Slafarquhar
FK6
3
83
TAKMADOON RD
Faughlin
Resr
Darrach Hill
2
Faughlin Burn
Denny Muir
Birns
1
82
73
A
B
74
C
D
75
E
F

7

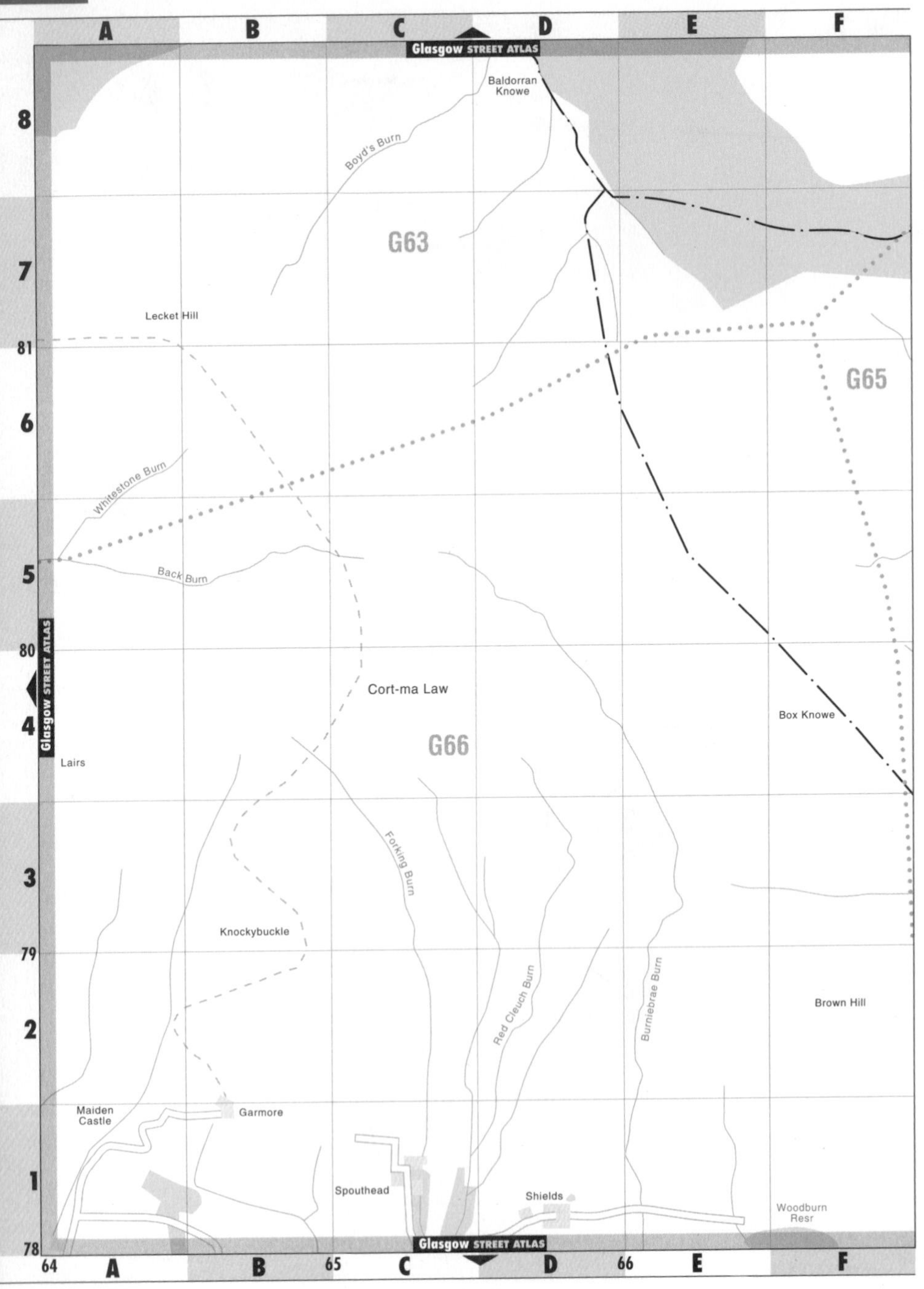
A
B
C
D
E
F
Glasgow STREET ATLAS
Baldorran Knowe
Boyd's Burn
G63
8
7
81
6
5
80
4
3
79
2
1
78
Lecket Hill
G65
Whitestone Burn
Back Burn
Glasgow STREET ATLAS
Cort-ma Law
Box Knowe
G66
Lairs
Forking Burn
Knockybuckle
Red Cleuch Burn
Burniebrae Burn
Brown Hill
Maiden Castle
Garmore
Spouthead
Shields
Woodburn Resr
Glasgow STREET ATLAS
64
65
66

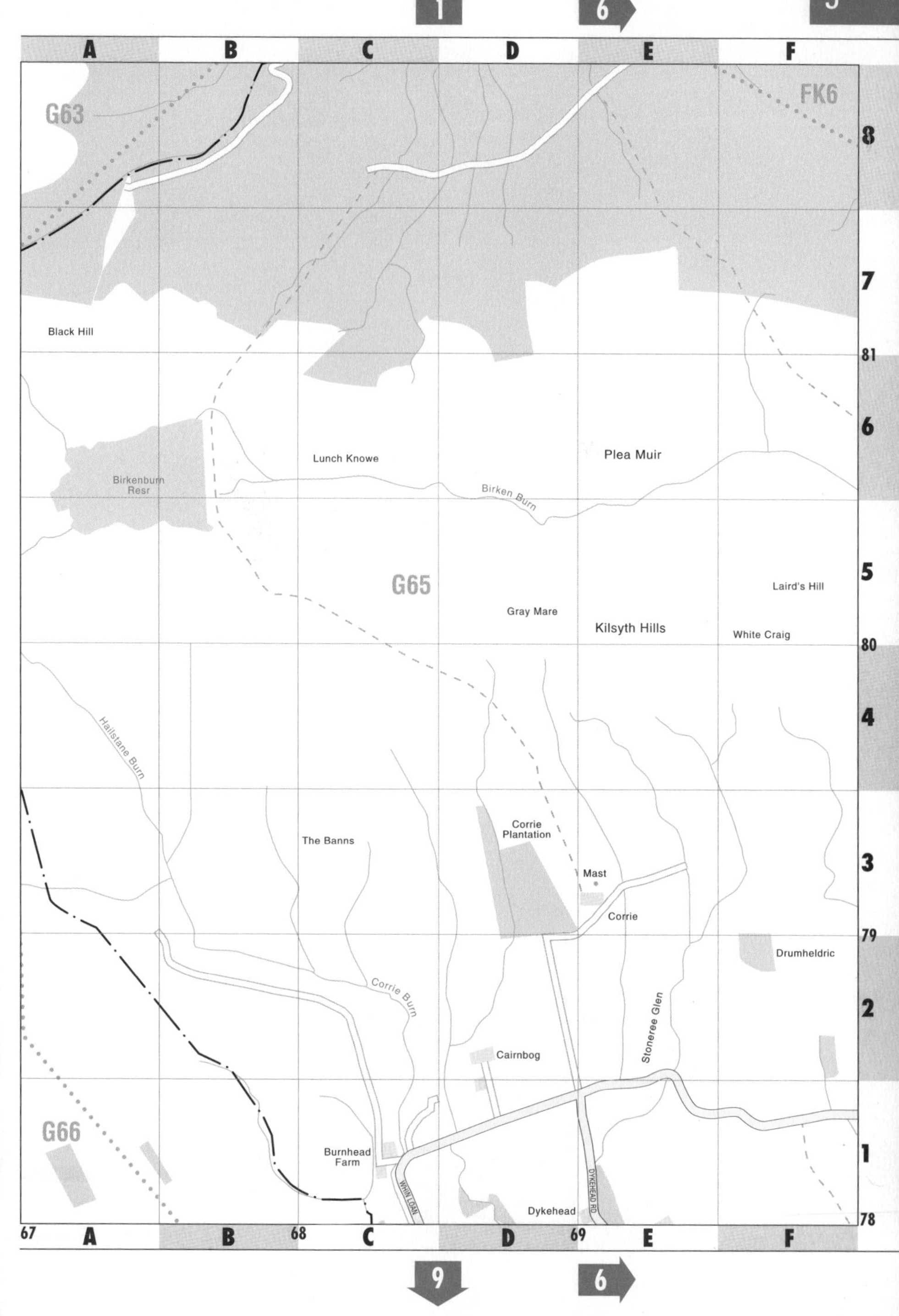
1
6
A
B
C
D
E
F
G63
FK6
8
7
Black Hill
81
6
Birkenburn
Resr
Lunch Knowe
Plea Muir
Birken Burn
5
G65
Laird's Hill
Gray Mare
Kilsyth Hills
White Craig
80
4
Hailstane Burn
Corrie
Plantation
The Banns
3
Mast
Corrie
79
Drumheldric
Corrie Burn
2
Stoneree Glen
Cairnbog
G66
1
Burnhead
Farm
WHIN LOAN
DYKEHEAD RD
Dykehead
78
67
68
69
9
6

5
2

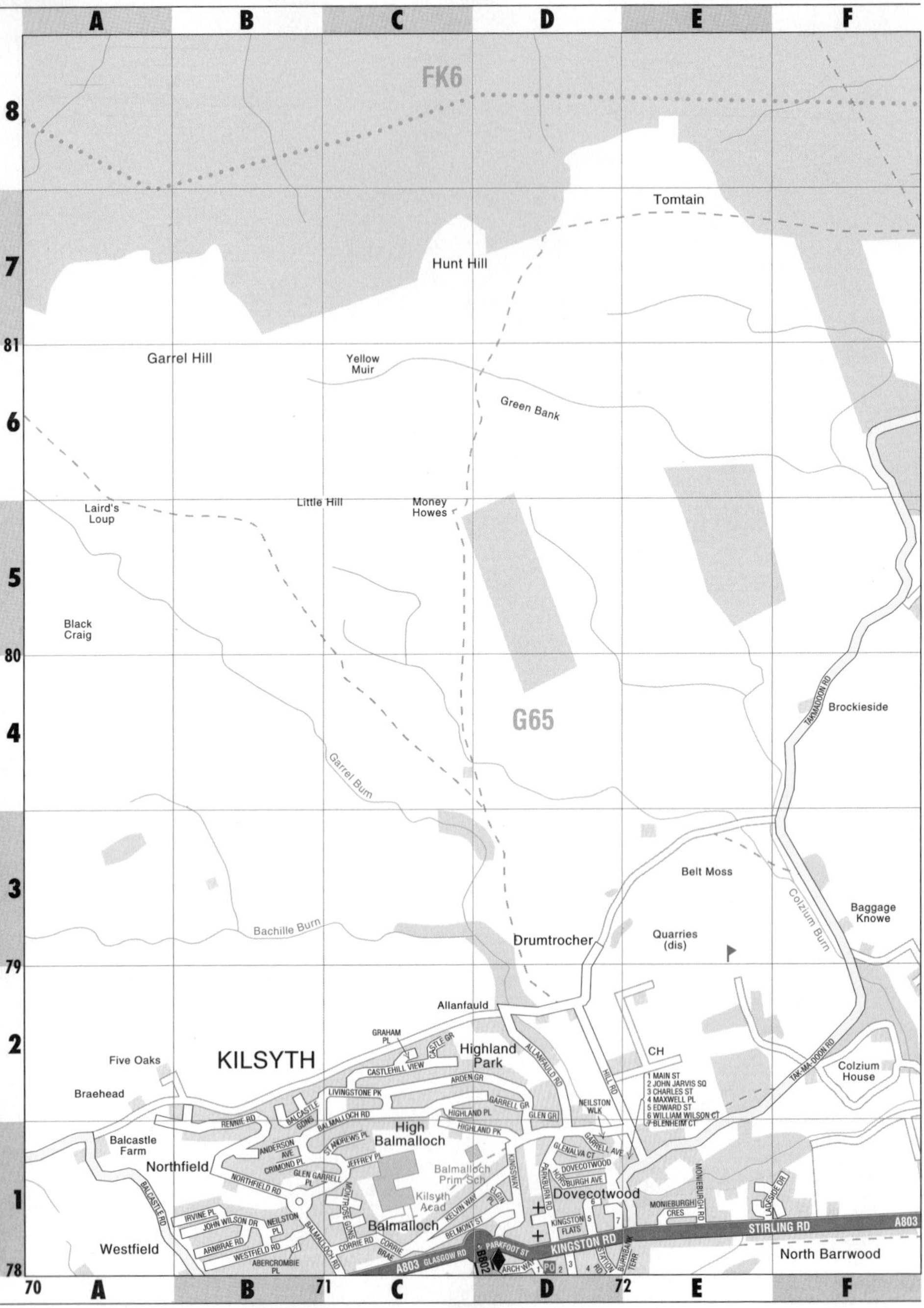

A B C D E F

FK6

8

Tomtain

7

Hunt Hill

81

Garrel Hill

Yellow Muir

6

Green Bank

Laird's Loup

Little Hill

Money Howes

5

Black Craig

80

G65

4

TAKMADOON RD

Brockieside

Garrel Burn

Belt Moss

3

Colzium Burn

Baggage Knowe

Bachille Burn

Drumtrocher

Quarries (dis)

79

Allanfauld

2

KILSYTH

Five Oaks

Braehead

Highland Park

GRAHAM PL

CASTLE GR

CASTLEHILL VIEW

ARDEN GR

LIVINGSTONE PK

GARRELL GR

HIGHLAND PL

HIGHLAND PK

GLEN GR

ALLANFAULD RD

HILL RD

CH

1 MAIN ST
2 JOHN JARVIS SQ
3 CHARLES ST
4 MAXWELL PL
5 EDWARD ST
6 WILLIAM WILSON CT
7 BLENHEIM CT

NEILSTON WLK

TAK-MA-DOON RD

Colzium House

RENNIE RD

BALCASTLE GDNS

BALMALLOCH RD

High Balmalloch

Balcastle Farm

Northfield

ANDERSON AVE

CRIMOND PL

ST ANDREWS PL

JEFFREY PL

GLEN GARRELL PL

NORTHFIELD RD

Balmalloch Prim Sch

Kilsyth Acad

KINGSWAY

GARRELL AVE

GLENALVA CT

DOVECOTWOOD

HORSBURGH AVE

PARKBURN RD

Dovecotwood

MONIEBURGH RD

MONIEBURGH CRES

LADESIDE DR

1

BALCASTLE RD

IRVINE PL

JOHN WILSON DR

NEILSTON PL

MONTROSE GDNS

KELVIN WAY

ELGIN PL

KINGSTON FLATS

Balmalloch

BELMONT ST

STIRLING RD

A803

Westfield

ARNBRAE RD

WESTFIELD RD

ABERCROMBIE PL

BALMALLOCH RD

CORRIE RD

CORRIE BRAE

A803 GLASGOW RD

B802

PARKFOOT ST

KINGSTON RD

ARCH WAY

PO

STATION RD

BURNBANK TERR

North Barrwood

78

70 A B 71 C D 72 E F

5
10

3
8
FK6
Doups
Mast
Drumnessie
Berryhill
Mast
Banton Burn
Glenhead
Banton Mains
High Banton
Binniemyre
Craigdouffie Burn
Bolling Glen
G65
Easter Auchinrivock
Wester Auchinrivock
Meadowside
THE MAILINGS
Banton Prim Sch
Slaughter Howe
Drum Burn
Auchinvalley
Banton
FK4
Riskend
Riskend Strip
Craigs
Dam Wood
Banton Loch
Kelvinhead Farm
Ruchill
Gateside
Speirs Island
Craigstone Wood
Castle Hill
Townhead
Girnal Hill
Bullet Knowes
River Kelvin
Forth & Clyde Canal
Kelvinhead Jetty
Back Drain
TAKMADOON RD
HIGH BANTON RD
MAILINGS RD
MAILINGS CT
HILLVIEW
MILL RD
MAIN ST
VALLEYBANK
LAMMERKNOWES RD
KELVIN CRES
ST MARGARET'S AVE
KELVINHEAD RD
BANTON RD
STIRLING RD
A803
KELVINHEAD
11
8

7

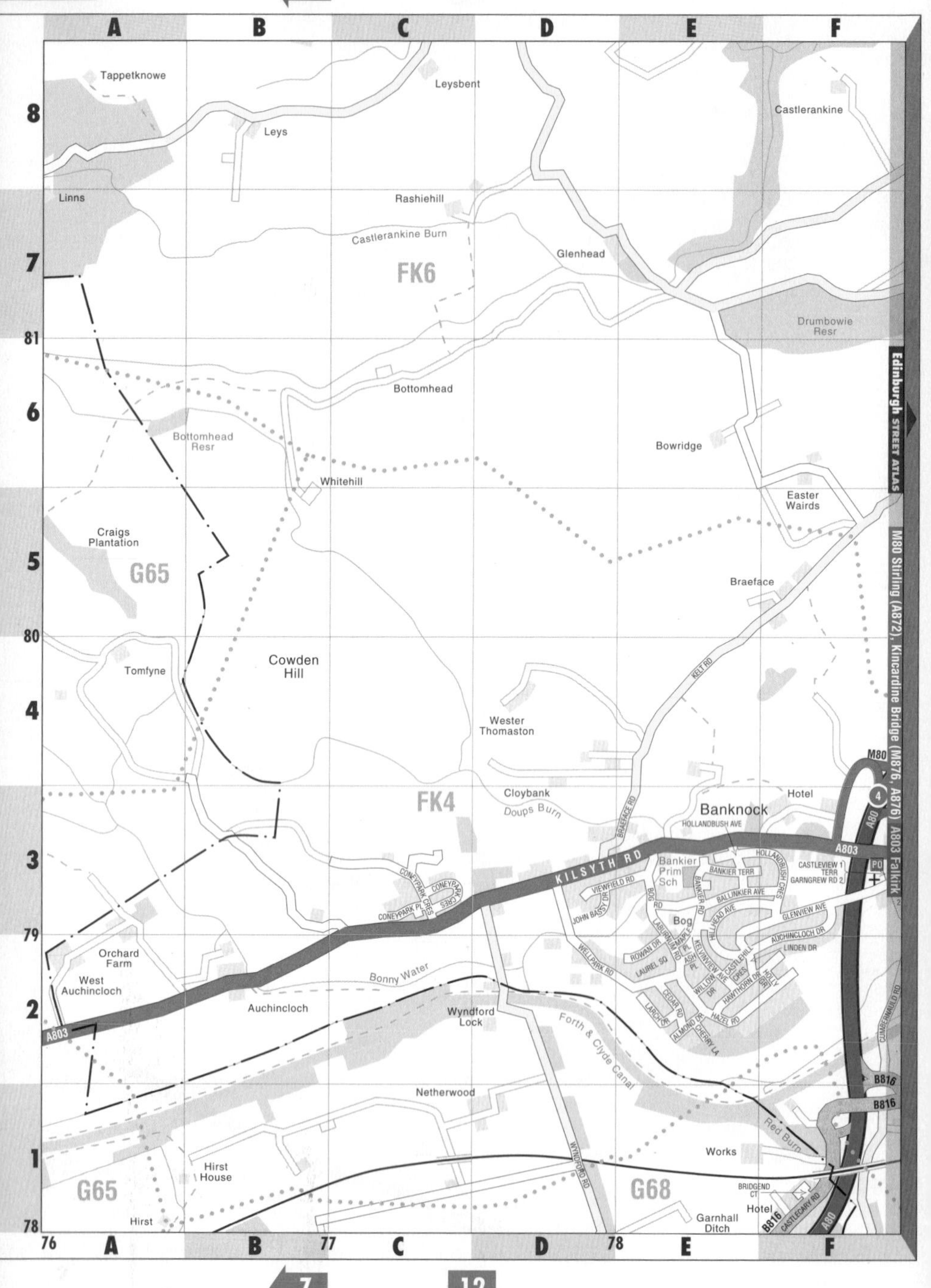

A
B
C
D
E
F
8
7
81
6
5
80
4
3
79
2
1
78
76
77
78
Tappetknowe
Leysbent
Leys
Castlerankine
Linns
Rashiehill
Castlerankine Burn
Glenhead
FK6
Drumbowie Resr
Bottomhead
Bottomhead Resr
Bowridge
Whitehill
Easter Wairds
Craigs Plantation
G65
Braeface
Cowden Hill
Tomfyne
KELT RD
Wester Thomaston
Cloybank
Doups Burn
FK4
BRAEFACE RD
Banknock
HOLLANDBUSH AVE
Hotel
M80
4
A80
A803
KILSYTH RD
CONEYPARK CRES
CONEYPARK PL
Bankier Prim Sch
BANKIER TERR
HOLLANDBUSH CRES
CASTLEVIEW TERR
GARNGREW RD
PO
VIEWFIELD RD
BALLINKIER AVE
JOHN BASSY DR
Bog
GLENVIEW AVE
AUCHINCLOCH DR
LINDEN DR
WELLPARK RD
ROWAN DR
LAUREL SQ
KELVINVIEW AVE
CASTLEHILL CRES
WILLOW DR
HAWTHORN DR
HAZEL RD
CEDAR RD
LARCH DR
ALMOND DR
CHERRY LA
Orchard Farm
West Auchincloch
Bonny Water
Auchincloch
Wyndford Lock
Forth & Clyde Canal
A803
CUMBERNAULD RD
B816
Netherwood
Red Burn
Works
Hirst House
WYNDFORD RD
G65
G68
BRIDGEND CT
Hotel
Hirst
Garnhall Ditch
B816
CASTLECARY RD
Edinburgh STREET ATLAS
M80 Stirling (A872), Kincardine Bridge (M876, A876) A803 Falkirk

7
12

5
10

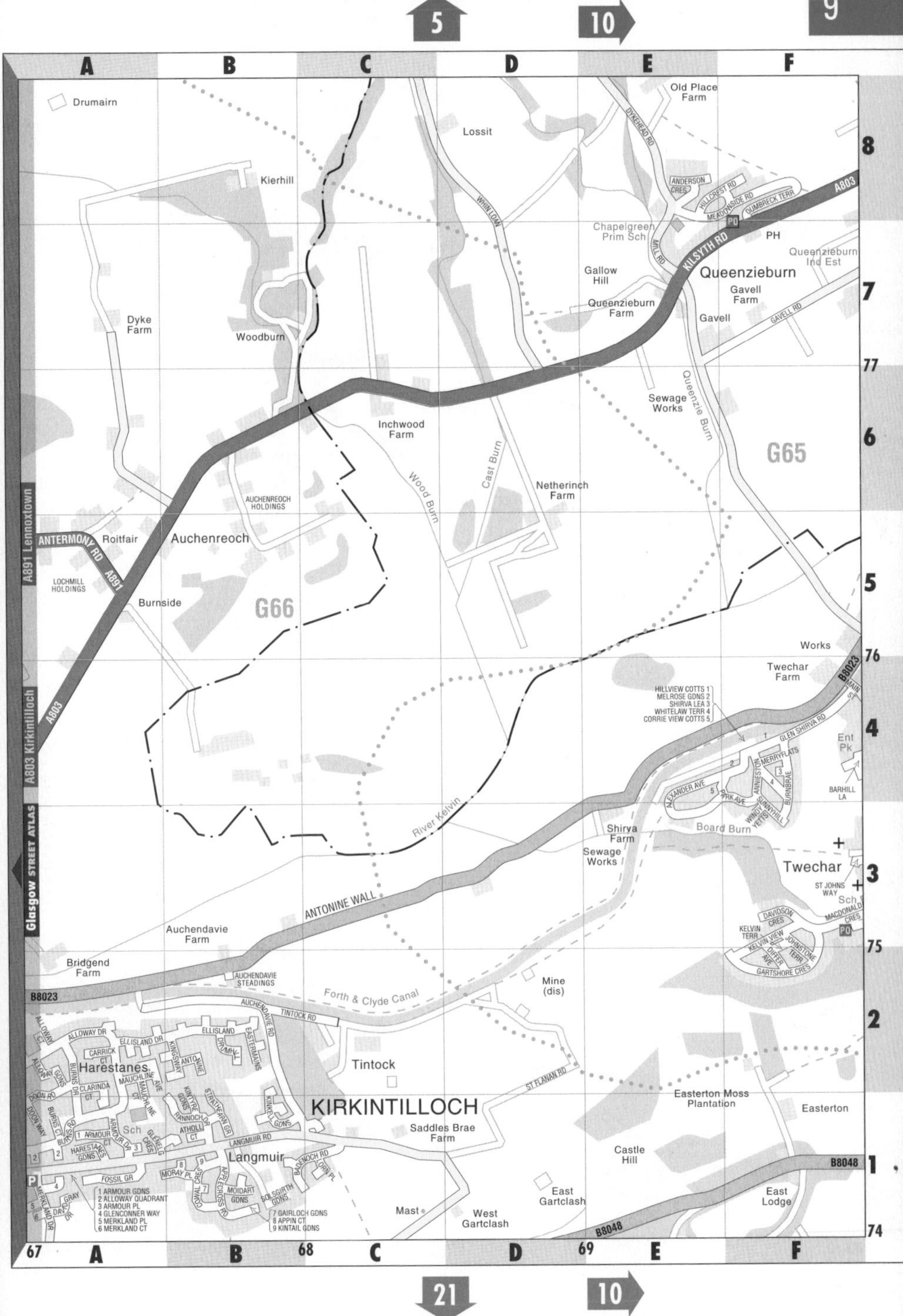
Drumairn
Lossit
Old Place Farm
Kierhill
DYKEHEAD RD
ANDERSON CRES
HILLCREST RD
MEADOWSIDE RD
DUMBRECK TERR
A803
WHIN LOAN
Chapelgreen Prim Sch
PH
Queenzieburn Ind Est
MILL RD
KILSYTH RD
Gallow Hill
Queenzieburn
Dyke Farm
Gavell Farm
Queenzieburn Farm
Woodburn
Gavell
GAVELL RD
Queenzie Burn
Sewage Works
Inchwood Farm
G65
Cast Burn
Wood Burn
Netherinch Farm
AUCHENREOCH HOLDINGS
A891 Lennoxtown
ANTERMONY RD
Roitfair
Auchenreoch
A891
LOCHMILL HOLDINGS
Burnside
G66
Works
Twechar Farm
B8023
HILLVIEW COTTS 1
MELROSE GDNS 2
SHIRVA LEA 3
WHITELAW TERR 4
CORRIE VIEW COTTS 5
GLEN SHIRVA RD
A803 Kirkintilloch
Ent Pk
MERRYFLATS
ANNIESTON
BURNBRAE
ALEXANDER AVE
PARK AVE
SUNNYHILL
WINDY YETTS
BARHILL LA
River Kelvin
Shirva Farm
Board Burn
Glasgow STREET ATLAS
Sewage Works
Twechar
ST JOHNS WAY
Sch
ANTONINE WALL
DAVIDSON CRES
MACDONALD CRES
KELVIN TERR
KELVIN VIEW
JOHNSTONE TERR
DIFFER AVE
GARTSHORE CRES
Auchendavie Farm
Bridgend Farm
AUCHENDAVIE STEADINGS
Mine (dis)
B8023
Forth & Clyde Canal
AUCHENDAVIE RD
TINTOCK RD
ALLOWAY DR
ELLISLAND
ELLISLAND DR
EASTERMAINS
CARRICK CT
KINGSWAY
ANTONINE
Harestanes
MAUCHLINE AVE
Tintock
CLARINDA CT
ST FLANAN RD
KINTYRE GDNS
STRATHEARN GR
Easterton Moss Plantation
KIRKINTILLOCH
Easterton
HANNOCH DR
KINKELL GDNS
ARMOUR
ATHOLL CT
Saddles Brae Farm
HARESTANES GDNS
LANGMUIR RD
Castle Hill
Langmuir
BADENOCH RD
B8048
FOSSIL GR
MORAY PL
APPLECROSS RD
MOIDART GDNS
SOLSGIRTH GDNS
ORN PL
East Gartclash
East Lodge
1 ARMOUR GDNS
2 ALLOWAY QUADRANT
3 ARMOUR PL
4 GLENCONNER WAY
5 MERKLAND PL
6 MERKLAND CT
7 GAIRLOCH GDNS
8 APPIN CT
9 KINTAIL GDNS
Mast
West Gartclash
B8048
MERKLAND DR
DAVA DR
GRAY
A B C D E F
8 7 77 6 5 76 4 3 75 2 1 74
67 68 69

21
10

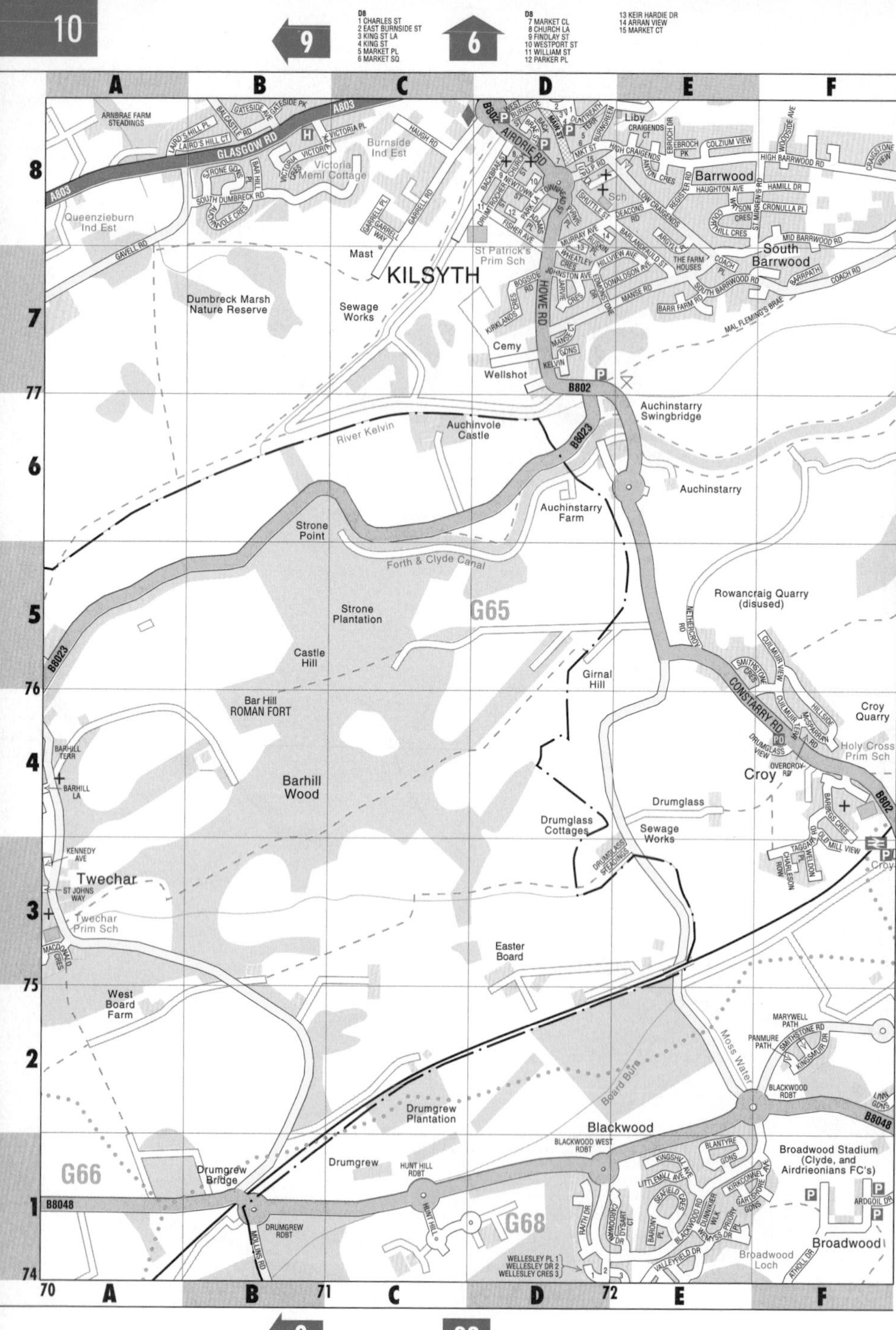
9
6
D8
1 CHARLES ST
2 EAST BURNSIDE ST
3 KING ST LA
4 KING ST
5 MARKET PL
6 MARKET SQ
D8
7 MARKET CL
8 CHURCH LA
9 FINDLAY ST
10 WESTPORT ST
11 WILLIAM ST
12 PARKER PL
13 KEIR HARDIE DR
14 ARRAN VIEW
15 MARKET CT
A
B
C
D
E
F
8
7
77
6
5
76
4
3
75
2
1
74
70
71
72
A803
GLASGOW RD
ARNBRAE FARM STEADINGS
Queenzieburn Ind Est
GAVELL RD
Burnside Ind Est
Victoria Meml Cottage
SOUTH DUMBRECK RD
HAUGH RD
GARRELL RD
Mast
KILSYTH
St Patrick's Prim Sch
Dumbreck Marsh Nature Reserve
Sewage Works
B802
AIRDRIE RD
MAIN ST
HOWE RD
Liby
Barrwood
South Barrwood
HIGH BARRWOOD RD
COACH RD
MAL FLEMING'S BRAE
Sch
Cemy
Wellshot
KELVIN
Auchinstarry Swingbridge
Auchinvole Castle
River Kelvin
B8023
Auchinstarry
Auchinstarry Farm
Strone Point
Forth & Clyde Canal
Strone Plantation
G65
Castle Hill
Rowancraig Quarry (disused)
NETHERCROY RD
Girnal Hill
CONSTARRY RD
Bar Hill ROMAN FORT
Croy Quarry
Holy Cross Prim Sch
Croy
Barhill Wood
BARHILL TERR
BARHILL LA
Drumglass
Drumglass Cottages
Sewage Works
KENNEDY AVE
Twechar
ST JOHNS WAY
Twechar Prim Sch
MACDONALD CRES
Easter Board
West Board Farm
Moss Water
Board Burn
MARYWELL PATH
PANMURE PATH
BLACKWOOD RDBT
B8048
Drumgrew Plantation
Blackwood
BLACKWOOD WEST RDBT
Broadwood Stadium (Clyde, and Airdrieonians FC's)
G66
Drumgrew Bridge
Drumgrew
HUNT HILL RDBT
DRUMGREW RDBT
G68
MOLLINS RD
WELLESLEY PL 1
WELLESLEY DR 2
WELLESLEY CRES 3
Broadwood Loch
Broadwood

7
12

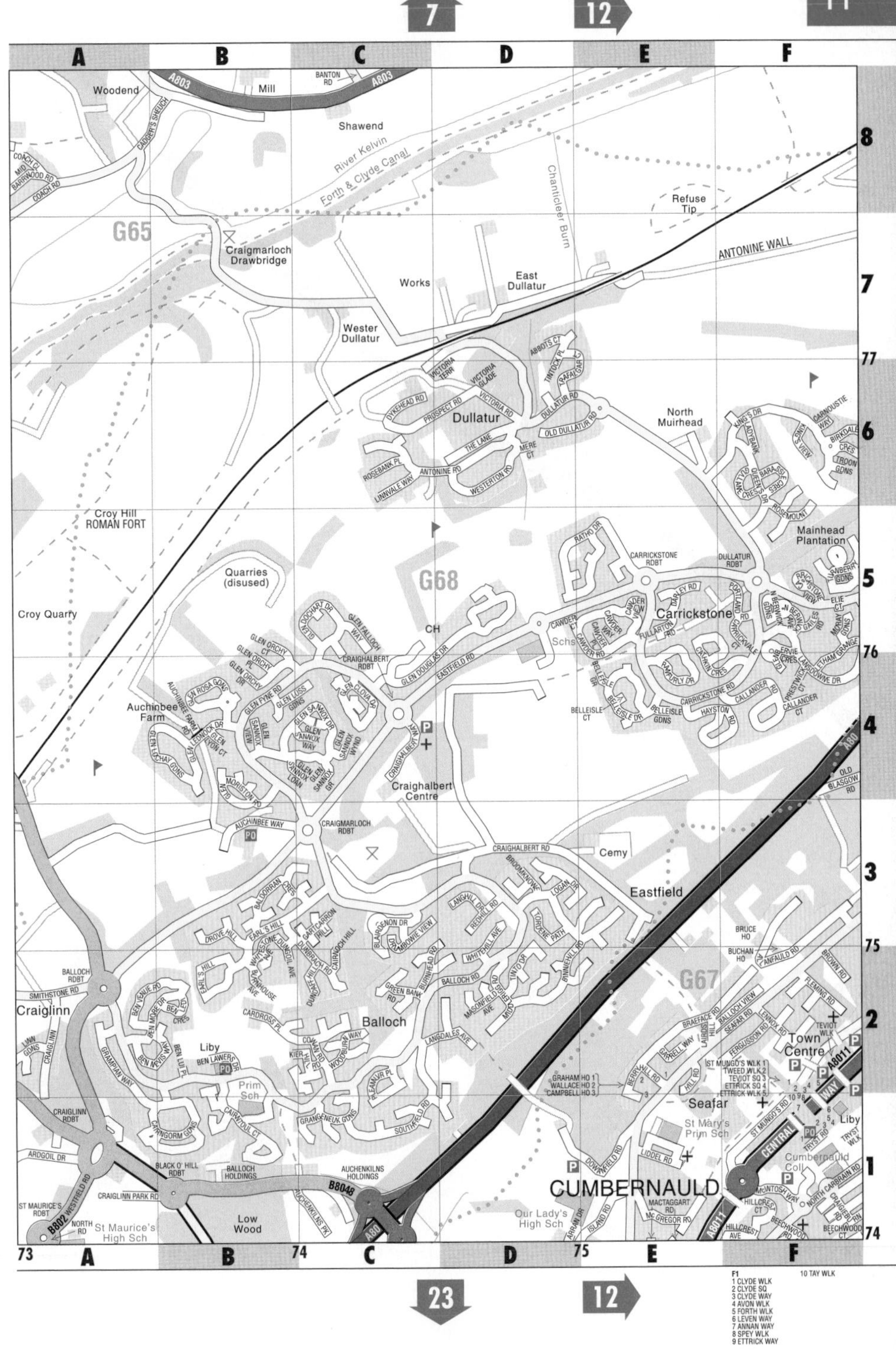

23
12

F1
1 CLYDE WLK
2 CLYDE SQ
3 CLYDE WAY
4 AVON WLK
5 FORTH WLK
6 LEVEN WAY
7 ANNAN WAY
8 SPEY WLK
9 ETTRICK WAY
10 TAY WLK

11 8

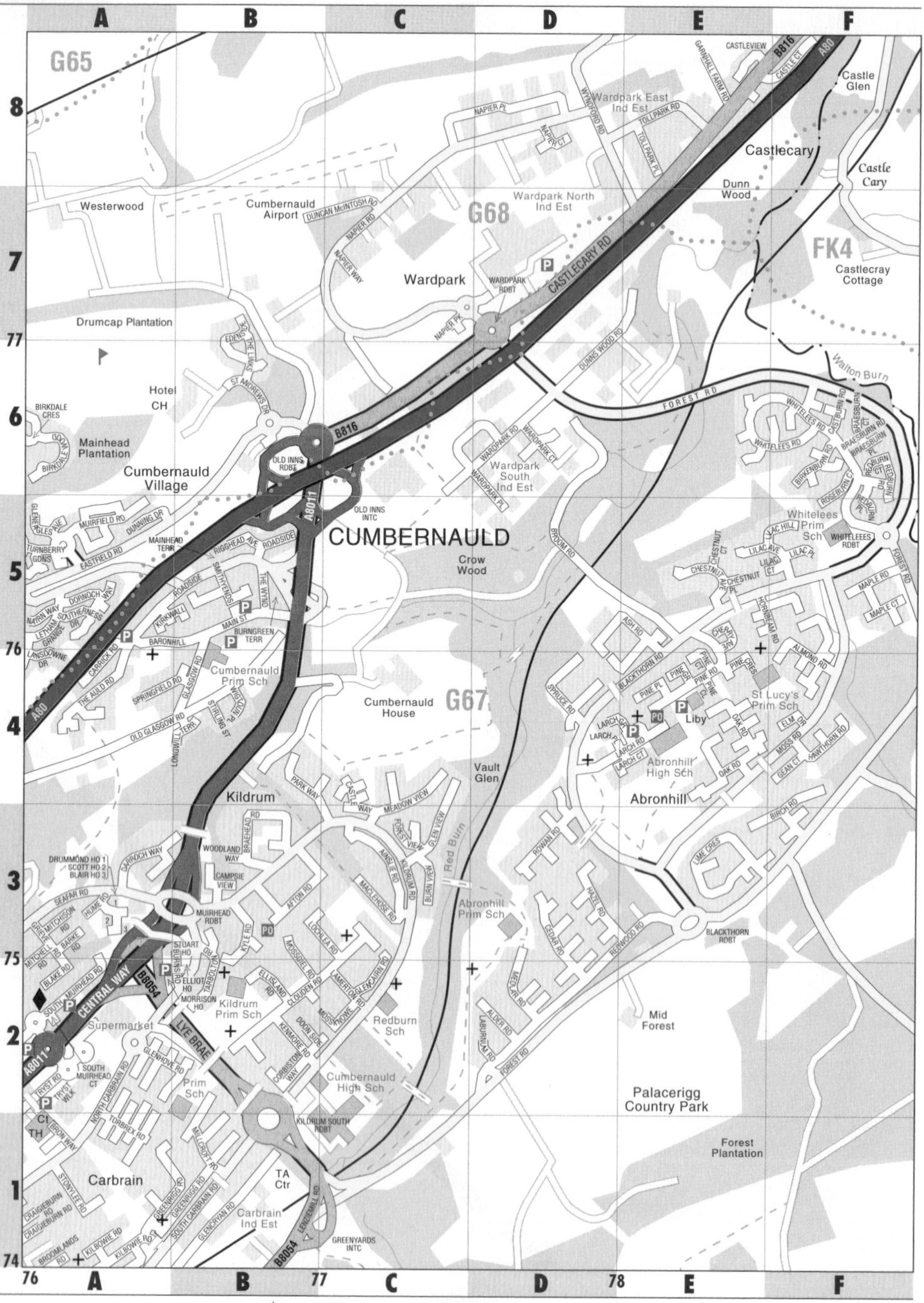

A B C D E F

8 7 77 6 5 76 4 3 75 2 1 74

G65 G68 G67 FK4

CUMBERNAULD

Westerwood
Cumbernauld Airport
Drumcap Plantation
Hotel
CH
Birkdale Cres
Mainhead Plantation
Cumbernauld Village
Wardpark
Wardpark East Ind Est
Wardpark North Ind Est
Wardpark South Ind Est
Wardpark Rdbt
Castlecary
Castle Glen
Castle Cary
Dunn Wood
Castlecray Cottage
Walton Burn
Old Inns Rdbt
Old Inns Intc
Crow Wood
Cumbernauld Prim Sch
Cumbernauld House
Vault Glen
Kildrum
Red Burn
Abronhill Prim Sch
Abronhill High Sch
Abronhill
St Lucy's Prim Sch
Liby
Whitelees Prim Sch
Whitelees Rdbt
Blackthorn Rdbt
Muirhead Rdbt
Kildrum Prim Sch
Redburn Sch
Cumbernauld High Sch
Kildrum South Rdbt
Supermarket
Prim Sch
South Muirhead Ct
Carbrain
TA Ctr
Carbrain Ind Est
Greenyards Intc
Mid Forest
Palacerigg Country Park
Forest Plantation
CT
TH
Drummond Ho 1
Scott Ho 2
Blair Ho 3
Stuart Ho
Elliot Ho
Morrison Ho

A80 B816 A8011 B8054
Castlecary Rd
Castleview
Garnhall Farm Rd
Castle Ct
Wyndford Rd
Tollpark Rd
Toll Park Pl
Napier Pl
Napier Ct
Napier Rd
Napier Way
Napier Pk
Duncan McIntosh Rd
Dunns Wood Rd
Forest Rd
Edens
The Links
St Andrews Dr
Birkdale Wood
Wardpark Rd
Wardpark Ct
Wardpark Pl
Whitelees Rd
Castburn Rd
Braesburn Ct
Braesburn Rd
Braesburn Pl
Birkenburn Rd
Redburn Ct
Redburn Rd
Roseburn Ct
Lilac Hill
Lilac Ave
Lilac Ct
Lilac Pl
Chestnut Ct
Chestnut Pl
Maple Rd
Maple Ct
Broom Rd
Ash Rd
Hornbeam Rd
Cherry Ave
Almond Rd
Blackthorn Rd
Pine Pl
Pine Ct
Pine Rd
Pine Cres
Spruce Rd
Larch Gr
Larch Pl
Larch Rd
Larch Ct
Oak Rd
Elm Dr
Moss Rd
Hawthorn Rd
Gean Ct
Birch Rd
Rowan Rd
Lime Cres
Hazel Rd
Cedar Rd
Redwood Rd
Medlar Rd
Alder Rd
Laburnum Rd
Gleneagles Gdns
Muirfield Rd
Dunning Dr
Turnberry Gdns
Eastfield Rd
Mainhead Terr
Rigghead Ave
Roadside
Smithyends
The Wynd
Main St
Burngreen Terr
Kirkwall
Dornoch Way
Nairn Way
Southerness Dr
Letham Grange
Lansdowne Dr
Baronhill
Carrick Rd
The Auld Rd
Springfield Rd
Glasgow Rd
Wigtoun Pl
Stirling St
Old Glasgow Rd
Longwill Terr
Park Way
Castle Way
Meadow View
Forest View
Glen View
Braehead Rd
Woodland Way
Campsie View
Garroch Way
Ainslie Rd
Kildrum Rd
Burn View
Maclehose Rd
Afton Rd
Lochlea Rd
Mossgiel Rd
Glencairn Rd
Amerton Rd
Ellisland Rd
Clouden Rd
Mossknowe
Doon Side
Kenmore Rd
Corbiston Way
Kyle Rd
Tarbolton
Burns Rd
Seafar Rd
Mitchison Rd
Hume Rd
Grieve Rd
Barke Rd
Mitchell Rd
Blake Rd
Muirhead Rd
Central Way
Lye Brae
Tryst Rd
Tryst Wlk
South Carbrain Rd
North Carbrain Rd
Glenhove Rd
Torbrex Rd
Millcroft Rd
Bron Way
Stoneylee Rd
Craigieburn Rd
Greenrigg Rd
Glencryan Rd
Kilbowie Rd
Broomlands Rd
Lenziemill Rd

76 77 78

11 24

14

A
B
C
D
E
F
Edinburgh STREET ATLAS
Burnhouse
Lochdrum
G68
8
Castlecary
Low Wood
Blackhill
Wester
Lochgreen
Loch
Green
Skipperton Burn
Mast
Lochgreen
7
Walton
FK4
Bandominie
77
Castlecary
High Wood
6
Kilt
Farm
5
Kilt Bridge
FORST RD
76
Walton Burn
G67
4
Graystone Knowe
Crowbank
Arns
Glenhead
Old
Shields
Garbethill
House
Mast
3
75
Garbet
2
Garbethill
Fannyside Muir
FK1
1
Easter
Fannyside
74
79
80
81

25
14

13

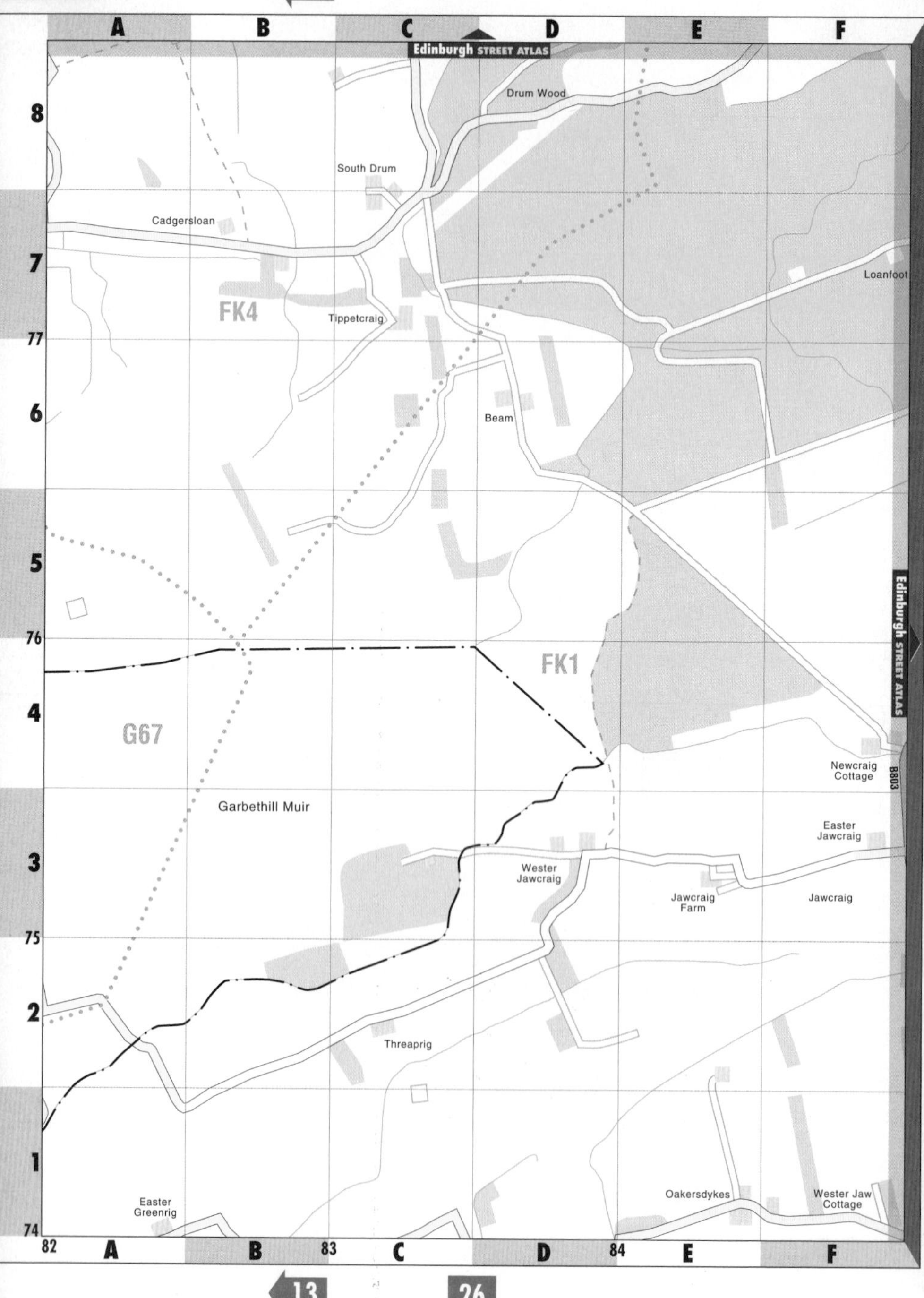

A
B
C
D
E
F
Edinburgh STREET ATLAS
Drum Wood
South Drum
Cadgersloan
Loanfoot
FK4
Tippetcraig
Beam
FK1
G67
Newcraig Cottage
B803
Garbethill Muir
Easter Jawcraig
Wester Jawcraig
Jawcraig Farm
Jawcraig
Threaprig
Oakersdykes
Wester Jaw Cottage
Easter Greenrig
8
7
77
6
5
76
4
3
75
2
1
74
82
83
84

13

26

16

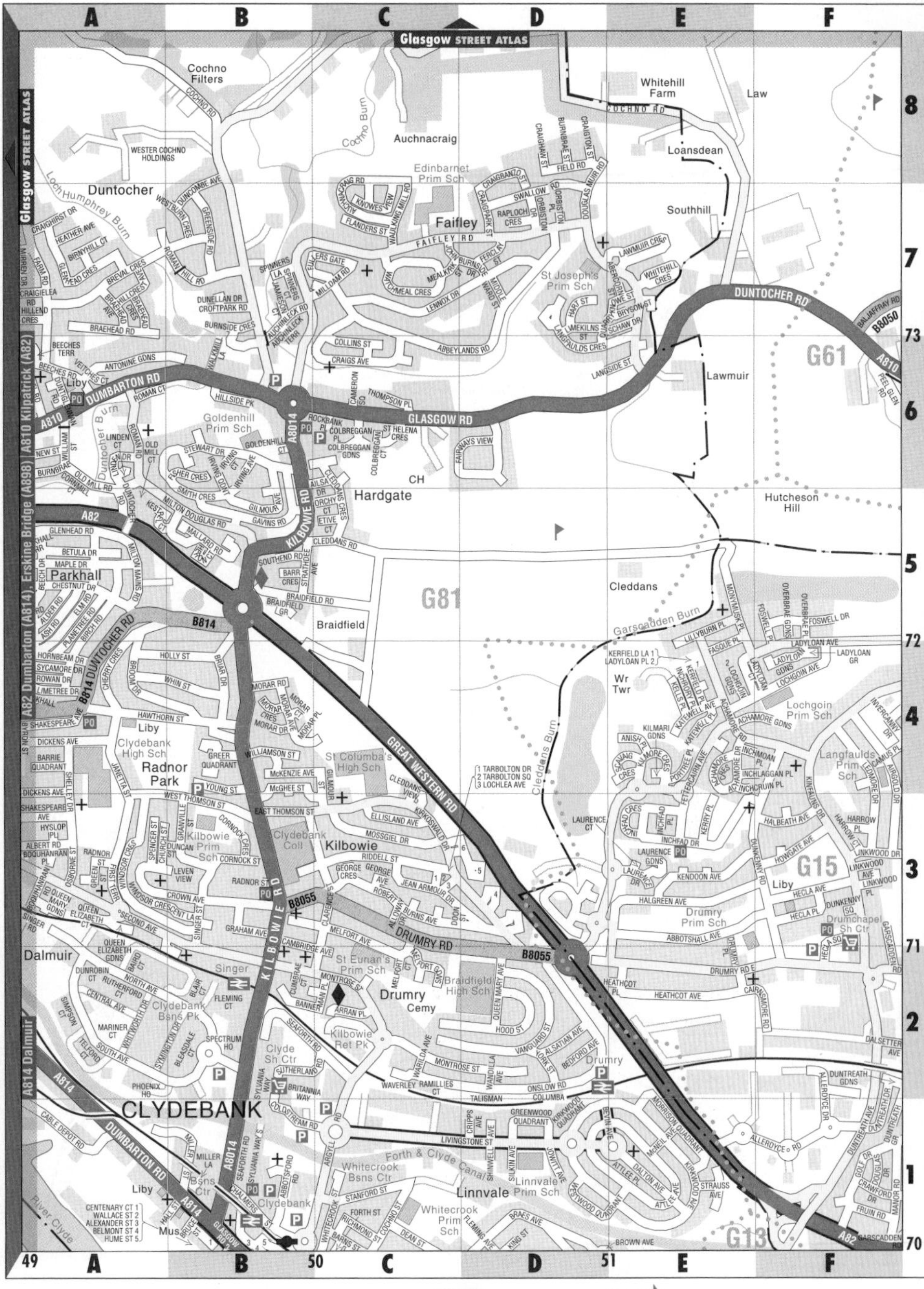

Glasgow STREET ATLAS

A B C D E F

8 7 73 6 5 72 4 3 71 2 1 70

Cochno Filters

WESTER COCHNO HOLDINGS

Duntocher

Loch Humphrey Burn

Cochno Burn

Auchnacraig

Edinbarnet Prim Sch

Faifley

FAIFLEY RD

Whitehill Farm

Law

COCHNO RD

Loansdean

Southhill

St Joseph's Prim Sch

DUNTOCHER RD

B8050

G61

A810

Lawmuir

DUMBARTON RD

GLASGOW RD

Goldenhill Prim Sch

A8014

KILBOWIE RD

Hardgate

CH

Hutcheson Hill

A82

Parkhall

G81

Cleddans

Garscadden Burn

Braidfield

B814

DUNTOCHER RD

Wr Twr

Lochgoin Prim Sch

Cleddans Burn

Liby

Clydebank High Sch

Radnor Park

St Columba's High Sch

GREAT WESTERN RD

1 TARBOLTON DR
2 TARBOLTON SQ
3 LOCHLEA AVE

Langfaulds Prim Sch

Kilbowie Prim Sch

Clydebank Coll

Kilbowie

G15

Liby

B8055

DRUMRY RD

Drumry Prim Sch

Drumchapel Sh Ctr

Dalmuir

Singer

St Eunan's Prim Sch

Braidfield High Sch

Clydebank Bsns Pk

Drumry Cemy

Kilbowie Ret Pk

Clyde Sh Ctr

Drumry

CLYDEBANK

Forth & Clyde Canal

Whitecrook Bsns Ctr

Linnvale

Linnvale Prim Sch

Whitecrook Prim Sch

Liby

Mus

River Clyde

G13

A814 DUMBARTON RD

A814 Dalmuir

A82 Dumbarton (A814), Erskine Bridge (A898) | A810 Kilpatrick (A82)

CENTENARY CT 1
WALLACE ST 2
ALEXANDER ST 3
BELMONT ST 4
HUME ST 5

49 A B 50 C D 51 E F

27

16

15

E5
1 DOUGLAS PL
2 KIRK LA
3 JEDWORTH CT
4 THE LOANING

B3
1 KINCLAVEN PL
2 KINCLAVEN GDNS
3 MERRYTON GDNS
4 LINKWOOD GR
5 SOUTHDEEN GR

15

28

18

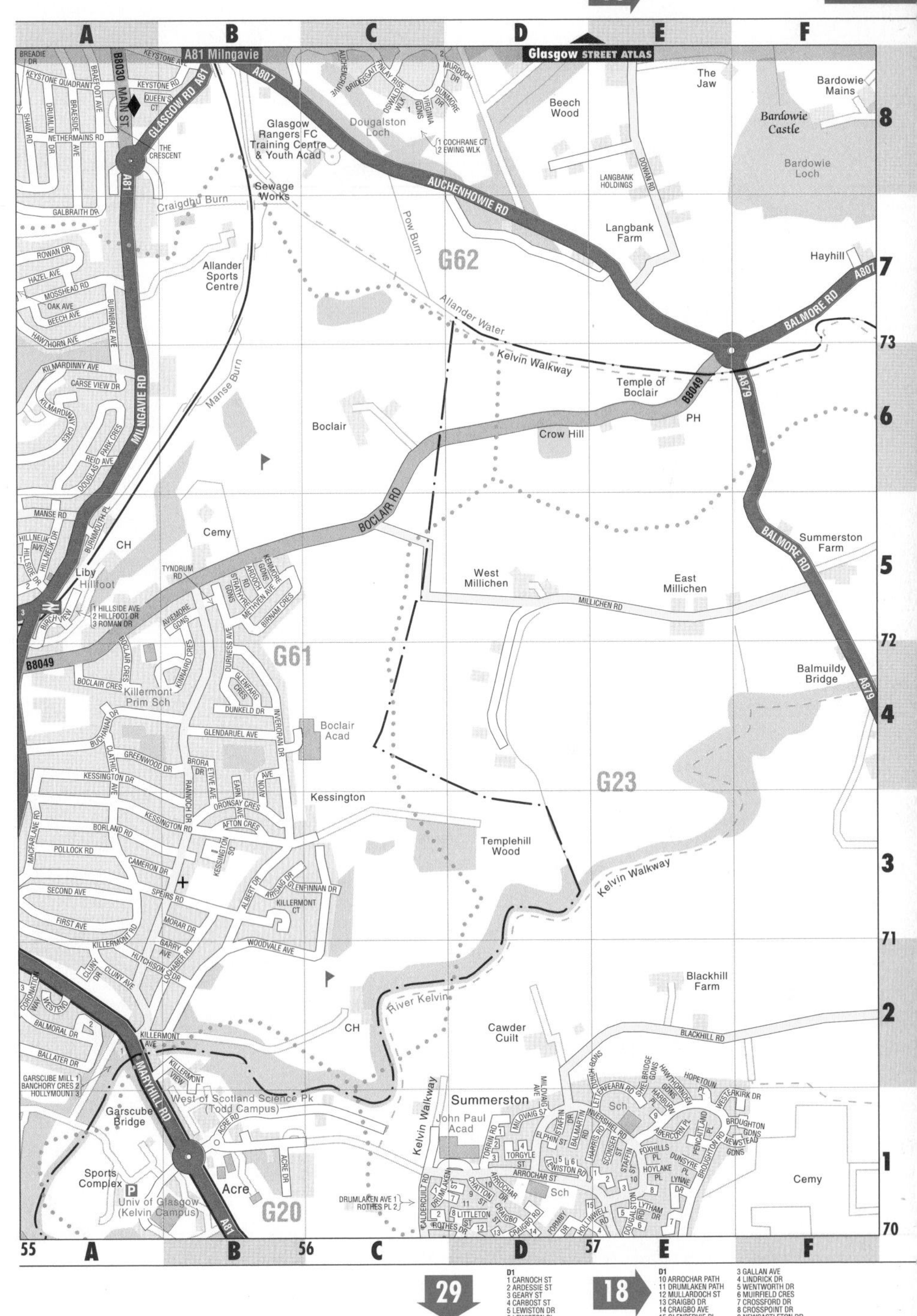

29

D1
1 CARNOCH ST
2 ARDESSIE ST
3 GEARY ST
4 CARBOST ST
5 LEWISTON DR
6 LEWISTON PL
7 DRUMLAKEN CT
8 LITTLETON DR
9 DRUMLAKEN PL

18

D1
10 ARROCHAR PATH
11 DRUMLAKEN PATH
12 MULLARDOCH ST
13 CRAIGBO DR
14 CRAIGBO AVE
15 GLENBERVIE PL

E1
1 FORRES ST
2 TOLSTA ST
3 GALLAN AVE
4 LINDRICK DR
5 WENTWORTH DR
6 MUIRFIELD CRES
7 CROSSFORD DR
8 CROSSPOINT DR
9 NEWCASTLETON DR
10 STAFFIN PATH

17

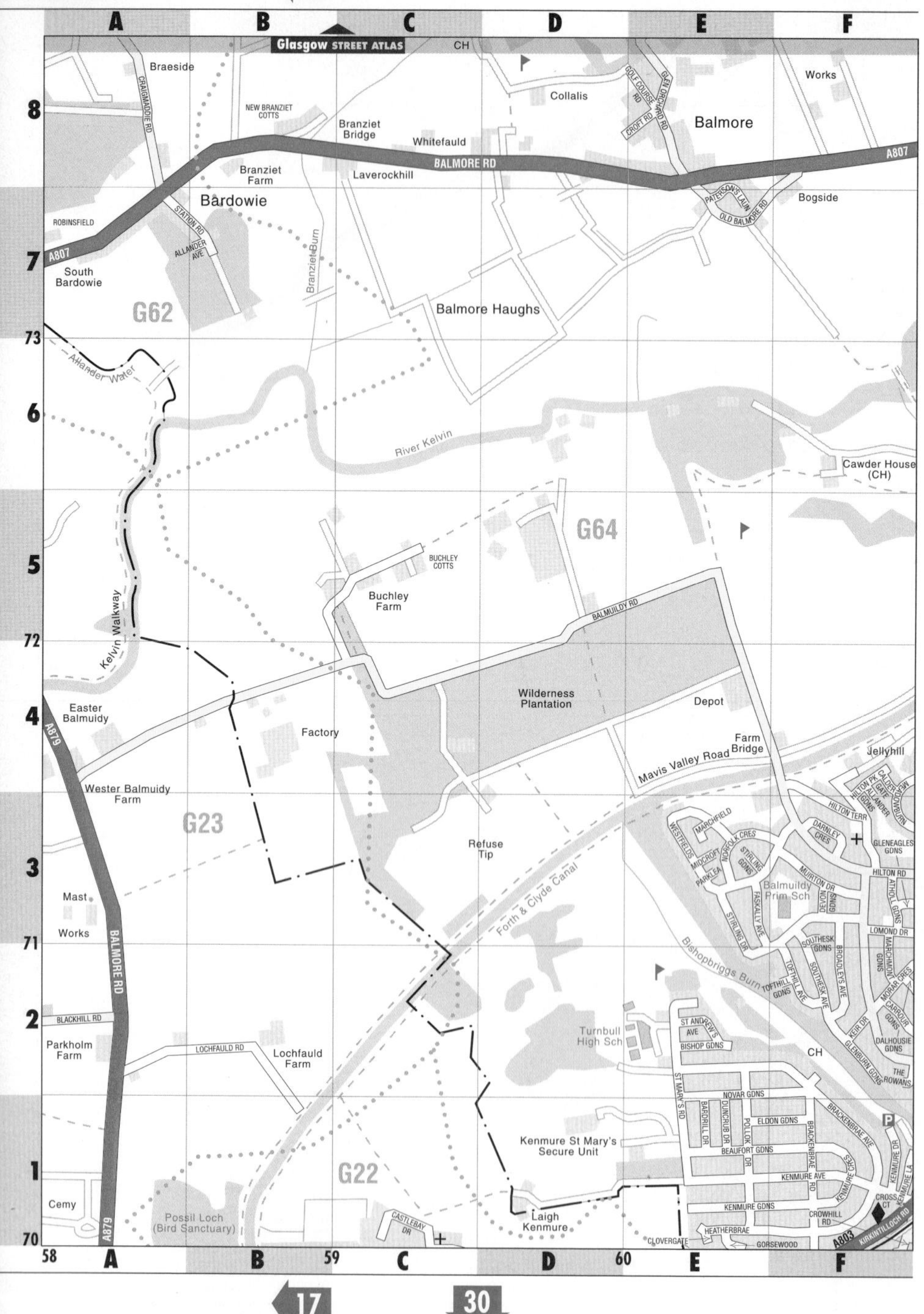

A
B
C
D
E
F
Glasgow STREET ATLAS
CH
Braeside
CRAIGMADDIE RD
NEW BRANZIET COTTS
Branziet Bridge
Whitefauld
Collalis
GOLF COURSE RD
GLEN ORCHARD RD
CROFT RD
Balmore
Works
BALMORE RD
A807
Branziet Farm
Laverockhill
Bardowie
ROBINSFIELD
STATION RD
ALLANDER AVE
PATERSON'S LAUN
OLD BALMORE RD
Bogside
South Bardowie
G62
Branziet Burn
Balmore Haughs
Allander Water
River Kelvin
Cawder House (CH)
G64
BUCHLEY COTTS
Buchley Farm
BALMUILDY RD
Kelvin Walkway
Easter Balmuidy
A879
Wilderness Plantation
Depot
Factory
Farm Bridge
Mavis Valley Road
Jellyhill
Wester Balmuidy Farm
G23
HILTON TERR
HILTON RD
Refuse Tip
MARCHFIELD
WESTFIELDS
MIDCROFT
PARKLEA
NORFOLK CRES
STIRLING GDNS
DARNLEY CRES
GLENEAGLES GDNS
MUIRTON DR
Balmuildy Prim Sch
FASKALLY AVE
STIRLING DR
SOUTHESK GDNS
BROADLEYS AVE
LOMOND DR
Mast
Works
Forth & Clyde Canal
Bishopbriggs Burn
TOFTHILL AVE
TOFTHILL GDNS
SOUTHESK AVE
KEIR DR
MORAR CRES
DALHOUSIE GDNS
GLENBURN GDNS
THE ROWANS
2
BLACKHILL RD
Parkholm Farm
LOCHFAULD RD
Lochfauld Farm
Turnbull High Sch
ST ANDREW'S AVE
BISHOP GDNS
CH
ST MARY'S RD
NOVAR GDNS
BARDRILL DR
DUNCRUB DR
POLLOK DR
ELDON GDNS
BRACKENBRAE RD
BRACKENBRAE AVE
BEAUFORT GDNS
Kenmure St Mary's Secure Unit
KENMURE AVE
KENMURE DR
KENMURE LA
KENMURE GDNS
CROWHILL RD
CROSS CT
G22
Cemy
Possil Loch (Bird Sanctuary)
CASTLEBAY DR
Laigh Kenmure
CLOVERGATE
HEATHERBRAE
GORSEWOOD
A803
KIRKINTILLOCH RD
8
7
73
6
5
72
4
3
71
2
1
70
58
59
60

17
30

20

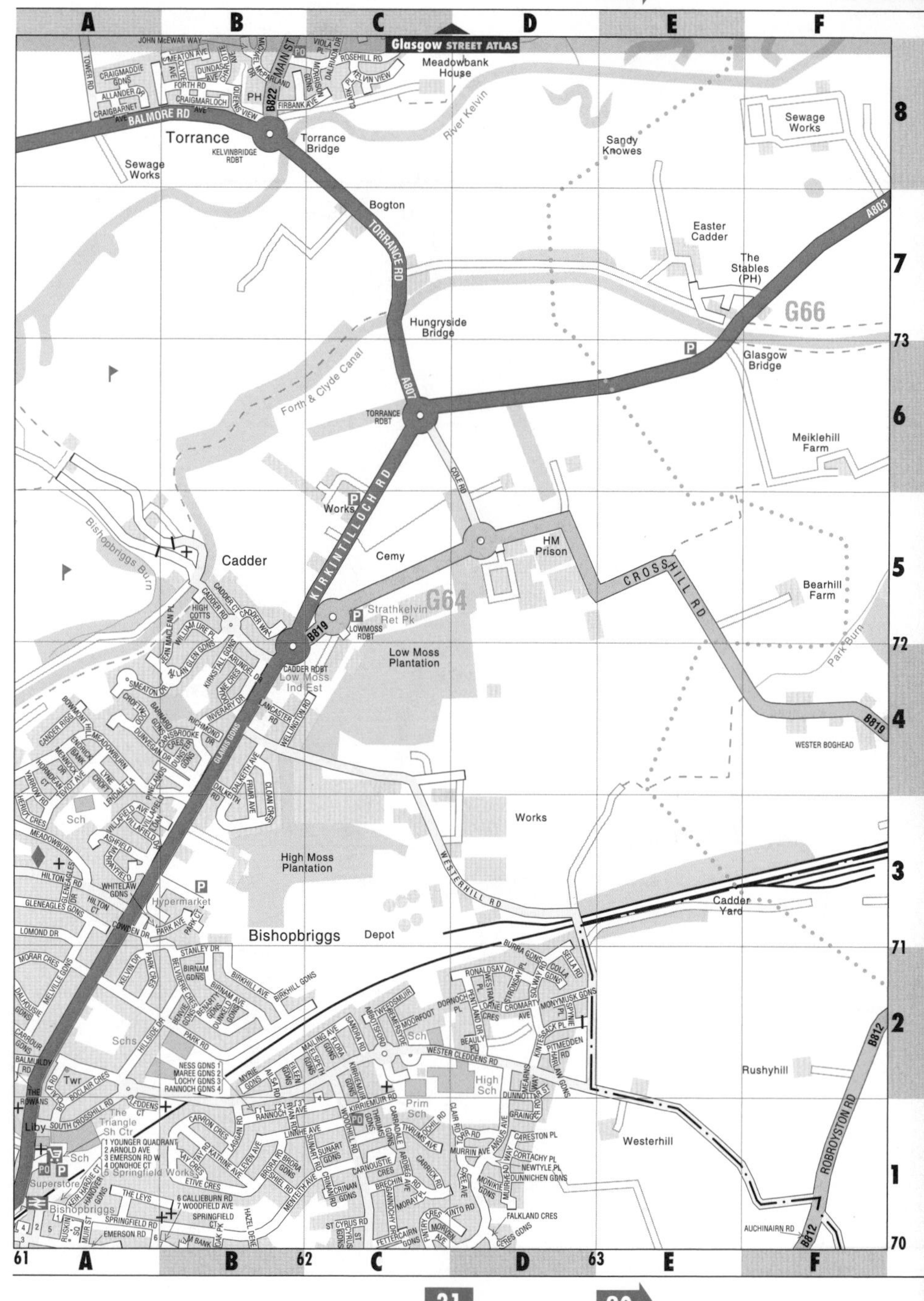

A
B
C
D
E
F
Glasgow STREET ATLAS
JOHN McEWAN WAY
TOWER RD
CRAIGMADDIE GDNS
ALLANDER DR
CRAIGBARNET AVE
MEATON AVE
CLYDE AVE
DUNDAS AVE
CHARLOTTE AV
FORTH RD
CRAIGMARLOCH AVE
QUEENS VIEW
MICHAEL McPARLAND DR
MAIN ST
B822
PO
PH
VIOLA PL
DALRIADA DR
MORRISON GDNS
ROSEHILL RD
KELVIN VIEW
PARK PL
FIRBANK AVE
Meadowbank House
BALMORE RD
Torrance
KELVINBRIDGE RDBT
Torrance Bridge
River Kelvin
Sewage Works
Sandy Knowes
Sewage Works
8
Bogton
TORRANCE RD
Easter Cadder
The Stables (PH)
A803
7
G66
Hungryside Bridge
73
Glasgow Bridge
Forth & Clyde Canal
A807
TORRANCE RDBT
6
Meiklehill Farm
COLE RD
Works
KIRKINTILLOCH RD
Cemy
HM Prison
CROSSHILL RD
Cadder
Bishopbriggs Burn
5
Bearhill Farm
G64
Strathkelvin Ret Pk
LOWMOSS RDBT
B819
CADDER CT
CADDER RD
HIGH COTTS
WILLIAM URE PL
JEAN MACLEAN PL
CADDER WAY
Park Burn
72
Low Moss Plantation
CADDER RDBT
Low Moss Ind Est
SMEATON DR
ALLAN GLEN GDNS
KIRKSTALL GDNS
ARUNDEL DR
INVERARY DR
LANCASTER RD
WELLINGTON RD
RICHMOND DR
CARISBROOKE CRES
DUNVEGAN DR
CROFTWOOD
BARNARD GDNS
GLAMIS GDNS
B819
4
WESTER BOGHEAD
CANDER RIGG
BOWMONT HILL
MEADOWBURN
ENDRICK BANK
MENNOCK DR
HORNDEAN CRES
TEVIOT AVE
YARROW RD
LYNE CROFT
LENDALE LA
PINELANDS
DALKEITH AVE
DALKEITH RD
FRIAR AVE
CLOAN CRES
Works
HERIOT CRES
Sch
VILLAFIELD AVE
VILLAFIELD DR
VILLAFIELD LOAN
ASHFIELD
MURRAYFIELD
MEADOWBURN
HILTON RD
GLENEAGLES DR
HILTON CT
WHITELAW GDNS
GLENEAGLES GDNS
High Moss Plantation
WESTERHILL RD
3
Hypermarket
Cadder Yard
COWDEN DR
PARK AVE
PARK CT
LOMOND DR
Bishopbriggs
Depot
71
MORAR CRES
STANLEY DR
KELVIN DR
PARK CRES
BELVIDERE CRES
BIRNAM GDNS
BIRKHILL AVE
BIRKHILL GDNS
BIRNAM AVE
BURRA GDNS
SELLA RD
COLL GDNS
RONALDSAY DR
STRONSAY PL
WESTRAY PL
SOLWAY RD
MELVILLE GDNS
DALHOUSIE GDNS
BENVIE GDNS
BENARTY GDNS
DUNKELD GDNS
TWEEDSMUIR
PENTLAND DR
LORNE CRES
CROMARTY AVE
MONYMUSK GDNS
SPYNIE PL
KINTESSACK PL
DORNOCH PL
MOORFOOT
ABBOTSFORD
BEMERSYDE
MAILING AVE
SANDRA RD
2
CARROUR GDNS
Schs
HILLSIDE DR
PARK RD
FLORA GDNS
ELSPETH GDNS
STUART
Sch
BEAULY PL
PITMEDDEN RD
B812
BALMUILDY RD
NESS GDNS 1
MAREE GDNS 2
LOCHY GDNS 3
RANNOCH GDNS 4
MYRIE GDNS
AILSA RD
EILEEN GDNS
WESTER CLEDDENS RD
HARLAW GDNS
Rushyhill
THE ROWANS
BOCLAIR CRES
Twr
KIRRIEMUIR GDNS
KIRRIEMUIR RD
High Sch
MEARNS WAY
DUNNOTTAR ST
CLEDDENS CT
Prim Sch
RANNOCH ST
WOODHILL RD
GRAINGER RD
SOUTH CROSSHILL RD
The Triangle Sh Ctr
CARRON CRES
LAGGAN RD
LINNHE AVE
THRUMS GDNS
THRUMS AVE
CARRADALE GDNS
OCHIL RD
TORR RD
CLAIR RD
ANGUS AVE
CARESTON PL
Liby
1 YOUNGER QUADRANT
2 ARNOLD AVE
3 EMERSON RD W
4 DONOHOE CT
5 Springfield Works
KATRINE AVE
LEVEN AVE
TAY CRES
SUNART GDNS
SUNART RD
MURRIN AVE
CORTACHY PL
NEWTYLE PL
DUNNICHEN GDNS
Westerhill
Sch
Superstore
ETIVE CRES
BRORA RD
BRORA GDNS
SHIEL RD
MENTEITH AVE
CRINAN GDNS
CRINAN RD
CARNOUSTIE CRES
ARDEG RD
CARRICK RD
CREE AVE
MONIKIE GDNS
MUIRHEAD WAY
1
Bishopbriggs
KEIR HARDIE CT
HANOVER GDNS
THE LEYS
6 CALLIEBURN RD
7 WOODFIELD AVE
BRECHIN RD
GLENOGIL RD
MORAY PL
FINTRY CRES
KINTO RD
FALKLAND CRES
ROBROYSTON RD
SPRINGFIELD RD
SPRINGFIELD CT
HAZEL DENE
OAK PK
ST CYRUS RD
ST CYRUS GDNS
FETTERCAIRN AVE
MORVEN AVE
CRES GDNS
AUCHINAIRN RD
B812
RUSKIN SQ
MUIR ST
EMERSON RD
ELM BANK
70
61
62
63

31

20

19

C8
1 YORK PL
2 The Regent Ctr

D8
1 GLENBURN CT
2 STRATHALLAN GDNS
3 BROOMFIELD WLK
4 BELMONT CT

19
32

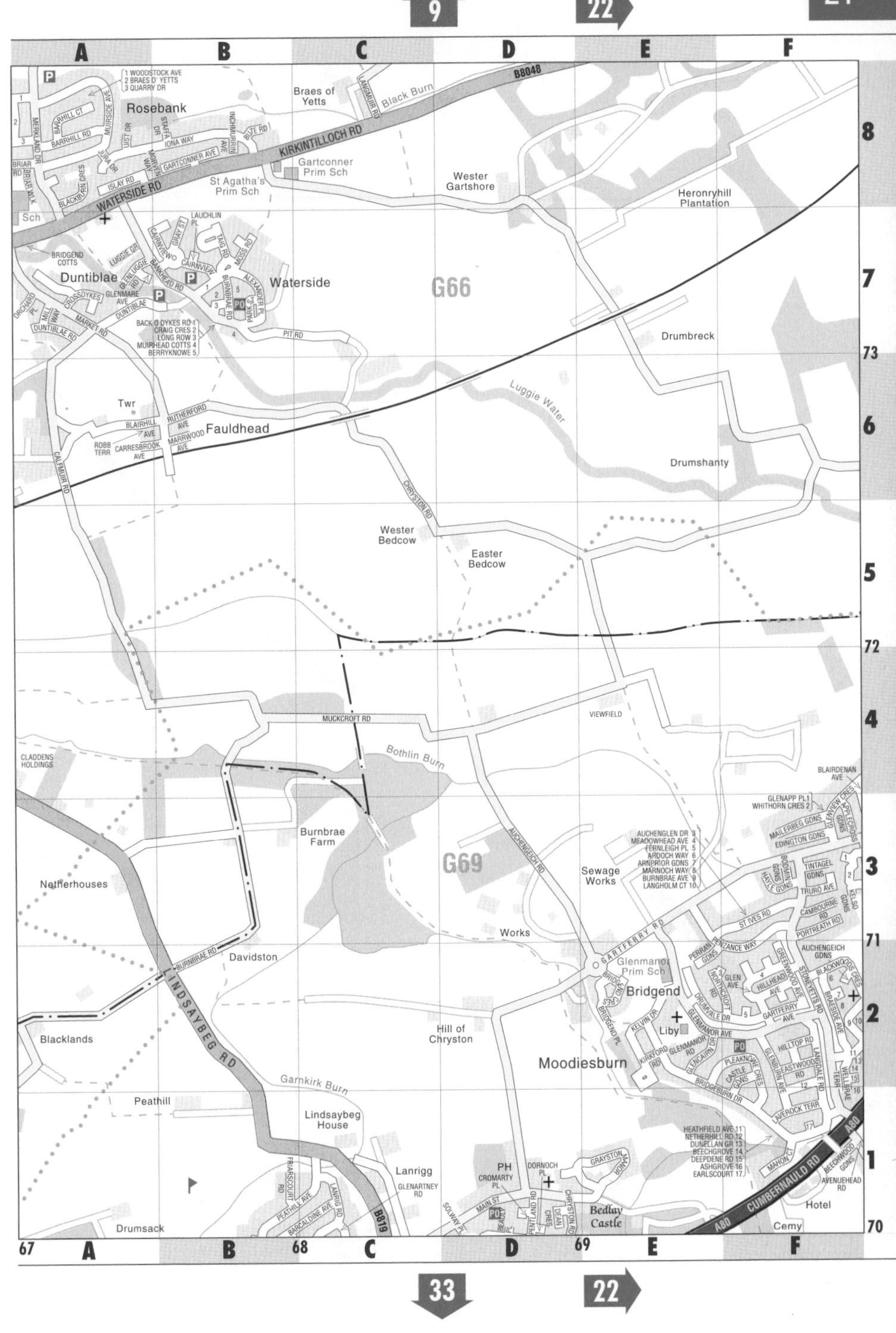
9
22
A B C D E F
8
7
73
6
5
72
4
3
71
2
1
70
67 68 69
33
22
1 WOODSTOCK AVE
2 BRAES O' YETTS
3 QUARRY DR
Rosebank
Braes of Yetts
Black Burn
B8048
KIRKINTILLOCH RD
WATERSIDE RD
Gartconner Prim Sch
St Agatha's Prim Sch
Wester Gartshore
Heronryhill Plantation
Duntiblae
Waterside
G66
BACK O DYKES RD 1
CRAIG CRES 2
LONG ROW 3
MUIRHEAD COTTS 4
BERRYKNOWE 5
Drumbreck
Luggie Water
Twr
Fauldhead
Drumshanty
Wester Bedcow
Easter Bedcow
MUCKCROFT RD
VIEWFIELD
Bothlin Burn
CLADDENS HOLDINGS
Burnbrae Farm
G69
AUCHENGLEN DR 3
MEADOWHEAD AVE 4
FERNLEIGH PL 5
ARDOCH WAY 6
ARNPRIOR GDNS 7
MARNOCH WAY 8
BURNBRAE AVE 9
LANGHOLM CT 10
Sewage Works
Netherhouses
Works
Davidston
Glenmanor Prim Sch
Bridgend
Moodiesburn
Hill of Chryston
Blacklands
LINDSAYBEG RD
Garnkirk Burn
Peathill
Lindsaybeg House
Lanrigg
HEATHFIELD AVE 11
NETHERHILL RD 12
DUNELLAN GR 13
BEECHGROVE 14
DEEPDENE RD 15
ASHGROVE 16
EARLSCOURT 17
CUMBERNAULD RD
A80
Hotel
Cemy
Drumsack
Bedlay Castle
PH
B819

21
10

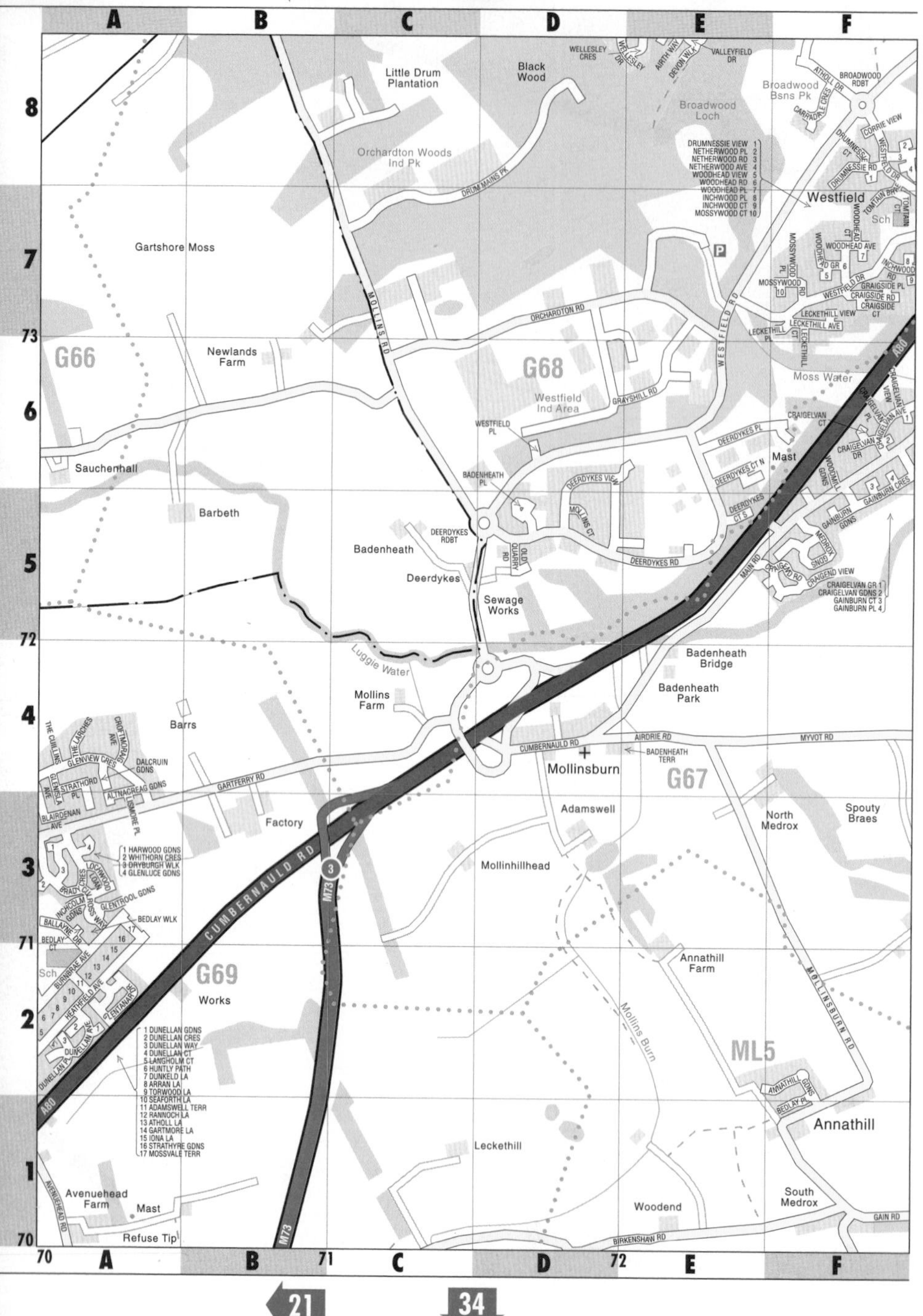
Little Drum Plantation
Black Wood
Broadwood Bsns Pk
Broadwood Loch
Orchardton Woods Ind Pk
Westfield
Gartshore Moss
G66
Newlands Farm
G68
Westfield Ind Area
Moss Water
Sauchenhall
Barbeth
Badenheath
Deerdykes
Sewage Works
Luggie Water
Mollins Farm
Badenheath Bridge
Badenheath Park
Barrs
Mollinsburn
G67
Adamswell
Factory
North Medrox
Spouty Braes
Mollinhillhead
CUMBERNAULD RD
Annathill Farm
G69
Works
Mollins Burn
ML5
Annathill
Leckethill
South Medrox
Avenuehead Farm
Mast
Refuse Tip
Woodend
BIRKENSHAW RD
GAIN RD
AIRDRIE RD
MYVOT RD
GARTFERRY RD
MOLLINS RD
WESTFIELD RD
ORCHARDTON RD
DRUM MAINS PK
DEERDYKES RD
MOLLINSBURN RD
DRUMNESSIE VIEW 1
NETHERWOOD PL 2
NETHERWOOD RD 3
NETHERWOOD AVE 4
WOODHEAD VIEW 5
WOODHEAD RD 6
WOODHEAD PL 7
INCHWOOD PL 8
INCHWOOD CT 9
MOSSYWOOD CT 10
CRAIGELVAN GR 1
CRAIGELVAN GDNS 2
GAINBURN CT 3
GAINBURN PL 4
1 HARWOOD GDNS
2 WHITHORN CRES
3 DRYBURGH WLK
4 GLENLUCE GDNS
1 DUNELLAN GDNS
2 DUNELLAN CRES
3 DUNELLAN WAY
4 DUNELLAN CT
5 LANGHOLM CT
6 HUNTLY PATH
7 DUNKELD LA
8 ARRAN LA
9 TORWOOD LA
10 SEAFORTH LA
11 ADAMSWELL TERR
12 RANNOCH LA
13 ATHOLL LA
14 GARTMORE LA
15 IONA LA
16 STRATHYRE GDNS
17 MOSSVALE TERR
A B C D E F
8 7 6 5 4 3 2 1
73 72 71 70

21
34

11
24

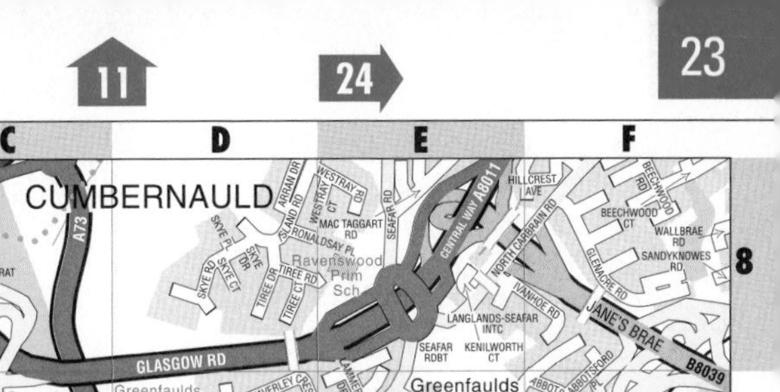
A
B
C
D
E
F
CUMBERNAULD
Low Wood
St Maurices High Sch
G68
A80
A73
A8011
B802
B8039
WESTFIELD RD
NORTH RD
GLASGOW RD
CONDORRAT INTC
1 NETHERWOOD RD
2 NETHERWOOD WAY
3 NETHERWOOD AVE
NETHERWOOD CT
2 NETHERWOOD GR
St Francis of Assisi Prim Sch
INCHWOOD RD
INCHWOOD CT
WESTFIELD DR
Liby
Condorrat
Condorrat Prim Sch
MOREE DR
MORAR CT
MORAR DR
BAIRD CRES
DALSHANNON WAY
TEMPLE COTTS
St Helen's Prim Sch
MAIN RD
KIRK PL
KIRKVIEW
LUGGIEVIEW
ROSE ST
PRIMROSE PL
JASMINE PL
RANNOCH DR
RANNOCH CT
CONDORRAT RING RD
LOMOND DR
LOMOND CRES
LOMOND VIEW
LOMOND GR
LOMOND CT
ACHRAY RD
ETIVE DR
ETIVE CRES
ETIVE PL
THORNIECROFT DR
THORNIECROFT PL
DRUMPELLIER AVE
DRUMPELLIER PL
DRUMPELLIER GDNS
AVONHEAD RD
AVONHEAD GDNS
AVONHEAD PL
1 AVONHEAD AVE
2 DRUMPELLIER GR
Sch
Greenfaulds High Sch
Nursery
AUCHENKILNS HOLDINGS
AUCHENKILNS RD
CHAPELTON RD
North Myvot
Luggie Water
MYVOT RD
MYVOT AVE
AIRDRIE RD
BARBETH RD
BARBETH GDNS
BARBETH PL
BARBETH WAY
LAIGHTOUN DR
LAIGHTOUN CT
LAIGHTOUN GDNS
SUMMERFIELD RD
GAINBURN VIEW
Dalshannon
SKYE RD
SKYE PL
SKYE CT
ARRAN DR
WESTRAY RD
WESTRAY CT
ISLAND RD
MAC TAGGART RD
RONALDSAY PL
TIREE DR
TIREE RD
TIREE CT
Ravenswood Prim Sch
SEAFAR RD
CENTRAL WAY
HILLCREST AVE
NORTH CARBRAIN RD
BEECHWOOD RD
BEECHWOOD CT
WALLBRAE RD
SANDYKNOWES RD
GLENACRE RD
IVANHOE RD
LANGLANDS-SEAFAR INTC
SEAFAR RDBT
KENILWORTH CT
JANE'S BRAE
JANE'S BRAE INTC
Greenfaulds
WAVERLEY CRES
LAMMERMOOR DR
MARMION PL
MARMION RD
ATHELSTANE DR
ABBOTSFORD RD
ABBOTSFORD PL
ABBOTSFORD CT
HALIDON AVE
Woodlands Prim Sch
MELROSE RD
LOCHINVAR RD
ASHIESTIEL PL
ASHIESTIEL RD
ASHIESTIEL CT
SCOTT CRES
SCOTT DR
FAIRFORD DR
GREENFAULDS RD
LOCKSLEY PL
LOCKSLEY AVE
LOCKSLEY RD
LOCKSLEY CRES
LENZIEMILL RD
TANNOCH DR
TANNOCH PL
BLAIRLINN RD
MID RD
Blairlinn Ind Est
BROOMLEE RD
GREENS RD
LIMEKILNS RD
BELSTANE RD
Garngibboch House
Wester Blairlinn
G67
North Myvot
MILLCROFT RD
Milncroft
SPAIRDRUM RD
South Myvot
WESTER MYVOT RD
Craigend Nursery
Wester Myvot
North Bellstane Plantation
SUMMERHILL & GARNGIBBOCK RD
Hallbrae
Gain Burn
Loanhead
CONDORRAT RD
Summerhill
Summerhill Strips
Shank Burn
Shank Bridge
Bellstane
BLACKBOG RD
Summerfield
Mossywood
GAIN & SHANKBURN RD
CULLOCHRIG RD
The Grain
South Bellstane Plantation
ML5
Gain Farm
YETTS HOLE RD
Cleddans
Douglas Glen
Douglas Plantation
ML6
GAIN RD
8
7
73
6
5
72
4
3
71
2
1
70
74
75

35
24

23 12

A B C D E F
8 7 73 6 5 72 4 3 71 2 1 70
76 77 78
CUMBERNAULD
Lenziemill
Cumbernauld
Glencryan Plantation
Glencryan Burn
GLENCRYAN RD
B8054
LENZIEMILL RD
KILBOWIE RD
BROOMLANDS RD
GREENFAULDS CRES
GREENFAULDS RD
SOUTH CARBRAIN RD
WALLBRAE RD
SANDYKNOWES RD
KELVIN RD
Ind Est
TELFORD PL
TELFORD RD
JANE'S BRAE
Greenside
West Waterhead
East Waterhead
CH
G67
Sandyknowes
Palacerigg Country Park
Visitor Ctr
Palacerigg Cottage
Tannoch
BROOMLEE RD
BLAIRLINN RD
Blairlinn Ind Est
TOWER RD
GREENS RD
BELSTANE RD
STIRLING RD
BLAIRLINN VIEW
Luggiebank
Luggie Water
Acrecroft Farm
Easter Blairlinn Cottages
Glenhove
Craigelvan
Fedderland
Wester Glentore
A73
Greens
Coathill
MILLCROFT RD
HULKS RD
SPAIRDRUM RD
Muirhead
Muirhead Glen
Boglea
Loanhead
Auldshields Bridge
Staylee Glen
Staylee
BRACKENKNOWE RD
ML6
BLACKBOG RD
Blacktongue
Whinrigg Farm
Cameron Burn
B8039
CAMERON RD
Cameron Glen
Cameron Farm
Greengairs Prim Sch
BLACKTONGUE FARM RD
RANKIN CRES
HILLVIEW
B803
AUREL GR
ANNANDALE
COALBURN ST
PO
GREENGAIRS RD
Greengairs
DRUMGRAY GDNS
OLD BIGGAR RD
Cullochrig Plantation
Drumgray Farm
MILL RD
DRUMGRAY LA
Berryhill Cottage
Riggend
BRACKENHIRST RD
MEIKLE DRUMGRAY RD
HILLRIGG

23 36

13
26

A
B
C
D
E
F
8
7
73
6
5
72
4
3
71
2
1
70
79
80
81
Palacerigg Country Park
Fannyside Lochs
Fannyside Mill
Garbethill Burn
Jawhills
River Avon
Fannyside Lodge
Thieves Hill
G67
Herd's Hill
West Fannyside
FK1
Scar Hill
Toddle Knowe
Bog Bridge
Luggie Water
Avon Water
Black Hill
Blackhill
Torbrex
Bogside
B803
HULKS RD
Netherton of Glentore
Easter Glentore
Shielhill Burn
Langdales
DERVAIG GDNS
LUCKENHILL DR
AVON AVE
SCAMADALE RD
HM Remand Inst
Easter Glentore
GREENGAIRS RD
ML6
Upperton Farm
THE CRESCENT
Meadowfield
PH
Avalon
Greendykeside
BRIDGE ST

37
26

25
14

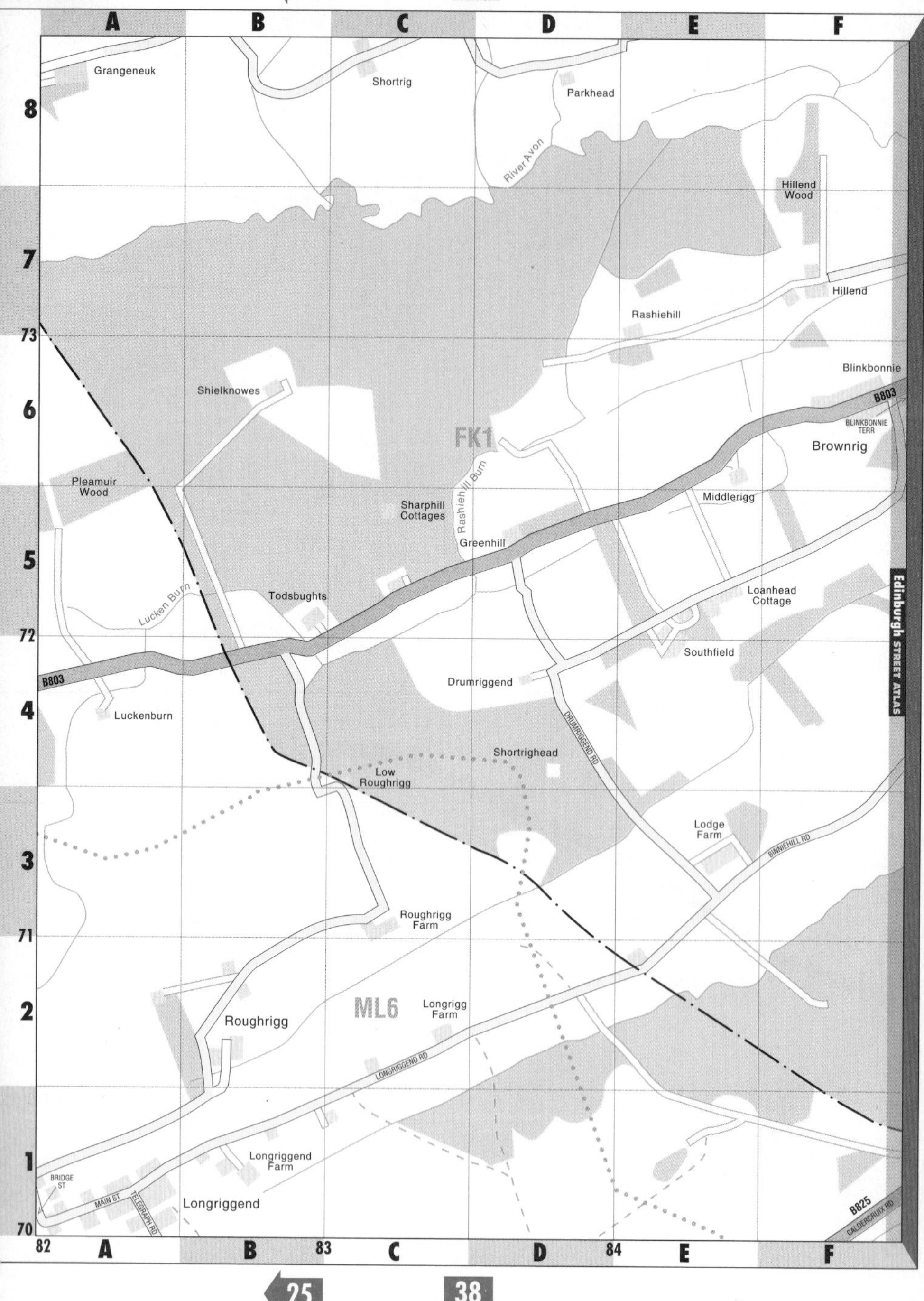
A
B
C
D
E
F
Grangeneuk
Shortrig
Parkhead
River Avon
Hillend Wood
Hillend
Rashiehill
Blinkbonnie
B803
BLINKBONNIE TERR
Brownrig
Shielknowes
FK1
Rashiehill Burn
Pleamuir Wood
Sharphill Cottages
Middlerigg
Greenhill
Lucken Burn
Todsbughts
Loanhead Cottage
Southfield
Drumriggend
Luckenburn
DRUMRIGGEND RD
Shortrighead
Low Roughrigg
Lodge Farm
BINNIEHILL RD
Roughrigg Farm
ML6
Longrigg Farm
Roughrigg
LONGRIGGEND RD
Longriggend Farm
BRIDGE ST
MAIN ST
TELEGRAPH RD
Longriggend
B825
CALDERCRUIX RD
8
7
73
6
5
72
4
3
71
2
1
70
82
83
84
Edinburgh STREET ATLAS

25
38

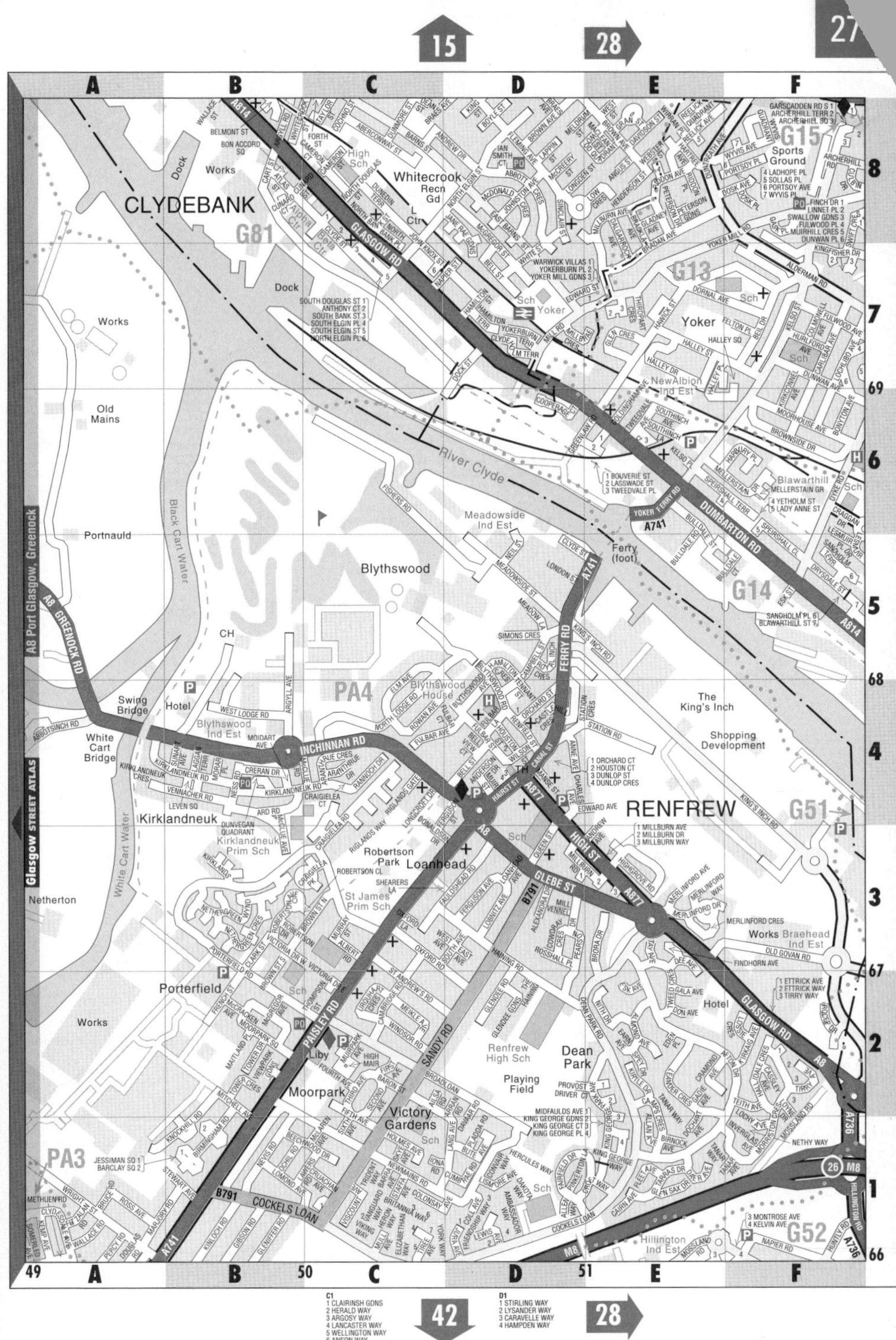

C1
1 CLAIRINSH GDNS
2 HERALD WAY
3 ARGOSY WAY
4 LANCASTER WAY
5 WELLINGTON WAY
6 ANSON WAY
7 HALIFAX WAY

D1
1 STIRLING WAY
2 LYSANDER WAY
3 CARAVELLE WAY
4 HAMPDEN WAY

42
28

27
16

D6
1 DUTHIE PARK PL
2 DUTHIE PARK GDNS
3 PRIORWOOD GDNS
4 BRANKLYN CL
5 BRANKLYN PL
6 BRANKLYN CT
7 PRIORWOOD CT

E5
1 CHAMBERLAIN LA
2 AUSTEN LA
3 BORDEN LA
4 SELBORNE PLACE LA
5 SELBORNE PL
6 WOODEND LA
7 MILNER LA
8 SOUTHBRAE LA

F5
1 KING EDWARD LA
2 FERN COTTS
3 ALBANY COTTS
4 AIGAS COTTS

F7
1 TEMPLE LOCKS CT
2 TEMPLE LOCKS PL
3 WALDO ST
4 STRATHCONA DR

F8
1 NETHERTON FARM LA
2 OLD FARM RD

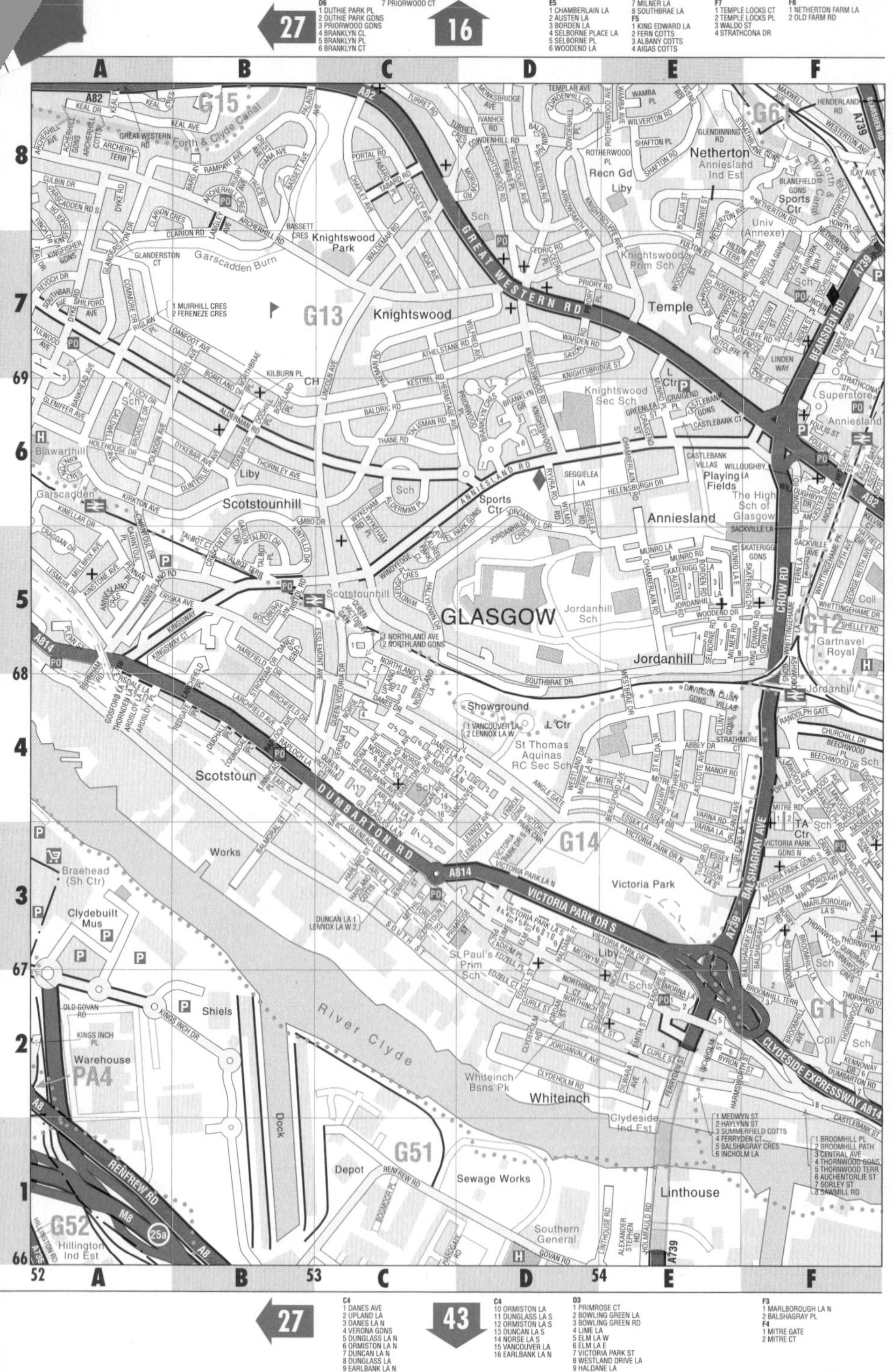

27
43

C4
1 DANES AVE
2 UPLAND LA
3 DANES LA N
4 VERONA GDNS
5 DUNGLASS LA N
6 ORMISTON LA N
7 DUNCAN LA N
8 DUNGLASS LA
9 EARLBANK LA N

C4
10 ORMISTON LA
11 DUNGLASS LA S
12 ORMISTON LA S
13 DUNCAN LA S
14 NORSE LA S
15 VANCOUVER LA
16 EARLBANK LA N

D3
1 PRIMROSE CT
2 BOWLING GREEN LA
3 BOWLING GREEN RD
4 LIME LA
5 ELM LA W
6 ELM LA E
7 VICTORIA PARK ST
8 WESTLAND DRIVE LA
9 HALDANE LA

F3
1 MARLBOROUGH LA N
2 BALSHAGRAY PL

F4
1 MITRE GATE
2 MITRE CT

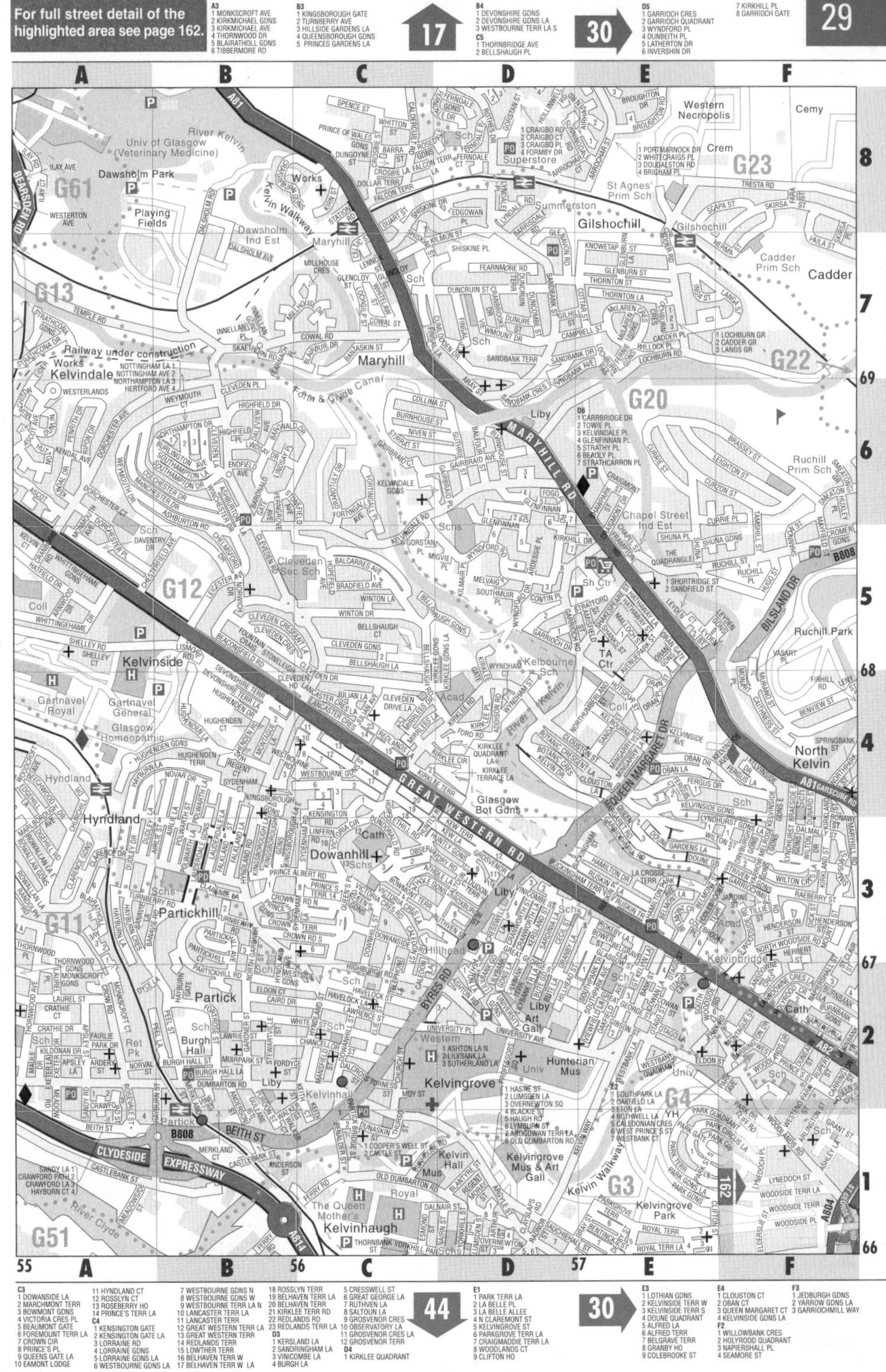

29
For full street detail of the highlighted area see page 162.
A3
1 MONKSCROFT AVE
2 KIRKMICHAEL GDNS
3 KIRKMICHAEL AVE
4 THORNWOOD DR
5 BLAIRATHOLL GDNS
6 TIBBERMORE RD
B3
1 KINGSBOROUGH GATE
2 TURNBERRY AVE
3 HILLSIDE GARDENS LA
4 QUEENSBOROUGH GDNS
5 PRINCES GARDENS LA
17
B4
1 DEVONSHIRE GDNS
2 DEVONSHIRE GDNS LA
3 WESTBOURNE TERR LA S
C5
1 THORNBRIDGE AVE
2 BELLSHAUGH PL
30
D5
1 GARRIOCH CRES
2 GARRIOCH QUADRANT
3 WYNDFORD PL
4 DUNBEITH PL
5 LATHERTON DR
6 INVERSHIN DR
7 KIRKHILL PL
8 GARRIOCH GATE
A B C D E F
8 7 69 6 5 68 4 3 67 2 1 66
55 A B 56 C D 57 E F
Western Necropolis
Cemy
Crem
G23
Univ of Glasgow (Veterinary Medicine)
River Kelvin
Dawsholm Park
Playing Fields
Dawsholm Ind Est
Kelvin Walkway
Works
Maryhill
Superstore
Summerston
St Agnes' Prim Sch
Gilshochill
Cadder Prim Sch
Cadder
G61
G13
G22
G20
Railway under construction
Kelvindale
Forth & Clyde Canal
Ruchill Prim Sch
Chapel Street Ind Est
Cleveden Sec Sch
G12
Sh Ctr
Ruchill Park
Kelvinside
Gartnavel Royal
Gartnavel General
Glasgow Homeopathic
Kelbourne Sch
TA Ctr
North Kelvin
Hyndland
Glasgow Bot Gdns
Dowanhill
GREAT WESTERN RD
MARYHILL RD
QUEEN MARGARET DR
Partickhill
G11
Hillhead
Kelvinbridge
Partick
Burgh Hall
Ret Pk
Western
Kelvingrove
Hunterian Mus
Univ
G4
Kelvinhall
CLYDESIDE EXPRESSWAY
River Clyde
G51
Kelvin Hall
Kelvingrove Mus & Art Gall
Kelvin Walkway
G3
Kelvingrove Park
Royal
The Queen Mother's
Kelvinhaugh
162
C3
1 DOWANSIDE LA
2 MARCHMONT TERR
3 BOWMONT GDNS
4 VICTORIA CRES PL
5 BEAUMONT GATE
6 FOREMOUNT TERR LA
7 CROWN CIR
8 PRINCE'S PL
9 QUEENS GATE LA
10 EAMONT LODGE
11 HYNDLAND CT
12 ROSSLYN CT
13 ROSEBERRY HO
14 PRINCE'S TERR LA
C4
1 KENSINGTON GATE
2 KENSINGTON GATE LA
3 LORRAINE RD
4 LORRAINE GDNS
5 LORRAINE GDNS LA
6 WESTBOURNE GDNS LA
7 WESTBOURNE GDNS N
8 WESTBOURNE GDNS W
9 WESTBOURNE TERR LA N
10 LANCASTER TERR LA
11 LANCASTER TERR
12 GREAT WESTERN TERR LA
13 GREAT WESTERN TERR
14 REDLANDS TERR
15 LOWTHER TERR
16 BELHAVEN TERR W
17 BELHAVEN TERR W LA
18 ROSSLYN TERR
19 BELHAVEN TERR LA
20 BELHAVEN TERR
21 KIRKLEE TERR RD
22 REDLANDS RD
23 REDLANDS TERR LA
D3
1 KERSLAND LA
2 SANDRINGHAM LA
3 VINICOMBE LA
4 BURGH LA
5 CRESSWELL ST
6 GREAT GEORGE LA
7 RUTHVEN LA
8 SALTOUN LA
9 GROSVENOR CRES
10 OBSERVATORY LA
11 GROSVENOR CRES LA
12 GROSVENOR TERR
D4
1 KIRKLEE QUADRANT
44
E1
1 PARK TERR LA
2 LA BELLE PL
3 LA BELLE ALLEE
4 N CLAREMONT ST
5 KELVINGROVE ST
6 PARKGROVE TERR LA
7 CRAIGMADDIE TERR LA
8 WOODLANDS CT
9 CLIFTON HO
30
E3
1 LOTHIAN GDNS
2 KELVINSIDE TERR W
3 KELVINSIDE TERR S
4 DOUNE QUADRANT
5 ALFRED LA
6 ALFRED TERR
7 BELGRAVE TERR
8 GRANBY HO
9 COLEBROOKE ST
E4
1 CLOUSTON CT
2 OBAN CT
3 QUEEN MARGARET CT
4 KELVINSIDE GDNS LA
F2
1 WILLOWBANK CRES
2 HOLYROOD QUADRANT
3 NAPIERSHALL PL
4 SEAMORE ST
F3
1 JEDBURGH GDNS
2 YARROW GDNS LA
3 GARRIOCHMILL WAY

29
18

E7
1 COLSTON PL
2 EVERARD PL
3 BISHOPSGATE PL

F7
1 MILTON DR
2 NEWBOLD AVE
3 SOUTHVIEW CT
4 STRATHKELVIN AVE

F8
1 FORRESTER CT
2 MUIRPARK TERR
3 HUNTERSHILL RD
4 FULMAR CT
5 RAVENS CT
6 HILLCROFT TERR

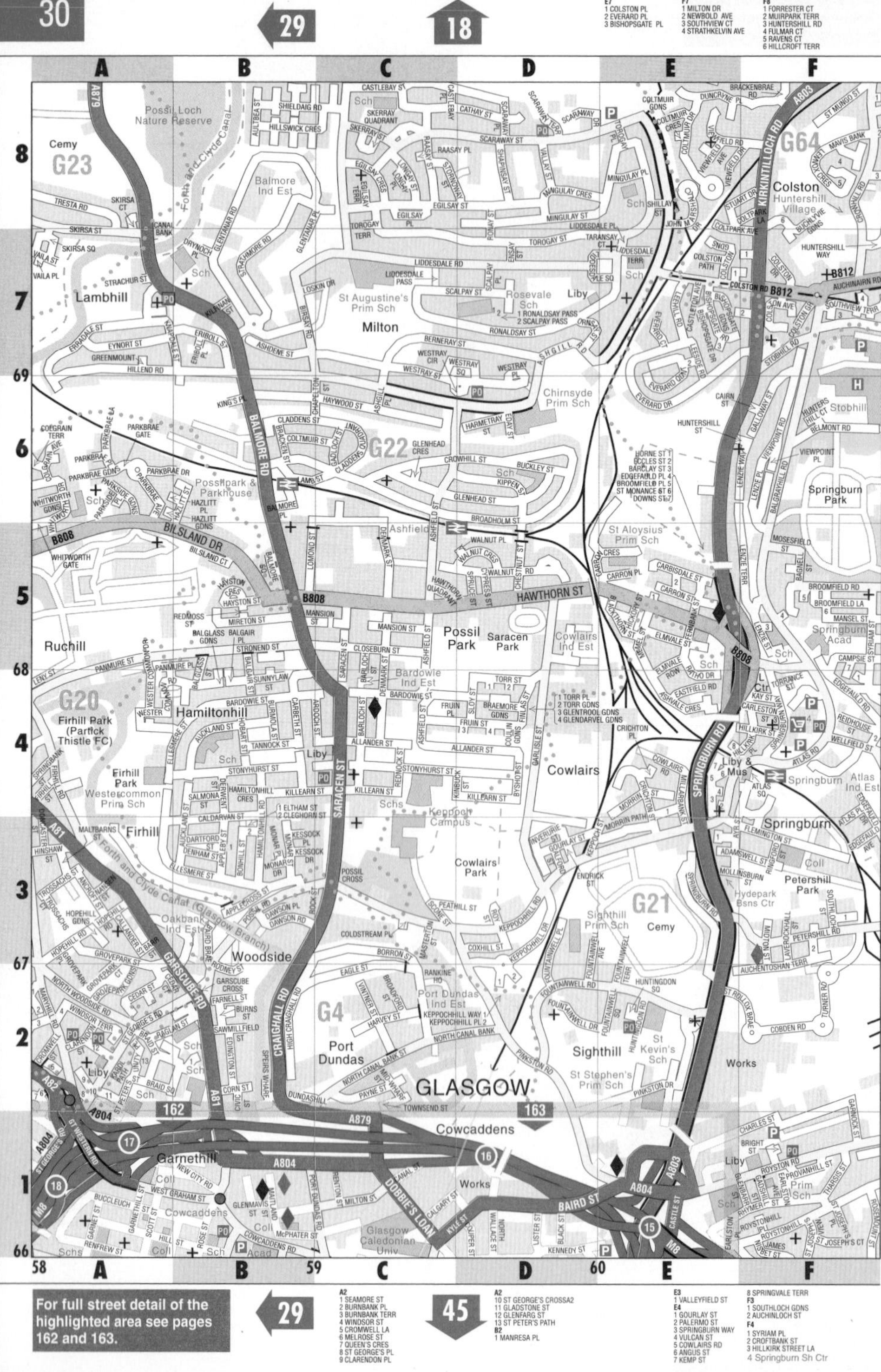

For full street detail of the highlighted area see pages 162 and 163.

29
45

A2
1 SEAMORE ST
2 BURNBANK PL
3 BURNBANK TERR
4 WINDSOR ST
5 CROMWELL LA
6 MELROSE ST
7 QUEEN'S CRES
8 ST GEORGE'S PL
9 CLARENDON PL

A2
10 ST GEORGE'S CROSSA2
11 GLADSTONE ST
12 GLENFARG ST
13 ST PETER'S PATH
B2
1 MANRESA PL

E3
1 VALLEYFIELD ST
E4
1 GOURLAY ST
2 PALERMO ST
3 SPRINGBURN WAY
4 VULCAN ST
5 COWLAIRS RD
6 ANGUS ST
7 KEMP ST

8 SPRINGVALE TERR
F3
1 SOUTHLOCH GDNS
2 AUCHINLOCH ST
F4
1 SYRIAM PL
2 CROFTBANK ST
3 HILLKIRK STREET LA
4 Springburn Sh Ctr

19
32

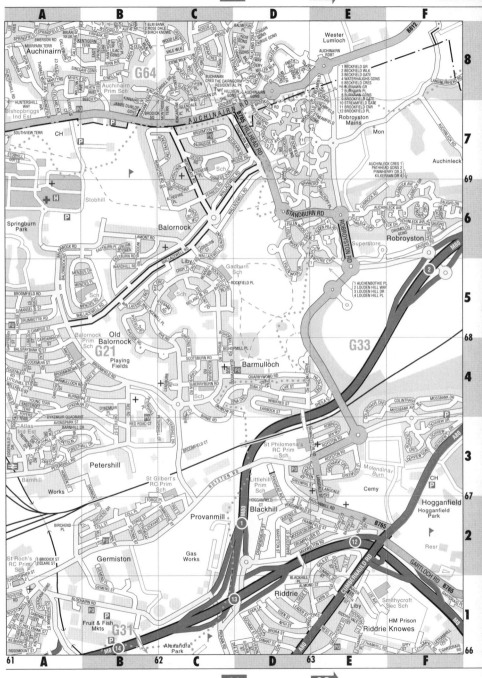

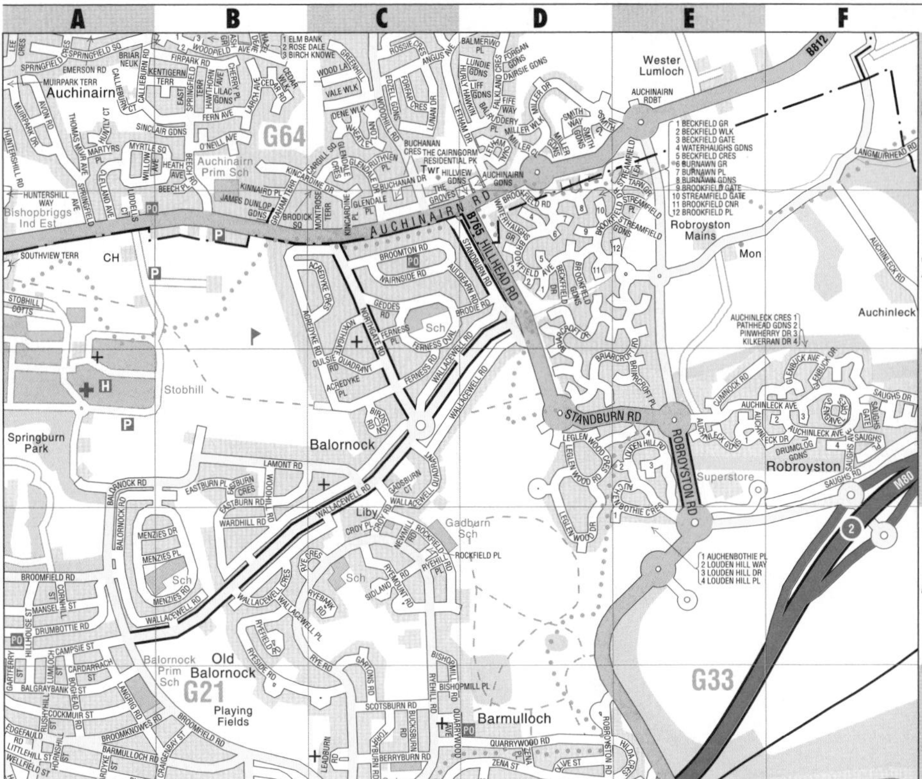
A B C D E F
8 7 6 5 4 3 2 1
69 68 67 66
61 62 63
Auchinairn
Wester Lumloch
G64
Auchinairn Prim Sch
Bishopbriggs Ind Est
AUCHINAIRN RD
B765 HILLHEAD RD
B812
Robroyston Mains
Mon
Auchinleck
CH
Stobhill
Springburn Park
Balornock
STANDBURN RD
ROBROYSTON RD
Robroyston
Superstore
M80
Liby
Gadburn Sch
Sch
Old Balornock
Balornock Prim Sch
G21
Playing Fields
G33
Barmulloch
Atlas Ind Est
Petershill
St Philomena's RC Prim Sch
Barnhill
Works
St Gilbert's RC Prim Sch
ROYSTON RD
Littlehill Prim Sch
Molendinar Burn
Cemy
Hogganfield
Hogganfield Park
Provanmill
Blackhill
B765
Resr
Germiston
Gas Works
GARTLOCH RD
St Roch's RC Prim Sch
Riddrie
CUMBERNAULD RD
Smithycroft Sec Sch
HM Prison
Riddrie Knowes
Fruit & Fish Mkts
G31
M8
A80
Alexandra Park

46
32

31
20

G64
G66
G69
G33
G34
Langmuirhead Farm
Cardyke Farm
Auchengree Farm
Arronhill Plantation
Hornshill
Glen Plantation
Gateside
Hotel
Recn Gd
Saughs
Whitehill Farm
Stepps
Buchanan Bsns Pk
Stepps Prim Sch
St Joseph's Prim Sch
Caravan Site
Craigendmuir
Frankfield Loch
Millerston
Cardowan Moss
Hogganfield Loch
Bird Sanctuary
Hogganfield Park
Ashcraig Sch
Sunnyside Prim Sch
Craigend
Blackfaulds Farm
Garthamlock
Croftcroighn Sch
Avenue End Prim Sch Annexe
St Rose of Lima Prim Sch
Wr Twr
Ruchazie
GLASGOW
Glasgow Fort
Provan Hall
Sp Ctr
CUMBERNAULD RD
GARTLOCH RD
STEPPS RD
M80
M8
A80
B765
B806

31
47

21
34

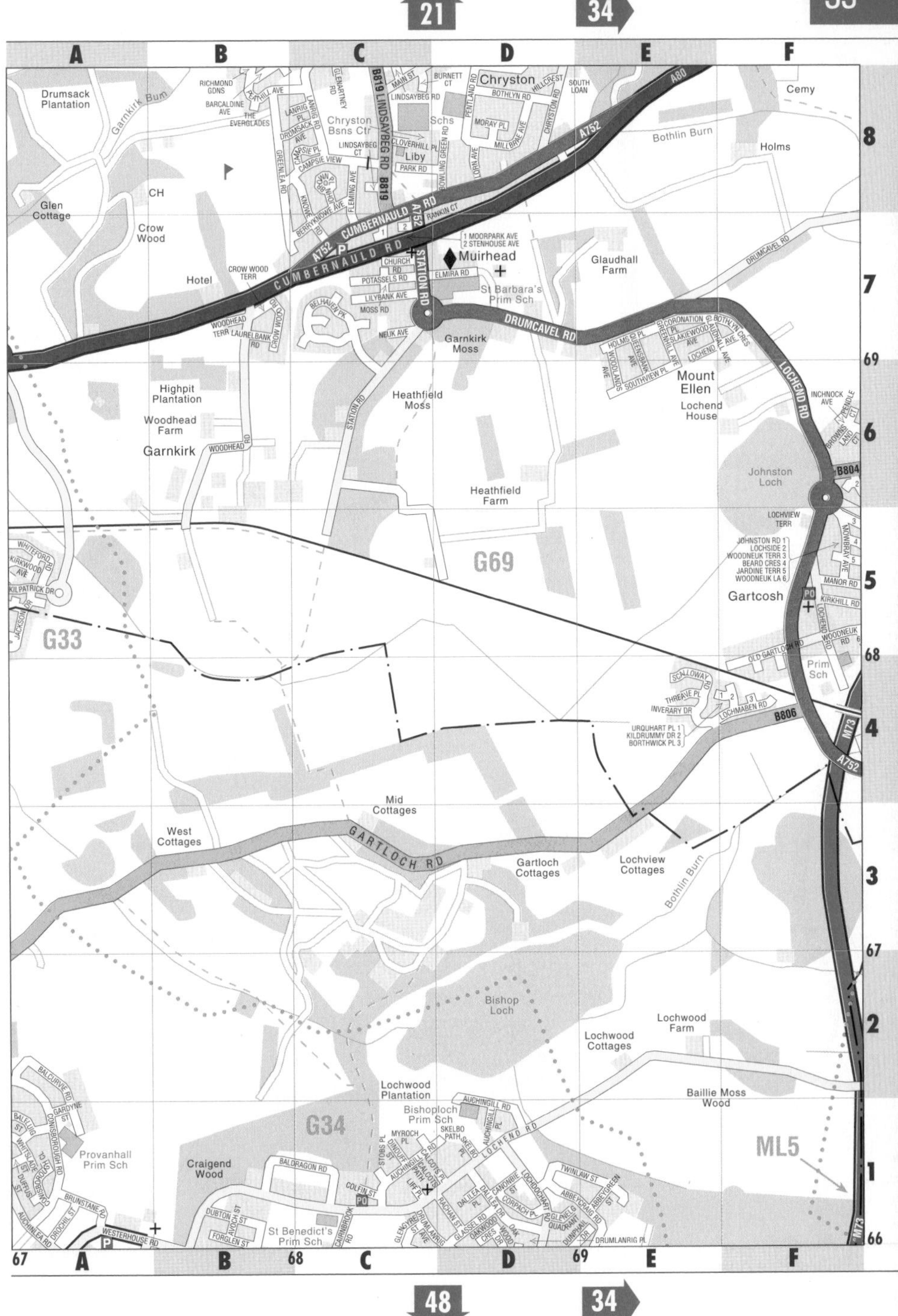
A
B
C
D
E
F
Drumsack Plantation
Garnkirk Burn
Chryston
Chryston Bsns Ctr
Schs
Liby
Cemy
Bothlin Burn
Holms
A80
A752
B819
CUMBERNAULD RD
Glen Cottage
CH
Crow Wood
Hotel
Muirhead
St Barbara's Prim Sch
Glaudhall Farm
DRUMCAVEL RD
STATION RD
Garnkirk Moss
Heathfield Moss
Highpit Plantation
Woodhead Farm
Garnkirk
Mount Ellen
Lochend House
LOCHEND RD
Johnston Loch
B804
Heathfield Farm
G69
G33
Gartcosh
Prim Sch
B806
M73
Mid Cottages
West Cottages
GARTLOCH RD
Gartloch Cottages
Lochview Cottages
Bishop Loch
Lochwood Farm
Lochwood Cottages
Lochwood Plantation
Baillie Moss Wood
Bishoploch Prim Sch
G34
ML5
Provanhall Prim Sch
Craigend Wood
St Benedict's Prim Sch
WESTERHOUSE RD
1
2
3
4
5
6
7
8
66
67
68
69

48
34

33
22

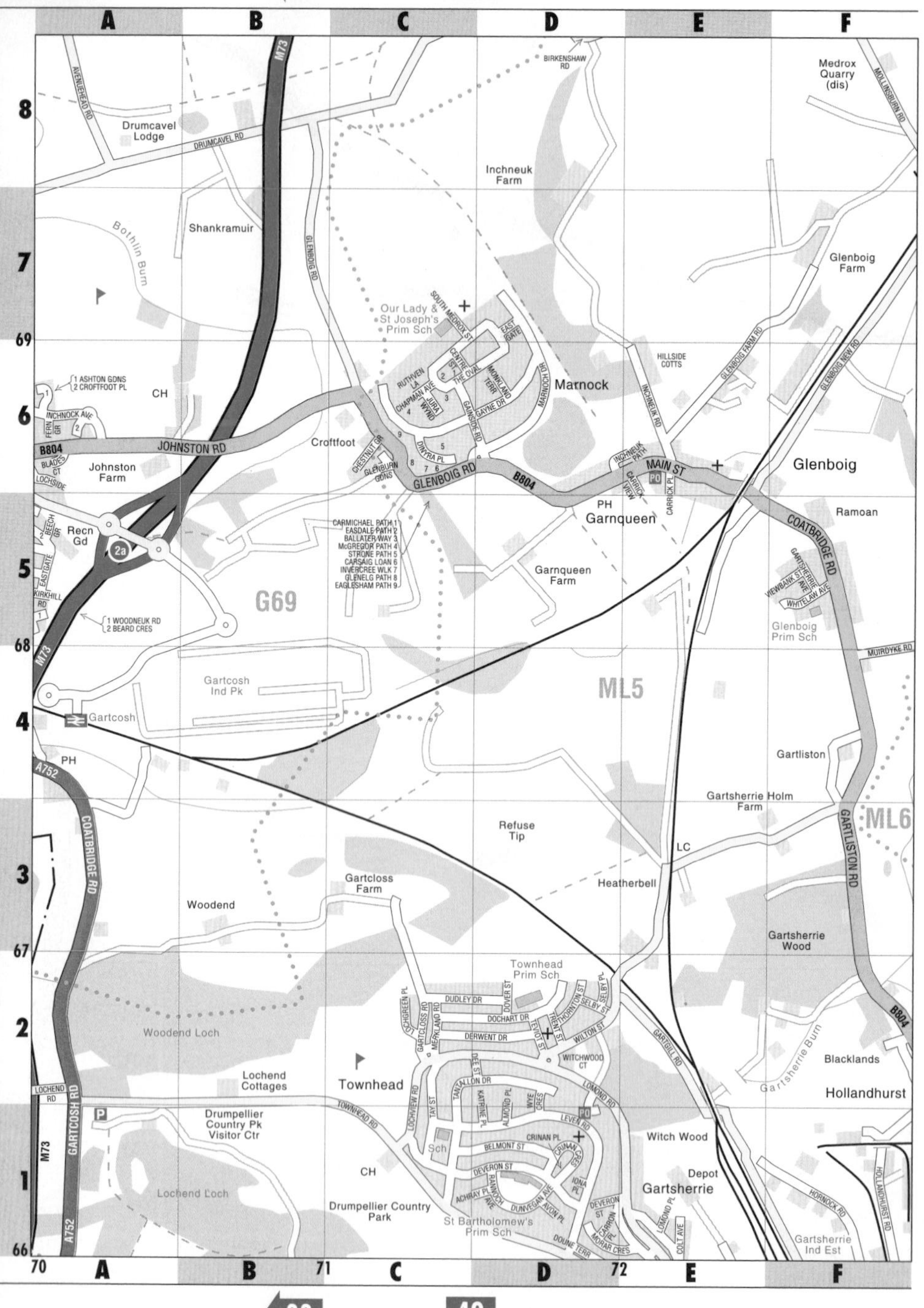
Medrox Quarry (dis)
Drumcavel Lodge
DRUMCAVEL RD
Inchneuk Farm
Shankramuir
Bothlin Burn
Glenboig Farm
Our Lady & St Joseph's Prim Sch
Marnock
HILLSIDE COTTS
Croftfoot
JOHNSTON RD
Johnston Farm
GLENBOIG RD
MAIN ST
Glenboig
Garnqueen
Ramoan
COATBRIDGE RD
Recn Gd
Garnqueen Farm
G69
1 ASHTON GDNS
2 CROFTFOOT PL
CARMICHAEL PATH 1
EASDALE PATH 2
BALLATER WAY 3
McGREGOR PATH 4
STRONE PATH 5
CARSAIG LOAN 6
INVERCREE WLK 7
GLENELG PATH 8
EAGLESHAM PATH 9
1 WOODNEUK RD
2 BEARD CRES
Glenboig Prim Sch
MUIRDYKE RD
Gartcosh Ind Pk
ML5
Gartcosh
Gartliston
Gartsherrie Holm Farm
Refuse Tip
ML6
GARTLISTON RD
LC
Heatherbell
Gartcloss Farm
Woodend
Gartsherrie Wood
Townhead Prim Sch
Woodend Loch
Lochend Cottages
Townhead
Blacklands
Hollandhurst
Drumpellier Country Pk Visitor Ctr
Witch Wood
Depot
Gartsherrie
Lochend Loch
Drumpellier Country Park
St Bartholomew's Prim Sch
Gartsherrie Ind Est
M73
A752
GARTCOSH RD
B804

33
49

23
36

A
B
C
D
E
F
G67
Gaindykehead
East Lodge Wood
Foot o' Loan Wood
East Gartmillan
Shank Burn
Callochrig
CULLOCHRIG RD
LC
GLENBOIG NEW RD
Greenfoot
West Gartmillan
Glenmill Wood
Drumbowie Farm
MOLLINSBURN RD
Ardaryth
BRACKENHIRST RD
ML5
CONDORRAT RD
MOLLINSBURN RD
Haggmuir Farm
Refuse Tip
BRACKENHIRST GDNS
Gas Storage Depot
Brackenhirst
MUIRDYKE RD
YETTS HOLE RD
DUNNET AVE 1
STRATHYRE GDNS 2
HAWKWOOD RD 3
Ryden Mains
New Monkland
Gartverrie Burn
ML6
Cemy
New Monkland Prim Sch
RAEBOG RD
B803
B802
Palace Farm
BURNLIP RD
Rochsoles Farm
RYDEN MAINS RD
CLEDDANS VIEW
QUARRYSIDE ST
LOCHBUIE LA
MELDRUM MAINS
PH
KIRKSTYLE PL
Gartverrie Farm
MACARTHUR AVE
Blackwalk Plantation
Copse Wood
Glenmavis
CROWNHILL CT
VIRTUE WELL VIEW
Cromlet
Braidenhill Farm
Dryflat
COATBRIDGE RD
STRATMUNGO CRES 1
STAINEYBRAES PL 2
DYKEHEAD CRES 3
CRAIGMOCHAN AVE 4
GLENMAVIS RD
CH
LOCHEARN CRES
BLUEBELL WAY
SPRINGHOLM DR
Virtuewell Glen
Golfhill Prim Sch
DYKEHEAD RD
BALLOCHNEY LA 5
LEVEN QUADRANT 6
LAIDON RD 7
KATRINE CRES 8
ML5
Kippsbyre
Burnfoot
ROCHSOLES DR
Kipps
North Burn
METHVEN TERR
LAGGAN QUADRANT
TAYSIDE
COMMONHEAD AVE
GARTLISTON RD
COLTSWOOD RD
B804
Greenhill Ind Est
Greenhill
Works
Greenhill Bsns Ctr
1 CHASSELS ST
2 BRUCE ST
3 GREENSIDE ST
4 BURNBANK ST
B803 WAVERLEY ST
NORTHBURN RD
BURNSIDE RD
CAMERON ST
WHINHALL RD
BALLOCHNEY ST
ARRAN VIEW
ARRAN DR
AIRDRIE
Sch
Acad
COMMONHEAD LA 9
SOUTH COMMONHEAD AVE 10
QUARRY RD 11
WHINHALL AVE
WILSON ST
BEECHBANK AVE
B802
8
7
69
6
5
68
4
3
67
2
1
66
73
74
75

50
36

35
24

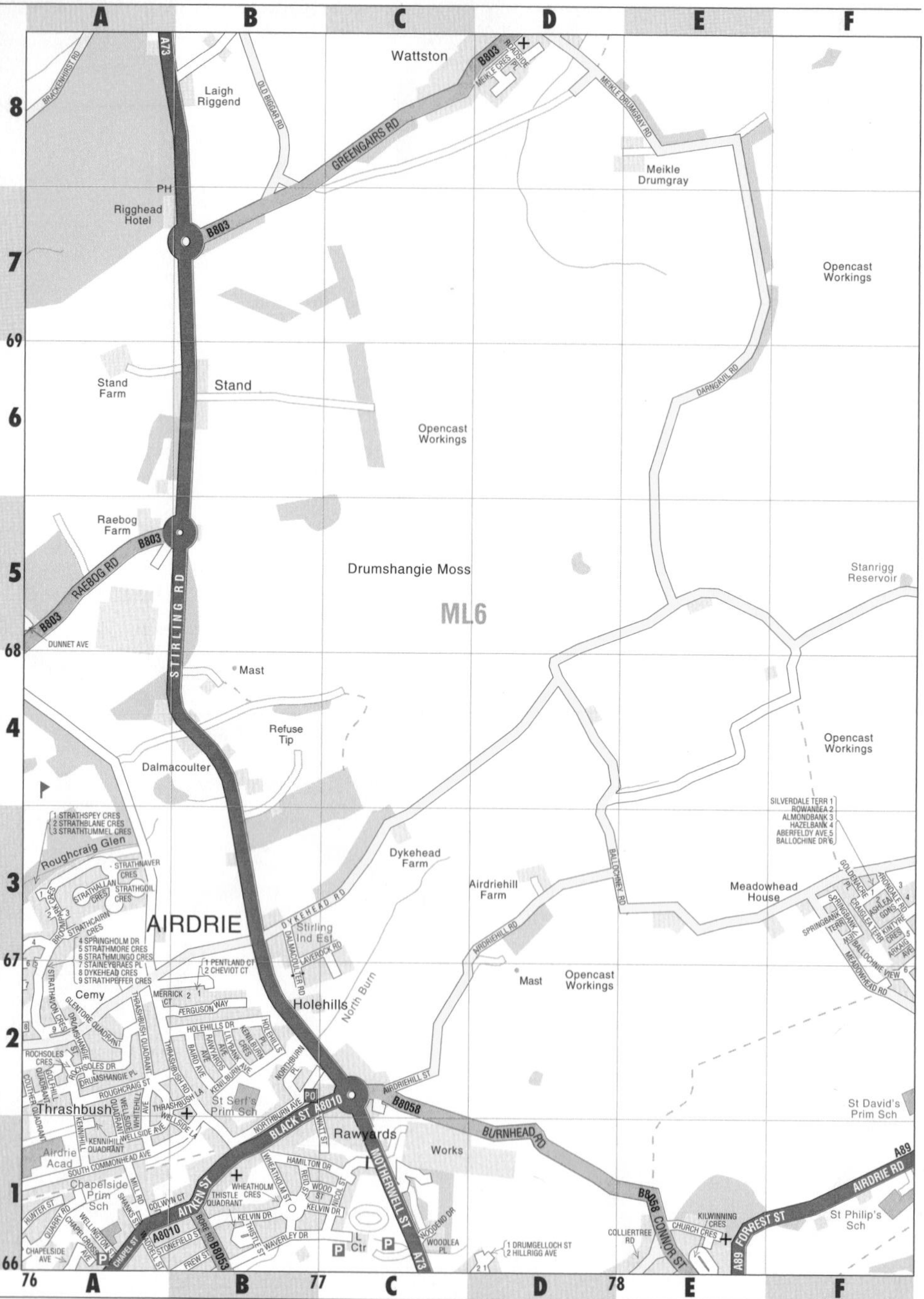
A
B
C
D
E
F
8
7
69
6
5
68
4
3
67
2
1
66
76
77
78
Wattston
Laigh Riggend
OLD BIGGAR RD
BRACKENHIRST RD
A73
B803
GREENGAIRS RD
ROADSIDE
MEIKLE CRES
MEIKLE DRUMGRAY RD
Meikle Drumgray
PH
Rigghead Hotel
Opencast Workings
Stand Farm
Stand
DARNGAVIL RD
Raebog Farm
RAEBOG RD
Drumshangie Moss
ML6
Stanrigg Reservoir
STIRLING RD
DUNNET AVE
Mast
Refuse Tip
Dalmacoulter
1 STRATHSPEY CRES
2 STRATHBLANE CRES
3 STRATHTUMMEL CRES
Roughcraig Glen
STRATHNAVER CRES
STRATHALLAN CRES
STRATHGOIL CRES
STRATHCAIRN CRES
AIRDRIE
4 SPRINGHOLM DR
5 STRATHMORE CRES
6 STRATHMUNGO CRES
7 STAINEYBRAES PL
8 DYKEHEAD CRES
9 STRATHPEFFER CRES
Dykehead Farm
DYKEHEAD RD
Stirling Ind Est
DALMACOULTER RD
LAVEROCK RD
Airdriehill Farm
AIRDRIEHILL RD
BALLOCHNEY RD
SILVERDALE TERR 1
ROWANLEA 2
ALMONDBANK 3
HAZELBANK 4
ABERFELDY AVE 5
BALLOCHINE DR 6
Meadowhead House
GOLDENACRE PL
ARONDALE RD
SPRINGBANK TERR
CRAIGLEA TERR
ASHLEA GDNS
KINTYRE CRES
ARKAIG AVE
BALLOCHNIE VIEW
MEADOWHEAD RD
1 PENTLAND CT
2 CHEVIOT CT
MERRICK CT
FERGUSON WAY
Cemy
GLENTORE QUADRANT
STRATHAVON CRES
THRASHBUSH QUADRANT
Holehills
North Burn
Mast
Opencast Workings
HOLEHILLS DR
HOLEHILLS PL
KENILBURN CRES
LILYBANK AVE
RAWYARDS AVE
BAIRD AVE
KENILBURN AVE
NORTHBURN PL
ROCHSOLES CRES
ROCHSOLES DR
DRUMSHANGIE PL
ROUGHCRAIG ST
THRASHBUSH RD
THRASHBUSH LA
St Serf's Prim Sch
AIRDRIEHILL ST
PO
NORTHBURN AVE
BLACK ST
A8010
B8058
BURNHEAD RD
Thrashbush
WELLSIDE QUADRANT
WELLSIDE AVE
WELLSIDE LA
KENNIHILL
KENNIHILL QUADRANT
WATT ST
Rawyards
Works
St David's Prim Sch
Airdrie Acad
SOUTH COMMONHEAD AVE
HAMILTON DR
WHEATHOLM ST
REID ST
WOOD ST
NICOL ST
MOTHERWELL ST
A89
AIRDRIE RD
Chapelside Prim Sch
MILL RD
COLWYN CT
AITKEN ST
WHEATHOLM CRES
THISTLE QUADRANT
KELVIN DR
HUNTER ST
QUARRY RD
WELLINGTON ST
CHAPELCROSS AVE
CHAPELSIDE AVE
CHAPEL ST
STONEFIELD ST
BORE RD
B8053
FREW ST
WAVERLEY DR
THISTLE ST
L Ctr
P
WOODEND DR
WOODLEA PL
1 DRUMGELLOCH ST
2 HILLRIGG AVE
COLLIERTREE RD
B8058
CONNOR ST
KILWINNING CRES
CHURCH CRES
FORREST ST
St Philip's Sch

35
51

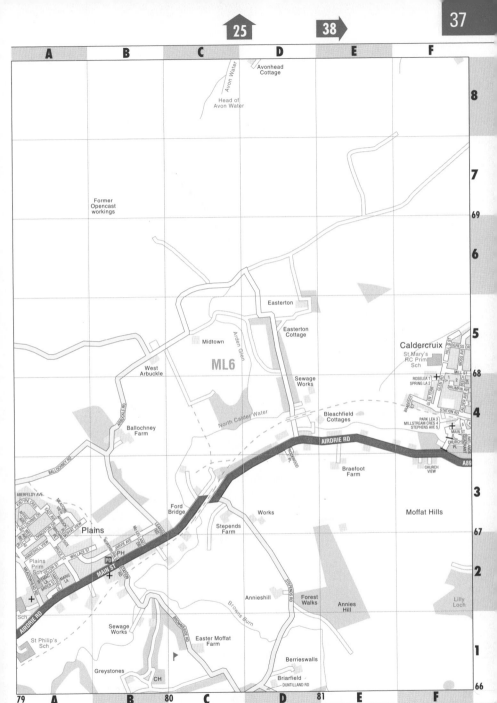

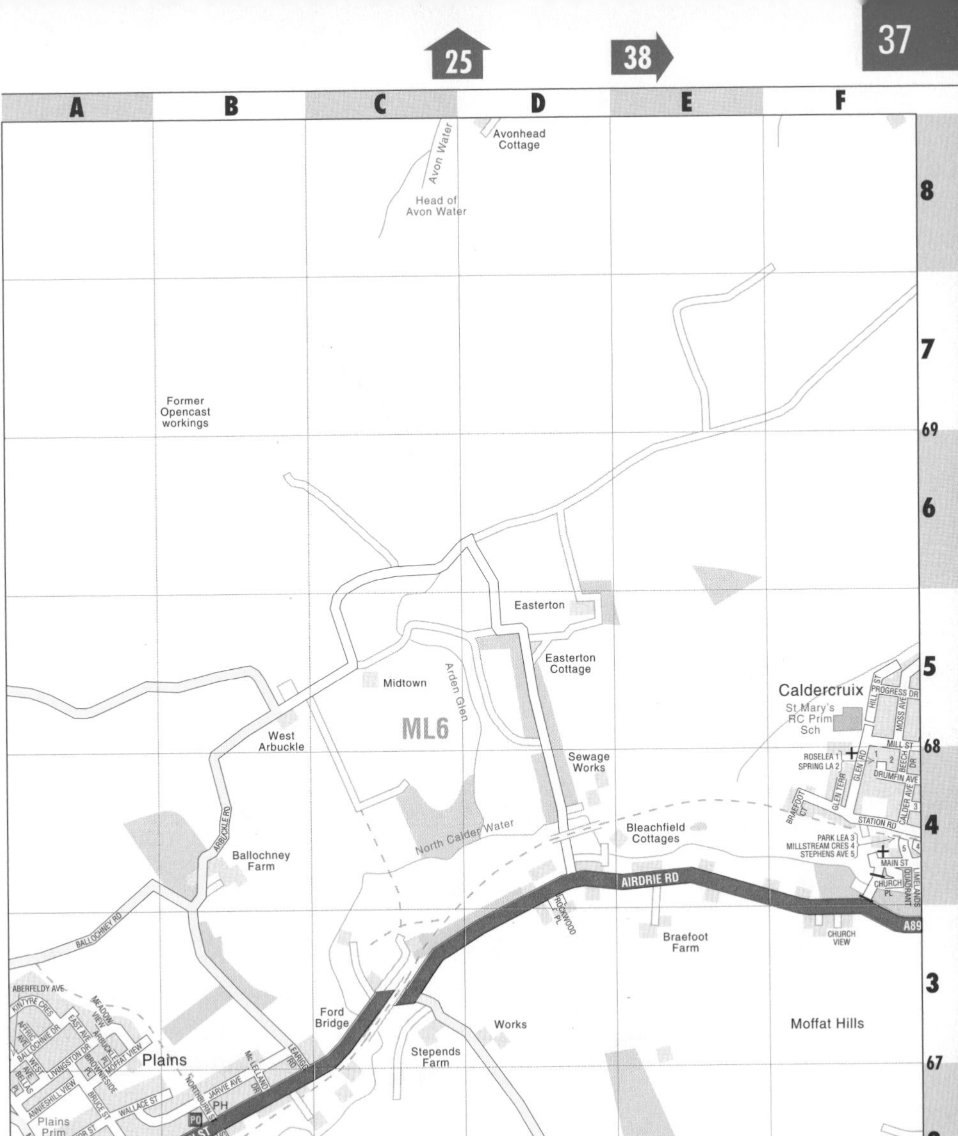

25
38
A
B
C
D
E
F
Avonhead Cottage
Avon Water
Head of Avon Water
8
7
69
6
5
68
4
3
67
2
1
66
Former Opencast workings
Easterton
Easterton Cottage
Midtown
Arden Glen
ML6
West Arbuckle
Caldercruix
St Mary's RC Prim Sch
Sewage Works
Bleachfield Cottages
North Calder Water
Ballochney Farm
ARBUCKLE RD
BALLOCHNEY RD
AIRDRIE RD
Braefoot Farm
CHURCH VIEW
A89
Ford Bridge
Works
Moffat Hills
Stepends Farm
Plains
Plains Prim Sch
MAIN ST
PH
PO
Annieshill
Forest Walks
Annies Hill
Browns Burn
STEPENDS RD
Sewage Works
St Philip's Sch
Easter Moffat Farm
BROWNIESIDE RD
Berrieswalls
Greystones
CH
Briarfield
DUNTILLAND RD
Lilly Loch
Sch
79
80
81

52
38

37
26

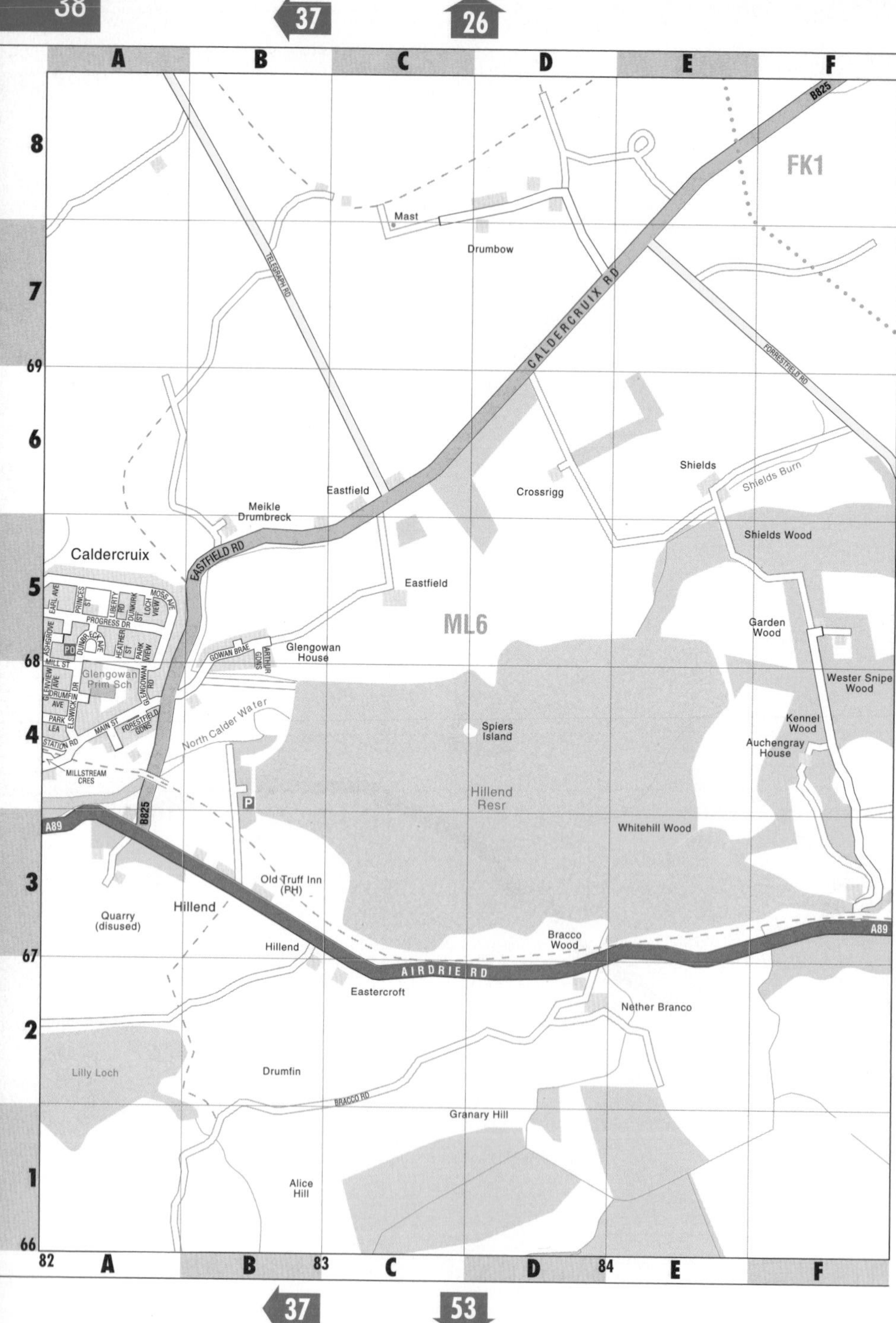
A
B
C
D
E
F
8
7
69
6
5
68
4
3
67
2
1
66
82
83
84
B825
FK1
Mast
Drumbow
TELEGRAPH RD
CALDERCRUIX RD
FORRESTFIELD RD
Shields
Shields Burn
Crossrigg
Eastfield
Meikle Drumbreck
Shields Wood
Caldercruix
EASTFIELD RD
Eastfield
ML6
Garden Wood
MOSS AVE
EARL AVE
PRINCES ST
LIBERTY RD
DUNKIRK ST
LOCH VIEW
PROGRESS DR
ASHGROVE
DUNBRECK AVE
HEATHER ST
PARK VIEW
PO
GOWAN BRAE
ARTHUR GDNS
Glengowan House
MILL ST
Glengowan Prim Sch
GLENVIEW AVE
ELSWICK DR
DRUMFIN AVE
GLENGOWAN RD
Wester Snipe Wood
PARK LEA
MAIN ST
FORESTFIELD GDNS
North Calder Water
Spiers Island
Kennel Wood
Auchengray House
STATION RD
MILLSTREAM CRES
P
Hillend Resr
B825
A89
Whitehill Wood
Old Truff Inn (PH)
Hillend
Quarry (disused)
Bracco Wood
A89
Hillend
AIRDRIE RD
Eastercroft
Nether Branco
Lilly Loch
Drumfin
BRACCO RD
Granary Hill
Alice Hill

37
53

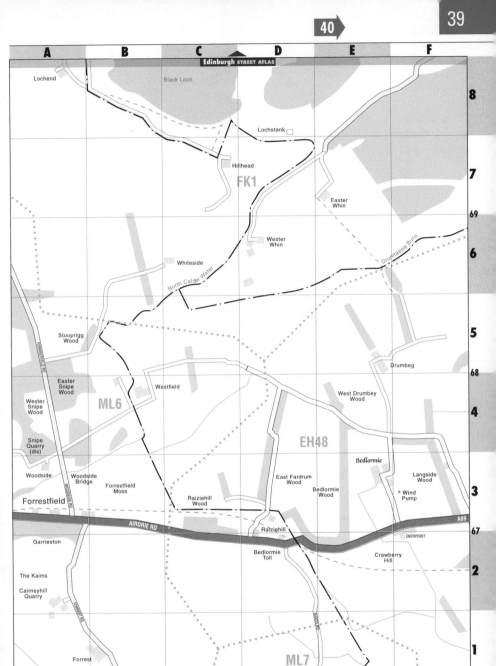

40

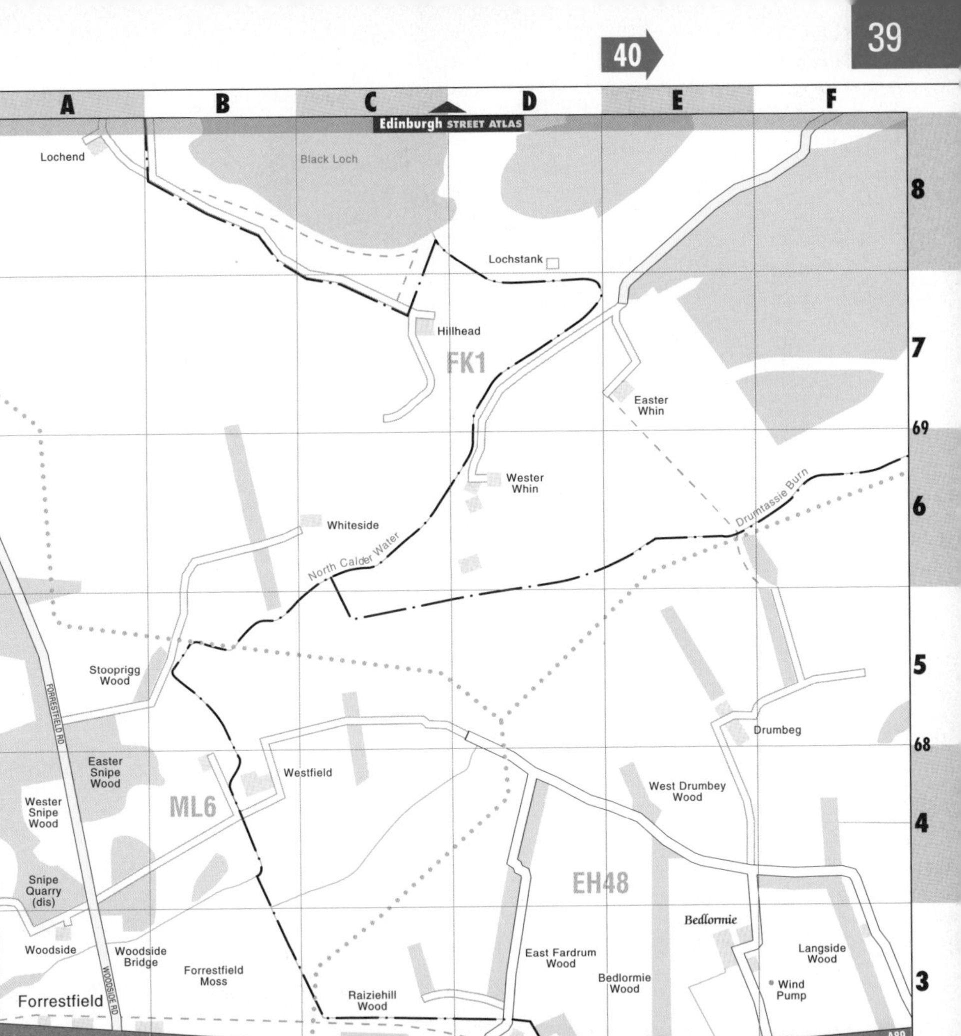

A
B
C
D
E
F
Edinburgh STREET ATLAS
Lochend
Black Loch
Lochstank
Hillhead
FK1
Easter Whin
Wester Whin
Whiteside
North Calder Water
Drumtassie Burn
Stooprigg Wood
FORRESTFIELD RD
Drumbeg
Easter Snipe Wood
Westfield
West Drumbey Wood
Wester Snipe Wood
ML6
EH48
Snipe Quarry (dis)
Bedlormie
Woodside
Woodside Bridge
Forrestfield Moss
East Fardrum Wood
Langside Wood
Bedlormie Wood
Wind Pump
Forrestfield
WOODSIDE RD
Raiziehill Wood
AIRDRIE RD
A89
Raiziehill
ENTRYFOOT
Garrieston
Bedlormie Toll
Crawberry Hill
The Kaims
Cairneyhill Quarry
FORREST RD
BAADS RD
Forrest
ML7
8
7
69
6
5
68
4
3
67
2
1
66
85
86
87

54

40

39

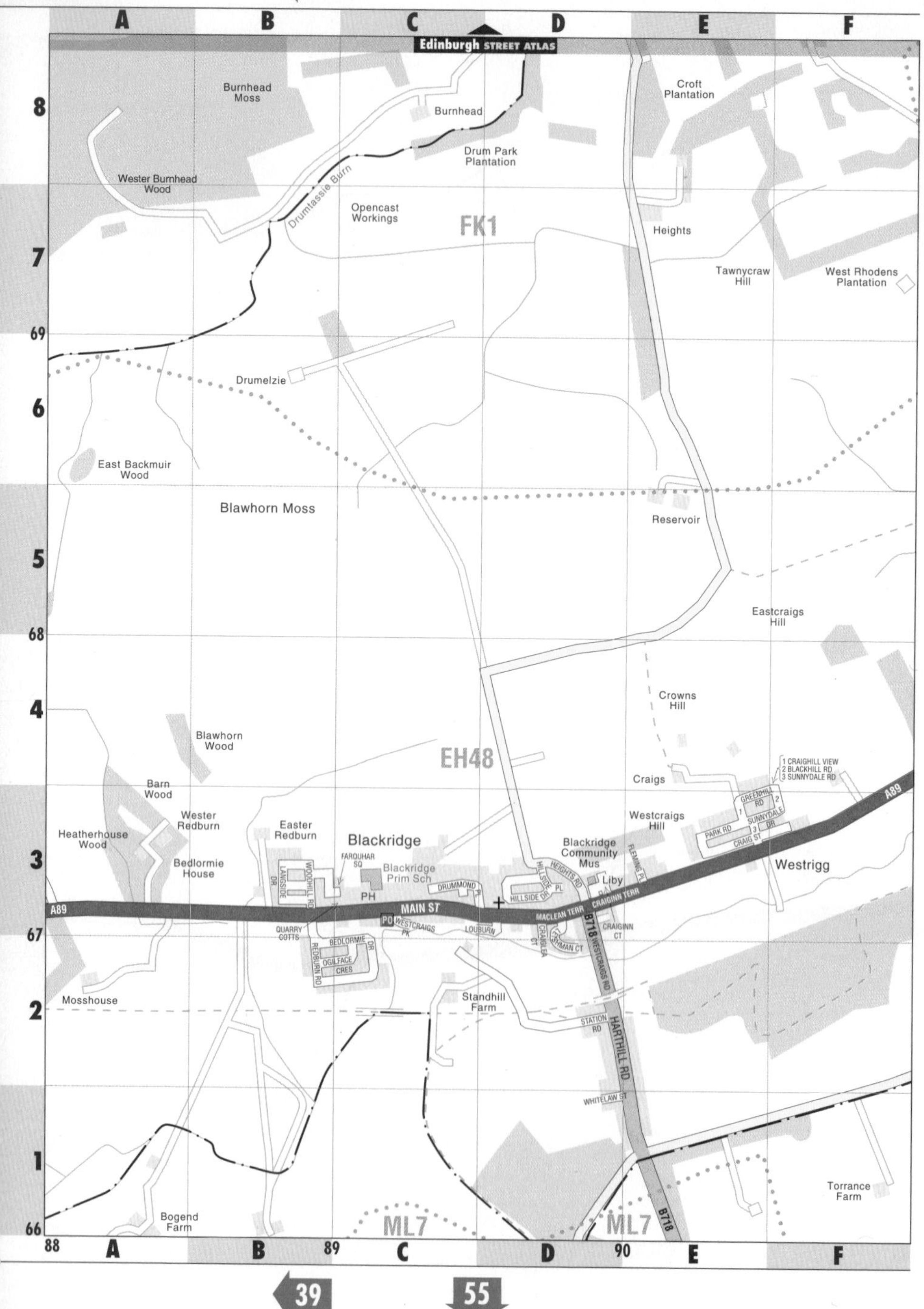
A
B
C
D
E
F
Edinburgh STREET ATLAS
8
7
69
6
5
68
4
3
67
2
1
66
88
89
90
Burnhead Moss
Burnhead
Drum Park Plantation
Croft Plantation
Wester Burnhead Wood
Drumtassie Burn
Opencast Workings
FK1
Heights
Tawnycraw Hill
West Rhodens Plantation
Drumelzie
East Backmuir Wood
Blawhorn Moss
Reservoir
Eastcraigs Hill
Crowns Hill
Blawhorn Wood
EH48
Craigs
1 CRAIGHILL VIEW
2 BLACKHILL RD
3 SUNNYDALE RD
Barn Wood
Wester Redburn
Westcraigs Hill
Heatherhouse Wood
Easter Redburn
Blackridge
Blackridge Community Mus
Bedlormie House
FARQUHAR SQ
Blackridge Prim Sch
PH
Liby
Westrigg
A89
MAIN ST
MACLEAN TERR
CRAIGINN TERR
CRAIGINN CT
B718
WESTCRAIGS RD
HEIGHTS RD
HILLSIDE DR
HILLSIDE PL
FLEMING PL
DRUMMOND PL
GREENHILL RD
SUNNYDALE DR
PARK RD
CRAIG ST
LANGSIDE DR
WOODHILL RD
QUARRY COTTS
PO
WESTCRAIGS PK
LOUBURN
CRAIGLEA CT
BEDLORMIE DR
REDBURN RD
OGILFACE CRES
Mosshouse
Standhill Farm
STATION RD
HARTHILL RD
WHITELAW ST
Torrance Farm
Bogend Farm
ML7
ML7
B718

39
55

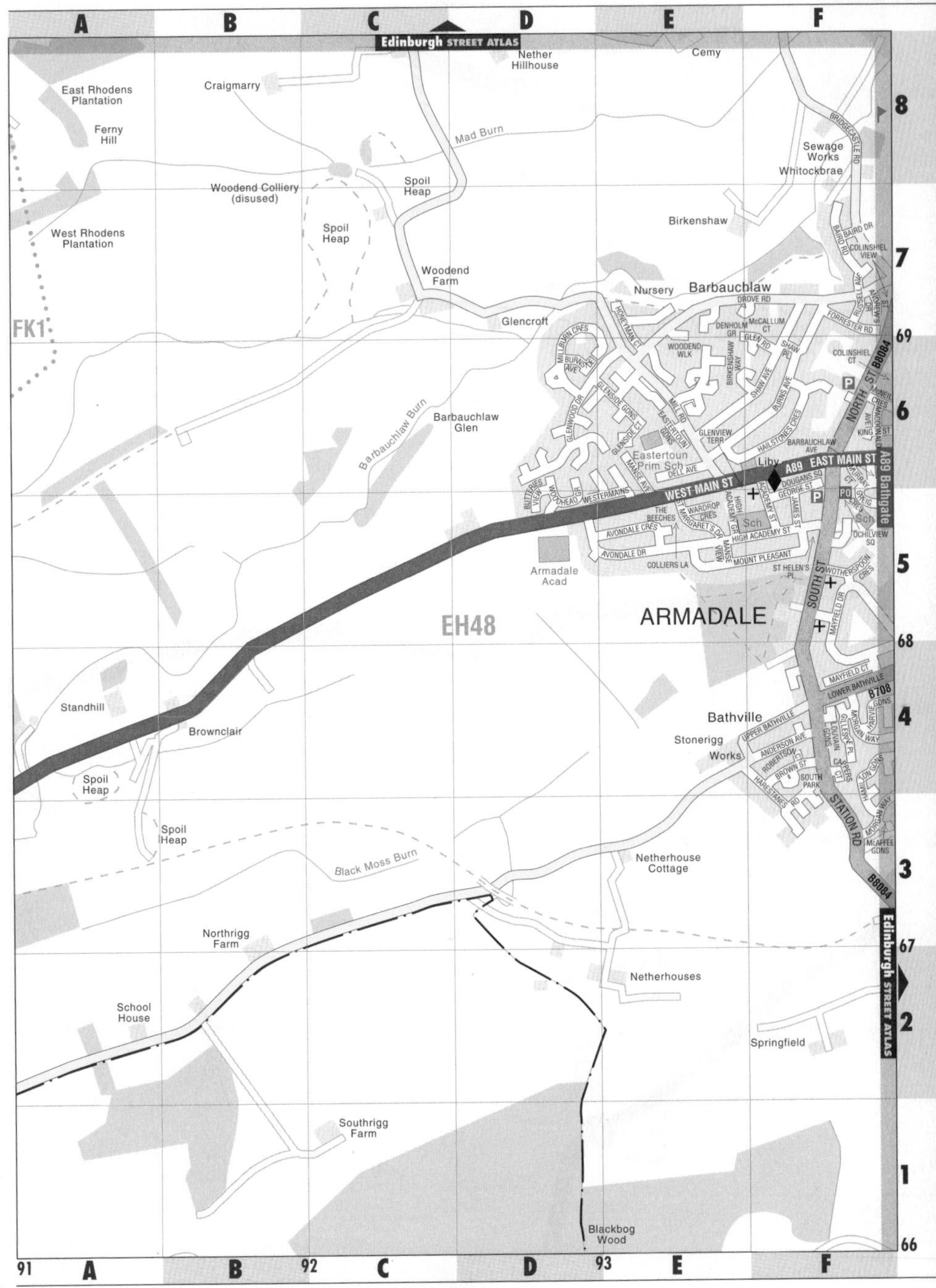
A
B
C
D
E
F
Edinburgh STREET ATLAS
Nether Hillhouse
Cemy
East Rhodens Plantation
Craigmarry
Ferny Hill
Mad Burn
Sewage Works
Whitockbrae
Woodend Colliery (disused)
Spoil Heap
West Rhodens Plantation
Spoil Heap
Birkenshaw
Woodend Farm
Nursery
Barbauchlaw
FK1
Glencroft
Barbauchlaw Burn
Barbauchlaw Glen
Eastertoun Prim Sch
Liby
A89 EAST MAIN ST
WEST MAIN ST
A89 Bathgate
Sch
Armadale Acad
EH48
ARMADALE
Standhill
Brownclair
Bathville
Stonerigg
Works
Spoil Heap
Spoil Heap
Black Moss Burn
Netherhouse Cottage
Northrigg Farm
Netherhouses
School House
Springfield
Southrigg Farm
Blackbog Wood
8
7
69
6
5
68
4
3
67
2
1
66
91
92
93
B8084
B708
SOUTH ST
STATION RD
NORTH ST

27

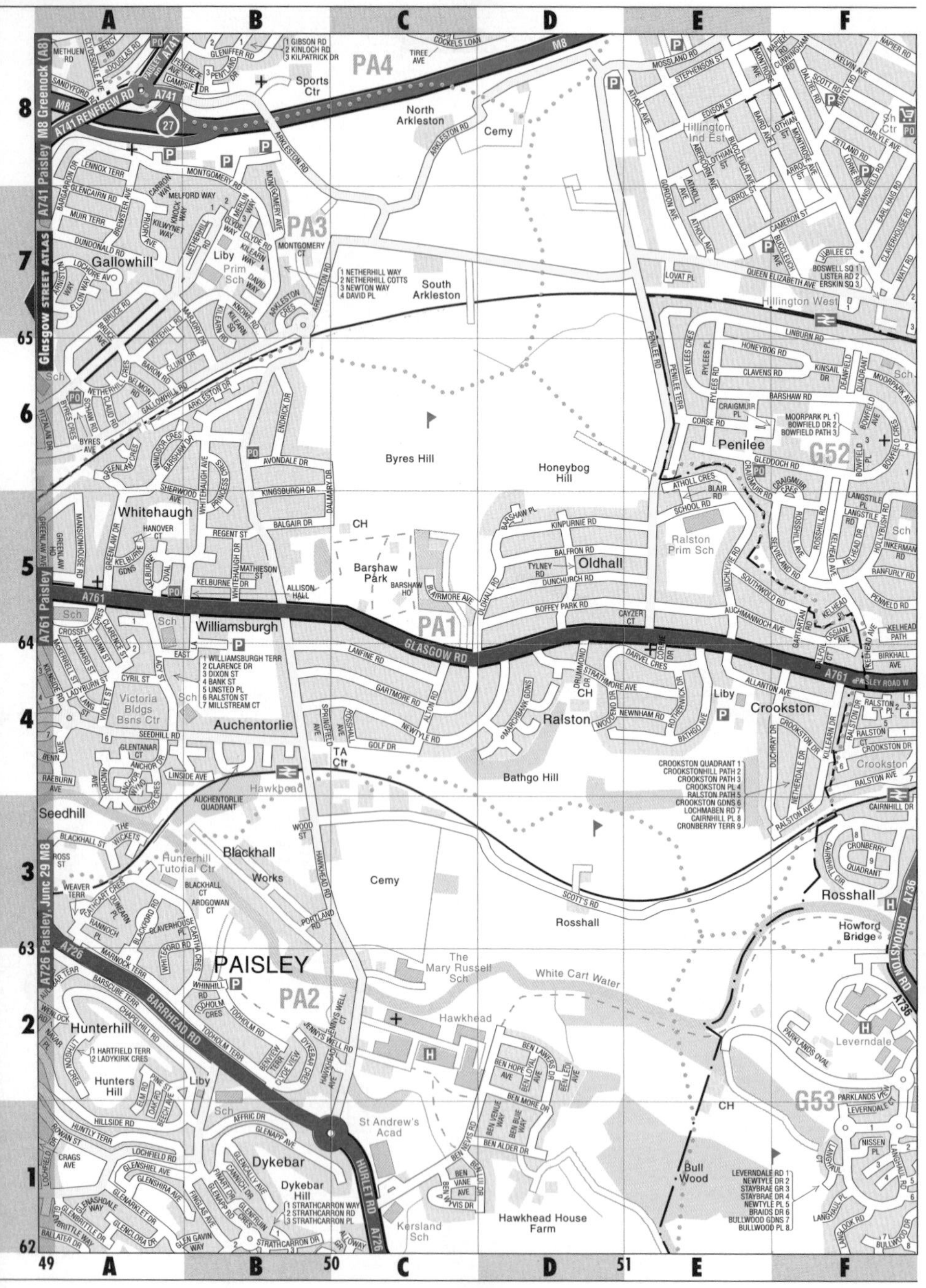

A
B
C
D
E
F
8
7
6
5
4
3
2
1
65
64
63
62
49
50
51
PA4
PA3
PA1
PA2
G52
G53
M8
M8 Greenock (A8)
A741 Paisley
A741 Paisley
Glasgow STREET ATLAS
A761 Paisley
A761
A761
A741 RENFREW RD
A741
A726
A726 Paisley, Junc 29 M8
A726
A736
1 GIBSON RD
2 KINLOCH RD
3 KILPATRICK DR
COCKELS LOAN
TIREE AVE
Sports Ctr
North Arkleston
Cemy
METHUEN RD
BERCY
CLYDESDALE AVE
DOUGLAS RD
SANDYFORD RD
GLENIFFER RD
PENTLAND DR
CAMPSIE DR
ARKLESTON RD
MOSSLAND RD
STEPHENSON ST
ATHOLL AVE
Hillington Ind Est
EDISON ST
NAPIER RD
CUNNINGHAM RD
KELVIN AVE
SCOTT RD
DALZIEL RD
LOTHIAN ST
BAIRD AVE
MONTROSE AVE
ABERCORN AVE
BUCCLEUCH AVE
ARROL ST
GORDON AVE
CAMERON ST
CARLYLE AVE
ZETLAND RD
LORNE RD
MANSFIELD RD
EARL HAIG RD
CLAVERHOUSE RD
WATT RD
Sh Ctr
JUBILEE CT
BOSWELL SQ 1
LISTER RD 2
ERSKIN SQ 3
LOVAT PL
QUEEN ELIZABETH AVE
Hillington West
LENNOX TERR
MONTGOMERY RD
GLENCAIRN RD
MELFORD WAY
MUIR TERR
DUNDONALD RD
BREWSTER AVE
PRIORY AVE
CARRON WAY
KNOCK WAY
KILWYNET WAY
NETHERHILL RD
CLYDE WAY
CLYDE RD
MERLIN WAY
KILEARN WAY
MONTGOMERY AVE
MONTGOMERY CT
Gallowhill
Liby
Prim Sch
DAVID WAY
1 NETHERHILL WAY
2 NETHERHILL COTTS
3 NEWTON WAY
4 DAVID PL
South Arkleston
LOCHORE AVE
ARNISTON WAY
ELLON WAY
BRUCE RD
MARJORY DR
KNOWE RD
KILEARN SQ
KILEARN RD
MOTEHILL RD
ARKLESTON CRES
CLUNY DR
BARON RD
BELMONT RD
NETHERHILL CRES
CLAUD RD
SCHAW RD
BYRES CRES
BYRES AVE
FITZALAN DR
GALLOWHILL RD
ARKLESTON DR
LINBURN RD
HONEYBOG RD
KINSAIL DR
CLAVENS RD
DEANFIELD
QUADRANT
MOORPARK AVE
BARSHAW RD
CRAIGMUIR PL
MOORPARK PL 1
BOWFIELD DR 2
BOWFIELD PATH 3
CORSE RD
RYLEES CRES
RYLEES PL
RYLEES RD
PENILEE TERR
PENILEE RD
Penilee
BOWFIELD PL
BOWFIELD AVE
BOWFIELD CRES
GLEDDOCH RD
CRAIGMUIR RD
CRAIGMUIR CRES
ENDRICK DR
AVONDALE DR
KINGSBURGH DR
DALMARY DR
BALGAIR DR
Byres Hill
Honeybog Hill
WINDSOR CRES
BARSHAW DR
GREENLAW CRES
WHITEHAUGH AVE
PRINCESS CRES
SHERWOOD AVE
Whitehaugh
HANOVER CT
REGENT ST
ATHOLL CRES
BLAIR RD
SCHOOL RD
Ralston Prim Sch
LANGSTILE PL
LANGSTILE RD
HOLLYBUSH RD
INKERMAN RD
RANFURLY RD
PENWELD RD
BARSHAW PL
KINPURNIE RD
BALFRON RD
TYLNEY RD
Oldhall
DUNCHURCH RD
ROFFEY PARK RD
CAYZER CT
CH
Barshaw Park
BARSHAW HO
BLAIRMORE AVE
OLDHALL RD
MANSIONHOUSE RD
GREENLAW RD
GREENLAW AVE
KELBURNE GDNS
KELBURNE OVAL
KELBURNE DR
WHITEHAUGH DR
MATHIESON ST
ALLISON HALL
BUCHLYVIE RD
SEYVELAND RD
ROSSHILL AVE
ROSSHILL RD
KELHEAD AVE
KELHEAD DR
SOUTHWOLD RD
AUCHMANNOCH AVE
GARTARTAN RD
KELHEAD PATH
BIRKHALL AVE
Sch
Williamsburgh
CROSSFLAT CRES
CLARENCE ST
HOWARD ST
DUNN ST
1 WILLIAMSBURGH TERR
2 CLARENCE DR
3 DIXON ST
4 BANK ST
5 UNSTED PL
6 RALSTON ST
7 MILLSTREAM CT
GLASGOW RD
LANFINE RD
GARTMORE RD
DARVEL CRES
STRATHMORE AVE
DRUMMOND DR
CORRIE DR
A761 PAISLEY ROAD W.
ALLANTON AVE
KILNSIDE RD
McKERRELL ST
CYRIL ST
Victoria Bldgs Bsns Ctr
LADYBURN ST
VIOLET ST
Auchentorlie
SEEDHILL RD
SPRINGFIELD AVE
ROSSHALL AVE
NEWTYLE RD
ALTON RD
GOLF DR
MARCHBANK GDNS
Ralston
WOODEND DR
NEWNHAM RD
ROTHERWICK DR
BATHGO AVE
Liby
Crookston
CROOKSTON DR
KILLEARN DR
RALSTON DR
RALSTON CT
RALSTON PL
RALSTON AVE
Crookston
CROOKSTON DR
BENN AVE
GLENTANAR CT
ANCHOR CT
ANCHOR DR
ANCHOR WYND
ANCHOR CRES
ANCHOR AVE
LINSIDE AVE
RAEBURN AVE
TA Ctr
Bathgo Hill
CROOKSTON QUADRANT 1
CROOKSTONHILL PATH 2
CROOKSTON PATH 3
CROOKSTON PL 4
RALSTON PATH 5
CROOKSTON GDNS 6
LOCHMABEN RD 7
CAIRNHILL PL 8
CRONBERRY TERR 9
DUCHRAY DR
NETHERDALE DR
CAIRNHILL DR
Hawkhead
AUCHENTORLIE QUADRANT
Seedhill
THE WICKETS
BLACKHALL ST
ROSS ST
WEAVER TERR
Hunterhill Tutorial Ctr
Blackhall
Works
BLACKHALL CT
ARDGOWAN CT
WOOD ST
HAWKHEAD RD
Cemy
SCOTT'S RD
Rosshall
CRONBERRY QUADRANT
CAIRNHILL CIR
Rosshall
CROOKSTON RD
Howford Bridge
CATHCART CRES
DUNEARN PL
RANNOCH PL
BLACKFORD RD
CLAVERHOUSE PL
WHITEFORD RD
CARTHA CRES
PORTLAND RD
MARNOCK TERR
PAISLEY
The Mary Russell Sch
White Cart Water
BARR TERR
BARSCUBE TERR
CHAPELHILL RD
WHINHILL RD
TODHOLM CRES
TODHOLM RD
TODHOLM TERR
BARRHEAD RD
WENLOCK RD
NAVAR PL
Hunterhill
1 HARTFIELD TERR
2 LADYKIRK CRES
JENNYS WELL CT
JENNYS WELL RD
DYKEBAR CRES
BENVIEW TERR
CLYDE VIEW
Hawkhead
BEN LAWERS DR
BEN HOPE AVE
BEN LOYAL AVE
BEN LEDI AVE
BEN MORE DR
BEN VENUE WAY
BEN BUIE WAY
BEN ALDER DR
Leverndale
PARKLANDS OVAL
Hunters Hill
ELM RD
PINE ST
OAK RD
BEECH AVE
Liby
HILLSIDE RD
Sch
AFFRIC DR
GLENAPP AVE
HUNTLY TERR
ROWAN ST
LOCHFIELD RD
St Andrew's Acad
BEN NEVIS RD
PARKLANDS VIEW
LEVERNDALE CT
CH
NISSEN PL
LANGHAUL PL
CRAGS AVE
Dykebar
GLENSHIEL AVE
GLENSHIRA AVE
GLENCALLY AVE
CANNICH DR
FINART DR
GLENAPP RD
FINGLAS AVE
GLENFRUIN CRES
BEN VANE AVE
BEN VORLICH DR
BEN LUI DR
Bull Wood
LEVERNDALE RD 1
NEWTYLE DR 2
STAYBRAE GR 3
STAYBRAE DR 4
NEWTYLE PL 5
BRAIDS DR 6
BULLWOOD GDNS 7
BULLWOOD PL 8
LOCHFIELD DR
GLENASHDALE WAY
GLENARKLET DR
GLENBRITTLE WAY
GLENBRITTLE DR
GLENCLORA DR
BALLATER DR
Dykebar Hill
1 STRATHCARRON WAY
2 STRATHCARRON RD
3 STRATHCARRON PL
GLEN GAVIN WAY
STRATHCARRON DR
ALTOWAY
HURLET RD
Kersland Sch
Hawkhead House Farm
LANGLOOK RD
BULLWOOD CT

57

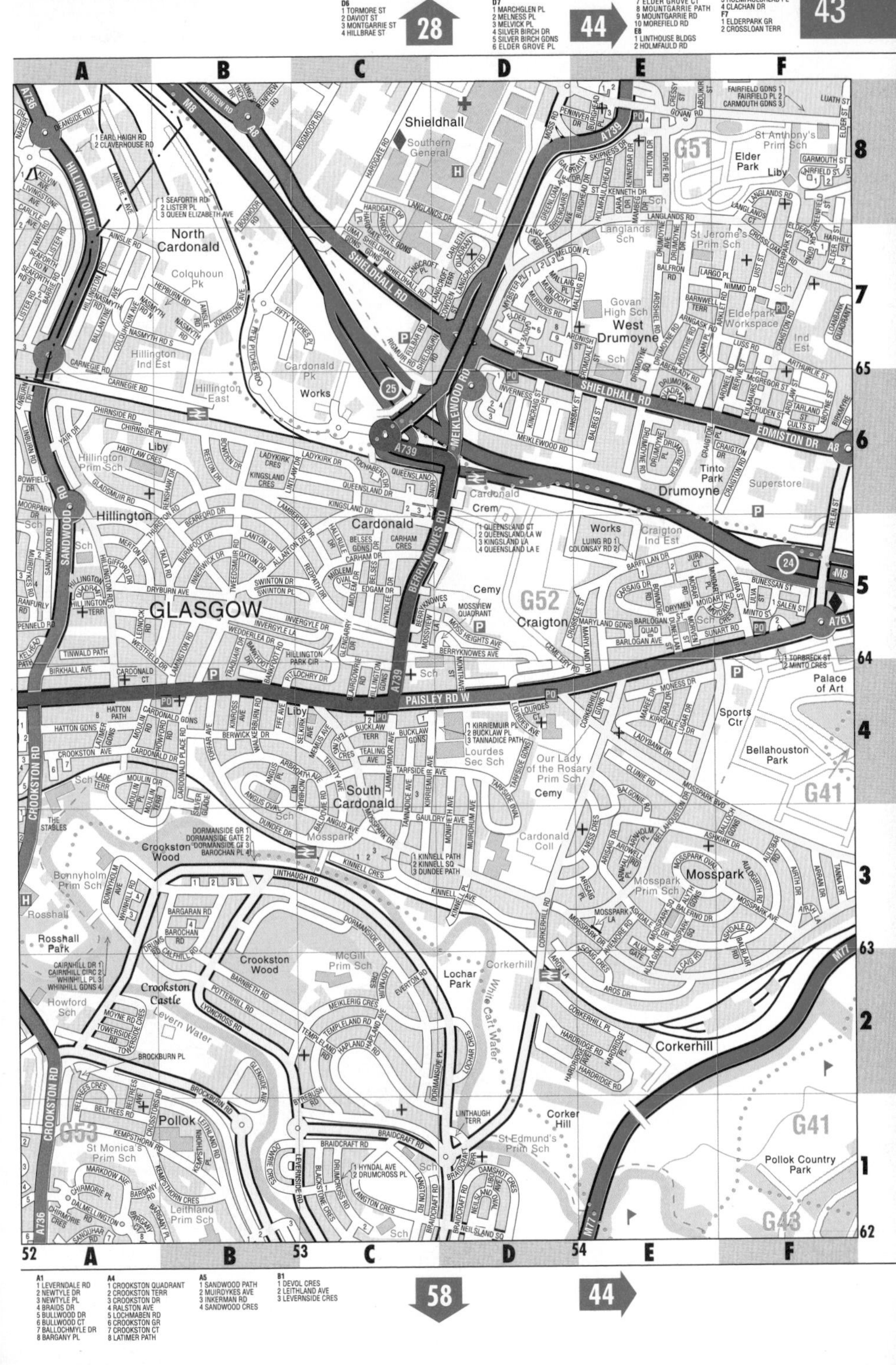
D6
1 TORMORE ST
2 DAVIOT ST
3 MONTGARRIE ST
4 HILLBRAE ST
28
D7
1 MARCHGLEN PL
2 MELNESS PL
3 MELVICK PL
4 SILVER BIRCH DR
5 SILVER BIRCH GDNS
6 ELDER GROVE PL
44
7 ELDER GROVE CT
8 MOUNTGARRIE PATH
9 MOUNTGARRIE RD
10 MOREFIELD RD
E8
1 LINTHOUSE BLDGS
2 HOLMFAULD RD
3 HOLMFAULDHEAD PL
4 CLACHAN DR
F7
1 ELDERPARK GR
2 CROSSLOAN TERR
Shieldhall
Southern General
North Cardonald
Colquhoun Pk
Hillington Ind Est
Hillington East
Cardonald Pk
Works
SHIELDHALL RD
West Drumoyne
Govan High Sch
Langlands Sch
St Jerome's Prim Sch
Elder Park
St Anthony's Prim Sch
Elderpark Workspace
Hillington Prim Sch
Hillington
GLASGOW
Cardonald
Cardonald Crem
Cemy
G52
Craigton
Tinto Park
Drumoyne
Superstore
Craigton Ind Est
EDMISTON DR
PAISLEY RD W
Palace of Art
Sports Ctr
Bellahouston Park
G41
South Cardonald
Mosspark
Lourdes Sec Sch
Our Lady of the Rosary Prim Sch
Cardonald Coll
Crookston Wood
Bonnyholm Prim Sch
Rosshall
Rosshall Park
Howford Sch
Crookston Castle
Levern Water
McGill Prim Sch
Lochar Park
Corkerhill
White Cart Water
Corker Hill
St Edmund's Prim Sch
Pollok
G53
St Monica's Prim Sch
Leithland Prim Sch
Pollok Country Park
G43
A1
1 LEVERNDALE RD
2 NEWTYLE DR
3 NEWTYLE PL
4 BRAIDS DR
5 BULLWOOD DR
6 BULLWOOD CT
7 BALLOCHMYLE DR
8 BARGANY PL
A4
1 CROOKSTON QUADRANT
2 CROOKSTON TERR
3 CROOKSTON DR
4 RALSTON AVE
5 LOCHMABEN RD
6 CROOKSTON GR
7 CROOKSTON CT
8 LATIMER PATH
A5
1 SANDWOOD PATH
2 MUIRDYKES AVE
3 INKERMAN RD
4 SANDWOOD CRES
B1
1 DEVOL CRES
2 LEITHLAND AVE
3 LEVERNSIDE CRES
58
44

A8
1 HARMONY ROW
2 WARDROP ST
3 GARMOUTH CT
4 GARMOUTH GDNS
D5
1 CLIFFORD PL
2 LANGSHOT ST
3 PLANTATION PARK GDNS
E5
1 MILNPARK GDNS
2 LAMBHILL QUADRANT
3 SEAWARD ST

43

E6
1 EAGLESHAM CT
2 EAGLESHAM PL
3 MIDDLESEX GDNS

29

E8
1 CLIFTON PL
2 FITZROY PL
3 WESTMINSTER TERR
4 DERBY TERRACE LA
5 CORUNNA ST
6 Stobcross Bsns Pk
7 HOULDSWORTH LA
8 Clydeway Ind Est
9 FINNIESTON SQ
10 MINERVA CT

For full street detail of the highlighted area see page 162.

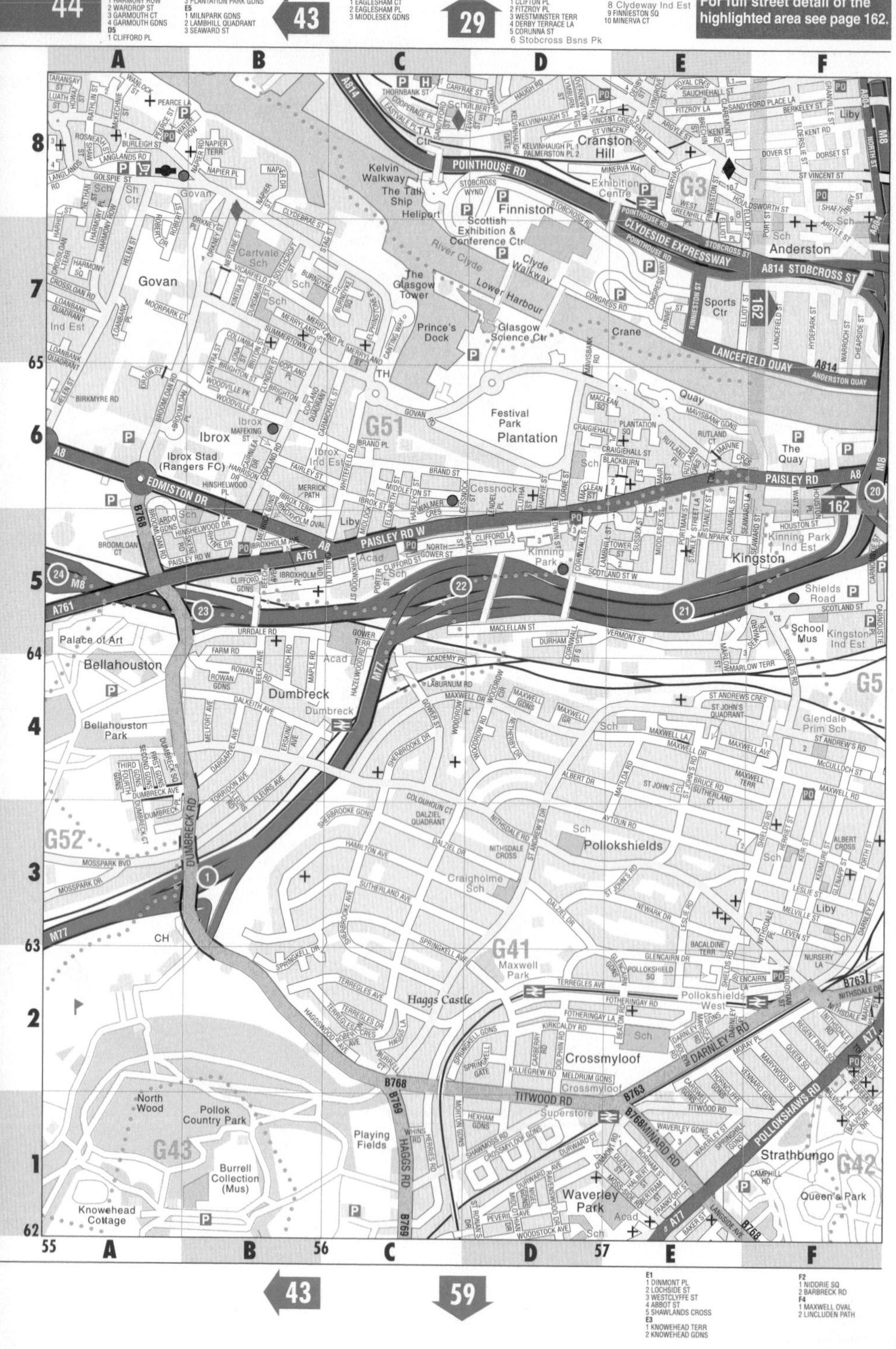

A B C D E F
55 56 57
62 63 64 65

43

59

E1
1 DINMONT PL
2 LOCHSIDE ST
3 WESTCLYFFE ST
4 ABBOT ST
5 SHAWLANDS CROSS
E3
1 KNOWEHEAD TERR
2 KNOWEHEAD GDNS

F2
1 NIDDRIE SQ
2 BARBRECK RD
F4
1 MAXWELL OVAL
2 LINCLUDEN PATH

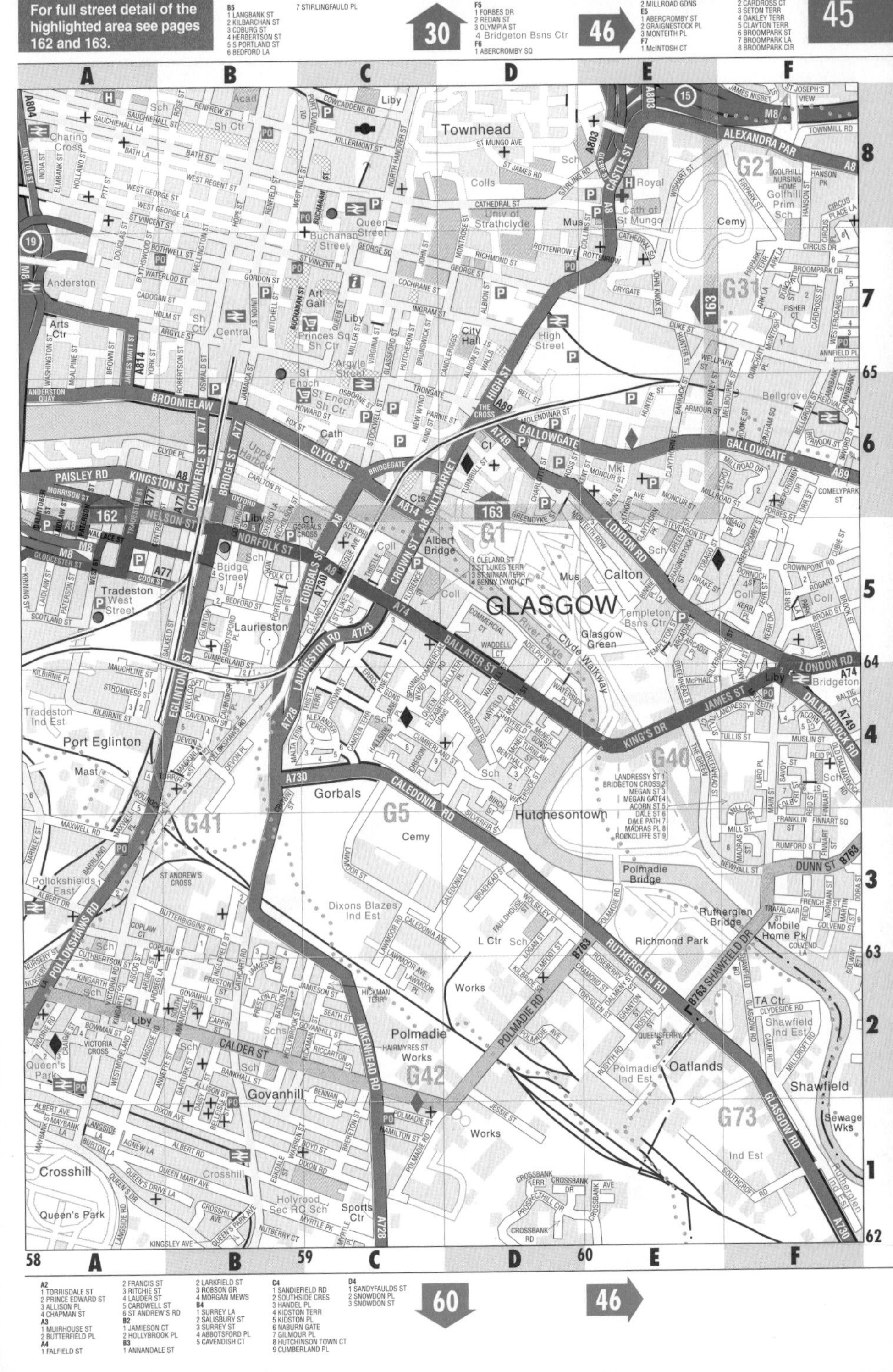
45
For full street detail of the highlighted area see pages 162 and 163.
B5
1 LANGBANK ST
2 KILBARCHAN ST
3 COBURG ST
4 HERBERTSON ST
5 S PORTLAND ST
6 BEDFORD LA
7 STIRLINGFAULD PL
30
F5
1 FORBES DR
2 REDAN ST
3 OLYMPIA ST
4 Bridgeton Bsns Ctr
F6
1 ABERCROMBY SQ
46
2 MILLROAD GDNS
E5
1 ABERCROMBY ST
2 GRAIGNESTOCK PL
3 MONTEITH PL
F7
1 McINTOSH CT
2 CARDROSS CT
3 SETON TERR
4 OAKLEY TERR
5 CLAYTON TERR
6 BROOMPARK ST
7 BROOMPARK LA
8 BROOMPARK CIR
Townhead
Charing Cross
Anderston
Arts Ctr
Queen Street
Buchanan Street
Art Gall
Central
Princes Sq Sh Ctr
St Enoch
St Enoch Sh Ctr
City Hall
High Street
Univ of Strathclyde
Royal
Cath of St Mungo
Cemy
Golfhill Prim Sch
Bellgrove
GALLOWGATE
BROOMIELAW
CLYDE ST
PAISLEY RD
KINGSTON ST
NELSON ST
NORFOLK ST
Tradeston
West Street
Bridge Street
Laurieston
Albert Bridge
GLASGOW
Calton
Mus
Templeton Bsns Ctr
Glasgow Green
River Clyde
Clyde Walkway
Bridgeton
LONDON RD
JAMES ST
KING'S DR
Tradeston Ind Est
Port Eglinton
Mast
Gorbals
CALEDONIA RD
Hutchesontown
Cemy
Polmadie Bridge
Pollokshields East
Dixons Blazes Ind Est
L Ctr
Works
Rutherglen Bridge
Richmond Park
Mobile Home Pk
SHAWFIELD DR
Shawfield Ind Est
TA Ctr
Polmadie
Polmadie Ind Est
Oatlands
Shawfield
Sewage Wks
Govanhill
CALDER ST
Queen's Park
Crosshill
Holyrood Sec RC Sch
Sports Ctr
Ind Est
Rutherglen Ind Est
RUTHERGLEN RD
GLASGOW RD
POLLOKSHAWS RD
AIKENHEAD RD
58
59
60
A2
1 TORRISDALE ST
2 PRINCE EDWARD ST
3 ALLISON PL
4 CHAPMAN ST
A3
1 MUIRHOUSE ST
2 BUTTERFIELD PL
A4
1 FALFIELD ST
2 FRANCIS ST
3 RITCHIE ST
4 LAUDER ST
5 CARDWELL ST
6 ST ANDREW'S RD
B2
1 JAMIESON CT
2 HOLLYBROOK PL
B3
1 ANNANDALE ST
2 LARKFIELD ST
3 ROBSON GR
4 MORGAN MEWS
B4
1 SURREY LA
2 SALISBURY ST
3 SURREY ST
4 ABBOTSFORD PL
5 CAVENDISH CT
C4
1 SANDIEFIELD RD
2 SOUTHSIDE CRES
3 HANDEL PL
4 KIDSTON TERR
5 KIDSTON PL
6 NABURN GATE
7 GILMOUR PL
8 HUTCHINSON TOWN CT
9 CUMBERLAND PL
D4
1 SANDYFAULDS ST
2 SNOWDON PL
3 SNOWDON ST
60
46

45
31

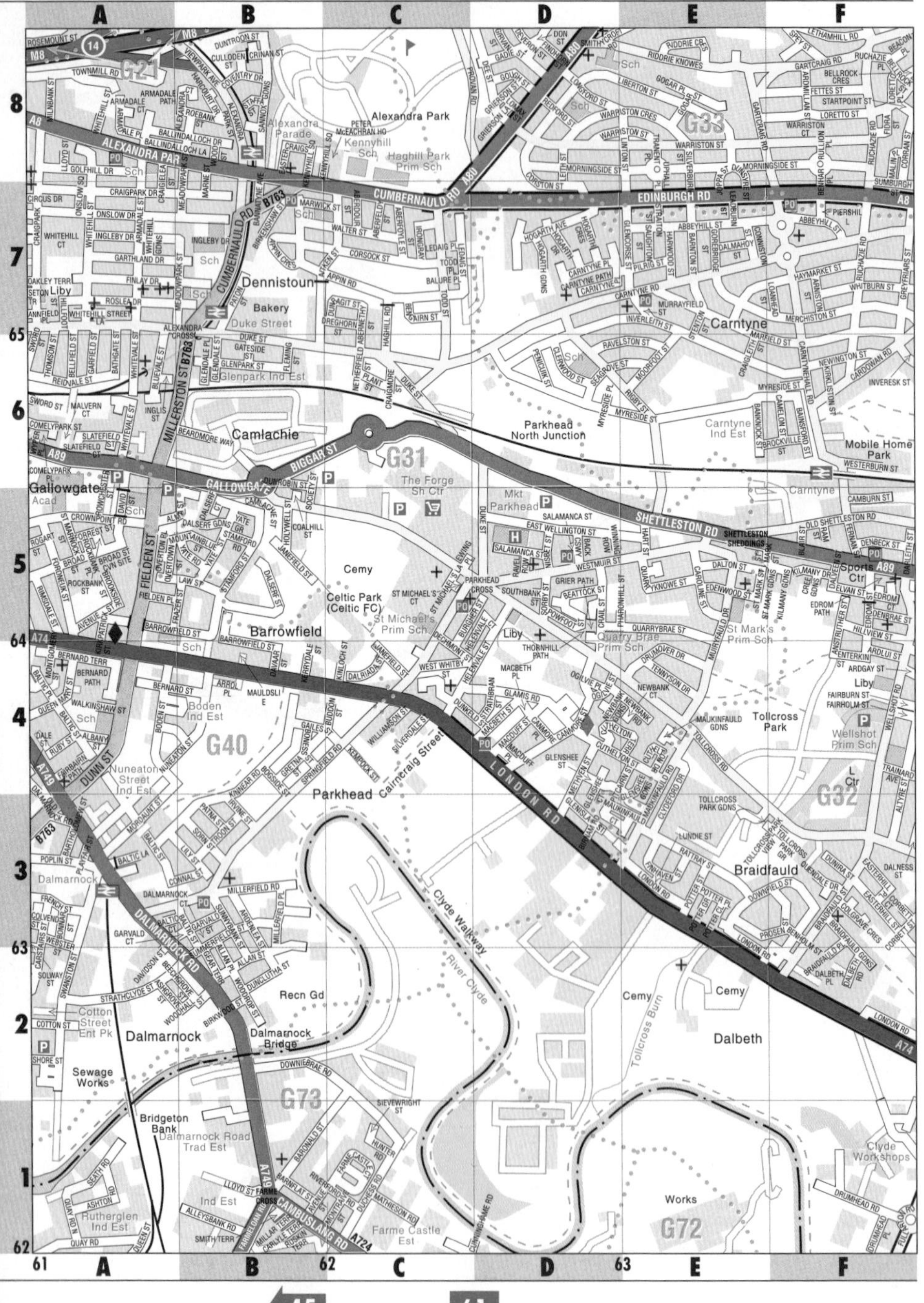
Alexandra Park
Dennistoun
Camlachie
Parkhead North Junction
Carntyne
Barrowfield
Celtic Park (Celtic FC)
Parkhead
Tollcross Park
Braidfauld
Dalmarnock
Dalbeth
Gallowgate
Carntyne Ind Est
Mobile Home Park
The Forge Sh Ctr
Cemy
Recn Gd
Sewage Works
Bridgeton Bank
Dalmarnock Road Trad Est
Rutherglen Ind Est
Farme Castle Est
Works
Clyde Workshops
River Clyde
Clyde Walkway
Tollcross Burn
ALEXANDRA PAR
CUMBERNAULD RD
EDINBURGH RD
GALLOWGATE
SHETTLESTON RD
LONDON RD
DALMARNOCK RD
CAMBUSLANG RD
MILLERSTON ST
FIELDEN ST
G21
G31
G32
G33
G40
G72
G73

32
48

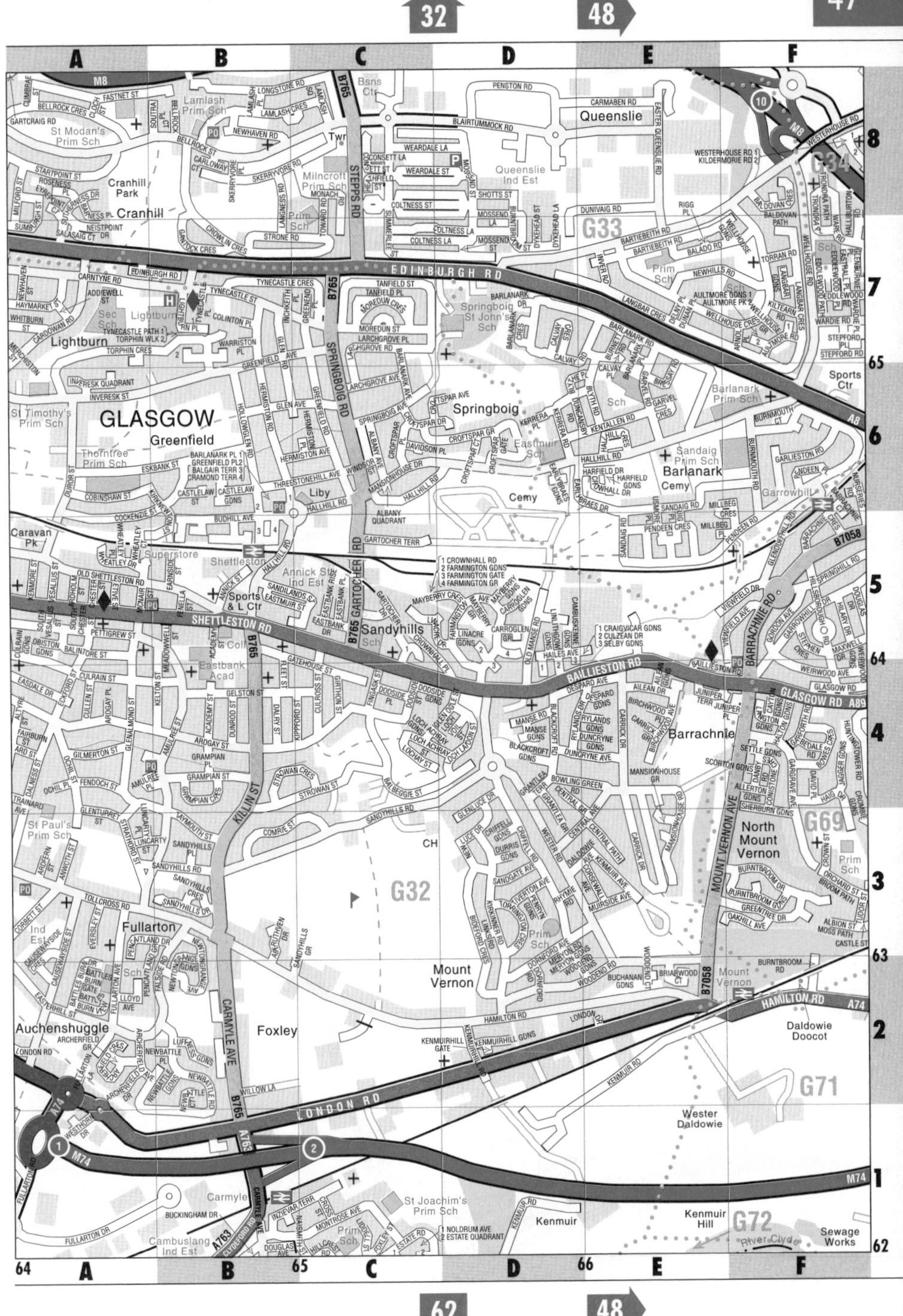
A
B
C
D
E
F
8
7
65
6
5
64
4
3
63
2
1
62
64
65
66
M8
Queenslie
Queenslie Ind Est
G33
G34
Cranhill Park
Cranhill
Lightburn
GLASGOW
Greenfield
Springboig
Barlanark
Cemy
Shettleston
Sandyhills
Barrachnie
North Mount Vernon
G69
G32
Mount Vernon
Fullarton
Auchenshuggle
Foxley
Carmyle
Kenmuir
Kenmuir Hill
Wester Daldowie
Daldowie Doocot
G71
G72
River Clyde
Sewage Works
Sports Ctr
Caravan Pk
Superstore
Sports & L Ctr
Annick St Ind Est
Cambuslang Ind Est
Eastbank Acad
St Joachim's Prim Sch
St Timothy's Prim Sch
Thorntree Prim Sch
St Paul's Prim Sch
St Modan's Prim Sch
Lamlash Prim Sch
Milncroft Prim Sch
Springboig St John's Sch
Eastmuir Sch
Sandaig Prim Sch
Barlanark Prim Sch
Garrowhill
EDINBURGH RD
SHETTLESTON RD
BAILLIESTON RD
GLASGOW RD
LONDON RD
HAMILTON RD
STEPPS RD
SPRINGBOIG RD
GARTOCHER RD
MOUNT VERNON AVE
KILLIN ST
CARMYLE AVE
BLAIRTUMMOCK RD
B765
B7058
A8
A89
A74
A763
M74

62
48

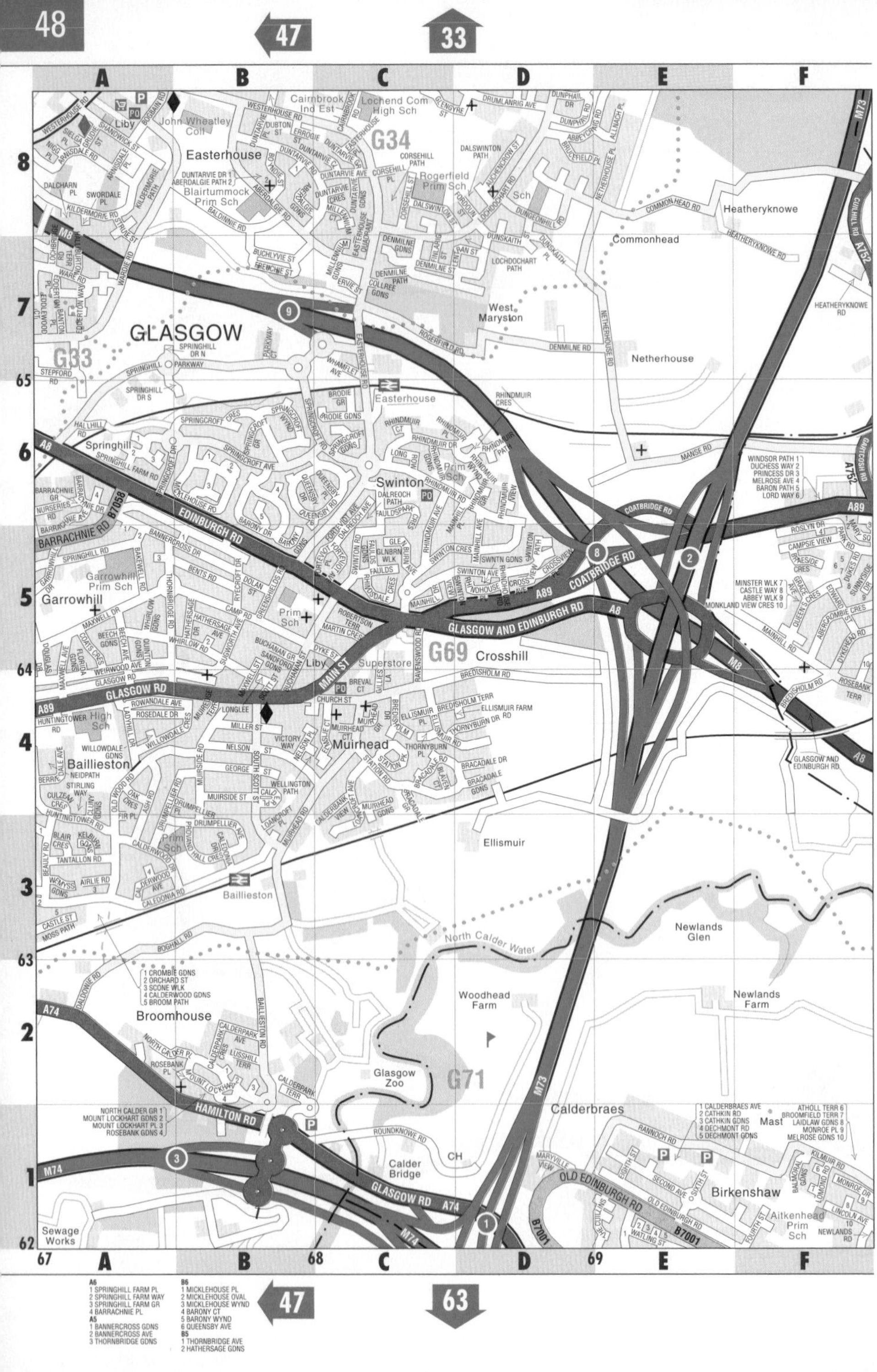

48
47
33
A
B
C
D
E
F
8
7
65
6
5
64
4
3
63
2
1
62
67
68
69
Easterhouse
GLASGOW
G33
G34
G69
G71
Liby
John Wheatley Coll
Cairnbrook Ind Est
Lochend Com High Sch
Blairtummock Prim Sch
Rogerfield Prim Sch
Sch
Heatheryknowe
Commonhead
West Maryston
Netherhouse
Springhill
Swinton
Prim Sch
Garrowhill
Garrowhill Prim Sch
Crosshill
Superstore
Muirhead
Baillieston
High Sch
Ellismuir
Newlands Glen
North Calder Water
Woodhead Farm
Newlands Farm
Broomhouse
Glasgow Zoo
Calderbraes
Mast
Calder Bridge
CH
Birkenshaw
Aitkenhead Prim Sch
Sewage Works
EDINBURGH RD
GLASGOW RD
GLASGOW AND EDINBURGH RD
COATBRIDGE RD
MAIN ST
HAMILTON RD
OLD EDINBURGH RD
BARRACHNIE RD
M8
M73
M74
A8
A89
A74
A752
B7058
B7001
WINDSOR PATH 1
DUCHESS WAY 2
PRINCESS DR 3
MELROSE AVE 4
BARON PATH 5
LORD WAY 6
MINSTER WLK 7
CASTLE WAY 8
ABBEY WLK 9
MONKLAND VIEW CRES 10
1 CROMBIE GDNS
2 ORCHARD ST
3 SCONE WLK
4 CALDERWOOD GDNS
5 BROOM PATH
NORTH CALDER GR 1
MOUNT LOCKHART GDNS 2
MOUNT LOCKHART PL 3
ROSEBANK GDNS 4
1 CALDERBRAES AVE
2 CATHKIN RD
3 CATHKIN GDNS
4 DECHMONT RD
5 DECHMONT GDNS
ATHOLL TERR 6
BROOMFIELD TERR 7
LAIDLAW GDNS 8
MONROE PL 9
MELROSE GDNS 10
A6
1 SPRINGHILL FARM PL
2 SPRINGHILL FARM WAY
3 SPRINGHILL FARM GR
4 BARRACHNIE PL
A5
1 BANNERCROSS GDNS
2 BANNERCROSS AVE
3 THORNBRIDGE GDNS
B6
1 MICKLEHOUSE PL
2 MICKLEHOUSE OVAL
3 MICKLEHOUSE WYND
4 BARONY CT
5 BARONY WYND
6 QUEENSBY AVE
B5
1 THORNBRIDGE AVE
2 HATHERSAGE GDNS
47
63

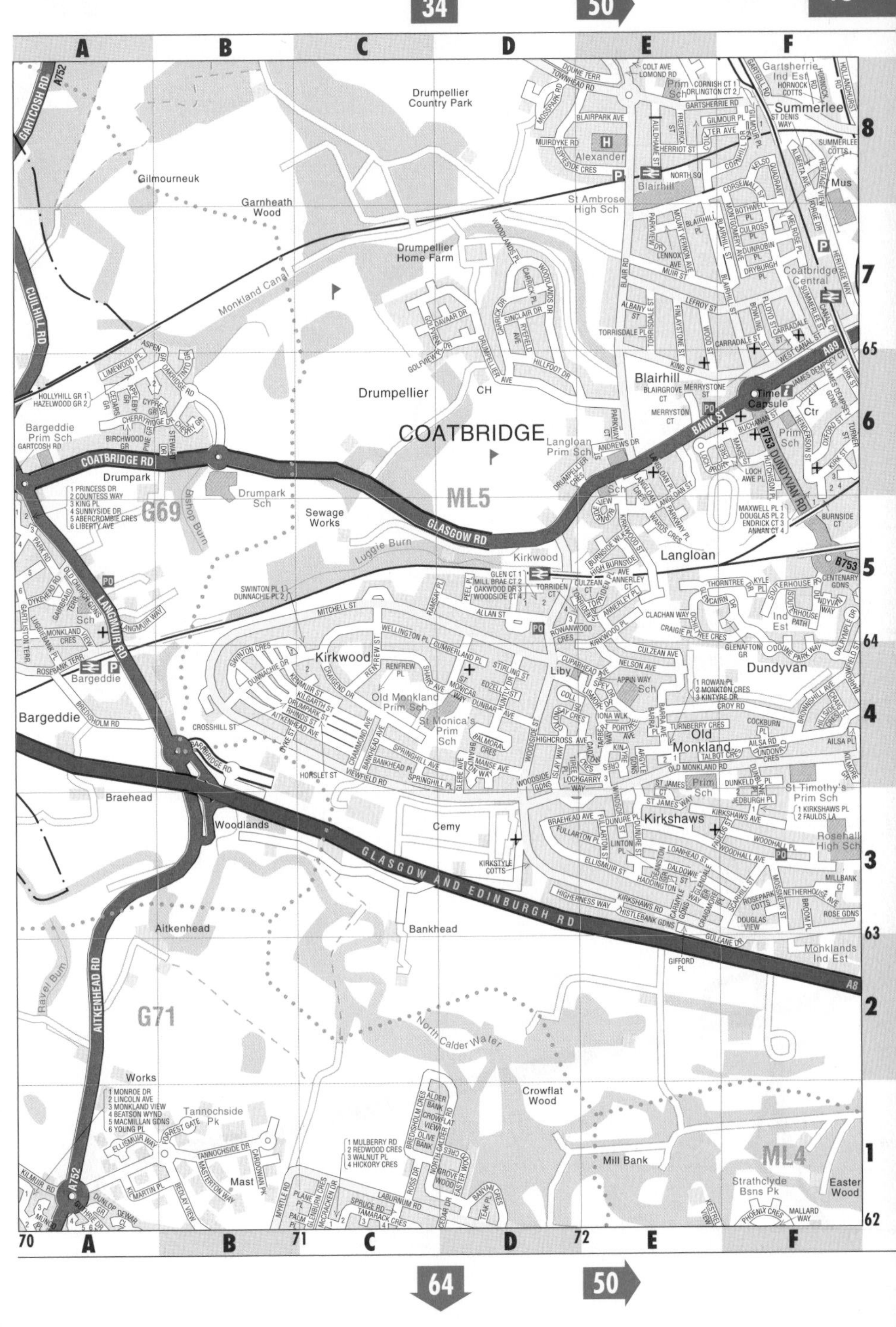
34
50
COATBRIDGE
Drumpellier
Drumpellier Country Park
Gilmourneuk
Garnheath Wood
Drumpellier Home Farm
Monkland Canal
Blairhill
Summerlee
Gartsherrie Ind Est
Alexander
St Ambrose High Sch
Coatbridge Central
Time Capsule
Langloan
Langloan Prim Sch
Kirkwood
Dundyvan
Old Monkland
Kirkshaws
St Timothy's Prim Sch
Rosehall High Sch
Monklands Ind Est
Bargeddie
Drumpark
Drumpark Sch
Sewage Works
Luggie Burn
Bishop Burn
Braehead
Woodlands
Cemy
Bankhead
Aitkenhead
North Calder Water
Crowflat Wood
Mill Bank
Strathclyde Bsns Pk
Easter Wood
Tannochside Pk
Works
Mast
Ravel Burn
ML5
G69
G71
ML4
COATBRIDGE RD
GLASGOW RD
GLASGOW AND EDINBURGH RD
BANK ST
DUNDYVAN RD
AITKENHEAD RD
LANGMUIR RD
CUILHILL RD
GARTCOSH RD
A752
A89
A8
B753
St Monica's Prim Sch
Old Monkland Prim Sch
64
50

A8
1 COLTSWOOD CT
2 RONALD ST
3 RED BRIDGE CT
4 LINCOLN CT

49
35

F8
1 NORTH BRIDGE ST
2 WELLWYND GDNS
3 WILLOWPARK CT
4 AITCHISON CT

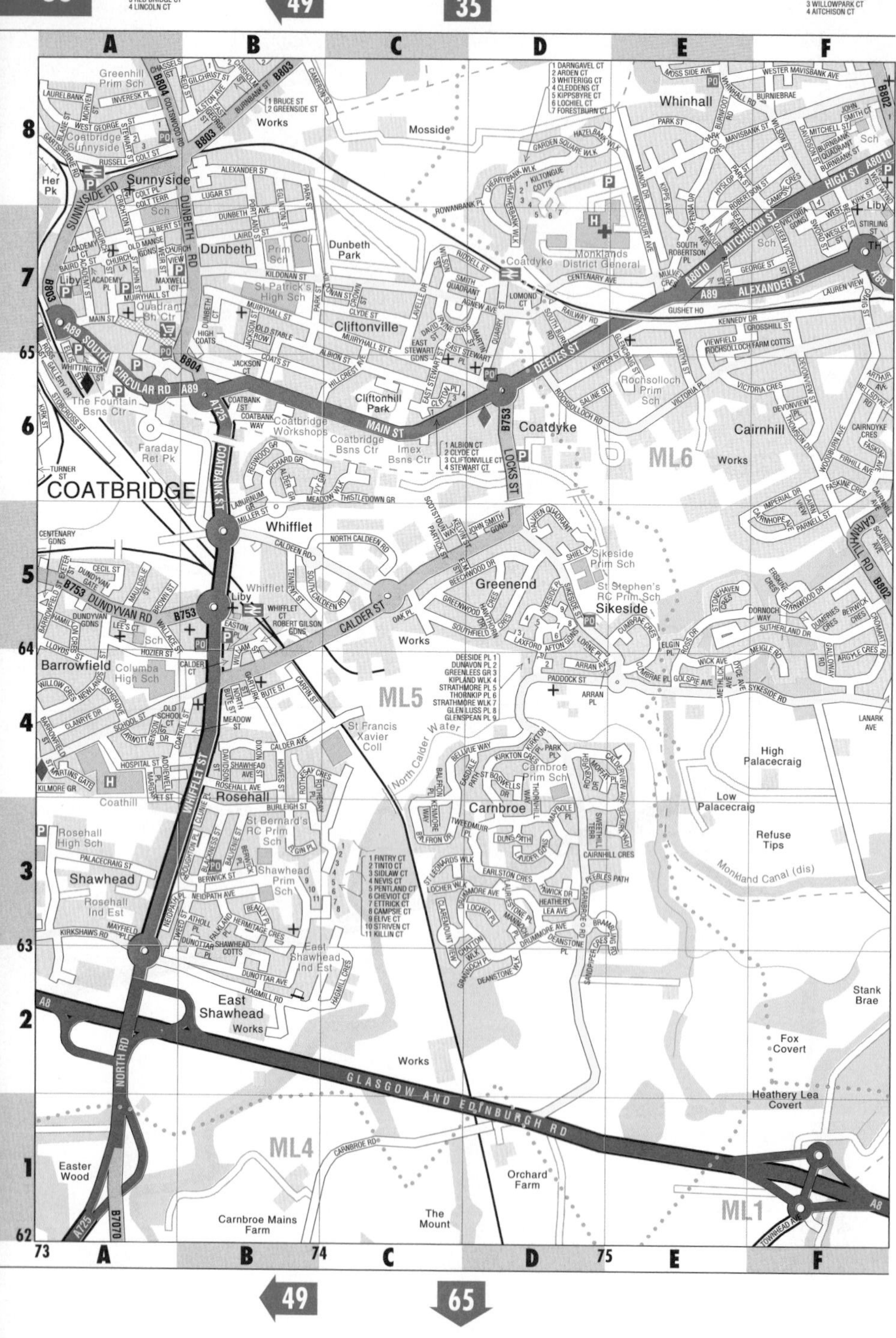

49
65

A8
1 ANDERSON LA
2 AULD'S BRAE
3 PARKHEAD LA
4 OLD CROSS
5 ANDERSON ST

B7
1 GARTLEA GDNS
2 SOUTH NIMMO ST
3 ALBERT CRES

C7
1 KINGSTON AVE
2 COLSTON PL
3 COLSTON ROW
4 COLSTON TERR

E7
1 FINLAYSON QUADRANT
2 WESTER MOFFAT CRES
3 MOORPARK AVE
4 CRAIGNURE CRES

36
52

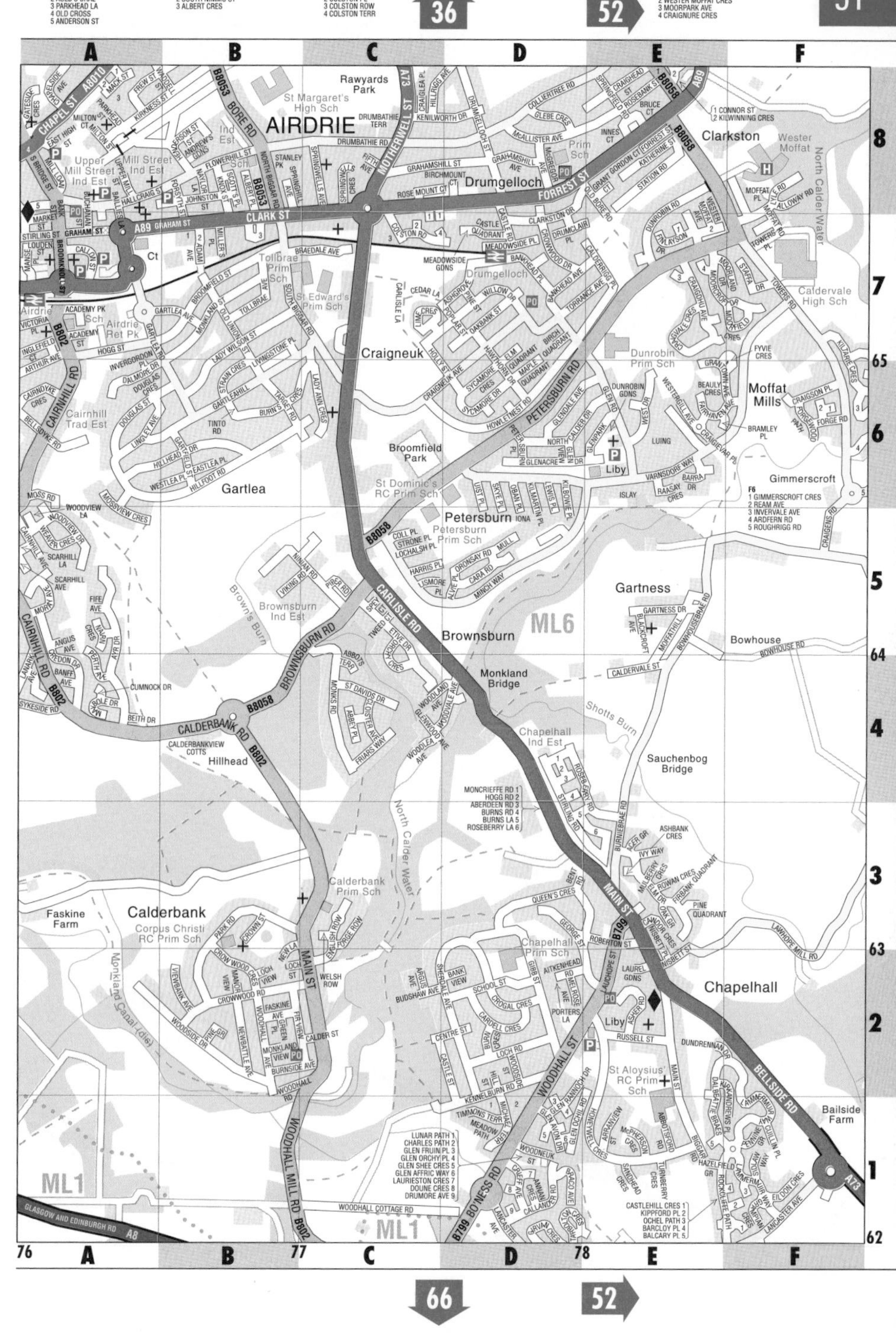

66
52

51
37

A
B
C
D
E
F
8
7
65
6
5
64
4
3
63
2
1
62
79
80
81
BROWNIESIDE RD
STEPENDS RD
Lochhill
DUNTILLAND RD
Browns Burn
Wester Bracco
Springbank Quarry (disused)
Lady Bell's Moss
BURNWOOD DR
INVERVALE AVE
ACHNASHEEN RD
ARDFERN RD
BALLOCH RD
DYSART WAY
Burn Wood
ROUGHRIGG RD
ML6
BOWHOUSE RD
Clattering Burn
Works
Roughrigg Resr
DUNSISTON RD
Easter Dunsyston
Craigends
Gartness Farm
GARTNESS RD
Turdees
Craigends Moss
CRAIGENS RD
Blackridge Farm
Wester Dunsyston
Langside
Bothwellshields
ML1
M8
Longacre Farm
Budshaw
BOTHWELLSHIELDS RD
Shotts Burn
Peatpots Farm
SPRINGFIELD RD
B7066
GLASGOW AND EDINBURGH RD
ML7
6
BELLSIDE RD
A73
WILSONS RD

51
67

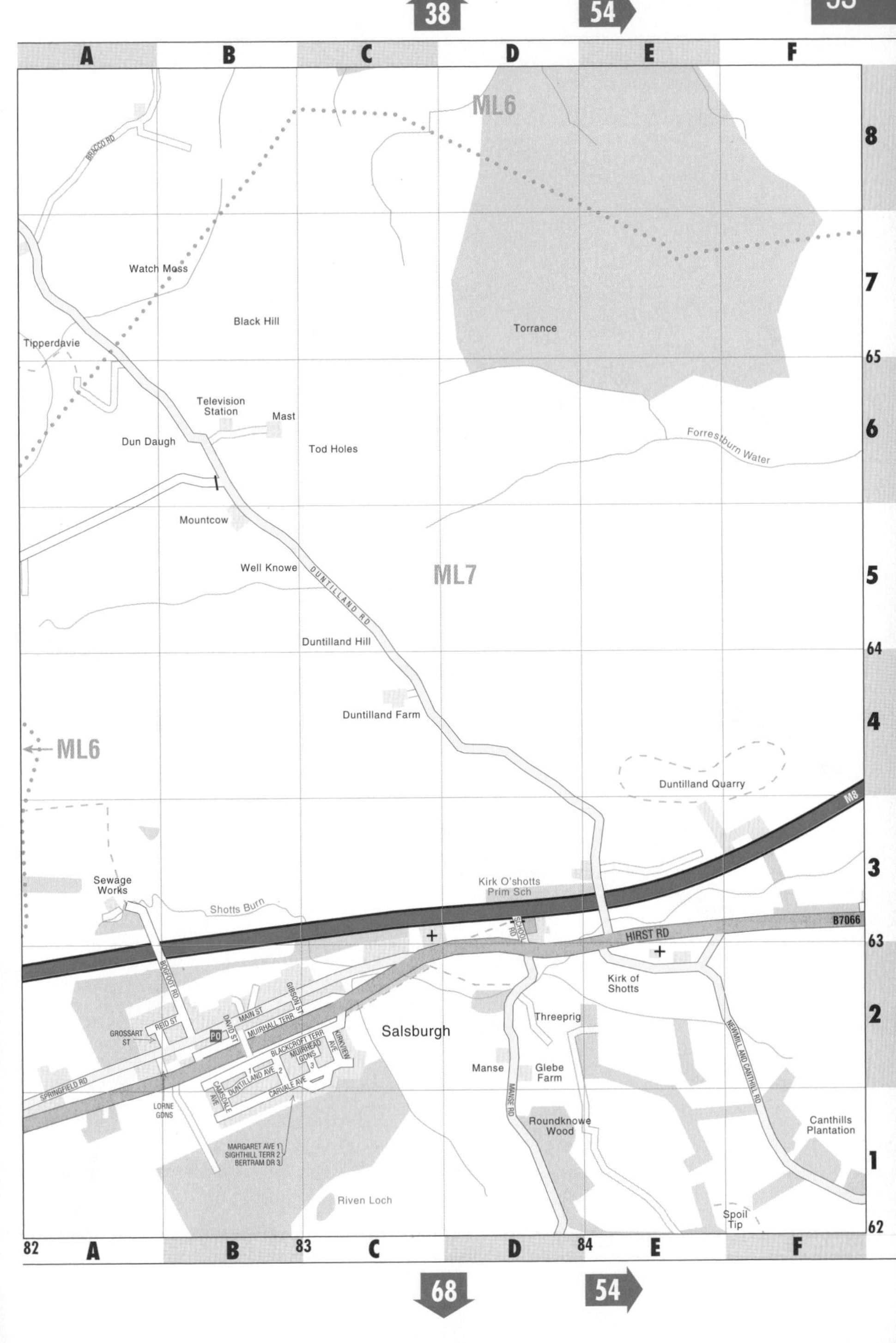
38
54
A
B
C
D
E
F
ML6
8
BRACCO RD
7
Watch Moss
Black Hill
Tipperdavie
Torrance
65
Television
Station
Mast
6
Dun Daugh
Tod Holes
Forrestburn Water
Mountcow
Well Knowe
DUNTILLAND RD
ML7
5
Duntilland Hill
64
Duntilland Farm
4
ML6
Duntilland Quarry
M8
3
Sewage
Works
Kirk O'shotts
Prim Sch
Shotts Burn
SCHOOL RD
B7066
HIRST RD
63
BOGFOOT RD
GIBSON ST
MAIN ST
DAVID ST
Kirk of
Shotts
2
Threeprig
GROSSART
ST
REID ST
PO
MUIRHALL TERR
Salsburgh
BLACKCROFT TERR
MUIRHEAD
GDNS
KIRKVIEW
AVE
NEWMILL AND CANTHILL RD
DUNTILLAND AVE
CAMSDALE
AVE
CARVALE AVE
Manse
Glebe
Farm
SPRINGFIELD RD
MANSE RD
LORNE
GDNS
Roundknowe
Wood
Canthills
Plantation
MARGARET AVE 1
SIGHTHILL TERR 2
BERTRAM DR 3
1
Riven Loch
Spoil
Tip
62
82
A
83
B
C
D
84
E
F
68
54

53
39

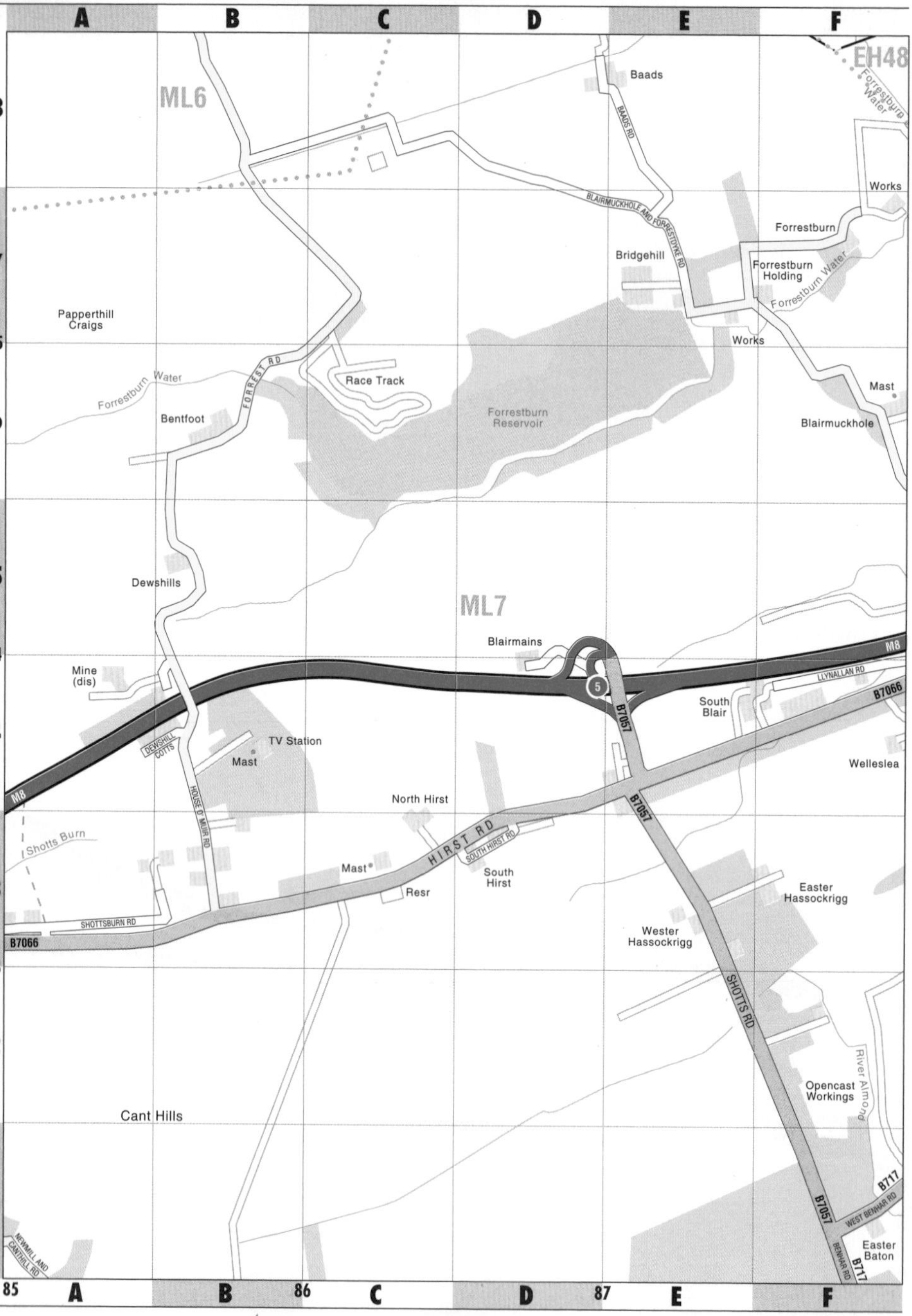

A B C D E F
8 7 65 6 5 64 4 3 63 2 1 62
ML6
ML7
EH48
Baads
BAADS RD
Forrestburn Water
Works
Forrestburn
BLAIRMUCKHOLE AND FORRESTDYKE RD
Bridgehill
Forrestburn Holding
Forrestburn Water
Papperthill Craigs
Works
FORREST RD
Race Track
Forrestburn Water
Bentfoot
Forrestburn Reservoir
Mast
Blairmuckhole
Dewshills
Blairmains
M8
5
LLYNALLAN RD
Mine (dis)
South Blair
B7066
B7057
DEWSHILL COTTS
TV Station
Mast
Welleslea
M8
North Hirst
B7057
Shotts Burn
HOUSE O' MUIR RD
HIRST RD
SOUTH HIRST RD
Mast
South Hirst
Resr
Easter Hassockrigg
SHOTTSBURN RD
B7066
Wester Hassockrigg
SHOTTS RD
River Almond
Opencast Workings
Cant Hills
B717
B7057
WEST BENHAR RD
NEWMILL AND CANTHILL RD
BENHAR RD
B717
Easter Baton
85 86 87
A B C D E F

53
69

40
56
A
B
C
D
E
F
Blairhill Quarry
EH48
Loan Farm
Hill Farm
Blairmuckhill
Netherton Farm
Knowehead
Mast
M8
Harthill Service Area
Sewage Works
Greenrigg Prim Sch
WESTCRAIGS RD
Treesbank Farm
Service Area
Harthill Ind Est
How Burn
WEST MAIN ST
EAST MAIN ST B7066
B718
B717
CHURCH ST
Alexander Peden Prim Sch
Harthill
HIRST RD
Tam's Loup Quarry
Eastfield
Paxtane
ML7
West Benhar
WEST BENHAR RD
Works
River Almond
Active Workings
Spoil Heap
Mon
Brownhill Farm
88
89
90
62
63
64
65
1
2
3
4
5
6
7
8
70
56

55
41

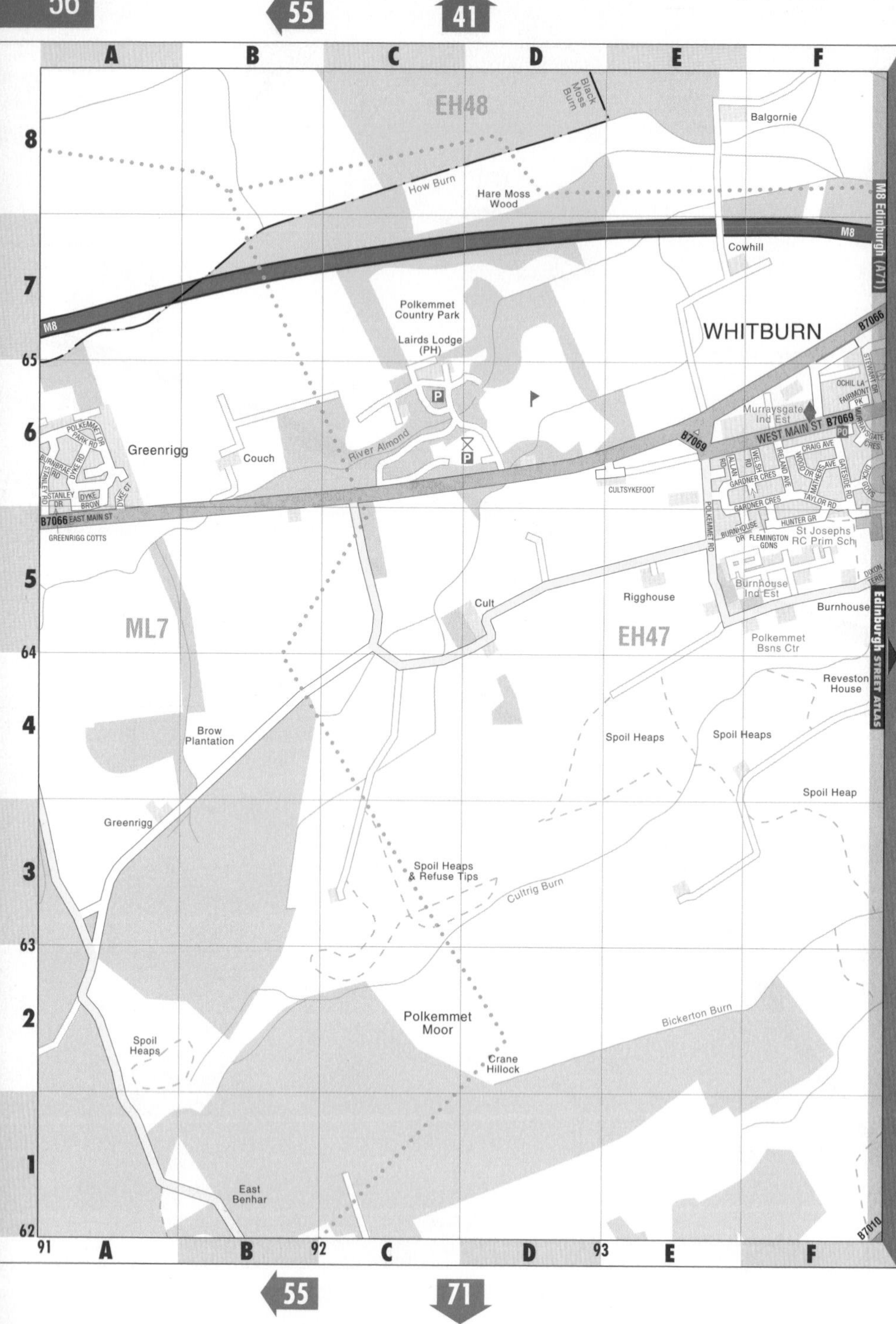
A
B
C
D
E
F
EH48
Black Moss Burn
Balgornie
How Burn
Hare Moss Wood
M8 Edinburgh (A71)
M8
Cowhill
Polkemmet Country Park
Lairds Lodge (PH)
WHITBURN
B7066
Greenrigg
Couch
River Almond
Murraysgate Ind Est
WEST MAIN ST
B7069
CULTSYKEFOOT
B7066 EAST MAIN ST
GREENRIGG COTTS
St Josephs RC Prim Sch
POLKEMMET RD
Rigghouse
Cult
Burnhouse Ind Est
Burnhouse
ML7
EH47
Polkemmet Bsns Ctr
Reveston House
Brow Plantation
Spoil Heaps
Spoil Heap
Greenrigg
Spoil Heaps & Refuse Tips
Cultrig Burn
Polkemmet Moor
Bickerton Burn
Spoil Heaps
Crane Hillock
East Benhar
B7010
Edinburgh STREET ATLAS
91
92
93
62
63
64
65

55
71

42
58

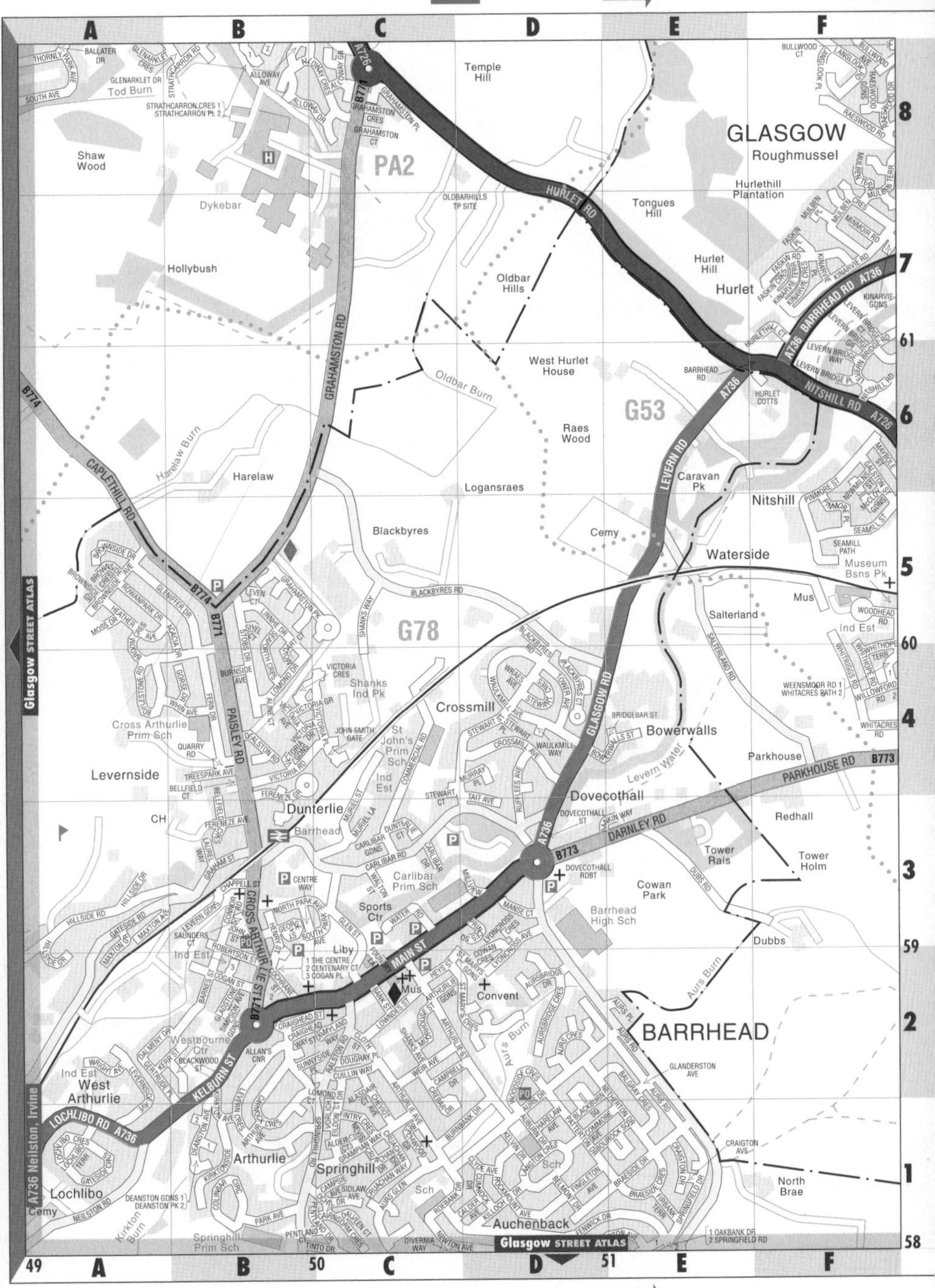
GLASGOW
Roughmussel
BARRHEAD
PA2
G53
G78
Temple Hill
Shaw Wood
Dykebar
Hollybush
Oldbar Hills
Tongues Hill
Hurlethill Plantation
Hurlet Hill
Hurlet
West Hurlet House
Oldbar Burn
Raes Wood
Harelaw Burn
Harelaw
Logansraes
Blackbyres
Caravan Pk
Nitshill
Cemy
Waterside
Museum Bsns Pk
Mus
Salterland
Ind Est
Shanks Ind Pk
Crossmill
Bowerwalls
Parkhouse
Levern Water
Cross Arthurlie Prim Sch
Leverside
St John's Prim Sch
Dunterlie
Barrhead
Dovecothall
Redhall
Tower Rais
Tower Holm
Cowan Park
Carlibar Prim Sch
Sports Ctr
Barrhead High Sch
Dubbs
Liby
Convent
Westbourne Ctr
Ind Est
West Arthurlie
Arthurlie
Springhill
Auchenback
Lochlibo
North Brae
Springhill Prim Sch
Kirkton Burn
Aurs Burn
Tod Burn
GRAHAMSTON RD
HURLET RD
NITSHILL RD
BARRHEAD RD
LEVERN RD
GLASGOW RD
PAISLEY RD
CROSS ARTHURLIE ST
MAIN ST
KELBURN ST
LOCHLIBO RD
CAPLETHILL RD
DARNLEY RD
PARKHOUSE RD
BLACKBYRES RD
A726
A736
B771
B773
B774
A736 Neilston, Irvine
Glasgow STREET ATLAS
A B C D E F
8 7 61 6 5 60 4 3 59 2 1 58
49 50 51

58

A8
1 SANQUHAR GDNS
2 SANQUHAR PL
3 RAESWOOD PL
4 POLQUHAP CT
5 POLQUHAP PL
6 POLQUHAP GDNS
7 CATRINE GDNS
8 CATRINE CT
9 DALMELLINGTON DR
10 LITTLEMILL GDNS
11 BALLOCHMYLE CRES
12 BALLOCHMYLE PL
13 MARLACH PL

A8
14 BALLOCHMYLE DR
15 BARGANY PL

57
43

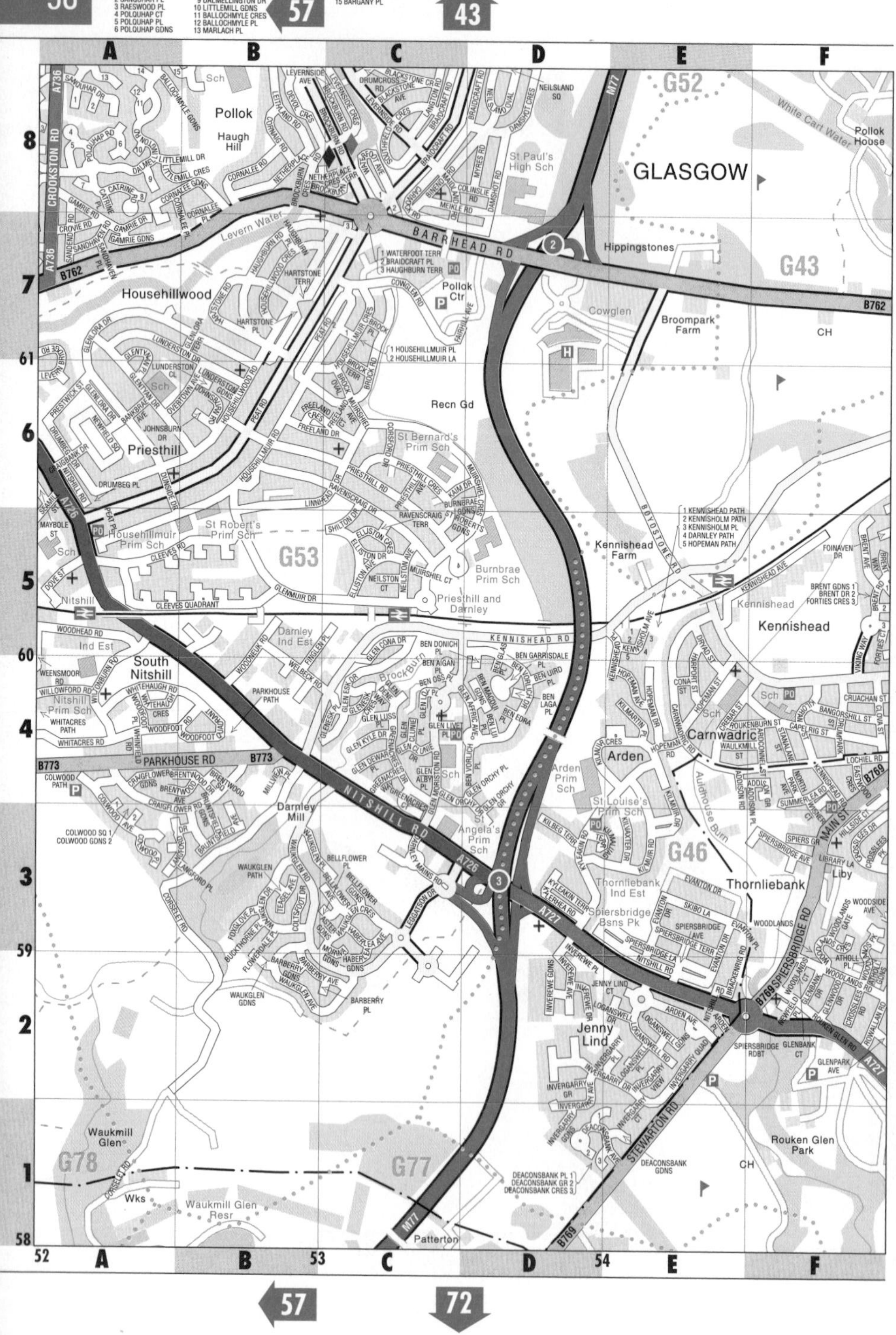

57
72

44
60

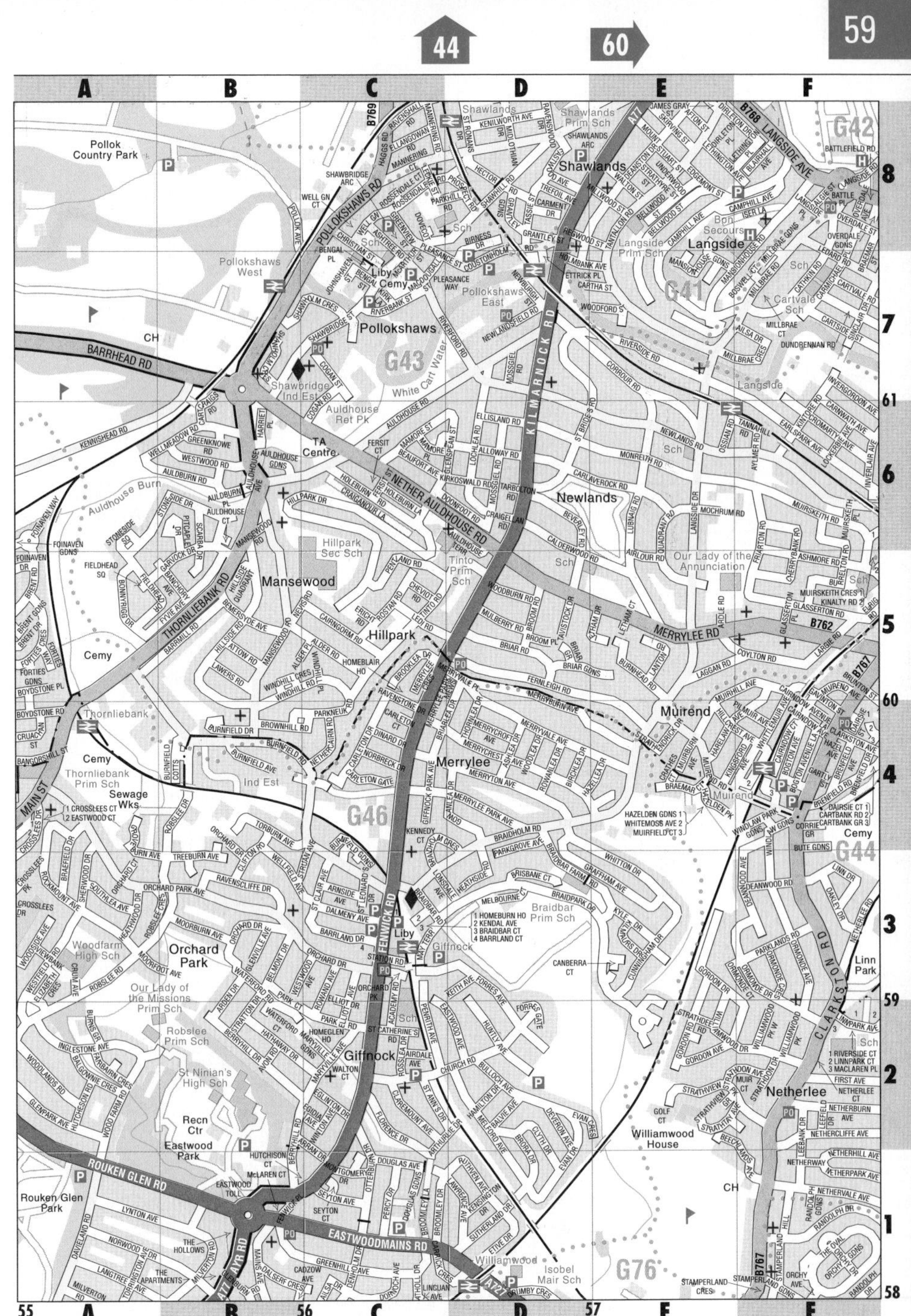
A
B
C
D
E
F
Pollok Country Park
Shawlands
Shawlands Prim Sch
Shawlands
Langside
Bon Secours
Langside Prim Sch
G42
G41
Cartvale Sch
Pollokshaws West
Pollokshaws
Liby Cemy
Pollokshaws East
G43
White Cart Water
Shawbridge Ind Est
Auldhouse Ret Pk
TA Centre
Langside
BARRHEAD RD
POLLOKSHAWS RD
KILMARNOCK RD
NETHER AULDHOUSE RD
Auldhouse Burn
Newlands
Hillpark Sec Sch
Tinto Prim Sch
Our Lady of the Annunciation
Mansewood
THORNLIEBANK RD
Hillpark
MERRYLEE RD
B762
B767
Cemy
Thornliebank
Muirend
Cemy
Thornliebank Prim Sch
Sewage Wks
Ind Est
Merrylee
G46
Muirend
G44
Cemy
Braidbar Prim Sch
Orchard Park
Woodfarm High Sch
Giffnock
Liby
Our Lady of the Missions Prim Sch
Robslee Prim Sch
Giffnock
St Ninian's High Sch
Netherlee
Linn Park
CLARKSTON RD
FENWICK RD
Recn Ctr
Eastwood Park
Williamwood House
ROUKEN GLEN RD
Rouken Glen Park
EASTWOODMAINS RD
Williamwood
Isobel Mair Sch
G76
AYR RD
A77
A727
B769
B768
CH
1 CROSSLEES CT
2 EASTWOOD CT
1 HOMEBURN HO
2 KENDAL AVE
3 BRAIDBAR CT
4 BARRLAND CT
HAZELDEN GDNS 1
WHITEMOSS AVE 2
MUIRFIELD CT 3
DAIRSIE CT 1
CARTBANK RD 2
CARTBANK GR 3
1 RIVERSIDE CT
2 LINNPARK CT
3 MACLAREN PL
8
7
61
6
5
60
4
3
59
2
1
58
55
56
57

73
60

59
45

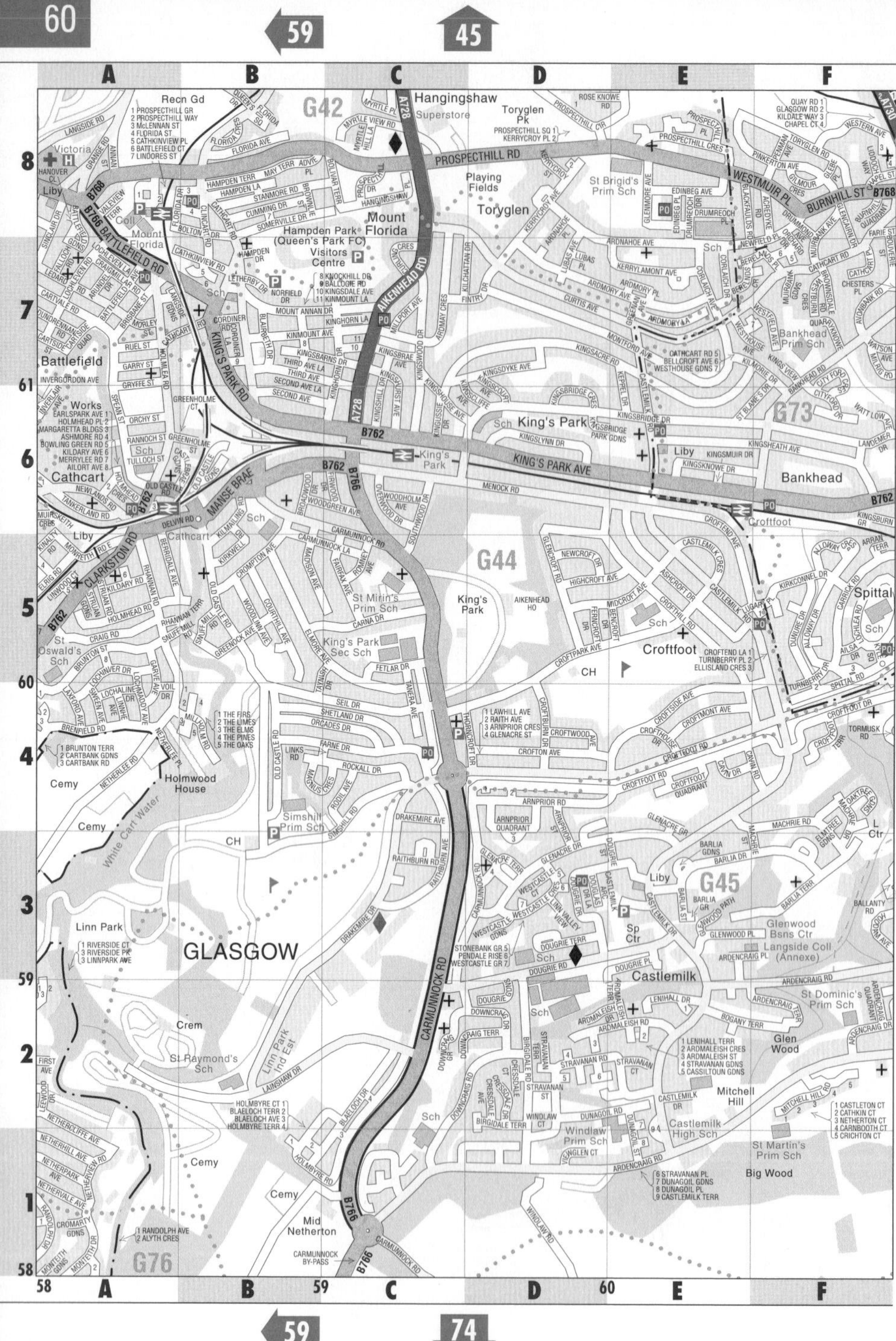
A
B
C
D
E
F
8
7
61
6
5
60
4
3
59
2
1
58
58
59
60
G42
G44
G45
G73
G76
Hangingshaw
Superstore
Toryglen Pk
Recn Gd
1 PROSPECTHILL GR
2 PROSPECTHILL WAY
3 McLENNAN ST
4 FLORIDA ST
5 CATHKINVIEW PL
6 BATTLEFIELD CT
7 LINDORES ST
PROSPECTHILL RD
Playing Fields
Toryglen
St Brigid's Prim Sch
Mount Florida
Hampden Park (Queen's Park FC)
Visitors Centre
8 KNOCKHILL DR
9 BALLOGIE RD
10 KINGSDALE AVE
11 KINMOUNT LA
AIKENHEAD RD
Victoria
Liby
Coll
Battlefield
Works
EARLSPARK AVE 1
HOLMHEAD PL 2
MARGARETTA BLDGS 3
ASHMORE RD 4
BOWLING GREEN RD 5
KILDARY AVE 6
MERRYLEE RD 7
AILORT AVE 8
Cathcart
KING'S PARK RD
KING'S PARK AVE
King's Park
MANSE BRAE
CLARKSTON RD
B762
B766
B768
A728
A730
WESTMUIR PL
BURNHILL ST
QUAY RD 1
GLASGOW RD 2
KILDALE WAY 3
CHAPEL CT 4
Bankhead Prim Sch
Bankhead
CATHCART RD 5
BELLCROFT AVE 6
WESTHOUSE GDNS 7
Croftfoot
CROFTEND LA 1
TURNBERRY PL 2
ELLISLAND CRES 3
Spittal
St Mirin's Prim Sch
King's Park Sec Sch
Aikenhead Ho
St Oswald's Sch
1 THE FIRS
2 THE LIMES
3 THE ELMS
4 THE PINES
5 THE OAKS
1 BRUNTON TERR
2 CARTBANK GDNS
3 CARTBANK RD
Cemy
Holmwood House
White Cart Water
Simshill Prim Sch
1 LAWHILL AVE
2 RAITH AVE
3 ARNPRIOR CRES
4 GLENACRE ST
Linn Park
1 RIVERSIDE CT
2 RIVERSIDE PK
3 LINNPARK AVE
GLASGOW
Crem
St Raymond's Sch
Linn Park Ind Est
CARMUNNOCK RD
STONEBANK GR 5
PENDALE RISE 6
WESTCASTLE GR 7
Sp Ctr
Castlemilk
G45
Glenwood Bsns Ctr
Langside Coll (Annexe)
St Dominic's Prim Sch
Glen Wood
1 LENIHALL TERR
2 ARDMALEISH CRES
3 ARDMALEISH ST
4 STRAVANAN GDNS
5 CASSILTOUN GDNS
Mitchell Hill
1 CASTLETON CT
2 CATHKIN CT
3 NETHERTON CT
4 CARNBOOTH CT
5 CRICHTON CT
HOLMBYRE CT 1
BLAELOCH TERR 2
BLAELOCH AVE 3
HOLMBYRE TERR 4
Windlaw Prim Sch
Castlemilk High Sch
St Martin's Prim Sch
Big Wood
6 STRAVANAN PL
7 DUNAGOIL GDNS
8 DUNAGOIL PL
9 CASTLEMILK TERR
Mid Netherton
CARMUNNOCK BY-PASS
1 RANDOLPH AVE
2 ALYTH CRES

59
74

A7
1 MACDONALD ST
2 BALVAIRD CRES
3 CHESTERS PL

A8
1 WESTERN AVE
2 CHAPEL ST
3 GREENBANK ST
4 VICTORIA PL
5 KING STREET LA

46
62

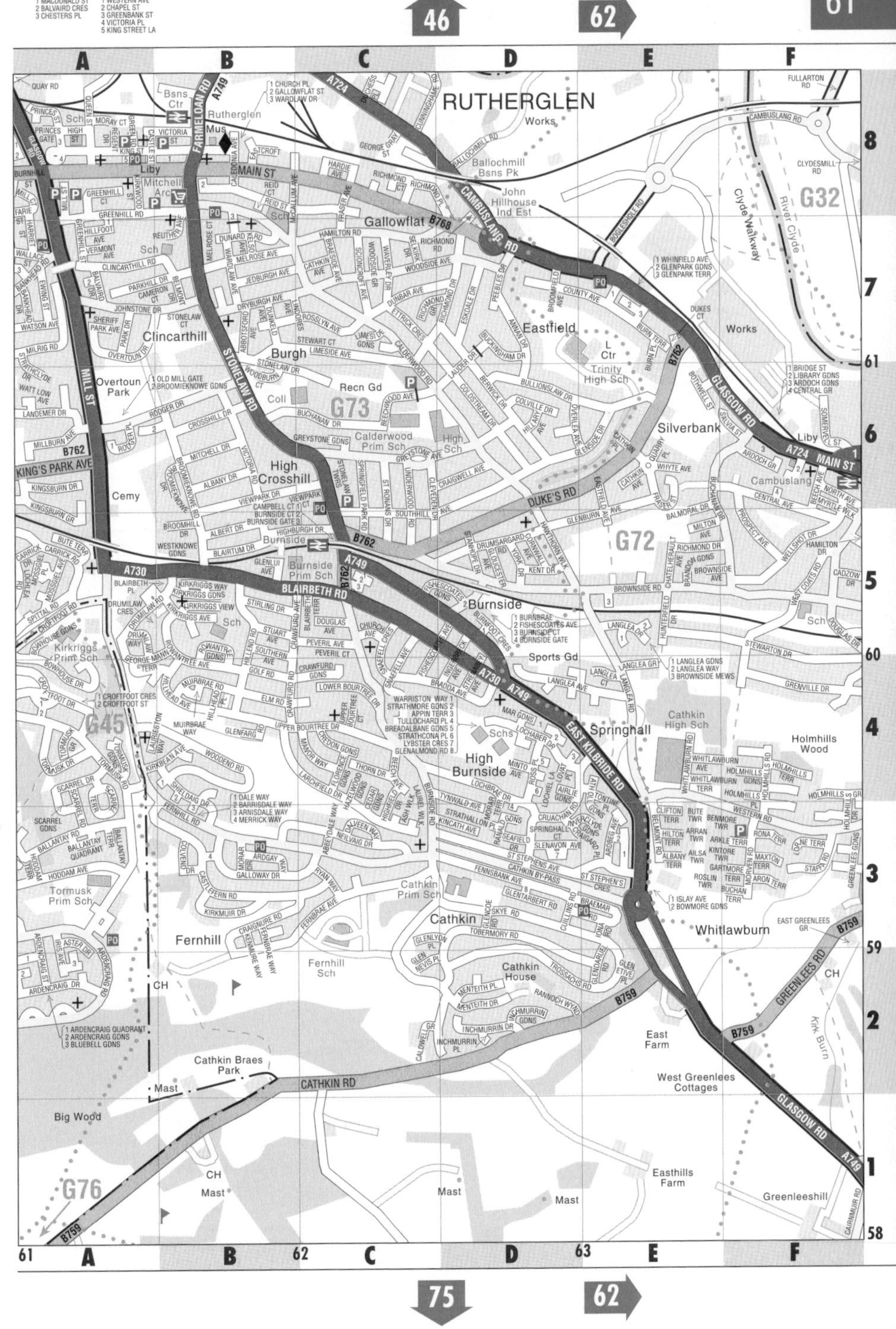

75
62

61
47

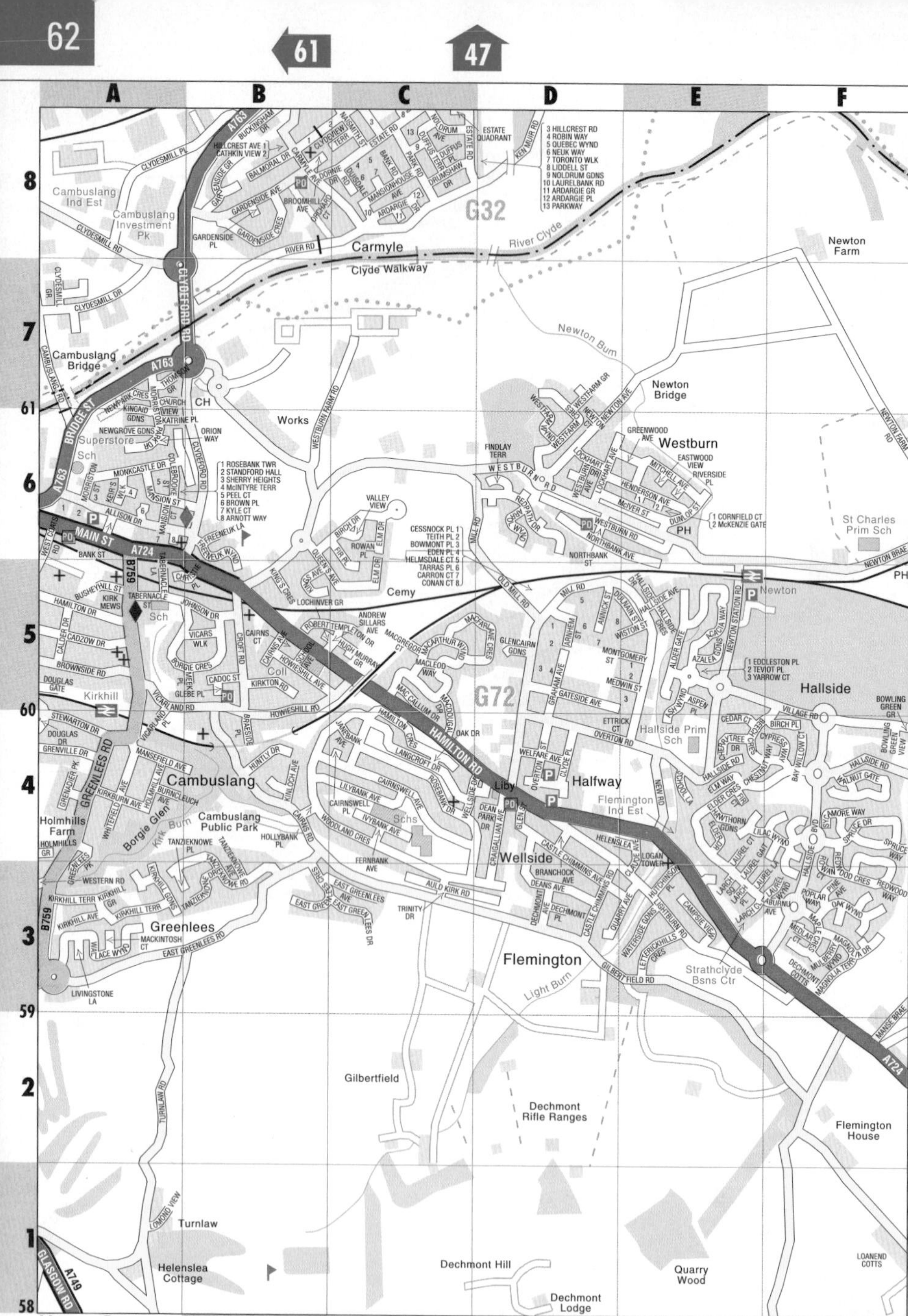
A
B
C
D
E
F
8
7
61
6
5
60
4
3
59
2
1
58
64
65
66
Cambuslang Ind Est
Cambuslang Investment Pk
Carmyle
River Clyde
Clyde Walkway
G32
Newton Farm
Newton Burn
Cambuslang Bridge
Newton Bridge
Works
Westburn
Superstore
Sch
CH
St Charles Prim Sch
Newton
Cemy
Kirkhill
Coll
G72
Hallside
Hallside Prim Sch
Cambuslang
Halfway
Flemington Ind Est
Holmhills Farm
Borgie Glen
Kirk Burn
Cambuslang Public Park
Schs
Wellside
Greenlees
Flemington
Strathclyde Bsns Ctr
Light Burn
Gilbertfield
Dechmont Rifle Ranges
Flemington House
Turnlaw
Helenslea Cottage
Dechmont Hill
Dechmont Lodge
Quarry Wood
LOANEND COTTS
CLYDEFORD RD
MAIN ST
A724
HAMILTON RD
A763
B759
GREENLEES RD
GLASGOW RD
A749
BRIDGE ST
WESTBURN RD
WESTBURN FARM RD
NEWTON AVE
NEWTON STATION RD
NEWTON FARM RD
NEWTON BRAE
MILL RD
OLD MILL RD
EAST GREENLEES RD
GILBERTFIELD RD
TURNLAW RD
RIVER RD
CLYDESMILL RD
CLYDESMILL DR
CLYDESMILL PL
CLYDESMILL GR
3 HILLCREST RD
4 ROBIN WAY
5 QUEBEC WYND
6 NEUK WAY
7 TORONTO WLK
8 LIDDELL ST
9 NOLDRUM GDNS
10 LAURELBANK RD
11 ARDARGIE GR
12 ARDARGIE PL
13 PARKWAY
1 ROSEBANK TWR
2 STANDFORD HALL
3 SHERRY HEIGHTS
4 McINTYRE TERR
5 PEEL CT
6 BROWN PL
7 KYLE CT
8 ARNOTT WAY
CESSNOCK PL 1
TEITH PL 2
BOWMONT PL 3
EDEN PL 4
HELMSDALE CT 5
TARRAS PL 6
CARRON CT 7
CONAN CT 8
1 CORNFIELD CT
2 McKENZIE GATE
1 EDDLESTON PL
2 TEVIOT PL
3 YARROW CT
HILLCREST AVE 1
CATHKIN VIEW 2

61
76

48 64

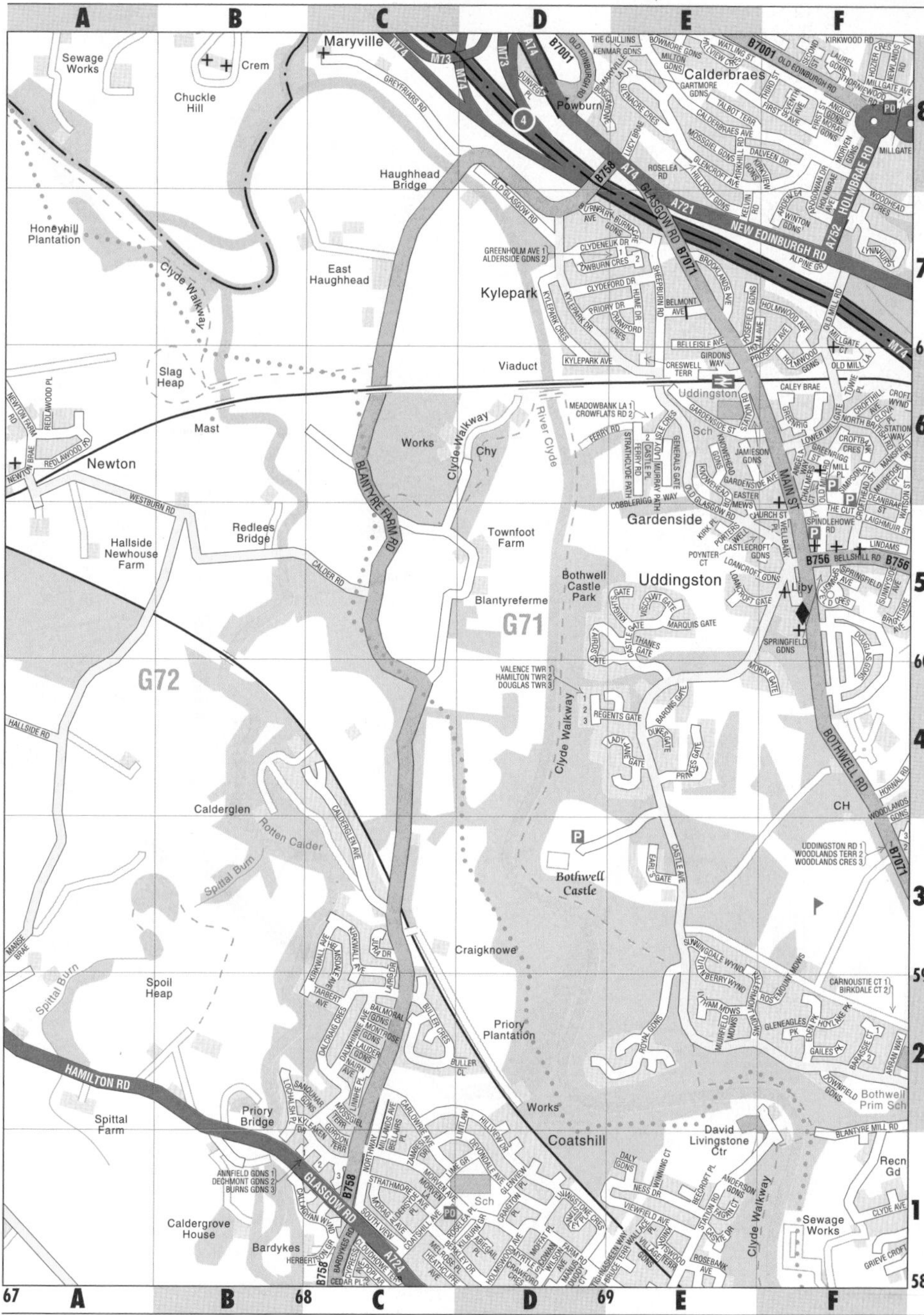

A B C D E F

8 7 61 6 5 60 4 3 59 2 1 58

Sewage Works
Crem
Chuckle Hill
Maryville
M74 M73 A74 B7001
GREYFRIARS RD
DUNVEGAN PL
Powburn
THE CUILLINS
KENMAR GDNS
BOWMORE GDNS
HILLVIEW CRES
WATLING ST
MILTON GDNS
Calderbraes
GARTMORE GDNS
GLENACRE CRES
TALBOT TERR
THIRD ST
FIRST ST
SEVENTH AVE
FIRST AVE
ANGUS GDNS
MORAY GDNS
CALDERBRAES AVE
MOSSGIEL GDNS
DALVEEN DR
LUCY BRAE
ROSELEA RD
GLENCROFT AVE
HILLFOOT GDNS
KIRKVIEW
MORVEN GDNS
HOLMBRAE RD
MILLGATE
KIRKWOOD RD
OLD EDINBURGH RD
B7001
LAUREL GDNS
THORNIEWOOD RD
HOZIER CRES
NEWLANDS RD
MILLGATE AVE
Haughhead Bridge
OLD GLASGOW RD
B758
A74
GLASGOW RD
B7071
A721
NEW EDINBURGH RD
A752
WOODHEAD CRES
LYNNHURST
ALPINE GR
WINTON GDNS
Honeyhill Plantation
Clyde Walkway
East Haughhead
GREENHOLM AVE 1
ALDERSIDE GDNS 2
BURNPARK AVE
CLYDENEUK DR
POWBURN CRES
CLYDEFORD DR
HUME DR
PRIORY DR
CRAWFORD CRES
Kylepark
KYLEPARK DR
KYLEPARK CRES
KYLEPARK AVE
SHEEPBURN RD
BELMONT AVE
BROOKLANDS AVE
ROSEFIELD GDNS
HOLMWOOD AVE
HOLM AVE
PROSPECT AVE
BELLEISLE AVE
GIRDONS WAY
CRESWELL TERR
OLD MILL RD
MILLGATE CT
OLD MILL LA
M74
Slag Heap
Viaduct
Uddingston
CALEY BRAE
TOWIE PL
CROFTHILL AVE
CROFT WYND
Mast
NEWTON FARM RD
REDLAWOOD PL
REDLAWOOD RD
NEWTON BRAE
Newton
Works
Clyde Walkway
Chy
River Clyde
MEADOWBANK LA 1
CROWFLATS RD 2
FERRY RD
CASTLE PL
STRATHCLYDE PATH
ISLE CRES
LADY ISLE CRES
MURRAY PATH
GENERALS GATE
COBBLERIGG WAY
GARDENSIDE ST
STATION RD
Sch
KNOWEHEAD GDNS
JAMIESON GDNS
GREENRIG
LOWER MILLGATE
NORTH BRITISH RD
STATION WAY
CROFTBANK CRES
GREENRIGG ST
MILL PL
OLD GLASGOW RD
GARDENSIDE AVE
EASTER MEWS
CHURCH ST
Gardenside
KIRK PL
PORTERS WELL
WELLBANK
SPINDLEHOWE RD
THE CUT
LAIGHMUIR ST
LINDAMS
MAIN ST
BLANTYRE FARM RD
WESTBURN RD
Redlees Bridge
Hallside Newhouse Farm
Townfoot Farm
CASTLECROFT GDNS
POYNTER CT
LOANCROFT GDNS
LOANCROFT GATE
B756
BELLSHILL RD
SPRINGFIELD AVE
SUNNYSIDE AVE
BRIGHTSIDE AVE
CALDER RD
Bothwell Castle Park
Uddingston
Liby
Blantyreferme
G71
KNIGHTS GATE
VISCOUNT GATE
MARQUIS GATE
CASTLE GATE
THANES GATE
LAIRDS GATE
SPRINGFIELD GDNS
DOUGLAS GDNS
MORAY GATE
G72
VALENCE TWR 1
HAMILTON TWR 2
DOUGLAS TWR 3
REGENTS GATE
BARONS GATE
LADY JANE GATE
DUKES GATE
PRINCES GATE
HALLSIDE RD
Clyde Walkway
BOTHWELL RD
HORNAL RD
CH
WOODLANDS GDNS
Calderglen
Rotten Calder
CALDERGLEN AVE
UDDINGSTON RD 1
WOODLANDS TERR 2
WOODLANDS CRES 3
B7071
Spittal Burn
CASTLE AVE
EARLS GATE
Bothwell Castle
MANSE BRAE
KIRKWALL AVE
Craigknowe
SUNNINGDALE WYND
TURNBERRY WYND
ROSEMOUNT MEWS
CARNOUSTIE CT 1
BIRKDALE CT 2
Spittal Burn
Spoil Heap
TARBERT AVE
JURA DR
LARGO PL
BALMORAL GDNS
MONTROSE GDNS
DALCRAIG CRES
DALWHINNIE AVE
LAUDER GDNS
NAIRN AVE
BULLER CRES
Priory Plantation
LYTHAM MEWS
MUIRFIELD MEWS
GLENEAGLES PK
EDEN PK
HOYLAKE PK
GAILES PK
BARASSIE CT
ARRAN WAY
ROYAL GDNS
BULLER CL
HAMILTON RD
Spittal Farm
Priory Bridge
SANQUHAR GDNS
LOCHALSH PL
KYLEAKEN DR
MOSSGIEL TERR
GORDON TERR
LINNHE PL
Works
DOWNFIELD GDNS
Bothwell Prim Sch
CARLOWRIE AVE
MILLANDS AVE
BELLAIRS PL
NORTHWAY
LINTLAW
HILLVIEW DR
DEVONDALE AVE
ZAMBESI DR
LIME GR
Coatshill
David Livingstone Ctr
BLANTYRE MILL RD
Recn Gd
ANNFIELD GDNS 1
DECHMONT GDNS 2
BURNS GDNS 3
GLASGOW RD
STRATHMORE AVE
MORVEN AVE
GLENVIEW
Sch
LIVINGSTONE CRES
DALY GDNS
WINNING CT
NESS DR
BEECROFT PL
ANDERSON GDNS
Caldergrove House
CALLAGHAN WYND
MORAG AVE
SOUTH VIEW
COATSHILL AVE
ROSELEA PL
KILBURN GR
ABIEGAIL PL
CRAIGTON PL
MOFFAT PL
VIEWFIELD AVE
STATION RD
TAGUS ST
Clyde Walkway
Sewage Works
CLYDE AVE
GRIEVE CROFT
Bardykes
HERBERTSON GR
BARDYKES RD
B758
CYPRESS CT
CEDAR PL
POPLAR
CLOUDHOWE TERR
A724
MELROSE PL
HEATHCLIFFE AVE
BERKELEY DR
HOLMSWOOD AVE
MYRTLE SQ
CRAWFORD CRES
COWAN WILSON AVE
FARM AVE
MANUS DUDDY CT
WALLACE GDNS
BRUCE TERR
HIGHMEADOW WAY
ROSEBANK AVE
ARDWOOD

67 A B 68 C D 69 E F

77 64

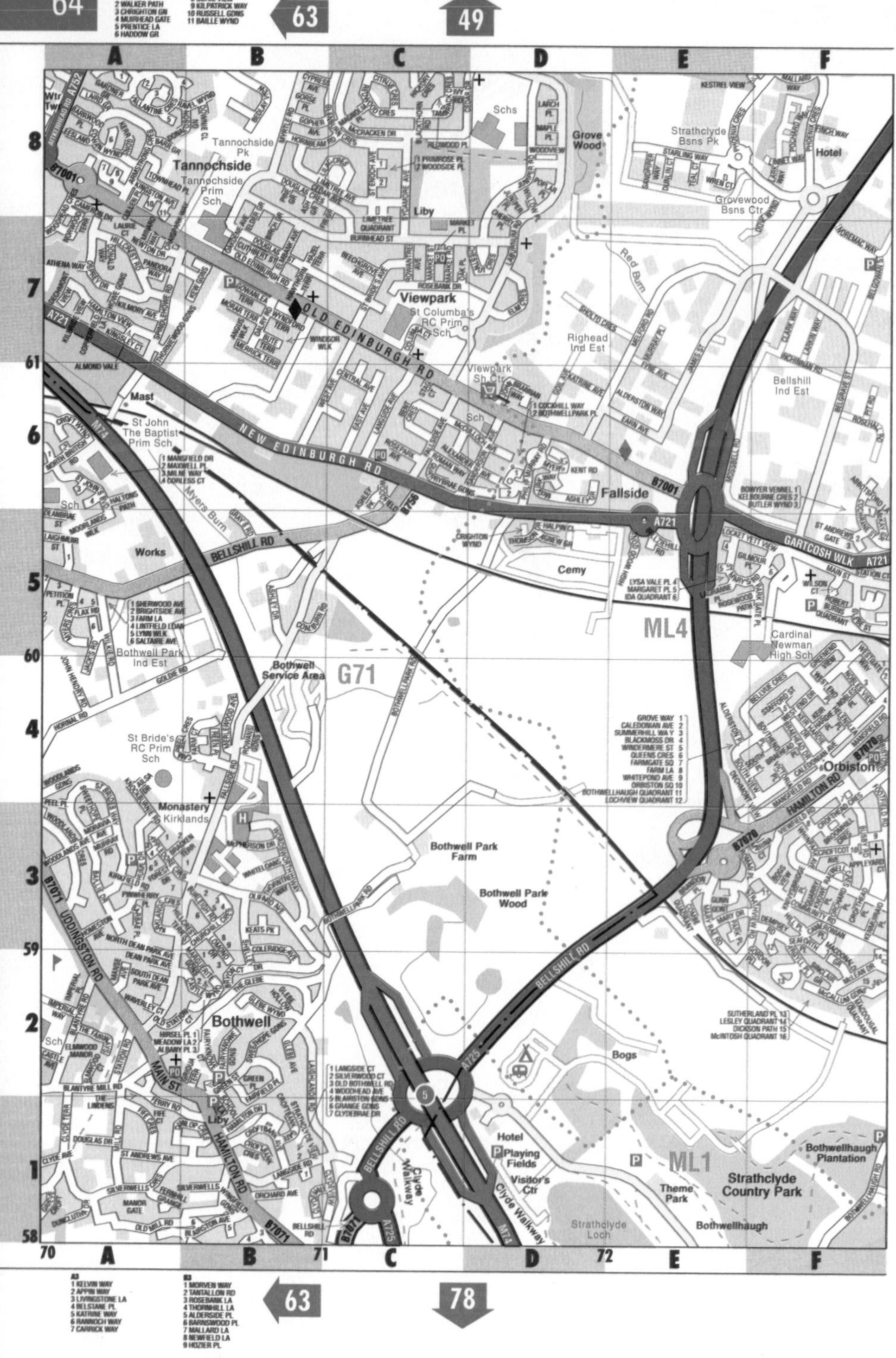
A8
1 YOUNG PL
2 WALKER PATH
3 CHRIGHTON GN
4 MUIRHEAD GATE
5 PRENTICE LA
6 HADDOW GR
7 CAMPSIE VIEW
8 OCHIL VIEW
9 KILPATRICK WAY
10 RUSSELL GDNS
11 BAILLIE WYND
63
49
A
B
C
D
E
F
8
7
61
6
5
60
4
3
59
2
1
58
70
71
72
Tannochside
Tannochside Pk
Tannochside Prim Sch
Schs
Grove Wood
Strathclyde Bsns Pk
Hotel
Grovewood Bsns Ctr
Liby
1 PRIMROSE PL
2 WOODSIDE PL
Viewpark
St Columba's RC Prim Sch
OLD EDINBURGH RD
NEW EDINBURGH RD
Righead Ind Est
Red Burn
Viewpark Sh Ctr
Sch
1 COCKHILL WAY
2 BOTHWELLPARK PL
Bellshill Ind Est
Mast
St John The Baptist Prim Sch
1 MANSFIELD DR
2 MAXWELL PL
3 MILNE WAY
4 CORLESS CT
Myers Burn
Fallside
B7001
A721
Works
BELLSHILL RD
Cemy
GARTCOSH WLK
BOWYER VENNEL 1
KELBOURNE CRES 2
BUTLER WYND 3
LYSA VALE PL 4
MARGARET PL 5
IDA QUADRANT 6
ML4
1 SHERWOOD AVE
2 BRIGHTSIDE AVE
3 FARM LA
4 LINTFIELD LOAN
5 LYNN WLK
6 SALTAIRE AVE
Bothwell Park Ind Est
Cardinal Newman High Sch
Bothwell Service Area
G71
St Bride's RC Prim Sch
GROVE WAY 1
CALEDONIAN AVE 2
SUMMERHILL WAY 3
BLACKMOSS DR 4
WINDERMERE ST 5
QUEENS CRES 6
FARMGATE SQ 7
FARM LA 8
WHITEPOND AVE 9
ORBISTON SQ 10
BOTHWELLHAUGH QUADRANT 11
LOCHVIEW QUADRANT 12
Orbiston
HAMILTON RD
B7070
Monastery
Kirklands
Bothwell Park Farm
Bothwell Park Wood
UDDINGSTON RD
B7071
BELLSHILL RD
SUTHERLAND PL 13
LESLEY QUADRANT 14
DICKSON PATH 15
McINTOSH QUADRANT 16
Bothwell
HIRSEL PL 1
MEADOW LA 2
ALBANY PL 3
1 LANGSIDE CT
2 SILVERWOOD CT
3 OLD BOTHWELL RD
4 WOODHEAD AVE
5 BLAIRSTON GDNS
6 GRANGE GDNS
7 CLYDEBRAE DR
Bogs
MAIN ST
HAMILTON RD
Hotel
Playing Fields
Visitor's Ctr
Clyde Walkway
ML1
Theme Park
Strathclyde Country Park
Bothwellhaugh Plantation
Strathclyde Loch
Bothwellhaugh
A725
M74
A
B
C
D
E
F
A3
1 KELVIN WAY
2 APPIN WAY
3 LIVINGSTONE LA
4 BELSTANE PL
5 KATRINE WAY
6 RANNOCH WAY
7 CARRICK WAY
B3
1 MORVEN WAY
2 TANTALLON RD
3 ROSEBANK LA
4 THORNHILL LA
5 ALDERSIDE PL
6 BARNSWOOD PL
7 MALLARD LA
8 NEWFIELD LA
9 HOZIER PL
63
78

50
66

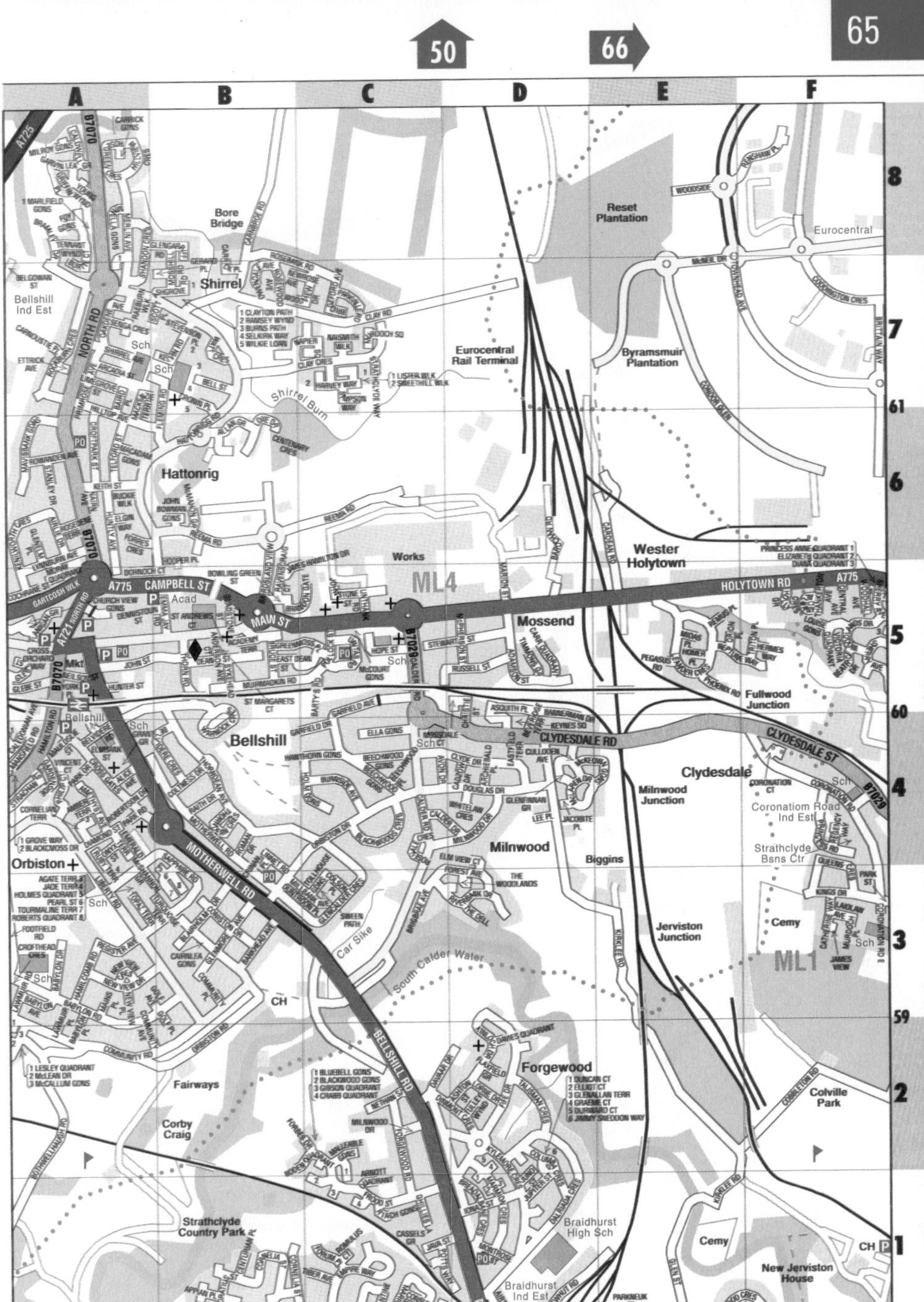
A
B
C
D
E
F
Bore Bridge
Shirrel
Reset Plantation
Eurocentral
Bellshill Ind Est
Eurocentral Rail Terminal
Byramsmuir Plantation
Shirrel Burn
Hattonrig
Works
ML4
Wester Holytown
CAMPBELL ST
MAIN ST
HOLYTOWN RD
Mossend
NORTH RD
Fullwood Junction
Bellshill
CLYDESDALE RD
CLYDESDALE ST
Clydesdale
Milnwood Junction
Coronatiom Road Ind Est
Strathclyde Bsns Ctr
Orbiston
MOTHERWELL RD
Milnwood
Biggins
Jerviston Junction
Cemy
ML1
South Calder Water
Car Sike
CH
BELLSHILL RD
Forgewood
Fairways
Corby Craig
Colville Park
Strathclyde Country Park
Braidhurst High Sch
Cemy
New Jerviston House
Braidhurst Ind Est
8
7
61
6
5
60
4
3
59
2
1
58
73
74
75

79
66

65
51

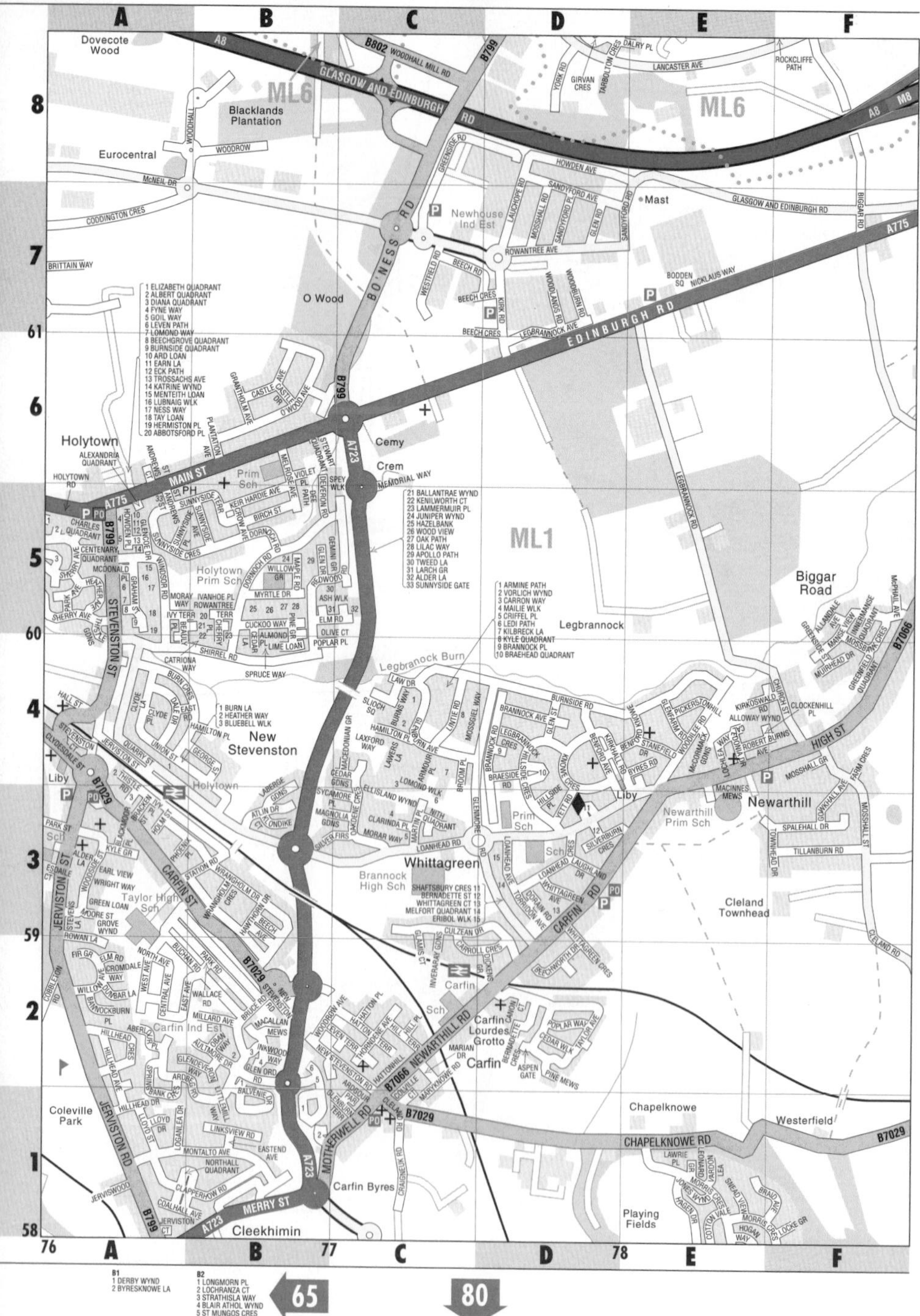
A
B
C
D
E
F
8
7
61
6
5
60
4
3
59
2
1
58
76
77
78
Dovecote Wood
A8
B802
WOODHALL MILL RD
B799
GLASGOW AND EDINBURGH RD
ML6
Blacklands Plantation
WOODHALL
WOODROW
Eurocentral
McNEIL DR
CODDINGTON CRES
BRITTAIN WAY
DALRY PL
LANCASTER AVE
ROCKCLIFFE PATH
YORK RD
GIRVAN CRES
TARBOLTON CRES
M8
HOWDEN AVE
SANDYFORD AVE
Mast
GLASGOW AND EDINBURGH RD
BIGGAR RD
A775
GREENSIDE RD
Newhouse Ind Est
LAUCHOPE RD
MOSSHALL RD
SANDYFORD PL
GLEN RD
SANDYFORD RD
ROWANTREE AVE
BO'NESS RD
WESTFIELD RD
BEECH RD
BEECH CRES
KIRK RD
WOODLANDS RD
WOODBURN RD
LEGBRANNOCK AVE
EDINBURGH RD
BODDEN SQ
NICKLAUS WAY
O Wood
1 ELIZABETH QUADRANT
2 ALBERT QUADRANT
3 DIANA QUADRANT
4 FYNE WAY
5 GOIL WAY
6 LEVEN PATH
7 LOMOND WAY
8 BEECHGROVE QUADRANT
9 BURNSIDE QUADRANT
10 ARD LOAN
11 EARN LA
12 ECK PATH
13 TROSSACHS AVE
14 KATRINE WYND
15 MENTEITH LOAN
16 LUBNAIG WLK
17 NESS WAY
18 TAY LOAN
19 HERMISTON PL
20 ABBOTSFORD PL
GRANTHOLM AVE
CASTLE AVE
O'WOOD AVE
PLANTATION AVE
A723
Cemy
Crem
MEMORIAL WAY
Holytown
ALEXANDRIA QUADRANT
HOLYTOWN RD
MAIN ST
Prim Sch
PH
MELROSE AVE
VIOLET PL
STEWART QUADRANT
DEVERON RD
SPEY WLK
DEE PATH
21 BALLANTRAE WYND
22 KENILWORTH CT
23 LAMMERMUIR PL
24 JUNIPER WYND
25 HAZELBANK
26 WOOD VIEW
27 OAK PATH
28 LILAC WAY
29 APOLLO PATH
30 TWEED LA
31 LARCH GR
32 ALDER LA
33 SUNNYSIDE GATE
ML1
LEGBRANNOCK RD
CHARLES QUADRANT
CENTENARY QUADRANT
SUNNYSIDE CRES
KEIR HARDIE AVE
BIRCH ST
Holytown Prim Sch
WILLOW GR
MAPLE RD
GEMINI GR
MYRTLE DR
ASH WLK
ELM RD
OLIVE CT
POPLAR PL
CUCKOO WAY
ALMOND PL
LIME LOAN
SPRUCE WAY
SHIRREL RD
CATRIONA WAY
MORAY WAY
IVANHOE PL
ROWANTREE TERR
IVY TERR
STEVENSTON ST
Biggar Road
Legbrannock
1 ARMINE PATH
2 VORLICH WYND
3 CARRON WAY
4 MAILIE WLK
5 CRIFFEL PL
6 LEDI PATH
7 KILBRECK LA
8 KYLE QUADRANT
9 BRANNOCK PL
10 BRAEHEAD QUADRANT
Legbranock Burn
B7066
1 BURN LA
2 HEATHER WAY
3 BLUEBELL WLK
New Stevenston
HALL ST
CLYDE LA
CLYDE PL
JERVISTON ST
QUARRY ST
UNION ST
HAMILTON PL
GEORGE ST
Holytown
LABERGE GDNS
ATLIN DR
KLONDIKE
LAW DR
SLIOCH SQ
BURNS WAY
HAMILTON PL
LAXFORD WAY
MACEDONIAN GR
LINTIE RD
MOSSGIEL WAY
BURNSIDE RD
BRANNOCK AVE
GLEN ST
KIRKHALL RD
BENFORD AVE
PICKERSTONHILL
STANEFIELD DR
BYRES RD
KIRKOSWALD RD
ALLOWAY WYND
ROBERT BURNS AVE
CLOCKENHILL PL
CHURCH ST
HIGH ST
Liby
Newarthill
Newarthill Prim Sch
MACINNES MEWS
MOSSHALL GR
SPALEHALL DR
TILLANBURN RD
MOSSHALL ST
TOWNHEAD DR
Cleland Townhead
CLELAND RD
B7029
Liby
THISTLE RD
CEDAR GDNS
SYCAMORE PL
MAGNOLIA GDNS
SILVER FIRS
ELLISLAND WYND
CLARINDA PL
MORAR WAY
LOMOND WLK
NITH QUADRANT
LOANHEAD RD
GLENMORE
Prim Sch
Sch
Whittagreen
Brannock High Sch
SHAFTSBURY CRES 11
BERNADETTE ST 12
WHITTAGREEN CT 13
MELFORT QUADRANT 14
ERIBOL WLK 15
SILVERBURN CRES
LAUGHLAND DR
WHITTAGREEN AVE
CARFIN RD
PARK ST
KYLE GR
ALDER LA
EARL VIEW
WRIGHT WAY
GREEN LOAN
MOORE ST
GROVE WYND
ROWAN LA
Taylor High Sch
CARFIN ST
STATION RD
WRANGHOLM DR
HAWTHORN DR
BEECH AVE
JERVISTON ST
CULZEAN CR
CARROLL CRES
GLAMIS CT
INVERARAY GDNS
DICKENS GR
Carfin
WHITTAGREEN CRES
FIR GR
ELM RD
CROMDALE WAY
DUNBAR LA
NORTH AVE
WEST AVE
CENTRAL AVE
EAST AVE
BUCHAN RD
PARK RD
WALLACE RD
MILLARD AVE
BRUCE RD
MACALLAN MEWS
BANNOCKBURN PL
HILLHEAD CRES
ABERLOUR PL
Carfin Ind Est
OBAN WAY
INKWOOD WAY
GLEN ORD
BALVENIE DR
WOODROW AVE
HATTON PL
LEVEN TERR
NEW STEVENSTON RD
NEWARTHILL RD
Sch
Carfin Lourdes Grotto
MARIAN DR
Carfin
POPLAR WAY
CEDAR WLK
ASPEN GATE
PINE MEWS
COBBLETON RD
Coleville Park
HILLHEAD AVE
HILLHEAD DR
LLOYD ST
LLOYD DR
LINKSVIEW RD
MONTALTO AVE
NORTHALL QUADRANT
EASTEND AVE
CLAPPERHOW RD
COALHALL AVE
JERVISTON RD
JERVISWOOD
JERVISTON CT
MERRY ST
Cleekhimin
MOTHERWELL RD
Carfin Byres
CRAIGNEUK RD
Chapelknowe
Westerfield
CHAPELKNOWE RD
LAWRIE PL
Playing Fields
B1
1 DERBY WYND
2 BYRESKNOWE LA
B2
1 LONGMORN PL
2 LOCHRANZA CT
3 STRATHISLA WAY
4 BLAIR ATHOL WYND
5 ST MUNGOS CRES
6 THE LAURELS

65
80

52
68

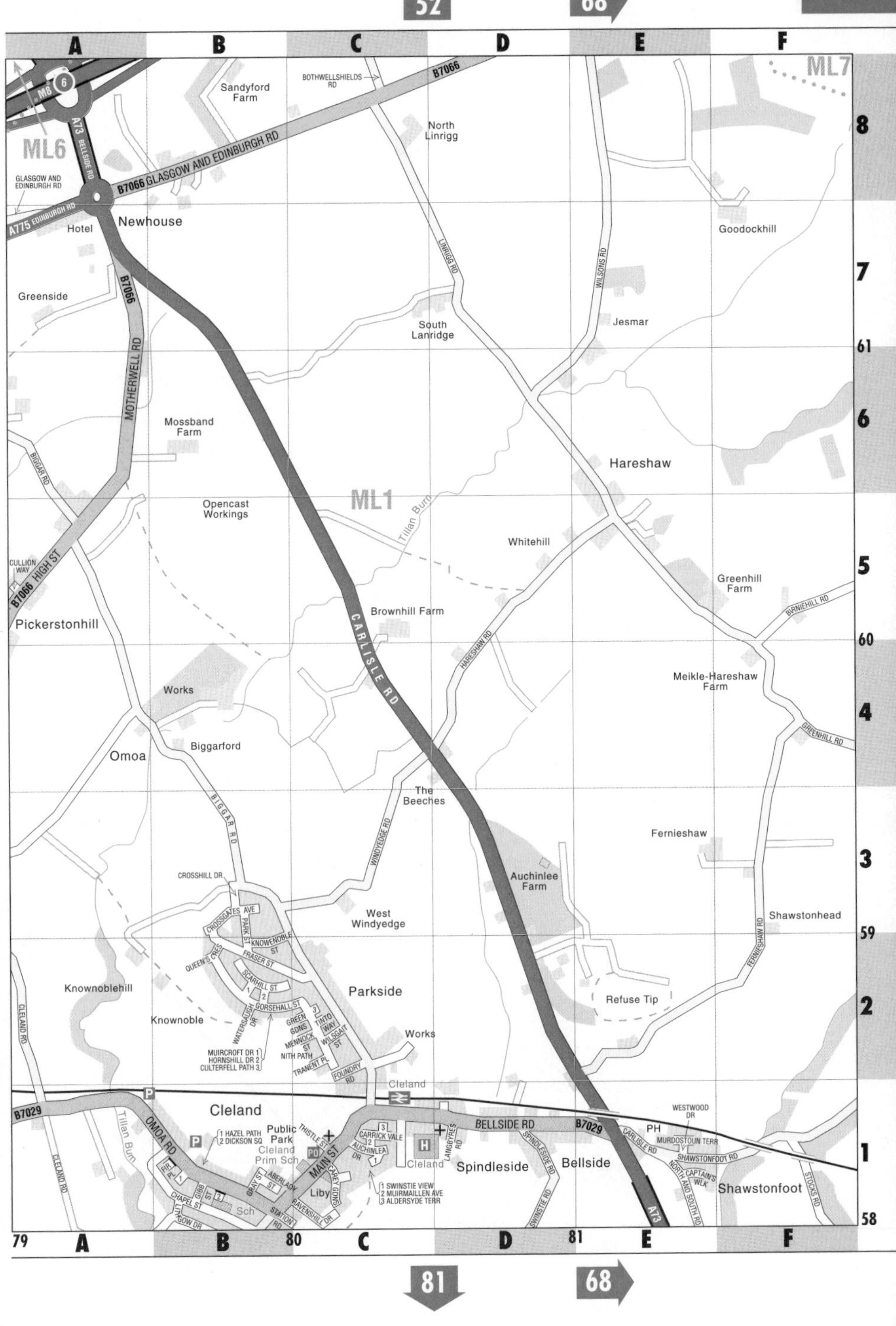
A
B
C
D
E
F
8
7
61
6
5
60
4
3
59
2
1
58
79
80
81
ML6
ML1
ML7
M8
6
A73
BELLSIDE RD
Sandyford Farm
BOTHWELLSHIELDS RD
B7066
North Linrigg
B7066 GLASGOW AND EDINBURGH RD
GLASGOW AND EDINBURGH RD
A775 EDINBURGH RD
Hotel
Newhouse
Goodockhill
LINRIGG RD
WILSONS RD
Greenside
B7066
MOTHERWELL RD
South Lanridge
Jesmar
Mossband Farm
BIGGAR RD
Hareshaw
Opencast Workings
Tillan Burn
Whitehill
CULLION WAY
B7066 HIGH ST
Greenhill Farm
Brownhill Farm
CARLISLE RD
BIRNIEHILL RD
Pickerstonhill
HARESHAW RD
Meikle-Hareshaw Farm
Works
GREENHILL RD
Omoa
Biggarford
The Beeches
BIGGAR RD
WINDYEDGE RD
Fernieshaw
CROSSHILL DR
Auchinlee Farm
West Windyedge
Shawstonhead
CROSSGATES AVE
PARK ST
KNOWENOBLE ST
FERNIESHAW RD
QUEEN'S CRES
FRASER ST
SCARHILL ST
Knownoblehill
Parkside
Refuse Tip
GORSEHALL ST
WATERSAUGH DR
Knownoble
GREEN GDNS
TINTO WAY
WILSGAIT ST
CLELAND RD
MENNOCK ST
NITH PATH
TRANENT PL
MUIRCROFT DR 1
HORNSHILL DR 2
CULTERFELL PATH 3
Works
FOUNDRY RD
Cleland
B7029
Cleland
WESTWOOD DR
1 HAZEL PATH
2 DICKSON SQ
Public Park
THISTLE ST
CARRICK VALE
BELLSIDE RD
B7029
PH
OMOA RD
Tillan Burn
Cleland Prim Sch
AUCHINLEA DR
LANGBYRES RD
SPINDLESIDE RD
CARLISLE RD
MURDOSTOUN TERR
SHAWSTONFOOT RD
CLELAND RD
FIR PL
MAIN ST
Cleland
Spindleside
Bellside
NORTH AND SOUTH RD
CAPTAIN'S WLK
Shawstonfoot
STOCKS RD
GRAY ST
ABERLADY ST
CAREY GDNS
Liby
1 SWINSTIE VIEW
2 MUIRMAILLEN AVE
3 ALDERSYDE TERR
CHAPEL ST
GIBB ST
Sch
STATION RD
RAVENSHILL DR
LITHGOW DR
SWINSTIE RD
A73

81
68

67
53
A
B
C
D
E
F
8
7
61
6
5
60
4
3
59
2
1
58
82
83
84
Spoil Tip
Well Hill
MANSE RD
Westfield
Fortissat View
Roughdike
Mains
Jersay
Law's Castle
Tillan Burn
ML7
Pell Hill
BIRNIEHILL RD
MUIREDGE AND JERSY RD
Muirhouse
Mine (dis)
Hareshaw Moss
Heatherhead Plantation
Pellhill Wood
ML1
Mast
GREENHILL RD
Home Farm
Hartwood
NEWMILL GDNS
CANTHILL GDNS
HARTWOOD GDNS
HARTWOOD RD
Penty
MUIREDGE AND JERSY RD
Hill of Murdostoun
Penty Wood
FOULBURN RD
BOWHOUSEBOG RD
Newmill Cottage
SHAWSTONFOOT RD
Big Wood
Newmill Wood
Muiredge Wood
MURDOSTOUN RD
ML2
HILL RD
ALLANTON RD
67
82

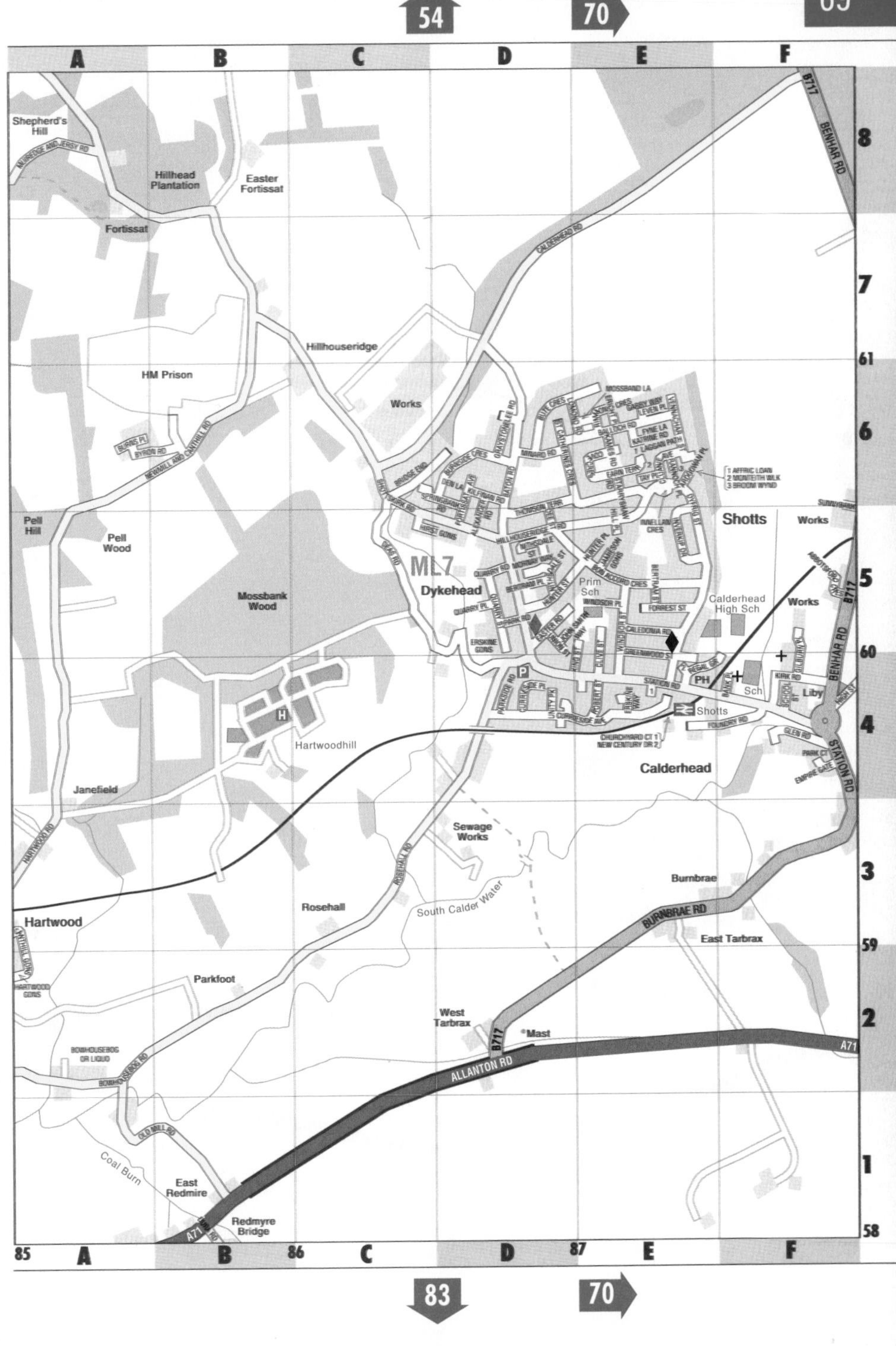
54
70
A
B
C
D
E
F
Shepherd's Hill
Hillhead Plantation
Easter Fortissat
Fortissat
CALDERHEAD RD
B717
BENHAR RD
Hillhouseridge
HM Prison
Works
BURNS PL
BYRON RD
NEWMILL AND CANTHILL RD
BRIDGE END
Pell Hill
Pell Wood
Shotts
Works
ML7
Dykehead
Mossbank Wood
Prim Sch
Calderhead High Sch
Works
STATION RD
PH
Sch
Liby
Shotts
FOUNDRY RD
Hartwoodhill
CHURCHYARD CT 1
NEW CENTURY DR 2
Calderhead
Janefield
HARTWOOD RD
Sewage Works
ROSEHALL RD
Burnbrae
BURNBRAE RD
Hartwood
Rosehall
South Calder Water
East Tarbrax
Parkfoot
West Tarbrax
Mast
B717
A71
ALLANTON RD
BOWHOUSEBOG RD
OLD MILL RD
Coal Burn
East Redmire
Redmyre Bridge
A71
8
7
61
6
5
60
4
3
59
2
1
58
85
86
87
83
70

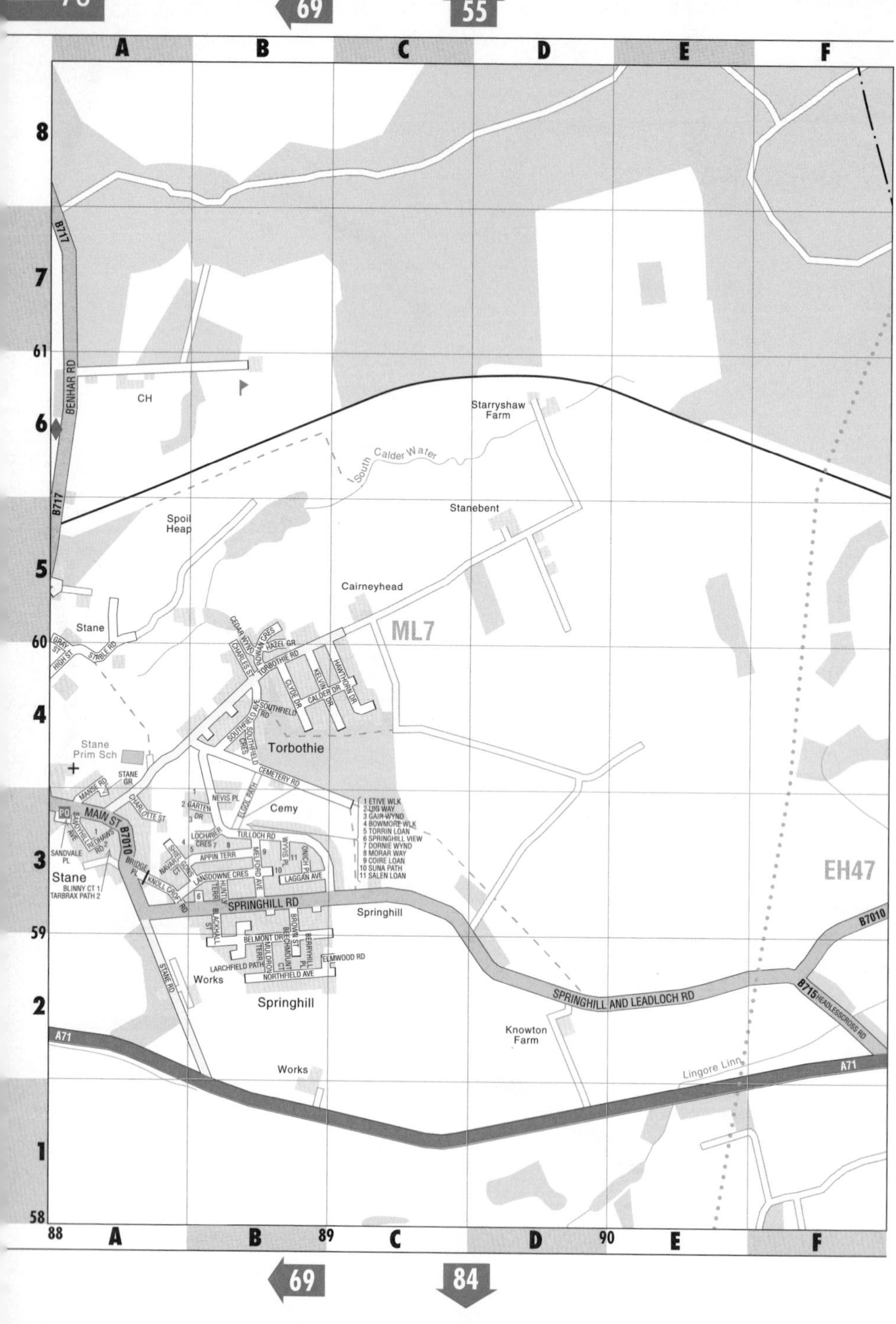
69
55
A
B
C
D
E
F
8
7
61
6
5
60
4
3
59
2
1
58
88
89
90
B717
BENHAR RD
CH
Starryshaw Farm
South Calder Water
Spoil Heap
Stanebent
Cairneyhead
ML7
Stane
GRAY ST
HIGH ST
STABLE RD
CEDAR WYND
ROWAN CRES
HAZEL GR
CHARLES ST
TORBOTHIE RD
CLYDE DR
KELVIN DR
CALDER DR
HAWTHORN DR
SOUTHFIELD RD
SOUTHFIELD AVE
SOUTHFIELD CRES
Torbothie
Stane Prim Sch
STANE GR
MANSE RD
CEMETERY RD
NEVIS PL
GARTEN DR
ELGOL PATH
Cemy
CHARLOTTE ST
MAIN ST
B7010
PO
SANDHILL AVE
REDHAWS RD
SANDVALE PL
Stane
BLINNY CT 1
TARBRAX PATH 2
BRIDGE PL
KNOLL CROFT RD
LOCHABER CRES
TULLOCH RD
SHIEL GDNS
NAVAR CT
APPIN TERR
MELFORD AVE
WYVIS PL
ONICH PL
LAGGAN AVE
LANSDOWNE CRES
HUNTLY TERR
1 ETIVE WLK
2 UIG WAY
3 GAIR WYND
4 BOWMORE WLK
5 TORRIN LOAN
6 SPRINGHILL VIEW
7 DORNIE WYND
8 MORAR WAY
9 COIRE LOAN
10 SUNA PATH
11 SALEN LOAN
SPRINGHILL RD
Springhill
BLACKHALL ST
BROWN ST
BEECHMOUNT CT
BERRYHILL PL
BELMONT DR
MULDRON TERR
ELMWOOD RD
LARCHFIELD PATH
NORTHFIELD AVE
STANE RD
Works
Springhill
SPRINGHILL AND LEADLOCH RD
EH47
B7010
B715
HEADLESSCROSS RD
Knowton Farm
A71
Works
Lingore Linn
A71
A
B
C
D
E
F
69
84

56
122

A
B
C
D
E
F
ML7
Spoil Heap
Fauldhouse Moor
B7010
8
Moss
Tippet Knowe
Fauldhouse Hills
7
61
St John the Baptist Prim Sch
Liby
Sports Ground
LANRIGG RD
SHEEPHOUSEHILL
B7015
6
Spoil Heap
Falla Hill Prim Sch
MAIN ST
PH
Benhar Junction
Warehouse
Fauldhouse
Greenburn
CH
Fauldhouse Bsns Ctr
Cemy
5
Leadloch
Braehead House
Fauldhouse
SHOTTS RD
60
Meadowfoot
Wayside
4
EH47
Levenseat Ind Est
A71
SPRINGHILL AND LEADLOCH RD
East Badallan
Meikle Eldrick
Works
Breich Water
3
Wee Eldrick
59
Lingore Linn
West Badallan
Muldron Bridge
2
Headlesscross
Risland Knowes
Muldron
Kitchen Linn
1
B715
58
91
92
93

85
122

58

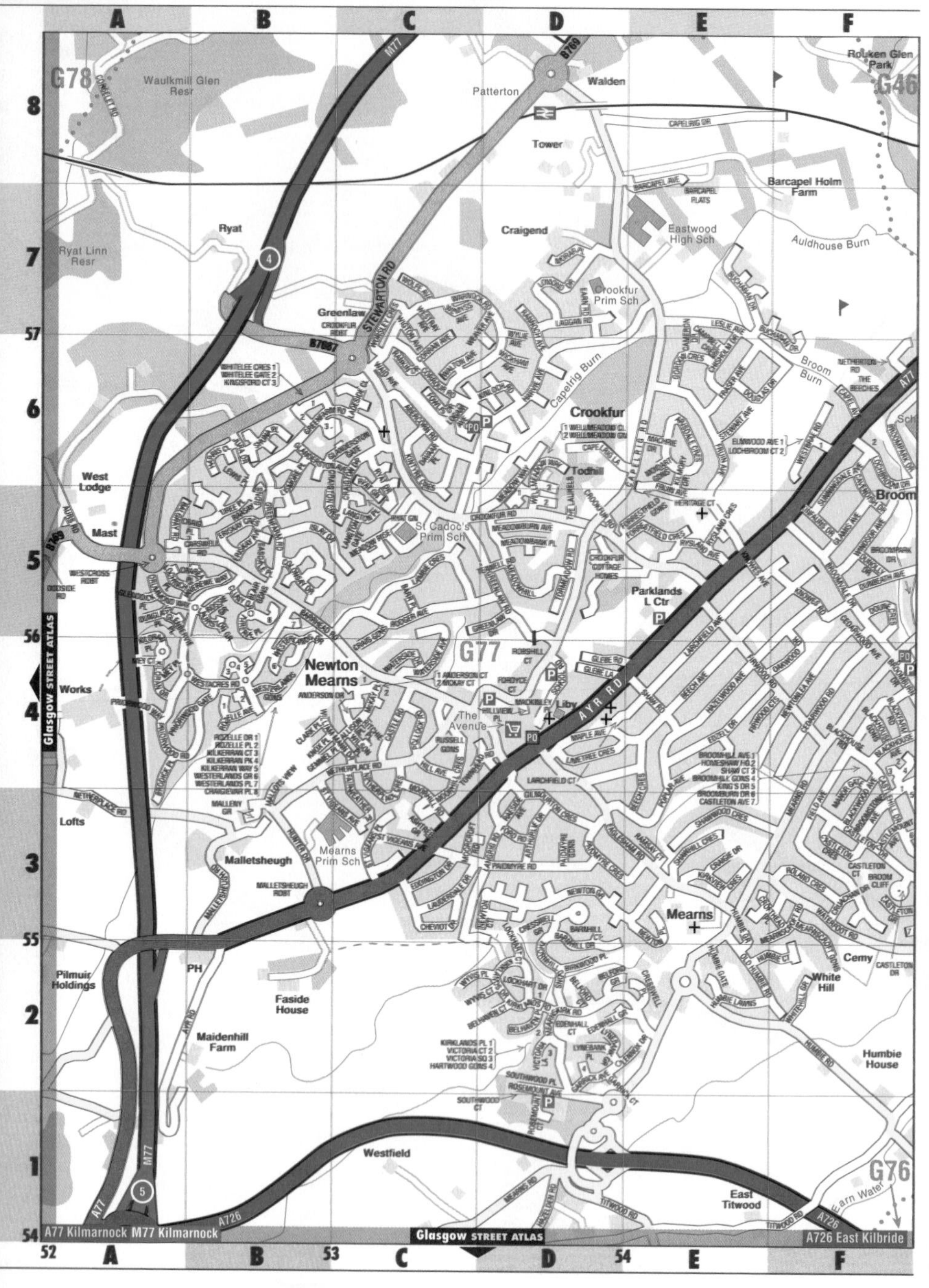

A
B
C
D
E
F
G78
Waulkmill Glen Resr
Patterton
Walden
Rouken Glen Park
G46
Tower
CAPELRIG DR
Barcapel Holm Farm
BARCAPEL AVE
BARCAPEL FLATS
Ryat
Craigend
Eastwood High Sch
Auldhouse Burn
Ryat Linn Resr
Crookfur Prim Sch
Greenlaw
CROOKFUR RDBT
STEWARTON RD
B7087
B769
M77
Broom Burn
Capelrig Burn
Crookfur
Todhill
West Lodge
Mast
B769
Broom
St Cadoc's Prim Sch
CROOKFUR RD
MEADOWBURN AVE
Parklands L Ctr
WESTCROSS RDBT
G77
Newton Mearns
Works
Glasgow STREET ATLAS
The Avenue
Liby
AYR RD
A77
Lofts
Malletsheugh
Mearns Prim Sch
MALLETSHEUGH RDBT
Mearns
Cemy
White Hill
Pilmuir Holdings
PH
Faside House
Maidenhill Farm
AYR RD
Humbie House
HUMBIE RD
Westfield
G76
East Titwood
Earn Water
A726
A77 Kilmarnock M77 Kilmarnock
Glasgow STREET ATLAS
A726 East Kilbride
52
53
54
8
7
57
6
5
56
4
3
55
2
1
54

59
74

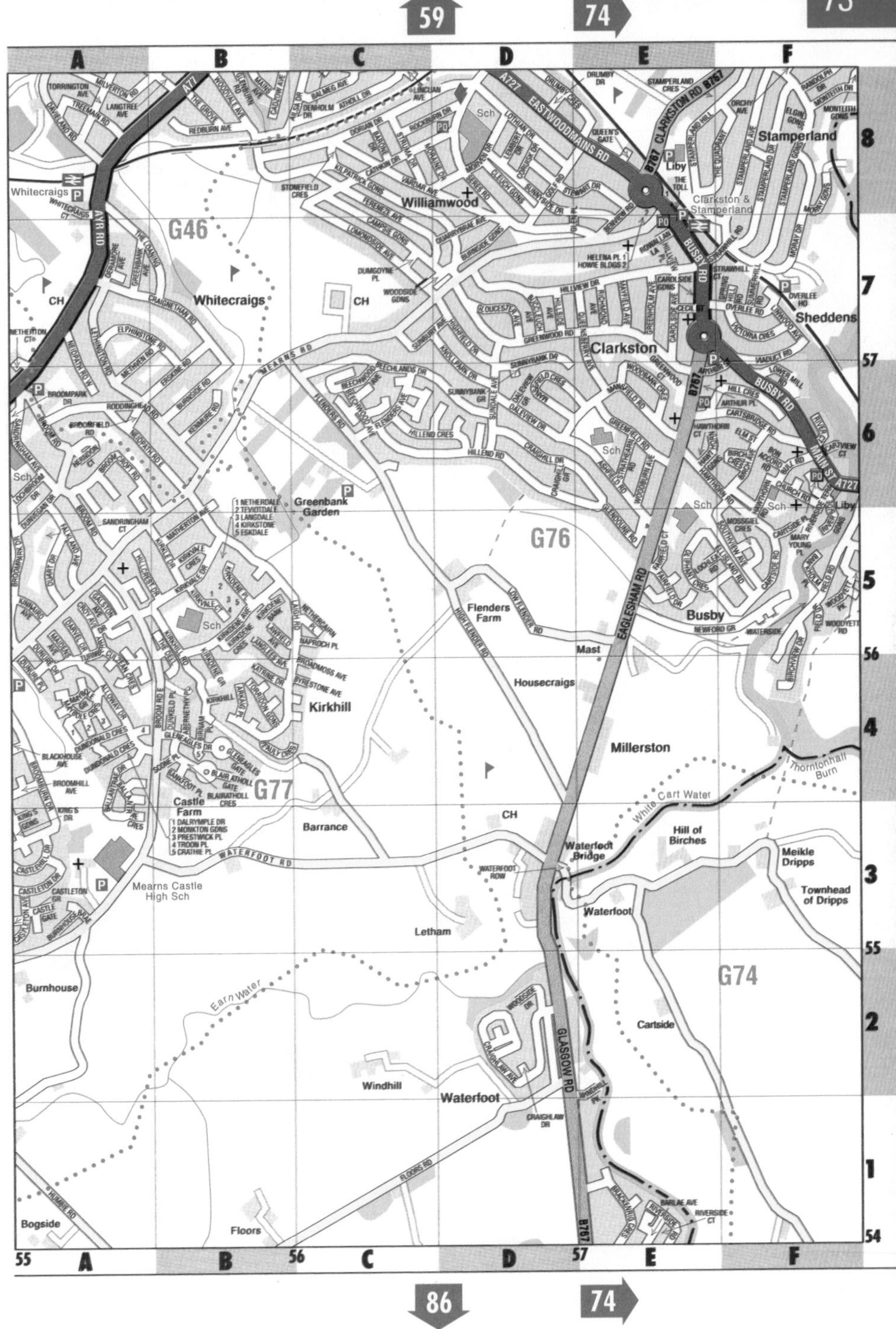
Whitecraigs
Williamwood
Stamperland
Clarkston
Sheddens
Busby
Kirkhill
Greenbank Garden
Flenders Farm
Housecraigs
Millerston
Castle Farm
Barrance
Mearns Castle High Sch
Waterfoot Bridge
Waterfoot
Hill of Birches
Meikle Dripps
Townhead of Dripps
Letham
Burnhouse
Cartside
Windhill
Bogside
Floors
G46
G76
G77
G74
White Cart Water
Earn Water
Thorntonhall Burn
EAGLESHAM RD
GLASGOW RD
AYR RD
MEARNS RD
WATERFOOT RD
EASTWOODMAINS RD
CLARKSTON RD
BUSBY RD
1 NETHERDALE
2 TEVIOTDALE
3 LANGDALE
4 KIRKSTONE
5 ESKDALE
1 DALRYMPLE DR
2 MONKTON GDNS
3 PRESTWICK PL
4 TROON PL
5 CRATHIE PL

86
74

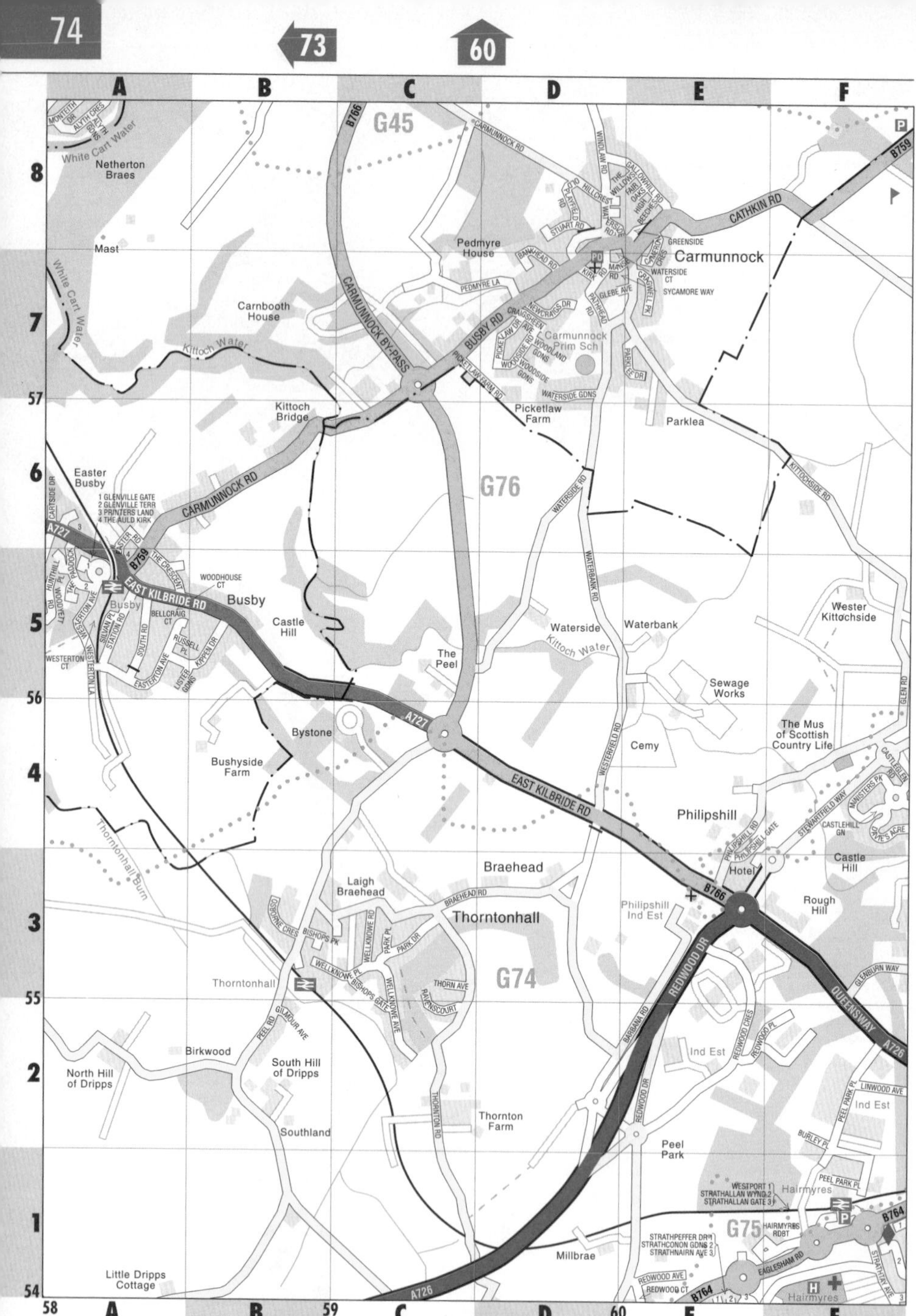
A
B
C
D
E
F
8
7
57
6
5
56
4
3
55
2
1
54
58
59
60
G45
G76
G74
G75
White Cart Water
Netherton Braes
Mast
Carnbooth House
Kittoch Water
Kittoch Bridge
Pedmyre House
Carmunnock
Carmunnock Prim Sch
Picketlaw Farm
Parklea
Easter Busby
1 GLENVILLE GATE
2 GLENVILLE TERR
3 PRINTERS LAND
4 THE AULD KIRK
CARMUNNOCK RD
CARMUNNOCK BY-PASS
BUSBY RD
CATHKIN RD
EAST KILBRIDE RD
Busby
Castle Hill
The Peel
Waterside
Waterbank
Sewage Works
Wester Kittochside
The Mus of Scottish Country Life
Bystone
Bushyside Farm
Cemy
Philipshill
Hotel
Castle Hill
Rough Hill
Braehead
Laigh Braehead
Thorntonhall
Philipshill Ind Est
Birkwood
North Hill of Dripps
South Hill of Dripps
Southland
Thornton Farm
Peel Park
Ind Est
Hairmyres
Millbrae
Little Dripps Cottage
A727
A726
B759
B766
B764
QUEENSWAY
REDWOOD DR
WATERBANK RD
WESTERFIELD RD
KITTOCHSIDE RD
EAGLESHAM RD
HAIRMYRES RDBT
STRATHPEFFER DR 1
STRATHCONON GDNS 2
STRATHNAIRN AVE 3
WESTPORT 1
STRATHALLAN WYND 2
STRATHALLAN GATE 3

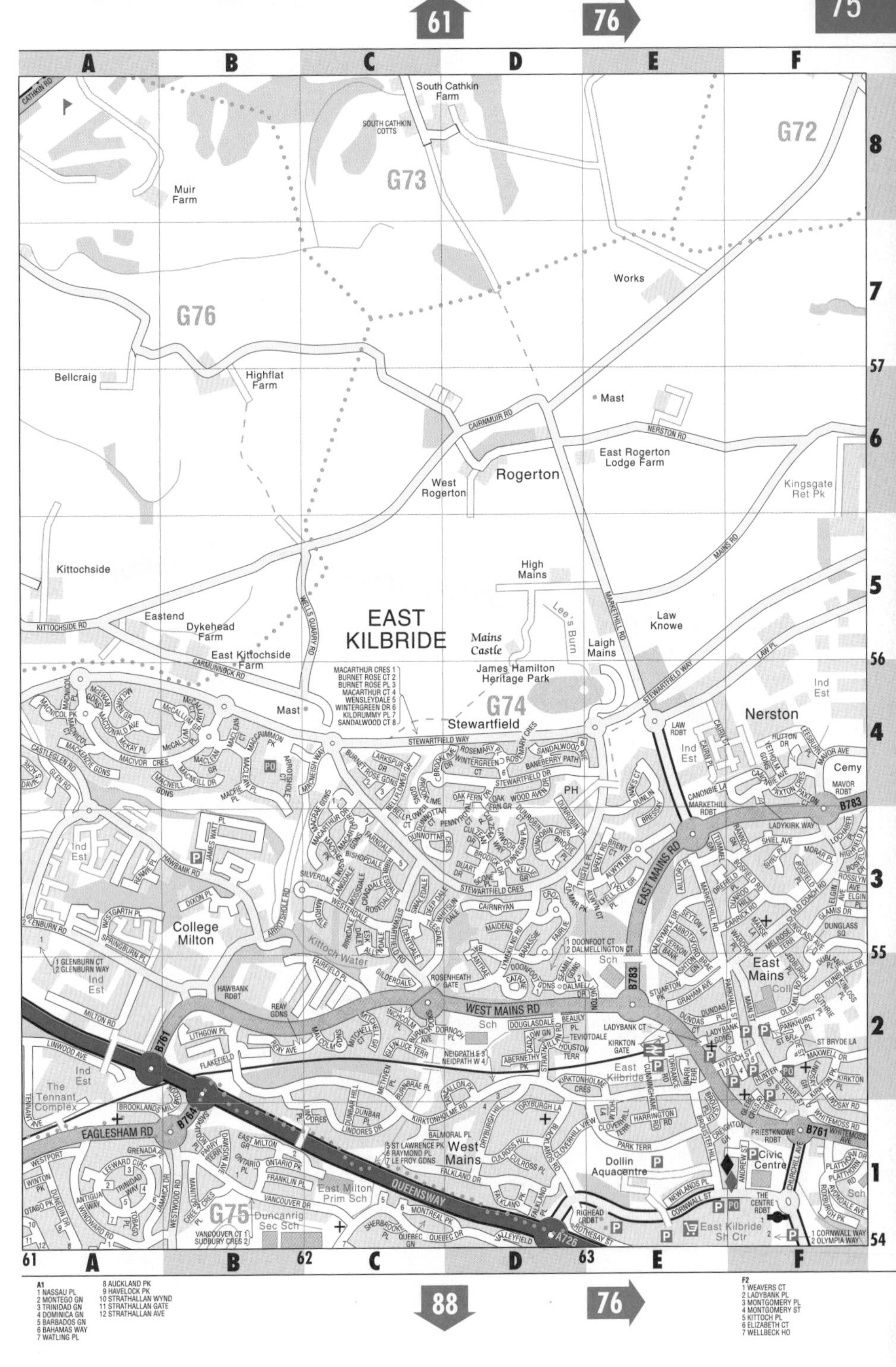

A1
1 NASSAU PL
2 MONTEGO GN
3 TRINIDAD GN
4 DOMINICA GN
5 BARBADOS GN
6 BAHAMAS WAY
7 WATLING PL
8 AUCKLAND PK
9 HAVELOCK PK
10 STRATHALLAN WYND
11 STRATHALLAN GATE
12 STRATHALLAN AVE

88
76

F2
1 WEAVERS CT
2 LADYBANK PL
3 MONTGOMERY PL
4 MONTGOMERY ST
5 KITTOCH PL
6 ELIZABETH CT
7 WELLBECK HO

75
62

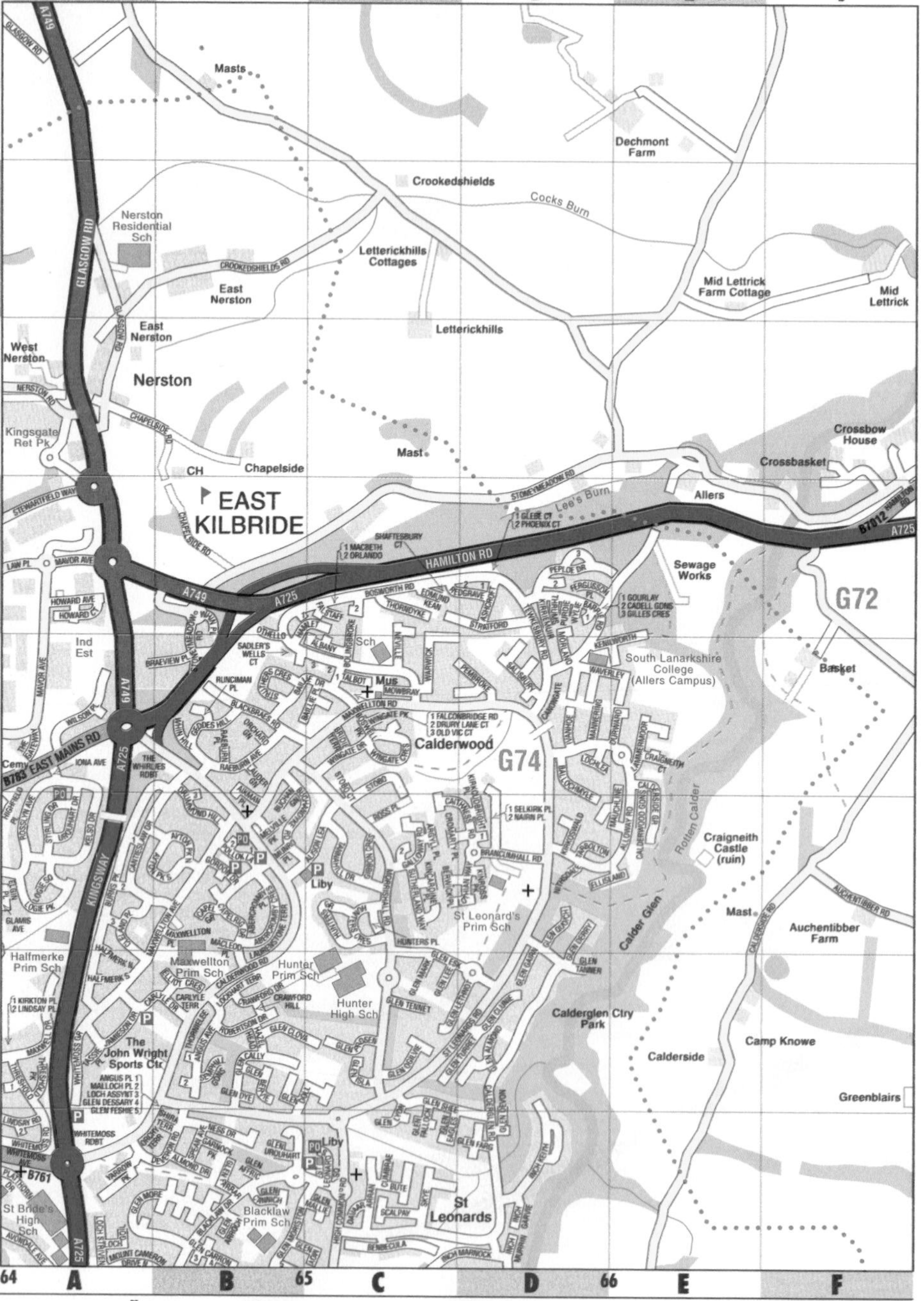

A B C D E F

8
7
57
6
5
56
4
3
55
2
1
54

Masts
Dechmont Farm
Crookedshields
Cocks Burn
Nerston Residential Sch
Letterickhills Cottages
Mid Lettrick Farm Cottage
Mid Lettrick
East Nerston
Letterickhills
West Nerston
Nerston
Kingsgate Ret Pk
Mast
Crossbow House
Crossbasket
CH
Chapelside
EAST KILBRIDE
Lee's Burn
Allers
Sewage Works
G72
Ind Est
South Lanarkshire College (Allers Campus)
Basket
Sch
Mus
Calderwood
G74
Cemy
Rotten Calder
Craigneith Castle (ruin)
Liby
St Leonard's Prim Sch
Calder Glen
Mast
Auchentibber Farm
Halfmerke Prim Sch
Maxwellton Prim Sch
Hunter Prim Sch
Hunter High Sch
Caldergien Ctry Park
The John Wright Sports Ctr
Camp Knowe
Calderside
Greenblairs
Liby
St Bride's High Sch
Blacklaw Prim Sch
St Leonards

GLASGOW RD
A749
A725
B7012
B783 EAST MAINS RD
B761
KINGSWAY
HAMILTON RD
STONEYMEADOW RD
CROOKEDSHIELDS RD
CHAPELSIDE RD
NERSTON RD
STEWARTFIELD WAY
MAVOR AVE
HOWARD AVE
THE WHIRLIES RDBT
WHITEMOSS RDBT
AUCHENTIBBER RD
CALDERSIDE RD
ST LEONARDS RD
BRANCUMHALL RD
KENILWORTH
WAVERLEY
BOSWORTH RD
STRATFORD
PEMBROKE
WARWICK
NEVILLE
MOWBRAY
MAXWELLTON RD
WINGATE DR
HUNTERS PL
GLEN CLOVA
GLEN ESK
GLEN SHEE

1 MACBETH
2 ORLANDO
SHAFTESBURY CT
1 GLEBE CT
2 PHOENIX CT
1 GOURLAY
2 CADELL GDNS
3 GILLIES CRES
1 FALCONBRIDGE RD
2 DRURY LANE CT
3 OLD VIC CT
1 SELKIRK PL
2 NAIRN PL
1 KIRKTON PL
2 LINDSAY PL
ANGUS PL 1
MALLOCH PL 2
LOCH ASSYNT 3
GLEN DESSARY 4
GLEN FESHIE 5

64 A B 65 C D 66 E F

B3
1 CALDERWOOD SQ
2 POLLOK PL
3 DRUMMOND PL
A3
1 SCOTT HILL
2 ETTRICK HILL
3 RAMSAY HILL

75
89

63
78

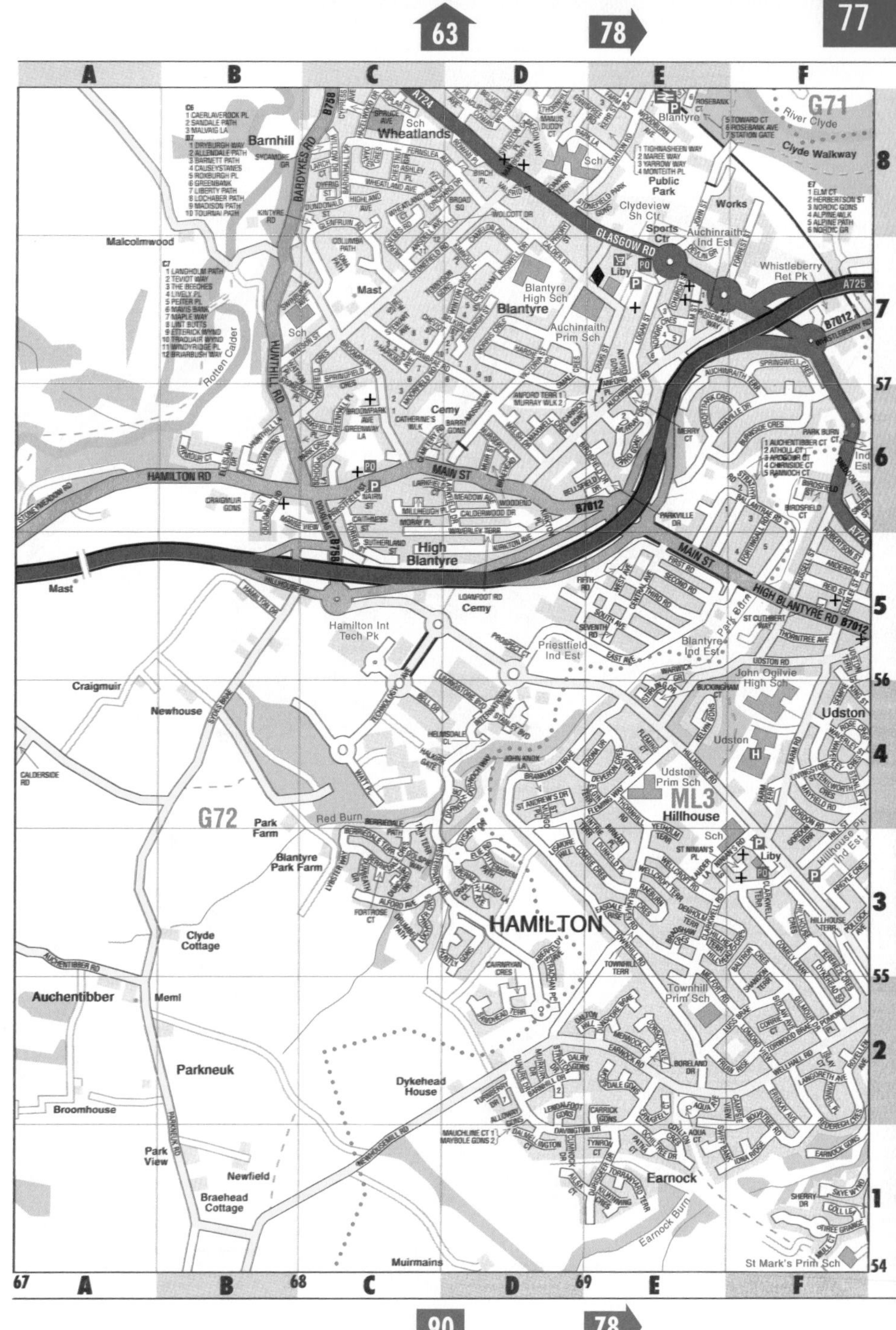
A
B
C
D
E
F
8
7
57
6
5
56
4
3
55
2
1
54
67
68
69
G71
G72
ML3
River Clyde
Clyde Walkway
Blantyre
Public Park
Works
Clydeview Sh Ctr
Sports Ctr
Auchinraith Ind Est
Whistleberry Ret Pk
Wheatlands
Barnhill
Malcolmwood
Mast
Sch
Blantyre High Sch
Auchinraith Prim Sch
Liby
PO
Cemy
High Blantyre
Rotten Calder
HAMILTON RD
MAIN ST
GLASGOW RD
HIGH BLANTYRE RD
BARDYKES RD
HUNTHILL RD
A724
A725
B7012
B758
Hamilton Int Tech Pk
Priestfield Ind Est
Blantyre Ind Est
John Ogilvie High Sch
Udston
Udston Prim Sch
Hillhouse
Hillhouse Pk Ind Est
Craigmuir
Newhouse
Park Farm
Blantyre Park Farm
Red Burn
Park Burn
HAMILTON
Clyde Cottage
Auchentibber
Meml
Parkneuk
Broomhouse
Park View
Newfield
Braehead Cottage
Dykehead House
Townhill Prim Sch
Earnock
Earnock Burn
Muirmains
St Mark's Prim Sch
C6
1 CAERLAVEROCK PL
2 SANDALE PATH
3 MALVAIG LA
B7
1 DRYBURGH WAY
2 ALLENDALE PATH
3 BARNETT PATH
4 CAUSEYSTANES
5 ROXBURGH PL
6 GREENBANK
7 LIBERTY PATH
8 LOCHABER PATH
9 MADISON PATH
10 TOURNAI PATH
C7
1 LANGHOLM PATH
2 TEVIOT WAY
3 THE BEECHES
4 LIVELY PL
5 PEITER PL
6 MAVIS BANK
7 MAPLE WAY
8 LINT BUTTS
9 ETTERICK WYND
10 TRAQUAIR WYND
11 WINDYRIDGE PL
12 BRIARBUSH WAY
1 TIGHNASHEEN WAY
2 MAREE WAY
3 YARROW WAY
4 MONTEITH PL
5 TOWARD CT
6 ROSEBANK AVE
7 STATION GATE
E7
1 ELM CT
2 HERBERTSON ST
3 NORDIC GDNS
4 ALPINE WALK
5 ALPINE PATH
6 NORDIC GR
1 AUCHENTIBBER CT
2 ATHOLL CT
3 ARDNOIR DR
4 CHIRNSIDE CT
5 RANNOCH CT
AMFORD TERR 1
MURRAY WALK 2
MAUCHLINE CT 1
MAYBOLE GDNS 2

90
78

77
64

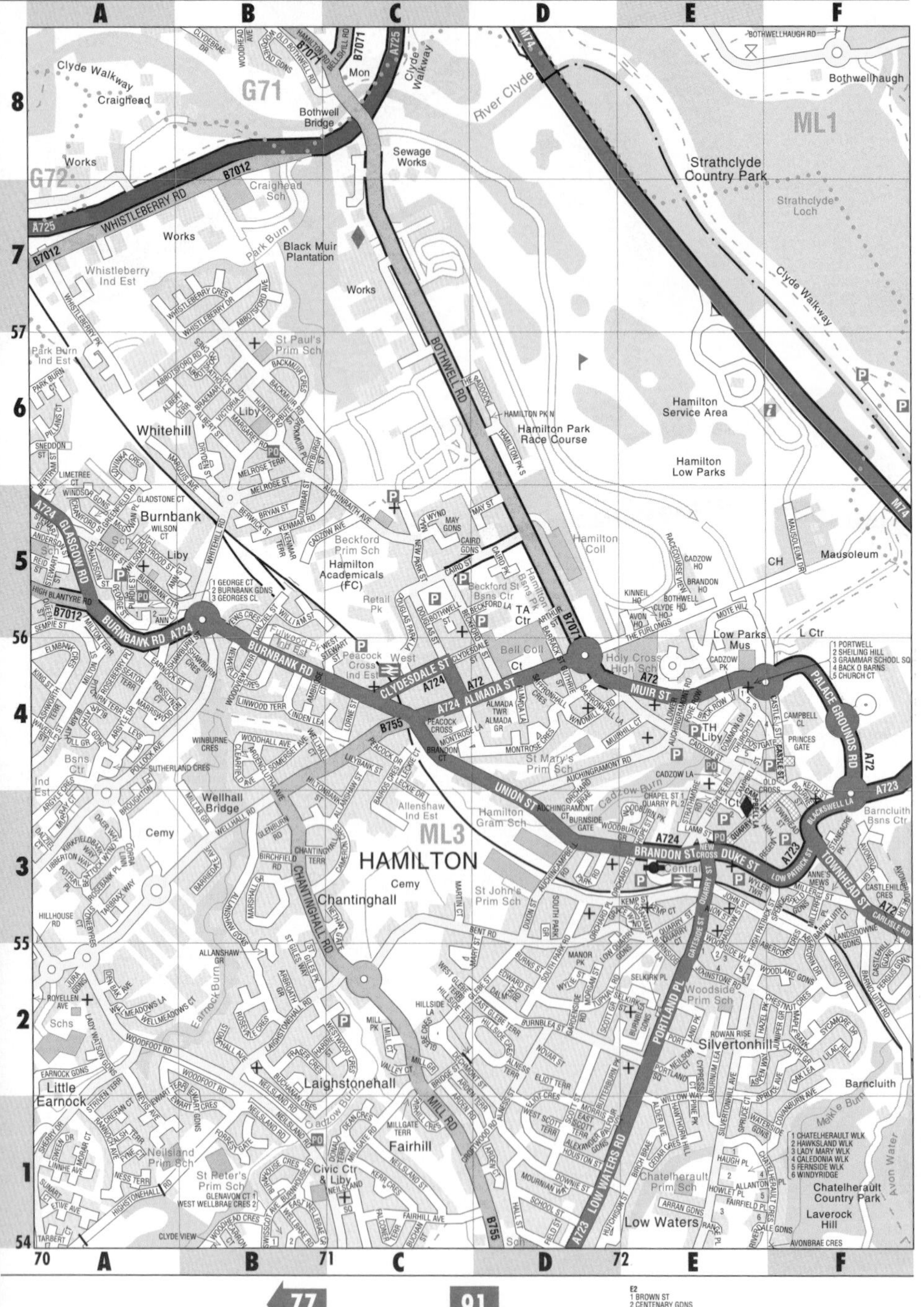

77
91

E2
1 BROWN ST
2 CENTENARY GDNS
3 WEAVERS CT
4 WOODSIDE CT
5 WOODSIDE AVE
6 CARLTON CT
7 HILTON CT

65
80

E5
1 OAKFIELD TWR
2 ALBION TWR
3 McCLURG CT
4 ELVAN TWR
5 KERR GRIEVE CT
6 CALDER TWR
7 AVON TWR
8 CLYDE TWR

E6
1 BRANDON ARC
2 OAKFIELD DR
3 WATSONVILLE PK

F5
1 GLENCAIRN TWR
2 CAIRN CT
3 MACDONALD ST
4 CIVIC SQ
5 BLAIR PATH
6 ELLIS WAY

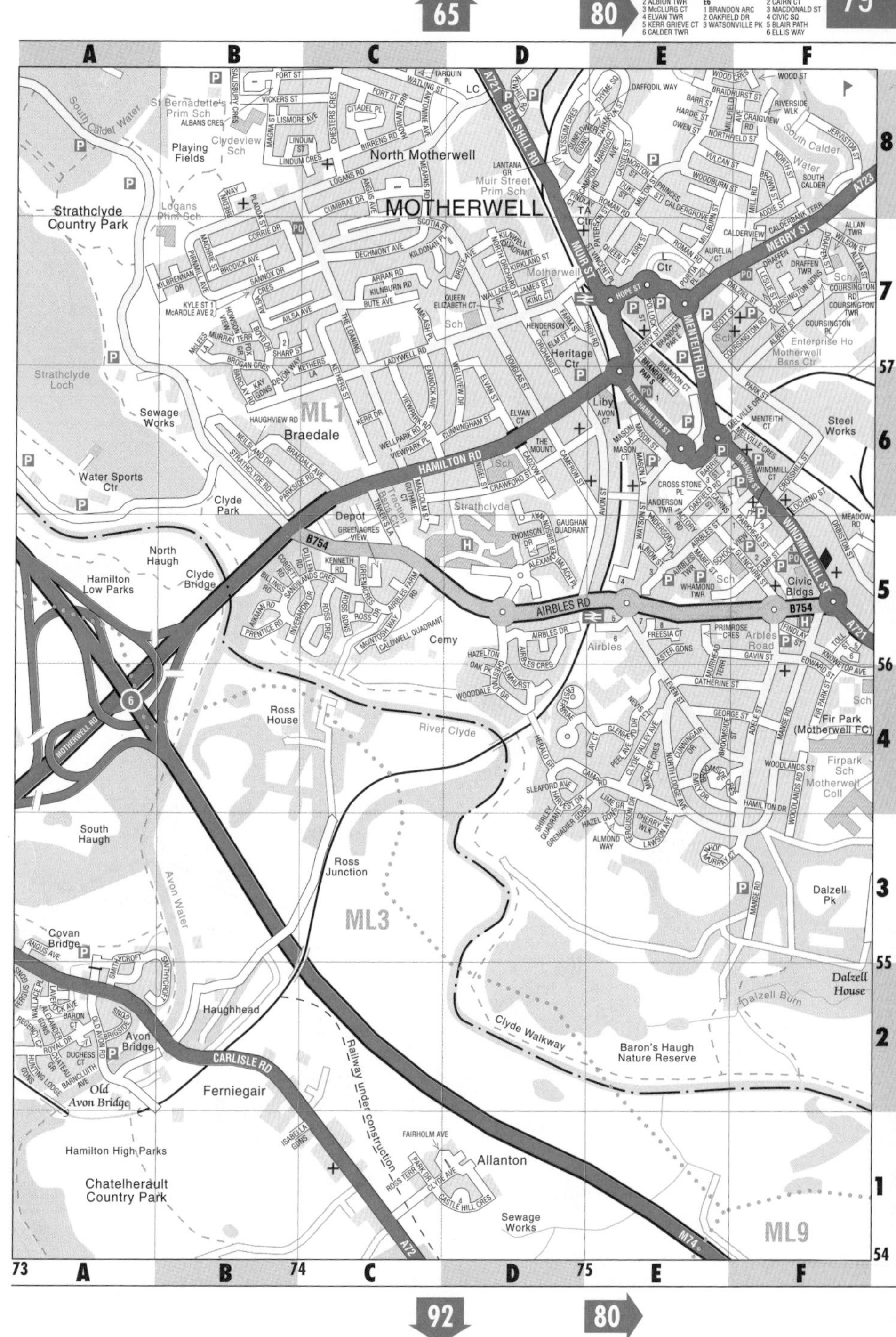

92
80

79
66

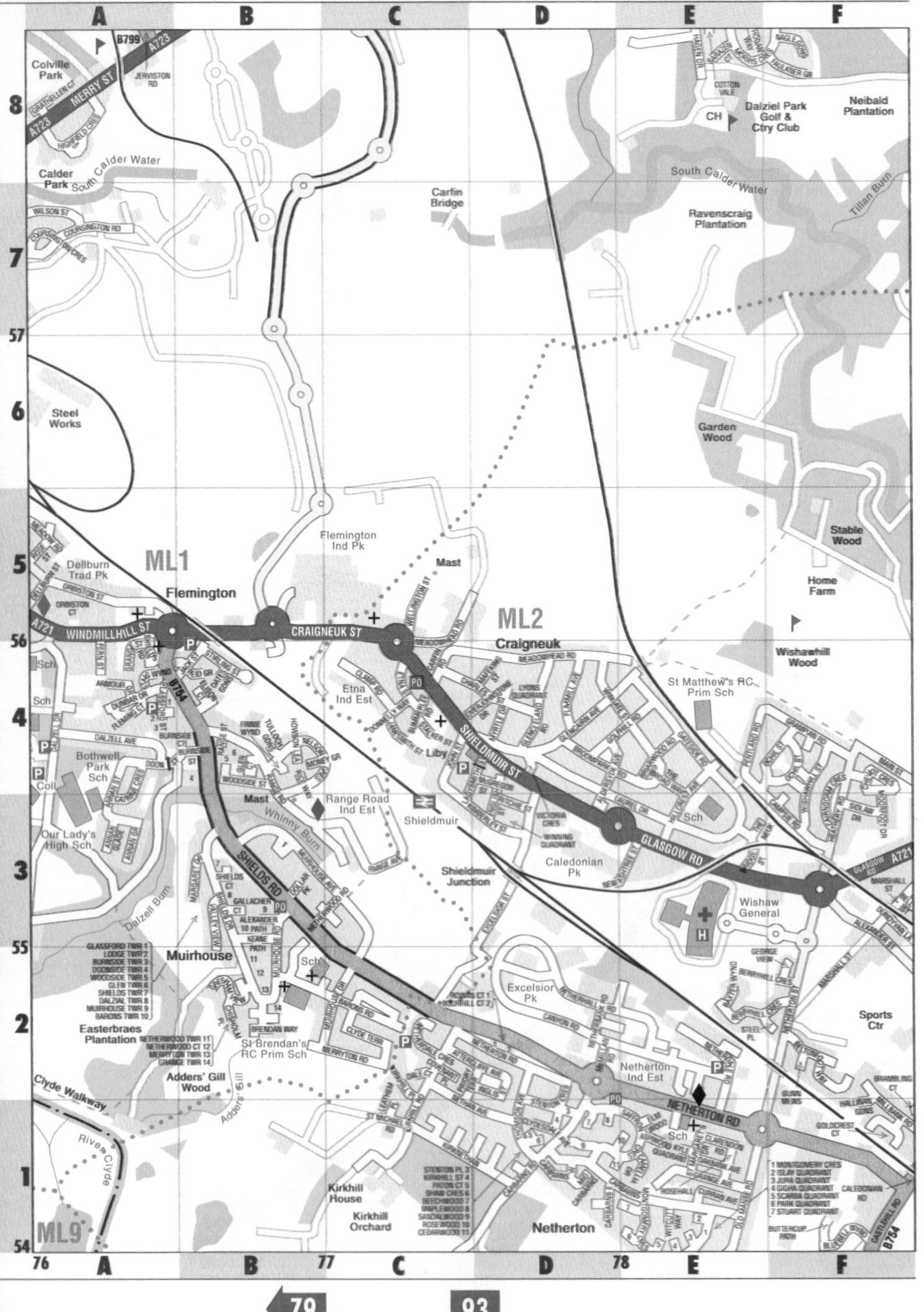
Colville Park
MERRY ST
A723
B799
Calder Park
South Calder Water
Carfin Bridge
Dalziel Park Golf & Ctry Club
Neibald Plantation
Ravenscraig Plantation
Tillan Burn
Steel Works
Garden Wood
Flemington Ind Pk
Mast
Stable Wood
Home Farm
ML1
Dellburn Trad Pk
Flemington
A721
WINDMILLHILL ST
CRAIGNEUK ST
ML2
Craigneuk
Wishawhill Wood
St Matthew's RC Prim Sch
Etna Ind Est
SHIELDMUIR ST
Bothwell Park Sch
Coll
Range Road Ind Est
Shieldmuir
Our Lady's High Sch
Whinny Burn
GLASGOW RD
Shieldmuir Junction
Caledonian Pk
SHIELDS RD
Wishaw General
Muirhouse
Excelsior Pk
Sports Ctr
Easterbraes Plantation
St Brendan's RC Prim Sch
Adders' Gill Wood
Netherton Ind Est
NETHERTON RD
Clyde Walkway
River Clyde
Kirkhill House
Kirkhill Orchard
Netherton
ML9
B754
A B C D E F
8 7 57 6 5 56 4 3 55 2 1 54
76 77 78

79
93

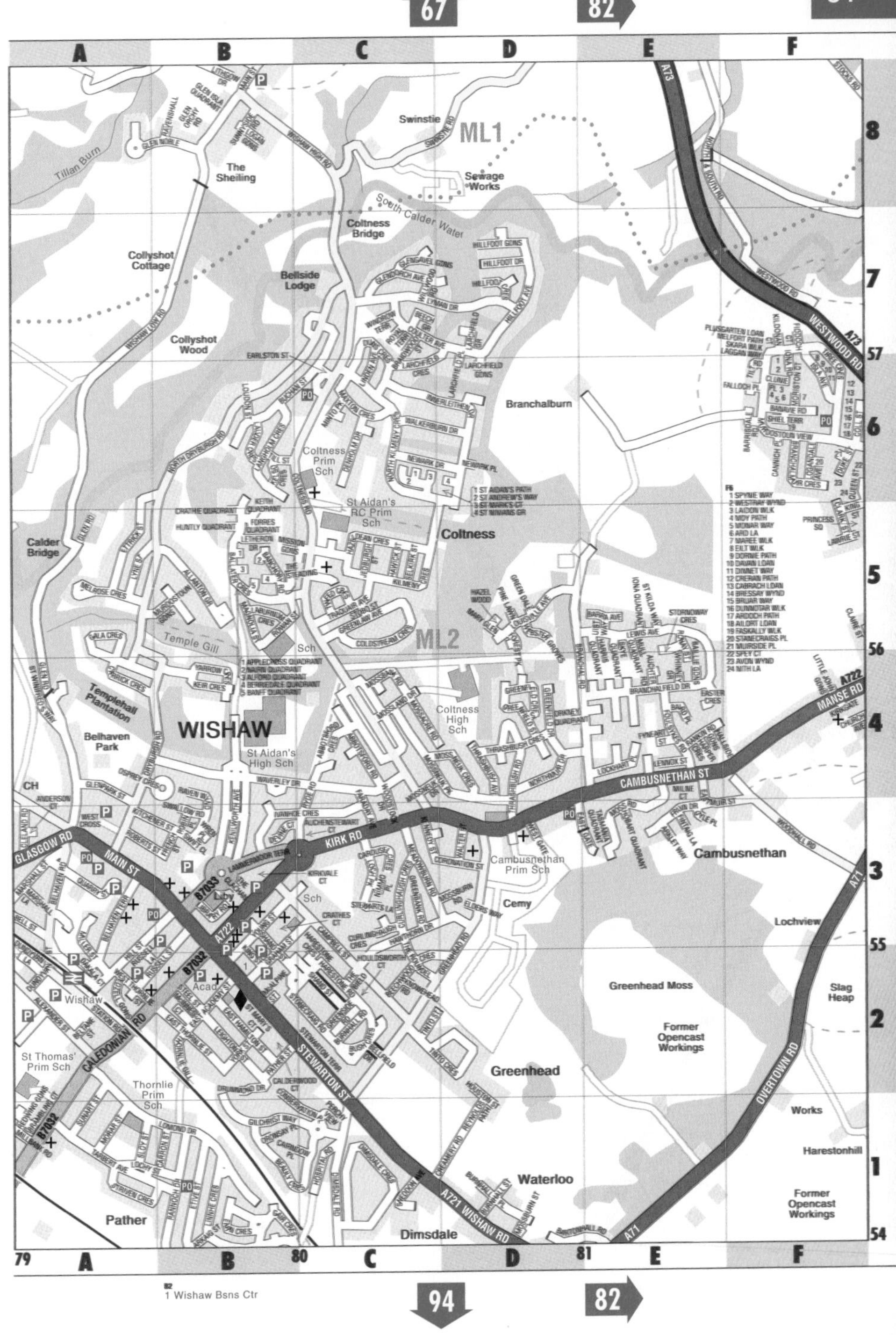

81
67
82
94
82
ML1
ML2
Swinstie
Sewage Works
The Sheiling
South Calder Water
Coltness Bridge
Collyshot Cottage
Bellside Lodge
Collyshot Wood
Tillan Burn
Branchalburn
Coltness Prim Sch
St Aidan's RC Prim Sch
Coltness
Calder Bridge
Temple Gill
Templehall Plantation
Belhaven Park
WISHAW
St Aidan's High Sch
Coltness High Sch
Cambusnethan Prim Sch
Cambusnethan
Cemy
Lochview
Greenhead Moss
Former Opencast Workings
Slag Heap
Greenhead
Works
Harestonhill
Waterloo
Dimsdale
Pather
Thornlie Prim Sch
St Thomas' Prim Sch
Wishaw
Acad
Lby
Sch
CH
A73
A71
A721 WISHAW RD
A722
B7033
B7032
WESTWOOD RD
CAMBUSNETHAN ST
KIRK RD
MAIN ST
GLASGOW RD
CALEDONIAN RD
STEWARTON ST
OVERTOWN RD
MANSE RD
WISHAW LOW RD
WISHAW HIGH RD
NORTH DRYBURGH RD
COLTNESS RD
GLEN RD
1 ST AIDAN'S PATH
2 ST ANDREW'S WAY
3 ST MARK'S CT
4 ST NINIANS GR
1 APPLECROSS QUADRANT
2 NAIRN QUADRANT
3 ALFORD QUADRANT
4 BERRIEDALE QUADRANT
5 BANFF QUADRANT
F6
1 SPYNIE WAY
2 WESTRAY WYND
3 LAIDON WLK
4 WDY PATH
5 MONAR WAY
6 ARD LA
7 MAREE WLK
8 EILT WLK
9 DORNIE PATH
10 DAVAN LOAN
11 DINMET WAY
12 CRERAN PATH
13 CABRACH LOAN
14 BRESSAY WYND
15 BRUAR WAY
16 DUNNOTAR WLK
17 ARDOCH PATH
18 AILORT LOAN
19 FASKALLY WLK
20 STANECRAIGS PL
21 MUIRSIDE PL
22 SPEY CT
23 AVON WYND
24 NITH LA
A B C D E F
1 2 3 4 5 6 7 8
54 55 56 57
79 80 81
B2
1 Wishaw Bsns Ctr

81
68

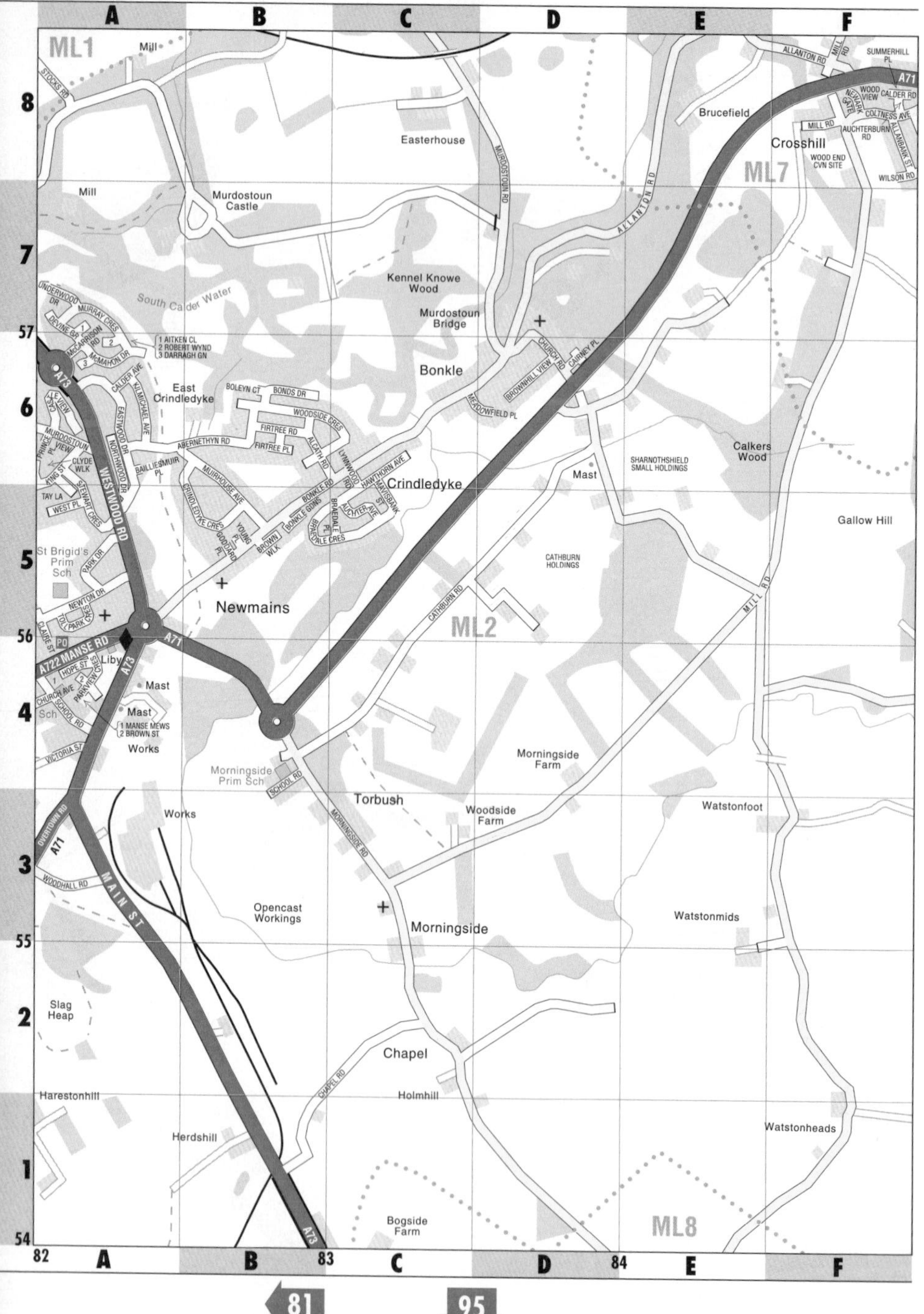
A
B
C
D
E
F
ML1
Mill
STOCKS RD
ALLANTON RD
MILL RD
SUMMERHILL PL
A71
WOOD VIEW
CALDER RD
NEWARK GATE
COLTNESS AVE
MILL RD
AUCHTERBURN RD
ALLANBANK ST
Brucefield
Easterhouse
Crosshill
WOOD END CVN SITE
WILSON RD
ML7
Mill
Murdostoun Castle
MURDOSTOUN RD
ALLANTON RD
Kennel Knowe Wood
South Calder Water
Murdostoun Bridge
UNDERWOOD DR
MURRAY CRES
DEVINE GR
McCARRISON RD
McMAHON DR
1 AITKEN CL
2 ROBERT WYND
3 DARRAGH GN
A73
CALDER AVE
KILMICHAEL AVE
East Crindledyke
BOLEYN CT
BONDS DR
Bonkle
CHURCH RD
CAIRNEY PL
BROWNHILL VIEW
MEADOWFIELD PL
WOODSIDE CRES
FIRTREE RD
FIRTREE PL
ALCATH RD
ABERNETHYN RD
EASTWOOD DR
NORTHWOOD DR
WESTWOOD RD
MURDOSTOUN VIEW
PRINCE PL
CLYDE WLK
BAILLIESMUIR PL
LYNNWOOD RD
HAWTHORN AVE
Crindledyke
MATTISBANK ST
BONKLE RD
BONKLE GDNS
BRAEDALE PL
AUCHTER AVE
BRAEDALE CRES
MUIRHOUSE AVE
CRINDLEDYKE CRES
YOUNG PL
GODDARD PL
BROWN WLK
STEWART CRES
TAY LA
WEST PL
SHARNOTHSHIELD SMALL HOLDINGS
Mast
Calkers Wood
Gallow Hill
St Brigid's Prim Sch
PARK DR
NEWTON DR
Newmains
CATHBURN HOLDINGS
CATHBURN RD
ML2
MILL RD
CLAIRE ST
PO
A722 MANSE RD
Liby
A71
HOPE ST
PARKVIEW
CHURCH AVE
SCHOOL RD
Sch
Mast
Mast
1 MANSE MEWS
2 BROWN ST
Works
VICTORIA ST
Morningside Prim Sch
SCHOOL RD
Morningside Farm
Torbush
Works
OVERTOWN RD
A71
Woodside Farm
Watstonfoot
MORNINGSIDE RD
MAIN ST
WOODHALL RD
Opencast Workings
Morningside
Watstonmids
Slag Heap
Chapel
CHAPEL RD
Holmhill
Harestonhill
Watstonheads
Herdshill
Bogside Farm
ML8
A73
8
7
57
6
5
56
4
3
55
2
1
54
82
83
84

81
95

69
84

A
B
C
D
E
F
COLTNESS AVE
P
PO
ALLANTON RD A71
Allanton Prim Sch
Damside (PH)
SCHOOL LA
REDMIRE CRES
DARMEID PL
HARTFIELD TERR
KINGSHILL RD
HOULDSWORTH CRES
SPRINGHEAD RD
KIRK PATH
WILSON RD
HAWTHORN PL
Allanton
Coal Burn
8
Opencast Workings
ML7
Hartfield
Netherhall
Blackhall Farm
7
57
6
Newark Plantation
5
Upper Daviesdykes
DURA RD
56
Kirkhall
ML2
4
Lower Daviesdykes
Lodge Hill
Winterhill
Dura
Brow Farm
Mountpleasant
Sunnyside
3
Auchterhead
55
Summerside
Kingshill
Auchter Water
2
1
ML8
54
85
86
87

96
84

83
70

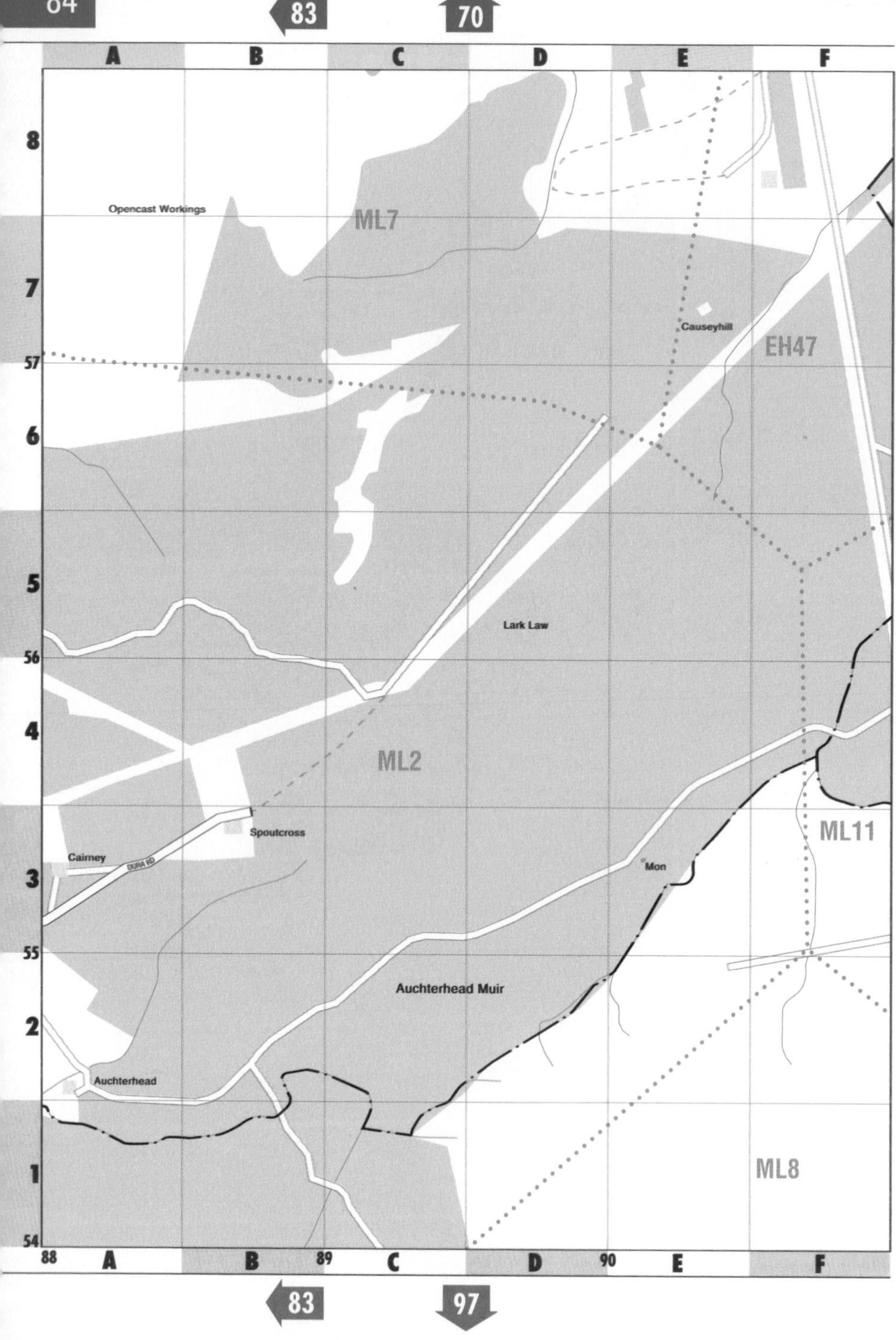
A
B
C
D
E
F
8
7
57
6
5
56
4
3
55
2
1
54
88
89
90
Opencast Workings
ML7
Causeyhill
EH47
Lark Law
ML2
Spoutcross
Cairney
ML11
Mon
Auchterhead Muir
Auchterhead
ML8

83
97

71
122

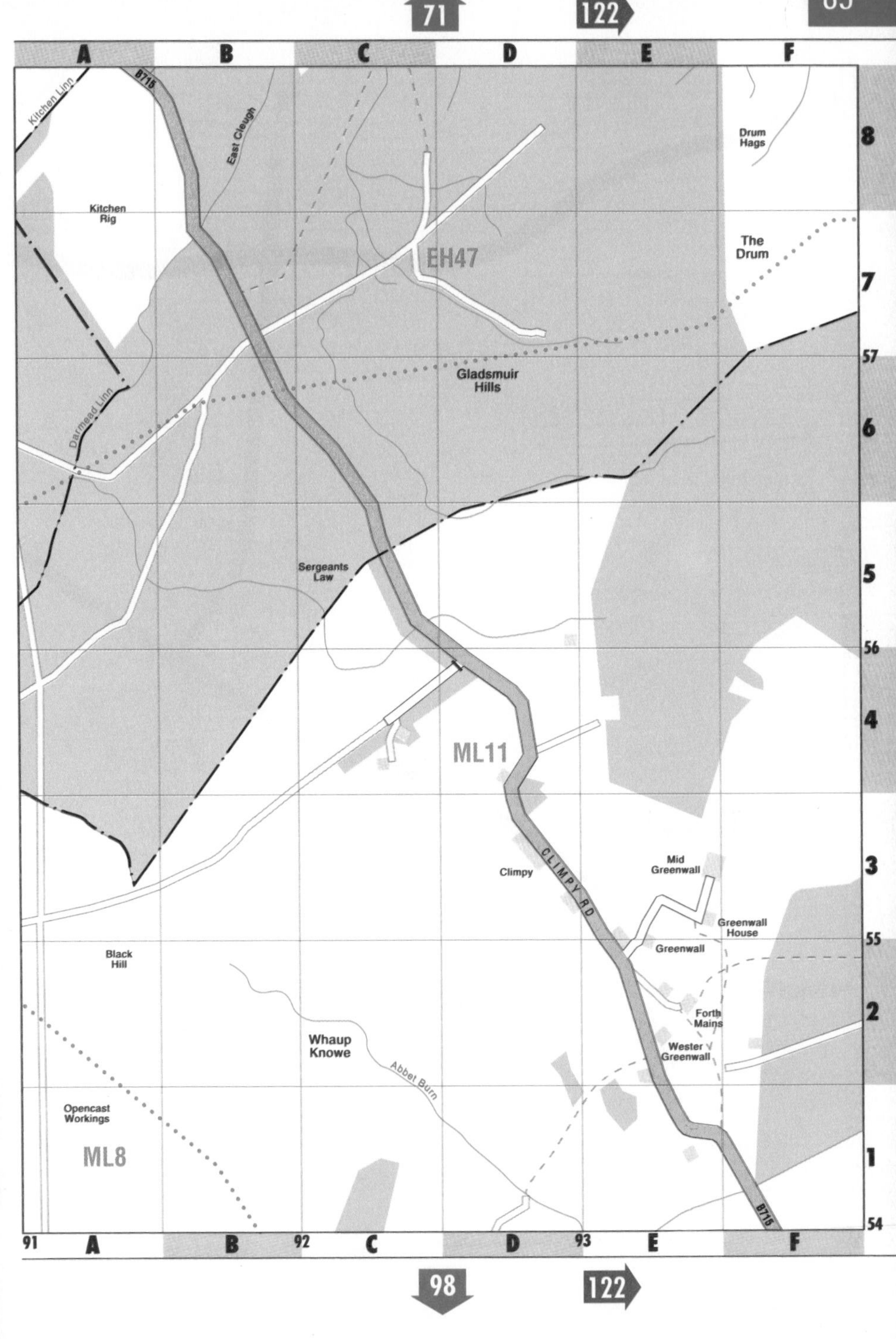
A
B
C
D
E
F
Kitchen Linn
B715
East Cleugh
Drum Hags
8
Kitchen Rig
The Drum
EH47
7
57
Gladsmuir Hills
Darmead Linn
6
Sergeants Law
5
56
4
ML11
3
Climpy
CLIMPY RD
Mid Greenwall
Greenwall House
Greenwall
55
Black Hill
2
Forth Mains
Whaup Knowe
Wester Greenwall
Abbet Burn
Opencast Workings
ML8
1
B715
54
91
92
93

98
122

73

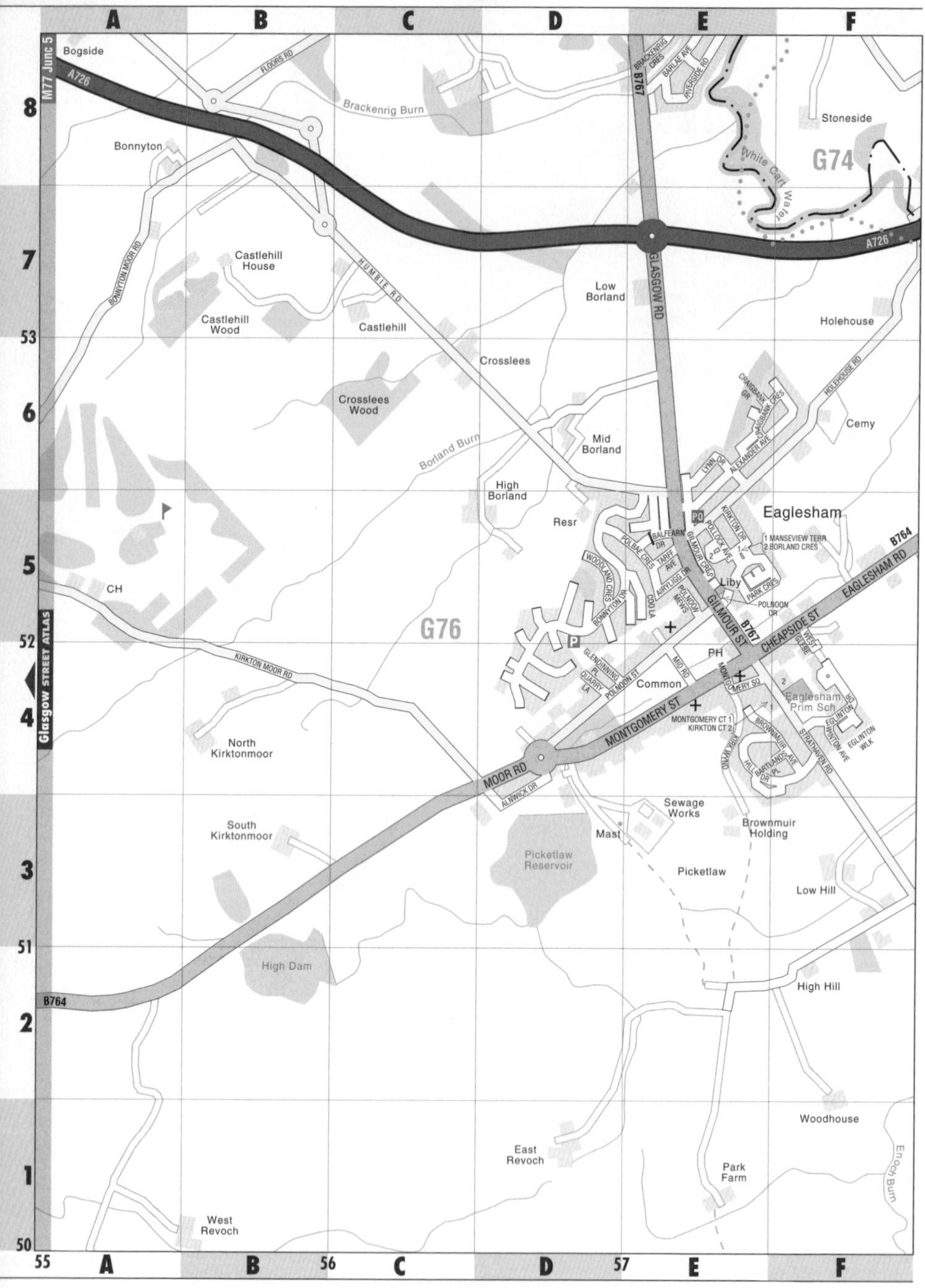

A
B
C
D
E
F
8
7
53
6
5
52
4
3
51
2
1
50
55
56
57
M77 Junc 5
Bogside
A726
FLOORS RD
Brackenrig Burn
BRACKENRIG CRES
BARLAE AVE
RIVERSIDE RD
B767
Stoneside
White Cart Water
G74
Bonnyton
Castlehill House
HUMBIE RD
BONNYTON MOOR RD
Low Borland
GLASGOW RD
Holehouse
Castlehill Wood
Castlehill
Crosslees
Crosslees Wood
CRAIGBANK GR
CRAIGBANK CRES
HOLEHOUSE RD
ALEXANDER AVE
LYNN DR
Cemy
Mid Borland
Borland Burn
High Borland
Resr
PO
KIRKTON DR
POLLOCK AVE
Eaglesham
1 MANSEVIEW TERR
2 BORLAND CRES
B764
BALFEARN DR
POLBAE CRES
TARFF AVE
AIRYLIGG DR
GILMOUR CRES
WOODLAND CRES
BONNYTON DR
COO LA
POLNOON MEWS
Liby
PARK CRES
POLNOON DR
EAGLESHAM RD
CH
G76
P
GILMOUR ST
CHEAPSIDE ST
WEST GLEBE
PH
GLENDINNING PL
QUARRY LA
POLNOON ST
MID RD
Common
MONTGOMERY SQ
KIRKTON MOOR RD
Eaglesham Prim Sch
MONTGOMERY ST
MONTGOMERY CT 1
KIRKTON CT 2
BROWNMUIR AVE
EGLINTON RD
WINTON AVE
EGLINTON WLK
North Kirktonmoor
KIRK WYND
HILL DR
BARTLANDS PL
STRATHAVEN RD
MOOR RD
ALNWICK DR
Sewage Works
Brownmuir Holding
Mast
Picketlaw Reservoir
Picketlaw
South Kirktonmoor
Low Hill
High Dam
High Hill
Woodhouse
East Revoch
Park Farm
Enoch Burn
West Revoch
Glasgow STREET ATLAS

74
88

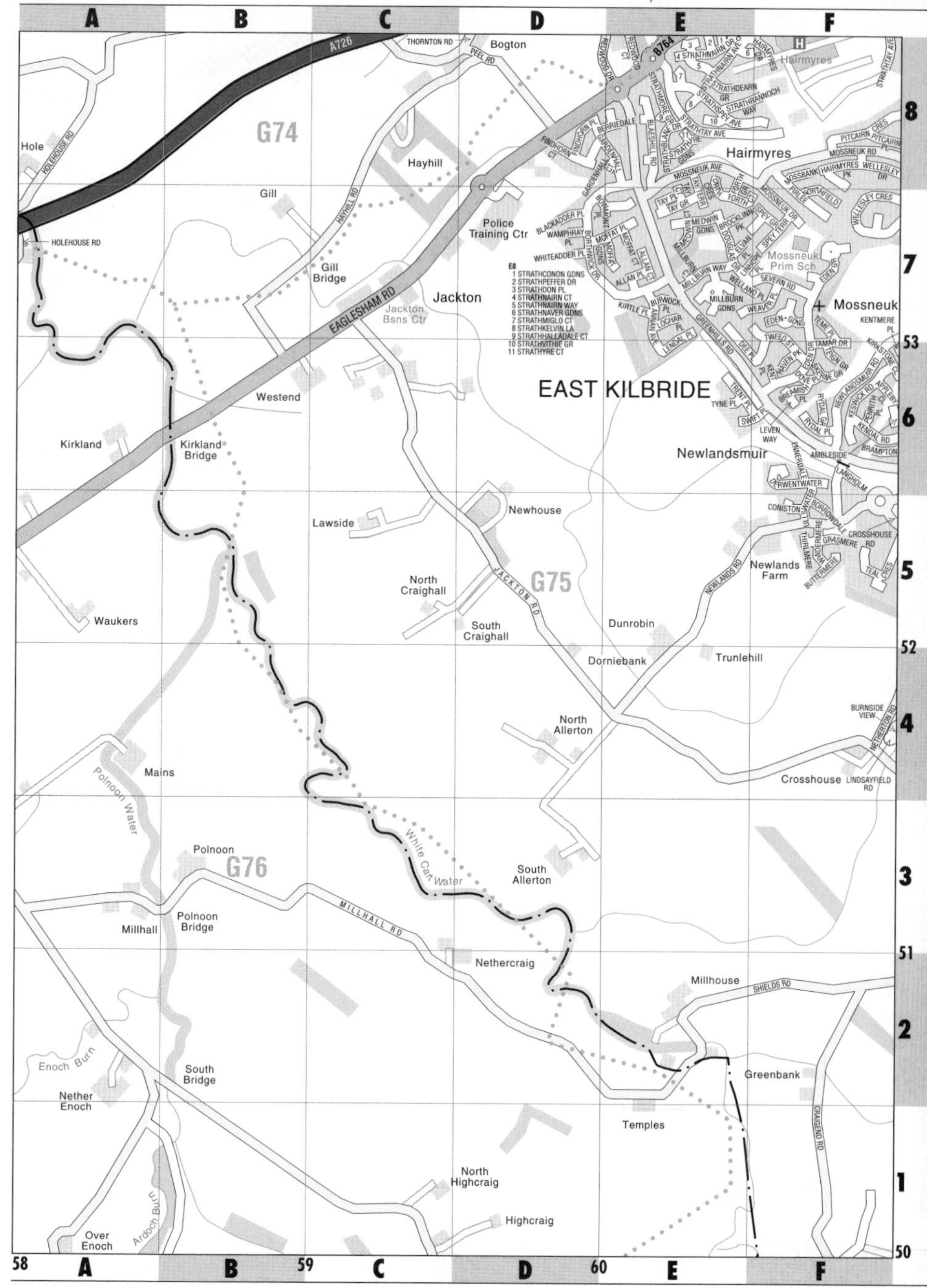
A726
G74
Hole
HOLEHOUSE RD
Gill
Gill Bridge
Hayhill
Bogton
THORNTON RD
PEEL RD
HAYHILL RD
Police Training Ctr
Jackton
Jackton Bsns Ctr
EAGLESHAM RD
Westend
Kirkland
Kirkland Bridge
Lawside
Newhouse
North Craighall
South Craighall
JACKTON RD
G75
Waukers
Mains
Polnoon Water
Polnoon
G76
Millhall
Polnoon Bridge
MILLHALL RD
White Cart Water
South Allerton
North Allerton
Dunrobin
Dorniebank
Trunlehill
Nethercraig
Millhouse
SHIELDS RD
Greenbank
Temples
CRAIGEND RD
Enoch Burn
Nether Enoch
South Bridge
North Highcraig
Highcraig
Over Enoch
Ardoch Burn
EAST KILBRIDE
Hairmyres
Mossneuk
Mossneuk Prim Sch
Newlandsmuir
Newlands Farm
NEWLANDS RD
Crosshouse
BURNSIDE VIEW
NETHERTON RD
LINDSAYFIELD RD
B764
E8
1 STRATHCONON GDNS
2 STRATHPEFFER DR
3 STRATHDON PL
4 STRATHNAIRN CT
5 STRATHNAIRN WAY
6 STRATHNAVER GDNS
7 STRATHMIGLO CT
8 STRATHKELVIN LA
9 STRATHALLADALE CT
10 STRATHVITHIE GR
11 STRATHYRE CT
A B C D E F
58 59 60
50 51 52 53
1 2 3 4 5 6 7 8

100
88

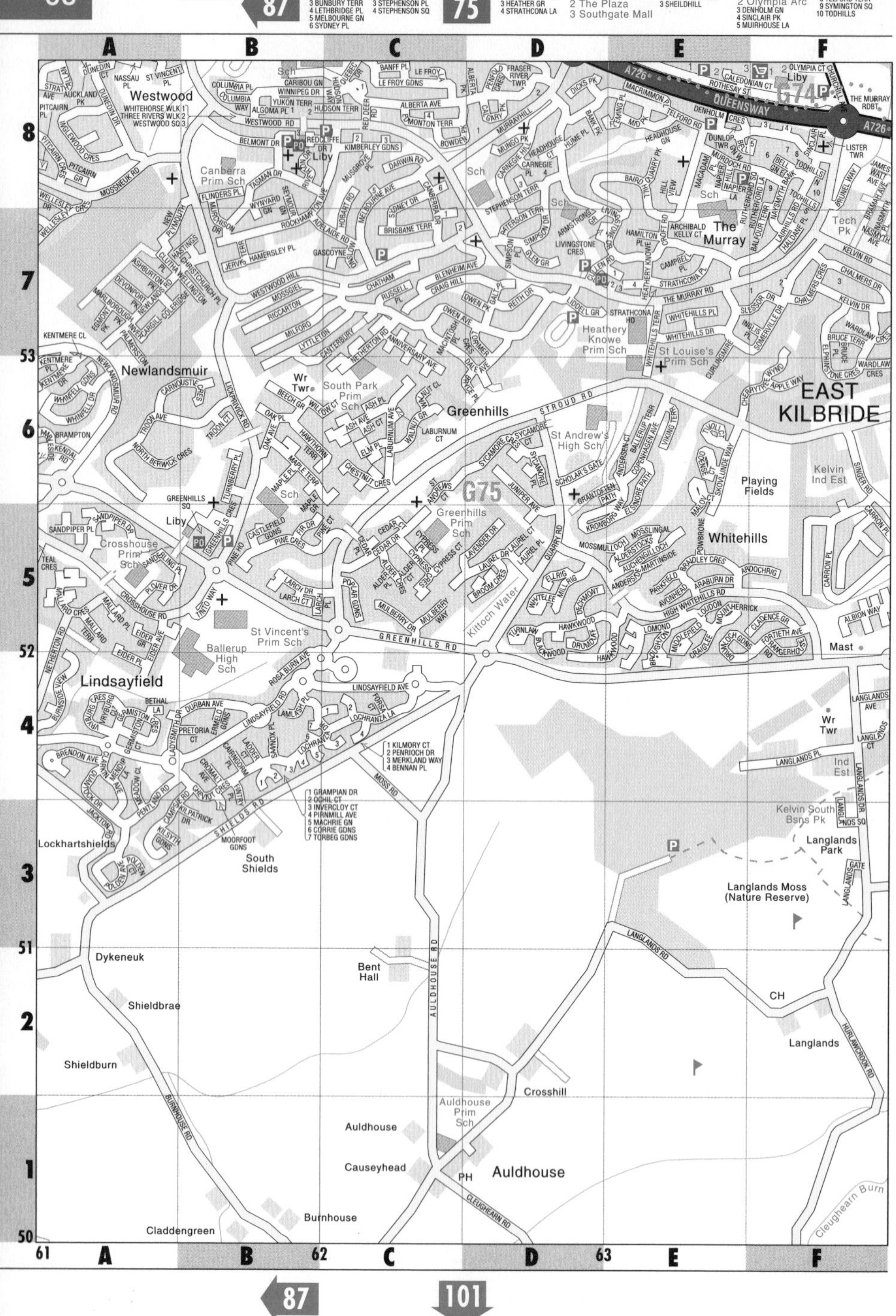
A
B
C
D
E
F
8
7
53
6
5
52
4
3
51
2
1
50
61
62
63
Westwood
Newlandsmuir
Lindsayfield
Lockhartshields
South Shields
Greenhills
EAST KILBRIDE
The Murray
Whitehills
Dykeneuk
Shieldbrae
Shieldburn
Bent Hall
Crosshill
Auldhouse
Causeyhead
Burnhouse
Claddengreen
Langlands
Langlands Park
Langlands Moss (Nature Reserve)
Kelvin South Bsns Pk
Kelvin Ind Est
Tech Pk
Playing Fields
Canberra Prim Sch
South Park Prim Sch
Greenhills Prim Sch
Crosshouse Prim Sch
St Vincent's Prim Sch
Ballerup High Sch
St Andrew's High Sch
Heathery Knowe Prim Sch
St Louise's Prim Sch
Auldhouse Prim Sch
G74
G75
A726
QUEENSWAY
STROUD RD
GREENHILLS RD
SHIELDS RD
AULDHOUSE RD
LANGLANDS RD
LANGLANDS DR
HURLAWCROOK RD
CLEUGHEARN RD
BURNHOUSE RD
MOSS RD
LICKPRIVICK RD
THE MURRAY RD
Kittoch Water
Cleughearn Burn
THE MURRAY RDBT
1 KILMORY CT
2 PENRIOCH DR
3 MERKLAND WAY
4 BENNAN PL
1 GRAMPIAN DR
2 OCHIL CT
3 INVERCLOY CT
4 PIRNMILL AVE
5 MACHRIE GN
6 CORRIE GDNS
7 TORBEG GDNS

76
90

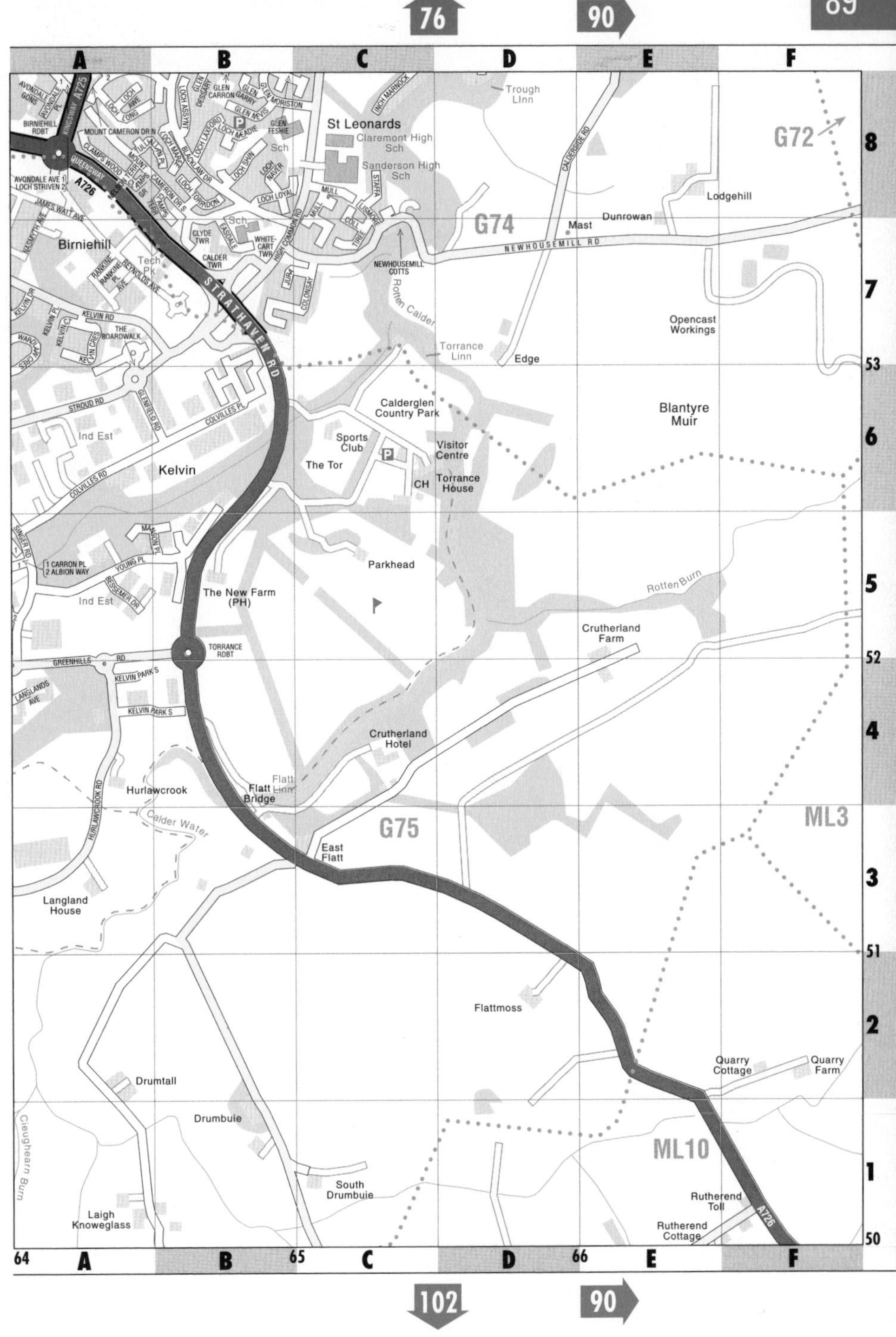
A
B
C
D
E
F
St Leonards
Claremont High Sch
Sanderson High Sch
Birniehill
Trough Linn
G72
Lodgehill
Dunrowan
Mast
G74
NEWHOUSEMILL RD
NEWHOUSEMILL COTTS
STRATHAVEN RD
Rotten Calder
Torrance Linn
Edge
Opencast Workings
Calderglen Country Park
Blantyre Muir
Sports Club
Visitor Centre
The Tor
Torrance House
CH
Kelvin
Ind Est
Parkhead
The New Farm (PH)
Rotten Burn
Crutherland Farm
TORRANCE RDBT
Crutherland Hotel
Hurlawcrook
Flatt Bridge
Flatt Linn
Calder Water
G75
East Flatt
ML3
Langland House
Flattmoss
Drumtall
Drumbuie
Quarry Cottage
Quarry Farm
ML10
South Drumbuie
Cleughearn Burn
Laigh Knoweglass
Rutherend Toll
Rutherend Cottage
A726
A725
KINGSWAY
QUEENSWAY
KELVIN RD
COLVILLES RD
COLVILLES PL
STROUD RD
GREENHILLS RD
KELVIN PARK S
HURLAWCROOK RD
CALDERSIDE RD
HIGH COMMON RD
8
7
53
6
5
52
4
3
51
2
1
50
64
65
66

102
90

89
77

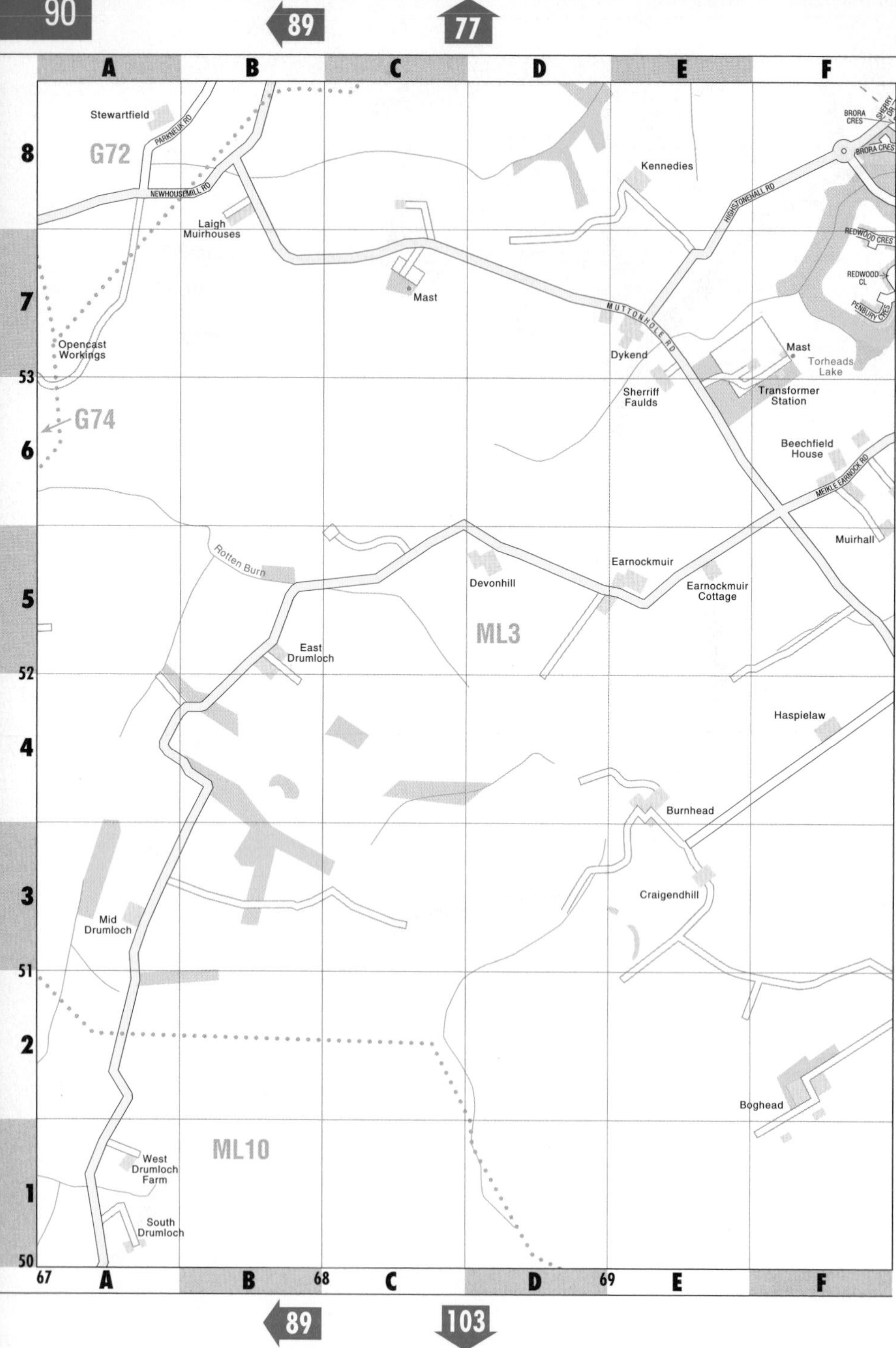
A
B
C
D
E
F
Stewartfield
PARKNEUK RD
G72
NEWHOUSEMILL RD
Laigh
Muirhouses
Mast
Kennedies
BRORA CRES
SHERRY DR
BRORA CRES
HIGHSTONEHALL RD
REDWOOD CRES
REDWOOD CL
PENBURY CRES
MUTTONHOLE RD
Dykend
Mast
Torheads
Lake
Sherriff
Faulds
Transformer
Station
Opencast
Workings
G74
Beechfield
House
MEIKLE EARNOCK RD
Muirhall
Rotten Burn
Devonhill
Earnockmuir
Earnockmuir
Cottage
ML3
East
Drumloch
Haspielaw
Burnhead
Craigendhill
Mid
Drumloch
Boghead
ML10
West
Drumloch
Farm
South
Drumloch
8
7
53
6
5
52
4
3
51
2
1
50
67
68
69

89
103

78
92

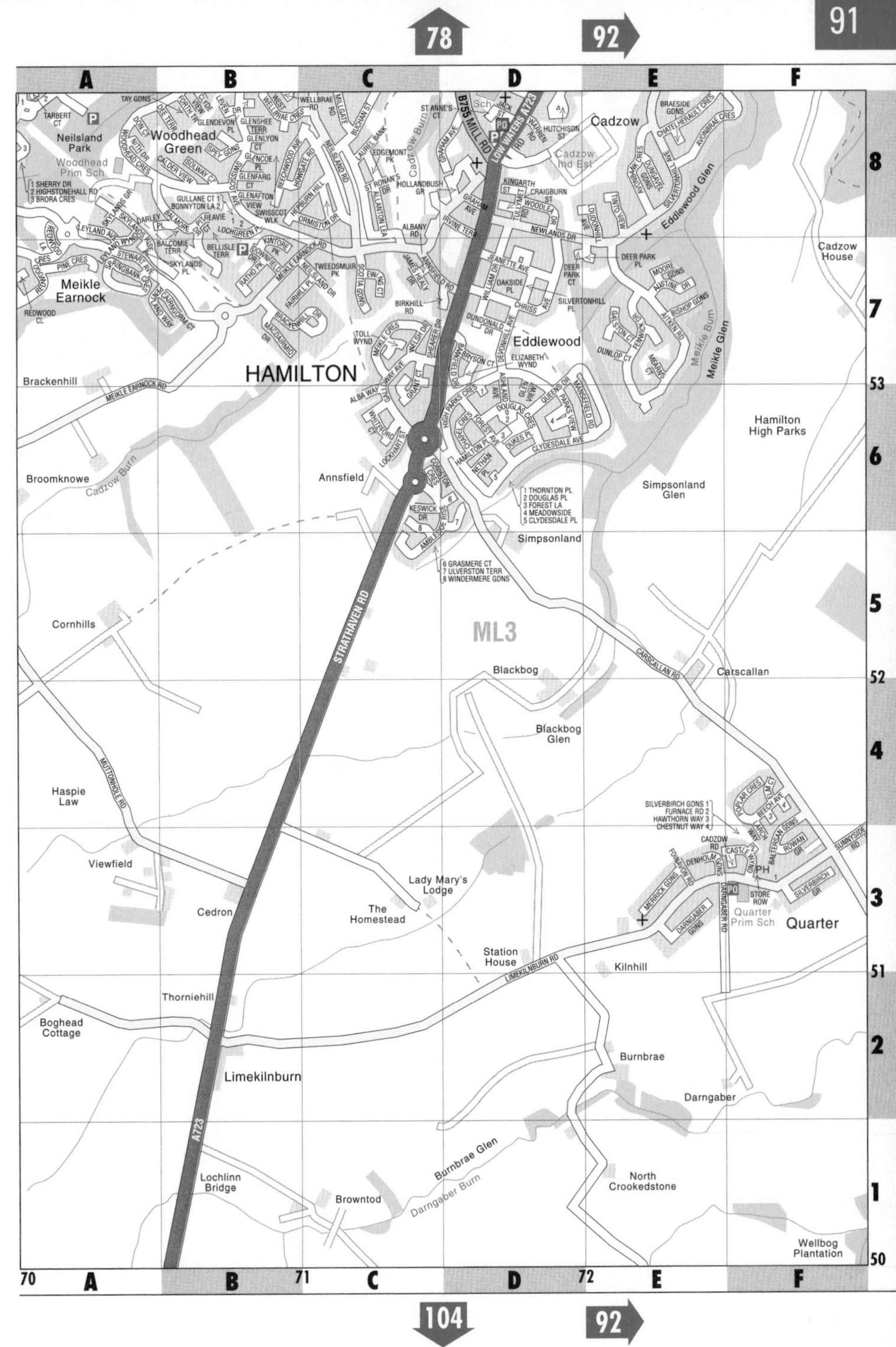
A
B
C
D
E
F
8
7
53
6
5
52
4
3
51
2
1
50
70
71
72
Neilsland Park
Woodhead Green
Woodhead Prim Sch
Meikle Earnock
HAMILTON
Cadzow
Cadzow Ind Est
Eddlewood
Edddlewood Glen
Meikle Glen
Meikle Burn
Cadzow House
Cadzow Burn
Brackenhill
MEIKLE EARNOCK RD
Broomknowe
Annsfield
Hamilton High Parks
Simpsonland Glen
Simpsonland
B755 MILL RD
LOW WATERS A723
1 SHERRY DR
2 HIGHSTONEHALL RD
3 BRORA CRES
1 THORNTON PL
2 DOUGLAS PL
3 FOREST LA
4 MEADOWSIDE
5 CLYDESDALE PL
6 GRASMERE CT
7 ULVERSTON TERR
8 WINDERMERE GDNS
STRATHAVEN RD
ML3
Cornhills
Blackbog
CARSCALLAN RD
Carscallan
Blackbog Glen
Haspie Law
MUTTONHOLE RD
SILVERBIRCH GDNS 1
FURNACE RD 2
HAWTHORN WAY 3
CHESTNUT WAY 4
Viewfield
Lady Mary's Lodge
Cedron
The Homestead
Quarter Prim Sch
Quarter
Station House
LIMEKILNBURN RD
Kilnhill
Thorniehill
Boghead Cottage
Burnbrae
Limekilnburn
Darngaber
A723
Burnbrae Glen
Darngaber Burn
Lochlinn Bridge
Browntod
North Crookedstone
Wellbog Plantation

104
92

91
79

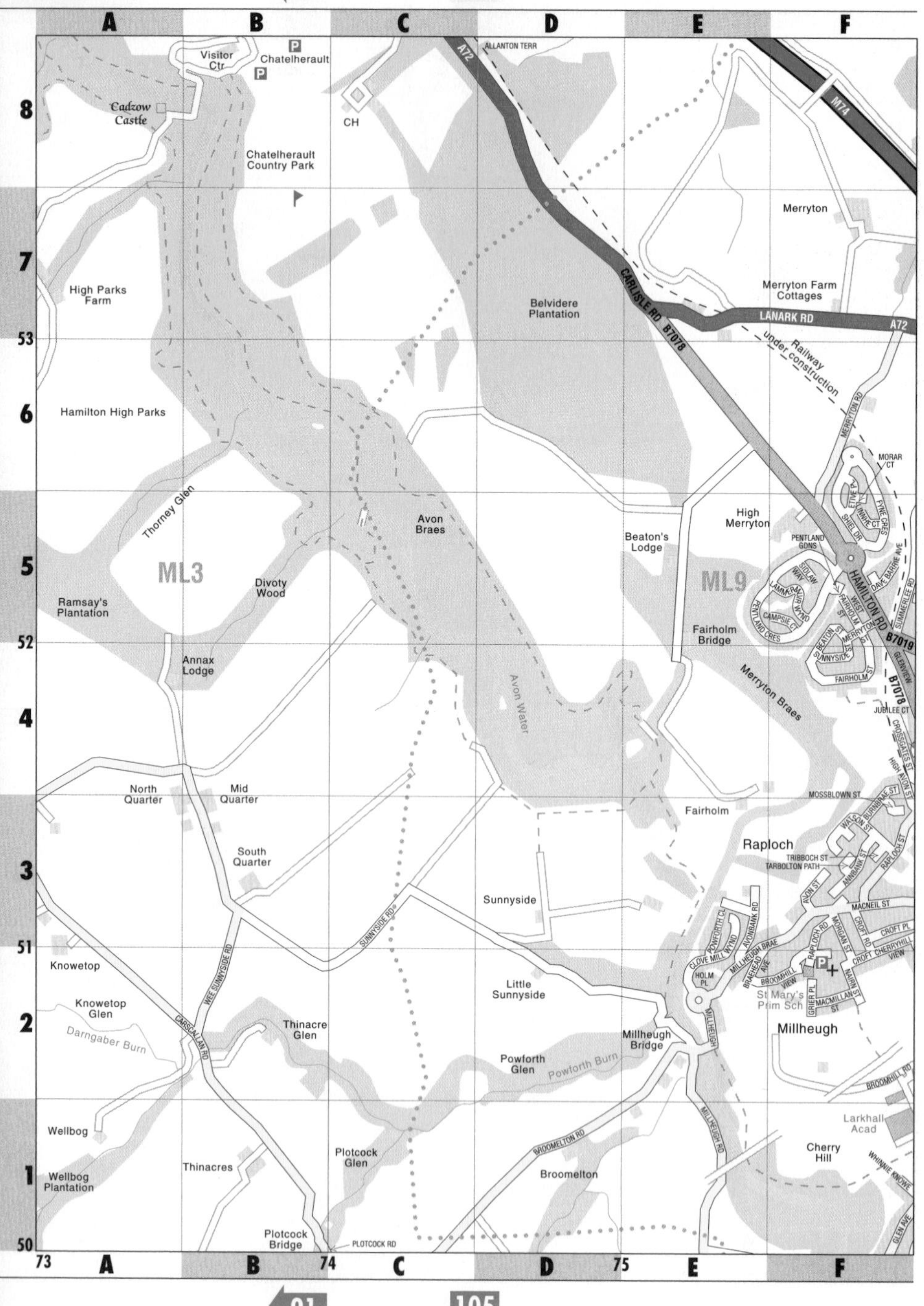
A
B
C
D
E
F
8
7
53
6
5
52
4
3
51
2
1
50
73
74
75
Visitor Ctr
Chatelherault
Cadzow Castle
CH
ALLANTON TERR
A72
M74
Chatelherault Country Park
Merryton
High Parks Farm
Merryton Farm Cottages
Belvidere Plantation
CARLISLE RD
B7078
LANARK RD
A72
Railway under construction
Hamilton High Parks
MERRYTON RD
MORAR CT
Thorney Glen
Avon Braes
High Merryton
Beaton's Lodge
PENTLAND GDNS
ML3
ML9
Divoty Wood
Ramsay's Plantation
HAMILTON RD
SUMMERLEE RD
CAMPSIE CT
PENTLAND CRES
Fairholm Bridge
B7019
SUNNYSIDE
FAIRHOLM
Annax Lodge
Avon Water
Merryton Braes
GLENVIEW
JUBILEE CT
CROSSGATES ST
HIGH AVON ST
North Quarter
Mid Quarter
MOSSBLOWN ST
Fairholm
Raploch
TRIBBOCH ST
TARBOLTON PATH
South Quarter
RAPLOCH ST
Sunnyside
MACNEIL ST
SUNNYSIDE RD
AVONBANK RD
CROFT PL
POWFORTH CL
CLOVE MILL WYND
MILLHEUGH BRAE
CHERRYHILL VIEW
HOLM PL
BROOMHILL VIEW
BRAEHEAD AVE
Knowetop
Little Sunnyside
St Mary's Prim Sch
MACMILLAN ST
GRIER PL
Knowetop Glen
WEE SUNNYSIDE RD
Millheugh
Darngaber Burn
CARSCALLAN RD
Thinacre Glen
Millheugh Bridge
MILLHEUGH
Powforth Glen
Powforth Burn
BROOMHILL RD
Larkhall Acad
Wellbog
BROOMELTON RD
MILLHEUGH RD
Cherry Hill
WHINNIE KNOWE
Plotcock Glen
Thinacres
Broomelton
Wellbog Plantation
GLEN AVE
Plotcock Bridge
PLOTCOCK RD

91
105

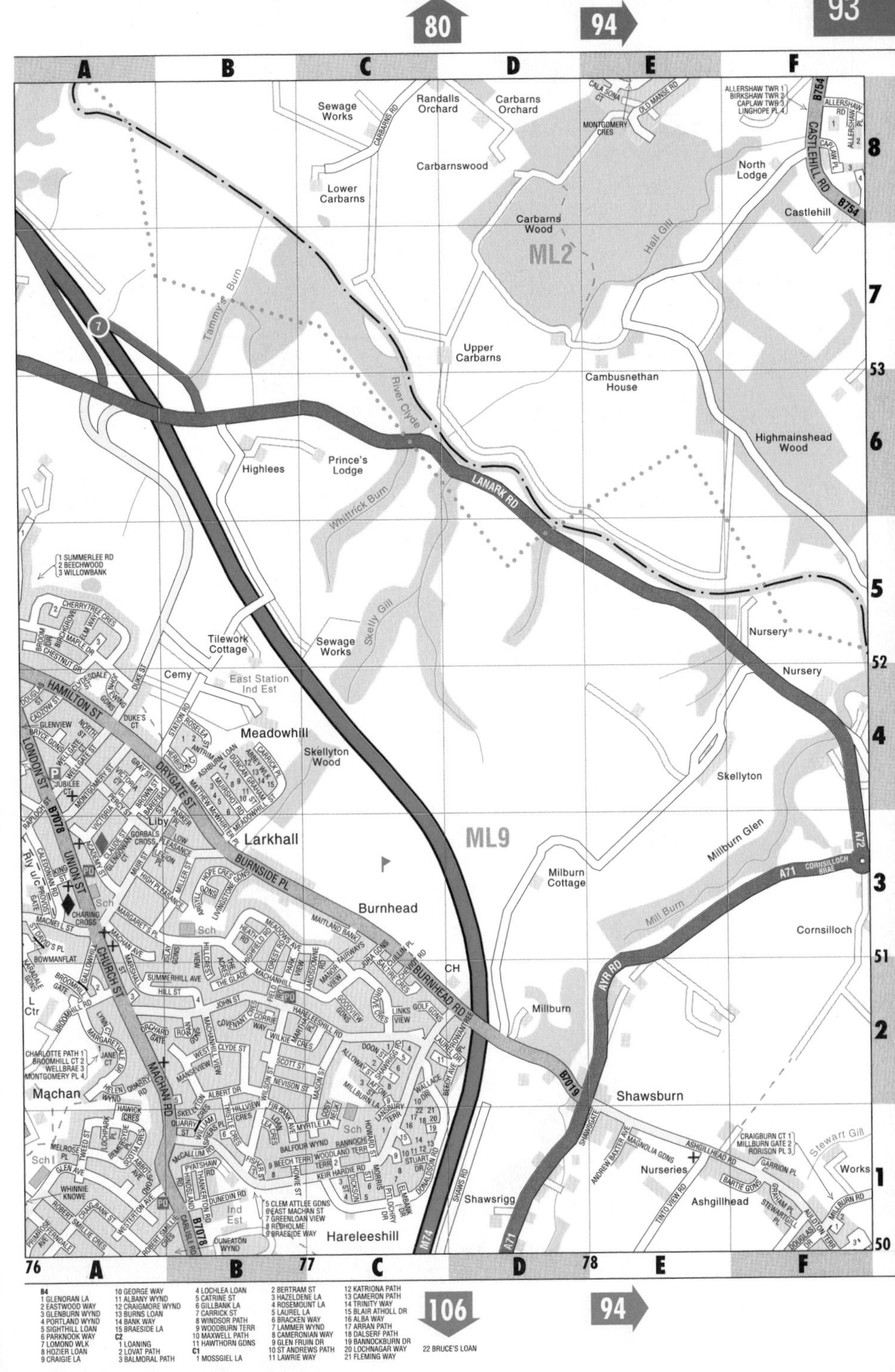

B4
1 GLENORAN LA
2 EASTWOOD WAY
3 GLENBURN WYND
4 PORTLAND WYND
5 SIGHTHILL LOAN
6 PARKNOOK WAY
7 LOMOND WLK
8 HOZIER LOAN
9 CRAIGIE LA
10 GEORGE WAY
11 ALBANY WYND
12 CRAIGMORE WYND
13 BURNS LOAN
14 BANK WAY
15 BRAESIDE LA
C2
1 LOANING
2 LOVAT PATH
3 BALMORAL PATH
4 LOCHLEA LOAN
5 CATRINE ST
6 GILLBANK LA
7 CARRICK ST
8 WINDSOR PATH
9 WOODBURN TERR
10 MAXWELL PATH
11 HAWTHORN GDNS
C1
1 MOSSGIEL LA
2 BERTRAM ST
3 HAZELDENE LA
4 ROSEMOUNT LA
5 LAUREL LA
6 BRACKEN WAY
7 LAMMER WYND
8 CAMERONIAN WAY
9 GLEN FRUIN DR
10 ST ANDREWS PATH
11 LAWRIE WAY
12 KATRIONA PATH
13 CAMERON PATH
14 TRINITY WAY
15 BLAIR ATHOLL DR
16 ALBA WAY
17 ARRAN PATH
18 DALSERF PATH
19 BANNOCKBURN DR
20 LOCHNAGAR WAY
21 FLEMING WAY
22 BRUCE'S LOAN

93
81

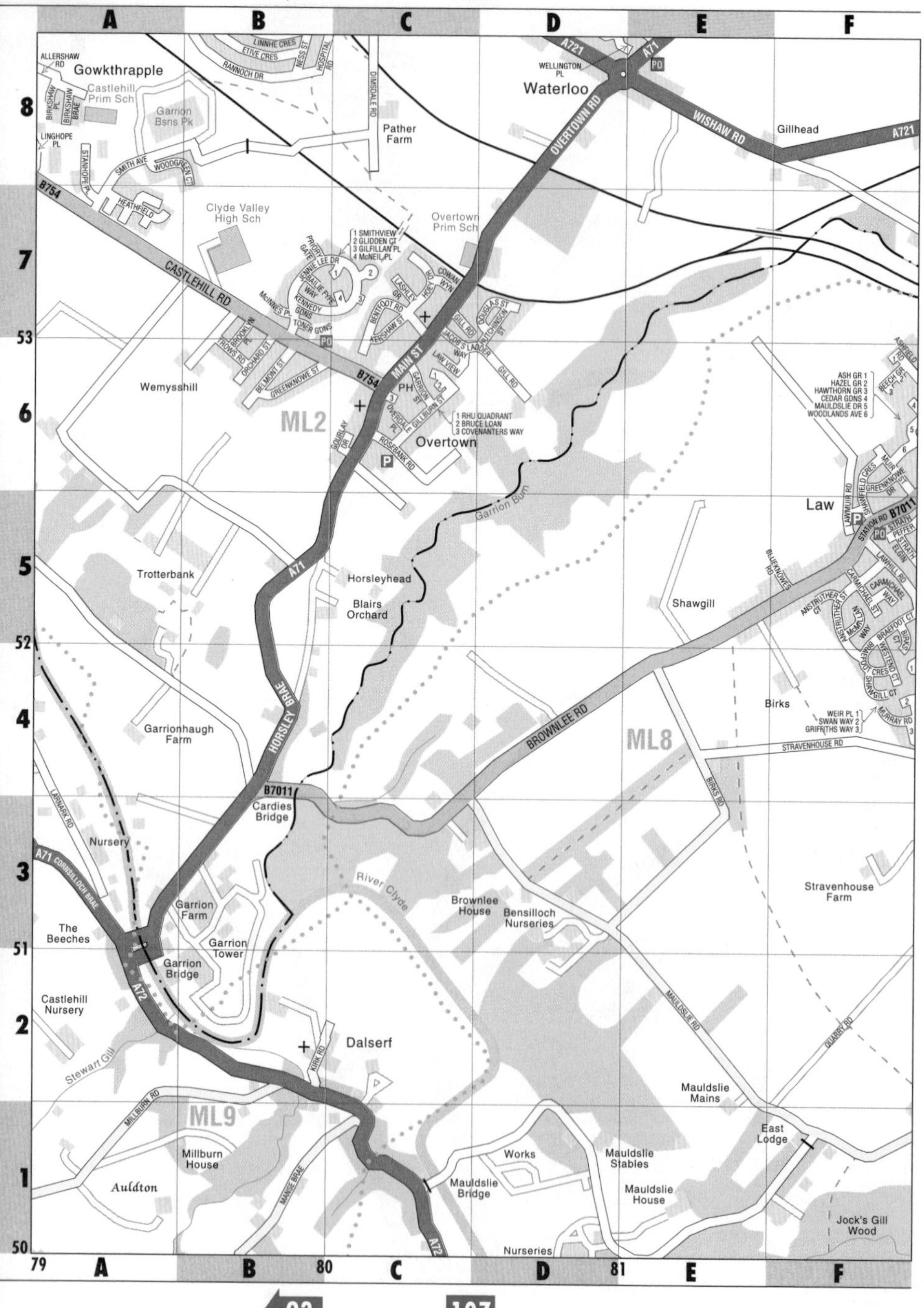
Gowkthrapple
Castlehill Prim Sch
Garrion Bsns Pk
Waterloo
Pather Farm
Gillhead
Clyde Valley High Sch
Overtown Prim Sch
CASTLEHILL RD
MAIN ST
OVERTOWN RD
WISHAW RD
Wemysshill
ML2
Overtown
Law
Trotterbank
Horsleyhead
Blairs Orchard
Shawgill
Garrion Burn
HORSLEY BRAE
BROWNLEE RD
Garrionhaugh Farm
Birks
ML8
Cardies Bridge
Nursery
River Clyde
Stravenhouse Farm
Garrion Farm
The Beeches
Brownlee House
Bensilloch Nurseries
Garrion Tower
Garrion Bridge
Castlehill Nursery
Dalserf
Stewart Gill
Mauldslie Mains
ML9
East Lodge
Millburn House
Works
Mauldslie Stables
Auldton
Mauldslie Bridge
Mauldslie House
Jock's Gill Wood
Nurseries

82
96

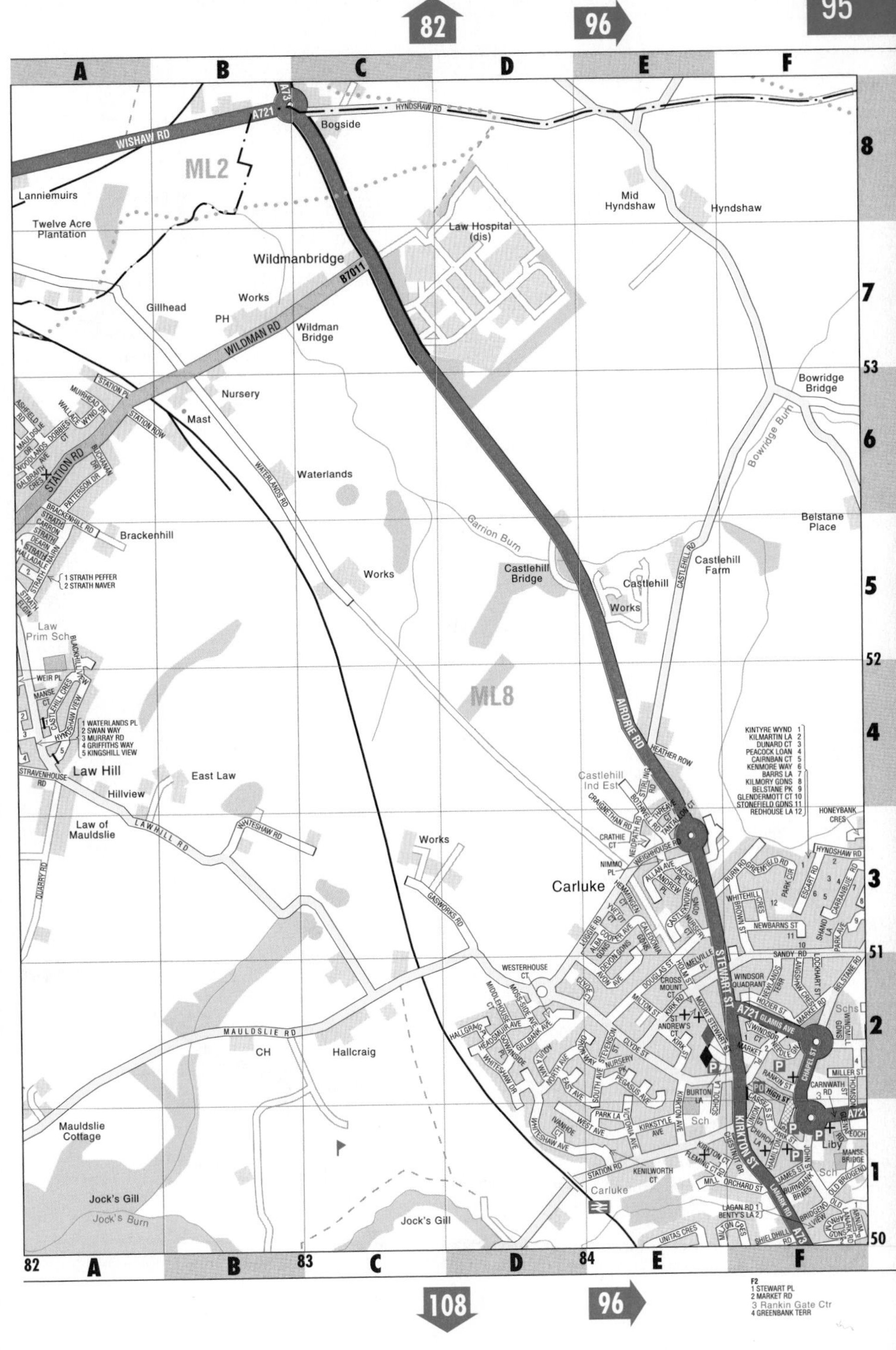
A
B
C
D
E
F
8
7
53
6
5
52
4
3
51
2
1
50
82
83
84
WISHAW RD
A721
A73
HYNDSHAW RD
Bogside
ML2
Lanniemuirs
Twelve Acre
Plantation
Wildmanbridge
B7011
Works
Gillhead
PH
WILDMAN RD
Wildman
Bridge
Law Hospital
(dis)
Mid
Hyndshaw
Hyndshaw
STATION PL
MUIRHEAD DR
WALLACE WYND
DOBBIES CT
ASHFIELD RD
MAULDSLIE DR
WOODLANDS AVE
GALBRAITH CRES
STATION RD
STATION ROW
BUCHANAN DR
PATTERSON DR
Nursery
Mast
Bowridge
Bridge
Bowridge Burn
WATERLANDS RD
Waterlands
BRACKENHILL RD
Brackenhill
1 STRATH PEFFER
2 STRATH NAVER
Garrion Burn
Belstane
Place
Castlehill
Bridge
Castlehill
Farm
Castlehill
CASTLEHILL RD
Works
Law
Prim Sch
BLACKHILL VIEW
WEIR PL
MANSE CT
CASTLEHILL CRES
HYNDSHAW VIEW
1 WATERLANDS PL
2 SWAN WAY
3 MURRAY RD
4 GRIFFITHS WAY
5 KINGSHILL VIEW
ML8
AIRDRIE RD
HEATHER ROW
KINTYRE WYND 1
KILMARTIN LA 2
DUNARD CT 3
PEACOCK LOAN 4
CAIRNBAN CT 5
KENMORE WAY 6
BARRS LA 7
KILMORY GDNS 8
BELSTANE PK 9
GLENDERMOTT CT 10
STONEFIELD GDNS 11
REDHOUSE LA 12
Law Hill
STRAVENHOUSE RD
East Law
Hillview
Castlehill
Ind Est
Law of
Mauldslie
LAWHILL RD
WHITESHAW RD
QUARRY RD
Works
CRAIGNETHAN RD
CRATHIE CT
NIMMO PL
WEIGHHOUSE RD
HONEYBANK CRES
HYNDSHAW RD
Carluke
GASWORKS RD
WESTERHOUSE CT
SANDY RD
NEWBARNS ST
WINDSOR QUADRANT
STEWART ST
A721 GLAMIS AVE
Schs
MAULDSLIE RD
CH
Hallcraig
MILLER ST
HIGH ST
CARNWATH RD
A721
Liby
KIRKTON ST
Mauldslie
Cottage
STATION RD
KENILWORTH CT
Carluke
Sch
Jock's Gill
Jock's Burn
Jock's Gill
UNITAS CRES
LANARK RD
A73
F2
1 STEWART PL
2 MARKET RD
3 Rankin Gate Ctr
4 GREENBANK TERR

108
96

95
83

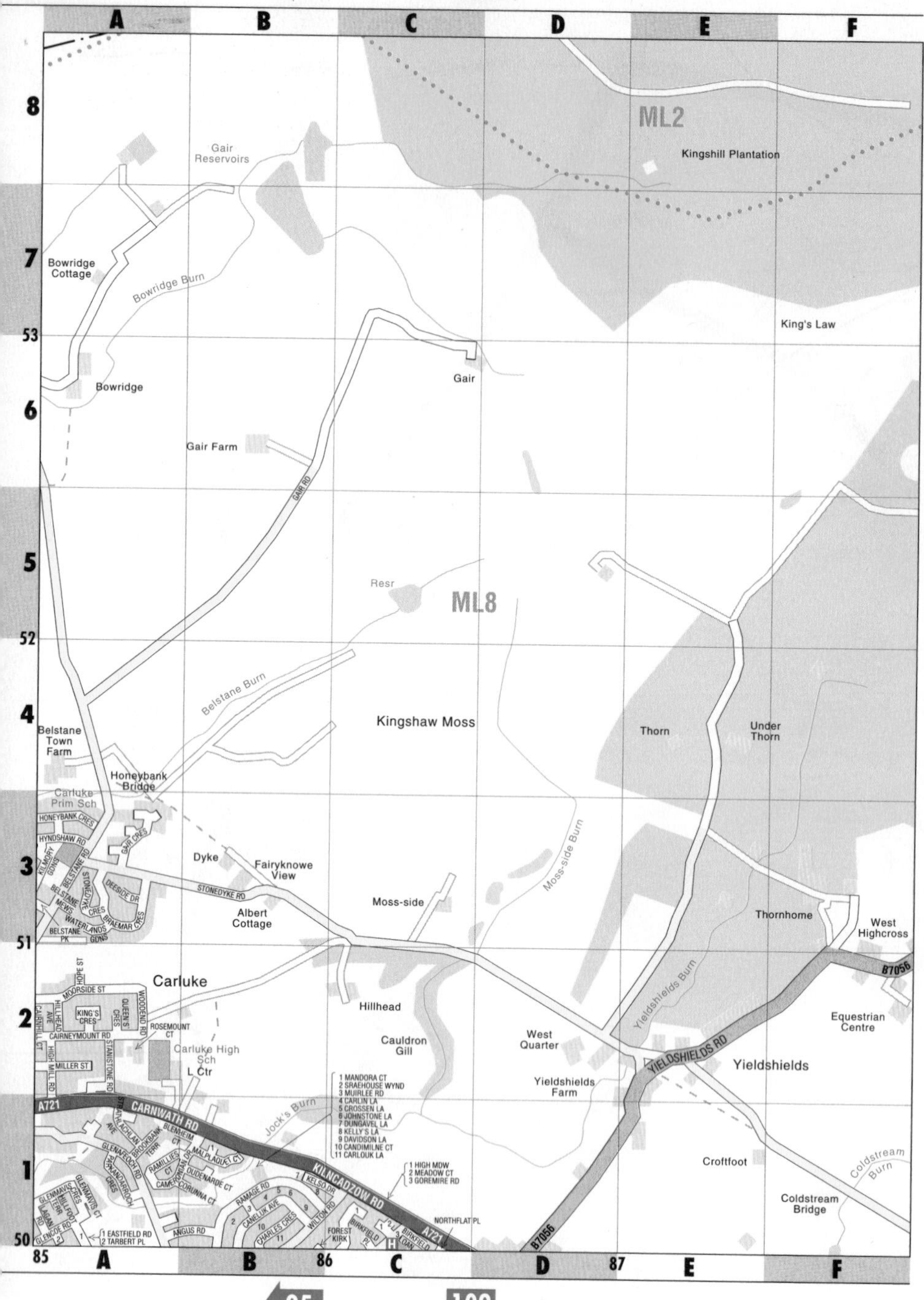
A
B
C
D
E
F
8
7
53
6
5
52
4
3
51
2
1
50
ML2
Kingshill Plantation
Gair
Reservoirs
Bowridge
Cottage
Bowridge Burn
King's Law
Bowridge
Gair
Gair Farm
GAIR RD
Resr
ML8
Belstane Burn
Kingshaw Moss
Thorn
Under
Thorn
Belstane
Town
Farm
Honeybank
Bridge
Carluke
Prim Sch
HONEYBANK CRES
HYNDSHAW RD
GAIR CRES
KILMORY
GDNS
BELSTANE RD
Dyke
Fairyknowe
View
Moss-side Burn
STONEDYKE CRES
DEESIDE DR
STONEDYKE RD
BELSTANE
MEWS
WATERLANDS
GDNS
BRAEMAR CRES
BELSTANE
PK
Albert
Cottage
Moss-side
Thornhome
West
Highcross
B7056
HOPE ST
MOORSIDE ST
Carluke
HILLHEAD
AVE
KING'S
CRES
QUEEN'S
CRES
WOODEND RD
CAIRNHILL CT
CAIRNEYMOUNT RD
ROSEMOUNT
CT
Carluke High
Sch
L Ctr
HIGH MILL RD
MILLER ST
STANISTONE RD
Hillhead
Cauldron
Gill
West
Quarter
Yieldshields Burn
Equestrian
Centre
YIELDSHIELDS RD
Yieldshields
Yieldshields
Farm
1 MANDORA CT
2 SRAEHOUSE WYND
3 MUIRLEE RD
4 CARLIN LA
5 CROSSEN LA
6 JOHNSTONE LA
7 DUNGAVEL LA
8 KELLY'S LA
9 DAVIDSON LA
10 CANDIMILNE CT
11 CARLOUK LA
A721
CARNWATH RD
STRATHLACHLAN
AVE
Jock's Burn
BROOKBANK
TERR
BLENHEIM
CT
GLENAFEOCH RD
PARKANDARROCH
CRES
RAMILLIES
CT
CAMERONIAN DR
MALPLAQUET CT
OUDENARDE CT
CORUNNA CT
KILNCADZOW RD
1 HIGH MDW
2 MEADOW CT
3 GOREMIRE RD
KELSO DR
RAMAGE RD
CANELUK AVE
CHARLES CRES
WILTON RD
GLENMAVIS
TERR
GLENMAVIS CRES
GLENMAVIS CT
HILLFOOT
LAGAN
RD
GLENCOE RD
1 EASTFIELD RD
2 TARBERT PL
ANGUS RD
FOREST
KIRK
BIRKFIELD
PL
BIRKFIELD
LOAN
NORTHFLAT PL
A721
B7056
Croftfoot
Coldstream
Bridge
Coldstream
Burn
85
A
B
86
C
D
87
E
F

95
109

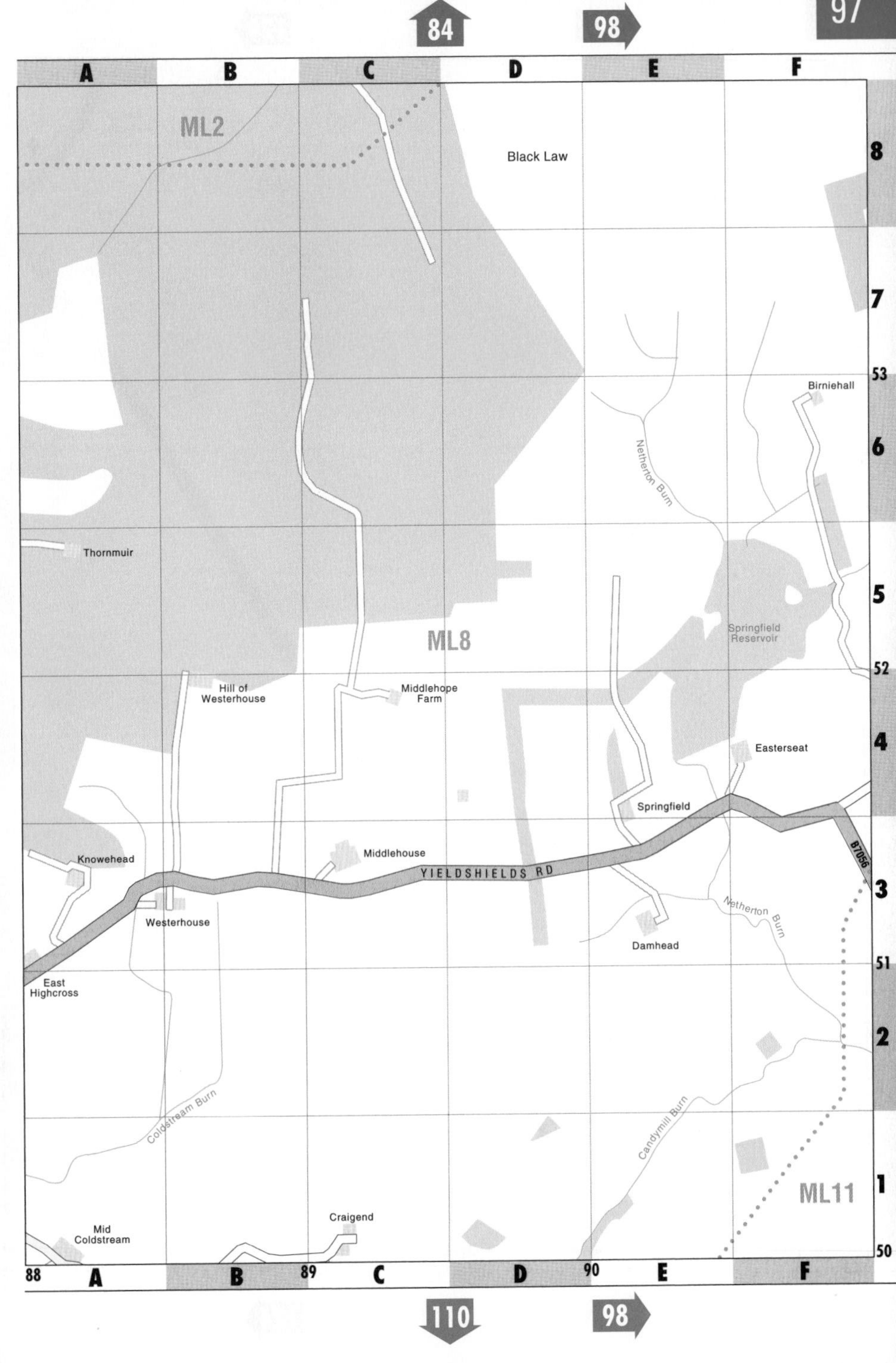
84
98
A
B
C
D
E
F
ML2
Black Law
8
7
53
Birniehall
6
Netherton Burn
Thornmuir
5
ML8
Springfield Reservoir
52
Hill of Westerhouse
Middlehope Farm
4
Easterseat
Springfield
Knowehead
Middlehouse
YIELDSHIELDS RD
B7056
3
Westerhouse
Netherton Burn
Damhead
51
East Highcross
2
Coldstream Burn
Candymill Burn
1
ML11
Mid Coldstream
Craigend
50
88
89
90
110
98

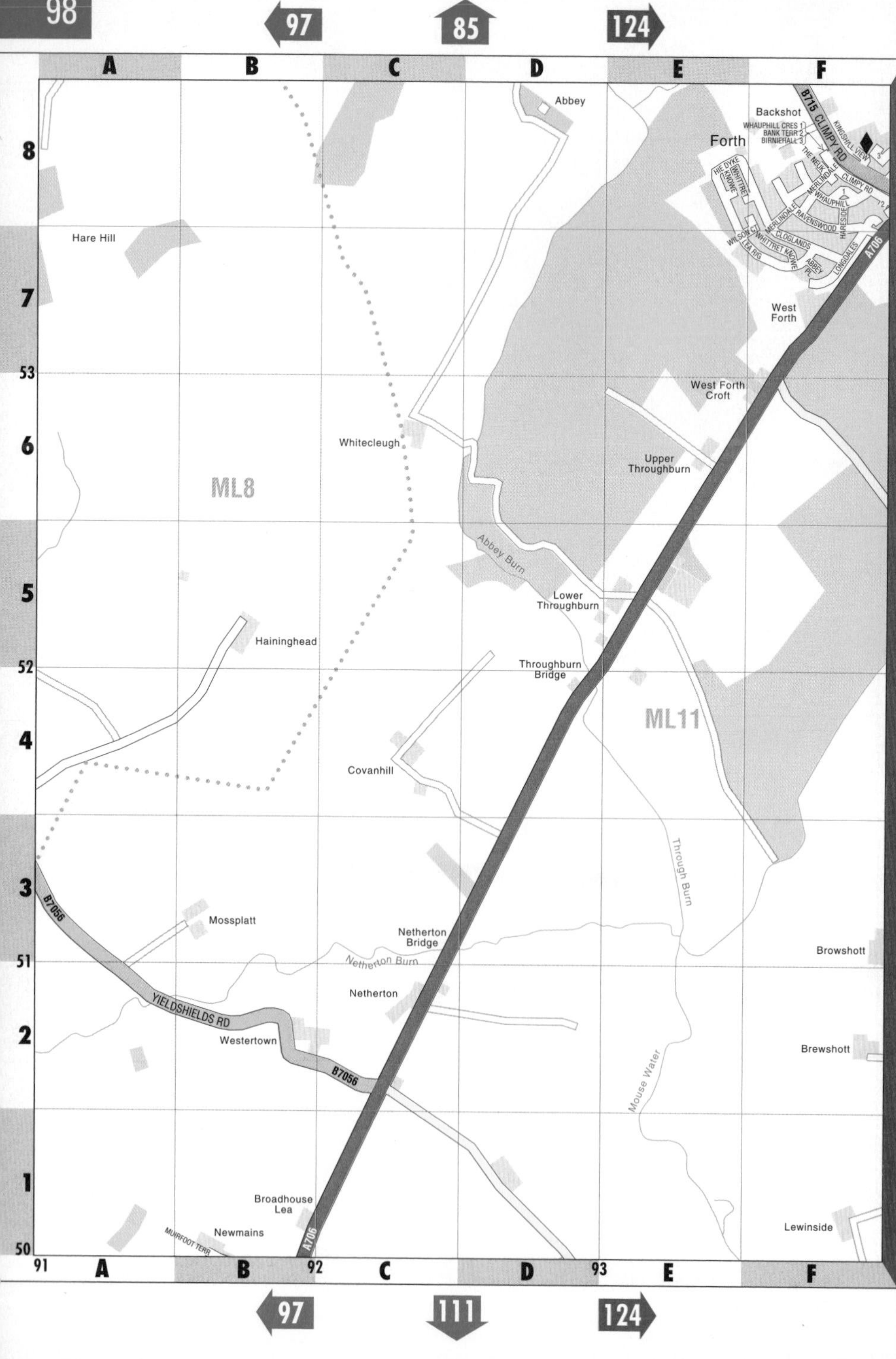
97
85
124
A
B
C
D
E
F
Abbey
Backshot
Forth
B715 CLIMPY RD
WHAUPHILL CRES 1
BANK TERR 2
BIRNIEHALL 3
KINGSHILL VIEW
THE NEUK
MERLINDALE
CLIMPY RD
HIE DYKE
KNOWE
WHITTRET
WHAUPHILL
RAVENSWOOD
HARESIDE
WILSON CT
LEA RIG
WHITTRET KNOWE
CLOGLANDS
ABBEY PL
LONGDALES
A706
8
Hare Hill
7
West Forth
53
West Forth Croft
6
Whitecleugh
Upper Throughburn
ML8
Abbey Burn
5
Lower Throughburn
Haininghead
52
Throughburn Bridge
ML11
4
Covanhill
Through Burn
3
B7056
Mossplatt
Netherton Bridge
Browshott
51
Netherton Burn
Netherton
YIELDSHIELDS RD
2
Westertown
Brewshott
B7056
Mouse Water
1
Broadhouse Lea
Newmains
MUIRFOOT TERR
Lewinside
A706
50
91
92
93
A
B
C
D
E
F
97
111
124

86
100
A
B
C
D
E
F
Dunwan Burn
8
Netherton
Dunwan Dam
7
Nethwerton Burn
49
Melowther Hill
6
Dunwan Burn
5
G76
Carrot House
48
Ayrshire STREET ATLAS
4
Carrot Burn
Loch Hill
3
47
Flow Moss
Mast
Myers Hill
2
Wind Farm
Mast
1
Myers Burn
46
Ayrshire STREET ATLAS
55
56
57
100

99
87

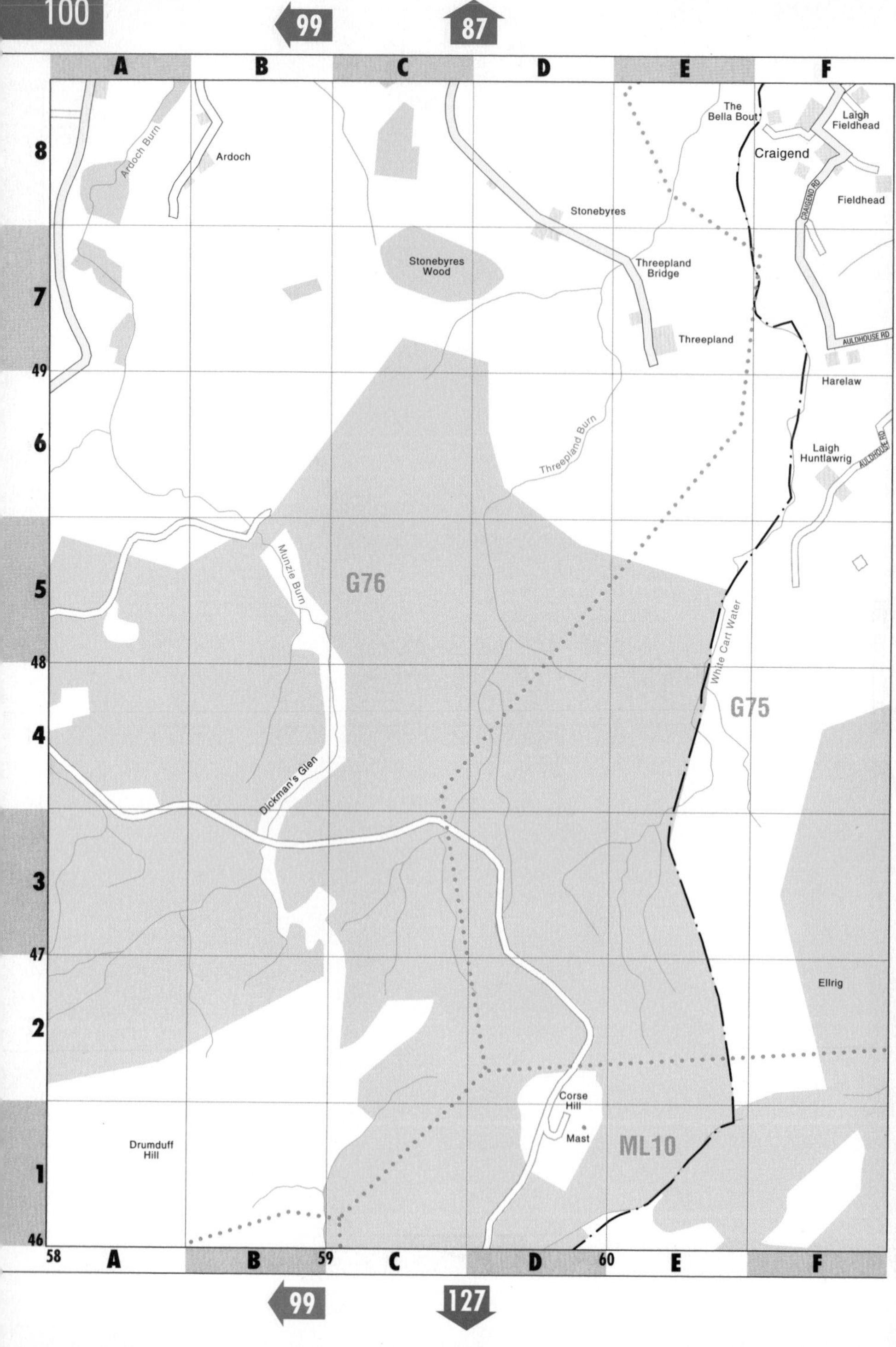
A
B
C
D
E
F
8
7
49
6
5
48
4
3
47
2
1
46
58
59
60
Ardoch Burn
Ardoch
Stonebyres
Stonebyres Wood
Threepland Bridge
Threepland
The Bella Bout
Laigh Fieldhead
Craigend
Fieldhead
CRAIGEND RD
AULDHOUSE RD
Harelaw
Laigh Huntlawrig
Threepland Burn
Munzie Burn
G76
White Cart Water
G75
Dickman's Glen
Ellrig
Corse Hill
Mast
ML10
Drumduff Hill

99
127

88
102

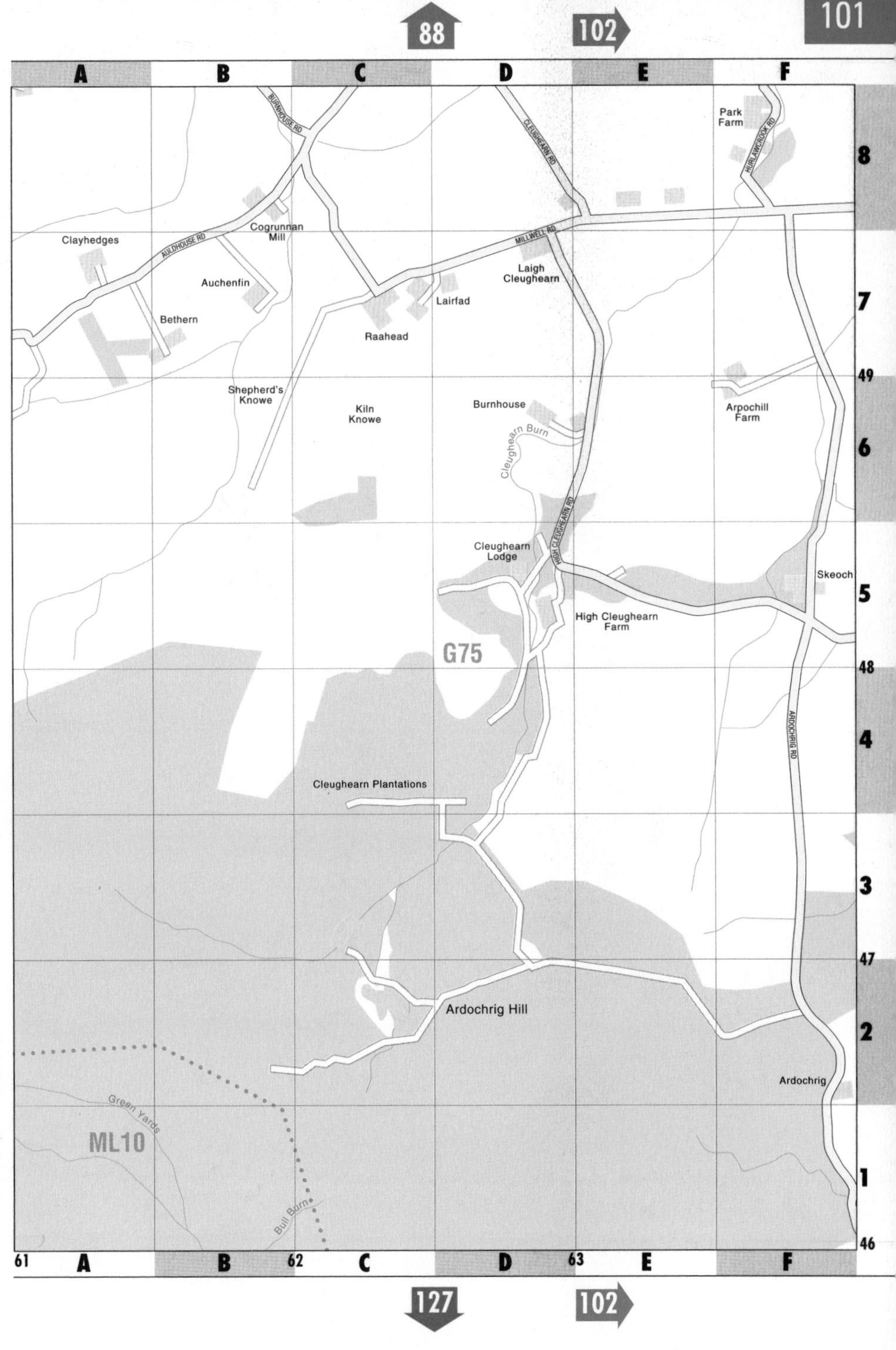

127
102

101
89

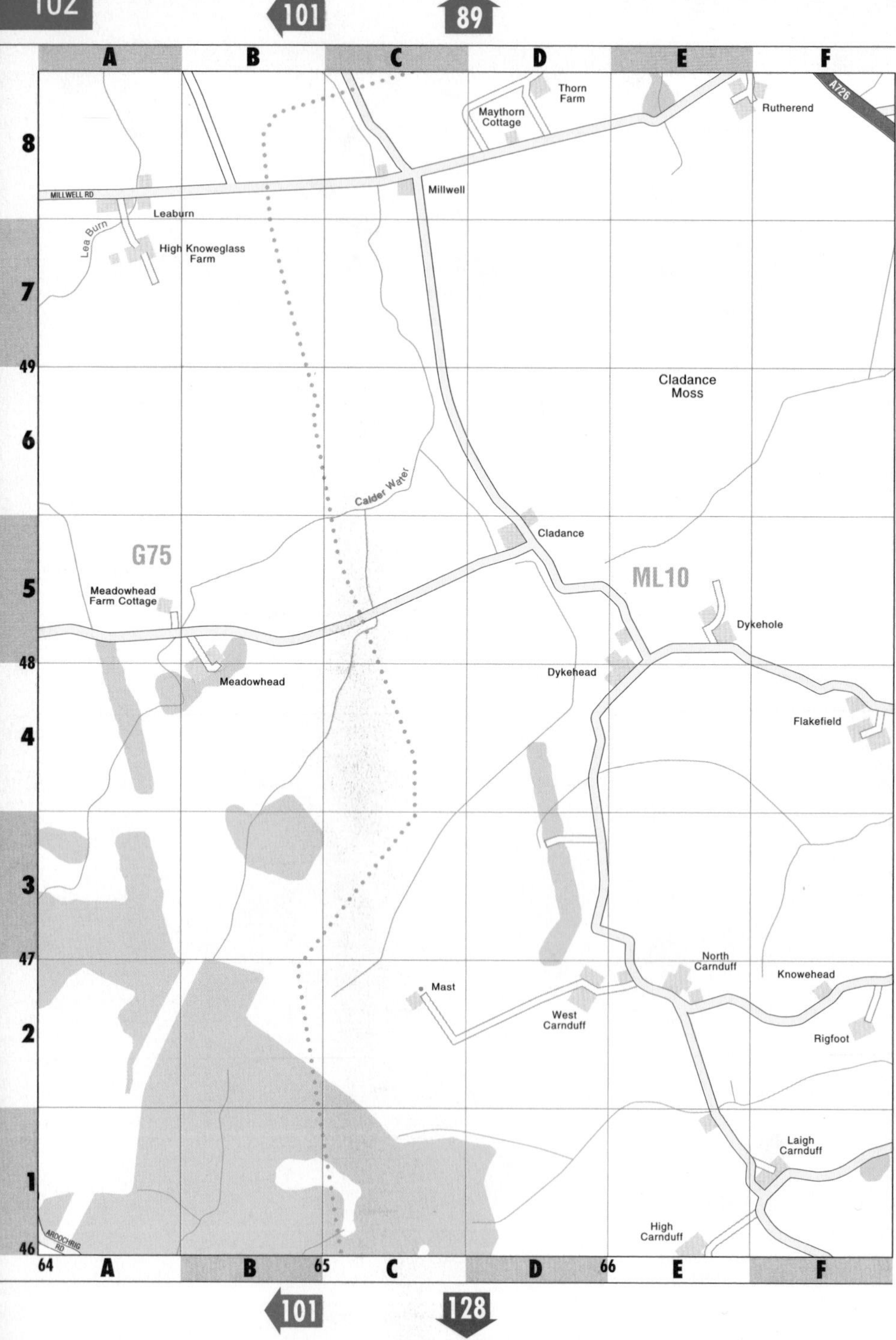

101
128

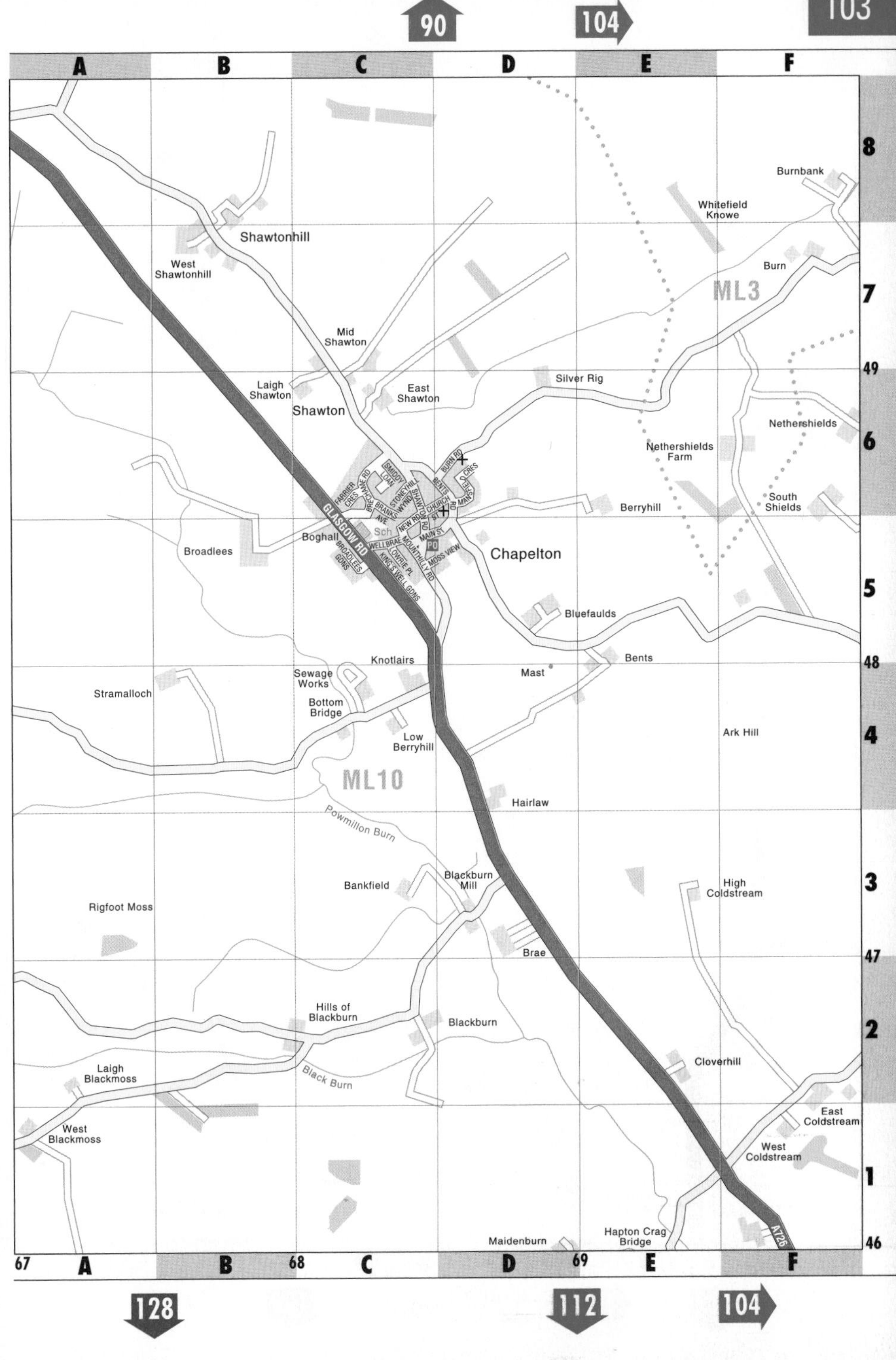
90
104
A
B
C
D
E
F
8
7
49
6
5
48
4
3
47
2
1
46
67
68
69
Burnbank
Whitefield Knowe
Shawtonhill
West Shawtonhill
Burn
ML3
Mid Shawton
Silver Rig
Laigh Shawton
East Shawton
Shawton
Nethershields
Nethershields Farm
Berryhill
South Shields
GLASGOW RD
Sch
Boghall
Broadlees
Chapelton
BROADLEES GDNS
WELLBRAE
LOWRIE PL
KINGS WELL GDNS
MOUNTHILLY RD
MOSS VIEW
MAIN ST
PO
NEW RD
CHURCH ST
SHAWTON RD
STONEYHILL WYND
BRANKS AVE
BRECHAN RD
FARRIER CRES
SMIDDY LOAN
BENTS RD
BURN RD
MANSFIELD CRES
Bluefaulds
Knotlairs
Bents
Mast
Sewage Works
Stramalloch
Bottom Bridge
Low Berryhill
Ark Hill
ML10
Hairlaw
Powmillon Burn
Bankfield
Blackburn Mill
High Coldstream
Rigfoot Moss
Brae
Hills of Blackburn
Blackburn
Cloverhill
Laigh Blackmoss
Black Burn
East Coldstream
West Blackmoss
West Coldstream
Maidenburn
Hapton Crag Bridge
A726
128
112
104

103
91

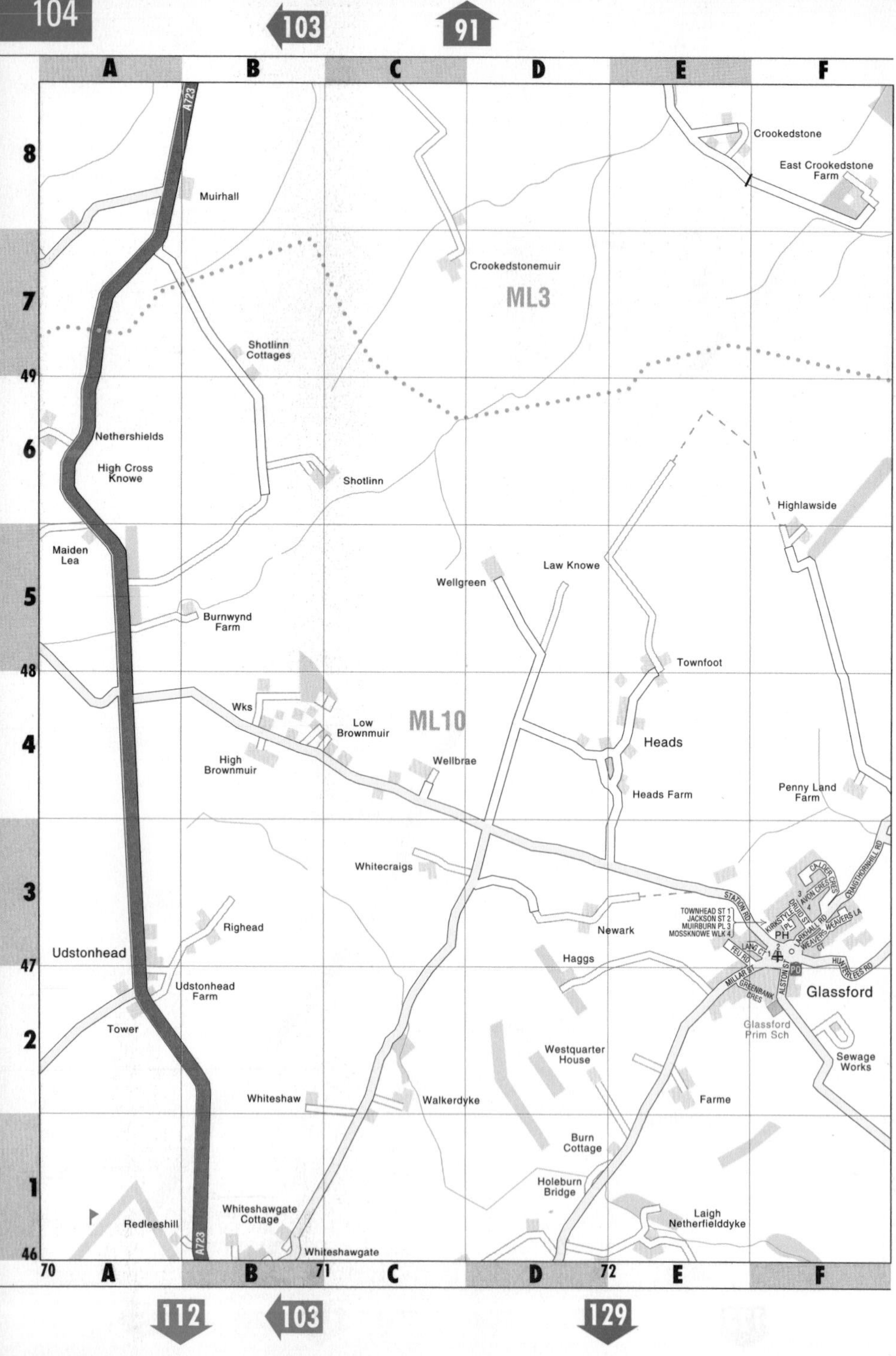
A
B
C
D
E
F
A723
Crookedstone
East Crookedstone Farm
Muirhall
Crookedstonemuir
ML3
Shotlinn Cottages
Nethershields
High Cross Knowe
Shotlinn
Highlawside
Maiden Lea
Law Knowe
Wellgreen
Burnwynd Farm
Townfoot
Wks
Low Brownmuir
ML10
Heads
High Brownmuir
Wellbrae
Heads Farm
Penny Land Farm
Whitecraigs
STATION RD
TOWNHEAD ST 1
JACKSON ST 2
MUIRBURN PL 3
MOSSKNOWE WLK 4
Righead
Newark
PH
Udstonhead
Haggs
FEU RD
MILLAR ST
GREENBANK CRES
ALSTON ST
Glassford
Udstonhead Farm
Glassford Prim Sch
Tower
Westquarter House
Sewage Works
Whiteshaw
Walkerdyke
Farme
Burn Cottage
Holeburn Bridge
Laigh Netherfielddyke
Whiteshawgate Cottage
Redleeshill
Whiteshawgate
8
7
49
6
5
48
4
3
47
2
1
46
70
71
72

112
103
129

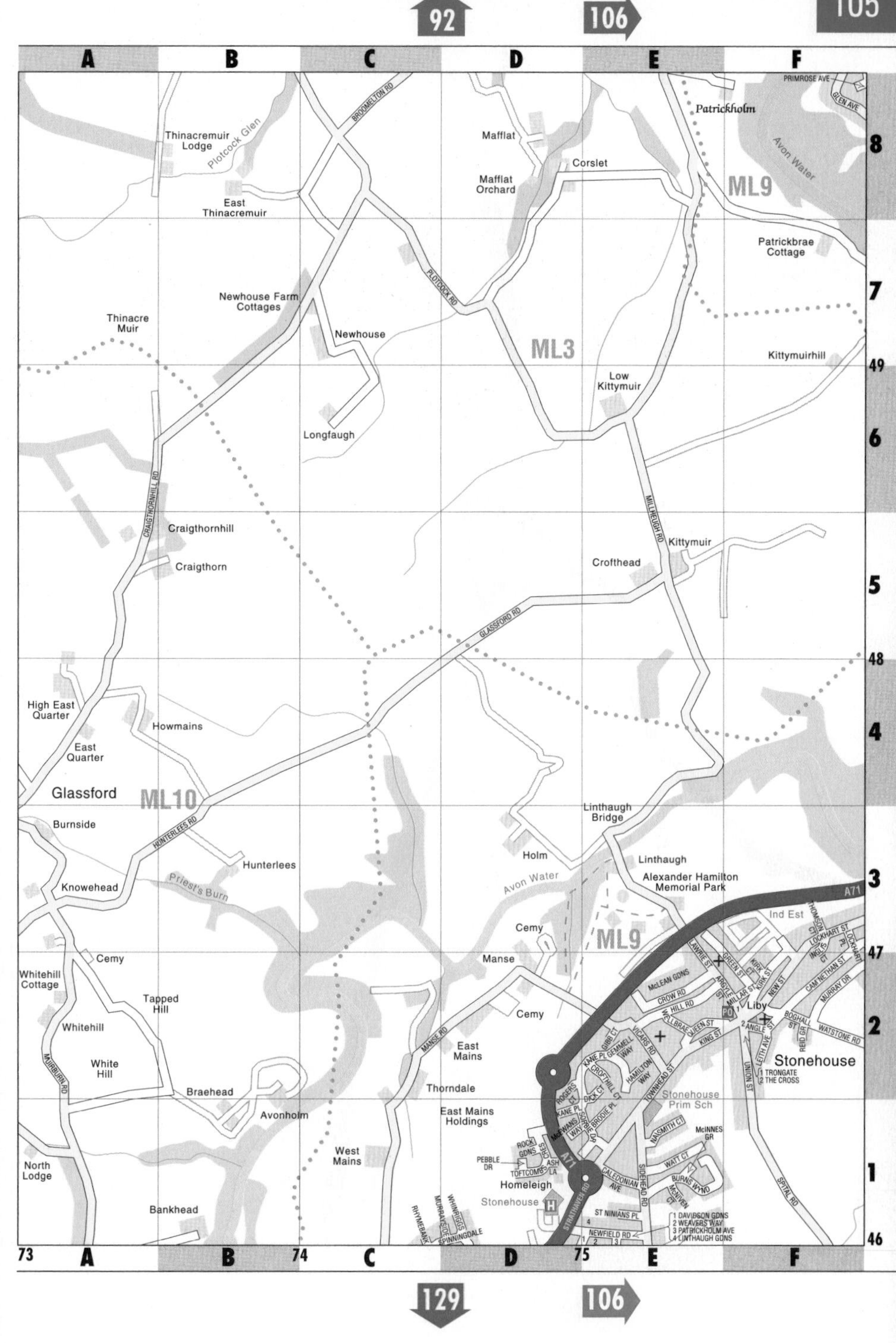

92
106
A
B
C
D
E
F
8
7
49
6
5
48
4
3
47
2
1
46
73
74
75
129
PRIMROSE AVE
GLEN AVE
Patrickholm
Avon Water
ML9
BROOMELTON RD
Thinacremuir Lodge
Plotcock Glen
East Thinacremuir
Mafflat
Corslet
Mafflat Orchard
Patrickbrae Cottage
PLOTCOCK RD
Newhouse Farm Cottages
Thinacre Muir
Newhouse
ML3
Kittymuirhill
Low Kittymuir
Longfaugh
CRAIGTHORNHILL RD
MILLHEUGH RD
Craigthornhill
Craigthorn
Kittymuir
Crofthead
GLASSFORD RD
High East Quarter
Howmains
East Quarter
Glassford
ML10
Linthaugh Bridge
Burnside
HUNTERLEES RD
Hunterlees
Holm
Linthaugh
Alexander Hamilton Memorial Park
Knowehead
Priest's Burn
Avon Water
A71
Ind Est
Cemy
ML9
Cemy
Manse
Whitehill Cottage
Tapped Hill
Cemy
Liby
Whitehill
MANSE RD
East Mains
Stonehouse
MUIRBURN RD
White Hill
Thorndale
1 TRONGATE
2 THE CROSS
Braehead
Avonholm
East Mains Holdings
Stonehouse Prim Sch
West Mains
Homeleigh
North Lodge
Stonehouse
STRATHAVEN RD
Bankhead
SPITAL RD
UNION ST
LEITH AVE
WATSTONE RD
BOGHALL ST
REID GR
MURRAY DR
CAMNETHAN ST
NEW ST
KIRK ST
LAWRIE ST
GREEN ST
ARGYLE ST
MILLAR ST
KING ST
QUEEN ST
HILL RD
CROW RD
McLEAN GDNS
VICARS RD
TOWNHEAD ST
HAMILTON WAY
GEMMELL WAY
CROFTHILL CT
KANE PL
KANE PL
DICK CT
BRODIE PL
ROGERS CT
McEWANS WAY
SIDEHEAD RD
NASMITH CT
WATT CT
BURNS WYND
McGIVEN CT
CALEDONIAN AVE
ROCK GDNS
PEBBLE DR
TOFTCOMBE
ASH LA
ST NINIANS PL
NEWFIELD RD
1 DAVIDSON GDNS
2 WEAVERS WAY
3 PATRICKHOLM AVE
4 LINTHAUGH GDNS
RHYMEBANK
MURRAYSIDE
WHINRIGGS
SPINNINGDALE
INGLIS CT
LOCKHART ST
THOMSON CT
LOCKHART PL
2 ANGLE ST

105
93

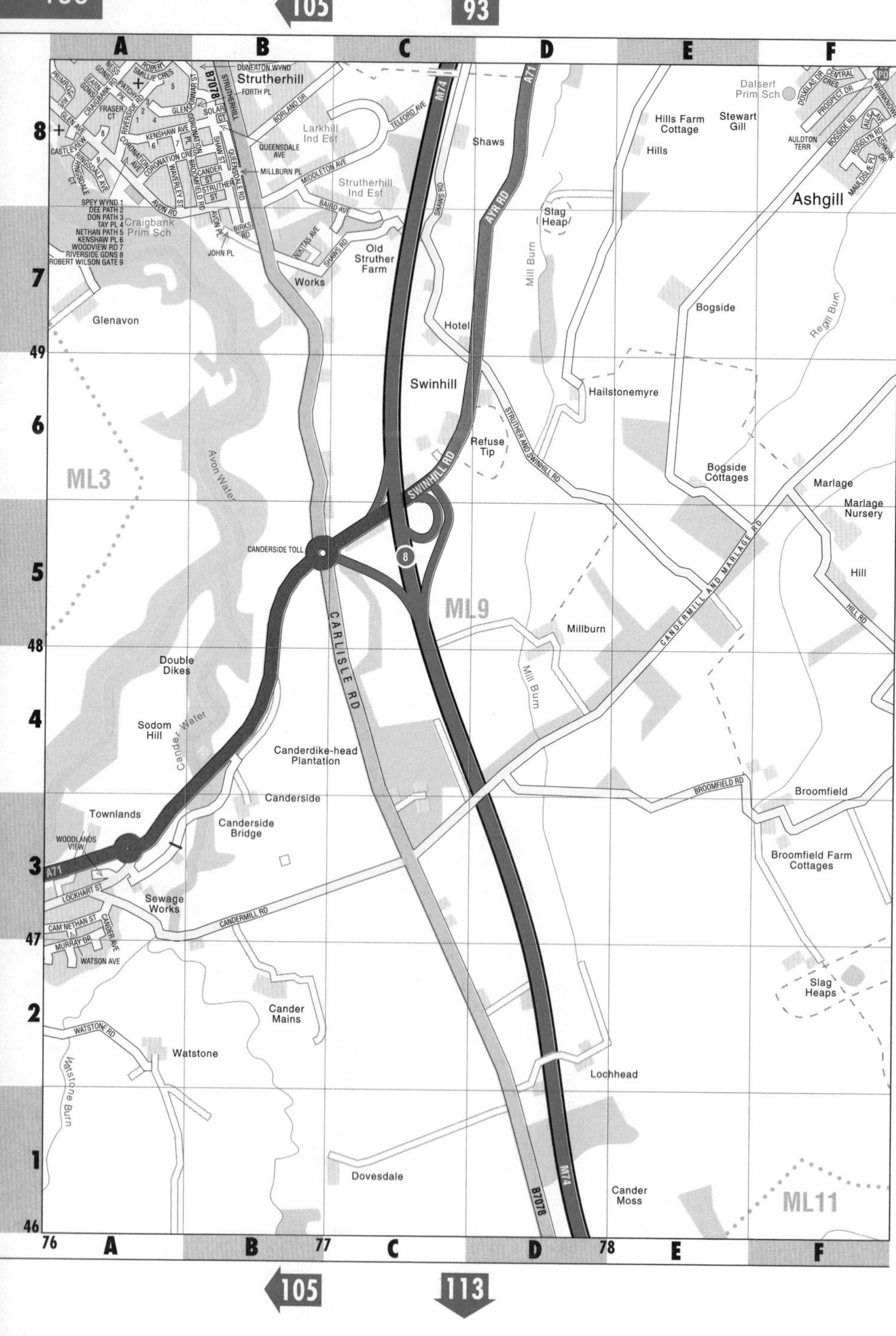

105
113

94
108

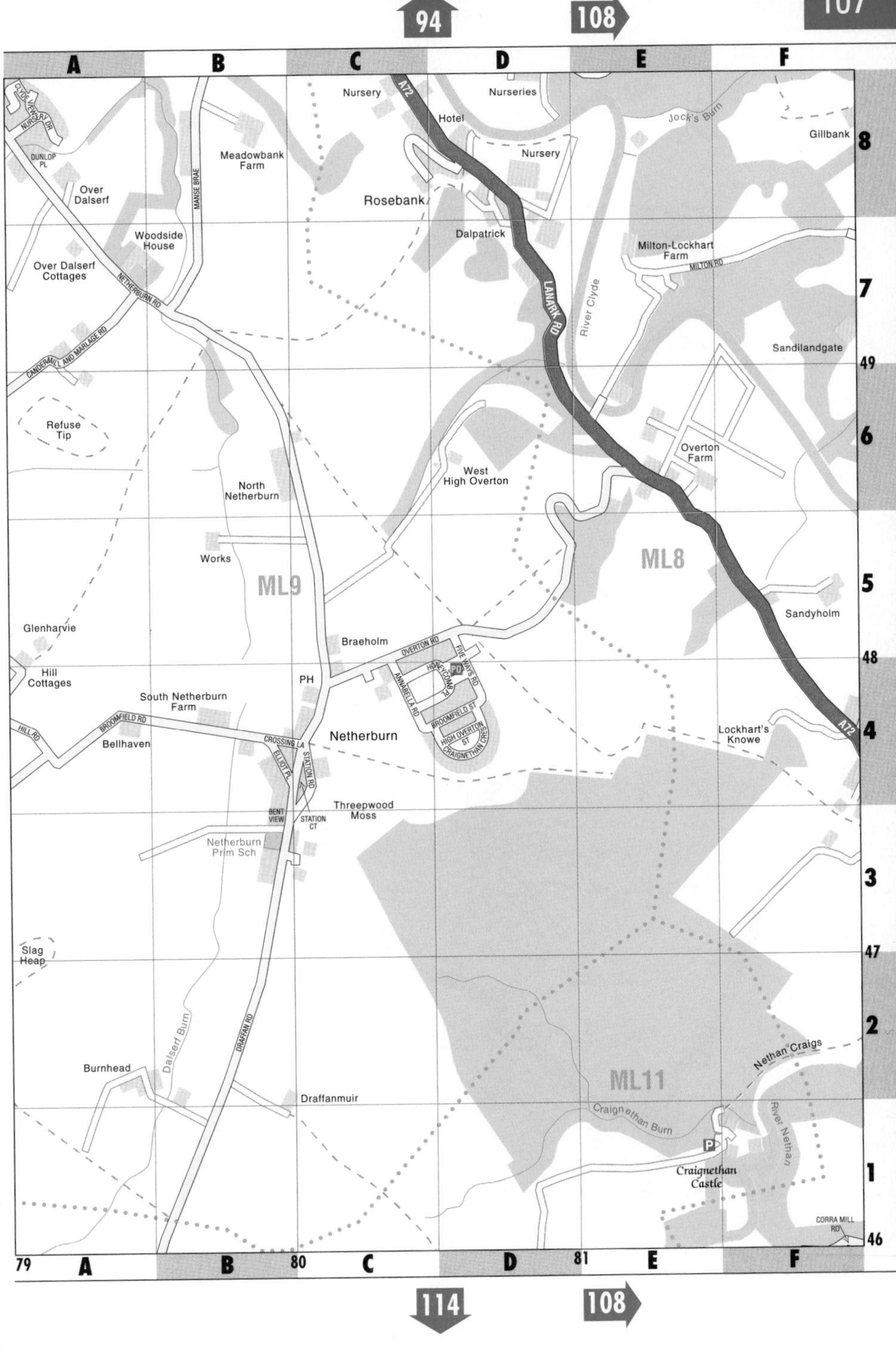

114
108

107
95

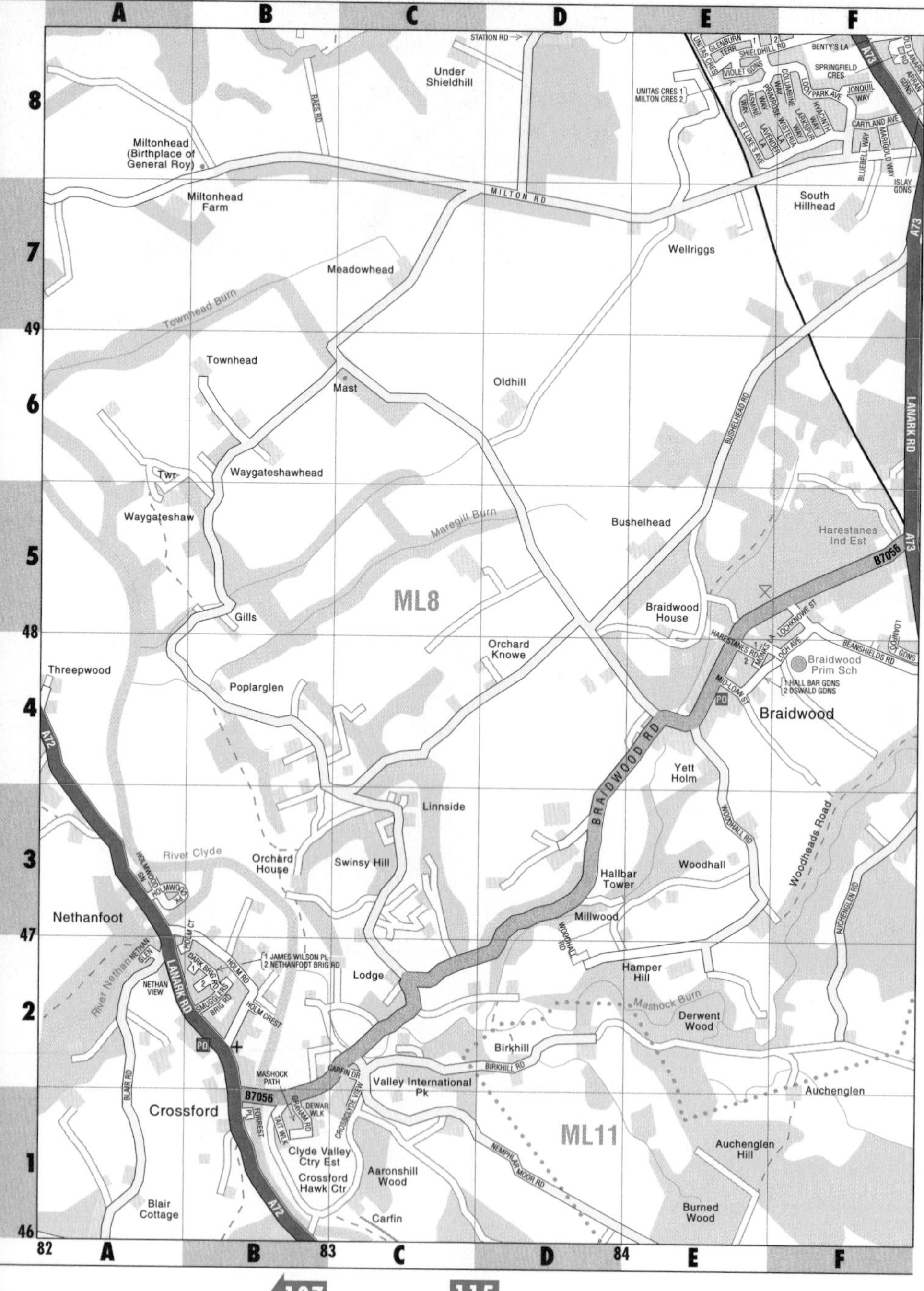

107
115

96
110

116
110

109
97

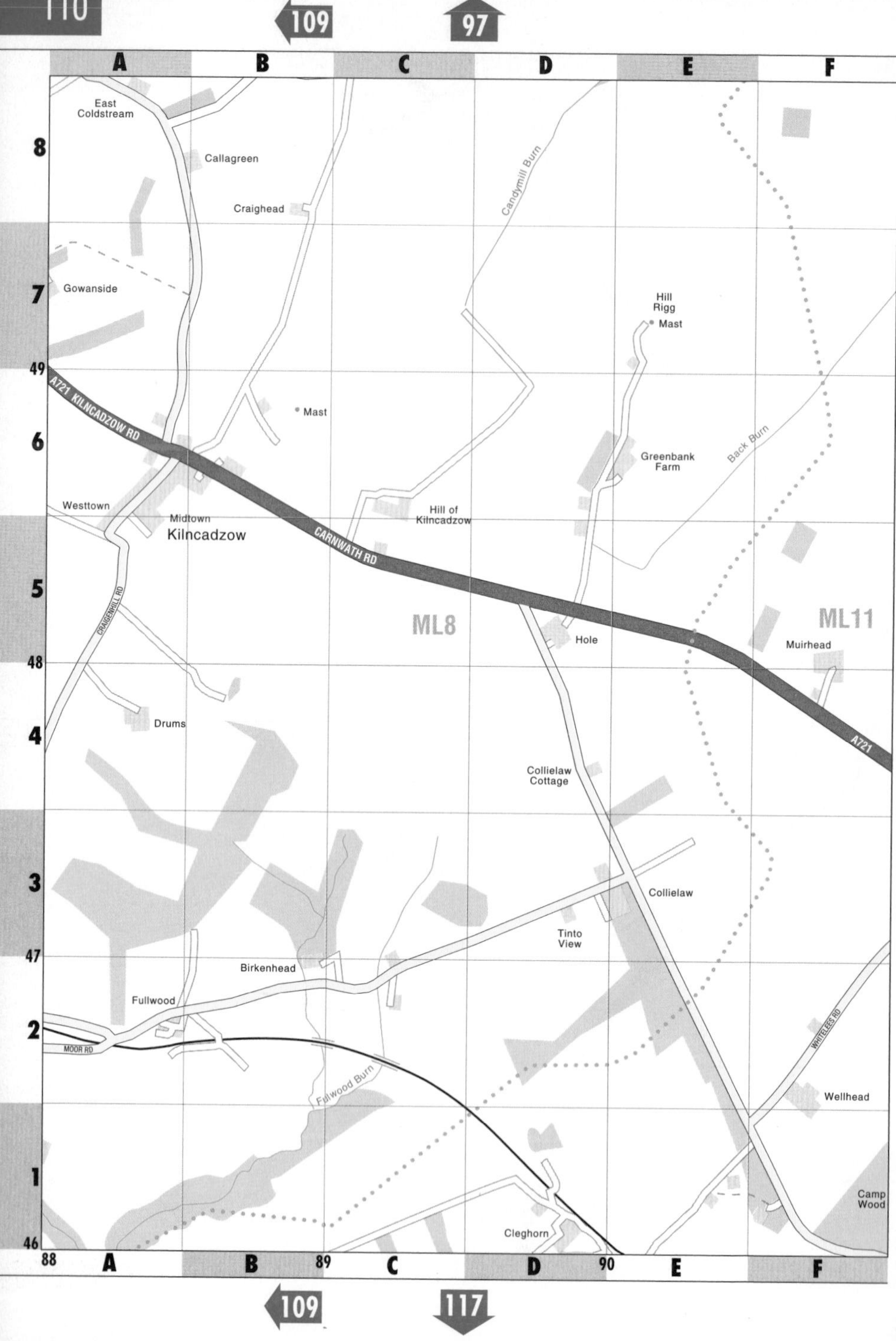

109
117

98
124

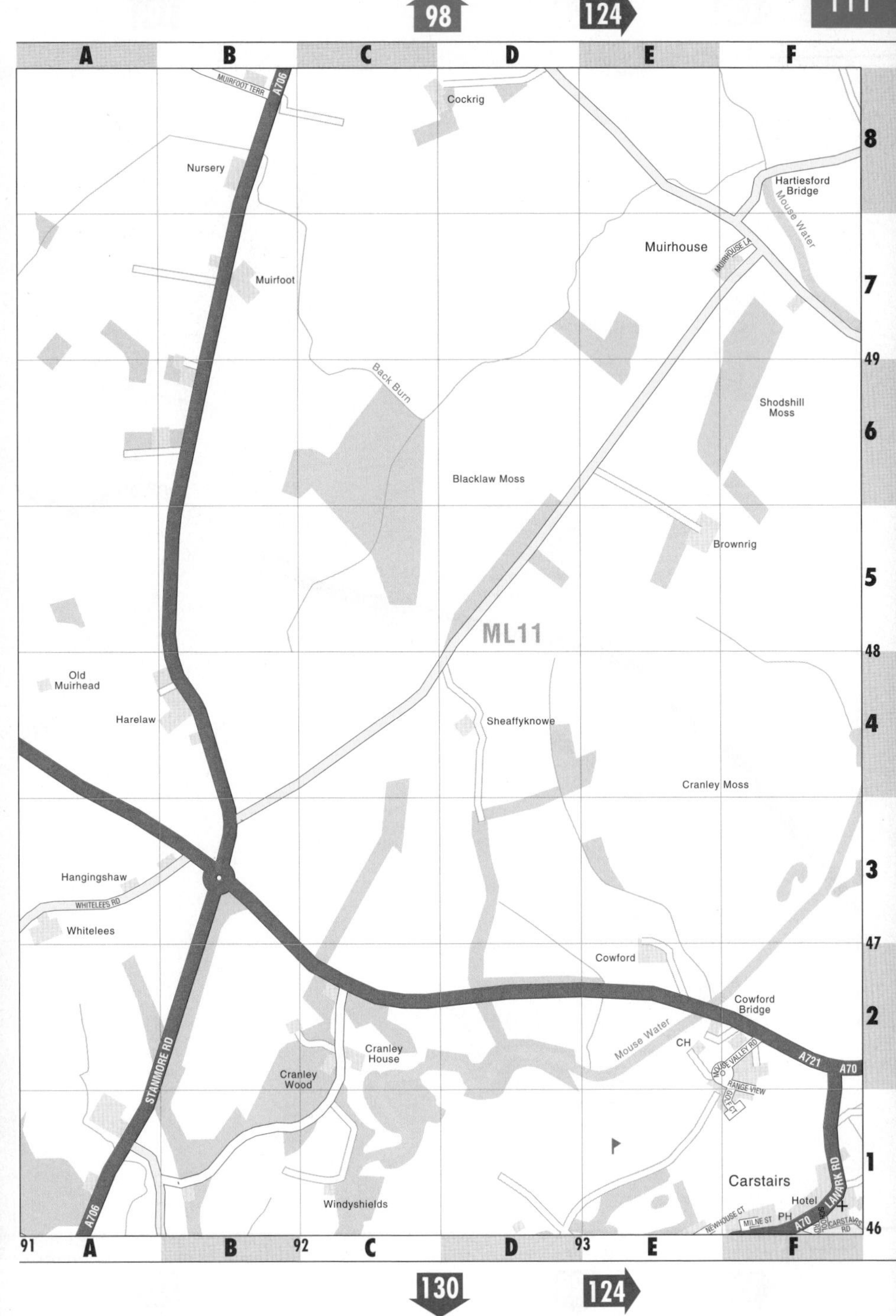

130
124

128
103
104

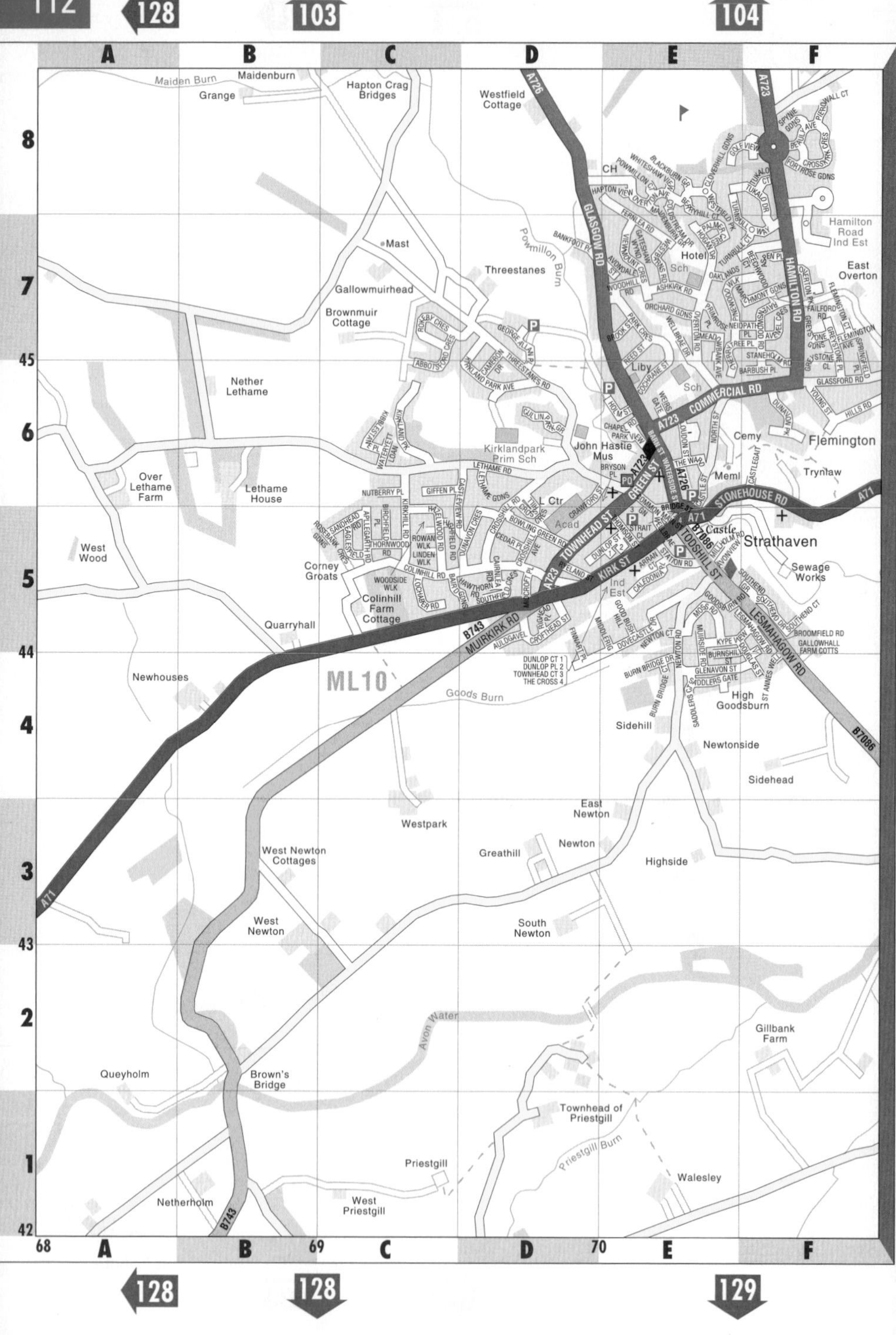

128
128
129

129
106
114

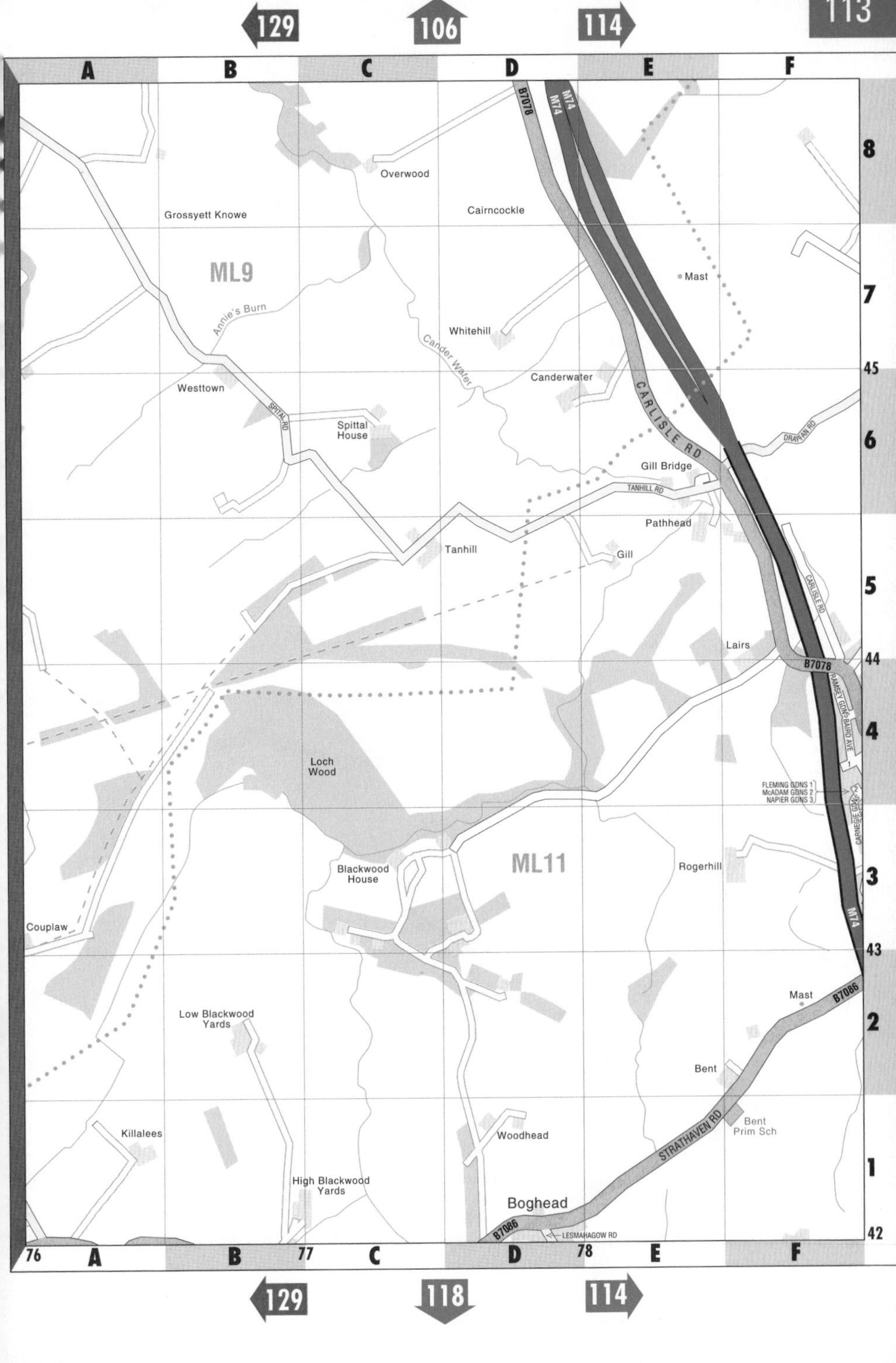

129
118
114

113
107

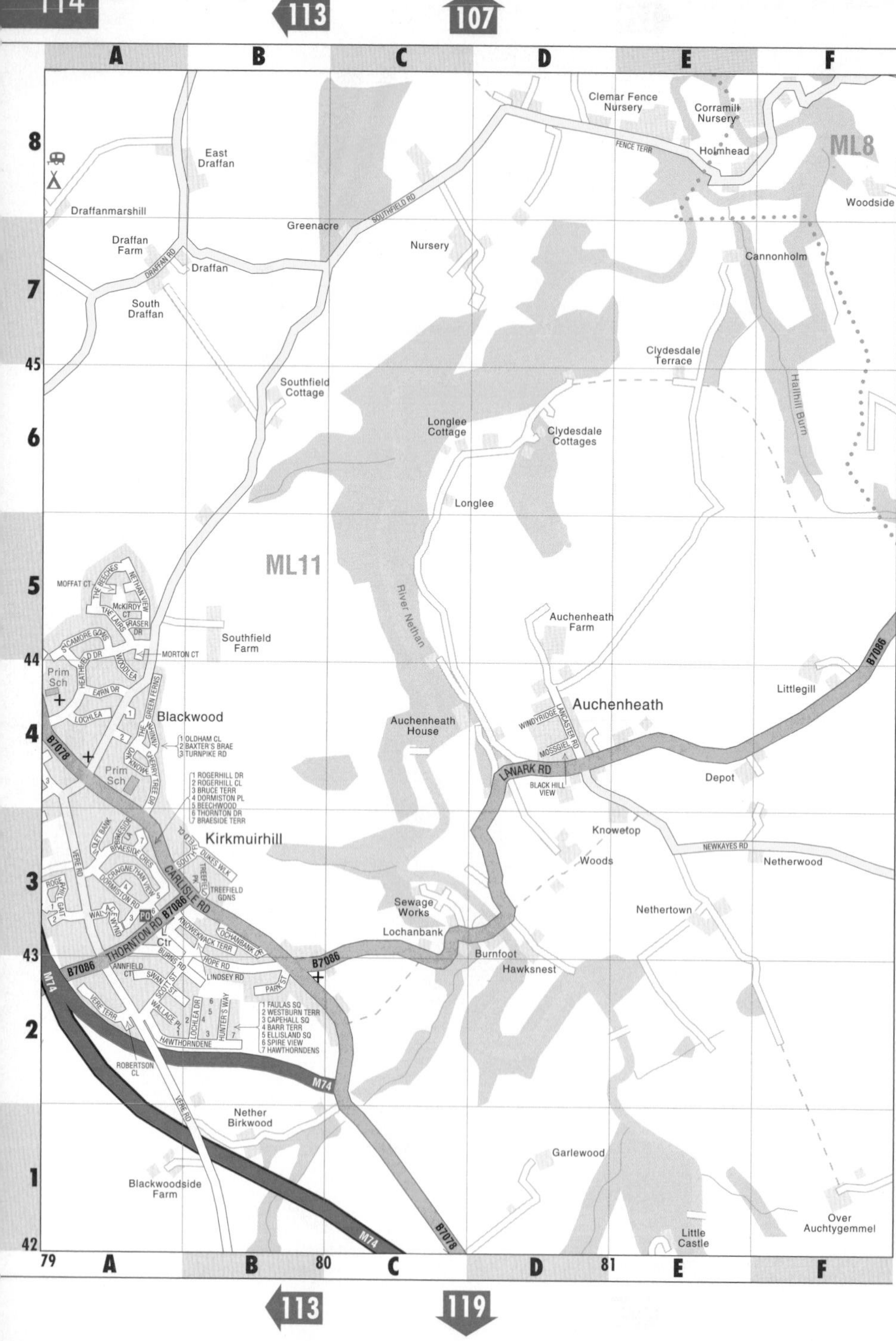

113
119

108
116
A
B
C
D
E
F
8
7
45
6
5
44
4
3
43
2
1
42
82
83
84
CORRA HILL RD
BLAIR RD
Crossbank
Underbank Prim Sch
Brodiehill
Underbank
Clydebank
Big Wood
NEMPHLAR MOOR RD
Westside of Nemphlar
Carlinside
West-town of Nemphlar
NEMPHLAR RD
Oakbank
A72
Clyde Walkway
Hazelbank
Hillend
ML8
Arthur's Craigs
LANARK RD
Hillend Cottage
HAZELBANK BRAES
River Clyde
Glendar
Hallhill
Hallhill Burn
Low Wood
Poplar Park
B7086
Stonebyres Bridge
Smugglers Bridge
Holehouse
Blackhill
AUCHNOTROCH RD
Stonebyres (remains of)
Dark Bridge
Auchnotroch
STONEBYRES HOLDINGS
Black Hill
The Cottage
Woodyett
ML11
Stonebyre Mains
BELLAS AVE
NEWKAYES RD
B7018
Vere Hills
Newkays
Nether Affleck
Clarkston Farm
Linn Burn
Linn Strip
Lesser Linn
Lesser Linn Cottage
Muirhouse
Clarkston Strip
Ben's Corner
Dillar's Corner
120
116

115 109

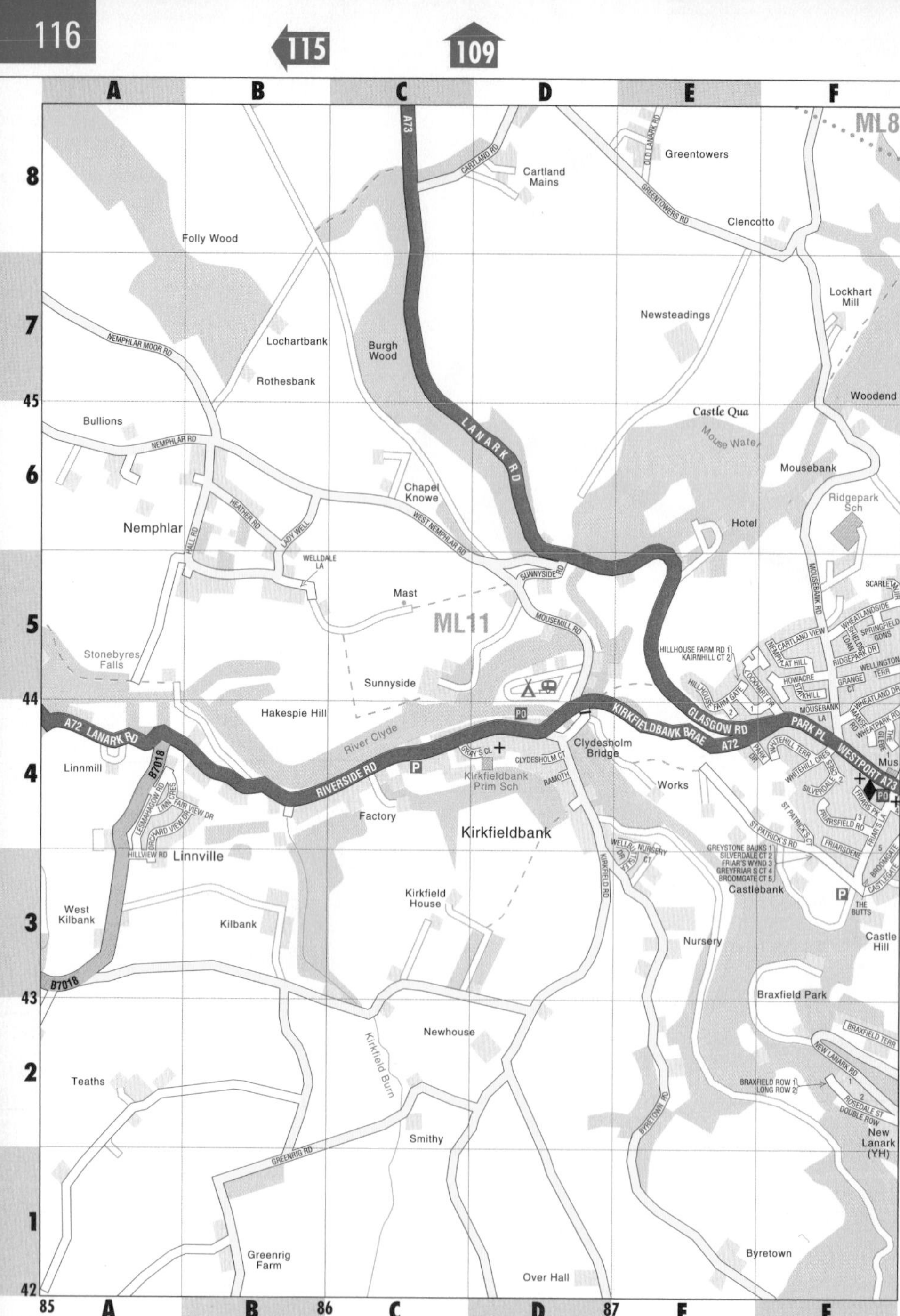

115 121

110
130

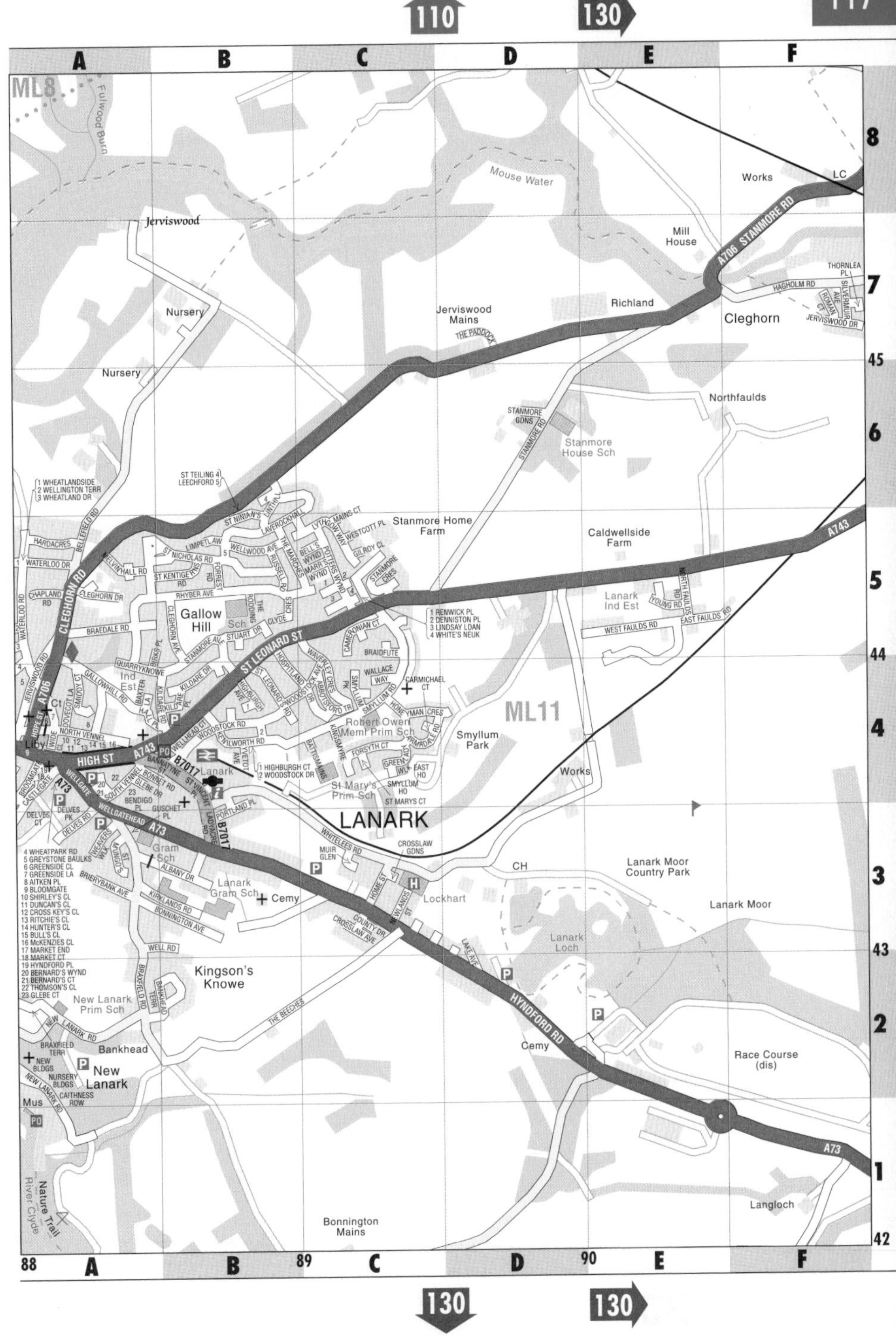

130
130

129
113

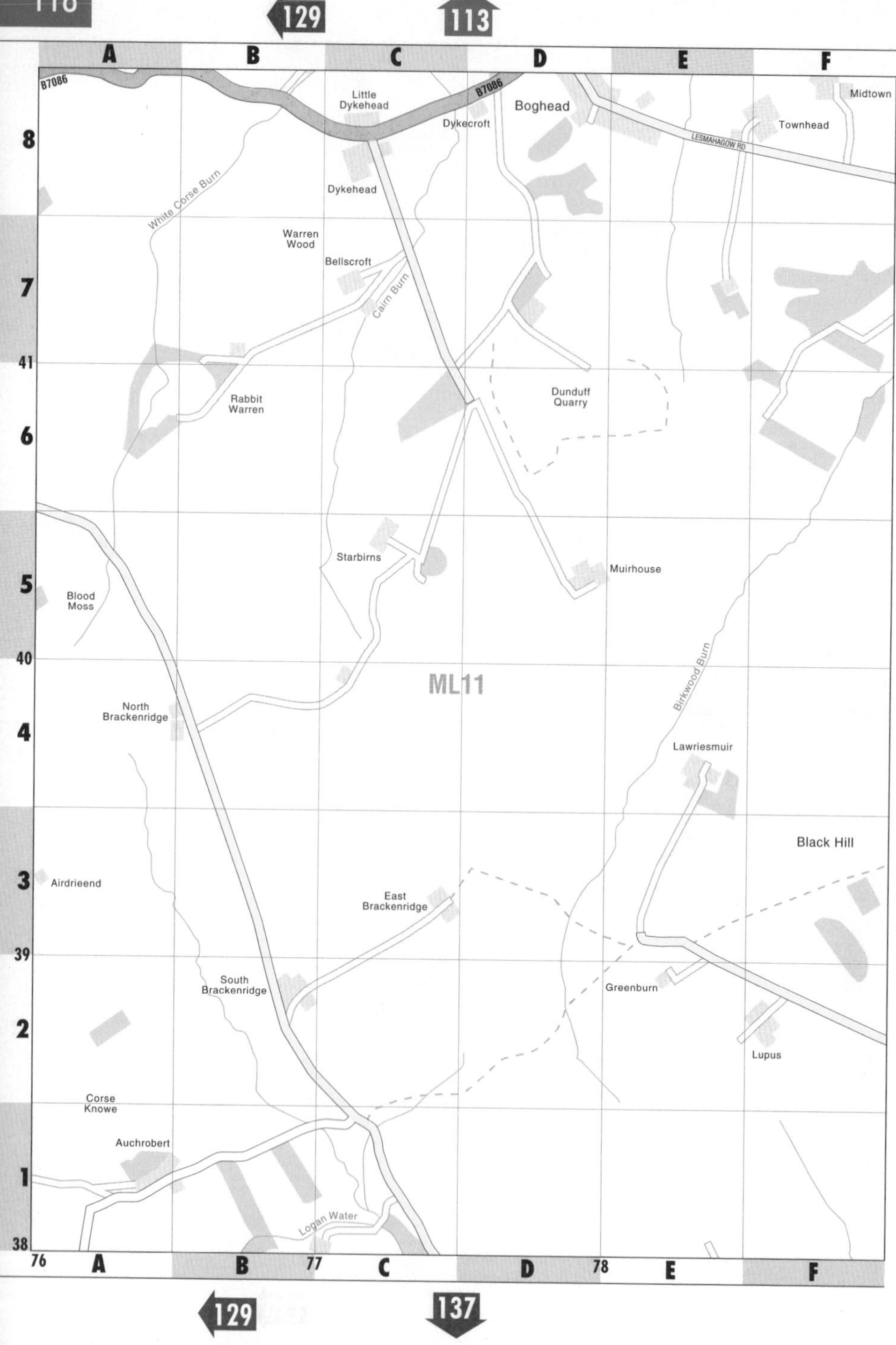

129
137

114
120

137
120

119
115

119
138

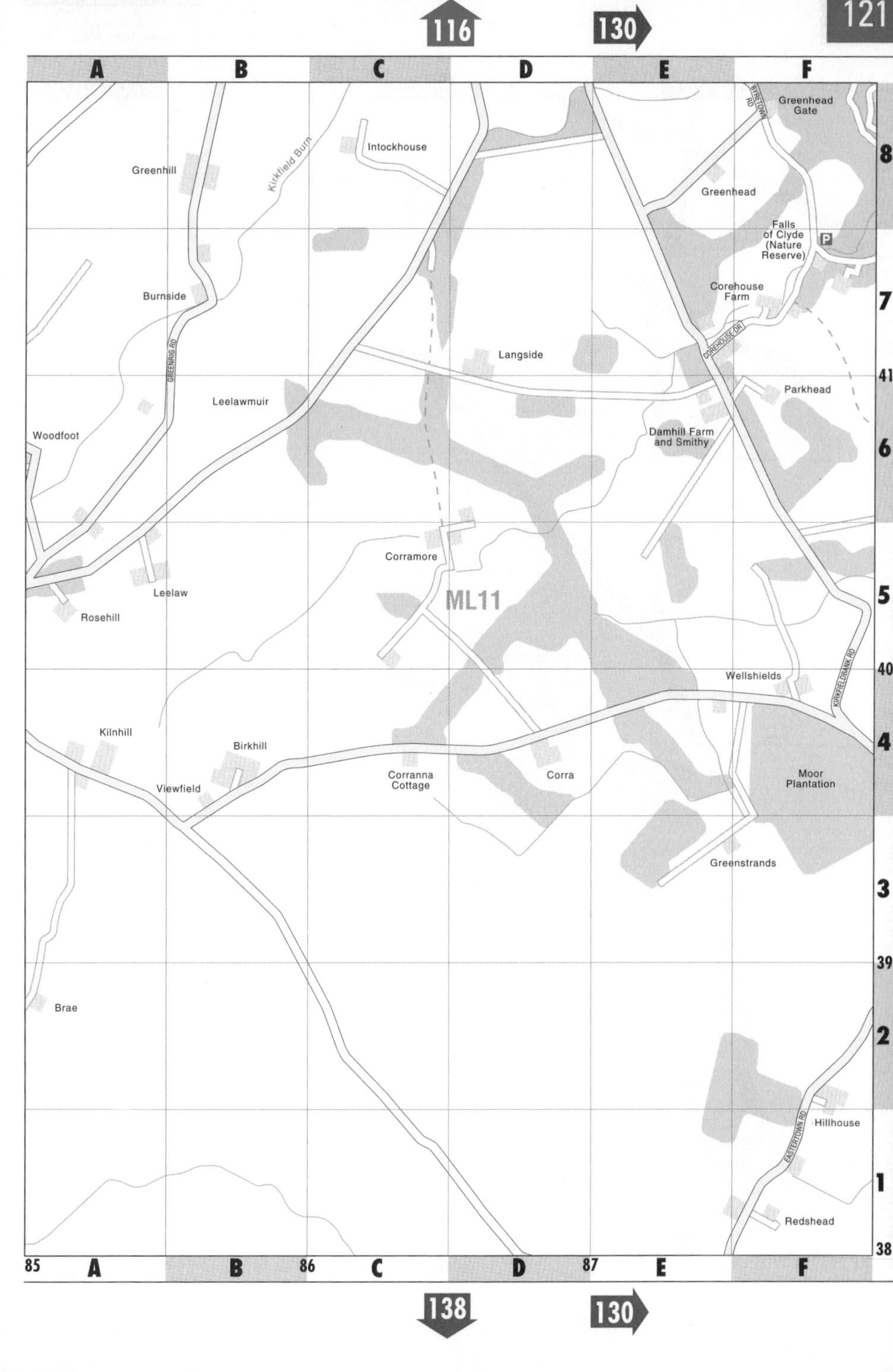
116
130
A
B
C
D
E
F
Greenhead Gate
BYRETOWN RD
Intockhouse
Greenhill
Kirkfield Burn
Greenhead
Falls of Clyde (Nature Reserve)
P
Burnside
Corehouse Farm
COREHOUSE DR
Langside
GREENRIG RD
Leelawmuir
Parkhead
Woodfoot
Damhill Farm and Smithy
Corramore
ML11
Leelaw
Rosehill
Wellshields
KIRKFIELDBANK RD
Kilnhill
Birkhill
Viewfield
Corranna Cottage
Corra
Moor Plantation
Greenstrands
Brae
EASTERTOWN RD
Hillhouse
Redshead
8
7
41
6
5
40
4
3
39
2
1
38
85
86
87
138
130

71

Scale: 1⅓ inches to 1 mile

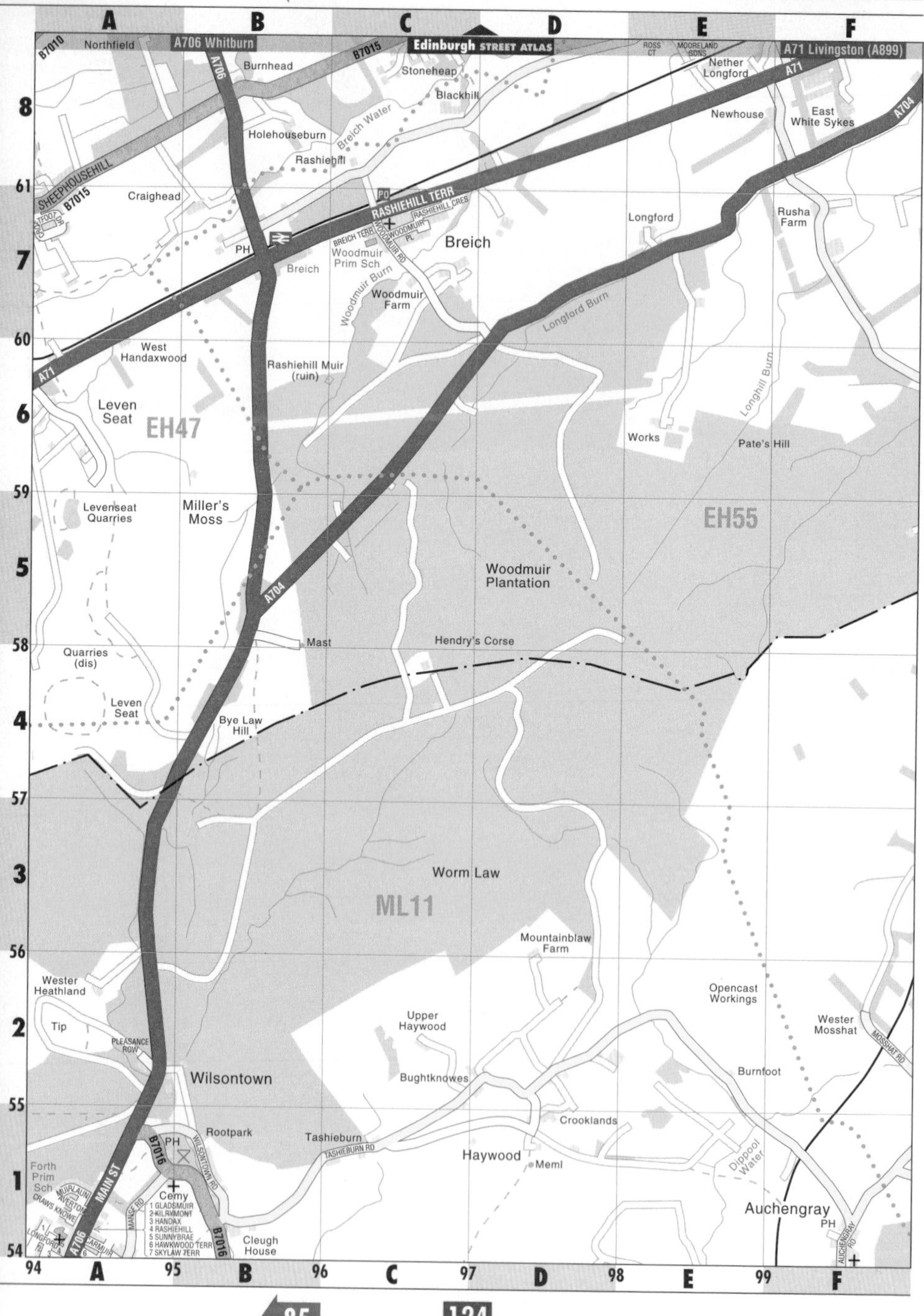

85

124

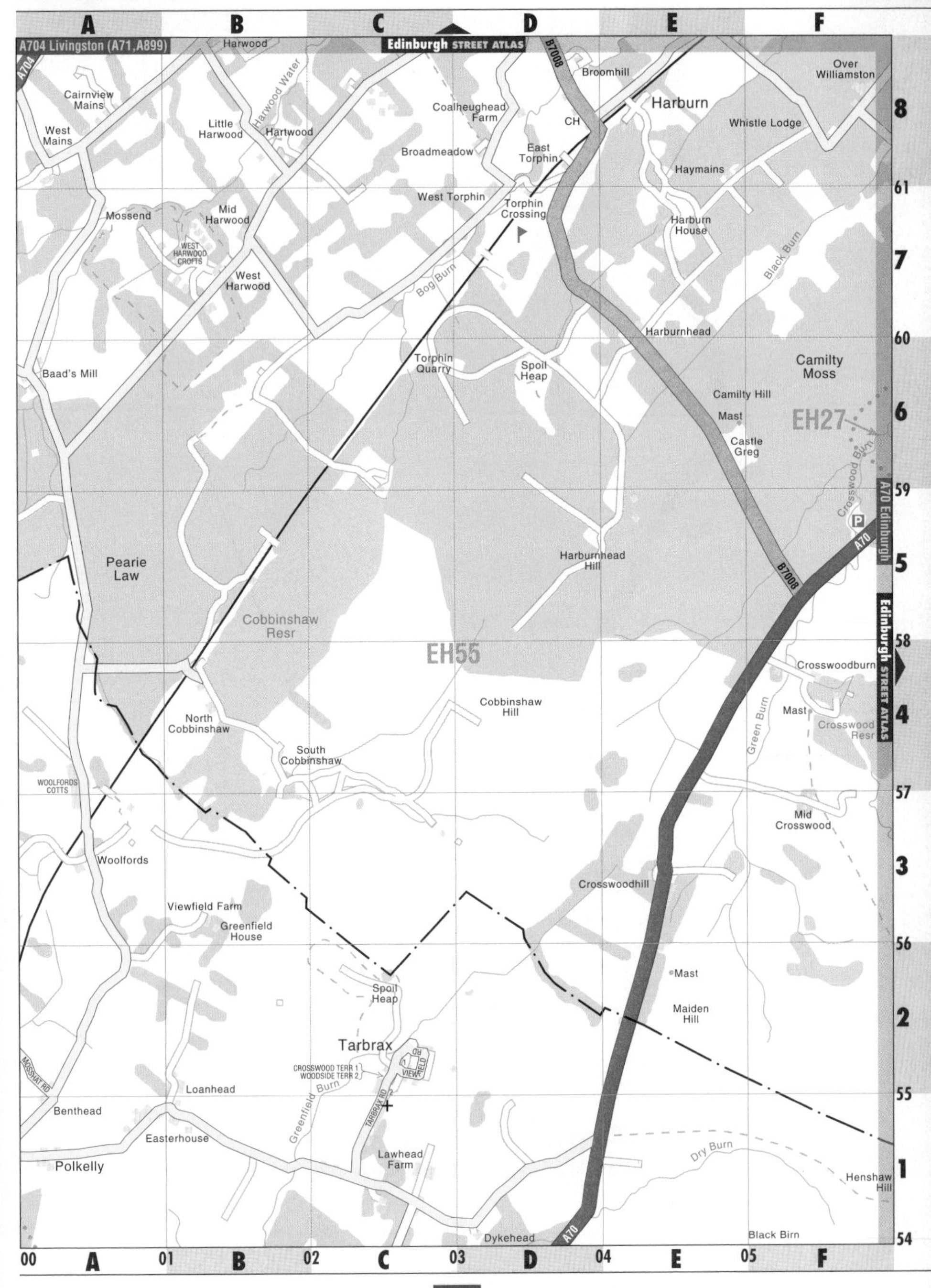
Scale: 1⅓ inches to 1 mile
A704 Livingston (A71,A899)
Edinburgh STREET ATLAS
Harwood
Broomhill
Over Williamston
Cairnview Mains
West Mains
Little Harwood
Harwood Water
Hartwood
Coalheughead Farm
Broadmeadow
CH
Harburn
Whistle Lodge
East Torphin
Haymains
West Torphin
Torphin Crossing
Mossend
Mid Harwood
WEST HARWOOD CROFTS
Harburn House
West Harwood
Bog Burn
Black Burn
Harburnhead
Baad's Mill
Torphin Quarry
Spoil Heap
Camilty Moss
Camilty Hill
Mast
EH27
Castle Greg
Crosswood Burn
A70 Edinburgh
Pearie Law
Harburnhead Hill
B7008
A70
Cobbinshaw Resr
EH55
Crosswoodburn
Cobbinshaw Hill
North Cobbinshaw
South Cobbinshaw
Green Burn
Crosswood Resr
WOOLFORDS COTTS
Mid Crosswood
Woolfords
Crosswoodhill
Viewfield Farm
Greenfield House
Spoil Heap
Maiden Hill
Tarbrax
CROSSWOOD TERR 1
WOODSIDE TERR 2
VIEWFIELD RD
TARBRAX RD
MOSSHAT RD
Loanhead
Benthead
Greenfield Burn
Easterhouse
Dry Burn
Polkelly
Lawhead Farm
Henshaw Hill
Dykehead
Black Birn

125

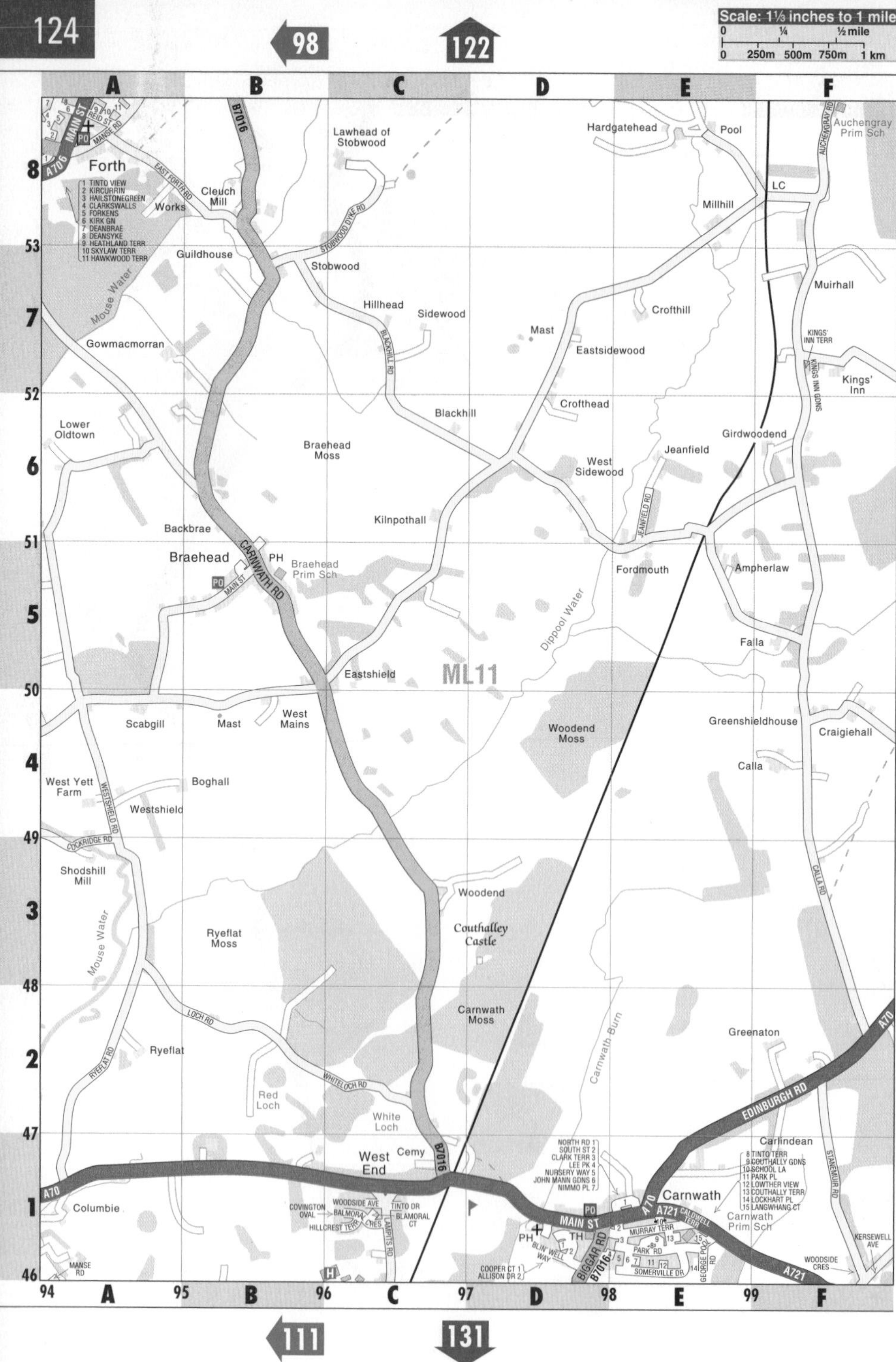

98
122
Scale: 1⅓ inches to 1 mile
0 ¼ ½ mile
0 250m 500m 750m 1 km
A
B
C
D
E
F
Forth
MAIN ST
REID ST
MANSE RD
A706
PO
1 TINTO VIEW
2 KIRCURRIN
3 HAILSTONEGREEN
4 CLARKSWALLS
5 FORKENS
6 KIRK GN
7 DEANBRAE
8 DEANSYKE
9 HEATHLAND TERR
10 SKYLAW TERR
11 HAWKWOOD TERR
EAST FORTH RD
Works
Cleuch Mill
B7016
Lawhead of Stobwood
STOBWOOD DYKE RD
Guildhouse
Stobwood
Mouse Water
Hillhead
Sidewood
BLACKHILL RD
Gowmacmorran
Hardgatehead
Pool
LC
Millhill
AUCHENGRAY RD
Auchengray Prim Sch
Muirhall
Crofthill
Mast
Eastsidewood
KINGS' INN TERR
KINGS INN GDNS
Kings' Inn
Crofthead
Blackhill
Lower Oldtown
Braehead Moss
Girdwoodend
Jeanfield
West Sidewood
JEANFIELD RD
Kilnpothall
Backbrae
Braehead
CARNWATH RD
PH
Braehead Prim Sch
PO
MAIN ST
Fordmouth
Ampherlaw
Dippool Water
Falla
Eastshield
ML11
Scabgill
Mast
West Mains
Woodend Moss
Greenshieldhouse
Craigiehall
Calla
West Yett Farm
Boghall
WESTSHIELD RD
Westshield
COCKRIDGE RD
Shodshill Mill
Woodend
Couthalley Castle
Ryeflat Moss
Mouse Water
CALLA RD
LOCH RD
Carnwath Moss
Carnwath Burn
Greenaton
A70
RYEFLAT RD
Ryeflat
WHITELOCH RD
Red Loch
White Loch
EDINBURGH RD
Carlindean
West End
Cemy
B7016
A70
Columbie
COVINGTON OVAL
WOODSIDE AVE
BALMORAL CRES
HILLCREST TERR
TINTO DR
BLAMORAL CT
LAMPITS RD
NORTH RD 1
SOUTH ST 2
CLARK TERR 3
LEE PK 4
NURSERY WAY 5
JOHN MANN GDNS 6
NIMMO PL 7
8 TINTO TERR
9 COUTHALLY GDNS
10 SCHOOL LA
11 PARK PL
12 LOWTHER VIEW
13 COUTHALLY TERR
14 LOCKHART PL
15 LANGWHANG CT
STANEMUIR RD
Carnwath
Carnwath Prim Sch
PO
MAIN ST
A721
CALDWELL TERR
MURRAY TERR
PARK RD
SOMERVILLE DR
GEORGE POOL RD
BIGGAR RD
B7016
PH
TH
BLIN' WELL WAY
COOPER CT 1
ALLISON DR 2
KERSEWELL AVE
WOODSIDE CRES
A721
MANSE RD
H
8
53
7
52
6
51
5
50
4
49
3
48
2
47
1
46
94
95
96
97
98
99
111
131

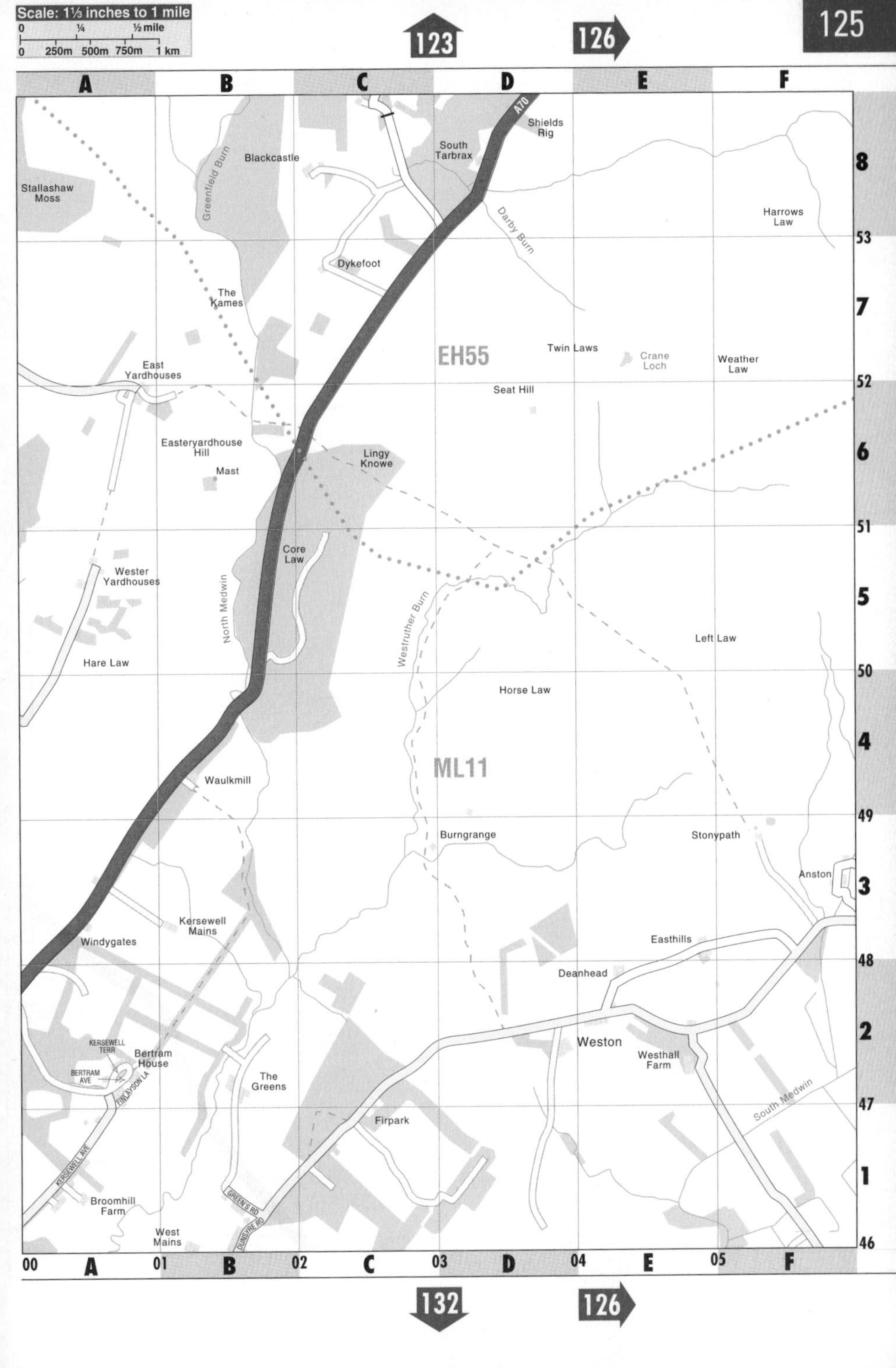
Scale: 1⅓ inches to 1 mile
0 ¼ ½ mile
0 250m 500m 750m 1 km
123
126
A
B
C
D
E
F
A70
Shields Rig
South Tarbrax
Blackcastle
Greenfield Burn
Stallashaw Moss
Darby Burn
Harrows Law
Dykefoot
The Kames
EH55
Twin Laws
Crane Loch
Weather Law
East Yardhouses
Seat Hill
Easteryardhouse Hill
Mast
Lingy Knowe
Core Law
Wester Yardhouses
North Medwin
Westruther Burn
Left Law
Hare Law
Horse Law
ML11
Waulkmill
Burngrange
Stonypath
Anston
Kersewell Mains
Windygates
Easthills
Deanhead
Weston
Westhall Farm
KERSEWELL TERR
Bertram House
BERTRAM AVE
FINLAYSON LA
The Greens
South Medwin
Firpark
KERSEWELL AVE
GREEN'S RD
Broomhill Farm
DUNSYRE RD
West Mains
8
53
7
52
6
51
5
50
4
49
3
48
2
47
1
46
00
01
02
03
04
05
132
126

125

Scale: 1⅓ inches to 1 mile
0 ¼ ½ mile
0 250m 500m 750m 1 km

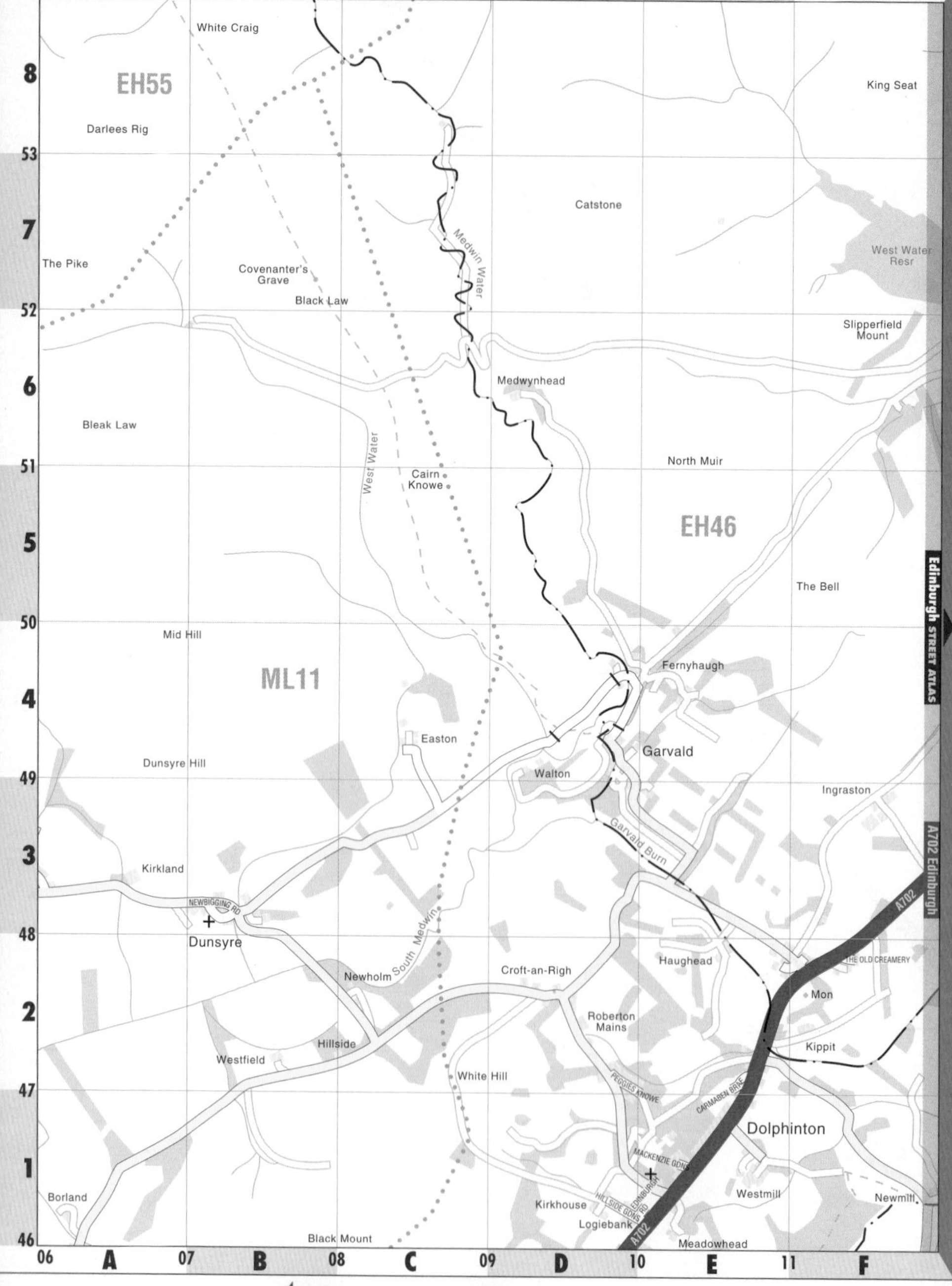

125
133

Scale: 1⅓ inches to 1 mile

100
101

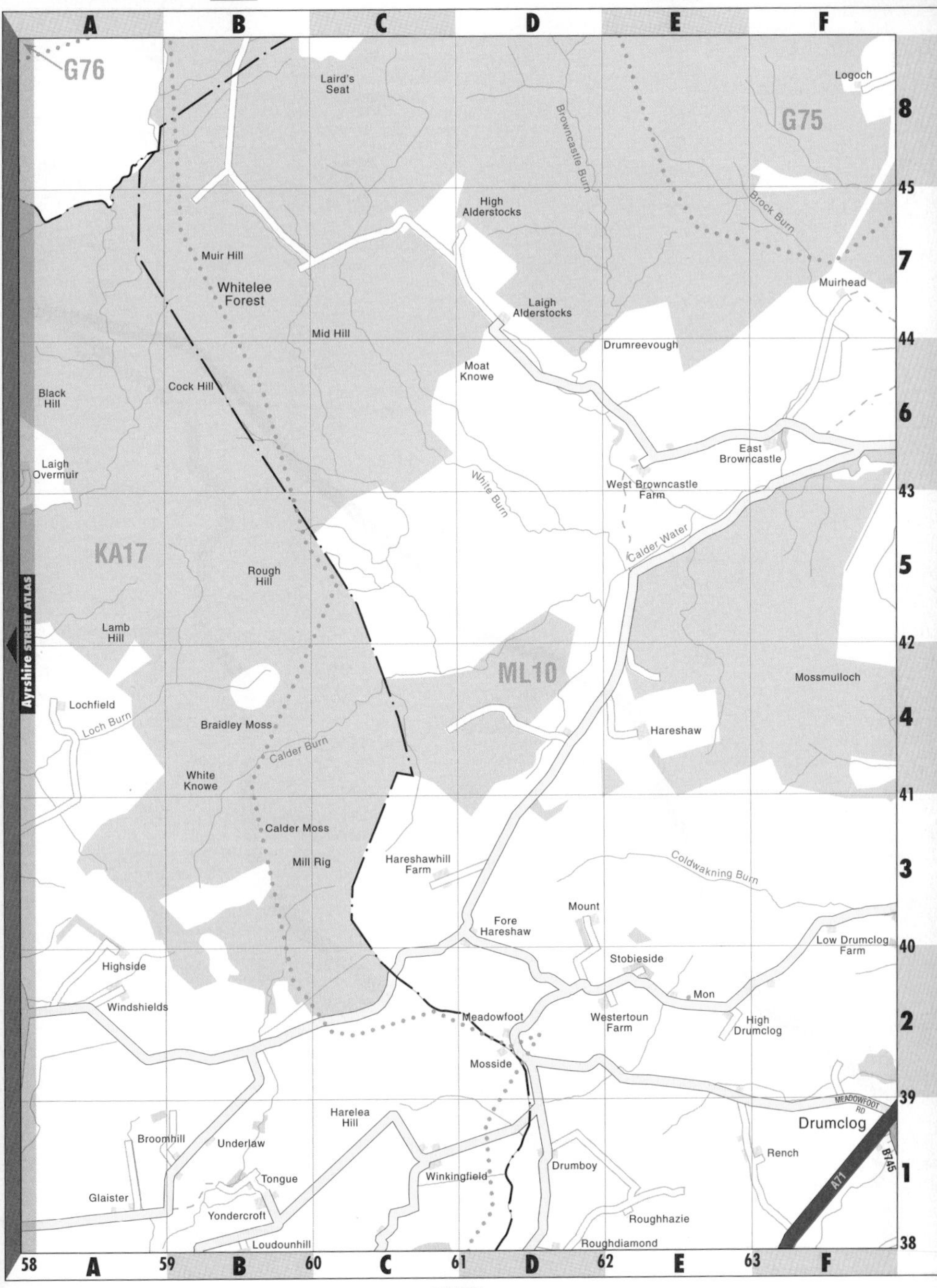

134

127 102 103

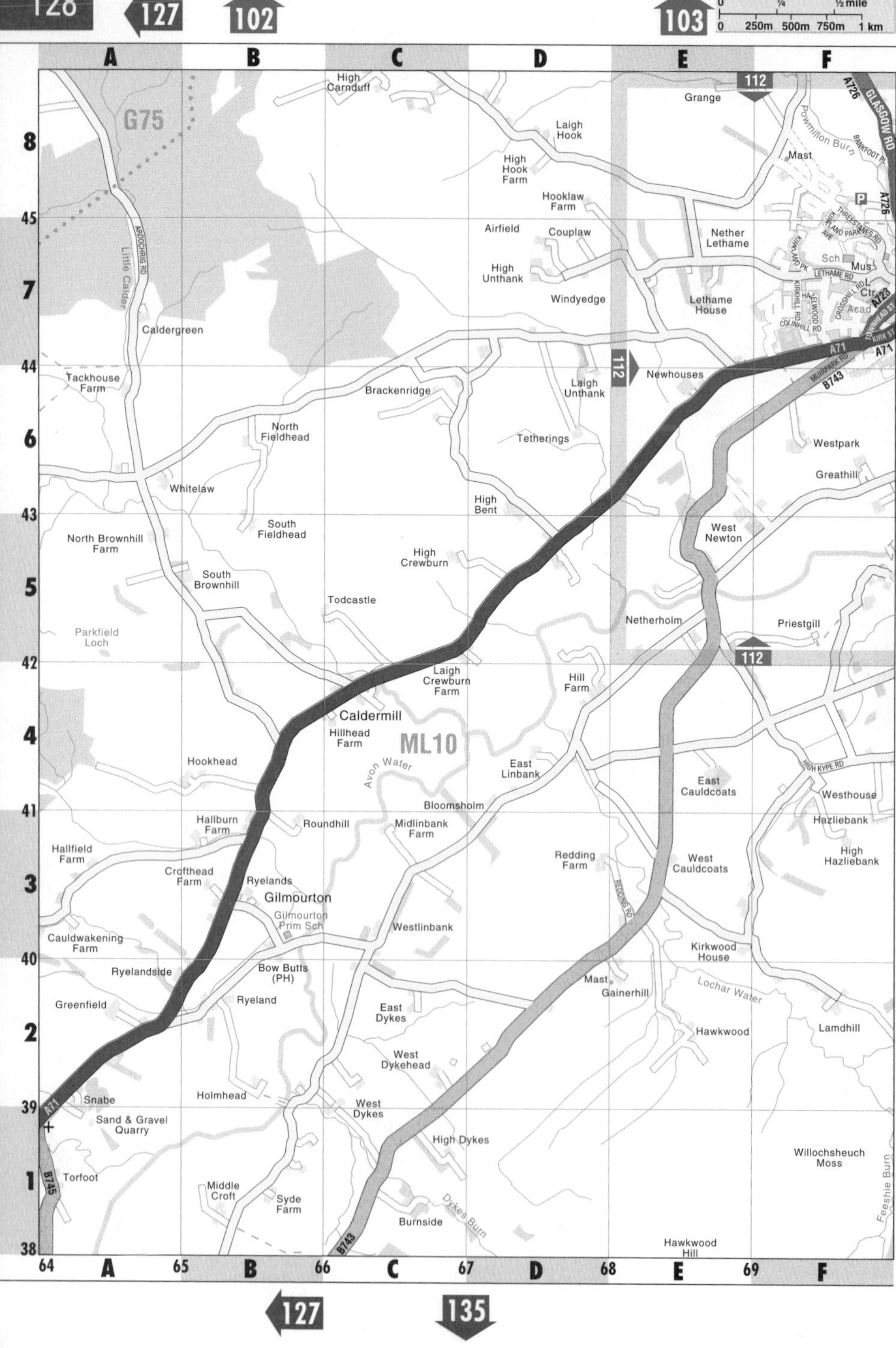

127 135

Scale: 1⅓ inches to 1 mile

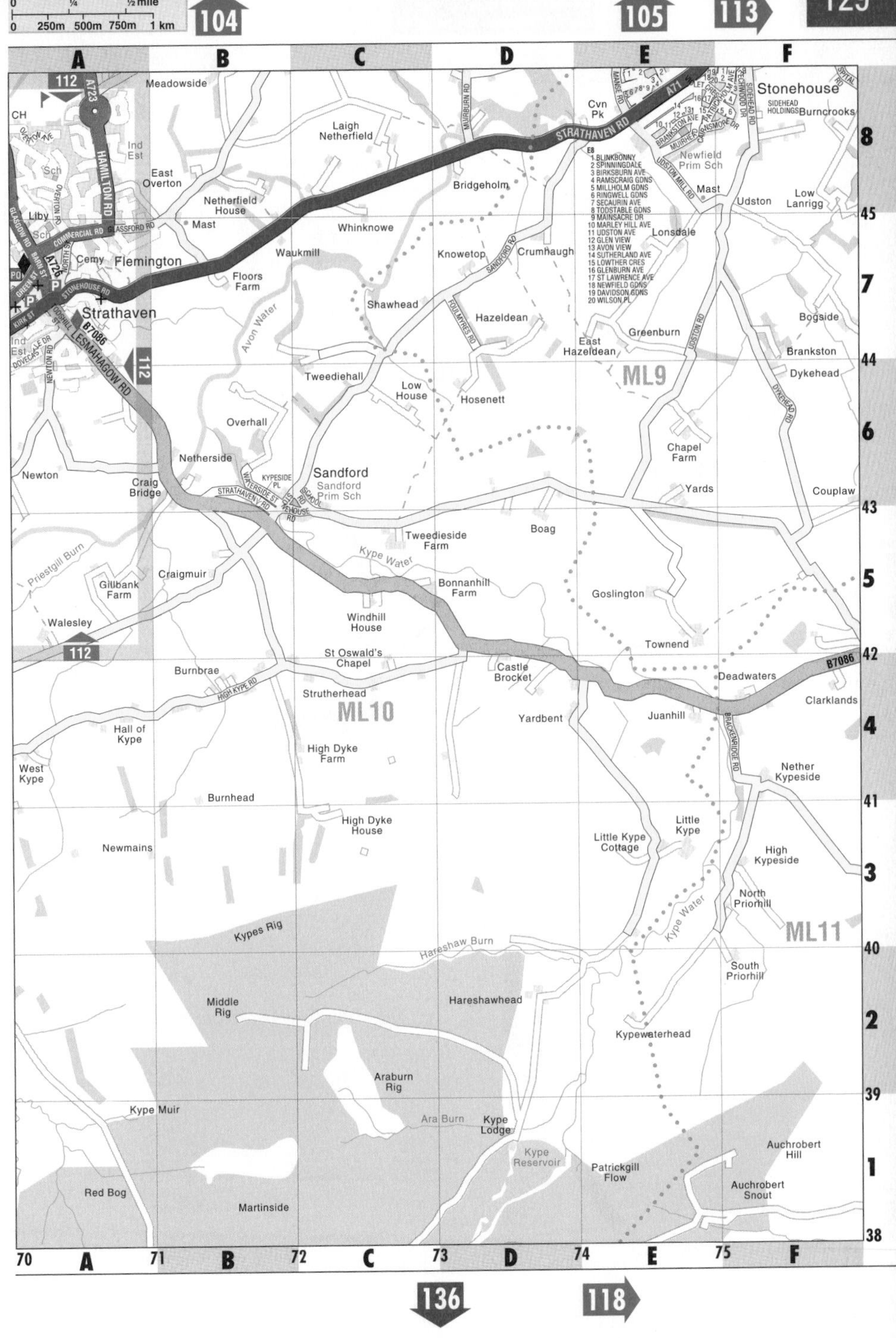

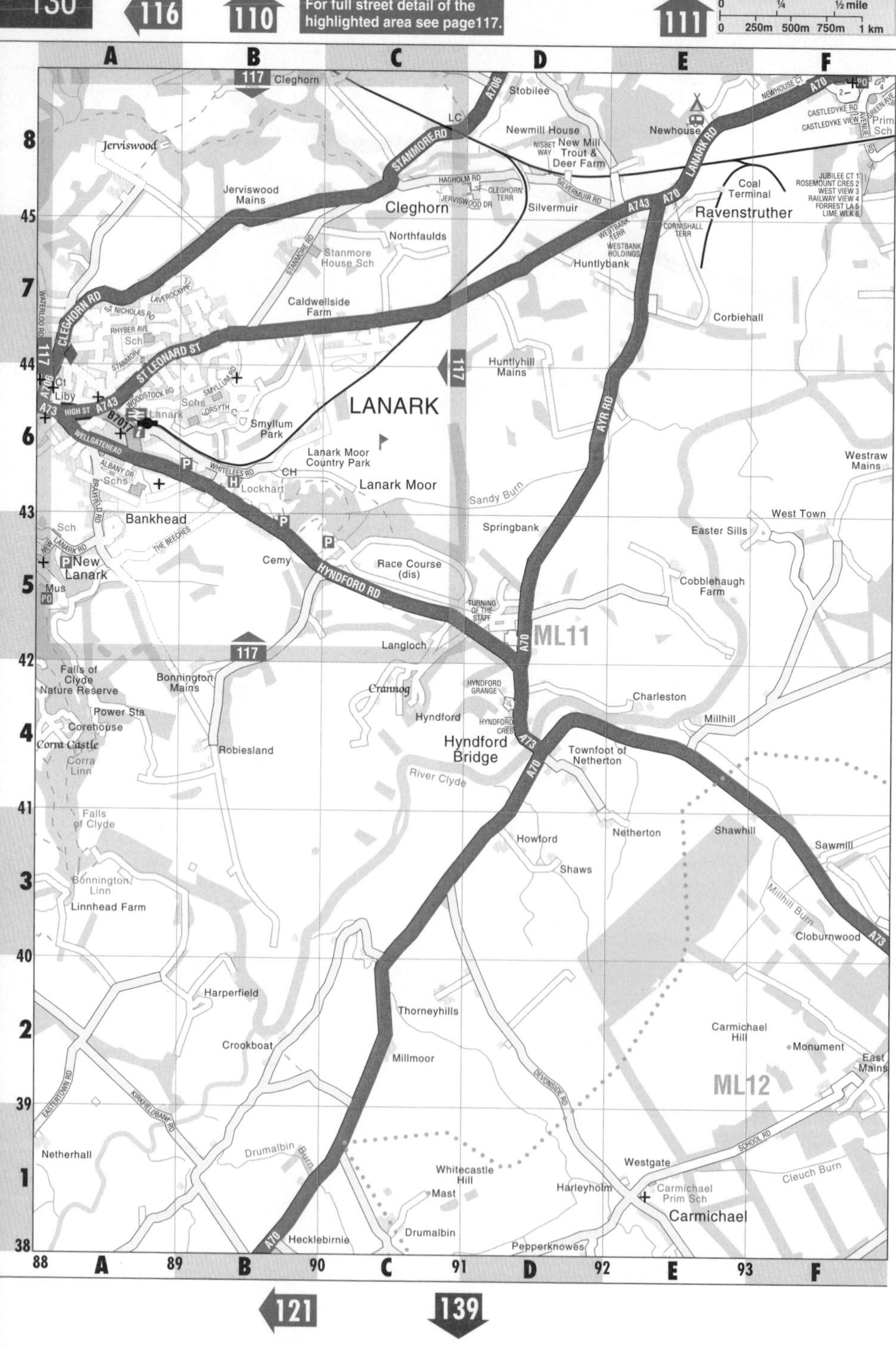
116
110
For full street detail of the highlighted area see page117.
111
Scale: 1⅓ inches to 1 mile
0 ¼ ½ mile
0 250m 500m 750m 1 km
A
B
C
D
E
F
117
Cleghorn
Stobilee
Newmill House
NISBET WAY
New Mill Trout & Deer Farm
Newhouse
NEWHOUSE CT
A70
CASTLEDYKE RD
CASTLEDYKE VIEW
AVENUE
GREEN AVE
Prim Sch
Jerviswood
A706
LC
STANMORE RD
HAGHOLM RD
CLEGHORN TERR
JERVISWOOD DR
SILVERMUIR RD
LANARK RD
Coal Terminal
JUBILEE CT 1
ROSEMOUNT CRES 2
WEST VIEW 3
RAILWAY VIEW 4
FORREST LA 5
LIME WLK 6
Jerviswood Mains
Cleghorn
Silvermuir
A743
Ravenstruther
CORNISHALL TERR
WESTBANK TERR
WESTBANK HOLDINGS
Northfaulds
STANMORE RD
Stanmore House Sch
Huntlybank
WATERLOO RD
CLEGHORN RD
LAVEROCKHILL
ST NICHOLAS RD
RHYBER AVE
Sch
Caldwellside Farm
Corbiehall
ST LEONARD ST
STANMORE
117
Huntlyhill Mains
Ct
Liby
A743
WOODSTOCK RD
SMYLLUM RD
Schs
ORSYTH
HIGH ST
A73
B7017
Lanark
LANARK
AYR RD
Smyllum Park
WELLGATEHEAD
Lanark Moor Country Park
Westraw Mains
ALBANY DR
Schs
P
WHITELEES RD
CH
H
Lockhart
Lanark Moor
Sandy Burn
BRAXFIELD RD
Bankhead
THE BEECHES
Springbank
West Town
Easter Sills
Sch
NEW LANARK RD
P
New Lanark
Cemy
P
Race Course (dis)
Cobblehaugh Farm
Mus
PO
HYNDFORD RD
TURNING OF THE STAFF
ML11
A70
117
Langloch
Falls of Clyde Nature Reserve
Bonnington Mains
Crannog
HYNDFORD GRANGE
Charleston
Power Sta
HYNDFORD CRES
Hyndford
Millhill
Corehouse
Corra Castle
Hyndford Bridge
A73
Robiesland
Townfoot of Netherton
Corra Linn
A70
River Clyde
Falls of Clyde
Howford
Netherton
Shawhill
Sawmill
Shaws
Bonnington Linn
Linnhead Farm
Millhill Burn
Cloburnwood
A73
Harperfield
Thorneyhills
Carmichael Hill
Monument
Crookboat
Millmoor
East Mains
EASTERTOWN RD
KIRKFIELDBANK RD
DEVONSIDE RD
ML12
SCHOOL RD
Netherhall
Drumalbin Burn
Whitecastle Hill
Westgate
Cleuch Burn
Mast
Harleyholm
Carmichael Prim Sch
Carmichael
A70
Hecklebirnie
Drumalbin
Pepperknowes
88
89
90
91
92
93
8
45
7
44
6
43
5
42
4
41
3
40
2
39
1
38
121
139

Scale: 1⅓ inches to 1 mile

124
132

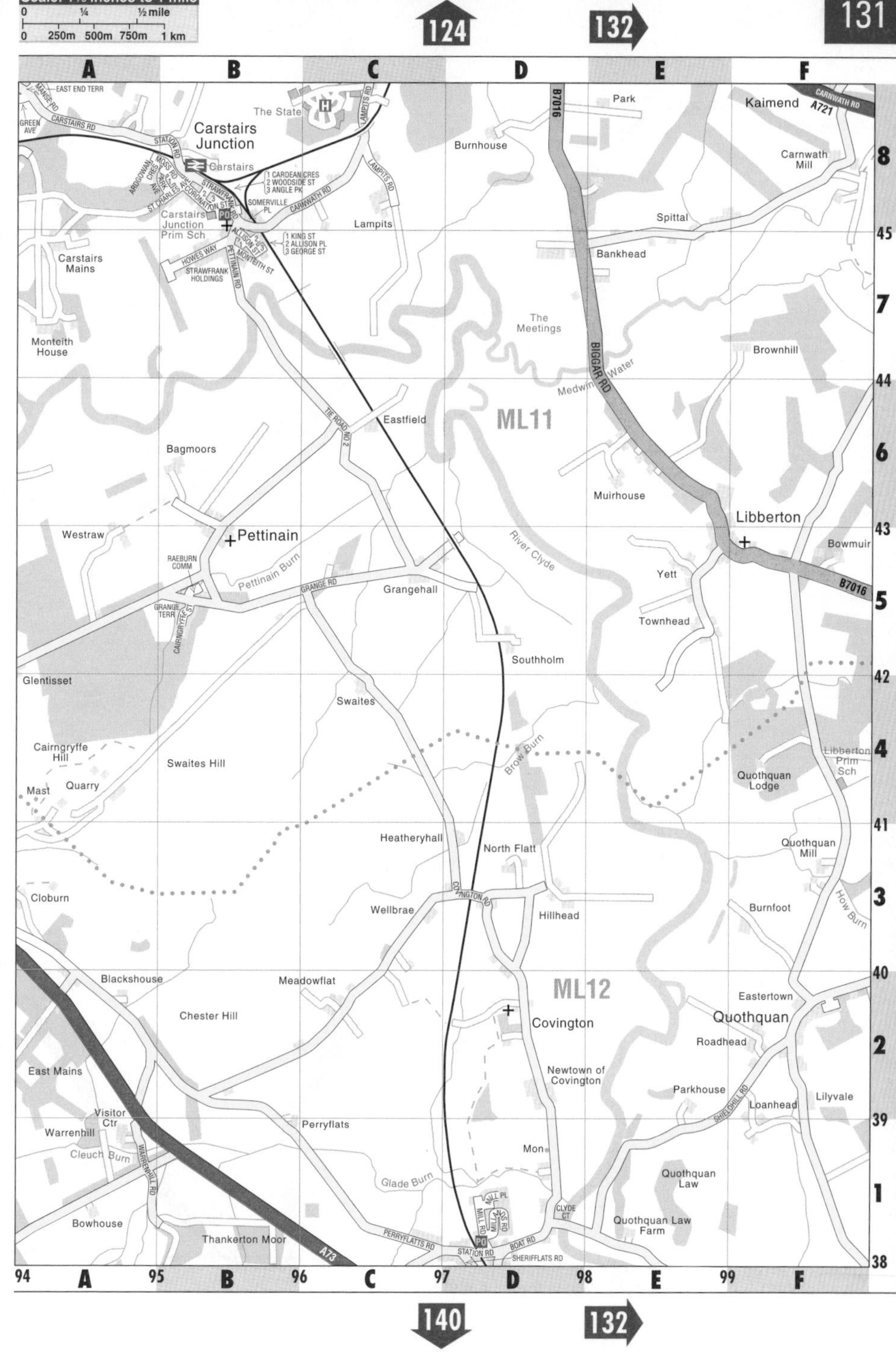

140
132

131
125

Scale: 1⅓ inches to 1 mile
0 ¼ ½ mile
0 250m 500m 750m 1 km

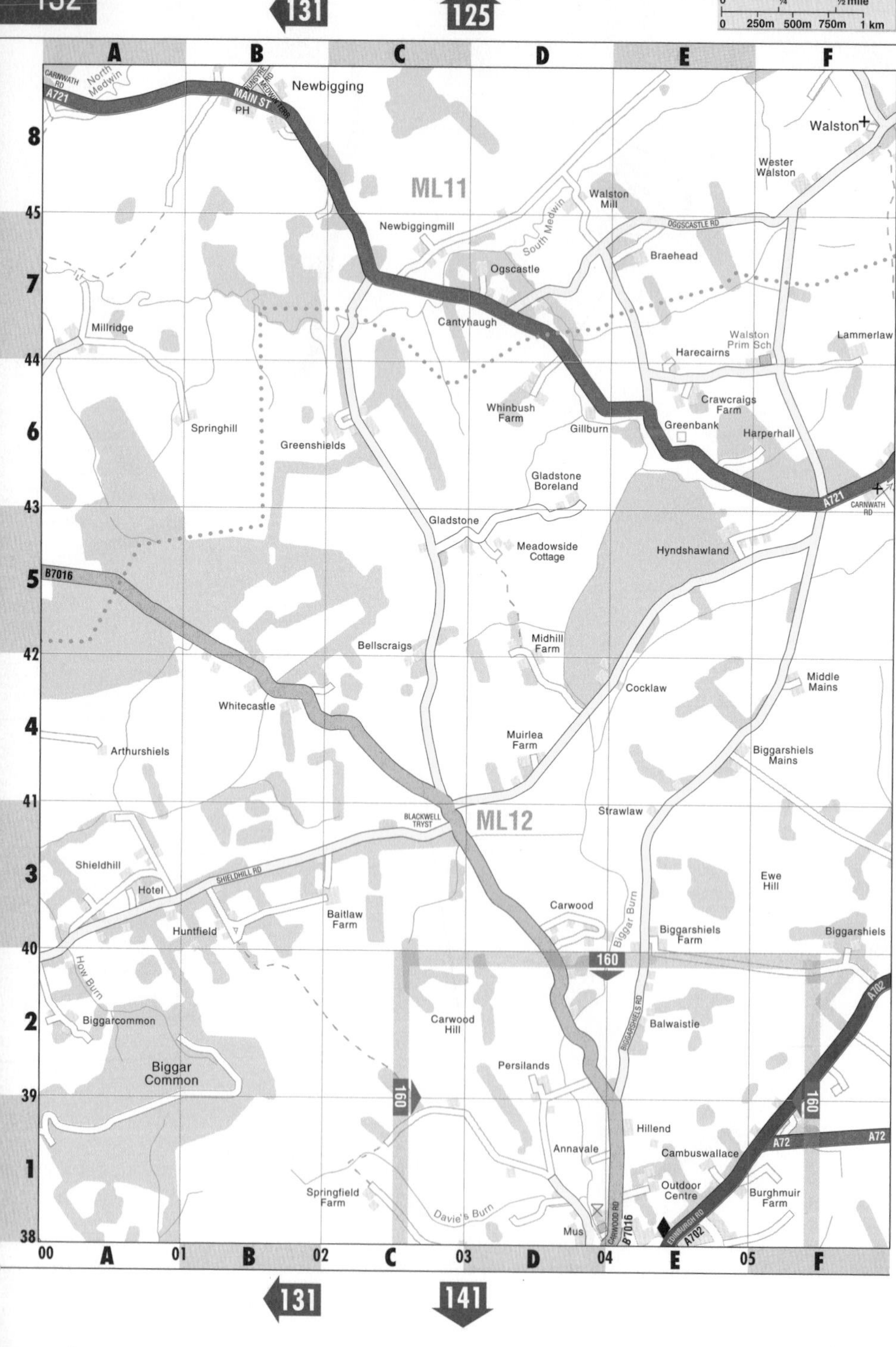

131
141

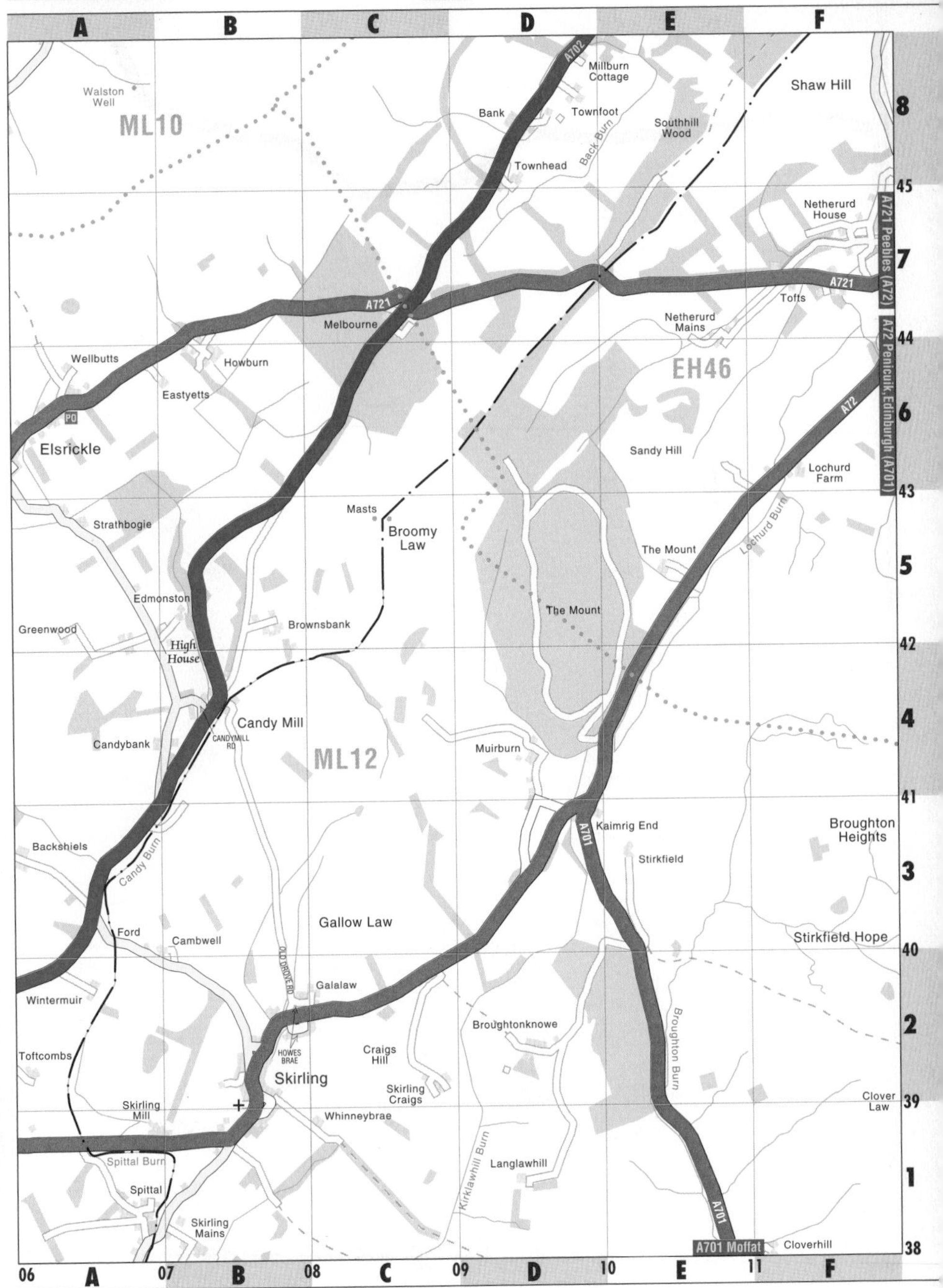
Scale: 1⅓ inches to 1 mile
0 ¼ ½ mile
0 250m 500m 750m 1 km
126
A B C D E F
8 7 6 5 4 3 2 1
45 44 43 42 41 40 39 38
06 07 08 09 10 11
ML10
ML12
EH46
Walston Well
Millburn Cottage
Bank
Townfoot
Shaw Hill
Southhill Wood
Back Burn
Townhead
Netherurd House
A702
A721
A721 Peebles (A72)
A72 Penicuik, Edinburgh (A701)
Melbourne
Tofts
Netherurd Mains
Wellbutts
Howburn
Eastyetts
PO
Elsrickle
A72
Sandy Hill
Lochurd Farm
Strathbogie
Masts
Broomy Law
Lochurd Burn
The Mount
Edmonston
The Mount
Greenwood
Brownsbank
High House
Candy Mill
CANDYMILL RD
Candybank
Muirburn
Backshiels
A701
Kaimrig End
Broughton Heights
Stirkfield
Candy Burn
Ford
Cambwell
Gallow Law
Stirkfield Hope
OLD DROVE RD
Galalaw
Wintermuir
Broughtonknowe
Broughton Burn
Toftcombs
HOWES BRAE
Craigs Hill
Skirling
Skirling Craigs
Skirling Mill
Whinneybrae
Clover Law
Spittal Burn
Kirklawhill Burn
Langlawhill
Spittal
Skirling Mains
A701
A701 Moffat
Cloverhill

127

Scale: 1⅓ inches to 1 mile

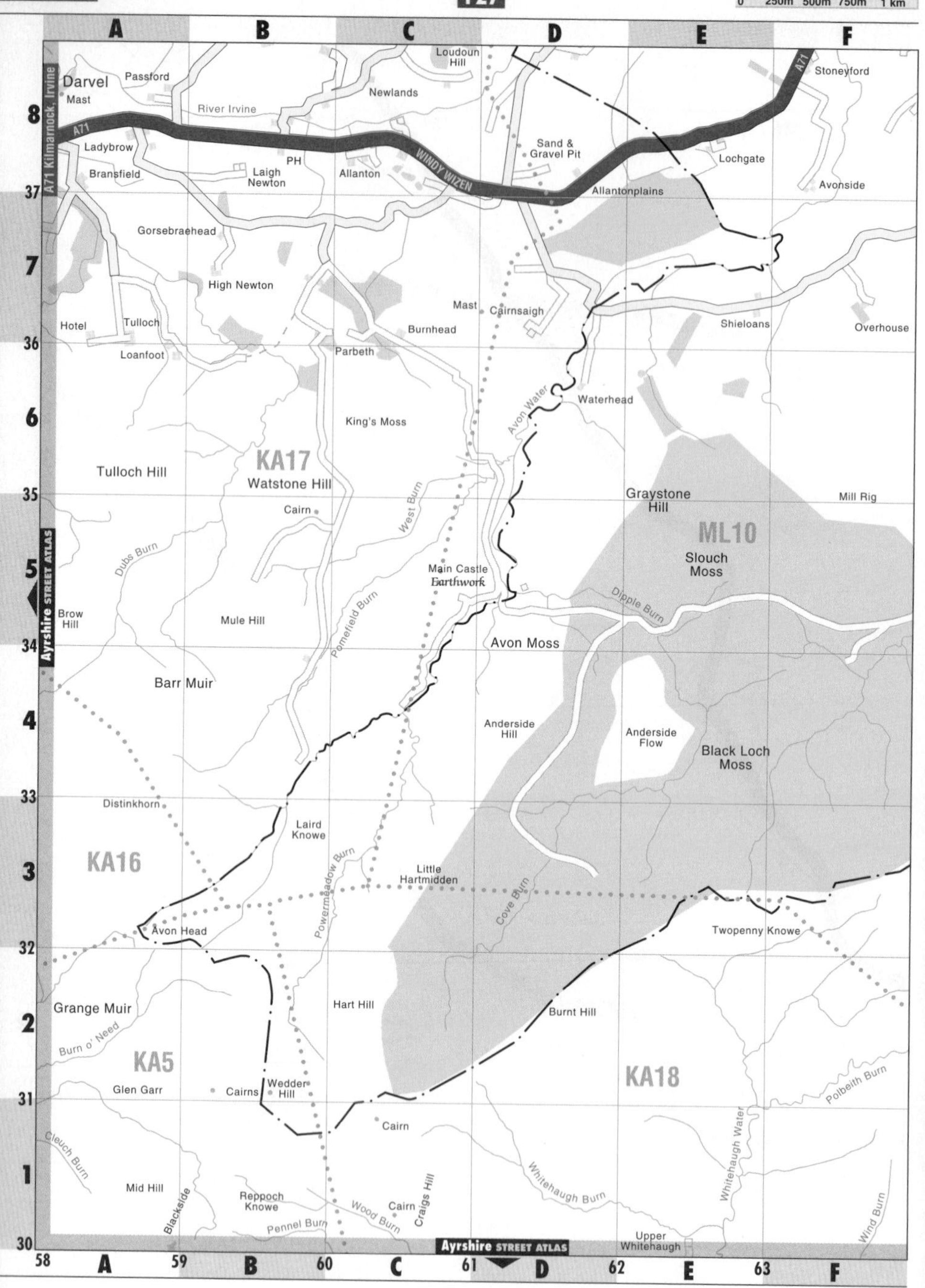

128
136

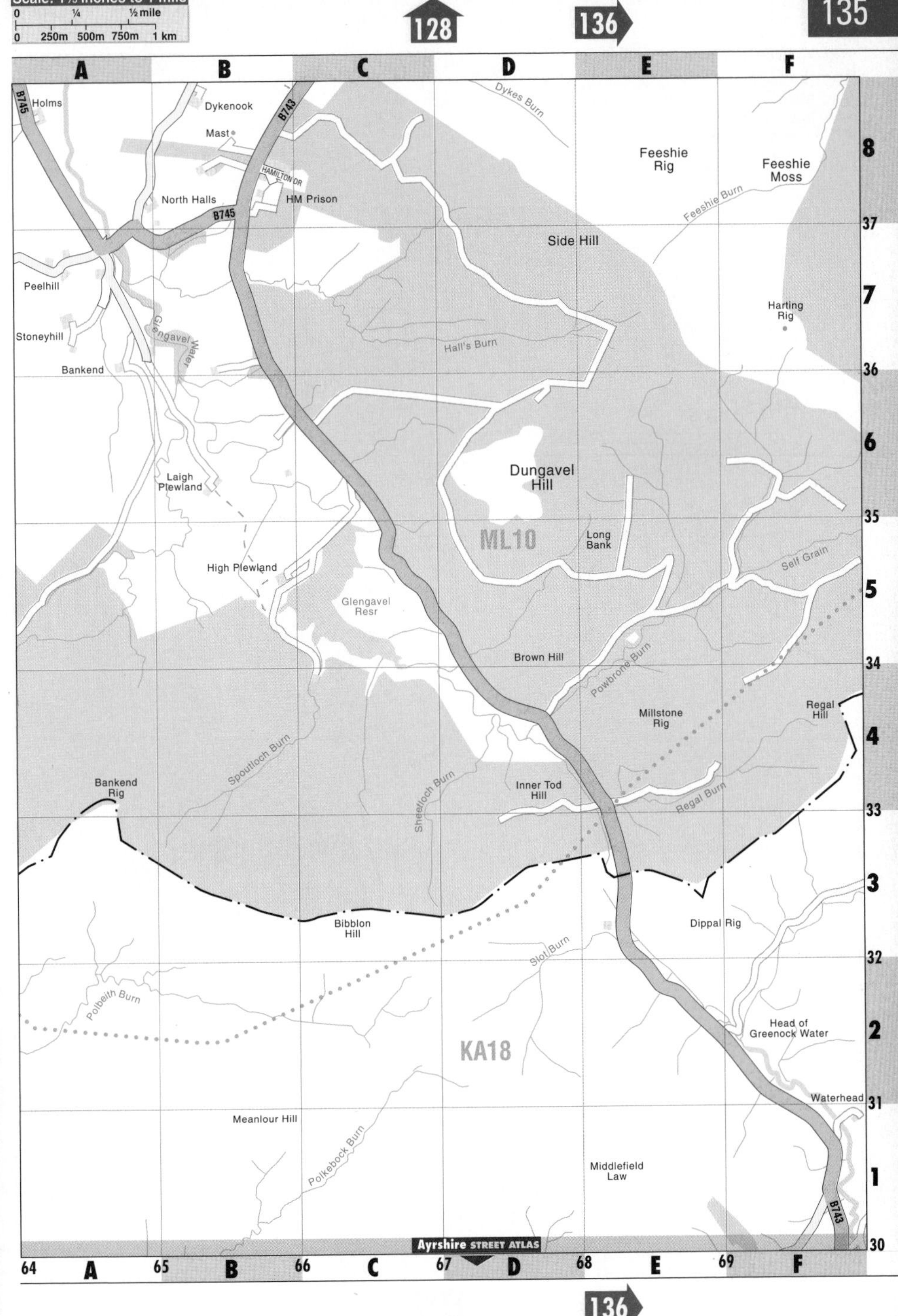
Scale: 1⅓ inches to 1 mile
0 ¼ ½ mile
0 250m 500m 750m 1 km
A
B
C
D
E
F
B745
Holms
Dykenook
B743
Dykes Burn
Mast
Feeshie Rig
Feeshie Moss
HAMILTON DR
North Halls
HM Prison
B745
Feeshie Burn
Side Hill
Peelhill
Harting Rig
Stoneyhill
Glengavel Water
Hall's Burn
Bankend
Dungavel Hill
Laigh Plewland
ML10
Long Bank
High Plewland
Self Grain
Glengavel Resr
Brown Hill
Powbrone Burn
Millstone Rig
Regal Hill
Spoutloch Burn
Sheeploch Burn
Bankend Rig
Inner Tod Hill
Regal Burn
Bibblon Hill
Dippal Rig
Slot Burn
Polbeith Burn
Head of Greenock Water
KA18
Waterhead
Meanlour Hill
Polkebock Burn
Middlefield Law
B743
8
37
7
36
6
35
5
34
4
33
3
32
2
31
1
30
64
65
66
67
68
69

136

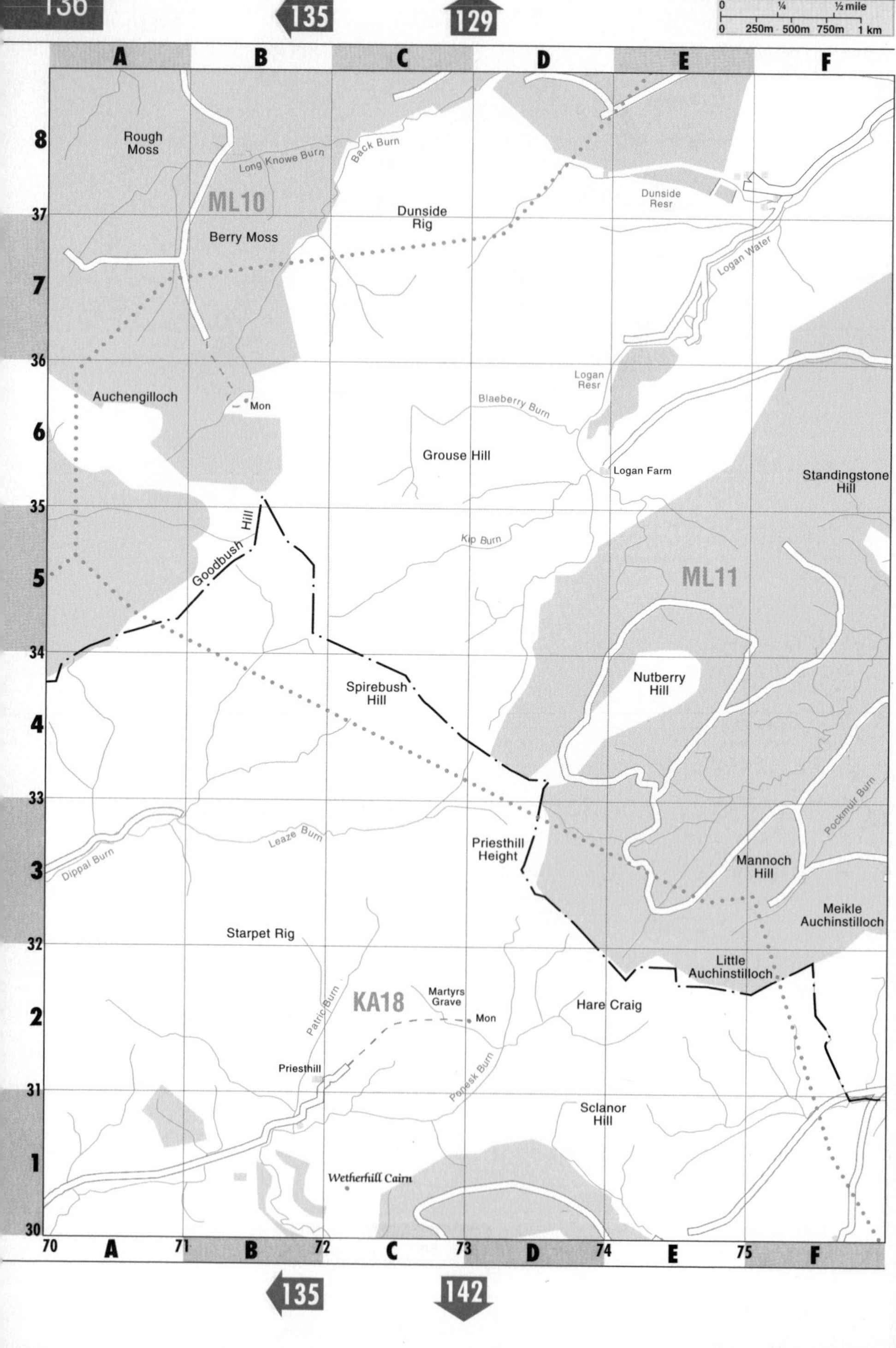
135
129
Scale: 1⅓ inches to 1 mile
0 ¼ ½ mile
0 250m 500m 750m 1 km
A B C D E F
8
7
6
5
4
3
2
1
37
36
35
34
33
32
31
30
Rough Moss
Long Knowe Burn
Back Burn
ML10
Berry Moss
Dunside Rig
Dunside Resr
Logan Water
Auchengilloch
Mon
Logan Resr
Blaeberry Burn
Grouse Hill
Logan Farm
Standingstone Hill
Goodbush Hill
Kip Burn
ML11
Nutberry Hill
Spirebush Hill
Leaze Burn
Dippal Burn
Priesthill Height
Pockmuir Burn
Mannoch Hill
Meikle Auchinstilloch
Starpet Rig
Little Auchinstilloch
Patric Burn
KA18
Martyrs Grave
Mon
Hare Craig
Priesthill
Ponesk Burn
Sclanor Hill
Wetherhill Cairn
70 71 72 73 74 75
135
142

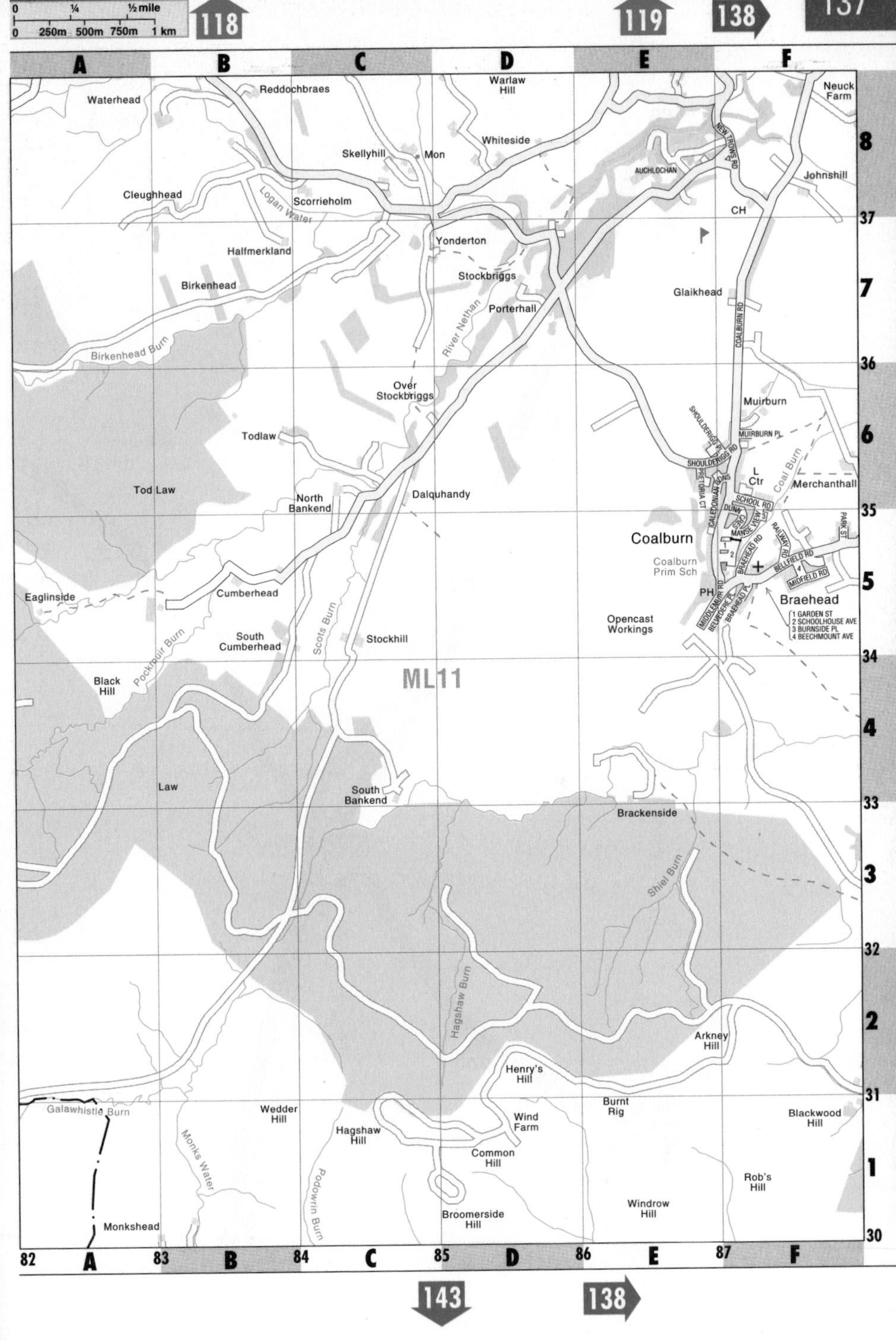

Scale: 1⅓ inches to 1 mile
0 ¼ ½ mile
0 250m 500m 750m 1 km
118
119
138
A B C D E F
Waterhead
Reddochbraes
Warlaw Hill
Neuck Farm
Whiteside
Skellyhill
Mon
AUCHLOCHAN
NEW TROWS RD
Johnshill
Cleughhead
Scorrieholm
Logan Water
CH
Yonderton
Halfmerkland
Stockbriggs
Birkenhead
Glaikhead
Porterhall
River Nethan
COALBURN RD
Birkenhead Burn
Over Stockbriggs
Muirburn
SHOULDERIGG PL
MUIRBURN PL
Todlaw
SHOULDERIGG RD
L
Ctr
Coal Burn
Merchanthall
Tod Law
PRETORIA CT
CALEDONIAN GDNS
Dalquhandy
North Bankend
SCHOOL RD
MANSE VIEW
PARK ST
Coalburn
RAILWAY RD
BRAEHEAD RD
BELLFIELD RD
Coalburn Prim Sch
MIDFIELD RD
Eaglinside
Cumberhead
PH
Braehead
MIDDLEMUIR RD
BELVEDERE PL
BRAEHEAD PL
Opencast Workings
1 GARDEN ST
2 SCHOOLHOUSE AVE
3 BURNSIDE PL
4 BEECHMOUNT AVE
South Cumberhead
Scots Burn
Stockhill
Pockmuir Burn
Black Hill
ML11
Law
South Bankend
Brackenside
Shiel Burn
Hagshaw Burn
Arkney Hill
Henry's Hill
Galawhistle Burn
Wedder Hill
Burnt Rig
Wind Farm
Blackwood Hill
Hagshaw Hill
Monks Water
Common Hill
Podowrin Burn
Rob's Hill
Windrow Hill
Broomerside Hill
Monkshead
8
37
7
36
6
35
5
34
4
33
3
32
2
31
1
30
82 83 84 85 86 87
143
138

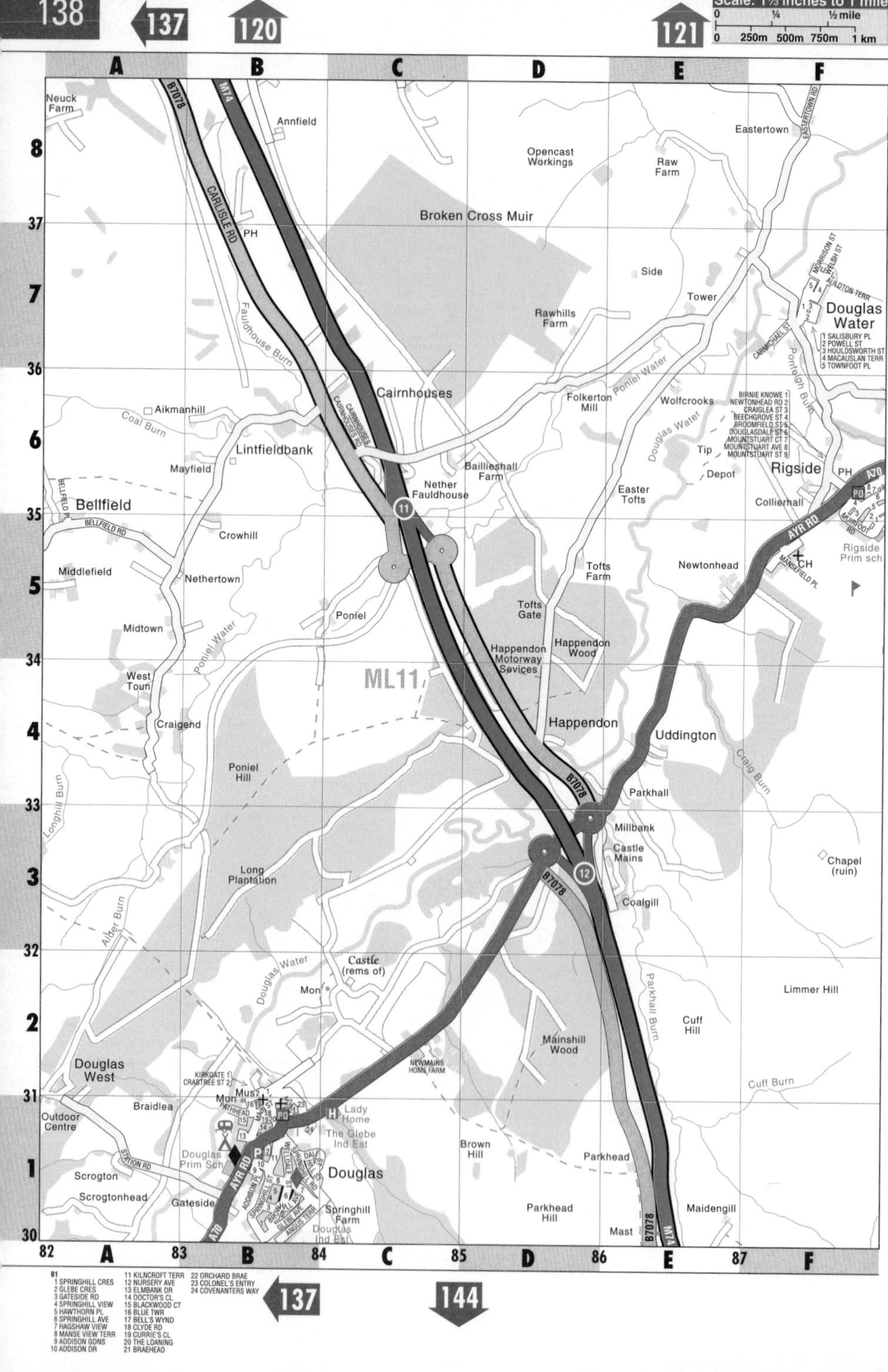

138
137
120
121
Scale: 1⅓ inches to 1 mile
0 ¼ ½ mile
0 250m 500m 750m 1 km
A B C D E F
8 37 7 36 6 35 5 34 4 33 3 32 2 31 1 30
82 83 84 85 86 87
Neuck Farm
Annfield
B7078
M74
CARLISLE RD
PH
Opencast Workings
Raw Farm
Eastertown
EASTERTOWN RD
Broken Cross Muir
Side
Tower
Rawhills Farm
Fauldhouse Burn
Douglas Water
MORRISON ST
WELSH ST
AULDTON TERR
CARMICHAEL ST
1 SALISBURY PL
2 POWELL ST
3 HOULDSWORTH ST
4 MACAUSLAN TERR
5 TOWNFOOT PL
Poniel Water
Ponfeigh Burn
Cairnhouses
CAIRNHOUSES
CAIRNHOUSES RD
Folkerton Mill
Wolfcrooks
BIRNIE KNOWE 1
NEWTONHEAD RD 2
CRAIGLEA ST 3
BEECHGROVE ST 4
BROOMFIELD ST 5
DOUGLASDALE ST 6
MOUNTSTUART CT 7
MOUNTSTUART AVE 8
MOUNTSTUART ST 9
Aikmanhill
Coal Burn
Lintfieldbank
Mayfield
Baillieshall Farm
Nether Fauldhouse
Tip
Depot
Rigside
PH
A70
PO
Collierhall
BELLFIELD PL
Bellfield
BELLFIELD RD
Crowhill
Easter Tofts
AYR RD
MUIRFOOT RD
Rigside Prim sch
CH
MANSEFIELD PL
Middlefield
Nethertown
Tofts Farm
Newtonhead
Poniel
Tofts Gate
Midtown
Poniel Water
Happendon Motorway Sevices
Happendon Wood
West Toun
ML11
Craigend
Happendon
Uddington
Craig Burn
Poniel Hill
Longhill Burn
Parkhall
Millbank
Castle Mains
Chapel (ruin)
Long Plantation
Coalgill
Alder Burn
Douglas Water
Castle (rems of)
Mon
Limmer Hill
Parkhall Burn
Cuff Hill
Mainshill Wood
NEWMAINS HOME FARM
Douglas West
KIRKGATE 1
CRABTREE ST 2
Mus
Mon
PATHHEAD
Cuff Burn
Outdoor Centre
Braidlea
Lady Home
The Glebe Ind Est
Brown Hill
Parkhead
Douglas Prim Sch
STATION RD
Douglas
Scrogton
Scrogtonhead
Gateside
ADDISON PL
SPRINGHILL ST
WELLDALE ST
DALE ST
SPRINGHILL RD
BROWNHILL AVE
GLEBE AVE
ANGUS TERR
Springhill Farm
Douglas Ind Est
Parkhead Hill
Maidengill
Mast
B7078
M74
B1
1 SPRINGHILL CRES
2 GLEBE CRES
3 GATESIDE RD
4 SPRINGHILL VIEW
5 HAWTHORN PL
6 SPRINGHILL AVE
7 HAGSHAW VIEW
8 MANSE VIEW TERR
9 ADDISON GDNS
10 ADDISON DR
11 KILNCROFT TERR
12 NURSERY AVE
13 ELMBANK DR
14 DOCTOR'S CL
15 BLACKWOOD CT
16 BLUE TWR
17 BELL'S WYND
18 CLYDE RD
19 CURRIE'S CL
20 THE LOANING
21 BRAEHEAD
22 ORCHARD BRAE
23 COLONEL'S ENTRY
24 COVENANTERS WAY
137
144

130
140

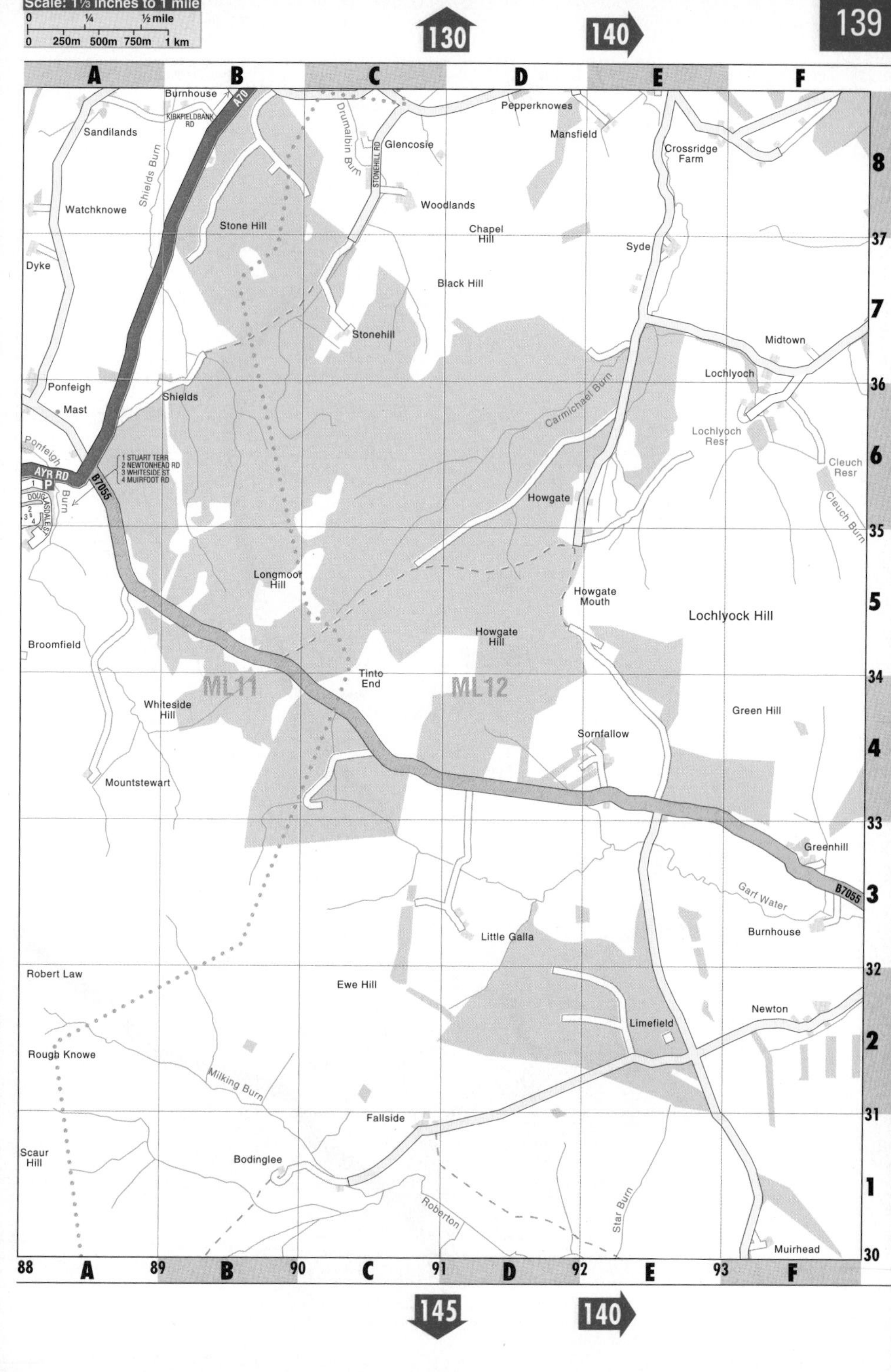

145
140

139
131

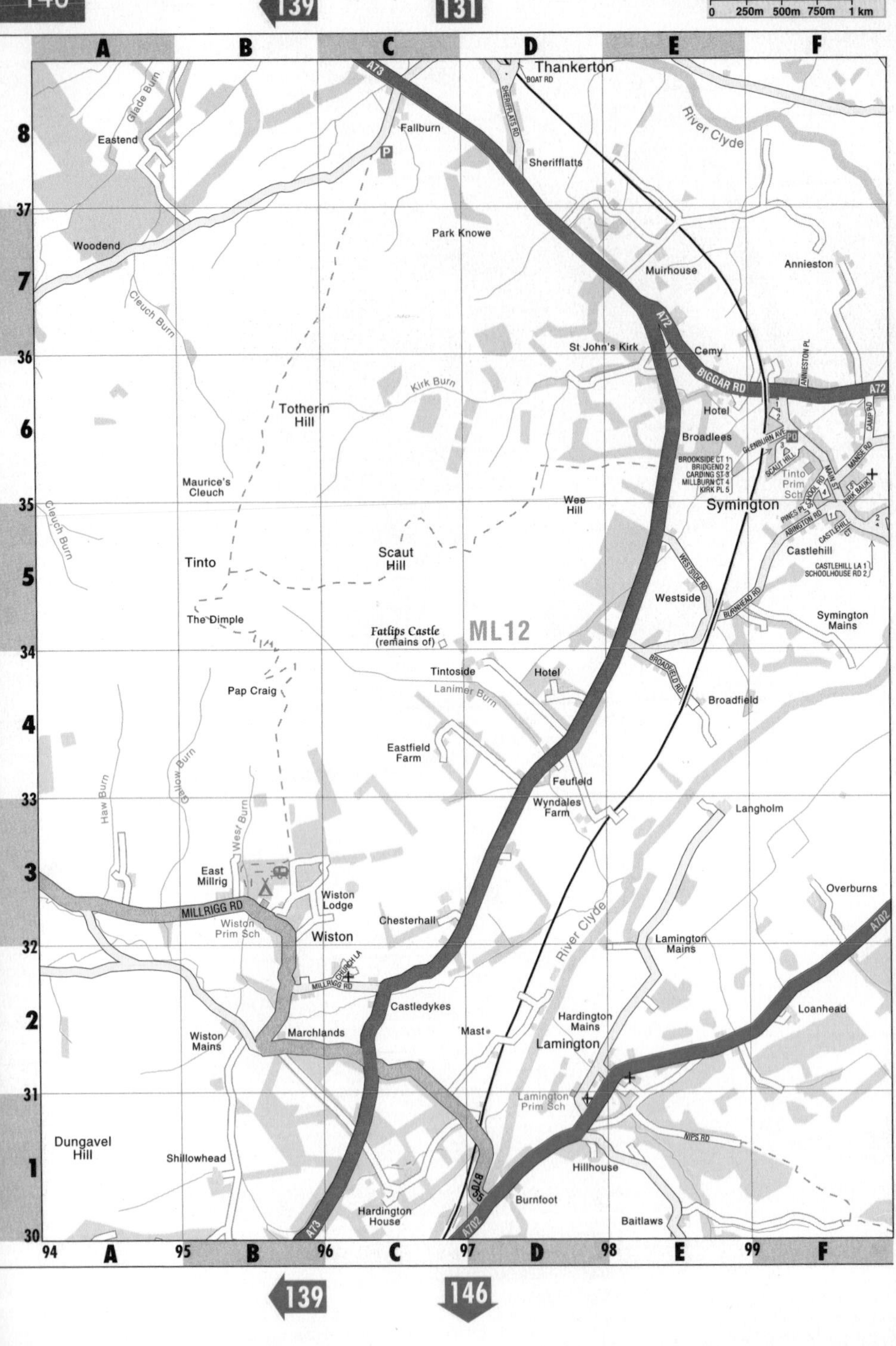

139
146

Scale: 1⅓ inches to 1 mile

132

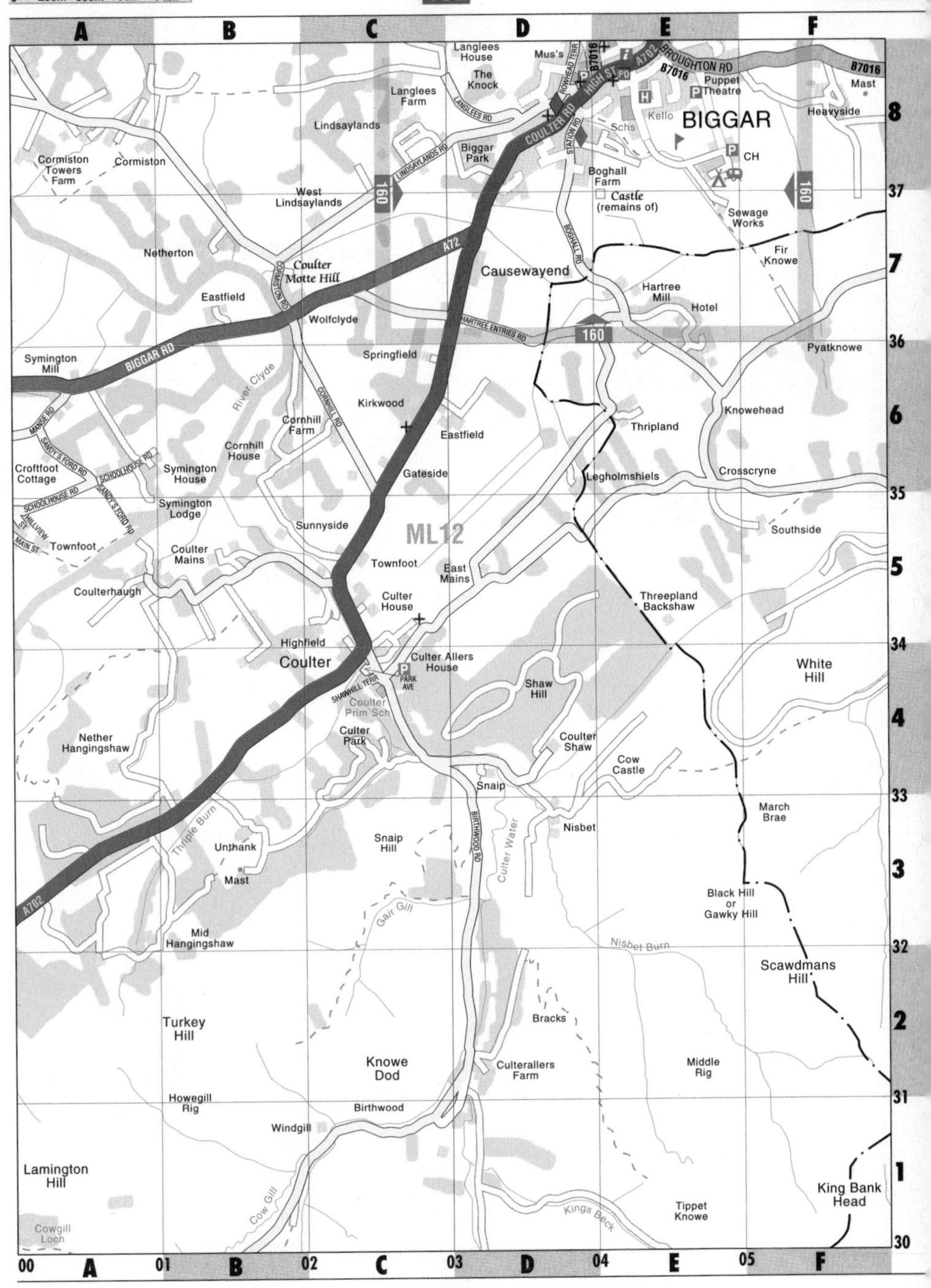

147

136

Scale: 1⅓ inches to 1 mile

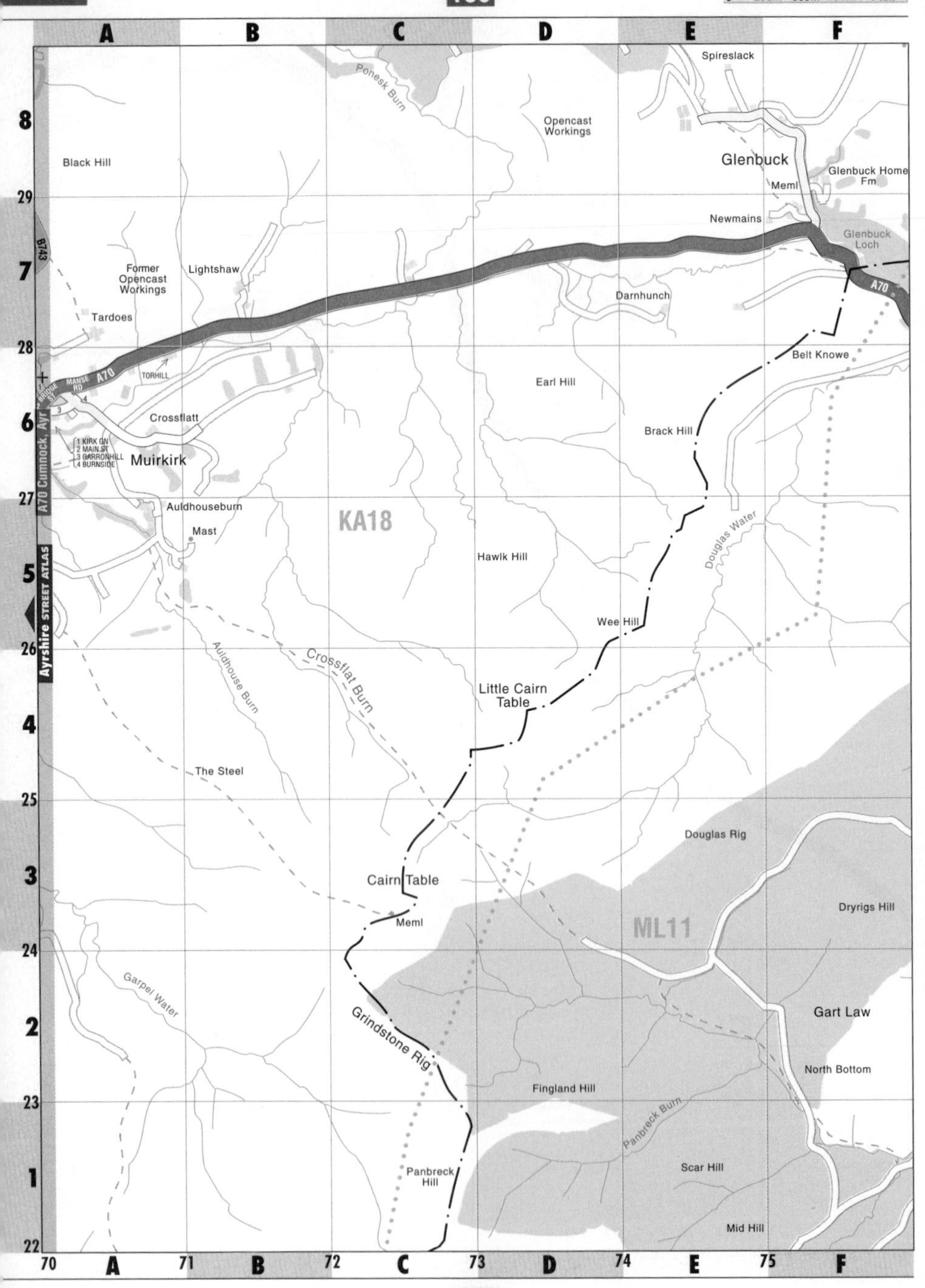

148

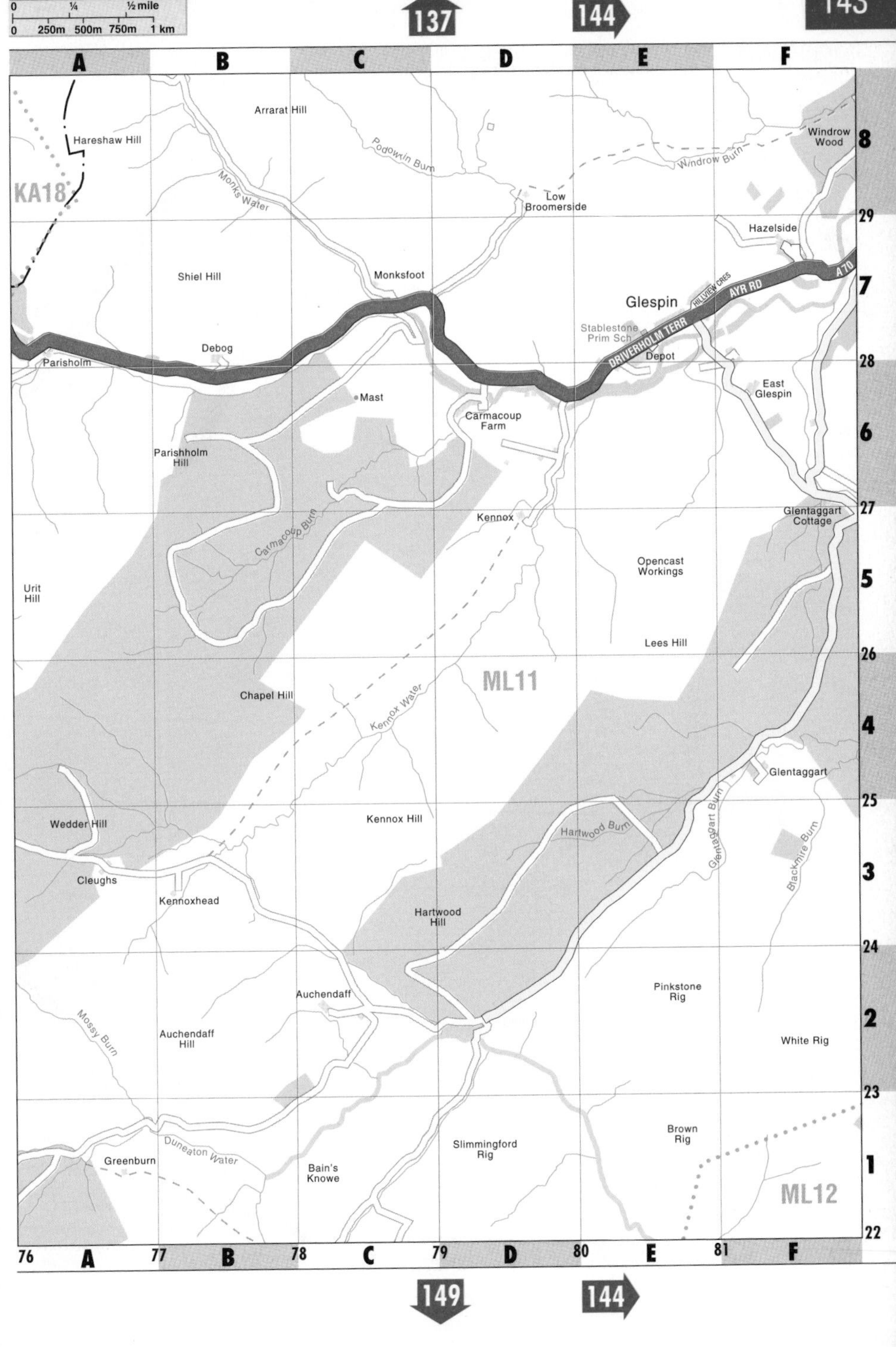
Scale: 1⅓ inches to 1 mile
0 ¼ ½ mile
0 250m 500m 750m 1 km
137
144
A B C D E F
Arrarat Hill
Hareshaw Hill
Podowrin Burn
Windrow Burn
Windrow Wood
KA18
Monks Water
Low Broomerside
Hazelside
Shiel Hill
Monksfoot
Glespin
HILLVIEW CRES
AYR RD
A70
Stablestone Prim Sch
DRIVERHOLM TERR
Depot
Debog
Parisholm
East Glespin
Mast
Carmacoup Farm
Parishholm Hill
Kennox
Glentaggart Cottage
Carmacoup Burn
Opencast Workings
Urit Hill
Lees Hill
ML11
Chapel Hill
Kennox Water
Glentaggart
Wedder Hill
Kennox Hill
Hartwood Burn
Glentaggart Burn
Blackmire Burn
Cleughs
Kennoxhead
Hartwood Hill
Auchendaff
Pinkstone Rig
Mossy Burn
Auchendaff Hill
White Rig
Brown Rig
Slimmingford Rig
Greenburn
Duneaton Water
Bain's Knowe
ML12
8 29 7 28 6 27 5 26 4 25 3 24 2 23 1 22
76 77 78 79 80 81
149
144

143
138

Scale: 1⅓ inches to 1 mile

143
150

Scale: 1⅓ inches to 1 mile

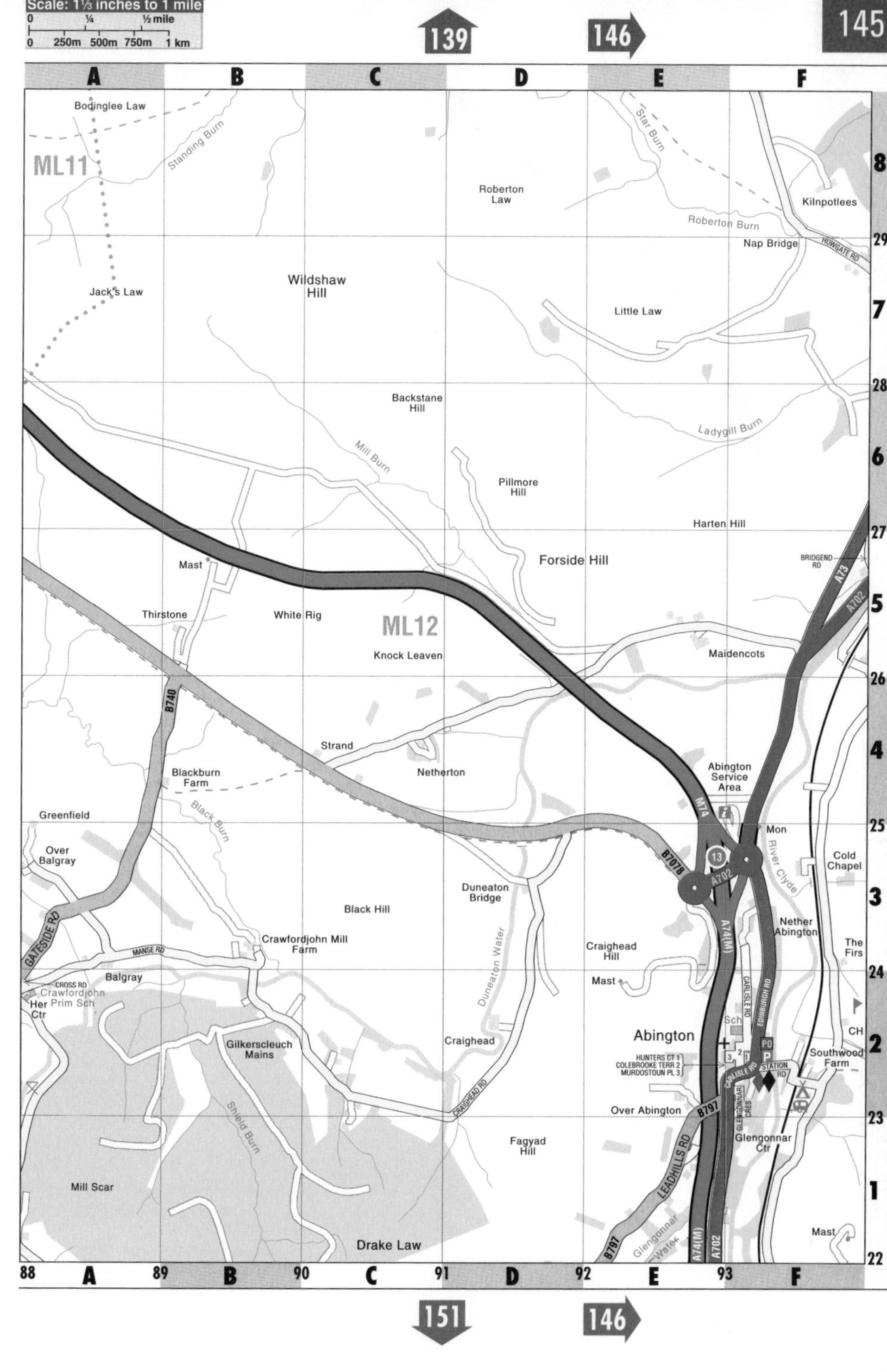

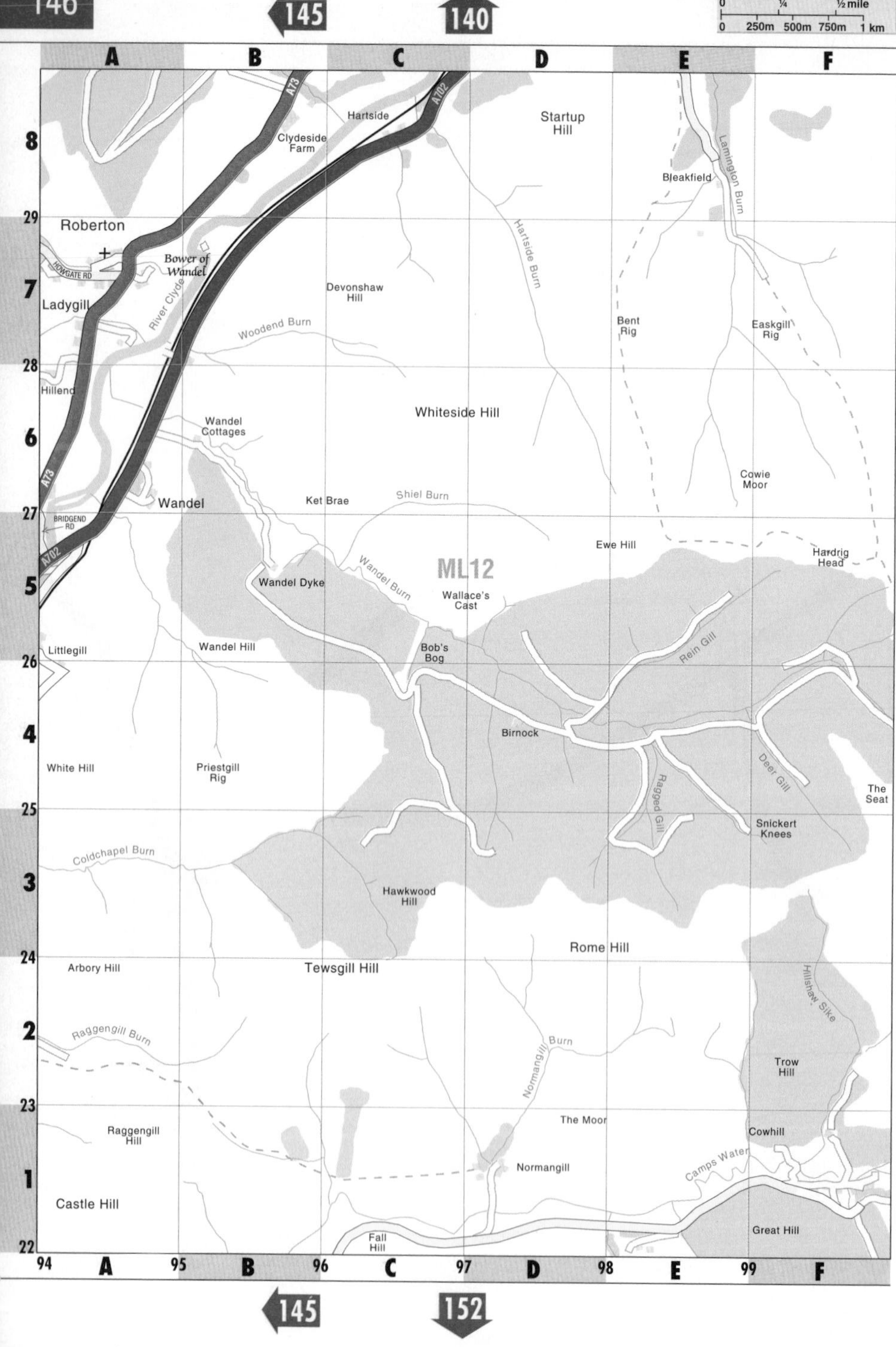
145
140
Scale: 1⅓ inches to 1 mile
0
¼
½ mile
0
250m
500m
750m
1 km
A
B
C
D
E
F
8
29
7
28
6
27
5
26
4
25
3
24
2
23
1
22
94
95
96
97
98
99
A73
A702
Hartside
Startup Hill
Clydeside Farm
Bleakfield
Lamington Burn
Roberton
Bower of Wandel
HOWGATE RD
River Clyde
Hartside Burn
Devonshaw Hill
Ladygill
Woodend Burn
Bent Rig
Easkgill Rig
Hillend
Whiteside Hill
Wandel Cottages
Cowie Moor
Wandel
Ket Brae
Shiel Burn
BRIDGEND RD
Ewe Hill
Hardrig Head
ML12
Wandel Dyke
Wandel Burn
Wallace's Cast
Bob's Bog
Rein Gill
Littlegill
Wandel Hill
Birnock
White Hill
Priestgill Rig
Ragged Gill
Deer Gill
The Seat
Snickert Knees
Coldchapel Burn
Hawkwood Hill
Rome Hill
Arbory Hill
Tewsgill Hill
Hillshaw Sike
Raggengill Burn
Normangill Burn
Trow Hill
The Moor
Raggengill Hill
Cowhill
Camps Water
Normangill
Castle Hill
Fall Hill
Great Hill
145
152

Scale: 1⅓ inches to 1 mile

141

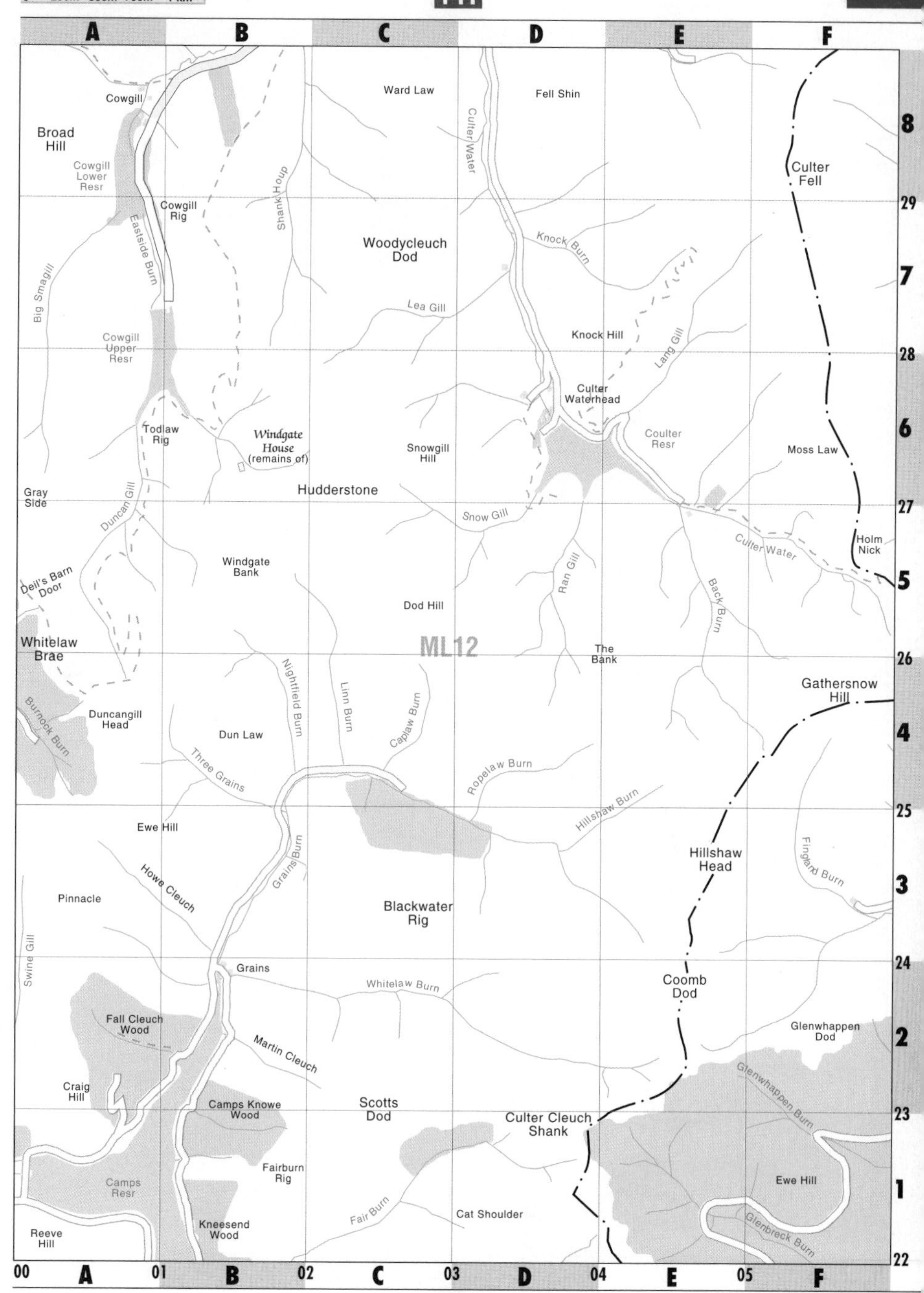
0
¼
½ mile
0
250m
500m
750m
1 km
A
B
C
D
E
F
Cowgill
Broad Hill
Cowgill Lower Resr
Ward Law
Fell Shin
Culter Water
Culter Fell
Cowgill Rig
Eastside Burn
Shank Houp
Woodycleuch Dod
Knock Burn
Big Smagill
Lea Gill
Cowgill Upper Resr
Knock Hill
Lang Gill
Culter Waterhead
Todlaw Rig
Windgate House (remains of)
Snowgill Hill
Coulter Resr
Moss Law
Gray Side
Hudderstone
Duncan Gill
Snow Gill
Culter Water
Holm Nick
Windgate Bank
Ran Gill
Back Burn
Deil's Barn Door
Dod Hill
Whitelaw Brae
ML12
The Bank
Gathersnow Hill
Burnock Burn
Duncangill Head
Nightfield Burn
Linn Burn
Caplaw Burn
Dun Law
Three Grains
Ropelaw Burn
Hillshaw Burn
Ewe Hill
Hillshaw Head
Fingland Burn
Howe Cleuch
Grains Burn
Pinnacle
Blackwater Rig
Swine Gill
Grains
Whitelaw Burn
Coomb Dod
Fall Cleuch Wood
Martin Cleuch
Glenwhappen Dod
Glenwhappen Burn
Craig Hill
Camps Knowe Wood
Scotts Dod
Culter Cleuch Shank
Fairburn Rig
Camps Resr
Ewe Hill
Fair Burn
Cat Shoulder
Kneesend Wood
Glenbreck Burn
Reeve Hill
8
29
7
28
6
27
5
26
4
25
3
24
2
23
1
22
00
01
02
03
04
05

153

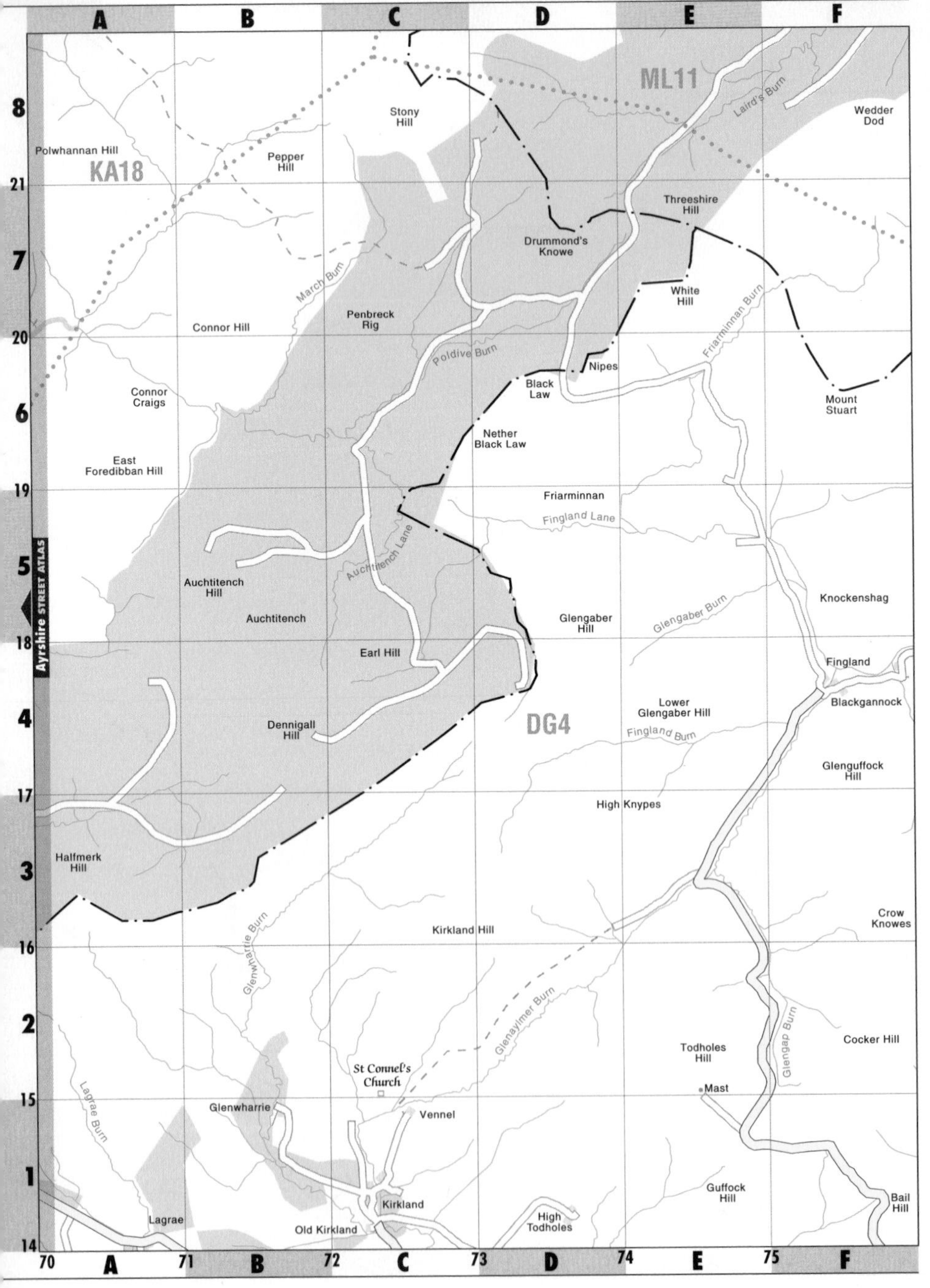
142
Scale: 1⅓ inches to 1 mile
0 ¼ ½ mile
0 250m 500m 750m 1 km
A B C D E F
8 21 7 20 6 19 5 18 4 17 3 16 2 15 1 14
70 71 72 73 74 75
ML11
KA18
DG4
Stony Hill
Polwhannan Hill
Pepper Hill
Wedder Dod
Laird's Burn
Threeshire Hill
Drummond's Knowe
March Burn
White Hill
Friarminnan Burn
Penbreck Rig
Connor Hill
Poldive Burn
Nipes
Black Law
Mount Stuart
Connor Craigs
Nether Black Law
East Foredibban Hill
Friarminnan
Fingland Lane
Auchtitench Lane
Auchtitench Hill
Auchtitench
Knockenshag
Glengaber Hill
Glengaber Burn
Earl Hill
Fingland
Blackgannock
Lower Glengaber Hill
Dennigall Hill
Fingland Burn
Glenguffock Hill
High Knypes
Halfmerk Hill
Crow Knowes
Kirkland Hill
Glenwharrie Burn
Glenaylmer Burn
Glengap Burn
Cocker Hill
Todholes Hill
St Connel's Church
Mast
Lagrae Burn
Glenwharrie
Vennel
Guffock Hill
Bail Hill
Kirkland
High Todholes
Lagrae
Old Kirkland
Ayrshire STREET ATLAS

Scale: 1⅓ inches to 1 mile

143
150

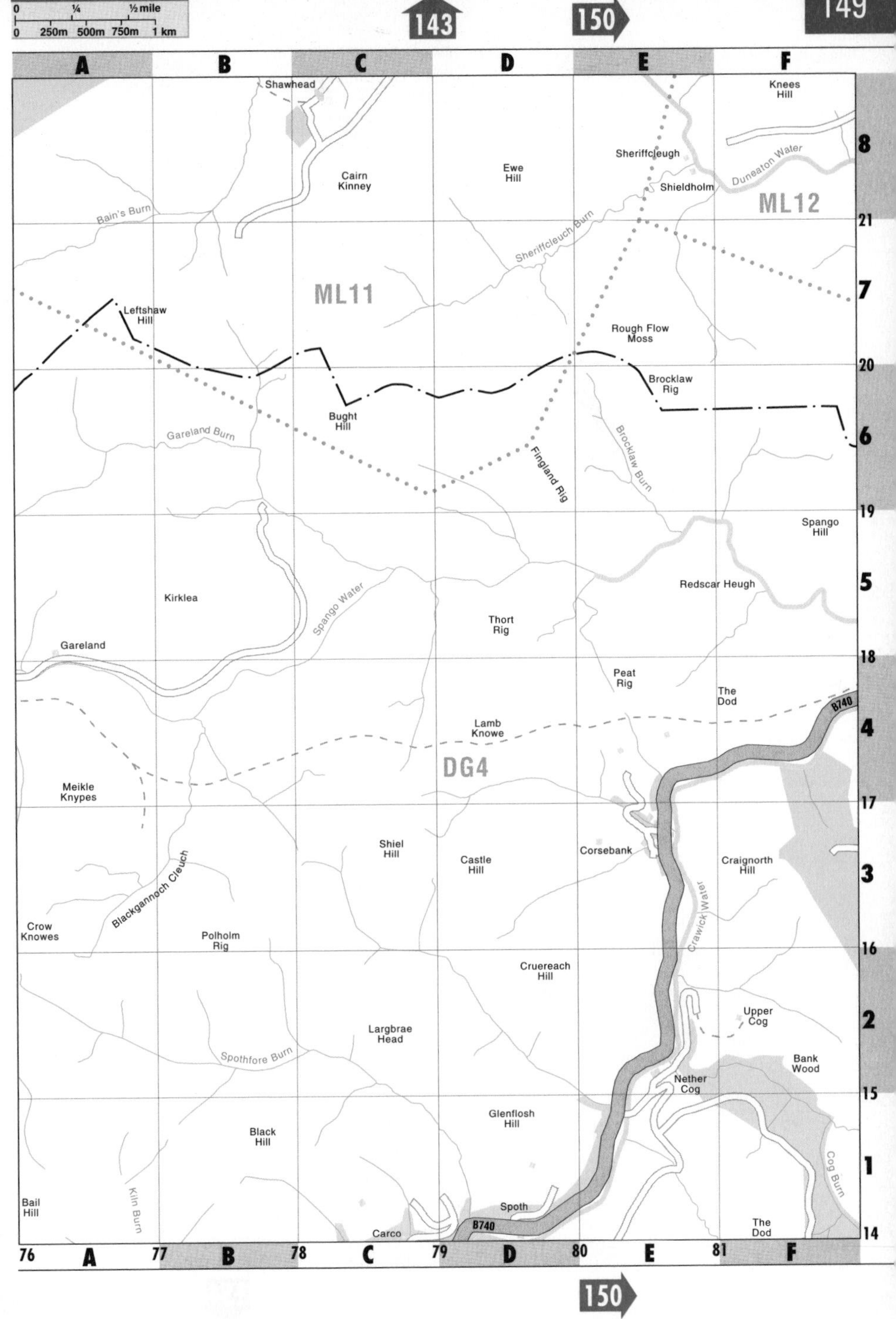

150

149
144

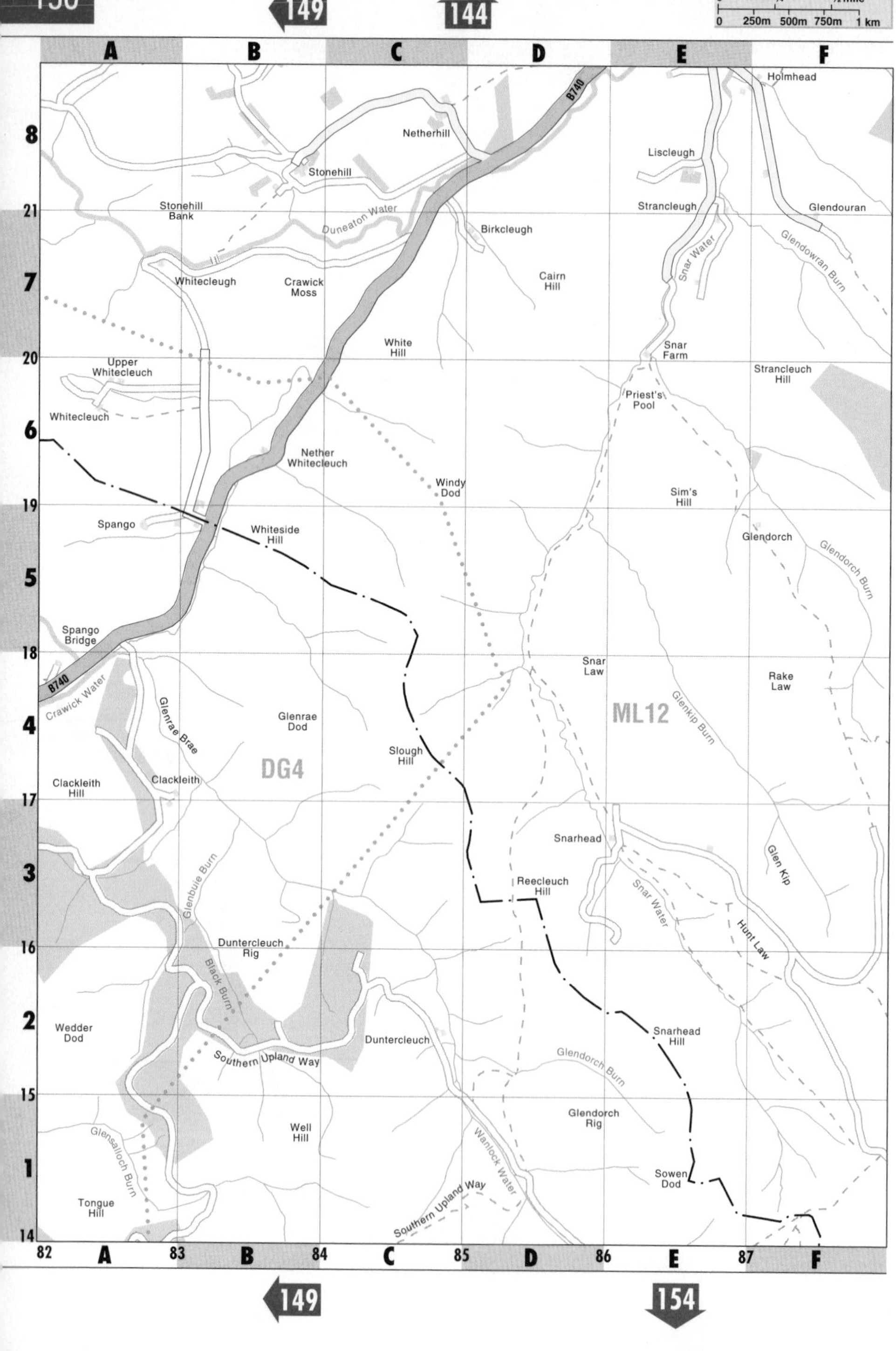

149
154

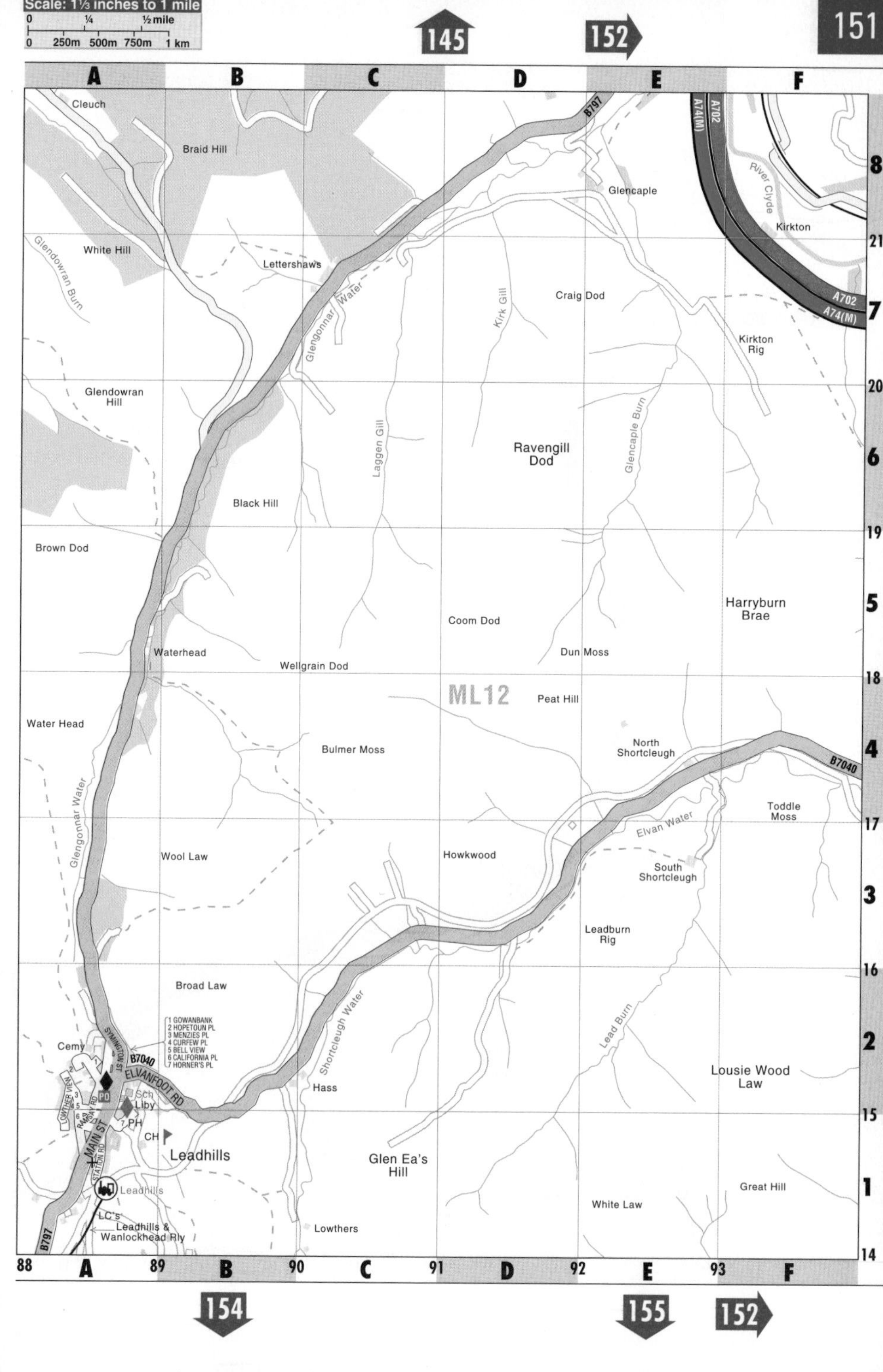
Scale: 1⅓ inches to 1 mile
0 ¼ ½ mile
0 250m 500m 750m 1 km
145
152
A B C D E F
8 21 7 20 6 19 5 18 4 17 3 16 2 15 1 14
Cleuch
Braid Hill
White Hill
Glendowran Burn
Lettershaws
Glengonnar Water
Glencaple
B797
A74(M)
A702
River Clyde
Kirkton
Kirk Gill
Craig Dod
Kirkton Rig
Glendowran Hill
Laggen Gill
Ravengill Dod
Glencaple Burn
Black Hill
Brown Dod
Coom Dod
Harryburn Brae
Waterhead
Wellgrain Dod
Dun Moss
ML12
Peat Hill
Water Head
Bulmer Moss
North Shortcleugh
B7040
Toddle Moss
Elvan Water
Wool Law
Howkwood
South Shortcleugh
Leadburn Rig
Broad Law
Shortcleugh Water
Lead Burn
Cemy
SYMINGTON ST
1 GOWANBANK
2 HOPETOUN PL
3 MENZIES PL
4 CURFEW PL
5 BELL VIEW
6 CALIFORNIA PL
7 HORNER'S PL
ELVANFOOT RD
PO
Sch
Liby
PH
CH
LOWTHER VIEW
RAMSAY RD
MAIN ST
STATION RD
Leadhills
Hass
Lousie Wood Law
Glen Ea's Hill
Great Hill
White Law
LC's
Leadhills & Wanlockhead Rly
Lowthers
88 89 90 91 92 93
154
155
152

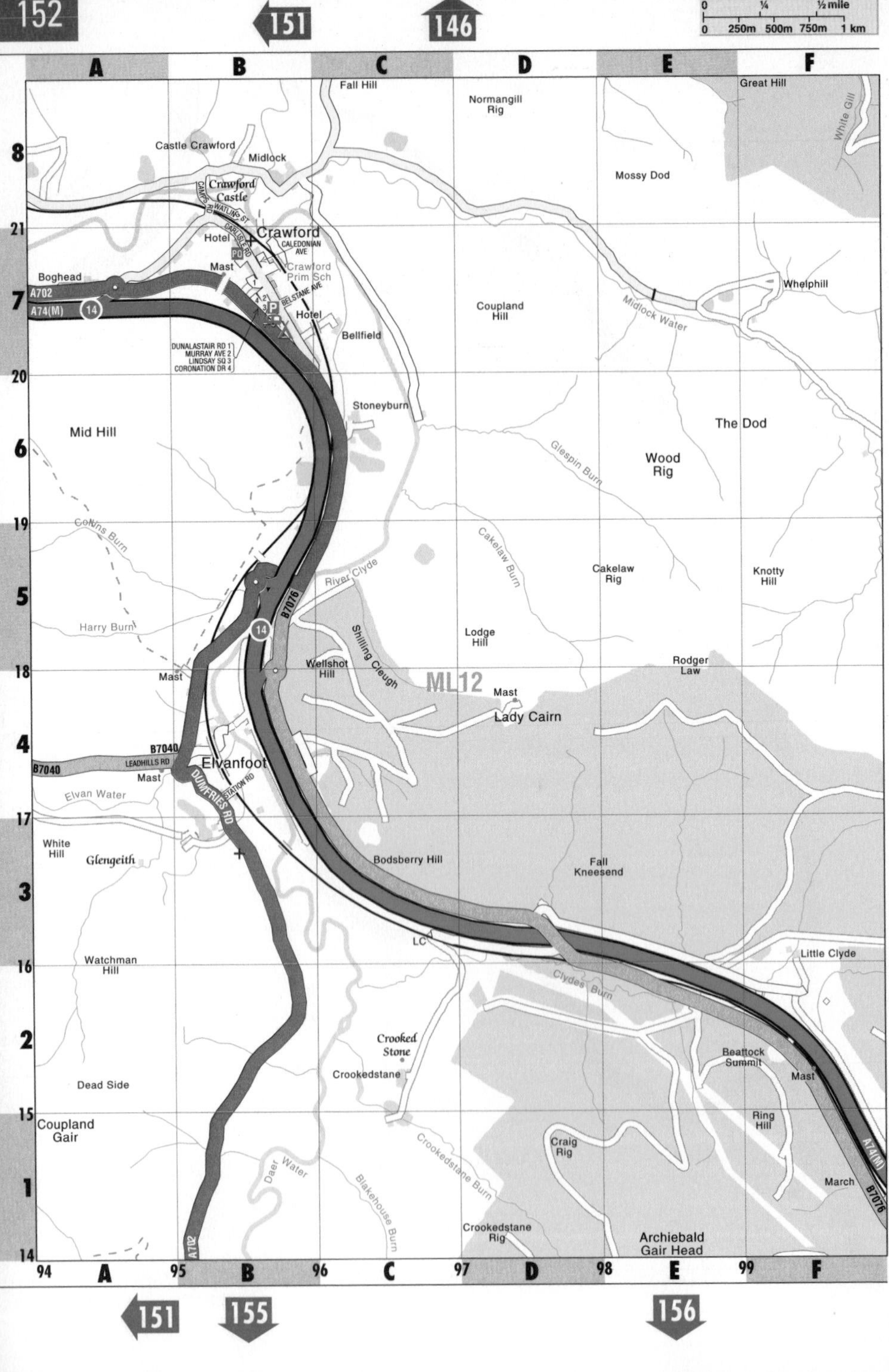
151
146
Scale: 1⅓ inches to 1 mile
0 ¼ ½ mile
0 250m 500m 750m 1 km
A B C D E F
Fall Hill
Normangill Rig
Great Hill
White Gill
Castle Crawford
Midlock
Mossy Dod
Crawford Castle
CAMPS RD
WATLING ST
Crawford
Hotel
CARLISLE RD
CALEDONIAN AVE
PO
Crawford Prim Sch
Boghead
Mast
A702
BELSTANE AVE
Whelphill
A74(M)
14
Hotel
Coupland Hill
Midlock Water
Bellfield
DUNALASTAIR RD 1
MURRAY AVE 2
LINDSAY SQ 3
CORONATION DR 4
Stoneyburn
Mid Hill
The Dod
Glespin Burn
Wood Rig
Collins Burn
Cakelaw Burn
Cakelaw Rig
Knotty Hill
River Clyde
B7076
Harry Burn
Shilling Cleugh
Lodge Hill
Rodger Law
Wellshot Hill
Mast
ML12
Mast
Lady Cairn
B7040
LEADHILLS RD
Elvanfoot
B7040
Mast
DUMFRIES RD
STATION RD
Elvan Water
White Hill
Glengeith
Bodsberry Hill
Fall Kneesend
LC
Little Clyde
Watchman Hill
Clydes Burn
Crooked Stone
Beattock Summit
Crookedstane
Mast
Dead Side
Ring Hill
Coupland Gair
Craig Rig
Crookedstane Burn
A74(M)
Daer Water
Blakehouse Burn
March
B7076
Crookedstane Rig
Archiebald Gair Head
A702
8 21 7 20 6 19 5 18 4 17 3 16 2 15 1 14
94 95 96 97 98 99

147

Scale: 1½ inches to 1 mile
0 ¼ ½ mile
0 250m 500m 750m 1 km
A B C D E F
Reeve Hill
Camps Resr
Campshead
Slate Brae
White Gill Wood
Midge Hill
Yearn Gill
Grip Shank
Petrifying Spring
Whitecamp Brae
Glenbreck Burn
Glenbreck
Peddirie Dod
A701 Penicuik (A72)
A701
Fore Brae
Great Hill
Risingclaw Burn
Wills Cleuch Head
Blackcleuch Burn
Whelphill Hope
Yearngill Head
Risingclaw Heights
Old Burn
Bank
Black Dod
Harecleuch
High Hogg Hill
Fingland
Broad Hill
Badlieu
ML12
Powskein Dod
River Tweed
Mid Hill
West Water
East Water
Badlieu Burn
Hare Cleuch Head
Badlieu Rig
Dun Law
Tweedhopefoot
Mast
Harleburn Head
Clyde Law
Pin Stane
Tippet Hill
Hazelbush Hill
Tweedhopefoot Rig
Smid Hope Burn
Clydes Burn
Middle Rig
Badenhay Rig
Nap Hill
Back Burn
Little Bog Hill
Upper Howecleuch
Fopperbeck Burn
The Rig
DG10
Bog Hill
P
Tweed's Well (source of River Tweed)
Williemont Hass
Errickstane Hill
Rowantree Grains
M74
B7076
8 21 7 20 6 19 5 18 4 17 3 16 2 15 1 14
00 01 02 03 04 05

156
157

150
151

Scale: 1⅓ inches to 1 mile
0 ¼ ½ mile
0 250m 500m 750m 1 km

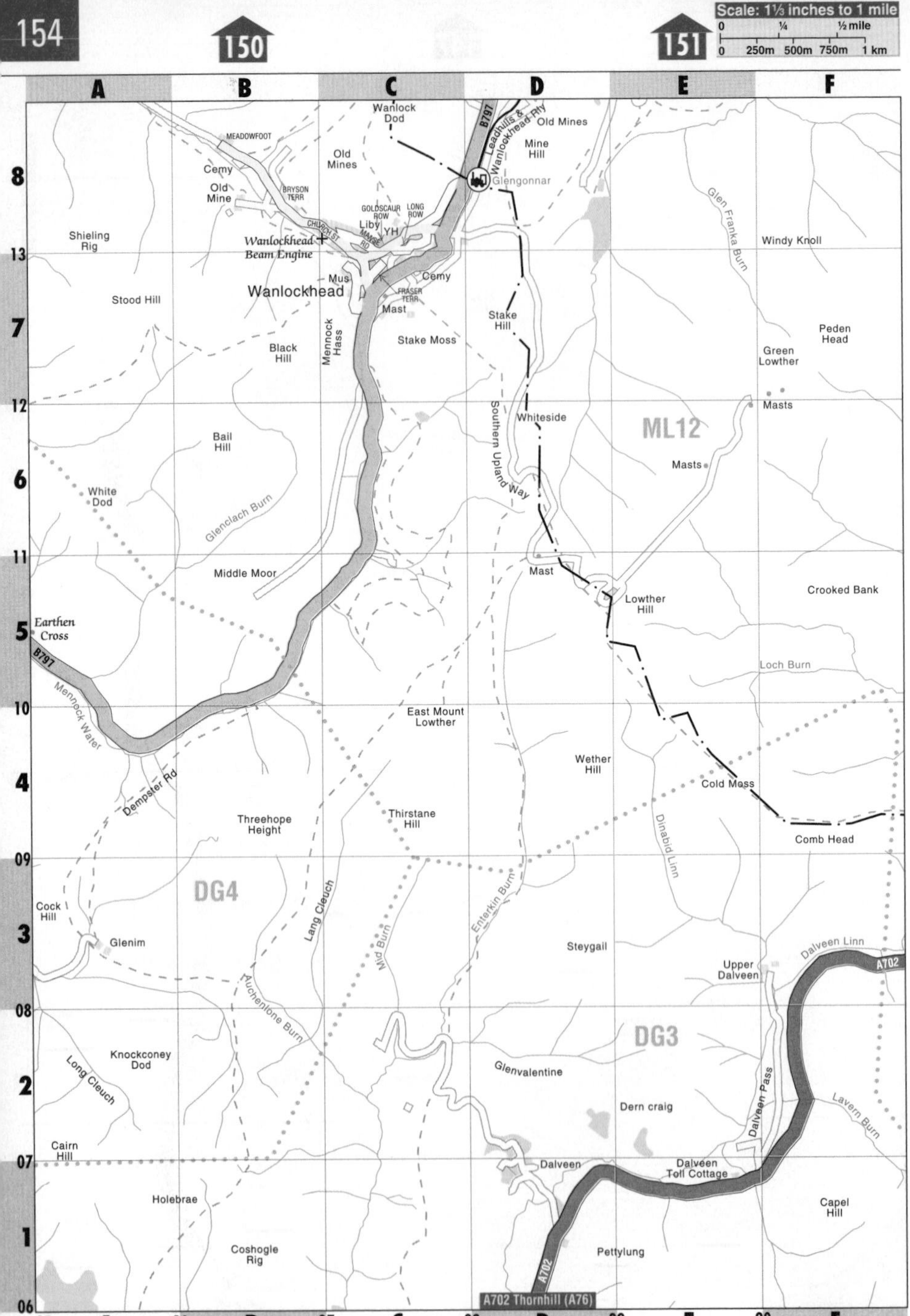

158

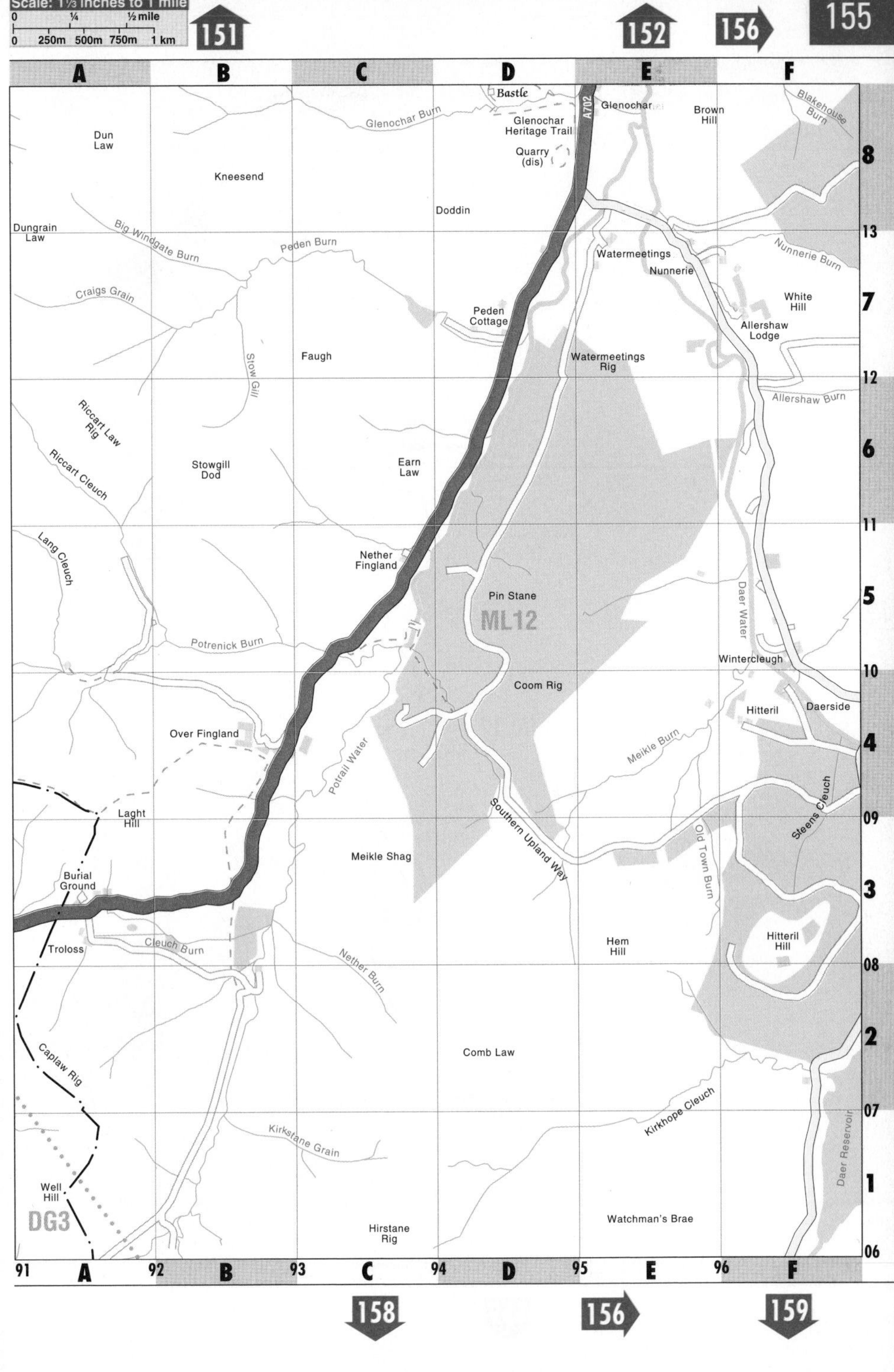

Scale: 1⅓ inches to 1 mile
0 ¼ ½ mile
0 250m 500m 750m 1 km
151
152
156
A B C D E F
Bastle
Glenochar Burn
Glenochar
Glenochar Heritage Trail
A702
Brown Hill
Blakehouse Burn
Dun Law
Kneesend
Quarry (dis)
Doddin
Dungrain Law
Big Windgate Burn
Peden Burn
Watermeetings
Nunnerie
Nunnerie Burn
Craigs Grain
White Hill
Peden Cottage
Allershaw Lodge
Stow Gill
Faugh
Watermeetings Rig
Allershaw Burn
Riccart Law Rig
Riccart Cleuch
Stowgill Dod
Earn Law
Lang Cleuch
Nether Fingland
Pin Stane
Daer Water
ML12
Potrenick Burn
Wintercleugh
Coom Rig
Hitteril
Daerside
Over Fingland
Meikle Burn
Potrail Water
Steens Cleuch
Laght Hill
Southern Upland Way
Old Town Burn
Meikle Shag
Burial Ground
Troloss
Cleuch Burn
Hem Hill
Hitteril Hill
Nether Burn
Caplaw Rig
Comb Law
Kirkhope Cleuch
Kirkstane Grain
Daer Reservoir
Well Hill
DG3
Hirstane Rig
Watchman's Brae
8
13
7
12
6
11
5
10
4
09
3
08
2
07
1
06
91
92
93
94
95
96
A B C D E F
158
156
159

152
153

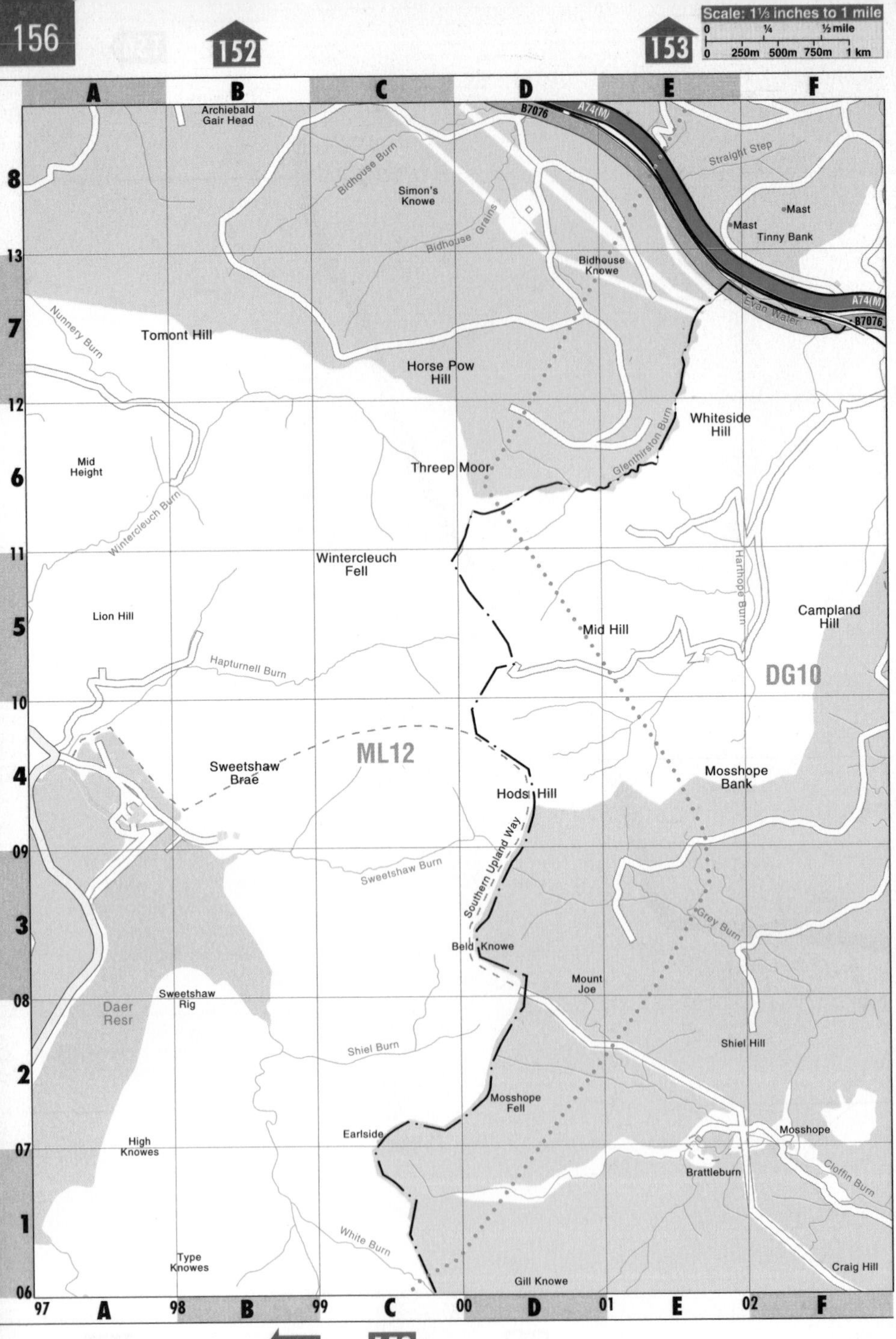

155
159

Scale: 1⅓ inches to 1 mile

153

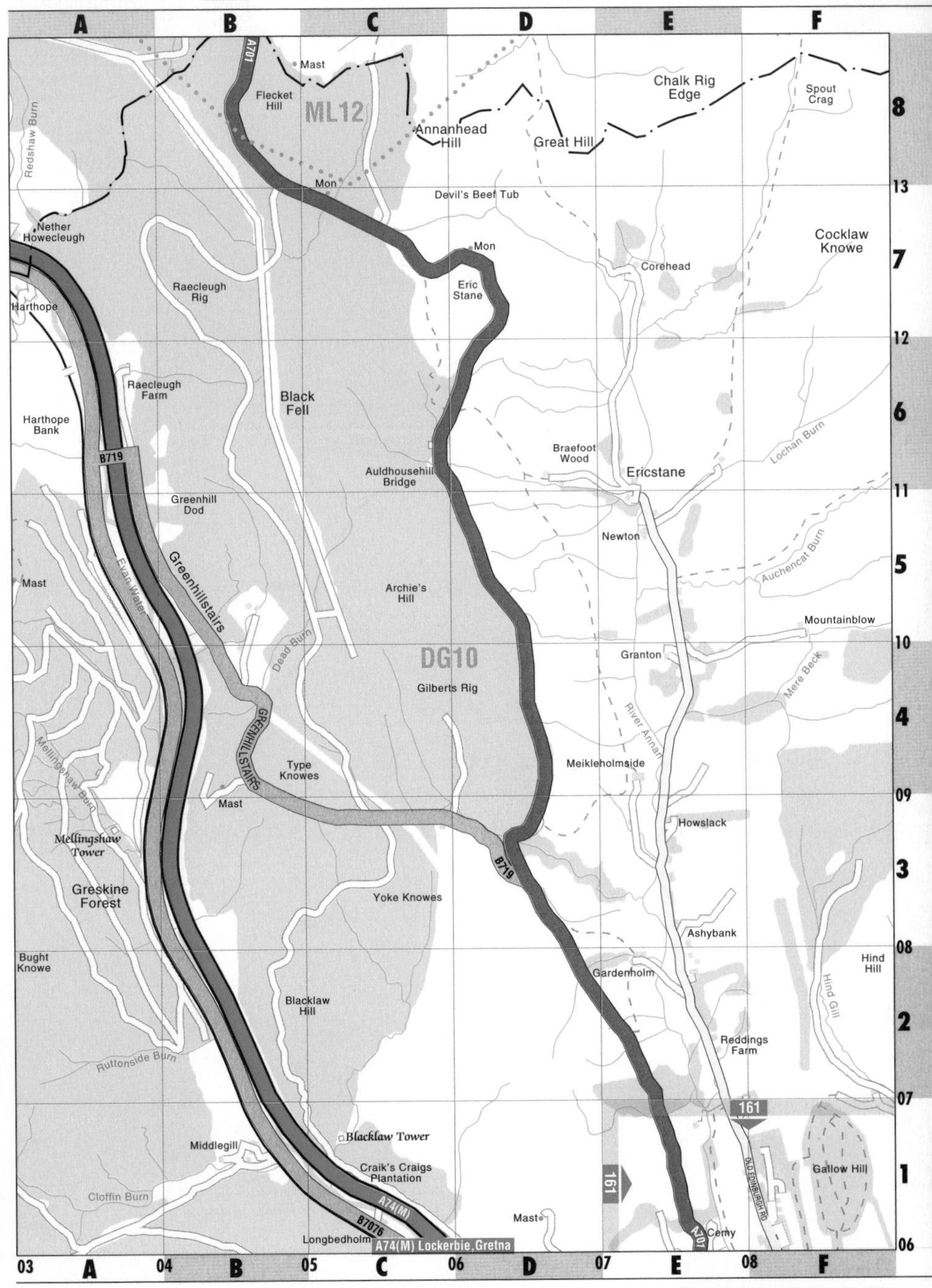

For full street detail of the highlighted area see page 161.

154

155

Scale: 1⅓ inches to 1 mile
0 ¼ ½ mile
0 250m 500m 750m 1 km

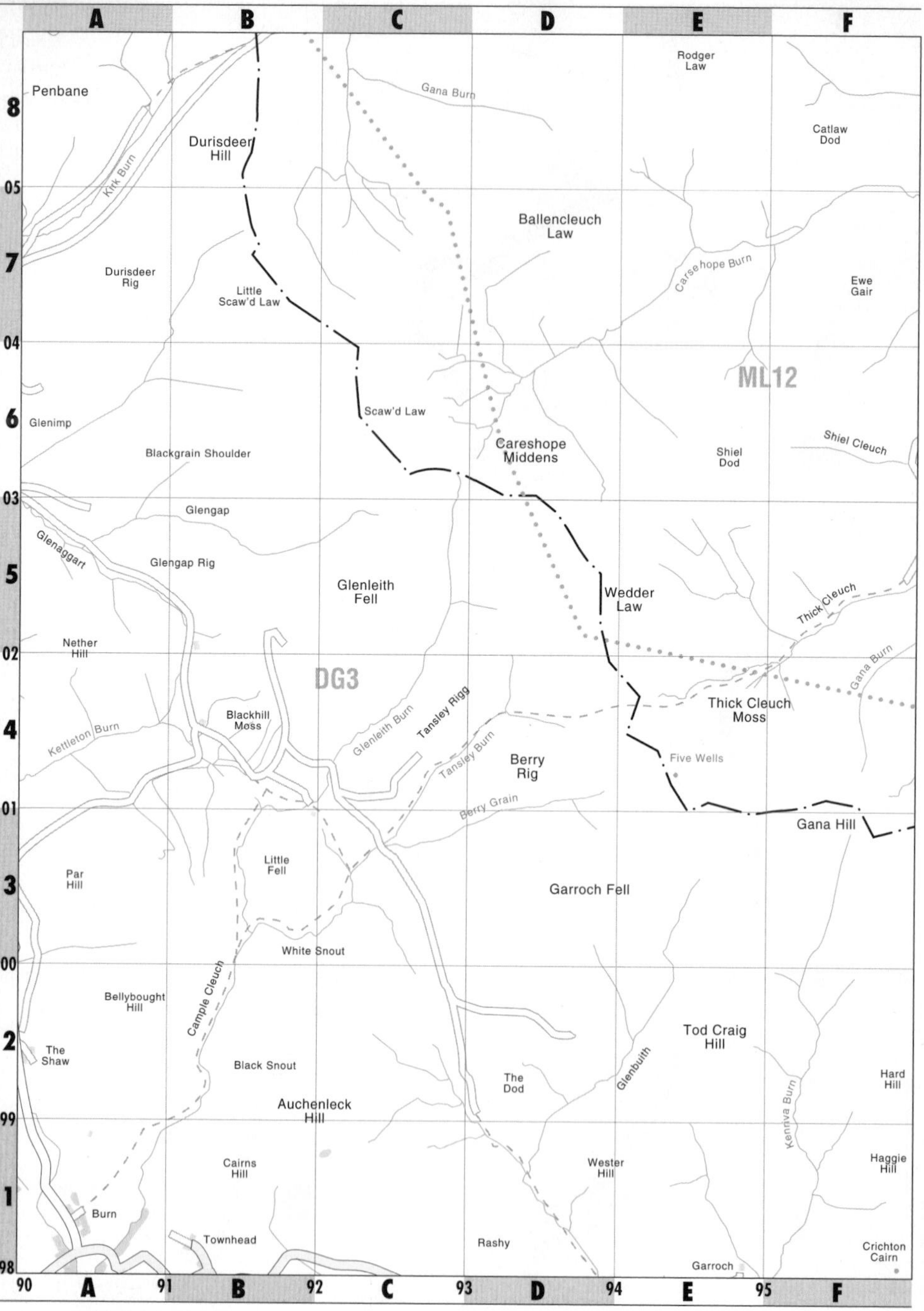

A B C D E F

8 05 7 04 6 03 5 02 4 01 3 00 2 99 1 98

Penbane
Kirk Burn
Durisdeer Hill
Gana Burn
Rodger Law
Catlaw Dod
Ballencleuch Law
Durisdeer Rig
Little Scaw'd Law
Carsehope Burn
Ewe Gair
ML12
Glenimp
Scaw'd Law
Careshope Middens
Shiel Dod
Shiel Cleuch
Blackgrain Shoulder
Glengap
Glenaggart
Glengap Rig
Glenleith Fell
Wedder Law
Thick Cleuch
Nether Hill
DG3
Gana Burn
Thick Cleuch Moss
Blackhill Moss
Kettleton Burn
Glenleith Burn
Tansley Rigg
Tansley Burn
Berry Rig
Five Wells
Berry Grain
Gana Hill
Par Hill
Little Fell
Garroch Fell
White Snout
Bellybought Hill
Campte Cleuch
The Shaw
Black Snout
Tod Craig Hill
The Dod
Glenbuith
Kenniva Burn
Hard Hill
Auchenleck Hill
Cairns Hill
Wester Hill
Haggie Hill
Burn
Townhead
Rashy
Garroch
Crichton Cairn

90 A 91 B 92 C 93 D 94 E 95 F

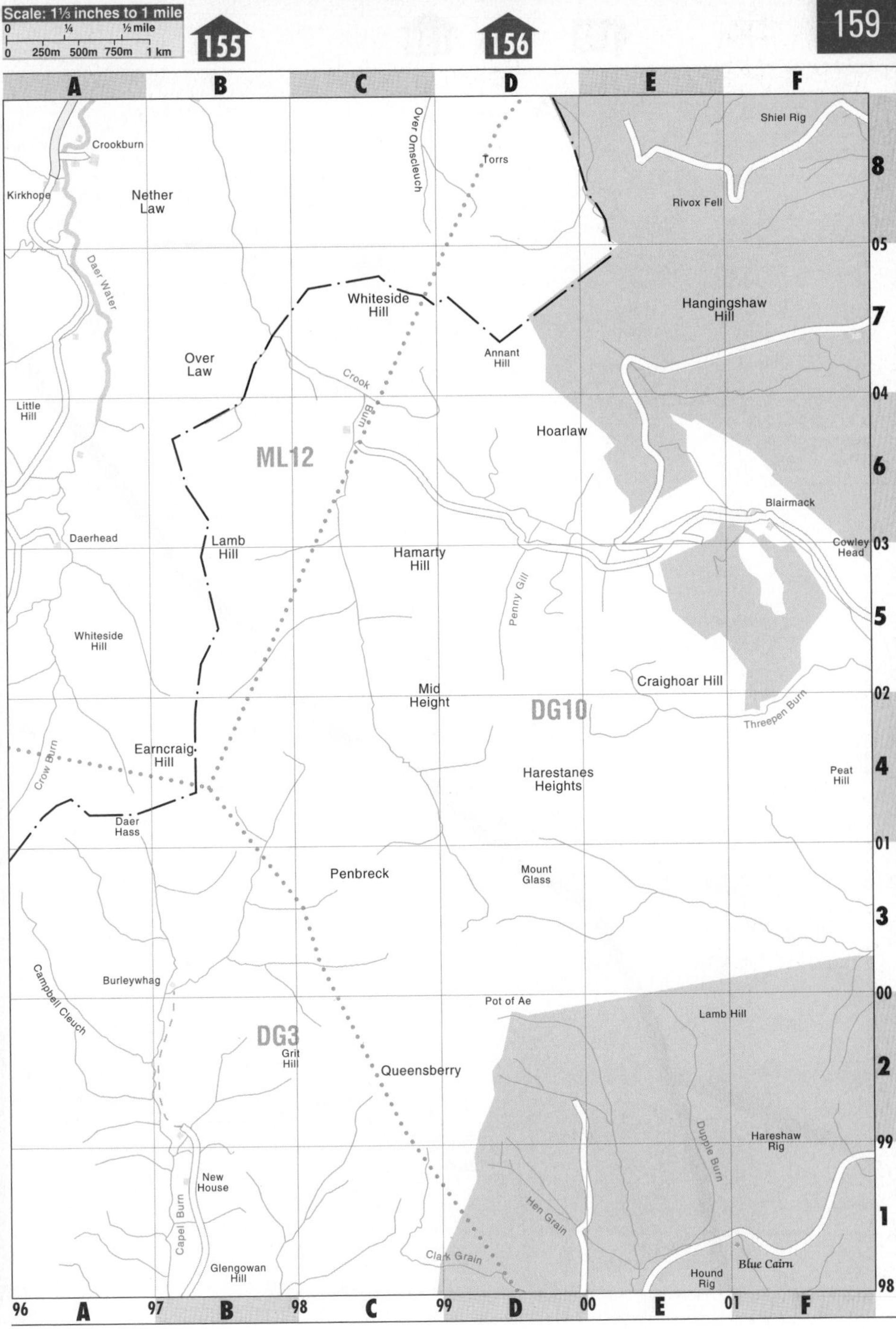

Scale: 1⅓ inches to 1 mile
0 ¼ ½ mile
0 250m 500m 750m 1 km
155
156
A
B
C
D
E
F
Crookburn
Kirkhope
Nether Law
Over Ormscleuch
Torrs
Shiel Rig
Rivox Fell
8
05
Daer Water
Whiteside Hill
Hangingshaw Hill
7
Annant Hill
Over Law
Crook Burn
04
Little Hill
Hoarlaw
ML12
6
Blairmack
Daerhead
Lamb Hill
Hamarty Hill
Cowley Head
03
Penny Gill
5
Whiteside Hill
Craighoar Hill
Mid Height
DG10
02
Threepen Burn
Crow Burn
Earncraig Hill
Harestanes Heights
Peat Hill
4
Daer Hass
01
Penbreck
Mount Glass
3
Campbell Cleuch
Burleywhag
00
Pot of Ae
Lamb Hill
DG3
Grit Hill
Queensberry
2
Dupple Burn
Hareshaw Rig
99
New House
Hen Grain
1
Capel Burn
Clark Grain
Blue Cairn
Glengowan Hill
Hound Rig
98
96
97
98
99
00
01

132
132

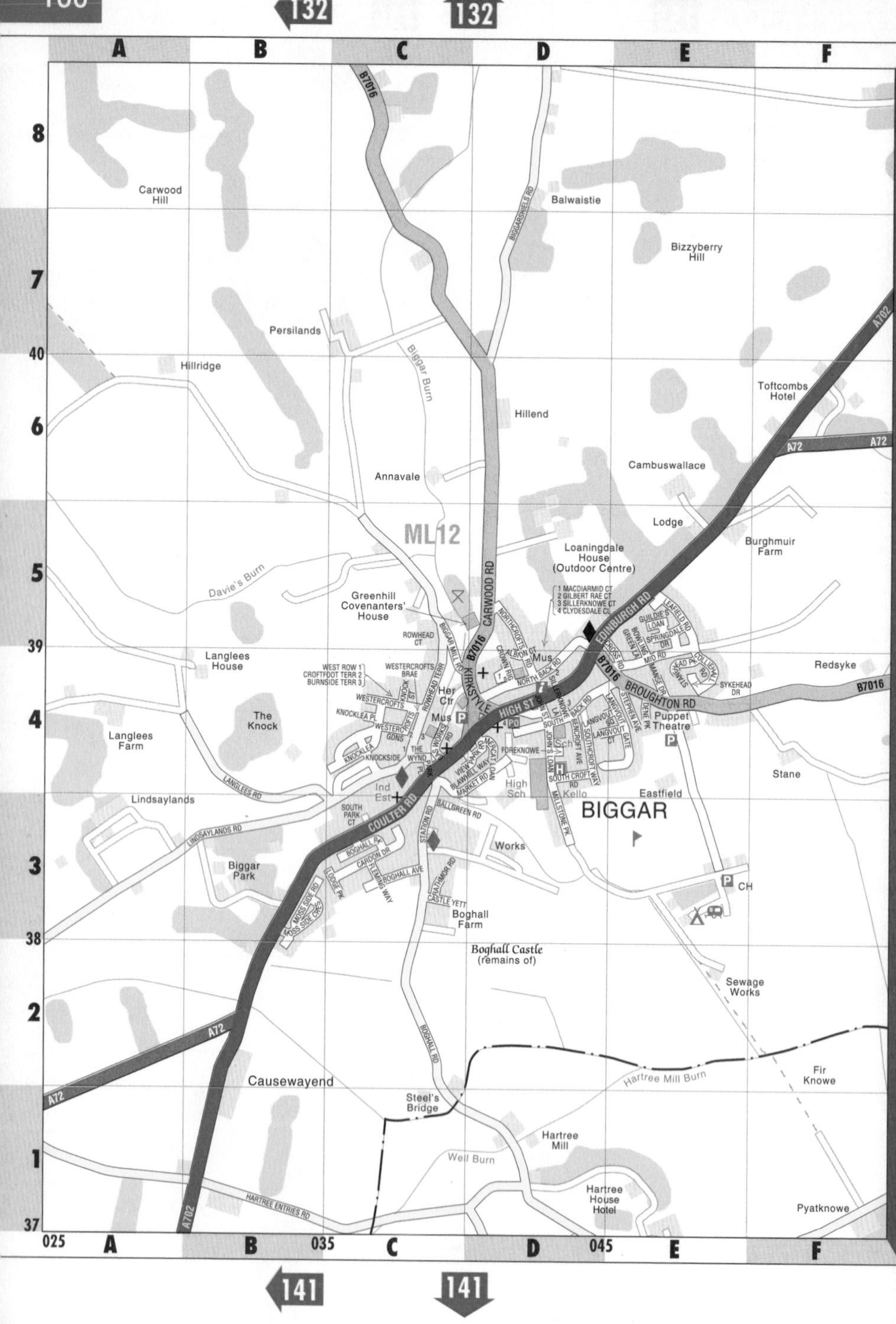

141
141

157
157

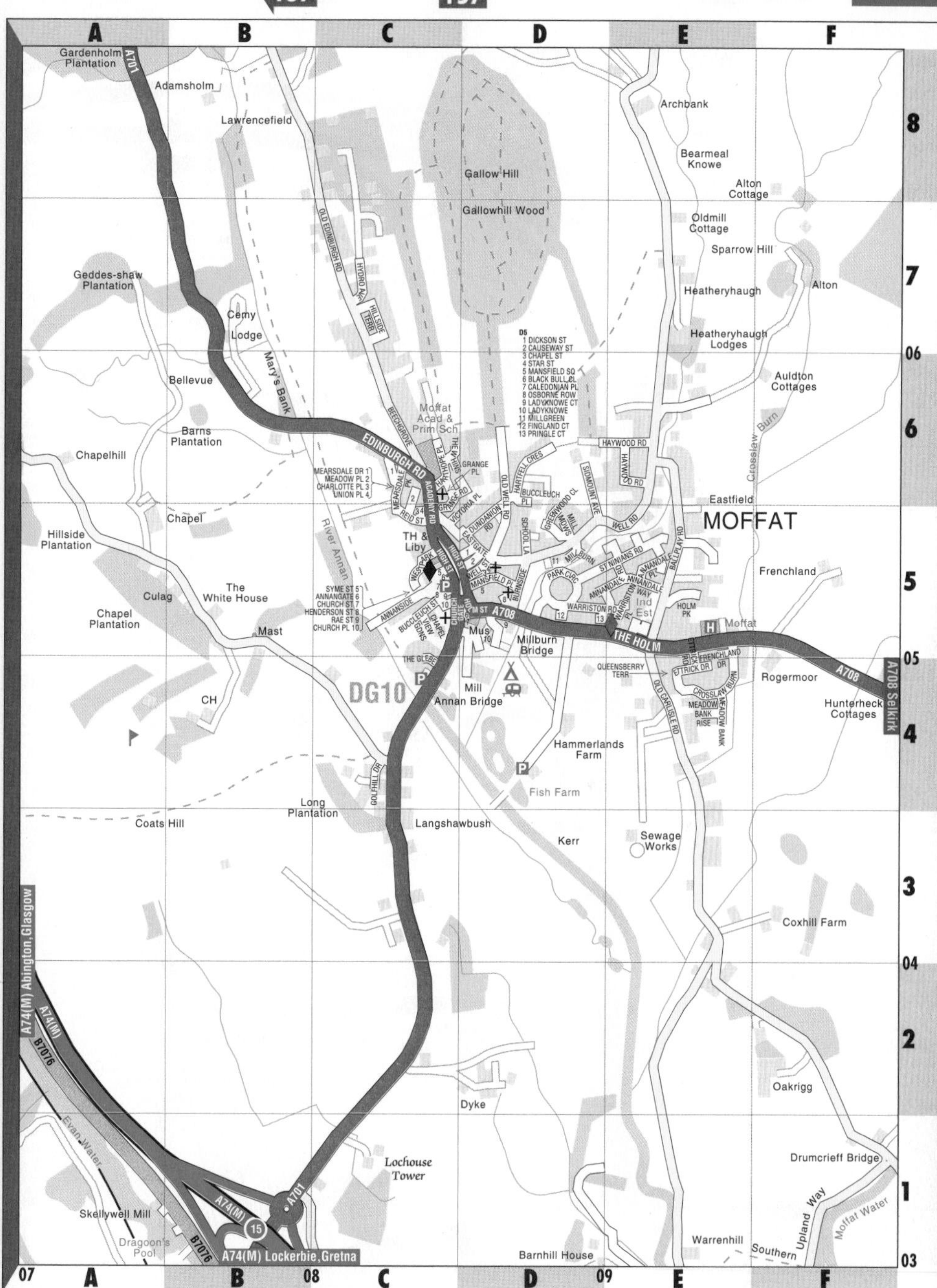
A
B
C
D
E
F
Gardenholm Plantation
A701
Adamsholm
Lawrencefield
Archbank
Bearmeal Knowe
Gallow Hill
Gallowhill Wood
Alton Cottage
Oldmill Cottage
Sparrow Hill
OLD EDINBURGH RD
HYDRO AV
HILLSIDE TERR
Geddes-shaw Plantation
Heatheryhaugh
Alton
Cemy Lodge
Heatheryhaugh Lodges
D5
1 DICKSON ST
2 CAUSEWAY ST
3 CHAPEL ST
4 STAR ST
5 MANSFIELD SQ
6 BLACK BULL CL
7 CALEDONIAN PL
8 OSBORNE ROW
9 LADYKNOWE CT
10 LADYKNOWE
11 MILLGREEN
12 FINGLAND CT
13 PRINGLE CT
Mary's Bank
Bellevue
Auldton Cottages
Moffat Acad & Prim Sch
Barns Plantation
EDINBURGH RD
HAYWOOD RD
Crosslaw Burn
Chapelhill
MEARSDALE DR 1
MEADOW PL 2
CHARLOTTE PL 3
UNION PL 4
Eastfield
MOFFAT
Chapel
Hillside Plantation
River Annan
TH & Liby
Frenchland
The White House
Culag
Chapel Plantation
SYME ST 5
ANNANGATE 6
CHURCH ST 7
HENDERSON ST 8
RAE ST 9
CHURCH PL 10
Mast
Mus
Millburn Bridge
A708
THE HOLM
Moffat
QUEENSBERRY TERR
Rogermoor
A708 Selkirk
Hunterheck Cottages
DG10
Mill
Annan Bridge
CH
Hammerlands Farm
Fish Farm
Long Plantation
Coats Hill
Langshawbush
Kerr
Sewage Works
Coxhill Farm
A74(M) Abington,Glasgow
B7076
Oakrigg
Dyke
Evan Water
Lochouse Tower
Drumcrieff Bridge
Skellywell Mill
Dragoon's Pool
A74(M) Lockerbie,Gretna
15
Warrenhill
Southern Upland Way
Moffat Water
Barnhill House
8
7
06
6
5
05
4
3
04
2
1
03
07
08
09

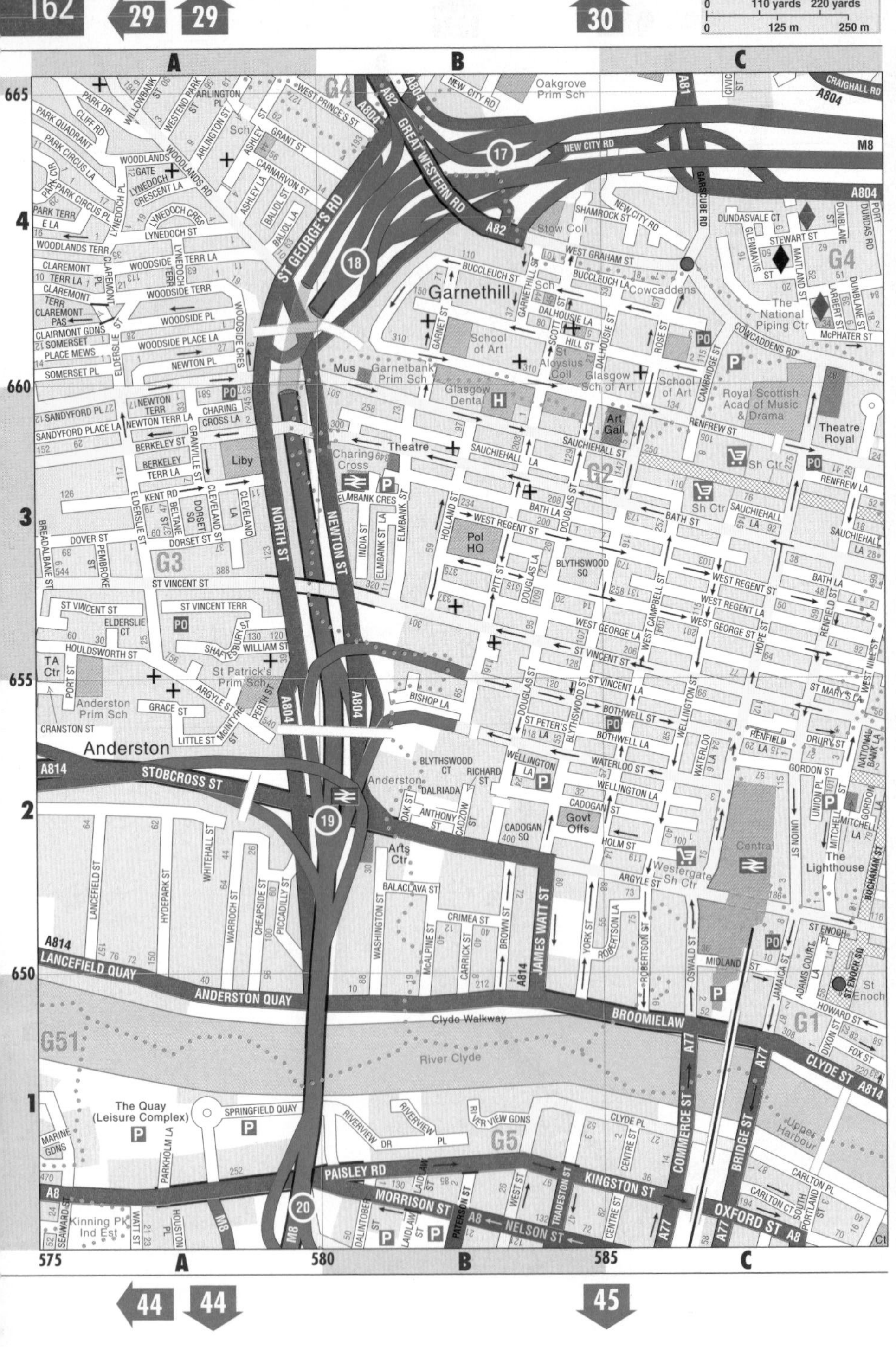

162
29
29
30
Scale: 5⅓ inches to 1 mile
0 110 yards 220 yards
0 125 m 250 m
A
B
C
665
660
655
650
4
3
2
1
575
580
585
44
44
45
Garnethill
Anderston
G4
G3
G2
G1
G5
G51
Oakgrove Prim Sch
Stow Coll
School of Art
Garnetbank Prim Sch
Glasgow Dental
St Aloysius Coll
Glasgow Sch of Art
Art Gall
Royal Scottish Acad of Music & Drama
Theatre Royal
The National Piping Ctr
Cowcaddens
Charing Cross
Theatre
Mus
Liby
Sh Ctr
Pol HQ
St Patrick's Prim Sch
Anderston Prim Sch
TA Ctr
Arts Ctr
Govt Offs
Central
The Lighthouse
Westergate Sh Ctr
St Enoch
Clyde Walkway
River Clyde
The Quay (Leisure Complex)
Upper Harbour
Kinning Pk Ind Est
M8
A804
A82
A81
A814
A8
A77
ST GEORGE'S RD
GREAT WESTERN RD
NEW CITY RD
NORTH ST
NEWTON ST
WOODLANDS RD
ST VINCENT ST
SAUCHIEHALL ST
RENFREW ST
BATH ST
WEST REGENT ST
WEST GEORGE ST
BOTHWELL ST
WATERLOO ST
ARGYLE ST
STOBCROSS ST
LANCEFIELD QUAY
ANDERSTON QUAY
BROOMIELAW
CLYDE ST
JAMES WATT ST
HOPE ST
WEST CAMPBELL ST
WELLINGTON ST
DOUGLAS ST
BLYTHSWOOD SQ
CAMBRIDGE ST
COWCADDENS RD
GARSCUBE RD
PAISLEY RD
KINGSTON ST
MORRISON ST
NELSON ST
COMMERCE ST
BRIDGE ST
OXFORD ST
SPRINGFIELD QUAY
UNION ST
BUCHANAN ST

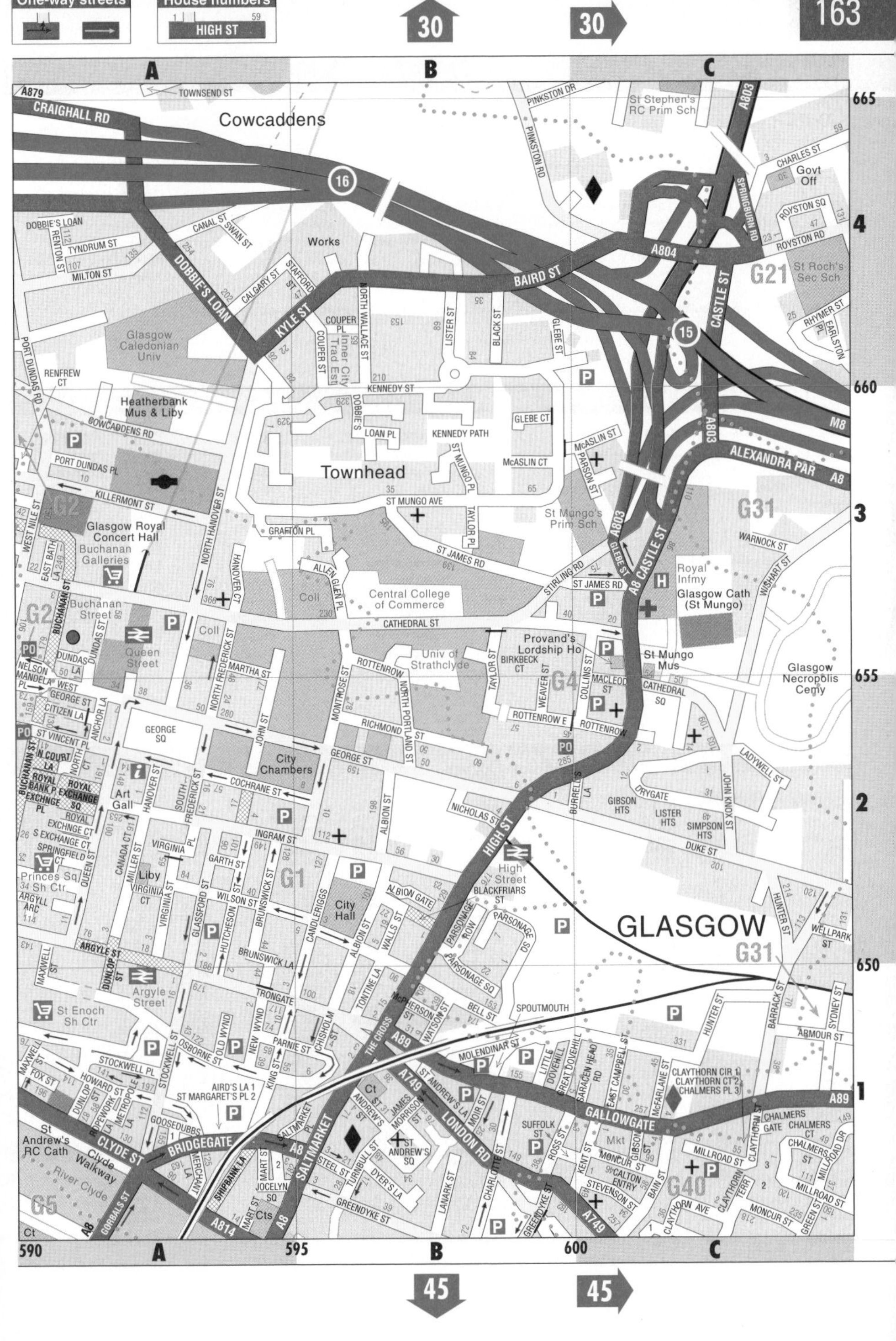
One-way streets
House numbers
HIGH ST
30
30
A
B
C
665
660
655
650
4
3
2
1
Cowcaddens
CRAIGHALL RD
A879
TOWNSEND ST
PINKSTON DR
PINKSTON RD
St Stephen's RC Prim Sch
A803
CHARLES ST
Govt Off
ROYSTON SQ
ROYSTON RD
SPRINGBURN RD
St Roch's Sec Sch
G21
RHYMER ST
EARLSTON PL
16
15
Works
DOBBIE'S LOAN
RENTON ST
TYNDRUM ST
MILTON ST
CANAL ST
SWAN ST
CALGARY ST
STAFFORD ST
KYLE ST
BAIRD ST
A804
CASTLE ST
COUPER PL
COUPER ST
NORTH WALLACE ST
Inner City Trad Est
LISTER ST
BLACK ST
GLEBE ST
Glasgow Caledonian Univ
PORT DUNDAS RD
RENFREW CT
Heatherbank Mus & Liby
COWCADDENS RD
PORT DUNDAS PL
KILLERMONT ST
KENNEDY ST
DOBBIE'S LOAN PL
KENNEDY PATH
GLEBE CT
McASLIN ST
McASLIN CT
PARSON ST
ST MUNGO PL
Townhead
M8
ALEXANDRA PAR
A8
G2
G31
WEST NILE ST
EAST BATH LA
Glasgow Royal Concert Hall
Buchanan Galleries
NORTH HANOVER ST
GRAFTON PL
ST MUNGO AVE
TAYLOR PL
St Mungo's Prim Sch
ST JAMES RD
ALLEN GLEN PL
HANOVER CT
Coll
Central College of Commerce
STIRLING RD
A8 CASTLE ST
Royal Infmy
Glasgow Cath (St Mungo)
WARNOCK ST
WISHART ST
BUCHANAN ST
Buchanan Street
DUNDAS ST
Queen Street
CATHEDRAL ST
Provand's Lordship Ho
St Mungo Mus
Univ of Strathclyde
NORTH FREDERICK ST
MARTHA ST
ROTTENROW
NORTH PORTLAND ST
BIRKBECK CT
TAYLOR ST
WEAVER ST
COLLINS ST
MACLEOD ST
G4
Glasgow Necropolis Cemy
NELSON MANDELA PL
DUNDAS LA
GEORGE ST
CITIZEN LA
ST VINCENT PL
ANCHOR LA
GEORGE SQ
JOHN ST
MONTROSE ST
RICHMOND ST
ROTTENROW E
City Chambers
NORTH CT
ROYAL BANK PL
ROYAL EXCHANGE SQ
EXCHNGE PL
HANOVER ST
SOUTH FREDERICK ST
COCHRANE ST
Art Gall
DRYGATE
GIBSON HTS
LISTER HTS
SIMPSON HTS
JOHN KNOX ST
LADYWELL ST
NICHOLAS ST
ALBION ST
INGRAM ST
HIGH ST
DUKE ST
S EXCHANGE CT
SPRINGFIELD CT
Princes Sq Sh Ctr
ARGYLL ARC
QUEEN ST
CANADA CT
MILLER ST
VIRGINIA PL
Liby
VIRGINIA ST
VIRGINIA CT
GARTH ST
WILSON ST
GLASSFORD ST
HUTCHESON ST
BRUNSWICK ST
G1
CANDLERIGGS
City Hall
ALBION GATE
High Street
BLACKFRIARS ST
PARSONAGE ROW
PARSONAGE SQ
GLASGOW
HUNTER ST
WELLPARK ST
ARGYLE ST
MAXWELL ST
DUNLOP ST
Argyle Street
BRUNSWICK LA
WALLS ST
TONTINE LA
TRONGATE
BELL ST
SPOUTMOUTH
St Enoch Sh Ctr
OLD WYND
NEW WYND
PARNIE ST
CHISHOLM ST
McPHERSON ST
WATSON ST
BARRACK ST
SYDNEY ST
ARMOUR ST
STOCKWELL ST
OSBORNE ST
KING ST
THE CROSS
A89
MOLENDINAR ST
LITTLE DOVEHILL
GREAT DOVEHILL
SARACEN HEAD RD
EAST CAMPBELL ST
McFARLANE ST
CLAYTHORN CIR
CLAYTHORN CT
CHALMERS PL
FOX ST
HOWARD ST
STOCKWELL PL
AIRD'S LA
ST MARGARET'S PL
A749
ST ANDREW'S LA
MOIR ST
LONDON RD
GALLOWGATE
CHALMERS GATE
CHALMERS CT
CHALMERS ST
DUNLOP ST
ROPEWORK LA
METROPOLE LA
GOOSEDUBBS
BRIDGEGATE
SALTMARKET
ST ANDREW'S ST
JAMES MORRISON ST
Ct
ST ANDREW'S SQ
SUFFOLK ST
ROSS ST
KENT ST
Mkt
MONCUR ST
CALTON ENTRY
GIBSON ST
BAIN ST
MILLROAD ST
CLAYTHORN ST
MILLROAD DR
St Andrew's RC Cath
CLYDE ST
Clyde Walkway
River Clyde
MERCHANT LA
SHIPBANK LA
MART ST
STEEL ST
TURNBULL ST
DYER'S LA
LANARK ST
CHARLOTTE ST
GREENDYKE ST
STEVENSON ST
G40
CLAYTHORN AVE
CLAYTHORN TERR
MONCUR ST
GREEN ST
JOCELYN SQ
Cts
G5
GORBALS ST
A814
590
595
600
45
45

Index

Church Rd 6 Beckenham BR2.......... **53** C6

Place name
May be abbreviated on the map

Location number
Present when a number indicates the place's position in a crowded area of mapping

Locality, town or village
Shown when more than one place has the same name

Postcode district
District for the indexed place

Page and grid square
Page number and grid reference for the standard mapping

Public and commercial buildings are highlighted in magenta **Places of interest** are highlighted in blue with a star★

Abbreviations used in the index

Acad	**Academy**	Comm	**Common**	Gd	**Ground**	L	**Leisure**	Prom	**Promenade**
App	**Approach**	Cott	**Cottage**	Gdn	**Garden**	La	**Lane**	Rd	**Road**
Arc	**Arcade**	Cres	**Crescent**	Gn	**Green**	Liby	**Library**	Recn	**Recreation**
Ave	**Avenue**	Cswy	**Causeway**	Gr	**Grove**	Mdw	**Meadow**	Ret	**Retail**
Bglw	**Bungalow**	Ct	**Court**	H	**Hall**	Meml	**Memorial**	Sh	**Shopping**
Bldg	**Building**	Ctr	**Centre**	Ho	**House**	Mkt	**Market**	Sq	**Square**
Bsns, Bus	**Business**	Ctry	**Country**	Hospl	**Hospital**	Mus	**Museum**	St	**Street**
Bvd	**Boulevard**	Cty	**County**	HQ	**Headquarters**	Orch	**Orchard**	Sta	**Station**
Cath	**Cathedral**	Dr	**Drive**	Hts	**Heights**	Pal	**Palace**	Terr	**Terrace**
Cir	**Circus**	Dro	**Drove**	Ind	**Industrial**	Par	**Parade**	TH	**Town Hall**
Cl	**Close**	Ed	**Education**	Inst	**Institute**	Pas	**Passage**	Univ	**University**
Cnr	**Corner**	Emb	**Embankment**	Int	**International**	Pk	**Park**	Wk, Wlk	**Walk**
Coll	**College**	Est	**Estate**	Intc	**Interchange**	Pl	**Place**	Wr	**Water**
Com	**Community**	Ex	**Exhibition**	Junc	**Junction**	Prec	**Precinct**	Yd	**Yard**

Index of localities, towns and villages

A

Abington **145** E2
Abronhill **12** E4
Acre **17** B1
Airdrie **51** B8
Allanton
Hamilton **79** D1
Wishaw **83** A8
Anderston **162** A2
Annathill **22** F1
Anniesland **28** E6
Arden **58** E4
Armadale **41** E5
Arthurlie **57** B1
Ashgill **106** F8
Auchenback **57** D1
Auchengray **122** F1
Auchenheath **114** D4
Auchenreoch **9** B5
Auchenshuggle **47** A2
Auchentibber **77** A2
Auchentorlie **42** B4
Auchinairn **31** A8
Auchinloch **20** D2
Auldhouse **88** D1

B

Baillieston **48** A4
Balloch **11** C2
Balmalloch **6** C1
Balmore **18** E8
Balornock **31** C6
Bankhead **60** F6
Banknock **8** E3
Banton **7** E3
Barbauchlaw **41** E7
Bardowie **18** B7
Bargeddie **49** A4
Barlanark **47** E6
Barleybank **20** D8
Barmulloch **31** D4
Barnhill **77** B8
Barrachnie **47** E4
Barrhead **57** E2
Barrowfield
Coatbridge **50** A4
Glasgow **46** B5
Barrwood **10** E8
Bathville **41** E4
Battlefield **60** A7
Bearsden **16** E6
Bellahouston **44** A4
Bellfield **138** A6
Bellshill **65** B4
Bellside **67** E1
Biggar **160** D3
Biggar Road **66** F5
Birkenshaw **48** F1
Birniehill **89** A7
Bishopbriggs **19** B3
Blackhall **42** B3
Blackhill **31** D2
Blackridge **40** C3
Blackwood
Cumbernauld **10** E2
Kirkmuirhill **114** B4
Blairdardie **16** B1
Blairhill **49** E6
Blantyre **77** D7
Blantyre Muir **89** E6
Blythswood **27** C5
Boghead
Kirkintilloch **20** A4
Kirkmuirhill **113** D1
Bonkle **82** C6
Bothwell **64** B2
Bowerwalls **57** E4
Brackenhirst **35** D5
Braedale **79** C6
Braehead
Douglas **137** F5
Forth **124** B5
Thorntonhall **74** D3
Braidfauld **46** E3
Braidwood **108** F4
Breich **122** C7
Broadwood **10** F1
Brocketsbrae **120** A4
Broom **72** F5
Broomhouse **48** B2
Brownrig **26** F6
Brownsburn **51** D5
Burgh **61** B7
Burnbank **78** A5
Burnfoot **35** E1
Burnhead **93** C3
Burnside **61** D5
Busby **74** B5

C

Cadder
Bishopbriggs **19** B5
Glasgow **29** F7
Cadzow **91** E8
Cairnhill **50** F6
Cairnhouses **138** C6
Calderbank **51** B3
Calderbraes **48** D1
Caldercruix **38** A5
Calderhead **69** E4
Caldermill **128** C4
Calderwood **76** C4
Calton **45** E5
Cambuslang **62** B4
Cambusnethan **81** E3
Camlachie **46** B6
Candy Mill **133** B4
Carbrain **12** A1
Cardonald **43** C5
Carfin **66** D2
Carluke **95** E3
Carmichael **130** E1
Carmunnock **74** E7
Carmyle **62** C8
Carnbroe **50** D3
Carntyne **46** E7
Carnwadric **58** E4
Carnwath **124** E1
Carrickstone **11** E5
Carron Bridge **3** C3
Carstairs **111** F1
Carstairs Junction **131** B8
Cartland **109** D1
Castlecary **12** F8
Castlemilk **60** E3
Cathcart **60** A6
Cathkin **61** D3
Causewayend **160** B2
Chantinghall **78** C3
Chapel **82** C2
Chapelhall **51** F2
Chapelton **103** D5
Chryston **33** D8
Claddens **20** F4
Clarkston
Airdrie **51** E8
Newton Mearns **73** E7
Cleekhimin **66** B1
Cleghorn **117** F7
Cleland **67** B1
Cliftonville **50** C7
Clincarthill **61** B7
Clydebank **15** B1
Clydesdale **65** E4
Coalburn **137** E5
Coatbridge **50** A6
Coatdyke **50** D6
Coatshill **63** D1
College Milton **75** B3
Colston **30** F8
Coltness **81** D5
Condorrat **23** B7
Corkerhill **43** E2
Coulter **141** C4
Covington **131** D2
Cowcaddens **163** A4
Cowlairs **30** D4
Craigend **32** D2
Craigendmuir **32** E4
Craiglinn **11** A2
Craigneuk
Airdrie **51** C7
Wishaw **80** D4
Craigton **43** D5
Cranhill **47** A8
Cranston Hill **44** D8
Crawford **152** B7
Crawfordjohn **144** F2
Crindledyke **82** C6
Croftfoot **60** E5
Crookfur **72** D6
Crookston **42** F4
Crossford **108** B1
Crosshill
Allanton **82** F8
Govanhill **45** A1
Muirhead **48** D5
Crossmill **57** C4
Crossmyloof **44** D2
Croy **10** F4
Cumbernauld **12** C5
Cumbernauld Village **12** A6

D

Dalbeth **46** E2
Dalmarnock **46** A2
Dalmuir **15** A2
Dalserf **94** C2
Dalshannon **23** A6
Darvel **134** A8
Dean Park **27** D2
Dennistoun **46** B7
Devonburn **120** C2

Dillarburn 120 B8
Dimsdale 81 C1
Dolphinton 126 E1
Douglas 138 C1
Douglas Water 138 F7
Douglas West 138 A2
Dovecothall 57 D3
Dovecotwood 6 D1
Dowanhill 29 C3
Drumchapel 16 A3
Drumclog 127 F1
Drumgelloch 51 D8
Drumoyne 43 E6
Drumpellier 49 C6
Drumry 15 C2
Drumtrocher 6 D3
Dullatur 11 D6
Dumbreck 44 B4
Dunbeth 50 B7
Dundyvan 49 F4
Dunsyre 126 B2
Dunterlie 57 C3
Duntiblae 21 A7
Duntocher 15 A7
Dykebar 42 B1
Dykehead 69 D5

E

Eaglesham 86 F5
Earnock 77 E1
Easterhouse 48 B8
Eastfield
- Cumbernauld 11 E3
- Harthill 55 C4
- Rutherglen 61 D7

East Kilbride 88 F6
East Mains 75 F2
East Shawhead 50 B2
Eddlewood 91 D7
Elsrickle 133 A6
Elvanfoot 152 B4
Ericstane 157 E6

F

Faifley 15 C7
Fairhill 78 C1
Fallside 64 D6
Fauldhead 21 B6
Fauldhouse 71 E5
Fernhill 61 B3
Ferniegair 79 B2
Finniston 44 D8
Firhill 30 A3
Flemington
- Cambuslang 62 D3
- Motherwell 80 B5
- Strathaven 112 F6

Forgewood 65 D2
Forrestfield 39 A3
Forth 98 E8
Foxley 47 B2
Fullarton 47 A3

G

Gallowflat 61 C7
Gallowgate 46 A5
Gallowhill 42 A7
Gallow Hill 117 B5
Gardenside 63 E5
Garnethill 162 B4
Garnkirk 33 B6
Garnqueen 34 E5
Garrowhill 48 A5
Gartcosh 33 F5
Garthamlock 32 E2
Gartlea 51 B6
Gartness 51 E5
Gartsherrie 34 E1
Garvald 126 E4
Germiston 31 B2
Giffnock 59 C2
Gilmourton 128 B3
Gilshochill 29 E8
Glasgow 163 C2
Glasgow 45 D5
Glassford 104 F2
Glenboig 34 F6
Glenbuck 142 E8
Glenmavis 35 E3
Glespin 143 E7
Gorbals 45 C4
Govan 44 A7
Govanhill 45 B2
Gowkthrapple 94 A8
Greenburn 71 F5
Greenend 50 D5
Greenfaulds 23 E7
Greenfield 47 B6
Greenfoot 35 A7
Greengairs 24 F1
Greenhead 81 D2
Greenhill 35 B1
Greenhills 88 C6
Greenlees 62 A3

H

Hairmyres 87 F8
Halfway 62 D4
Hallside 62 F5
Hamilton 78 C3
Hamiltonhill 30 B4
Hangingshaw 60 C8
Happendon 138 D4
Harburn 123 E8
Hardgate 15 C5
Hareleeshill 93 C1
Hareshaw 67 E6
Harestanes 9 A2
Harthill 55 F5
Hartwood 69 A3
Hattonrig 65 B6
Hawksland 120 F4
Hayston 20 A8
Haywood 122 D1
Hazelbank 115 D7
Heads 104 E4
High Balmalloch 6 C1
High Blantyre 77 C5
High Burnside 61 D4
High Crosshill 61 B6
High Gallowhill 20 A6
Highland Park 6 D2
Hillend 38 B3
Hillhead 20 E8
Hillhouse 77 E4
Hillington 43 A5
Hillpark 59 C5
Hogganfield 31 F2
Holehills 36 B2
Hollandhurst 34 F2
Holytown 66 A6
Househillwood 58 A7
Hunterhill 42 A2
Hurlet 57 E7
Hutchesontown 45 D3
Hyndford Bridge 130 D4
Hyndland 29 A3

I

Ibrox 44 B6

J

Jackton 87 C7
Jenny Lind 58 D2
Jordanhill 28 E5

K

Kaimend 131 F8
Kelvin 89 B6
Kelvindale 29 A7
Kelvingrove 29 D2
Kelvinhaugh 29 C1
Kelvinside 29 A5
Kennishead 58 F5
Kilbowie 15 C3
Kildrum 12 B4
Kilncadzow 110 A5
Kilsyth 6 B2
Kingson's Knowe 117 B2
King's Park 60 D6
Kingston 44 F5
Kirkfieldbank 116 D4
Kirkhill 73 C4
Kirkintilloch 20 F7
Kirklandneuk 27 B4
Kirkmuirhill 114 B3
Kirkshaws 49 E3
Kirkwood 49 C4
Knightswood 28 C7
Kylepark 63 D7

L

Ladygill 146 A7
Laighstonehall 78 C2
Lambhill 30 A7
Lamington 140 D2
Lanark 117 C3
Langloan 49 E5
Langmuir 9 B1
Langside 59 E8
Larkhall 93 B3
Laurieston 45 B5
Law 94 F5
Law Hill 95 A4
Leadhills 151 B1
Lenzie 20 D5
Lenziemill 24 B8
Lesmahagow 119 E3
Levernside 57 A4
Libberton 131 F6
Lightburn 47 A7
Limekilnburn 91 B2
Lindsayfield 88 A4
Linnvale 15 D1
Linnville 116 B3
Lintfieldbank 138 B6
Linthouse 28 E1
Little Earnock 78 A2
Loanhead 27 C3
Lochlibo 57 A1
Longriggend 26 B1
Low Waters 78 E1
Luggiebank 24 B6

M

Machan 93 A2
Mansewood 59 B5
Marnock 34 D6
Maryhill 29 C7
Maryville 63 C8
Meadowhill 93 B4
Mearns 72 E3
Meikle Earnock 91 A7
Merrylee 59 D4
Millersneuk 20 F5
Millerston
- Busby 73 E4
- Stepps 32 A4

Millheugh 92 F2
Milngavie 16 E8
Milnwood 65 D4
Milton
- Glasgow 30 C7
- Lesmahagow 119 E5

Moffat 161 E5
Moffat Mills 51 F6
Mollinsburn 22 D4
Moodiesburn 21 E2
Moorpark 27 B2
Morningside 82 C3
Mossend 65 D5
Mossneuk 87 F7
Mosspark 43 E3
Motherwell 79 D8
Mount Ellen 33 E6
Mount Florida 60 C8
Mount Vernon 47 D2
Muirend 59 E4
Muirhead
- Baillieston 48 C4
- Chryston 33 D7

Muirhouse
- Carstairs 111 E7
- Motherwell 80 B2

Muirkirk 142 A6

N

Nemphlar 116 A6
Nerston 75 F4
Nethanfoot 108 A3
Netherburn 107 C4
Netherlee 59 F2
Netherton
- Glasgow 28 E8
- Motherwell 80 D1

Newarthill 66 E3
Newbigging 132 B8
Newhouse 67 A7
New Lanark 117 A2
Newlands 59 D6
Newlandsmuir 88 A6
Newmains 82 B5
New Monkland 35 E5
New Stevenston 66 B4
Newton 63 A6
Newton Mearns 72 B4
New Trows 119 D1
Nitshill 57 F5
North Barrwood 6 F1
North Cardonald 43 B7
Northfield 6 B1
North Kelvin 29 F4
North Motherwell 79 C8
North Mount Vernon 47 F3

O

Oatlands 45 E2
Old Balornock 31 B5
Old Drumchapel 16 A1
Oldhall 42 D5
Old Monkland 49 E4
Omoa 67 A4
Orbiston 64 F4
Orchard Park 59 B3
Overtown 94 C6
Oxgang 20 F7

P

Paisley 42 B2
Parkhall 15 A5
Parkhead 46 C3
Parkneuk 77 B2
Parkside 67 C2
Partick 29 B2
Partickhill 29 B3
Pather 81 A1
Penilee 42 E6
Petersburn 51 D5
Petershill 31 B3
Pettinain 131 B5
Philipshill 74 E4
Pickerstonhill 67 A5
Plains 37 A3
Plantation 44 D6
Polkelly 123 A1
Pollok 58 B8
Pollokshaws 59 C7
Pollokshields 44 E3
Polmadie 45 C2
Port Dundas 30 C2
Port Eglington 45 A4
Possil Park 30 D5
Potterfield 27 B2
Priesthill 58 A6
Provanmill 31 C2

Q

Quarter 91 F3
Queenslie 47 E8
Queenzieburn 9 F7
Quothquan 131 F2

R

Radnor Park 15 A4
Ralston 42 D4
Raploch 92 F3
Ravenstruther 130 F8
Rawyards 36 C1
Renfrew 27 E4
Riddrie 31 D1
Riddrie Knowes 31 E1
Riggend 24 B1
Rigside 138 F6
Roadmeetings 109 D8
Roberton 146 A7
Robroyston 31 F6
Rogerton 75 D6
Rosebank
- Crossford 107 C8
- Kirkintilloch 21 A8

Rosehall 50 B4
Rosshall 42 F3
Roughmussel 57 F8
Roughrigg 26 B2
Ruchazie 32 B1
Ruchill 30 A5
Rutherglen 61 D8

S

St Leonards 89 C8
Salsburgh 53 C2
Sandford 129 C6
Sandilands 139 A8
Sandyhills 47 C5
Scotstoun 28 B4
Scotstounhill 28 B6
Seafar 11 E1
Seedhill 42 A3
Shawfield 45 F2
Shawhead 50 A3
Shawlands 59 E8
Shawsburn 93 E2
Shawstonefoot 67 F1
Shawton 103 C6
Shawtonhill 103 B7
Sheddens 73 F7
Shieldhall 43 D8
Shirrel 65 B7
Shotts 69 F5
Sighthill 30 D2
Sikeside 50 E5
Silverbank 61 E6
Silvertonhill 78 E2
Skirling 133 B2
South Barrwood 10 F7
South Cardonald 43 C4
South Nitshill 58 A4
Spindleside 67 D1
Spittal 60 F5
Springboig 47 D6
Springburn 30 F3
Springhall 61 E4
Springhill
- Barrhead 57 C1
- Shotts 70 B2

Stamperland 73 F8
Stand 36 B6
Stane 70 A3
Stepps 32 C6
Stewartfield 75 D4
Stonehouse 105 F2
Strathaven 112 F5
Strathbungo 44 F1
Strutherhill 106 B8
Summerlee 49 F8
Summerston 17 D1
Sunnyside 50 A8
Swinhill 106 C6
Swinton 48 C6
Symington 140 E5

T

Tannochside 64 B8
Tarbrax 123 C2
Temple 28 E7
Thankerton 140 D8
The Greens 20 B6
The Murray 88 E7
Thornliebank 58 F3
Thorntonhall 74 C3
Thrashbush 36 A2
Tintock 9 C2
Torbothie 70 B4
Torbush 82 C3
Torrance 19 B8
Toryglen 60 D8
Townhead
- Coatbridge 34 C2
- Glasgow 163 B3
- Kirkintilloch 20 C8

Tradeston 45 A5
Turfholm 119 F4
Twechar 10 A3

U

Uddingston 63 E5
Uddington 138 E4
Udston 77 F4
Udstonhead 104 A3

V

Victoria Gardens 27 C1
Viewpark 64 C7

W

Walston 132 F8
Wandel 146 A6
Wanlockhead 154 B7
Wardpark 12 C7
Waterfoot 73 D2
Waterloo 81 D1
Waterside
- Glasgow 57 E5
- Kirkintilloch 21 B7

Wattston 36 C8
Waverley Park 44 D1
Wellside 62 D4
West Arthurlie 57 A2
West Benhar 55 B4
Westburn 62 E6
West Drumoyne 43 E7
West End 124 C1
Wester Auchinloch 20 C2
Wester Holytown 65 E6
Westermains 20 B8
Westfield
- Cumbernauld 22 F7
- Kilsyth 6 A1

West Mains 75 D1
Weston 125 E2
Westrigg 40 F3
Westwood 88 A8
Wheatlands 77 C8
Whifflet 50 B5
Whinhall 50 E8
Whitburn 56 F7
Whitecraigs 73 B7
Whitecrook 27 C8
Whitehaugh 42 A5
Whitehill 78 A6
Whitehills 88 E5
Whiteinch 28 D2
Whitlawburn 61 F3
Whittagreen 66 C3
Wildmanbridge 95 C7
Williamsburgh 42 B5
Williamwood 73 D8
Wilsontown 122 B2
Wishaw 81 B4
Wiston 140 C3
Woodhead Green 91 B8
Woodside 30 B3

Y

Yieldshields 96 E2
Yoker 27 E7

A

Abbey Dr G14 28 E4
Abbey Pl Airdrie ML6 51 C4
Forth ML11 98 F7
Abbey Wlk Coatbridge G69 48 F5
Larkhall ML9 93 B4
Abbeycraig Rd G34 33 E1
Abbeydale Way G73 61 C3
Abbeygreen ML11 119 E4
Abbeygreen Rd ML11 119 E3
Abbeygreen St G34 33 E1
Abbeyhill Cres ML11 119 F3
Abbeyhill Rd ML11 119 F3
Abbeyhill St G32 46 E7
Abbeylands Rd G81 15 D6
Abbot St 4 G41 44 E1
Abbots Ct G68 11 D7
Abbots Knowe ML11 119 F3
Abbots Terr ML6 51 C4
Abbots Way ML11 119 F3
Abbotsford G64 19 C2
Abbotsford Ave
Hamilton ML3 78 B7
Larkhall ML9 93 A1
Rutherglen G73 61 B7
Abbotsford Brae G74 75 E3
Abbotsford Cres
Hamilton ML3 78 B6
Shotts ML7 69 F5
Strathaven ML10 112 C6
Wishaw ML2 81 C4
Abbotsford Ct G67 23 F7
Abbotsford Dr G66 20 E8
Abbotsford La ML4 64 F6
Abbotsford Pl
Cumbernauld G67 23 F7
4 Glasgow G5 45 B4
Glasgow,Laurieston G5 45 B5
Motherwell ML1 66 B5
Abbotsford Rd
Bearsden G61 16 C6
Chapelhall ML6 51 E1
Clydebank G81 15 B1
Cumbernauld G67 23 F7
Hamilton ML3 78 B6
Wishaw ML2 81 C4
Abbotsford Terr ML11 117 C4
Abbotshall Ave G15 15 E3
Abbotsinch Rd PA4 27 A4
Abbott Cres G81 27 D8
Aberconway St G81 27 C8
Abercorn Ave G52 42 E8
Abercorn Cres ML3 78 F2
Abercorn Dr ML3 78 F2
Abercorn Pl G23 17 E1
Abercorn Rd G77 72 C6
Abercorn Sch G4 30 B2
Abercorn St G81 15 E7
Abercrombie Cres G69 48 F5
Abercrombie Dr G61 16 B8
Abercrombie Pl G65 6 B1
Abercromby Cres G74 76 B3
Abercromby Dr G40 45 F6
Abercromby Pl G74 76 B3
Abercromby Sq 1 G40 45 F6
Abercromby St 1 G40 45 E5
Aberdalgie Gdns G34 48 B8
Aberdalgie Path G34 48 B8
Aberdalgie Rd G34 48 B8
Aberdeen Rd ML6 51 D4
Aberdour St G31 46 C7
Aberfeldy Ave
Hamilton G72 77 D3
Plains ML6 36 F3
Aberfeldy St G31 46 C7
Aberfoyle St G31 46 C7
Aberlady Rd G51 43 E6
Aberlady St ML1 67 B1
Aberlour Pl ML1 66 A2
Abernethy Ave G72 77 D3
Abernethy Pk G74 75 D2
Abernethy Pl G77 73 B4
Abernethy St G31 46 C7
Abernethyn Rd ML2 82 B6
Aberuthven Dr G32 47 B3
Abiegail Pl G72 63 D1
Abington Prim Sch ML12 145 F2
Abington Rd ML12 140 F5
Aboukir St G51 43 E8
Aboyne St G51 43 F6
Abronhill High Sch G67 12 E4
Abronhill Prim Sch G67 12 D3
Acacia Dr G78 57 B5
Acacia Way G72 62 E5
Academy Ct ML5 50 A7
Academy Pk Airdrie ML6 51 A7
Glasgow G51 44 C4
Academy Pl ML5 50 A7
Academy Rd Glasgow G46 59 C2
Moffat DG10 161 C6
Academy St Airdrie ML6 51 A7
Armadale EH48 41 F5
Coatbridge ML5 50 A7
Glasgow G32 47 B4
Larkhall ML9 93 A3
Academy Terr ML4 65 B5
Acer Gr ML6 51 E3
Achamore Cres G15 15 E4
Achamore Dr G15 15 E4
Achamore Gdns G15 15 E4
Achamore Rd G15 15 E4
Achnasheen Rd ML6 52 A6
Achray Pl ML5 34 D1
Achray Rd G67 23 C6
Acorn Ct G40 45 F4
Acorn St G40 45 F4
Acre Dr G20 17 B1
Acre Rd G20 17 B1
Acredyke Cres G21 31 C7
Acredyke Pl G21 31 C6
Acredyke Rd Glasgow G21 31 C7
Rutherglen G73 60 F8
Acres The ML9 93 B2
Adam Ave ML6 51 B7
Adams Court La G1 162 C1
Adams Pl G65 10 D8
Adamslie Cres G66 20 A8
Adamslie Dr G66 20 A8
Adamson St ML4 65 D5
Adamswell St G21 30 F3
Adamswell Terr G69 22 A2
Addie St ML1 79 F8
Addiewell Pl ML5 50 A4
Addiewell St G32 47 A7
Addison Dr 10 ML11 138 B1
Addison Gdns 9 ML11 138 B1
Addison Gr G46 58 F4
Addison Pl Douglas ML11 138 B1
Glasgow G46 58 F4
Addison Rd Glasgow G12 29 D4
Glasgow,Thornliebank G46 58 E4
Adelaide Rd G75 88 C7
Adele St ML1 79 F4
Adelphi St Glasgow G5 45 C5
Glasgow G5 45 D5
Admiral St G41 44 E5
Advie Pl G42 60 B8
Affric Ave ML6 37 A3
Affric Dr PA2 42 B1
Affric Loan ML7 69 E6
Afton Cres G61 17 B3
Afton Dr PA4 27 F2
Afton Gdns
Coatbridge ML5 50 D5
Hamilton G72 77 B6
Afton Rd G67 12 B3
Afton St Glasgow G41 59 E8
Larkhall ML9 93 C2
Agate Terr ML4 65 A4
Agnew Ave ML5 50 D7
Agnew Gr ML4 64 D5
Agnew La G42 45 A1
Aigas Cotts 4 G13 28 F5
Aikenhead Ho G44 60 D5
Aikenhead Rd
Glasgow,Mount Florida G44 60 C7
Glasgow,Polmadie G42 45 C2
Aikman Pl G74 76 B4
Aikman Rd ML1 79 B5
Ailean Dr G32 47 E4
Ailean Gdns G32 47 E4
Aillort Pl G74 75 E3
Ailort Ave G44 60 A5
Ailort Loan 18 ML2 81 F6
Ailsa Ave Ashgill ML9 106 F8
Motherwell ML1 79 B7
Ailsa Cres ML1 79 B7
Ailsa Ct ML3 77 D1
Ailsa Dr Bothwell G71 64 A4
Clydebank G81 15 C6
Giffnock G46 59 C1
Glasgow G42 59 F7
Rutherglen G46 73 C8
Rutherglen,Croftfoot G73 60 F5
Ailsa Pl ML5 49 F4
Ailsa Rd Bishopbriggs G64 19 B2
Coatbridge ML5 49 F4
Renfrew PA4 27 C2
Ailsa Twr G72 61 E3
Ainslie Ave G52 43 A8
Ainslie Rd
Cumbernauld G67 12 C3
Glasgow G52 43 A7
Glasgow G52 43 B7
Airbles Cres ML1 79 D5
Airbles Dr ML1 79 D5
Airbles Farm Rd ML1 79 C5
Airbles Rd ML1 79 D5
Airbles St ML1 79 E5
Airbles Sta ML1 79 E5
Airbles Twr ML1 79 E5
Aird's La G1 163 A1
Airdale Ave G46 59 C2
Airdrie Acad ML6 36 A1
Airdrie Rd Caldercruix ML6 38 C2
Carluke ML8 95 E4
Cumbernauld G67 23 A7
Cumbernauld G67 23 B6
Cumbernauld,Mollinsburn G67 22 E4
Kilsyth G65 10 D8
Plains ML6 36 F1
Airdrie Ret Pk ML6 51 A7
Airdrie Sta ML6 51 A7
Airdriehill Rd ML6 36 D3
Airdriehill St ML6 36 C2
Airgold Dr G15 15 F4
Airlie Ave G61 16 E7
Airlie Dr ML4 65 A6
Airlie Gdns G73 61 D4
Airlie La G12 29 B3
Airlie Rd G69 48 A3
Airlie St G12 29 B3
Airlour Rd G44 59 E5
Airth Ct ML1 65 D1
Airth Dr G52 43 F3
Airth La G52 43 F3
Airth Way G68 22 E8
Airthrey Ave G14 28 E4
Airthrey La G14 28 E4
Airyligg Dr G76 86 E5
Aitchison Ct 4 ML6 50 F8
Aitchison St ML6 50 E7
Aitken Cl ML2 82 A7
Aitken Pl ML11 117 A4
Aitken Rd ML3 91 E7
Aitken St Airdrie ML6 36 B1
Glasgow G31 46 C7
Aitkenhead Ave ML5 49 B4
Aitkenhead Prim Sch G71 48 F1
Aitkenhead Rd
Chapelhall ML6 51 D2
Uddingston G71 49 A2
Alasdair Ct G78 57 C2
Alba Gdns ML8 95 E3
Alba Way Hamilton ML3 91 C6
18 Larkhall ML9 93 C1
Albans Cres ML1 79 B8
Albany G74 76 C4
Albany Ave G32 47 C6
Albany Cotts 3 G13 28 F5
Albany Dr Lanark ML11 117 B3
Rutherglen G73 61 B6
Albany Pl G71 64 B2
Albany Quadrant G32 47 C6
Albany Rd ML3 91 C7
Albany St Coatbridge ML5 49 E7
Glasgow G40 46 A4
Albany Terr G72 61 E3
Albany Wynd 11 ML9 93 B4
Albert Ave G42 45 A1
Albert Cres 3 ML6 51 B7
Albert Cross G41 44 F3
Albert Dr Bearsden G61 17 B3
Glasgow G41 44 D4
Larkhall ML9 93 B2
Rutherglen G73 61 B5
Albert Pk ML8 109 A6
Albert Pl ML6 51 B8
Albert Prim Sch
Airdrie ML6 51 B8
Glasgow G21 30 F5
Albert Quadrant ML1 66 A5
Albert Rd Clydebank G81 15 A3
Glasgow G42 45 B1
Harthill ML7 55 E5
Kirkintilloch G66 20 C3
Renfrew PA4 27 C3
Albert St Coatbridge ML5 50 A7
Hamilton ML3 78 B6
Motherwell ML1 79 F7
Albert Terr ML3 78 A6
Alberta Ave
Coatbridge ML5 49 F8
East Kilbride G75 88 C8
Alberta Cres 1 G75 88 C8
Alberta Pk G75 88 D8
Alberta Pl 2 G75 88 D8
Albion Ct Biggar ML12 160 D4
Coatbridge ML5 50 C6
Albion Gate G1 163 B2
Albion St Coatbridge ML5 50 C6
Glasgow G1 163 B2
Glasgow,North Mount Vernon G69 47 F3
Motherwell ML1 79 E5
Albion Twr 2 ML1 79 E5
Albion Way G75 88 F5
Alcaig Rd G52 43 E2
Alcath Rd ML2 82 B6
Alder Ave Hamilton ML3 78 E1
Kirkintilloch G66 20 B5
Alder Bank G71 49 C1
Alder Cres G75 88 C5
Alder Ct Barrhead G78 57 C1
East Kilbride G75 88 C5
Alder Gate G72 62 E5
Alder Gr ML5 50 B6
Alder La
Motherwell,Holytown ML1 66 C5
Motherwell,New Stevenston ML1 66 A3
Alder Pl East Kilbride G75 88 C5
Glasgow G43 59 C5
Alder Rd Clydebank G81 15 A5
Cumbernauld G67 12 D2
Glasgow G43 59 C5
Alderman Pl G13 28 C6
Alderman Rd G13 28 B6
Alderside Gdns G71 63 E7
Alderside Pl 5 G71 64 B3
Alderstocks G75 88 E5
Alderston Pl ML4 64 E4
Alderston Way ML4 64 E6
Aldersyde Ave ML2 80 D4
Aldersyde Pl G72 63 C1
Aldersyde Terr ML1 67 C1
Alexander Ave
Eaglesham G76 86 E6
Twechar G65 9 E4
Uddingston G71 64 C6
Alexander Balfour Gdns ML3 78 D1
Alexander Cres G5 45 C4
Alexander Gdns ML3 79 A2
Alexander Gibson Way ML1 79 D5
Alexander Hospl ML5 49 E8
Alexander Path ML1 80 B3
Alexander Peden Prim Sch ML7 55 E5
Alexander Pl G66 21 B7
Alexander Rd ML7 69 D6
Alexander St Airdrie ML6 50 F7
Clydebank G81 15 B1
Coatbridge ML5 50 B8
Alexander St *continued*
Wishaw ML2 81 A2
Alexander Stephen Ho G51 28 E1
Alexandra Ave
Kirkintilloch G66 20 C4
Stepps G33 32 D6
Alexandra Cross G31 46 B7
Alexandra Ct G31 46 B8
Alexandra Dr PA4 27 D3
Alexandra Gdns G66 20 C4
Alexandra Par G31 46 A8
Alexandra Parade Prim Sch G31 46 A8
Alexandra Parade Sta G31 46 B8
Alexandra Park St G31 46 B8
Alexandra Pk G66 20 C4
Alexandra Prim Sch ML6 51 A7
Alexandra Rd G66 20 C4
Alexandra St G66 20 C8
Alexandria Quadrant ML1 66 A5
Alford Ave Hamilton G72 77 C3
Kirkintilloch G66 20 B8
Alford Quadrant ML2 81 B5
Alford St G21 30 D3
Alfred La 5 G12 29 E3
Alfred Terr 6 G12 29 E3
Algie St G41 59 F8
Algoma Pl G75 88 B8
Alice Ave ML4 65 A4
Aline Ct G78 57 B4
Alison Lea G74 76 C3
Allan Ave Carluke ML8 95 E3
Renfrew PA4 27 E1
Allan Ct G75 87 E7
Allan Glen Gdns G64 19 B4
Allan Gr ML4 65 B6
Allan Pl East Kilbride G75 87 E7
Glasgow G40 46 B2
Allan Rd EH47 56 E6
Allan St Coatbridge ML5 49 D5
Glasgow G40 46 B2
Motherwell ML1 79 F7
Allan Twr ML1 79 F7
Allan's Cnr G78 57 B2
Allanbank St ML7 82 F8
Allandale Ave ML1 66 F5
Allander Ave G62 18 B7
Allander Dr G64 19 A8
Allander Gdns G64 18 F4
Allander Rd G61 16 D2
Allander St Glasgow G22 30 C4
Glasgow G22 30 D4
Allanfauld Rd
Cumbernauld G67 11 F2
Kilsyth G65 6 D2
Allanshaw Gdns ML3 78 B3
Allanshaw Gr ML3 78 B2
Allanshaw St ML3 78 C3
Allanton Ave PA1 42 E4
Allanton Dr G52 43 C5
Allanton Gr ML2 81 B5
Allanton Lea ML3 91 C8
Allanton Pl ML3 78 E1
Allanton Prim Sch ML7 83 B8
Allanton Rd
Crosshill ML2,ML7 82 E7
Shotts ML7 69 D2
Allanton Terr ML3 92 D8
Allbany Cres ML1 65 F5
Allen Glen Pl G4 163 B3
Allen Way PA4 27 D1
Allendale G74 75 C3
Allendale Path 2 G72 77 D7
Allenshaw Ind Est ML3 78 C3
Allerdyce Dr G15 15 F1
Allerdyce Rd G15 15 F1
Allershaw Pl ML2 93 F8
Allershaw Rd ML2 93 F8
Allershaw Twr ML2 93 F8
Allerton Gdns G69 47 F4
Alleysbank Rd G73 46 B1
Allison Dr
Cambuslang G72 62 A6
Carnwath ML11 124 D1
Allison Hall PA1 42 B5
Allison Pl 3 Glasgow G42 45 A2
Newton Mearns G77 72 C4
Allison St
Carstairs Junction ML11 131 B7
Glasgow G42 45 B2
Allnach Pl G34 48 E8
Alloway Ave PA2 57 B8
Alloway Cres Paisley PA2 57 C8
Rutherglen G73 60 F5
Alloway Ct G66 9 A2
Alloway Dr Clydebank G81 15 C3
Kirkintilloch G66 9 A2
Newton Mearns G77 73 A4
Paisley PA2 57 B8
Rutherglen G73 60 F5
Alloway Gdns
Hamilton ML3 77 D2
Kirkintilloch G66 9 A2
Alloway Gr Paisley PA2 42 C1
Paisley PA2 57 C8
Alloway Quadrant G66 9 A1
Alloway Rd Airdrie ML6 51 F8
East Kilbride G74 76 E3
Glasgow G43 59 D6
Alloway St ML9 93 C2
Alloway Wynd ML1 66 E4
Alma St G31 46 B5
Almada Gr ML3 78 D4
Almada La ML3 78 D4
Almada St ML3 78 D4
Almada Twr ML3 78 D4
Almond Ave PA4 27 E2
Almond Bank G61 16 C2
Almond Dr Banknock FK4 8 E2
East Kilbride G74 76 B1
Kirkintilloch G66 20 B5
Almond Pl Coatbridge ML5 34 D1
Motherwell ML1 66 B5
Almond Rd Bearsden G61 16 D2
Cumbernauld G67 12 F4
Stepps G33 32 C5
Almond St G33 31 D1
Almond Terr ML7 55 C5
Almond Vale G71 64 A7
Almond Way ML1 79 E3
Almondbank ML6 36 F3
Alness Cres G52 43 E3
Alness St ML3 78 D1
Alness Terr ML3 78 D2
Alnwick Dr G76 86 D4
Alpha Ctr G81 27 C8
Alpine Gr G71 63 F7
Alpine Path 5 G72 77 E7
Alpine Wlk 4 G72 77 E7
Alsatian Ave G81 15 D2
Alsh Terr ML3 78 A1
Alston Ave ML5 50 B8
Alston Gdns G61 16 B8
Alston St ML10 104 F2
Altnacreag Gdns G69 22 A3
Alton Rd PA1 42 C4
Altyre St G32 46 F4
Alva Gate G52 43 E3
Alva Gdns Bearsden G61 16 D8
Glasgow G52 43 E2
Alva Pl G66 20 E4
Alvie Pl ML6 51 D5
Alwyn Ct G74 75 E3
Alwyn Dr G74 75 E3
Alyssum Cres ML1 79 D8
Alyth Cres G76 74 A8
Alyth Gdns Clarkston G76 74 A8
Glasgow G52 43 E3
Ambassador Way PA4 27 D1
Amber Terr ML4 65 A4
Ambleside G75 88 A6
Ambleside Rise ML3 91 D6
Ambrose Ct ML3 78 B4
Amethyst Ave ML4 65 A4
Amisfield St G20 29 E5
Amulree Pl G32 47 A4
Amulree St G32 47 B4
Ancaster Dr G13 28 F6
Ancaster La G13 28 F6
Anchor Ave PA1 42 A4
Anchor Cres PA1 42 A3
Anchor Dr PA1 42 A4
Anchor La G1 163 A2
Anchor Wynd PA1 42 A4
Ancroft St G20 30 A3
Andersen Ct G75 88 E6
Anderside G75 88 E5
Anderson Ave
Armadale EH48 41 F4
Kilsyth G65 6 B1
Anderson Cres G65 9 E8
Anderson Ct Bellshill ML4 65 B5
Newton Mearns G77 72 C4
Wishaw ML2 81 A3
Anderson Dr
Newton Mearns G77 72 C4
Renfrew PA4 27 D4
Anderson Gdns G72 63 E1
Anderson La 1 ML6 51 A8
Anderson St
5 Airdrie ML6 51 A8
Glasgow G11 29 B1
Glasgow G11 29 B2
Hamilton ML3 77 F5
Motherwell ML1 79 E5
Anderson Twr ML1 79 E6
Anderston Prim Sch G3 162 A2
Anderston Quay G3 162 A1
Anderston Sta G3 162 B2
Andrew Ave
Kirkintilloch G66 20 D3
Renfrew PA4 27 E3
Andrew Baxter Ave ML9 93 E1
Andrew Dr G81 27 D8
Andrew Pl ML8 95 E3
Andrew Sillars Ave G72 62 C5
Andrew St G74 75 F1
Anford Gdns G72 77 E7
Anford Pl G72 77 E7
Anford Terr G72 77 E6
Angela Way G71 63 F6
Angle Gate G14 28 D4
Angle Pk ML11 131 B8
Angle St ML11 105 F2
Angus Ave Airdrie ML6 51 A5
Bishopbriggs G64 19 D1
East Kilbride G74 76 B2
Glasgow G52 43 C3
Hamilton ML3 79 A3
Motherwell ML1 79 C8
Angus Gdns G71 63 F8
Angus Oval G52 43 B4
Angus Pl East Kilbride G74 76 B2
Glasgow G52 43 B4
Angus Rd ML8 96 B1
Angus St Clydebank G81 27 E8
6 Glasgow G21 30 E4
Angus Terr ML11 138 B1
Angus Wlk G71 64 B7
Anish Pl G15 15 E4
Ann Ct ML3 78 A5
Ann St ML3 78 A5
Annabella Rd ML9 107 C4

Annan Ave G75 .87 E7
Annan Cres ML6 .51 D1
Annan Ct ML5 .49 F6
Annan Dr Bearsden G61 .16 D3
Rutherglen G73 .61 D7
Annan Glade ML1 .80 A3
Annan Gr ML1 .80 A3
Annan St Glasgow G42 .60 A8
Motherwell ML1 .80 A3
Annan Way 7 G67 .11 F1
Annandale ML6 .24 F2
Annandale Pl DG10 .161 E5
Annandale Rd DG10 .161 E5
Annandale St 1 G42 .45 B3
Annandale Way DG10 .161 E5
Annangate DG10 .161 C5
Annanside DG10 .161 C5
Annathill Gdns ML5 .22 F2
Annbank Pl G31 .45 F6
Annbank St Glasgow G31 .45 F6
Larkhall ML9 .92 F3
Anne Ave PA4 .27 D4
Anne Cres G66 .20 D3
Anne's Mews ML3 .78 F3
Annerley Ct ML5 .49 E5
Annerley Pl ML5 .49 E5
Annette St G42 .45 A2
Annette Street Prim Sch G42 .45 B2
Annfield Ct ML11 .114 A2
Annfield Gdns G72 .63 C1
Annfield Pl G31 .45 F7
Annick Dr G61 .16 C2
Annick St Cambuslang G72 .62 D5
Glasgow G32 .47 B5
Annick St Ind Est G32 .47 C5
Anniesdale Ave G33 .32 D6
Annieshill Forest Walks* ML6 .37 D2
Annieshill View ML6 .37 A2
Anniesland Coll G12 .29 A5
Anniesland Coll (Balshagray Campus) G11 .28 F2
Anniesland Cres G14 .28 A5
Anniesland Ind Est G13 .28 E8
Anniesland Rd
Glasgow,Anniesland G14 .28 C5
Glasgow,Scotstounhill G14 .28 A5
Anniesland Sta G13 .28 F6
Annieston G65 .9 F4
Annieston Pl ML12 .140 F6
Anniversary Ave G75 .88 C7
Annsfield Rd ML3 .91 D7
Ansdell Ave G72 .77 C8
Anson St G40 .45 F4
Anson Way 6 PA4 .27 C1
Anstruther Ct ML8 .94 F5
Anstruther St
Glasgow G32 .46 F5
Law ML8 .94 F5
Anthony Ct G81 .27 C8
Anthony St G2 .162 B2
Antigua Way G75 .75 A1
Antimony Rd G66 .9 A5
Anton Cres G65 .10 E8
Antonine G66 .9 B2
Antonine Ave ML1 .79 C8
Antonine Gdns G81 .15 A6
Antonine Rd
Bearsden G61 .16 B6
Dullatur G68 .11 D6
Antonine Wall* G66 .9 C3
Antrim La ML9 .93 B4
Anwoth St G32 .47 A3
Apartments The G46 .59 B1
Apllegarth Rd ML10 .112 C5
Apollo Path ML1 .66 B5
Appian Pl ML1 .65 B1
Appin Cres G31 .46 B7
Appin Ct G66 .9 B1
Appin Rd G31 .46 C7
Appin Terr Hamilton ML3 .77 E4
Rutherglen G73 .61 D4
Shotts ML7 .70 B3
Appin Way
2 Bothwell G71 .64 A3
Coatbridge ML5 .49 E4
Glenmavis ML6 .35 F4
Apple Way G75 .88 F6
Appleby Cl G75 .87 F6
Appleby Gr G69 .49 A6
Appleby St G22 .30 B3
Applecross Gdns G69 .21 F3
Applecross Quadrant ML2 .81 B5
Applecross Rd G66 .9 B1
Applecross St G4,G22 .30 B3
Appledore Cres G71 .64 A3
Appleyard Ct ML4 .64 F3
Apsley La G11 .29 A2
Apsley St G11 .29 A2
Aqua Ave ML3 .77 E2
Aqua Ct ML3 .77 E2
Aquila Way ML8 .95 D2
Araburn Dr G75 .88 E5
Aranthrue Cres PA4 .27 C4
Aranthrue Dr PA4 .27 C4
Aray St G20 .29 D6
Arbles Road Hospl ML1 .79 F5
Arbroath Ave G52 .43 B4
Arbroath Gr ML3 .78 B2
Arbuckle Pl ML6 .37 A3
Arbuckle Rd ML6 .37 B4
Arcadia Bsns Ctr G81 .15 B1
Arcadia Pl G40 .45 E5
Arcadia St Bellshill ML4 .65 A7
Glasgow G40 .45 E5
Arcan Cres G15 .16 B2
Arch Way G65 .6 D1
Archerfield Ave G32 .47 A2
Archerfield Cres G32 .47 A2
Archerfield Dr G32 .47 A2
Archerfield Gr G32 .47 A2
Archerhill Ave G13 .28 A8
Archerhill Cotts G13 .28 A8
Archerhill Cres G13 .28 B8
Archerhill Gdns G13 .28 A8
Archerhill Rd G13 .28 B7
Archerhill Sq G13 .27 F8
Archerhill Terr G13 .28 A8
Archibald Kelly Ct G75 .88 E7
Archiebald Pl ML4 .65 D4
Ard La 6 ML2 .81 F6
Ard Loan ML1 .66 A5
Ard Rd PA4 .27 B4
Ard St G32 .47 A4
Ardargie Dr G32 .62 C8
Ardargie Gr G32 .62 C8
Ardargie Pl G32 .62 C8
Ardbeg Ave
Bishopbriggs G64 .19 C1
Rutherglen G73 .61 E3
Ardbeg La G42 .45 A2
Ardbeg Rd ML1 .66 B2
Ardbeg St G42 .45 A2
Ardconnel St G46 .58 F4
Arden Ave G46 .58 E2
Arden Ct Airdrie ML6 .50 D8
Hamilton ML3 .78 D1
Arden Dr G46 .59 B3
Arden Gr G65 .6 C2
Arden Pl G46 .58 E2
Arden Prim Sch G46 .58 D4
Arden Rd ML3 .78 C1
Arden St ML6 .37 A2
Arden Terr ML3 .78 C2
Ardenclutha Ave ML3 .78 B4
Ardencraig Cres G45 .60 C1
Ardencraig Dr G45 .61 A2
Ardencraig Gdns G45 .61 A2
Ardencraig Pl G45 .60 E3
Ardencraig Quadrant G45 .60 F2
Ardencraig Rd
Glasgow G45 .60 E1
Glasgow G45 .60 F3
Ardencraig St G45 .61 A2
Ardencraig Terr G45 .60 F2
Ardenlea G71 .63 F7
Ardenlea St G40 .46 B3
Ardery St G11 .29 A2
Ardessie Pl G20 .29 D5
Ardessie St 2 G23 .17 D1
Ardfern Rd ML6 .52 A6
Ardfern St G32 .47 A3
Ardgay Pl G32 .47 A4
Ardgay St G32 .47 B4
Ardgay Way G73 .61 B3
Ardgoil Dr G68 .11 A1
Ardgour Ct G72 .77 F6
Ardgour Par ML1 .66 C1
Ardgowan Cres ML11 .131 A8
Ardgowan Ct PA2 .42 B3
Ardgowan Dr G71 .63 F7
Ardgowan Pl ML7 .69 E6
Ardgowan Terrace La G3 .29 D1
Ardholm St G32 .47 A5
Ardhu Pl G15 .16 A4
Ardlaw St G51 .43 F6
Ardle Rd G43 .59 E5
Ardlui St G32 .46 F4
Ardmaleish Cres G45 .60 E2
Ardmaleish Dr G45 .60 D2
Ardmaleish Rd G45 .60 E2
Ardmaleish St G45 .60 D2
Ardmaleish Terr G45 .60 E2
Ardmay Cres G44 .60 C7
Ardmillan St G33 .46 F8
Ardmory Ave G42 .60 D7
Ardmory La G42 .60 E7
Ardmory Pl G42 .60 E7
Ardnahoe Ave G42 .60 E7
Ardnahoe Pl G42 .60 D8
Ardneil Rd G51 .43 F6
Ardnish St G51 .43 E7
Ardo Gdns G51 .44 A5
Ardoch Gdns G72 .61 F6
Ardoch Gr G72 .61 F6
Ardoch Path 17 ML2 .81 F6
Ardoch Rd G61 .17 B5
Ardoch St G22 .30 C4
Ardoch Way G69 .21 F2
Ardochrig G75 .88 F5
Ardochrig Rd G75 .101 F4
Ardshiel Rd G51 .43 E7
Ardsloy La G14 .28 A4
Ardsloy Pl G14 .28 A4
Ardtoe Cres G33 .32 E5
Ardtoe Pl G33 .32 E5
Arduthie Rd G51 .43 E7
Ardwell Rd G52 .43 E3
Argosy Way 3 PA4 .27 C1
Argus Ave ML6 .51 C2
Argyle Cres Airdrie ML6 .50 F5
Hamilton ML3 .78 A3
Argyle Dr ML3 .78 A4
Argyle Gdns ML5 .49 E4
Argyle St Glasgow G2 .162 C2
Glasgow,Anderston G3 .162 A2
Glasgow,Cranston Hill G3 .44 E8
Stonehouse ML9 .105 F2
Argyle Street Sta G1 .163 A1
Argyll Arc G1 .163 A2
Argyll Ave PA4 .27 B4
Argyll Ct ML7 .55 F5
Argyll Gdns ML9 .93 B3
Argyll Pl Bellshill ML4 .64 F2
East Kilbride G74 .76 C3
Kilsyth G65 .10 E8
Argyll Rd Bearsden G61 .16 E7
Clydebank G81 .15 C1
Arisaig Dr Bearsden G61 .17 B3
Glasgow G52 .43 E3
Arisaig Pl G52 .43 E3
Arisdale Cres G77 .72 E6
Ark La G31 .45 F7
Arkaig Ave ML6 .36 F3
Arkaig Pl G77 .73 B4
Arkaig St ML2 .81 B1
Arkle Terr G72 .61 F3
Arkleston Cres PA3 .42 B7
Arkleston Dr PA1 .42 B6
Arkleston Prim Sch PA4 .27 D1
Arkleston Rd Paisley PA3 .42 B7
Paisley PA4,PA3 .42 B8
Paisley PA4,PA3 .42 C8
Arklet Rd G51 .43 F7
Arklet Way ML2 .81 E3
Arlington Pl G3 .162 A4
Arlington St G3 .162 A4
Armadale Acad EH48 .41 D5
Armadale Ct G31 .46 A8
Armadale Path G31 .46 A8
Armadale Pl G31 .46 A8
Armadale Prim Sch EH48 .41 F5
Armadale Rd ML11 .117 C4
Armadale St G31 .46 A7
Armine Path ML1 .66 C4
Armour Ave ML6 .50 E7
Armour Ct Hamilton G72 .77 B6
Kirkintilloch G66 .9 A1
Armour Dr G66 .9 A1
Armour Gdns G66 .9 A1
Armour Gr ML1 .80 A4
Armour Pl Kirkintilloch G66 .9 A1
Motherwell ML1 .66 C4
Armour St G4,G31 .163 C1
Armstrong Cres G71 .64 A8
Armstrong Gr G75 .88 D7
Arnbrae Farm Steadings G65 .10 A8
Arnbrae Rd G65 .6 B1
Arngask Rd G51 .43 E7
Arnhall Pl G52 .43 E3
Arnhem St G72 .62 D5
Arnholm Pl G52 .43 E3
Arnisdale Pl G34 .48 A8
Arnisdale Rd G34 .48 A8
Arnisdale Way G73 .61 B3
Arniston St G32 .46 F7
Arniston Way PA3 .42 A7
Arnol Pl G33 .47 F7
Arnold Ave G64 .19 A1
Arnott Dr ML5 .50 A4
Arnott Quadrant ML1 .65 C1
Arnott Way G72 .62 A6
Arnprior Cres G45 .60 D3
Arnprior Gdns G69 .21 F2
Arnprior Quadrant G45 .60 D4
Arnprior Rd G45 .60 D4
Arnprior St G45 .60 D4
Arnside Ave G46 .59 C3
Arnum Gdns ML8 .95 F1
Arnum Pl ML8 .95 F1
Arnwood Dr G12 .29 A5
Aron Terr G72 .61 F3
Arondale Rd ML6 .36 F3
Aros Dr G52 .43 E2
Aros La G52 .43 D2
Arran G74 .76 C1
Arran Ave ML5 .50 D4
Arran Ct ML10 .112 E5
Arran Dr Airdrie ML6 .35 F1
Cumbernauld G67 .23 D8
Glasgow G52 .43 F3
Glasgow,Giffnock G46 .59 C2
Glenmavis ML6 .35 F5
Arran Gdns Carluke ML8 .108 F8
Hamilton ML3 .78 E1
Arran La G69 .22 A2
Arran Path 17 ML9 .93 C1
Arran Pl Clydebank G81 .15 C2
Coatbridge ML5 .50 D4
Arran Rd Motherwell ML1 .79 C7
Renfrew PA4 .27 D2
Arran Terr G73 .60 F5
Arran Twr G72 .61 E3
Arran View Airdrie ML6 .35 F1
14 Kilsyth G65 .10 D8
Arran Way G71 .63 F2
Arranview St ML6 .51 E1
Arrochar Ct G23 .29 E8
Arrochar Dr G23 .17 D1
Arrochar Path 10 G23 .17 D1
Arrochar St G23 .17 D1
Arrol Pl G40 .46 B4
Arrol St Glasgow G52 .42 E7
Glasgow G52 .42 F8
Arrol Wynd G72 .62 D6
Arrotshole Ct G74 .75 B4
Arrotshole Rd G74 .75 B3
Arrowsmith Ave G13 .28 D8
Arthur Ave Airdrie ML6 .51 A6
Barrhead G78 .57 B1
Arthur Gdns ML6 .38 B4
Arthur Pl G76 .73 E6
Arthur St Clarkston G76 .73 E6
Glasgow G3 .29 D1
Hamilton ML3 .78 D5
Arthurlie Ave G78 .57 C1
Arthurlie Dr Glasgow G46 .59 C2
Newton Mearns G77 .72 D3
Arthurlie Gdns G78 .57 C2
Arthurlie St Barrhead G78 .57 C2
Glasgow G51 .43 F6
Arundel Dr
Bishopbriggs G64 .19 B4
Glasgow G42 .60 A7
Ascaig Cres G52 .43 E2
Ascog Rd G61 .16 F2
Ascog St G42 .45 A2
Ascot G12 .29 A6
Ascot Ave G12 .28 F6
Ascot Gate G12 .28 F6
Ash Ave G75 .88 C6
Ash Ct G75 .88 C6
Ash Gr Bishopbriggs G64 .31 B8
Kirkintilloch G66 .20 B5
Law ML8 .94 F6
Uddingston G71 .64 B8
Ash La ML9 .105 D1
Ash Pl Banknock FK4 .8 E2
East Kilbride G75 .88 C6
Ash Rd Clydebank G81 .15 A5
Cumbernauld G67 .12 E5
Glasgow G69 .48 A4
Ash Wlk Motherwell ML1 .66 B5
Rutherglen G73 .61 C3
Ash Wynd G72 .62 E5
Ashbank Cres ML6 .51 E3
Ashburn Loan ML9 .93 B4
Ashburton La G12 .29 B6
Ashburton Pk G75 .88 A7
Ashburton Rd G12 .29 B6
Ashby Cres G13 .16 E1
Ashcraig Sch G33 .32 B3
Ashcroft G74 .76 D5
Ashcroft Dr G44 .60 E5
Ashdale Dr G52 .43 E3
Ashdene St G22 .30 B7
Asher Rd ML6 .51 E2
Ashfield G64 .19 A3
Ashfield Rd G76 .73 E6
Ashfield St Glasgow G22 .30 C4
Glasgow G22 .30 C5
Ashfield Sta G22 .30 C5
Ashgill Pl G22 .30 C6
Ashgill Rd G22 .30 D7
Ashgillhead Rd ML9 .93 E1
Ashgrove Airdrie ML6 .51 D7
Caldercruix ML6 .38 A5
Coatbridge ML5 .50 A4
Hartwood ML7 .68 F3
Moodiesburn G69 .21 F1
Ashgrove Rd ML4 .65 B7
Ashgrove St G40 .46 A2
Ashiestiel Ct G67 .23 E7
Ashiestiel Pl G67 .23 E7
Ashiestiel Rd G67 .23 E7
Ashkirk Dr Ashgill ML9 .106 F8
Glasgow G52 .43 F3
Ashkirk Rd ML10 .112 E7
Ashland Ave ML3 .91 D6
Ashlea Dr G46 .59 D4
Ashlea Gdns ML6 .36 F3
Ashley Dr G71 .64 B5
Ashley Gr ML4 .64 D6
Ashley La G3 .162 A4
Ashley Pk G71 .64 C6
Ashley Pl G72 .77 C8
Ashley St G3 .162 A4
Ashmore Rd G44 .59 F5
Ashton Gdns G69 .34 A6
Ashton Gn G74 .75 E2
Ashton La G12 .29 D2
Ashton La N G12 .29 D2
Ashton Rd
Glasgow,Dalmarnock G73 .46 A1
Glasgow,Kelvingrove G12 .29 D2
Ashton St ML1 .65 D2
Ashtree Gr G77 .72 C3
Ashtree Rd G43 .59 C8
Ashvale Cres G21 .30 E4
Ashwood ML2 .80 E1
Ashwood Gdns G13 .28 F5
Ashworth Terr ML3 .78 A4
Aspen Dr G21 .31 A3
Aspen Gate ML1 .66 D2
Aspen Gr G69 .49 B6
Aspen Pl Cambuslang G72 .62 E5
Strathaven ML10 .112 F7
Aspen Way ML3 .78 E2
Asquith Pl ML4 .65 D5
Aster Dr G45 .61 A3
Aster Gdns Glasgow G53 .58 C3
Motherwell ML1 .79 E5
Athelstane Dr G67 .23 D7
Athelstane Rd G13 .28 C7
Athena Way G71 .64 A7
Athole Gdns G12 .29 C3
Athole La G12 .29 D3
Atholl Ave Glasgow G52 .42 E7
Glasgow G52 .42 E8
Atholl Cres PA1 .42 E6
Atholl Ct Hamilton G72 .77 F6
Kirkintilloch G66 .9 B1
Atholl Dr Cumbernauld G68 .22 F8
Giffnock G46 .59 C1
Rutherglen G46 .73 C8
Atholl Gdns Bearsden G61 .16 E7
Bishopbriggs G64 .18 F3
Glasgow G46 .58 F2
Rutherglen G73 .61 E4
Atholl La G69 .22 A2
Atholl Pl Coatbridge ML5 .50 B3
Glasgow G46 .58 F2
Atholl St ML3 .78 B6
Atholl Terr G71 .48 F1
Atlas Ind Est G21 .30 E4
Atlas Pl G21 .30 F4
Atlas Rd G21 .30 F4
Atlas Sq G21 .30 F4
Atlas St G81 .27 B8
Atlin Dr ML1 .66 B3
Attercliffe Ave ML2 .80 D2
Attlee Ave G81 .15 E1
Attlee Pl G81 .15 E1
Attow Rd G43 .59 B5
Auburn Dr G78 .57 D1
Auchenback Prim Sch G78 .57 D1
Auchenbothie Cres G33 .31 E5
Auchenbothie Pl G33 .31 E5
Auchencrow St G34 .48 D8
Auchencruive G62 .17 C8
Auchendavie Rd G66 .9 B2
Auchendavie Steadings G66 .9 B2
Auchengeich Gdns G69 .21 F2
Auchengeich Rd G69 .21 D3
Auchengilloch G75 .88 E5
Auchenglen Dr G69 .21 E2
Auchenglen Rd ML8 .108 F3
Auchengray Prim Sch ML11 .124 F8
Auchengray Rd ML11 .122 F1
Auchenhowie Rd G62 .17 D7
Auchenkilns Holdings
Cumbernauld,Balloch G68 .11 C1
Cumbernauld,Condorrat G67 .23 D6
Auchenkilns Pk G68 .11 C1
Auchenkilns Rd G67 .23 D6
Auchenreoch Holdings G66 .9 B6
Auchenstewart Ct ML2 .81 C3
Auchentibber Ct G72 .77 F6
Auchentibber Rd G72 .77 A3
Auchentorlie Quadrant PA1 .42 B4
Auchentorlie St G11 .28 F2
Auchentoshan Terr G21 .30 F2
Auchinairn Gdns G64 .31 D8
Auchinairn Prim Sch G64 .31 B8
Auchinairn Rd G64 .31 C7
Auchinairn Rdbt G64 .31 E8
Auchinbee Farm Rd G68 .11 B4
Auchinbee Way G68 .11 B3
Auchincampbell Rd ML3 .78 D3
Auchincloch Dr FK4 .8 F3
Auchineden Ct G61 .16 C7
Auchingill Pl G34 .33 D1
Auchingill Rd
Glasgow G34 .33 C1
Glasgow G34 .33 D1
Auchingramont Ct ML3 .78 D3
Auchingramont Rd ML3 .78 D4
Auchinlea Dr ML1 .67 C1
Auchinlea Rd G34 .32 F1
Auchinleck Ave G33 .31 F6
Auchinleck Cres G33 .31 E6
Auchinleck Dr G33 .31 E6
Auchinleck Gdns G33 .31 E6
Auchinleck Rd
Clydebank G81 .15 B7
Glasgow G33 .31 F7
Auchinleck Terr G81 .15 B7
Auchinloch Prim Sch G66 .20 D2
Auchinloch Rd G66 .20 D4
Auchinloch St 2 G21 .30 F3
Auchinraith Ave ML3 .78 C5
Auchinraith Ind Est G72 .77 E7
Auchinraith Prim Sch G72 .77 D7
Auchinraith Rd G72 .77 E6
Auchinraith Terr G72 .77 F7
Auchinvole Cres G65 .10 B8
Auchmannoch Ave PA1 .42 E5
Auchnacraig Rd G81 .15 C7
Auchnotroch Rd ML8, ML11 .115 A4
Auchter Ave ML2 .82 C5
Auchter Rd ML2 .81 E4
Auchterburn Rd ML7 .82 F8
Auckland Pk 8 G75 .75 A1
Auckland St
Glasgow,Firhill G22 .30 B3
Glasgow,Hamiltonhill G22 .30 B4
Auld Kirk Rd G72 .62 C3
Auld Kirk The G76 .74 A5
Auld Rd The G67 .12 A4
Auld's Brae 2 ML6 .51 A8
Auldbar Rd G52 .43 F3
Auldbar Terr PA2 .42 A2
Auldburn Pl G43 .59 B6
Auldburn Rd G43 .59 B6
Auldearn Rd G21 .31 D7
Auldgavel ML10 .112 D5
Auldgirth Rd G52 .43 F3
Auldhame St ML5 .49 E8
Auldhouse Ave G43 .59 B6
Auldhouse Ct G43 .59 B6
Auldhouse Gdns G43 .59 B6
Auldhouse Prim Sch G75 .88 C1
Auldhouse Rd
East Kilbride G75 .88 C2
Glasgow G43 .59 C6
Auldhouse Ret Pk G43 .59 C6
Auldhouse Terr G43 .59 D6
Auldton Dr ML11 .119 F2
Auldton Gdns ML11 .119 F3
Auldton Terr Ashgill ML9 .93 F1
Douglas Water ML11 .138 F7
Aultbea St G22 .30 B8

Aultmore Dr ML1 66 B2
Aultmore Gdns G33 47 F7
Aultmore Pk G33 47 F7
Aultmore Rd G33 47 F7
Aurelia Ct ML1 79 E7
Aurs Cres G78 57 D2
Aurs Dr G78 57 D2
Aurs Glen G78 57 C1
Aurs Pl G78 57 E2
Aurs Rd Barrhead G78 57 E2
Newton Mearns G77 72 A5
Aursbridge Cres G78 57 D2
Aursbridge Dr G78 57 D2
Austen La 2 G13 28 E5
Austen Rd G13 28 E5
Austine Dr ML3 91 E7
Avenel Cres ML10 112 F7
Avenel Rd G13 16 E1
Avenue End Prim Sch G33 32 C1
Avenue End Prim Sch Annexe G33 32 A1
Avenue End Rd G33 32 B3
Avenue Rd ML11 130 F8
Avenue St Glasgow G40 46 A5
Rutherglen G73 46 B1
Avenuehead Rd
Moodiesburn G69 22 A1
Muirhead G69 34 A8
Avenuepark St G20 29 E5
Averton ML11 122 A1
Aviemore Gdns G61 17 B5
Aviemore Rd G52 43 E3
Avoch St G34 33 B1
Avon Ave Bearsden G61 17 B4
Carluke ML8 95 E2
Longriggend ML6 25 D3
Avon Cres ML10 104 F3
Avon Ct ML1 79 E6
Avon Dr ML4 65 C4
Avon Ho ML3 78 E5
Avon Pl Coatbridge ML5 34 D1
Larkhall ML9 106 B7
Avon Rd Bishopbriggs G64 31 A8
Glasgow G46 59 B2
Larkhall ML9 106 A7
Avon St Hamilton ML3 78 E3
Larkhall ML9 92 F3
Motherwell ML1 79 E6
Avon Twr 7 ML1 79 E5
Avon View 13 ML9 129 E8
Avon Wlk 4 G67 11 F1
Avon Wynd 23 ML2 81 F6
Avonbank Cres ML3 91 E8
Avonbank Rd Larkhall ML9 92 E3
Rutherglen G73 60 F7
Avonbrae Cres ML3 91 E8
Avonbridge Dr ML3 78 F3
Avondale Ave G74 75 F1
Avondale Cres EH48 41 E5
Avondale Dr
Armadale EH48 41 E5
Paisley PA1 42 B6
Avondale Gdns G74 89 A8
Avondale Pl G74 89 A8
Avondale St Glasgow G33 32 A1
Strathaven ML10 112 E7
Avonhead G75 88 E5
Avonhead Ave G67 23 C7
Avonhead Gdns G67 23 C7
Avonhead Pl G67 23 C7
Avonhead Rd G67 23 C7
Avonside Gr ML3 78 F3
Avonspark St G21 31 A3
Avonview ML10 112 E5
Aylmer Rd G43 59 F6
Ayr Dr ML6 51 A5
Ayr Rd Ashgill ML9 93 E2
Douglas ML11 144 A8
Giffnock G46 59 B1
Newton Mearns G77 72 B2
Newton Mearns G77 72 D4
Ravenstruther ML11 130 D6
Rigside ML11 138 F5
Rutherglen G77 73 A7
Ayr St G21 30 E3
Ayton Pk N G74 76 B3
Ayton Pk S G74 76 A3
Aytoun Rd G41 44 E3
Azalea Gdns G72 62 E5

B

Baads Rd ML7 54 E8
Babylon Ave ML4 65 A3
Babylon Dr ML4 65 A3
Babylon Pl ML4 65 A3
Babylon Rd ML4 65 A3
Back Cswy G31 46 D5
Back O Barns ML3 78 E4
Back O Dykes Rd G66 21 B7
Back Row ML3 78 E4
Backbrae St G65 10 D8
Backmuir Cres ML3 78 B6
Backmuir Pl ML3 78 B6
Backmuir Rd
Clydebank G15 16 B4
Hamilton ML3 78 B6
Badallan Pl EH47 71 E6
Badenheath Pl G68 22 D5
Badenheath Terr G67 22 E4
Badenoch Rd G66 9 C1
Bagnell St G21 30 F5
Bahamas Way 6 G75 75 A1
Bailie Dr G61 16 D7
Bailie Fyfe Way ML2 94 B7
Baillie Ave ML7 55 F5
Baillie Dr Bothwell G71 64 A3
East Kilbride G74 76 C4
Baillie Gdns ML2 81 E4
Baillie Pl G74 76 C4
Baillie Wynd 11 G71 64 A8
Baillies La ML6 51 A8
Bailliesmuir Pl ML2 82 A6
Baillieston Rd
Glasgow,Barrachnie G32 47 E4
Glasgow,Broomhouse G71 48 B2
Baillieston Sta G69 48 B3
Bain St G40 163 C1
Bainsford St G32 46 F6
Baird Ave Airdrie ML6 36 B2
Glasgow G52 42 E8
Kirkmuirhill ML11 113 F4
Larkhall ML9 106 C8
Baird Brae G4 30 B3
Baird Cres G67 23 B7
Baird Ct G81 15 A2
Baird Dr Armadale EH48 41 F7
Bearsden G61 16 D5
Baird Gdns Hamilton G72 77 E6
Strathaven ML10 112 C5
Baird Hill G75 88 E8
Baird Meml Prim Sch G67 23 C7
Baird Pl Bellshill ML4 65 A7
Wishaw ML2 81 E4
Baird Rd EH48 41 F7
Baird St Coatbridge ML5 50 A7
Glasgow G4 163 B4
Baird Terr ML7 55 C5
Bairds Cres ML3 78 C3
Bairdsland View ML4 65 B6
Baker St G41 44 E1
Baker's Brae ML11 119 E4
Bakewell Rd G69 48 A5
Balaclava St G2,G3 162 B2
Balado Rd G33 47 E7
Balbakie Rd ML7 55 E5
Balbeg St G51 43 E6
Balbeggie St G32 47 C4
Balblair Rd G52 43 F2
Balcarres Ave G12 29 C5
Balcary Pl ML6 51 E1
Balcastle Gdns G65 6 B2
Balcastle Rd G65 6 A1
Balcomie St G33 32 A1
Balcomie Terr ML3 91 B8
Balcurvie Rd G34 33 A2
Baldinnie Rd G34 48 B8
Baldorran Cres G68 11 B3
Baldovan Cres G33 47 F8
Baldovan Path G33 47 F7
Baldovie Rd G52 43 C3
Baldragon Rd G34 33 C1
Baldric Rd G13 28 C6
Baldwin Ave G13 28 D8
Balerno Dr G52 43 E3
Balfearn Dr G76 86 E5
Balfluig St G34 32 F1
Balfour St G20 29 D6
Balfour Terr G75 88 F7
Balfour Wynd ML9 93 B1
Balfron Cres ML3 77 F3
Balfron Dr ML5 50 C3
Balfron Pl ML5 50 C4
Balfron Rd Glasgow G51 43 E7
Paisley PA1 42 D5
Balgair Dr PA1 42 B5
Balgair Pl G22 30 B5
Balgair St G22 30 B4
Balgair Terr G32 47 B5
Balglass Gdns G22 30 B4
Balglass St G22 30 B4
Balgonie Rd G52 43 E4
Balgownie Cres G46 59 A2
Balgray Cres G78 57 E2
Balgray Rd
Lesmahagow ML11 119 F2
Lesmahagow ML11 119 F3
Newton Mearns G77 72 A5
Balgraybank St G21 31 A4
Balgrayhill Rd G21 30 F6
Balintore St G32 47 A5
Baliol La G3 162 A4
Baliol St G3 162 A4
Baljaffray Prim Sch G61 16 C8
Baljaffray Rd G61 16 B8
Ballaig Ave G61 16 D5
Ballaig Cres G33 32 C5
Ballantay Quadrant G45 61 A3
Ballantay Rd G45 61 A3
Ballantay Terr G45 61 A3
Ballantine Ave G52 43 A7
Ballantrae G74 75 D2
Ballantrae Cres G77 73 A4
Ballantrae Dr G77 73 A4
Ballantrae Rd G72 77 F6
Ballantrae Wynd ML1 66 B5
Ballater Cres ML2 81 B5
Ballater Dr Bearsden G61 17 A2
Paisley PA2 42 A1
Ballater Pl G5 45 D4
Ballater St G5 45 D5
Ballater Way ML5 34 C6
Ballayne Dr G69 22 A3
Ballerup High Sch G75 88 B4
Ballerup Terr G75 88 E6
Ballgreen Rd ML12 160 C3
Ballindalloch Dr G31 46 B8
Ballindalloch La G31 46 A8
Ballinkier Ave FK4 8 E3
Balloch Gdns G52 43 F3
Balloch Holdings G68 11 B1
Balloch Rd Airdrie ML6 52 A6
Cumbernauld G68 11 D2
Shotts ML7 69 E6
Balloch Rdbt G68 11 A2
Balloch View G67 11 F2
Ballochmill Bsns Pk G73 61 D8
Ballochmill Rd G73 61 D8
Ballochmyle G74 76 D4
Ballochmyle Cres 11 G53 58 A8
Ballochmyle Dr 14 G53 58 A8
Ballochmyle Gdns G53 58 A8
Ballochmyle Pl 12 G53 58 A8
Ballochney La ML6 35 E2
Ballochney Rd ML6 36 E3
Ballochney St Airdrie ML6 35 F1
Airdrie ML6 35 F2
Ballochnie Dr ML6 37 A3
Ballochnie View ML6 36 F2
Ballogie Rd G44 60 B7
Ballplay Rd DG10 161 E5
Balmalloch Prim Sch G65 6 C1
Balmalloch Rd G65 6 B1
Balmartin Rd G23 17 D1
Balmeg Ave G46 73 C8
Balmerino Pl G64 31 D8
Balmoral Ave ML6 35 F5
Balmoral Cres
Carstairs Junction ML11 124 C1
Coatbridge ML5 49 D4
Balmoral Ct ML11 124 C1
Balmoral Dr Bearsden G61 17 A2
Cambuslang G72 61 E6
Carstairs Junction ML11 124 C1
Glasgow G32 62 B8
Balmoral Gdns
Blantyre G72 63 C2
Uddingston G71 48 F1
Balmoral Path 3 ML9 93 C2
Balmoral Pl G74 75 C1
Balmoral St G14 28 B3
Balmore Dr ML3 91 B8
Balmore Ind Est G22 30 B8
Balmore Pl G22 30 B6
Balmore Rd
Balmore G62,G64 18 C8
Glasgow G22,G23 18 A2
Bardowie G62,G64 18 C8
Balmore Sq G22 30 B5
Balmuildy Prim Sch G64 18 F3
Balmuildy Rd G64 18 D5
Balornock Prim Sch G21 31 A4
Balornock Rd G64 31 A6
Balruddery Pl G64 31 D8
Balshagray Ave G11 28 F3
Balshagray Cres G14 28 E2
Balshagray Dr G11 28 F3
Balshagray La G11 28 F3
Balshagray Pl 2 G11 28 F3
Baltersan Gdns ML3 91 F3
Baltic Ct G40 46 A3
Baltic La G40 46 A3
Baltic Pl G40 46 A4
Baltic St Glasgow G40 46 A3
Glasgow G40 46 A4
Glasgow G40 46 B3
Balure Pl G31 46 C7
Balvaird Cres 2 G73 61 A7
Balvaird Dr G73 61 A7
Balvenie Dr ML1 66 B1
Balvenie St ML5 50 B3
Balveny St G33 32 D2
Balvicar Dr G42 44 F1
Balvicar St G42 44 F1
Balvie Ave Clydebank G15 16 A1
Glasgow,Giffnock G46 59 D2
Banavie La G11 29 A3
Banavie Rd Glasgow G11 29 A3
Wishaw ML2 81 F6
Banchory Ave
Glasgow G43 59 B5
Glenmavis ML6 35 F5
Banchory Cres G61 17 A2
Banchory Rd ML2 81 B5
Baneberry Path G74 75 D4
Banff Ave ML6 51 A4
Banff Pl G75 88 C8
Banff Quadrant ML2 81 B5
Banff St G33 32 B2
Bangorshill St
Glasgow G46 58 F4
Thornliebank G46 59 A4
Bank Pk G75 88 D8
Bank Pl ML7 69 F4
Bank Rd Glasgow G32 62 C8
Harthill ML7 55 E5
Bank St Airdrie ML6 51 A8
Barrhead G78 57 C2
Cambuslang G72 62 A6
Coatbridge ML5 49 E6
Glasgow G12 29 E2
Paisley PA1 42 A4
Bank Terr ML11 98 F8
Bank View ML6 51 D2
Bank Way 14 ML9 93 B4
Bankbrae Ave G53 58 A6
Bankend St G33 32 A1
Bankfield Dr ML3 91 D7
Bankfoot Dr G52 43 B4
Bankfoot Pl
Newton Mearns G77 73 B4
Strathaven ML10 112 D7
Bankfoot Rd G52 43 B4
Bankglen Rd G15 16 B4
Bankhall St G42 45 B2
Bankhead Ave
Airdrie ML6 51 D7
Bellshill ML4 65 B3
Bankhead Ave *continued*
Coatbridge ML5 49 C4
Glasgow G13 28 A6
Lesmahagow ML11 119 F3
Bankhead Dr G73 61 A7
Bankhead Pl Airdrie ML6 51 D7
Coatbridge ML5 49 C4
Bankhead Prim Sch
Glasgow G13 28 A6
Rutherglen G73 60 F7
Bankhead Rd
Carmunnock G76 74 D7
Kirkintilloch G66 21 B7
Lesmahagow ML11 119 F3
Rutherglen G73 60 F7
Bankhead Terr ML11 117 B2
Bankholm Pl G76 73 F5
Bankhouse Rd ML11 119 E4
Bankier Prim Sch FK4 8 E3
Bankier Rd FK4 8 E3
Bankier Terr FK4 8 E3
Banknock St G32 46 E6
Bankview Cres G66 20 A8
Bankview Dr G66 20 A8
Bannatyne Ave G31 46 B7
Bannatyne St ML11 117 B4
Banner Dr G13 16 C1
Banner Rd G13 16 D1
Bannercross Ave 2 G69 48 A5
Bannercross Dr G69 48 A5
Bannercross Gdns 1 G69 48 A5
Bannerman Dr ML4 65 D5
Bannerman High Sch G69 48 A4
Bannerman Pl G81 15 B2
Bannockburn Dr 19 ML9 93 C1
Bannockburn Pl ML1 66 A2
Bantaskin St G20 29 C7
Banton Pl G33 48 A7
Banton Prim Sch G65 7 E3
Banton Rd G65 7 D2
Banyan Cres G71 49 D1
Bar Hill Pl G65 10 B8
Bar Hill Roman Fort* G65 10 B4
Barassie G74 75 D3
Barassie Cres G68 11 F6
Barassie Ct G71 63 F2
Barbados Gn 5 G75 75 A1
Barbae Pl G71 64 A3
Barbana Rd G74 74 E2
Barbauchlaw Ave EH48 41 F6
Barbegs Cres G65 10 F4
Barberry Ave G53 58 B2
Barberry Gdns G53 58 B2
Barberry Pl G53 58 C2
Barbeth Gdns G67 23 B6
Barbeth Pl G67 23 B6
Barbeth Rd G67 23 B6
Barbeth Way G67 23 A6
Barbreck Rd 7 G42 44 F2
Barbush Pl ML10 112 F6
Barcaldine Ave G69 21 B1
Barcaldine Terr G41 44 F2
Barcapel Ave G77 72 E8
Barcapel Flats G77 72 E7
Barclay Rd ML1 79 B6
Barclay Sq PA4 27 B1
Barclay St G21 30 F5
Barcloy Pl ML6 51 F1
Bard Ave G13 28 B8
Bardowie Ind Est G22 30 C4
Bardowie St Glasgow G22 30 B4
Glasgow G22 30 C4
Bardrill Dr G64 18 E1
Bardykes Rd Blantyre G72 63 C1
Hamilton G72 77 B8
Barefield St ML9 93 A4
Barfillan Dr G52 43 E5
Bargany Ct G53 43 A1
Bargany Pl
8 Glasgow G53 43 A1
Glasgow G53 43 B1
Bargany Rd G53 43 A1
Bargaran Rd G53 43 B3
Bargarron Dr PA3 42 A8
Bargeddie Prim Sch G69 49 A6
Bargeddie St G33 31 D2
Bargeddie Sta G69 49 A4
Barhill La G65 9 F4
Barhill Terr G65 10 A4
Barholm Sq G33 32 D1
Barke Rd G67 12 A3
Barkly Terr 2 G75 88 C8
Barlae Ave G76 86 E8
Barlanark Ave G32 47 C6
Barlanark Cres G33 47 D7
Barlanark Dr G33 47 D7
Barlanark Pl Glasgow G33 47 E7
Glasgow,Greenfield G32 47 B6
Barlanark Prim Sch G33 47 F6
Barlanark Rd G33 47 E7
Barlandfauld St G65 10 E7
Barlia Dr G45 60 E3
Barlia Gdns G45 60 E3
Barlia Gr G45 60 E3
Barlia St G45 60 E3
Barlia Terr G45 60 F3
Barloch St Glasgow G22 30 C4
Glasgow G22 30 C5
Barlogan Ave G52 43 E5
Barlogan Quadrant G52 43 E5
Barmore Ave ML8 109 A8
Barmulloch Prim Sch G21 31 C4
Barmulloch Rd G21 31 B4
Barn St ML10 112 E6
Barnard Gdns G64 19 B4
Barnbeth Rd G53 43 B2
Barncluith Ave ML3 79 A2
Barncluith Bsns Ctr ML3 78 F3
Barncluith Ct ML3 78 F3
Barncluith Rd ML3 78 F2
Barnes St G78 57 B2
Barness Pl G33 47 A8
Barnett Path 3 G72 77 D7
Barnflat St G73 46 B1
Barnhill Ct G77 72 D3
Barnhill Dr Glasgow G21 31 A3
Hamilton ML3 77 D2
Newton Mearns G77 72 D2
Barnhill Sta G21 31 A3
Barnkirk Ave G15 16 A3
Barns St G81 27 C8
Barnswood Pl 6 G71 64 B3
Barnton St G32 46 E7
Barnwell Terr G51 43 E7
Barochan Pl G53 43 B3
Barochan Rd Bellshill ML4 65 D6
Glasgow G53 43 B3
Baron Ct ML3 79 A2
Baron Path G69 48 F5
Baron Rd PA3 42 A6
Baron St PA4 27 C2
Baron's Haugh Nature Reserve* ML1 79 E2
Baronald Dr G12 29 B6
Baronald Gate G12 29 B6
Baronald St G73 46 B1
Barone Dr G76 73 C8
Baronhall Dr G72 77 C8
Baronhill G67 12 B5
Barons Gate G71 63 E4
Barons Rd ML1 80 C2
Barons Twr ML1 80 B3
Barony Ct 4 G69 48 B6
Barony Dr G69 48 B5
Barony Gdns G69 48 B5
Barony Pl G68 10 E1
Barony Wynd 5 G69 48 B6
Barr Cres G81 15 B5
Barr Farm Rd G65 10 E7
Barr Gr G71 64 A8
Barr Pl G77 72 C5
Barr St Glasgow G20 30 A3
Motherwell ML1 79 E8
Barr Terr East Kilbride G74 75 E2
Kirkmuirhill ML11 114 B2
Barra Ave Coatbridge ML5 49 E4
Renfrew PA4 27 C1
Wishaw ML2 81 E5
Barra Dr ML6 51 E6
Barra Pl ML5 49 E4
Barra St G20 29 C8
Barrachnie Ave G69 48 A6
Barrachnie Cres G69 47 F5
Barrachnie Ct G69 47 F6
Barrachnie Dr G69 48 A5
Barrachnie Gr G69 48 A6
Barrachnie Pl 4 G69 48 A6
Barrachnie Rd G69 47 F5
Barrack St Glasgow G4 163 C1
Hamilton ML3 78 D4
Barras Mkt G4 163 C1
Barrbridge Rd ML5 49 B4
Barrhead High Sch G78 57 D3
Barrhead Mus G78 57 C2
Barrhead Rd
Glasgow G43,G53 58 C7
Newton Mearns G77 72 B5
Paisley PA2 42 A2
Barrhead Sta G78 57 B3
Barrhill Ct G66 21 A8
Barrhill Rd G66 21 A8
Barrie Quadrant G81 15 A4
Barrie Rd
East Kilbride G74 76 D5
Glasgow G52 43 A7
Barrie St ML1 79 E6
Barriedale Ave ML3 78 B3
Barrington Dr G4 29 F2
Barrisdale Rd
Glasgow G20 29 D8
Wishaw ML2 81 F6
Barrisdale Way G73 61 B4
Barrland Ct G46 59 C3
Barrland Dr G46 59 C3
Barrland St G41 45 A3
Barrmill Rd G43 59 B5
Barrowfield Prim Sch G40 46 A5
Barrowfield St
Coatbridge ML5 49 F4
Glasgow G40 46 A5
Barrpath G65 10 F7
Barrs La ML8 95 F3
Barrwood Pl G71 64 A8
Barrwood St G33 31 E2
Barry Gdns G72 77 D6
Barscube Terr PA2 42 A2
Barshaw Dr PA1 42 A6
Barshaw Ho PA1 42 C5
Barshaw Pl PA1 42 D5
Barshaw Rd G52 42 F6
Bartholomew St G40 46 A3
Bartie Gdns ML9 93 F1
Bartiebeith Rd G33 47 E7
Bartlands Pl G76 86 F4
Barton Ct EH47 71 E6
Barton Terr EH47 71 F6
Bartonhall Rd ML2 81 D1
Barty's Rd ML4 65 C5
Bassett Ave G13 28 B8
Bassett Cres G13 28 B8
Bath La G2 162 B3

Bath St G2 162 C3
Bathgate St G31 46 A6
Bathgo Ave PA1 42 E4
Baton Rd ML7 69 D6
Batson St G42 45 B2
Battismains ML11 117 C4
Battle Pl G42 59 F8
Battlefield Ave G42 60 A7
Battlefield Ct G42 60 B7
Battlefield Gdns G42 60 A8
Battlefield Prim Sch G42 59 F7
Battlefield Rd G42 60 A7
Battles Burn Dr G32 47 A2
Battles Burn Gate G32 47 A2
Battles Burn View G32 47 A2
Bavelaw St G33 32 D2
Baxter La ML11 117 A4
Baxter Wynd ML2 80 E2
Baxter's Brae ML11 114 A4
Bay Willow Ct G72 62 F4
Bayfield Ave G15 16 A3
Bayfield Terr G15 16 A3
Beacon Pl G33 46 F8
Beaconsfield Rd G12 29 B5
Beanshields Rd ML8 108 F4
Beard Cres G69 34 A5
Beardmore Way G31 46 B6
Bearford Dr G52 43 B6
Bearsden Acad G61 16 E6
Bearsden Bath Ho* G61 16 F5
Bearsden Prim Sch G61 16 E5
Bearsden Rd
Bearsden G61 28 F7
Bearsden G61 28 F8
Bearsden Sta G61 16 E4
Beaton Rd G41 44 E2
Beaton St ML9 92 F5
Beatrice Dr ML1 65 F5
Beatson Wynd G71 49 A1
Beattock St G31 46 D5
Beattock Wynd ML3 78 A3
Beaufort Ave G43 59 C6
Beaufort Dr G66 20 B8
Beaufort Gdns G64 18 E1
Beauly Ave ML10 112 F8
Beauly Cres Airdrie ML6 51 E6
Newton Mearns G77 73 B4
Wishaw ML2 81 B1
Beauly Pl
Bishopbriggs G64 19 D2
Chryston G69 21 D1
Coatbridge ML5 50 B3
East Kilbride G74 75 D2
6 Glasgow G20 29 D6
Motherwell ML1 66 A5
Beauly Rd G69 48 A3
Beaumont Gate 5 G12 29 C3
Beckfield Cres G33 31 D7
Beckfield Dr G33 31 D7
Beckfield Gate G33 31 D7
Beckfield Gr G33 31 D7
Beckfield Wlk G33 31 D7
Beckford La ML3 78 D5
Beckford Prim Sch ML3 78 C5
Beckford St ML3 78 D5
Beckford St Bsns Ctr ML3 78 D5
Bedale Rd G69 47 F4
Bedcow View G66 20 F7
Bedford Ave G81 15 D2
Bedford La 6 G5 45 B5
Bedford St G5 45 B5
Bedlay Ct G69 22 A3
Bedlay Pl ML5 22 F1
Bedlay View G71 64 B8
Bedlay Wlk G69 22 A3
Bedlormie Dr EH48 40 C2
Beech Ave Bearsden G61 17 A7
Cambuslang G72 61 F6
Glasgow,Dumbreck G41 44 B4
Glasgow,Garrowhill G69 48 A5
Glasgow,Ibrox G41 44 B5
Larkhall ML9 93 D2
Motherwell ML1 66 B3
Newton Mearns G77 72 E4
Paisley PA2 42 A1
Quarter ML3 91 F4
Rutherglen G73 61 C4
Beech Cres
Cambuslang G72 62 E4
Motherwell ML1 66 D7
Newton Mearns G77 72 E4
Beech Dr Caldercruix ML6 37 F4
Clydebank G81 15 A5
Beech Gdns G69 48 A5
Beech Gr East Kilbride G75 88 B6
Gartcosh G69 34 A5
Law ML8 94 F6
Wishaw ML2 81 C7
Beech Pl G64 31 B8
Beech Rd
Bishopbriggs G64 31 B8
Kirkintilloch G66 20 C6
Motherwell ML1 66 C7
Beech Terr ML9 93 B1
Beechbank Ave ML6 35 F1
Beeches Rd G81 15 A6
Beeches Terr G81 15 A6
Beeches The
Armadale EH48 41 E5
3 Hamilton G72 77 C7
Kirkmuirhill ML11 114 A5
Lanark ML11 117 B2
Newton Mearns G77 72 F6
Beechfield Dr ML8 109 A8
Beechgrove Moffat DG10 161 C6
Moodiesburn G69 21 F2
Beechgrove Ave G71 64 C7
Beechgrove Quadrant ML1 66 A5
Beechgrove St
Glasgow G40 46 B2
Rigside ML11 138 F6
Beechlands Ave G44 59 F1
Beechlands Dr G76 73 C6
Beechmount Ave 137 F5
Beechmount Ct ML7 70 B2
Beechmount Rd G66 20 D4
Beechwood
Kirkmuirhill ML11 114 A3
Larkhall ML9 93 A5
Wishaw ML2 80 D1
Beechwood Ave
Clarkston G76 73 C6
Hamilton ML3 91 B8
Rutherglen G73 61 C6
Beechwood Cres
Lesmahagow ML11 119 E4
Wishaw ML2 81 C2
Beechwood Ct
Bearsden G61 16 F3
Cumbernauld G67 23 F8
Strathaven ML10 112 F7
Beechwood Dr
Coatbridge ML5 50 D5
Glasgow G11 28 F4
Renfrew PA4 27 C1
Stonehouse ML9 129 F8
Beechwood Gdns
Bellshill ML4 65 C4
Moodiesburn G69 21 F1
Beechwood Gr G78 57 C1
Beechwood La G61 16 F3
Beechwood Pl
Bellshill ML4 65 C4
Glasgow G11 28 F4
Beechwood Rd G67 23 F8
Beechworth Dr ML1 66 D2
Beecroft Pl G72 63 E1
Beil Dr G13 27 F7
Beith Dr ML6 51 A4
Beith St G11 29 B1
Belford Ct G77 72 D2
Belford Gr G77 72 D2
Belgowan St ML4 64 F7
Belgrave La G12 29 E3
Belgrave St ML4 64 F6
Belgrave Terr 7 G12 29 E3
Belhaven Ct G77 72 D2
Belhaven Pk G69 33 C7
Belhaven Pl G77 72 D2
Belhaven Rd Hamilton ML3 77 E3
Wishaw ML2 81 A3
Belhaven Terr
20 Glasgow G12 29 C4
Wishaw ML2 81 A3
Belhaven Terr W 16 G12 29 C4
Belhaven Terrace La 19 G12 29 C4
Belhaven Terrace West La 17 G12 29 C4
Bell Coll ML3 78 D4
Bell Dr G72 77 C4
Bell Gn E G75 88 F8
Bell Gn W G75 88 E8
Bell St Airdrie ML6 50 F7
Bellshill ML4 65 B7
Clydebank G81 27 D7
Glasgow G1 163 B1
Renfrew PA4 27 D4
Wishaw ML2 81 A3
Bell View ML12 151 A2
Bell View Ct PA4 27 D4
Bell's Wynd
17 Douglas ML11 138 B1
Lanark ML11 117 C5
Bellahouston Acad G41 44 C5
Bellahouston Acad Annexe G51 44 C5
Bellahouston Dr G52 43 E3
Bellahouston Prim Sch G51 44 C5
Bellairs Pl G72 63 C1
Bellas Ave ML11 115 E3
Bellas Pl ML6 37 A2
Bellcraig Ct G76 74 A5
Bellefield Rd ML11 117 A5
Belleisle Ave G71 63 E7
Belleisle Ct G68 11 E4
Belleisle Dr G68 11 E4
Belleisle Gdns G68 11 E4
Belleisle Gr G68 11 E4
Belleisle St G42 45 B1
Bellevue Ave G66 20 B8
Bellevue Rd G66 20 B8
Bellfield Cres G78 57 B3
Bellfield Ct G78 57 B4
Bellfield Dr ML2 81 C1
Bellfield Pl ML11 138 A5
Bellfield Rd
Bellfield ML11 138 A5
Kirkintilloch G66 20 B8
137 F5
Bellfield St G31 46 A6
Bellflower Ave G53 58 C3
Bellflower Ct G74 75 C3
Bellflower Gdns G53 58 C3
Bellflower Gr G74 75 C4
Bellflower Pl G53 58 C3
Bellgrove St G31 46 A5
Bellgrove Sta G31 45 F6
Bellisle Terr ML3 91 B8
Bellona Terr EH47 71 F6
Bellrock Cres G33 47 A8
Bellrock Ct G33 47 B8
Bellrock St G33 47 B8
Bells Wynd ML11 117 C5
Bellscroft Ave G73 60 F7
Bellsdyke Rd ML6 51 A6
Bellsfield Dr G72 77 E6
Bellshaugh Ct G12 29 C5
Bellshaugh Gdns G12 29 C5
Bellshaugh La G12 29 C5
Bellshaugh Pl 2 G12 29 C5
Bellshaugh Rd G12 29 C4
Bellshill Acad ML4 65 B5
Bellshill Ind Est ML4 64 F6
Bellshill Rd
Bellshill G71,ML1,ML4 64 D2
Bothwell G71 64 B5
Motherwell ML1 65 C2
Bellshill Sta ML4 65 A5
Bellside Rd Chapelhall ML6 51 F2
Cleland ML1 67 D1
Motherwell ML1 67 A8
Bellvue Cres ML4 64 F4
Bellvue Way ML5 50 D4
Bellwood St G41 59 E8
Bellziehill Rd ML4 64 E5
Belmont Ave G71 63 E7
Belmont Cres G12 29 E3
Belmont Ct 6 G66 20 D8
Belmont Dr Barrhead G78 57 D1
East Kilbride G75 88 B8
Glasgow G46 59 B3
Rutherglen G73 61 B7
Shotts ML7 70 B2
Belmont House Sch G77 73 A6
Belmont La G12 29 E3
Belmont Rd
Cambuslang G72 61 E3
Glasgow G21 30 F6
Paisley PA3 42 A6
Belmont St Clydebank G81 27 B8
Coatbridge ML5 34 D1
Glasgow G12 29 E3
Kilsyth G65 6 C1
Overtown ML2 94 B6
Belses Dr G52 43 C5
Belses Gdns G52 43 C5
Belstane Ave ML12 152 B7
Belstane Mews ML8 96 A3
Belstane Pk ML8 95 F3
Belstane Pl 4 G71 64 A3
Belstane Rd Carluke ML8 96 A3
Cumbernauld G67 23 F5
Belsyde Ave G15 16 B2
Beltane St Glasgow G3 162 A3
Wishaw ML2 81 A2
Beltonfoot Way ML2 80 F2
Beltrees Ave G53 43 A2
Beltrees Cres G53 43 A2
Beltrees Rd G53 43 A1
Belvedere Pl 137 F5
Belvidere Cres
Bellshill ML4 65 B4
Bishopbriggs G64 19 B2
Belvidere Prim Sch ML4 65 A4
Belvidere Rd ML4 65 A4
Belvoir Pl G72 77 D8
Bemersyde G64 19 C2
Bemersyde Ave G43 59 B5
Bemersyde Pl ML9 93 A1
Ben Aigan Pl G53 58 C4
Ben Alder Dr PA2 42 D1
Ben Buie Way PA2 42 D1
Ben Donich Pl G53 58 D4
Ben Edra Pl G53 58 D4
Ben Garrisdale Pl G53 58 D4
Ben Glas Pl G53 58 D4
Ben Hope Ave PA2 42 D2
Ben Laga Pl G53 58 D4
Ben Lawers Dr
Cumbernauld G68 11 B2
Paisley PA2 42 D2
Ben Ledi Ave PA2 42 D2
Ben Ledi Cres G68 11 B2
Ben Loyal Ave PA2 42 D2
Ben Lui Dr PA2 42 D1
Ben Lui Pl
Cumbernauld G68 11 B2
Glasgow G53 58 D4
Ben MacDui Gdns G53 58 D4
Ben More Dr
Cumbernauld G68 11 A2
Paisley PA2 42 D1
Ben Nevis Rd PA2 42 C1
Ben Nevis Way G68 11 B2
Ben Oss Pl G53 58 C4
Ben Uird Pl G53 58 D4
Ben Vane Ave PA2 42 C1
Ben Venue Rd G68 11 A2
Ben Venue Way PA2 42 D1
Ben Vorlich Dr G53 58 D4
Ben Vorlich Pl G53 58 D4
Ben Wyvis Dr PA2 42 C1
Benalder St G11 29 C1
Benarty Gdns G64 19 B2
Benbecula G74 76 C1
Bencroft Ave ML12 160 D4
Bencroft Dr G44 60 E5
Bendigo Pl ML11 117 A4
Benford Ave ML1 66 D4
Benford Knowe ML1 66 E4
Bengairn St G31 46 C7
Bengal Pl G43 59 C7
Bengal St G43 59 C7
Benhar Pl G33 46 F8
Benhar Rd ML7 70 A6
Benholm St G32 46 F3
Benmore Twr G72 61 E3
Benn Ave PA1 42 A4
Bennan Pl G75 88 C4
Bennan Sq G42 45 C2
Benny Lynch Ct G5 45 C5
Benson St ML5 50 A4
Bent Cres G71 64 C3
Bent Prim Sch ML11 113 F1
Bent Rd Chapelhall ML6 51 D3
Hamilton ML3 78 D3
Bent View ML9 107 B3
Bentfoot Rd ML2 94 C7
Benthall St G5 45 D4
Bentinck St G3 29 E1
Bents Rd Chapelton ML10 103 D6
Glasgow G69 48 B5
Benty's La ML8 108 F8
Benvie Gdns G64 19 B2
Benview Rd G76 73 E7
Benview St G20 29 F4
Benview Terr PA2 42 B2
Bereholm ML11 119 E4
Berelands Cres G73 60 E7
Berelands Pl G73 60 F7
Beresford Ave G14 28 E4
Berkeley St G3 162 A3
Berkeley Terrace La G3 162 A3
Berkley Dr G72 63 D1
Bernadette Cres ML1 66 D2
Bernadette St ML1 66 D3
Bernard Path G40 46 A4
Bernard St G40 46 A4
Bernard Terr G40 46 A4
Bernard's Ct ML11 117 A4
Bernard's Wynd ML11 117 A4
Berneray St G22 30 C7
Bernisdale Pl 1 G15 15 D3
Berridale Ave G44 60 A5
Berriedale G75 87 E8
Berriedale Ave G69 48 A4
Berriedale Cres G72 77 C3
Berriedale Path G72 77 C3
Berriedale Quadrant ML2 81 B5
Berriedale Terr G72 77 C3
Berryburn Rd G21 31 C4
Berryhill Cres ML2 80 F2
Berryhill Ct ML10 112 E8
Berryhill Dr G46 59 B2
Berryhill Pl ML7 70 B2
Berryhill Prim Sch ML2 80 E3
Berryhill Rd
Cumbernauld G67 11 E2
Glasgow G46 59 B2
Berryknowe G66 21 B7
Berryknowe Ave G69 33 C7
Berryknowes Ave G52 43 D5
Berryknowes La G52 43 C5
Berryknowes Rd G52 43 C5
Bertram Ave ML11 125 A2
Bertram Dr ML7 53 C2
Bertram Pl ML7 69 D5
Bertram St Glasgow G41 44 E1
Hamilton ML3 78 A6
Harthill ML7 55 C5
2 Larkhall ML9 93 C1
Shotts ML7 69 E5
Bervie St G51 43 F6
Berwick Cres ML6 50 F5
Berwick Dr Glasgow G52 43 B4
Rutherglen G73 61 D6
Berwick Pl Coatbridge ML5 50 B3
East Kilbride G74 76 C3
Berwick St Coatbridge ML5 50 B3
Hamilton ML3 78 B5
Bessemer Dr G75 89 A5
Beta Ctr G81 27 C8
Bethal La G75 88 A4
Betula Dr G81 15 A5
Beveridge Terr ML4 65 D4
Beverley Rd G43 59 D6
Bevin Ave G81 15 D1
Bideford Cres G32 47 D3
Bield The ML2 81 C2
Biggar Gasworks Mus* ML12 160 C4
Biggar High Sch ML12 160 D4
Biggar Mill Rd ML12 160 C4
Biggar Prim Sch ML12 160 D4
Biggar Puppet Theatre* ML12 160 E4
Biggar Rd
Biggar Road ML1 67 A6
Chapelhall ML6 51 E1
Libberton ML11 131 E7
Newhouse ML1,ML6 66 F7
Parkside ML1 67 B3
Symington ML12 140 E6
Biggar St G31 46 B6
Biggarshiels Rd ML12 160 D7
Bigton St G33 32 B2
Billings Rd ML1 79 B5
Bilsland Ct G20 30 B5
Bilsland Dr G20 30 A5
Binend Rd G53 58 C8
Binnie Pl G40 45 E5
Binniehill Rd
Brownrigg FK1 26 F3
Cumbernauld G68 11 D2
Binns Rd G33 32 C2
Birch Ave G76 73 F6
Birch Brae ML3 78 E1
Birch Cres G76 73 F6
Birch Dr Cambuslang G72 62 C6
Kirkintilloch G66 20 D5
Birch Gr G71 64 B7
Birch Knowe G64 31 B8
Birch Pl Cambuslang G72 62 F4
Hamilton G72 77 D8
Birch Quadrant ML6 51 D7
Birch Rd Clydebank G81 15 A5
Cumbernauld G67 12 F3
Birch St Glasgow G5 45 D3
Motherwell ML1 66 B5
Birch View G61 17 A5
Birchend Dr G21 31 B2
Birchend Pl G21 31 B2
Birchfield Dr G14 28 B4
Birchfield Pl ML10 112 C5
Birchfield Rd ML3 78 B3
Birchgrove ML9 93 A5
Birchlea Dr G46 59 D4
Birchmount Ct ML6 51 D8
Birchview Dr G76 73 F4
Birchwood Ave G32 47 E4
Birchwood Gr G69 49 A6
Birchwood Pl G32 47 E4
Birdsfield Ct G72 77 F6
Birdsfield Dr G72 77 E6
Birdsfield St ML3 77 F6
Birdston Rd G21 31 C6
Birgidale Rd G45 60 D2
Birgidale Terr G45 60 D2
Birkbeck Ct G4 163 B3
Birkdale G74 75 C3
Birkdale Cres G68 11 F6
Birkdale Ct G71 63 F2
Birkdale Wood G68 12 A6
Birken Rd G66 20 E4
Birkenburn Rd G67 12 F6
Birkenshaw Rd ML5 22 E1
Birkenshaw St G31 46 B7
Birkenshaw Way EH48 41 E6
Birkfield Loan ML8 96 C1
Birkfield Pl ML8 96 C1
Birkhall Ave G52 43 A4
Birkhall Dr G61 16 F2
Birkhill Ave G64 19 B2
Birkhill Gdns G64 19 B2
Birkhill Rd
Crossford ML8,ML11 108 D2
Hamilton ML3 91 D7
Birks Ct ML8 94 F5
Birks Pl ML11 117 A5
Birks Rd Larkhall ML9 106 B7
Law ML8 94 E3
Birksburn Ave 3 ML9 129 E8
Birkshaw Brae ML2 94 A8
Birkshaw Pl ML2 94 A8
Birkshaw Twr ML2 93 F8
Birkwood Pl G77 72 D2
Birkwood St G40 46 B2
Birmingham Rd PA4 27 B1
Birnam Ave G64 19 B2
Birnam Cres G61 17 B5
Birnam Gdns G64 19 B2
Birnam Pl Hamilton ML3 77 E3
Newton Mearns G77 73 B4
Birnam Rd G31 46 D3
Birness Dr G43 59 D7
Birnie Ct G21 31 C4
Birnie Knowe ML11 138 F6
Birnie Rd G21 31 C3
Birniehall ML11 98 F8
Birniehill Rd ML1 68 A5
Birniehill Rdbt G74 89 A8
Birnock Ave PA4 27 E1
Birnyhill Ct G81 15 A7
Birrens Rd ML1 79 C8
Birsay Rd G22 30 B7
Birthwood Rd ML12 141 D3
Bishop Gdns
Bishopbriggs G64 18 E2
Hamilton ML3 91 E7
Bishop La G2 162 B2
Bishopbriggs High Sch G64 19 A1
Bishopbriggs Ind Est G21 31 A7
Bishopbriggs Sta G64 19 A1
Bishopdale G74 75 C3
Bishoploch Prim Sch G34 33 D1
Bishopmill Pl G21 31 C4
Bishopmill Rd G21 31 C4
Bishops Gate G74 74 C3
Bishops Pk G74 74 B3
Bishopsgate Dr G21 30 E7
Bishopsgate Gdns G21 30 E7
Bishopsgate Pl 3 G21 30 E7
Bishopsgate Rd G21 30 E7
Black Bull Cl 6 DG10 161 D5
Black Hill View ML11 114 D4
Black O' Hill Rdbt G68 11 B1
Black St Airdrie ML6 36 B1
Glasgow G4 163 B4
Blackadder Pl G75 87 D7
Blackbog Rd ML6 23 F2
Blackbraes Rd G74 76 B4
Blackburn Cres G66 21 A8
Blackburn Gr ML10 112 E8
Blackburn Sq G78 57 D1
Blackburn St G51 44 E6
Blackbyres Ct G78 57 D4
Blackbyres Rd G78 57 C5
Blackcraig Ave G15 16 A3
Blackcroft Ave ML6 51 E5
Blackcroft Gdns G32 47 D4
Blackcroft Rd G32 47 D4
Blackcroft Terr ML7 53 B2
Blackdyke Rd G66 20 E8
Blackfarm Rd G77 72 F4
Blackfaulds Ct EH47 71 E6
Blackfaulds Dr EH47 71 E6
Blackfaulds Pl EH47 71 E6
Blackfaulds Rd G73 60 E8
Blackford Rd PA2 42 A3

Blackfriars Prim Sch G5 ... 45 C4
Blackfriars St G1 ... 163 B2
Blackhall Ct PA2 ... 42 B3
Blackhall St Paisley PA1 ... 42 A3
Shotts ML7 ... 70 B3
Blackhill Pl G33 ... 31 D2
Blackhill Rd
Blackridge EH48 ... 40 F3
Forth ML11 ... 124 C7
Glasgow G23 ... 17 E2
Blackhill View ML8 ... 95 A4
Blackhouse Ave G77 ... 72 F4
Blackhouse Gdns G77 ... 72 F4
Blackhouse Rd G77 ... 72 F4
Blackie St G3 ... 29 D1
Blacklands Pl G66 ... 20 F4
Blacklands Rd G74 ... 75 D1
Blacklaw Dr G74 ... 89 B8
Blacklaw Prim Sch G74 ... 76 B1
Blackmoor Pl ML1 ... 66 A3
Blackmoss Dr ML4 ... 64 F4
Blackness St ML5 ... 50 B3
Blackridge Community Mus* EH48 ... 40 C3
Blackridge Prim Sch EH48 ... 40 C3
Blackstone Ave G53 ... 58 C8
Blackstone Cres G53 ... 43 C1
Blackswell La ML3 ... 78 F3
Blackthorn Ave G66 ... 20 B5
Blackthorn Gr G66 ... 20 B5
Blackthorn Rd
Cumbernauld G67 ... 12 E4
Uddingston G71 ... 64 C8
Blackthorn Rdbt G67 ... 12 E3
Blackthorn St G22 ... 30 E5
Blacktongue Farm Rd ML6 ... 24 E2
Blackwell Tryst ML11 ... 132 C3
Blackwood G75 ... 88 D5
Blackwood Ave G77 ... 72 F3
Blackwood Ct [15] ML11 ... 138 B1
Blackwood Gdns ML1 ... 65 C2
Blackwood Prim Sch ML11 ... 114 A4
Blackwood Rd G68 ... 10 E1
Blackwood Rdbt G68 ... 10 F2
Blackwood St
Barrhead G78 ... 57 B2
Glasgow G13 ... 28 E7
Blackwood West Rdbt G68 ... 10 D1
Blackwoods Cres
Bellshill ML4 ... 65 C4
Moodiesburn G69 ... 21 F2
Blades Ct G69 ... 34 A6
Bladnoch Dr G15 ... 16 C2
Blaeloch Ave G45 ... 60 C1
Blaeloch Dr G45 ... 60 C2
Blaeloch Terr G45 ... 60 B1
Blaeshill Rd G75 ... 87 E8
Blair Athol Wynd [4] ML1 ... 66 B2
Blair Atholl Dr [15] ML9 ... 93 C1
Blair Atholl Gate G77 ... 73 B4
Blair Atholl Gdns ML3 ... 78 A4
Blair Atholl Gr ML3 ... 78 A4
Blair Cres G69 ... 48 A3
Blair Ct G81 ... 15 B2
Blair Gdns G77 ... 72 B5
Blair Ho G67 ... 12 A3
Blair Path [5] ML1 ... 79 F5
Blair Rd Coatbridge ML5 ... 49 E7
Crossford ML8 ... 108 A1
Paisley PA1 ... 42 E5
Blair St G32 ... 46 F5
Blairatholl Ave G11 ... 29 A3
Blairatholl Cres G77 ... 73 B4
Blairatholl Gdns [5] G11 ... 29 A3
Blairbeth Dr G44 ... 60 B7
Blairbeth Pl G73 ... 61 A5
Blairbeth Rd G73 ... 61 C5
Blairbeth Terr G73 ... 61 C5
Blairbuie Dr G20 ... 29 C7
Blairdardie Prim Sch G15 ... 16 B1
Blairdardie Rd
Clydebank G15 ... 16 B1
Glasgow G13 ... 16 C1
Blairdenan Ave G69 ... 22 A3
Blairdenon Dr G68 ... 11 C3
Blairgowrie Rd G52 ... 43 C4
Blairgrove Ct ML5 ... 49 E6
Blairhall Ave G41 ... 59 F8
Blairhill Ave G66 ... 21 A6
Blairhill Pl ML5 ... 49 E7
Blairhill St ML5 ... 49 F7
Blairhill Sta ML5 ... 49 E8
Blairholm Dr ML4 ... 65 B3
Blairlinn Ind Est G67 ... 23 F6
Blairlinn Rd G67 ... 23 F6
Blairlinn View G67 ... 24 A6
Blairlogie St G33 ... 32 B2
Blairmore Ave PA1 ... 42 C5
Blairmuckhole & Forrestdyke Rd ML7 ... 54 E7
Blairpark Ave ML5 ... 49 E8
Blairston Ave G71 ... 64 B1
Blairston Gdns G71 ... 64 B1
Blairtum Dr G73 ... 61 B5
Blairtummock Prim Sch G34 ... 48 B8
Blairtummock Rd G33 ... 47 D8
Blake Rd G67 ... 12 A2
Blane St ML5 ... 50 A8
Blanefield Gdns G13 ... 28 F8
Blaneview G33 ... 32 D4
Blantyre Farm Rd G71, G72 ... 63 C5
Blantyre Gdns G68 ... 10 E1
Blantyre High Sch G72 ... 77 D7
Blantyre Ind Est G72 ... 77 E5
Blantyre Mill Rd G71 ... 64 A2
Blantyre Rd G71 ... 64 A2
Blantyre St G3 ... 29 D1
Blantyre Sta G72 ... 77 E8
Blaven Ct G69 ... 48 C4
Blawarthill Hospl G14 ... 28 A6
Blawarthill St G14 ... 27 F5
Blawhill Way ML12 ... 160 C4
Bleasdale Ct G81 ... 15 B2
Blenheim Ave
East Kilbride G75 ... 88 C7
Stepps G33 ... 32 E6
Blenheim Ct Carluke ML8 ... 96 B1
Kilsyth G65 ... 6 D1
Stepps G33 ... 32 C5
Blin' Well Way ML11 ... 124 D1
Blinkbonny [1] ML9 ... 129 E8
Blinny Ct ML7 ... 70 A3
Blochairn Rd G21 ... 31 B1
Bloomfield Rd ML11 ... 119 E5
Bloomgate ML11 ... 117 A4
Blue Twr [16] ML11 ... 138 B1
Bluebell Gdns
Glasgow G45 ... 61 A2
Motherwell ML1 ... 65 C2
Bluebell Way Airdrie ML6 ... 35 F2
Carluke ML8 ... 108 F8
Bluebell Wlk ML1 ... 66 A3
Bluebell Wynd ML2 ... 80 F1
Blueknowes Rd ML8 ... 94 F5
Bluevale St G31 ... 46 A6
Blyth Rd G33 ... 47 E6
Blythe Pl G33 ... 47 D6
Blythswood Ave PA4 ... 27 D4
Blythswood Ct G2 ... 162 B2
Blythswood Ho Hospl PA4 ... 27 D4
Blythswood Ind Est PA4 ... 27 B4
Blythswood Rd PA4 ... 27 D4
Blythswood Sq G2 ... 162 B3
Blythswood St G2 ... 162 B2
Bo'ness Rd Chapelhall ML6 ... 51 D1
Motherwell ML1 ... 66 C7
Boardwalk The G75 ... 89 A7
Boat Rd ML12 ... 131 D1
Boclair Acad G61 ... 17 C4
Boclair Ave G61 ... 16 F4
Boclair Cres
Bearsden G61 ... 17 A4
Bishopbriggs G64 ... 19 A2
Boclair Rd Bearsden G62 ... 17 C5
Bishopbriggs G64 ... 19 A2
Boclair St G13 ... 28 E8
Bodden Sq ML1 ... 66 E7
Boden Ind Est G40 ... 46 B4
Boden Quadrant ML1 ... 65 C2
Boden St G40 ... 46 A4
Bodmin Gdns G69 ... 21 F3
Bog Rd Banknock FK4 ... 8 E3
Lesmahagow ML11 ... 120 B2
Lesmahagow ML11 ... 120 C3
Bogany Terr G45 ... 60 E2
Bogbain Rd G34 ... 48 A8
Bogfoot Rd ML7 ... 53 B2
Boggknowe G71 ... 63 D8
Boghall Ave ML12 ... 160 C3
Boghall Pk ML12 ... 160 C3
Boghall Rd Biggar ML12 ... 160 C2
Carluke ML8 ... 109 B7
Glasgow G69 ... 48 B3
Boghall St Glasgow G33 ... 32 B1
Stonehouse ML9 ... 105 F2
Boghead Rd Glasgow G21 ... 31 A4
Kirkintilloch G66 ... 20 A5
Bogleshole Rd G72 ... 61 E7
Bogmoor Pl G51 ... 28 C1
Bogmoor Rd G51 ... 43 C8
Bogs View ML4 ... 64 F3
Bogside Rd Ashgill ML9 ... 106 F8
Kilsyth G65 ... 10 D7
Millerston G33 ... 32 A5
Bogside St G40 ... 46 B4
Bogton Ave G44 ... 59 F4
Bogton Avenue La G44 ... 59 F4
Boleyn Ct ML2 ... 82 B6
Boleyn Rd G41 ... 44 E2
Bolingbroke G74 ... 76 C4
Bolivar Terr G42 ... 60 C8
Bolton Dr G42 ... 60 B8
Bon Accord Cres ML7 ... 69 E5
Bon Accord Rd G76 ... 73 F6
Bon Accord Sq G81 ... 27 B8
Bon Secours Hospl G41 ... 59 F8
Bonawe St G20 ... 29 F3
Bonds Dr ML2 ... 82 B6
Boness St G40 ... 46 B4
Bonhill St G22 ... 30 B3
Bonkle Gdns ML2 ... 82 B5
Bonkle Rd ML2 ... 82 B5
Bonnar St G40 ... 46 A3
Bonnaughton Rd G61 ... 16 B6
Bonnet Rd ML11 ... 117 A4
Bonnington Ave ML11 ... 117 B3
Bonnyholm Ave G53 ... 43 A3
Bonnyholm Prim Sch G53 ... 43 A3
Bonnyrigg Dr G43 ... 59 A5
Bonnyton Dr G76 ... 86 D5
Bonnyton La ML3 ... 91 B8
Bonnyton Moor Rd G76 ... 86 A7
Bonyton Ave G13 ... 27 F6
Boon Dr G15 ... 16 B2
Boquhanran Pl G81 ... 15 A3
Boquhanran Rd G81 ... 15 A3
Borden La [3] G13 ... 28 E5
Borden Rd G13 ... 28 E5
Border Way G66 ... 20 F8
Bore Rd ML6 ... 51 B8
Boreland Dr Glasgow G13 ... 28 B6
Hamilton ML3 ... 77 E2
Boreland Pl G13 ... 28 B6
Borgie Cres G72 ... 62 B5
Borland Cres G76 ... 86 E5
Borland Dr ML9 ... 106 B8
Borland Rd G61 ... 17 A3
Borron St G4 ... 30 C3
Borrowdale G75 ... 87 F5
Borthwick Dr G75 ... 87 D7
Borthwick Pl G69 ... 33 F4
Borthwick St G33 ... 32 B1
Bosfield Cnr G74 ... 75 F3
Bosfield Pl G74 ... 75 F3
Bosfield Rd G74 ... 75 F3
Boswell Ct G42 ... 59 F7
Boswell Dr G72 ... 77 D7
Boswell Pk G74 ... 76 C4
Boswell Sq G52 ... 42 F7
Bosworth Rd G74 ... 76 C5
Botanic Cres G20 ... 29 D4
Botanic Crescent La G20 ... 29 D4
Bothlin Dr G33 ... 32 D6
Bothlyn Ave G66 ... 20 E7
Bothlyn Cres G69 ... 33 F7
Bothlyn Rd G69 ... 33 D8
Bothwell Castle* G72 ... 63 D3
Bothwell Ho ML3 ... 78 E5
Bothwell La Glasgow G2 ... 162 C2
[4] Glasgow,Kelvingrove G12 ... 29 E2
Bothwell Park Ind Est G71 ... 64 A5
Bothwell Park Sch ML1 ... 80 A4
Bothwell Pl ML5 ... 49 F7
Bothwell Prim Sch G71 ... 64 A2
Bothwell Rd Bothwell G71 ... 63 F4
Carluke ML8 ... 95 E3
Hamilton ML3 ... 78 C6
Bothwell St
Cambuslang G72 ... 61 E6
Glasgow G2 ... 162 C2
Hamilton ML3 ... 78 C5
Bothwellhaugh Quadrant ML4 ... 64 F3
Bothwellhaugh Rd ML4 ... 65 A2
Bothwellpark Pl ML4 ... 64 D6
Bothwellpark Rd
Bothwell G71 ... 64 C3
Fallside G71,ML4 ... 64 C4
Bothwellshields Rd ML1 ... 52 C2
Boughden Way ML11 ... 119 F2
Bourhill Ct ML2 ... 80 D2
Bourne St ML3 ... 78 F3
Bourock Sq G78 ... 57 E1
Bourtree Rd ML3 ... 77 F2
Bouverie St Glasgow G14 ... 27 E6
Rutherglen G73 ... 60 F7
Bowden Dr G52 ... 43 B6
Bowden Pk G75 ... 88 C8
Bower St G12 ... 29 E3
Bowerwalls St G78 ... 57 E4
Bowes Cres G69 ... 47 F4
Bowfield Ave G52 ... 42 F6
Bowfield Cres G52 ... 42 F6
Bowfield Dr G52 ... 43 A6
Bowfield Path G52 ... 42 F6
Bowfield Pl G52 ... 42 F6
Bowhouse Dr G45 ... 61 A4
Bowhouse Gdns G45 ... 61 A5
Bowhouse Rd ML6 ... 51 F5
Bowhousebog or Liquo ML7 ... 69 A2
Bowhousebog Rd ML7 ... 69 A2
Bowhousebrae Rd ML6 ... 51 E5
Bowling Green Gr G72 ... 62 F4
Bowling Green La
Biggar ML12 ... 160 E5
[2] Glasgow G14 ... 28 D3
Bowling Green Rd
Chryston G69 ... 33 D8
Glasgow G44 ... 60 A5
Glasgow,Barrachnie G32 ... 47 D4
[3] Glasgow,Whiteinch G14 ... 28 D3
Strathaven ML10 ... 112 D5
Bowling Green St ML4 ... 65 B5
Bowling Green View G72 ... 62 F4
Bowling St ML5 ... 49 F7
Bowman St G42 ... 45 A2
Bowmanflat ML9 ... 93 A3
Bowmont Gdns [3] G12 ... 29 C3
Bowmont Hill G64 ... 19 A4
Bowmont Pl
Cambuslang G72 ... 62 D5
East Kilbride G75 ... 87 D7
Bowmont Terr G12 ... 29 C3
Bowmore Gdns
Rutherglen G73 ... 61 E3
Uddingston G71 ... 63 E8
Bowmore Rd G52 ... 43 E5
Bowmore Wlk ML7 ... 70 A3
Bowyer Vennel ML4 ... 64 F6
Boyd Dr ML1 ... 79 B7
Boyd St G42 ... 45 C1
Boydstone Pl G46 ... 59 A5
Boydstone Rd
Glasgow G53,G46,G43 ... 58 E5
Thornliebank G46 ... 59 A4
Boyle St G81 ... 27 D8
Boylestone Rd G78 ... 57 A4
Boyndie St G34 ... 48 B8
Bracadale Dr G69 ... 48 D4
Bracadale Gdns G69 ... 48 D4
Bracadale Gr G69 ... 48 C4
Bracadale Rd G69 ... 48 C4
Bracco Rd ML6 ... 38 C2
Bracken Brae ML11 ... 119 F2
Bracken St Glasgow G22 ... 30 B6
Motherwell ML1 ... 66 A3
Bracken Terr G71 ... 64 A3
Bracken Way [6] ML9 ... 93 C1
Brackenbrae Ave G64 ... 18 F1
Brackenbrae Rd G64 ... 18 F1
Brackenhill Dr ML3 ... 91 C7
Brackenhill Rd ML8 ... 95 A6
Brackenhirst Gdns ML6 ... 35 D6
Brackenhirst Rd ML6 ... 35 E7
Brackenknowe Rd ML6 ... 24 D3
Brackenridge Rd ML11 ... 129 F4
Brackenrig Cres G76 ... 73 E1
Brackenrig Rd G46 ... 58 E2
Brackla Ave G13,G81 ... 27 E8
Braco Ave ML6 ... 51 D1
Bradan Ave G13 ... 27 E7
Bradda Ave G73 ... 61 D4
Bradfield Ave G12 ... 29 C5
Bradley Ct G33 ... 32 F5
Bradshaw Cres ML3 ... 77 E3
Brady Cres G69 ... 22 A3
Braedale Ave Airdrie ML6 ... 51 C7
Motherwell ML1 ... 79 C6
Braedale Cres ML2 ... 82 B5
Braedale Pl ML2 ... 82 C5
Braedale Rd ML11 ... 117 A5
Braeface Rd Banknock FK4 ... 8 E3
Cumbernauld G67 ... 11 E2
Braefield Dr G46 ... 59 A3
Braefoot Ave G62 ... 17 A8
Braefoot Cres ML8 ... 94 F4
Braefoot Ct
Caldercruix ML6 ... 37 F4
Law ML8 ... 94 F5
Braehead
[21] Douglas ML11 ... 138 B1
Hamilton G72 ... 77 D6
Braehead (Sh Ctr) G51 ... 28 A3
Braehead Ave
Clydebank G81 ... 15 A7
Coatbridge ML5 ... 49 D3
Larkhall ML9 ... 92 E2
Braehead Cres G81 ... 15 A7
Braehead Dr ML4 ... 64 F4
Braehead Ind Est PA4 ... 27 F3
Braehead Loan ML8 ... 109 B8
Braehead Pl Bellshill ML4 ... 64 F4
... 137 F5
Braehead Prim Sch ML11 ... 124 B5
Braehead Quadrant ML1 ... 66 D4
Braehead Rd
Clydebank G81 ... 15 A7
Cumbernauld G67 ... 12 B3
Thorntonhall G74 ... 74 C3
... 137 F5
Braehead St G5 ... 45 D3
Braemar Cres
Bearsden G61 ... 16 F2
Carluke ML8 ... 96 A3
Braemar Ct G44 ... 59 E4
Braemar Rd G73 ... 61 E3
Braemar St Glasgow G42 ... 59 F7
Hamilton ML3 ... 78 B6
Braemore Gdns G22 ... 30 D4
Braes Ave G81 ... 15 D1
Braes O' Yetts G66 ... 21 A8
Braesburn Ct G67 ... 12 F6
Braesburn Pl G67 ... 12 F6
Braesburn Rd G67 ... 12 F6
Braeside Ave
Milngavie G62 ... 17 A8
Moodiesburn G69 ... 21 F2
Rutherglen G73 ... 61 C7
Braeside Cres
Barrhead G78 ... 57 E1
Coatbridge G69 ... 48 F5
Fauldhouse EH47 ... 71 D5
Kirkmuirhill ML11 ... 114 A3
Braeside Dr G78 ... 57 E1
Braeside Gdns ML3 ... 91 E8
Braeside La
Kirkmuirhill ML11 ... 114 A3
[15] Larkhall ML9 ... 93 B4
Braeside Pl G72 ... 62 B4
Braeside Rd ML1 ... 66 D4
Braeside St G20 ... 29 F4
Braeside Terr ML11 ... 114 A3
Braeside Way ML9 ... 93 B1
Braeval Way G33 ... 32 E5
Braeview Pl G74 ... 76 B4
Braid Ave ML1 ... 66 F1
Braid Sq G4 ... 30 A2
Braid St G4 ... 30 A2
Braidbar Ct G46 ... 59 C3
Braidbar Farm Rd G46 ... 59 D3
Braidbar Prim Sch G46 ... 59 D3
Braidbar Rd G46 ... 59 C3
Braidcraft Pl G53 ... 58 C8
Braidcraft Rd
Glasgow G53 ... 43 C1
Glasgow G53 ... 43 D1
Braidcraft Terr G53 ... 43 D1
Braidfauld Gdns G32 ... 46 F3
Braidfauld Pl G32 ... 46 F2
Braidfauld St G32 ... 46 F3
Braidfield Gr G81 ... 15 B5
Braidfield High Sch G81 ... 15 D2
Braidfield Rd G81 ... 15 B5
Braidfute ML11 ... 117 C5
Braidholm Cres G46 ... 59 C4
Braidholm Rd G46 ... 59 D4
Braidhurst High Sch ML1 ... 65 D1
Braidhurst Ind Est ML1 ... 65 D1
Braidhurst St ML1 ... 79 E8
Braidley Cres G75 ... 88 E5
Braidpark Dr G46 ... 59 D3
Braids Dr G53 ... 42 F1
Braidwood Prim Sch ML8 ... 108 F4
Braidwood Rd ML8 ... 108 D4
Braidwood St ML2 ... 81 C7
Bramah Ave G75 ... 88 F8
Brambling Ct ML2 ... 81 A1
Brambling Rd ML5 ... 50 D3
Bramley Dr ML4 ... 65 A8
Bramley Pl Airdrie ML6 ... 51 E6
Kirkintilloch G66 ... 20 E4
Brampton G75 ... 87 F6
Branchal Rd ML2 ... 81 E4
Branchalfield Dr ML2 ... 81 E4
Branchalmuir Cres ML2 ... 81 F6
Branchock Ave G72 ... 62 D4
Brancumhall Rd G74 ... 76 D3
Brand Pl G51 ... 44 C6
Brand St G51 ... 44 C6
Brandon Arc [1] ML1 ... 79 E6
Brandon Ct Hamilton ML3 ... 78 C4
Motherwell ML1 ... 79 E6
Brandon Dr G61 ... 16 E7
Brandon Gate ML4 ... 65 B5
Brandon Gdns G72 ... 61 E5
Brandon Ho ML3 ... 78 E5
Brandon Par E ML1 ... 79 E7
Brandon Par S ML1 ... 79 E6
Brandon Pl ML4 ... 64 E3
Brandon St Glasgow G31 ... 45 F6
Hamilton ML3 ... 78 E3
Motherwell ML1 ... 79 F6
Brandon Way ML5 ... 49 D4
Brankholm Brae ML3 ... 77 D4
Branklyn Cl [4] G13 ... 28 D6
Branklyn Cres G13 ... 28 D6
Branklyn Ct [6] G13 ... 28 D6
Branklyn Gr G13 ... 28 D6
Branklyn Pl [5] G13 ... 28 D6
Branks Ave ML10 ... 103 C6
Brankston Ave ML9 ... 129 E8
Brannock Ave ML1 ... 66 D4
Brannock High Sch ML1 ... 66 C3
Brannock Pl ML1 ... 66 D4
Brannock Rd ML1 ... 66 D4
Brassey St G20 ... 29 F6
Braxfield Rd ML11 ... 117 A2
Braxfield Row ML11 ... 116 F2
Braxfield Terr ML11 ... 116 F2
Breadalbane Cres ML1 ... 65 D1
Breadalbane Gdns G73 ... 61 D4
Breadalbane St G3 ... 162 A3
Breadie Dr G62 ... 16 F8
Breamish Pl G75 ... 87 F6
Brechame Rd ML10 ... 103 C6
Brechin Rd G64 ... 19 C1
Brechin St G3 ... 44 E8
Bredin Way ML1 ... 79 B8
Bredisholm Cres G71 ... 49 C1
Bredisholm Dr G69 ... 48 C4
Bredisholm Rd
Coatbridge G69 ... 48 F4
Coatbridge G69 ... 49 A4
Glasgow G69 ... 48 D4
Bredisholm Terr G69 ... 48 D4
Breich Sta EH55 ... 122 B7
Breich Terr EH55 ... 122 C7
Brendan Way ML1 ... 80 B2
Brendon Ave G75 ... 88 A4
Brenfield Ave G44 ... 59 F4
Brenfield Dr G44 ... 59 F4
Brenfield Rd G44 ... 59 F4
Brent Ave G46 ... 58 F5
Brent Ct G74 ... 75 E3
Brent Dr Glasgow G46 ... 58 F5
Thornliebank G46 ... 59 A5
Brent Gdns Glasgow G46 ... 58 F5
Thornliebank G46 ... 59 A5
Brent Rd East Kilbride G74 ... 75 E3
Glasgow G46 ... 58 F5
Thornliebank G46 ... 59 A5
Brent Way G46 ... 58 F5
Brentwood Ave G53 ... 58 B4
Brentwood Dr G53 ... 58 B4
Brentwood Sq G53 ... 58 B4
Brereton St G42 ... 45 C1
Breslin Terr ML7 ... 55 C5
Bressay G74 ... 75 E4
Bressay Rd G33 ... 47 E6
Bressay Wynd [14] ML2 ... 81 F6
Breval Cres G81 ... 15 A7
Breval Ct G69 ... 48 C4
Brewster Ave PA3 ... 42 A7
Briar Bank ML11 ... 119 F2
Briar Dr G81 ... 15 B4
Briar Gdns G43 ... 59 D5
Briar Gr G43 ... 59 D5
Briar Neuk G64 ... 31 B8
Briar Rd Glasgow G43 ... 59 D5
Kirkintilloch G66 ... 20 F8
Briar Wlk G66 ... 21 A8
Briarbush Way [12] G72 ... 77 C7
Briarcroft Dr G33 ... 31 D7
Briarcroft Pl G33 ... 31 E6
Briarcroft Rd G33 ... 31 D6
Briarlea Dr G46 ... 59 C4
Briarwood Ct G32 ... 47 E2
Briarwood Rd ML2 ... 80 E4
Bridge End ML7 ... 69 C6
Bridge Pl ML7 ... 70 A3
Bridge St Cambuslang G72 ... 62 A6
Fauldhouse EH47 ... 71 E6

Bridge St *continued*
Glasgow G5 .162 C1
Hamilton ML3 .78 C2
Longriggend ML6 .25 F1
Muirkirk KA18 .142 A6
Strathaven ML10 .112 E6
Wishaw ML2 .80 E3
Bridge Street Underground Sta G5 .45 B5
Bridgebar St G78 .57 E4
Bridgeburn Dr G69 .21 F1
Bridgecastle Rd EH48 .41 F8
Bridgeford Ave ML4 .65 C7
Bridgegait G62 .17 C8
Bridgegate G1 .163 A1
Bridgend ML12 .140 F6
Bridgend Cotts G66 .21 A7
Bridgend Cres G69 .21 E2
Bridgend Ct G68 .8 F1
Bridgend Pl G69 .21 E2
Bridgend Rd ML12 .146 A5
Bridgend View ML8 .95 F1
Bridgeton Bsns Ctr 4 G40 .45 F5
Bridgeton Cross G40 .45 F4
Bridgeton Sta G40 .45 F4
Bridgeway Ct G66 .20 F7
Bridgeway Pl G66 .20 F7
Bridgeway Rd G66 .20 F7
Bridgeway Terr G66 .20 F7
Bridie Terr G74 .76 C4
Brierybank Ave ML11 .117 A3
Brigbrae Ave ML4 .65 C3
Brigham Pl G23 .29 E8
Bright St G21 .30 F1
Brighton Pl G51 .44 B6
Brighton St G51 .44 B6
Brightside Ave G71 .63 F5
Brigside Gdns ML3 .79 A2
Brisbane Ct G46 .59 D3
Brisbane St G42 .60 A7
Brisbane Terr G75 .88 C7
Britannia Way
Clydebank G81 .15 B2
Renfrew PA4 .27 C1
Briton St G51 .44 B7
Brittain Way ML1 .65 F7
Broad Sq G72 .77 D8
Broad St G40 .46 A5
Broad St Cvn Site G40 .46 A5
Broad Way The ML2 .80 E4
Broadfield Rd ML12 .140 E4
Broadford St G4 .30 C2
Broadholm St G22 .30 C6
Broadlees Gdns ML10 .103 C5
Broadleys Ave G64 .18 F2
Broadlie Dr G13 .28 A6
Broadloan PA4 .27 C2
Broadmoss Ave G77 .73 C4
Broadwood Bsns Pk G68 .22 F8
Broadwood Dr G44 .60 B6
Broadwood Rdbt G68 .22 F8
Broadwood Stad (Clyde, & Airdrieonians FC's) G68 .10 F1
Brock Oval G53 .58 C6
Brock Pl G53 .58 C7
Brock Rd G53 .58 C6
Brock Terr G53 .58 C6
Brockburn Cres G53 .58 B8
Brockburn Pl G53 .43 A2
Brockburn Rd G53 .43 B1
Brockburn Terr G53 .58 C8
Brocketsbrae Rd
Lesmahagow,Brocketsbrae ML11 .120 A4
Lesmahagow,Milton ML11 .119 F5
Brocklinn Pk G75 .87 E7
Brockville St G32 .46 F6
Brodick Ave ML1 .79 B7
Brodick Dr G74 .75 D3
Brodick Pl G77 .72 A4
Brodick Sq G64 .31 C7
Brodick St G21 .31 A1
Brodie Gdns G69 .48 C6
Brodie Gr G69 .48 C6
Brodie Pl East Kilbride G74 .75 D3
Stonehouse ML9 .105 E1
Brodie Rd G21 .31 D7
Brogan Cres ML1 .79 B7
Bron Way G67 .12 A1
Brook St Glasgow G40 .45 F5
Strathaven ML10 .112 E7
Brookbank Terr ML8 .96 A1
Brookfield Ave G33 .31 D7
Brookfield Cnr G33 .31 D7
Brookfield Dr G33 .31 D7
Brookfield Gate G33 .31 D8
Brookfield Gdns G33 .31 D7
Brookfield Pl G33 .31 E7
Brookfield Rd G33 .31 D7
Brooklands G74 .75 A1
Brooklands Ave G71 .63 E7
Brooklea Dr G46 .59 C5
Brooklime Dr G74 .75 D4
Brooklime Gdns G74 .75 C4
Brooklyn Pl ML2 .94 B7
Brookside Ct ML12 .140 F6
Brookside St G40 .46 A5
Broom Cliff G77 .72 F3
Broom Cres Barrhead G78 .57 A5
East Kilbride G75 .88 D5
Broom Dr Clydebank G81 .15 A4
Larkhall ML9 .93 A5
Broom Gdns G66 .20 B6
Broom Park Dr ML11 .119 E5
Broom Path G69 .47 F3
Broom Pl Coatbridge ML5 .49 F3
Glasgow G43 .59 D5
Broom Pl *continued*
Motherwell ML1 .66 C4
Broom Rd
Cumbernauld G67 .12 D5
Glasgow G43 .59 D5
Newton Mearns G77 .73 A6
Broom Rd E G77 .73 B4
Broom Wynd ML7 .69 E6
Broomburn Dr G77 .73 A4
Broomcroft Rd G46 .73 A6
Broomelton Rd ML3,ML9 .92 D1
Broomfield Ave
Cambuslang G72 .61 D7
Newton Mearns G77 .72 F3
Broomfield Ct G21 .31 C3
Broomfield La G21 .30 F5
Broomfield Pl G21 .30 F5
Broomfield Rd
Glasgow G21 .31 B4
Larkhall ML9 .106 B8
Netherburn ML9 .106 E4
Rutherglen G46 .73 A6
Strathaven ML10 .112 F5
Broomfield St Airdrie ML6 .51 B7
Netherburn ML9 .107 D4
Rigside ML11 .138 F6
Broomfield Terr G71 .48 F1
Broomfield Wlk 5 G66 .20 D8
Broomgate ML11 .117 A4
Broomgate Ct ML11 .116 F4
Broomhill Ave
Glasgow G32 .62 B8
Glasgow,Whiteinch G11 .28 F2
Newton Mearns G77 .72 F4
Broomhill Cres ML4 .64 F3
Broomhill Ct ML9 .93 A2
Broomhill Dr Glasgow G11 .28 F3
Rutherglen G73 .61 B5
Broomhill Gate ML9 .93 A2
Broomhill Gdns
Glasgow G11 .28 F3
Newton Mearns G77 .72 F4
Broomhill La G11 .28 F3
Broomhill Path G11 .28 F2
Broomhill Pl G11 .28 F2
Broomhill Prim Sch G11 .28 F4
Broomhill Prim Sch Annexe G11 .28 F4
Broomhill Rd ML9 .93 A2
Broomhill St ML7 .55 C5
Broomhill Terr G11 .28 F2
Broomhill View ML9 .92 F2
Broomieknowe Dr G73 .61 B6
Broomieknowe Gdns G73 .61 B6
Broomieknowe Rd G73 .61 B6
Broomielaw G1,G2 .162 C1
Broomknoll St ML6 .51 A7
Broomknowe G68 .11 D3
Broomknowes Ave G66 .20 E4
Broomknowes Rd G21 .31 A4
Broomlands Rd G67 .24 A8
Broomlea Sch G11 .28 F3
Broomlee Rd G67 .23 F6
Broomley Dr G46 .59 C1
Broomley La G46 .59 C1
Broomloan Ct G51 .44 A5
Broomloan Pl G51 .44 B6
Broomloan Rd
Glasgow G51 .44 A5
Glasgow G51 .44 A6
Broompark Ave G72 .77 C6
Broompark Cir 8 G31 .45 F7
Broompark Cres ML6 .36 A3
Broompark Dr
Glasgow G31 .45 F7
Newton Mearns G77 .73 A5
Broompark La 7 G31 .45 F7
Broompark Rd
Hamilton G72 .77 C7
Wishaw ML2 .80 D4
Broompark St 6 G31 .45 F7
Broomside Cres ML1 .79 E4
Broomside St ML1 .79 E4
Broomstone Ave G77 .72 F3
Broomton Rd G21 .31 C7
Broomvale Dr G77 .72 F5
Brora Cres ML3 .90 F8
Brora Dr Bearsden G61 .17 B4
Glasgow G46 .59 D2
Renfrew PA4 .27 E3
Brora Gdns G64 .19 B1
Brora Rd G64 .19 B1
Brora St G33 .31 D1
Broughton G75 .88 E5
Broughton Dr G23 .29 E8
Broughton Gdns G23 .17 F1
Broughton Pl
Coatbridge ML5 .50 B3
Hamilton ML3 .78 A3
Broughton Rd
Biggar ML12 .160 E4
Glasgow G23 .17 E1
Brouster Hill G74 .75 E1
Brouster Pl G74 .75 E1
Browhill Ave ML11 .138 B1
Brown Ave G81 .27 E8
Brown Pl G72 .62 A6
Brown Rd G67 .11 F2
Brown St Armadale EH48 .41 F4
Carluke ML8 .95 F3
Coatbridge ML5 .50 A5
Glasgow G2 .162 B2
1 Hamilton ML3 .78 E2
Larkhall ML9 .93 A4
Motherwell ML1 .79 F8
Shotts ML7 .70 B3
Wishaw ML2 .82 A4
Brown St N PA4 .27 C3
Brown St S PA4 .27 B3
Brown Wlk ML2 .82 B5
Brownhill Rd G43 .59 B4
Brownhill View ML2 .82 D6
Brownieside Pl ML6 .37 A3
Brownieside Rd ML6 .37 C1
Brownlee Rd ML8 .94 D4
Brownlie St G42 .60 B8
Brownmuir Ave G76 .86 F4
Brownsburn Ind Est ML6 .51 B5
Brownsburn Rd ML6 .51 C5
Brownsdale Rd G73 .60 F7
Brownshill Ave ML5 .49 F4
Brownside Ave
Barrhead G78 .57 A5
Cambuslang G72 .61 E5
Brownside Cres G78 .57 A5
Brownside Dr
Barrhead G78 .57 A5
Glasgow G13 .27 F6
Brownside Gr G78 .57 A5
Brownside Mews G72 .61 E5
Brownside Rd G72,G73 .61 E5
Brownsland Ct G69 .33 F6
Bruar Way 15 ML2 .81 F6
Bruce Ave Motherwell ML1 .79 D7
Paisley PA3 .42 A7
Bruce Ct ML6 .51 E8
Bruce Ho G67 .11 F3
Bruce Loan ML2 .94 C6
Bruce Pl G75 .88 F7
Bruce Rd Glasgow G41 .44 E4
Motherwell ML1 .66 B2
Paisley PA3 .42 A7
Renfrew PA4 .27 A1
Bruce St Bellshill ML4 .65 B5
Clydebank G81 .15 B1
Coatbridge ML5 .50 B8
Plains ML6 .37 A2
Bruce Terr Blantyre G72 .63 E1
East Kilbride G75 .88 F7
Kirkmuirhill ML11 .114 A3
Bruce's Loan 22 ML9 .93 C1
Brucefield Pl G34 .48 D8
Brunel Way G75 .88 F8
Brunstane Rd G34 .33 A1
Brunswick La G1 .163 A2
Brunswick St G1 .163 A2
Brunton St G44 .60 A5
Brunton Terr G44 .60 A4
Bruntsfield Ave G53 .58 B3
Bruntsfield Gdns G53 .58 B3
Bryan St ML3 .78 B5
Bryce Gdns ML9 .93 A4
Bryce Pl G75 .88 D6
Bryon Ct G71 .64 B2
Bryson Ct ML3 .91 D7
Bryson Pl ML10 .112 E6
Bryson St G81 .15 E7
Bryson Terr ML12 .154 B8
Buccleuch Ave
Clarkston G76 .73 D7
Glasgow G52 .42 E8
Glasgow G52 .42 F7
Buccleuch Ct G61 .16 E7
Buccleuch Dr G61 .16 E7
Buccleuch La G3 .162 B4
Buccleuch Pl DG10 .161 D6
Buccleuch St
Glasgow G3 .162 B4
Moffat DG10 .161 C5
Buchan Gn G74 .76 B3
Buchan Ho G67 .11 F2
Buchan Rd ML1 .66 B2
Buchan St Hamilton ML3 .91 C8
Wishaw ML2 .81 B6
Buchan Terr G72 .61 F3
Buchanan Bsns Pk G33 .32 E6
Buchanan Cres
Bishopbriggs G64 .31 C7
Hamilton ML3 .78 B2
Buchanan Ct G33 .32 F6
Buchanan Dr
Bearsden G61 .17 A4
Bishopbriggs G64 .31 C8
Cambuslang G72 .61 E6
Carluke ML8 .109 C8
Kirkintilloch G66 .20 D3
Law ML8 .95 A6
Newton Mearns G77 .72 E7
Rutherglen G73 .61 C6
Buchanan Galleries G1 .163 A3
Buchanan Gate G33 .32 F6
Buchanan Gdns G32 .47 E2
Buchanan Gr G69 .48 B5
Buchanan St Airdrie ML6 .51 A7
Coatbridge ML5 .49 F6
Glasgow G1 .162 C2
Glasgow G1 .163 A3
Glasgow,Garrowhill G69 .48 B4
Buchanan Street Underground Sta G1 .163 A3
Buchandyke Rd G74 .76 B3
Buchley Cotts G64 .18 C5
Buchlyvie Gdns G64 .30 F8
Buchlyvie Rd PA1 .42 E5
Buchlyvie St G34 .48 B7
Buckie Wlk ML4 .65 A6
Buckingham Ct ML3 .77 E4
Buckingham Dr
Glasgow G32 .62 B8
Rutherglen G73 .61 D7
Buckingham St G12 .29 D3
Buckingham Terr G12 .29 D3
Bucklaw Gdns G52 .43 C4
Bucklaw Pl G52 .43 C4
Bucklaw Terr G52 .43 C4
Buckley St G22 .30 D6
Bucksburn Rd G21 .31 C4
Buckthorne Pl G53 .58 B3
Buddon St G31 .46 C4
Budhill Ave G32 .47 B5
Budshaw Ave ML6 .51 C2
Bull Rd G76 .73 F6
Bull's Cl ML11 .117 A4
Bulldale Ct G14 .27 F5
Bulldale Rd G14 .27 E5
Bulldale St G14 .27 E6
Buller Cl G72 .63 D2
Buller Cres G72 .63 C2
Bullionslaw Dr G73 .61 D6
Bulloch Ave G46 .59 D2
Bullwood Ave G53 .57 F8
Bullwood Ct G53 .57 F8
Bullwood Dr G53 .42 F1
Bullwood Gdns G53 .42 F1
Bullwood Pl G53 .42 F1
Bunbury Terr 3 G75 .88 C8
Bunessan St G52 .43 F5
Bunhouse Rd G3 .29 C1
Burgh Hall La G11 .29 B2
Burgh Hall St G11 .29 B2
Burgh La 4 G12 .29 D3
Burgh Prim Sch G73 .61 A8
Burghead Dr G51 .43 E8
Burghead Pl G51 .43 E8
Burgher St G31 .46 C5
Burleigh Rd G71 .64 B3
Burleigh St
Coatbridge ML5 .50 B3
Glasgow G51 .44 A8
Burley Pl G74 .74 F2
Burlington Ave G12 .29 B6
Burmola St G22 .30 B4
Burn Bridge Ct ML10 .112 E4
Burn Bridge Dr ML10 .112 E4
Burn Cres Chapelhall ML6 .51 D2
Motherwell ML1 .66 B4
Burn La ML1 .66 A4
Burn Pl G72 .61 E7
Burn Rd Carluke ML8 .95 F3
Chapelton ML10 .103 D6
Burn Terr G72 .61 E7
Burn View G67 .12 C3
Burn's Cres ML6 .51 B6
Burnacre Gdns G71 .63 E7
Burnawn Gdns G33 .31 D7
Burnawn Gr G33 .31 D7
Burnawn Pl G33 .31 D7
Burnbank Braes ML8 .95 F1
Burnbank Ctr ML3 .78 A5
Burnbank Dr G78 .57 D1
Burnbank Gdns
Hamilton ML3 .78 A5
Glasgow G20 .29 F2
Burnbank La G20 .29 F2
Burnbank Pl 2 G20 .30 A2
Burnbank Quadrant ML6 .50 F8
Burnbank Rd ML3 .78 B4
Burnbank St Airdrie ML6 .50 F8
Coatbridge ML5 .50 B8
Burnbank Terr
Glasgow G20 .29 F2
Kilsyth G65 .6 D1
Burnblea Gdns ML3 .78 E2
Burnblea St ML3 .78 D2
Burnbrae Clydebank G81 .15 A6
Fauldhouse EH47 .71 F5
Twechar G65 .9 F4
Burnbrae Ave
Bearsden G61 .17 A7
Moodiesburn G69 .22 A2
Burnbrae Dr G73 .61 D5
Burnbrae Gdns G53 .58 D6
Burnbrae Pl G74 .75 C2
Burnbrae Prim Sch G53 .58 D5
Burnbrae Rd
Hamilton G72 .77 C7
Harthill ML7 .56 A6
Kirkintilloch G66 .21 B2
Kirkintilloch,Auchinloch G66 .20 F2
Kirkintilloch,Waterside G66 .21 B7
Shotts ML7 .69 E3
Burnbrae St
Clydebank G81 .15 D8
Glasgow G21 .31 A4
Larkhall ML9 .92 F3
Burncleuch Ave G72 .62 A4
Burncrooks Ave
Bearsden G61 .16 D7
East Kilbride G74 .75 C2
Burndyke Ct G51 .44 C7
Burndyke Sq G51 .44 C7
Burnet Rose Ct G74 .75 C4
Burnet Rose Gdns G74 .75 C4
Burnet Rose Pl G74 .75 C4
Burnett Ct G69 .33 C8
Burnett Rd G33 .47 E7
Burnfield Ave G46 .59 B4
Burnfield Cotts G46 .59 B4
Burnfield Dr G43 .59 B4
Burnfield Gdns G46 .59 C4
Burnfield Rd G46 .59 B4
Burnfoot Cres G73 .61 D5
Burnfoot Dr G52 .43 B5
Burnfoot Rd ML6 .50 E8
Burngreen G65 .10 D8
Burngreen Terr G67 .12 B5
Burnhall Pl ML2 .81 D1
Burnhall Rd ML2 .81 C2
Burnhall St ML2 .81 D1
Burnham Rd G14 .28 A4
Burnhead Prim Sch G71 .64 D8
Burnhead Rd Airdrie ML6 .36 D1
Cumbernauld G68 .11 C2
Burnhead Rd *continued*
Glasgow G43 .59 E5
Larkhall ML9 .93 C2
Symington ML12 .140 E5
Burnhead St G71 .64 C7
Burnhill Quadrant G73 .60 F8
Burnhill St G73 .60 F8
Burnhouse Ave G68 .11 B2
Burnhouse Brae G77 .73 A3
Burnhouse Cres ML3 .78 B1
Burnhouse Dr EH47 .56 F5
Burnhouse Ind Est EH47 .56 F5
Burnhouse Rd
East Kilbride G75 .88 A1
Hamilton ML3 .78 B1
Burnhouse St
Glasgow G20 .29 C6
Glasgow G20 .29 D6
Burniebrae ML6 .50 F8
Burniebrae Rd ML6 .51 E3
Burnlip Rd ML6 .35 A4
Burnmouth Ct G33 .47 F6
Burnmouth Pl G61 .17 A5
Burnmouth Rd G33 .47 F6
Burnock Pl G75 .87 E7
Burnpark Ave G71 .63 D7
Burns Ave EH48 .41 F6
Burns Cres ML7 .55 F6
Burns Ct G66 .9 A1
Burns Dr G66 .9 A2
Burns Gdns G72 .63 C1
Burns Gr G46 .59 A2
Burns La ML6 .51 D3
Burns Loan 13 ML9 .93 B4
Burns Path ML4 .65 B7
Burns Pk G74 .76 A3
Burns Pl ML7 .69 A6
Burns Rd Chapelhall ML6 .51 D4
Cumbernauld G67 .12 B2
Kirkintilloch G66 .9 A1
Kirkmuirhill ML11 .114 A2
Burns St Glasgow G4 .30 B2
Hamilton ML3 .78 D2
Burns Way ML1 .66 C4
Burns Wynd ML9 .105 E1
Burnshill St ML10 .112 E4
Burnside Bearsden G61 .16 C7
Moffat DG10 .161 D5
Muirkirk KA18 .142 A6
Burnside Ave
Armadale EH48 .41 D6
Barrhead G78 .57 B4
Bellshill ML4 .65 C4
Calderbank ML6 .51 B2
Kirkintilloch G66 .20 B7
Burnside Cres
Clydebank G81 .15 B7
Fauldhouse EH47 .71 E6
Hamilton G72 .77 F6
Shotts ML7 .69 D6
Burnside Ct Bearsden G61 .16 C7
Coatbridge ML5 .49 F5
Motherwell ML1 .80 B4
Rutherglen G73 .61 C5
Burnside Gate
Hamilton ML3 .78 D3
Rutherglen G73 .61 C5
Burnside Gdns G76 .73 D7
Burnside Ind Est G65 .10 C8
Burnside La ML3 .78 E2
Burnside Pl Larkhall ML9 .93 B3
.137 F5
Burnside Prim Sch G73 .61 B5
Burnside Quadrant ML1 .66 A5
Burnside Rd
Glenmavis ML5 .35 C1
Motherwell ML1 .66 D4
Rutherglen G46 .73 B6
Rutherglen,High Burnside G73 .61 C4
Burnside St ML1 .80 B4
Burnside Sta G73 .61 C5
Burnside Terr
Biggar ML12 .160 C4
Fauldhouse EH47 .71 E6
Burnside Twr ML1 .80 B3
Burnside View
Coatbridge ML5 .49 E5
East Kilbride G75 .88 A4
Burnside Wlk
Bearsden G61 .16 C7
Coatbridge ML5 .49 E5
Burntbroom Dr G69 .47 F3
Burntbroom Gdns G69 .47 F3
Burntbroom Rd G69 .47 F2
Burntbroom St G33 .47 D7
Burnwood Dr ML6 .52 A6
Burra Gdns G64 .19 D2
Burrell Collection (Mus)* G43 .44 B1
Burrell Ct G41 .44 C2
Burrell's La G4 .163 C2
Burrelton Rd G43 .59 F5
Burte Ct ML4 .65 A7
Burton La Carluke ML8 .95 E2
Glasgow G42 .45 A1
Busby Prim Sch G76 .73 F6
Busby Rd Bellshill ML4 .64 F3
Carmunnock G76 .74 C7
Clarkston G76 .73 E7
Busby Sta G76 .74 A5
Bush Cres ML2 .81 C2
Bushelhead Rd ML8 .108 E6
Busheyhill St G72 .62 A5
Bute G74 .76 C1

Bute Ave Motherwell ML1 ..79 C7
Renfrew PA4 ..27 D1
Bute Cres Bearsden G61 ..16 F2
Shotts ML7 ..69 D6
Bute Gdns Glasgow G44 ..59 F4
Glasgow,Kelvingrove G12 ..29 D2
Bute La G12 ..29 D2
Bute Rd G66 ..21 B8
Bute St Coatbridge ML5 ..50 B4
Hamilton ML3 ..78 B6
Bute Terr Rutherglen G73 ..61 A5
Uddingston G71 ..64 B7
Bute Twr G72 ..61 E3
Butler Wynd ML4 ..64 F5
Butterbiggins Rd G42 ..45 B3
Butterburnpark St ML3 ..78 D2
Buttercup Path ML2 ..80 F1
Butterfield Pl 2 G41 ..45 A3
Butteries View EH48 ..41 D5
Buttermere G75 ..87 F5
Butts The ML11 ..116 F3
Buttsley Ct ML11 ..116 E4
Byars Rd G66 ..20 B8
Byrebush Rd G53 ..43 C1
Byres Ave PA3 ..42 A6
Byres Cres PA3 ..42 A6
Byres Rd Glasgow G12 ..29 C2
Motherwell ML1 ..66 E4
Byresknowe La 2 ML1 ..66 B1
Byrestone Ave G77 ..73 C4
Byretown Rd ML11 ..116 E2
Byron Rd ML7 ..69 B6
Byron St Clydebank G81 ..15 A4
Glasgow G11 ..28 F2
Byshot St G22 ..30 D4

C

Cable Depot Rd G81 ..15 A1
Cabrach Loan 13 ML2 ..81 F6
Cadder Ct G64 ..19 B5
Cadder Gr G20 ..29 E7
Cadder Pl G20 ..29 E7
Cadder Prim Sch G23 ..29 F7
Cadder Rd
Bishopbriggs G64 ..19 B5
Glasgow G23 ..29 E7
Cadder Rdbt G64 ..19 B4
Cadder Way G64 ..19 B5
Cadell Gdns G74 ..76 D5
Cadell Pl EH47 ..71 E6
Cadger's Sheuch G68 ..11 B8
Cadoc St G72 ..62 B5
Cadogan Sq G2 ..162 B2
Cadogan St G2 ..162 B2
Cadzow Ave Hamilton ML3 ..78 C5
Rutherglen G46 ..73 B8
Cadzow Cres ML5 ..49 E4
Cadzow Dr Bellshill ML4 ..65 D4
Cambuslang G72 ..62 A5
Cadzow Gn G74 ..75 D2
Cadzow Ho ML3 ..78 E5
Cadzow Ind Est ML3 ..91 D8
Cadzow La ML3 ..78 E4
Cadzow Pk ML3 ..78 E4
Cadzow Rd ML3 ..91 F3
Cadzow St Glasgow G2 ..162 B2
Hamilton ML3 ..78 E4
Larkhall ML9 ..93 A4
Motherwell ML1 ..79 D6
Caerlaverock Pl 1 G72 ..77 C6
Caird Dr G11 ..29 B2
Caird Gdns ML3 ..78 D5
Caird Pk ML3 ..78 D5
Caird St ML3 ..78 C5
Caird Terr G61 ..16 D7
Cairn Ave PA4 ..27 E1
Cairn Ct East Kilbride G74 ..75 E4
2 Motherwell ML1 ..79 F5
Cairn Pl G74 ..75 E4
Cairn St G21 ..30 F6
Cairn View ML6 ..50 F6
Cairnban Ct ML8 ..95 F3
Cairnbrook Ind Est G34 ..48 C8
Cairnbrook Rd G34 ..48 C8
Cairncross Cres ML11 ..119 D6
Cairndow Ave G44 ..59 F4
Cairndow Avenue La G44 ..59 F4
Cairndow Ct G44 ..59 F4
Cairndow Pl ML2 ..81 C1
Cairndyke Cres ML6 ..51 A6
Cairney Pl ML2 ..82 D6
Cairneymount Rd ML8 ..96 A2
Cairngorm Cres
Barrhead G78 ..57 C1
Bearsden G61 ..16 B6
Wishaw ML2 ..80 F3
Cairngorm Ct ML3 ..91 B7
Cairngorm Gdns G68 ..11 B1
Cairngorm Pl G75 ..88 B4
Cairngorm Rd G43 ..59 C5
Cairngorm Residential Pk
The G64 ..31 C8
Cairngryffe St ML11 ..131 B5
Cairnhill Ave ML6 ..51 A5
Cairnhill Cir G53 ..42 F3
Cairnhill Cres ML5 ..50 D3
Cairnhill Ct ML8 ..96 A2
Cairnhill Dr G53 ..42 F3
Cairnhill Pl G53 ..42 F3
Cairnhill Rd Airdrie ML6 ..51 A6
Bearsden G61 ..16 F1
Cairnhill Trad Est ML6 ..51 A6
Cairnhope Ave ML6 ..50 F5
Cairnhouses ML11 ..138 C6
Cairnhouses Rd ML11 ..138 C6
Cairnlea Dr G51 ..44 B6
Cairnlea Gdns ML4 ..65 B3
Cairnlea Rd ML10 ..112 D5
Cairnmuir Rd G74 ..75 D6
Cairnoch Hill G68 ..11 C2
Cairnryan G74 ..75 D3
Cairnryan Cres G72 ..77 D2
Cairns Ave G72 ..62 B5
Cairns Ct G72 ..62 B5
Cairns Prim Sch G72 ..62 C4
Cairns Rd G72 ..62 B4
Cairns St ML1 ..79 E6
Cairnsmore Dr
Bearsden G61 ..16 B7
Stonehouse ML9 ..129 E8
Cairnsmore Rd G15 ..15 F2
Cairnswell Ave G72 ..62 C4
Cairnswell Pl G72 ..62 C4
Cairntoul Ct G68 ..11 B1
Cairntoul Dr G14 ..28 A5
Cairntoul Pl G14 ..28 A5
Cairnview G66 ..21 B7
Cairnwood Dr ML6 ..50 F5
Caithness Rd G74 ..76 D3
Caithness Row ML11 ..117 A2
Caithness St Glasgow G20 ..29 F4
Hamilton G72 ..77 C6
Cala Sona Ct ML2 ..93 E8
Calcots Path G34 ..33 C1
Calcots Pl G34 ..33 D1
Caldarvan St G22 ..30 B3
Caldeen Rd ML5 ..50 B5
Calder Ave Barrhead G78 ..57 D1
Caldercruix ML6 ..37 F4
Coatbridge ML5 ..50 B4
Wishaw ML2 ..82 A6
Calder Cres ML10 ..104 F3
Calder Ct ML5 ..50 B4
Calder Dr Bellshill ML4 ..65 C4
Cambuslang G72 ..62 A5
Shotts ML7 ..70 B4
Calder Gate G64 ..18 F4
Calder Pl G69 ..48 B4
Calder Prim Sch ML1 ..79 F7
Calder Rd Bellshill ML4 ..65 C4
Shotts ML7 ..82 F8
Uddingston G71,G72 ..63 C5
Calder St Calderbank ML6 ..51 C2
Coatbridge ML5 ..50 C5
Glasgow G42 ..45 B2
Hamilton G72 ..77 D7
Calder Twr
East Kilbride G74 ..89 B7
6 Motherwell ML1 ..79 E5
Calder View ML3 ..91 B8
Calderbank Prim Sch
ML6 ..51 C3
Calderbank Rd ML6 ..51 B4
Calderbank Terr ML1 ..79 F7
Calderbank View G69 ..48 C4
Calderbankview Cotts
ML6 ..51 B4
Calderbraes Ave G71 ..63 E8
Caldercruix Rd ML6 ..38 D7
Caldercuilt Prim Sch
G23 ..17 E1
Caldercuilt Rd G20 ..29 C8
Calderglen Ave G72 ..63 C3
Calderglen Ctry Pk*
G75 ..89 C6
Calderglen Ctry Pk Visitor
Ctr* G75 ..89 C6
Calderglen Rd G74 ..76 D1
Caldergrove ML1 ..79 E8
Calderhead High Sch
ML7 ..69 F5
Calderhead Rd ML7 ..69 D7
Calderpark Ave G71 ..48 B2
Calderpark Cres G71 ..48 B2
Calderpark Terr G71 ..48 B2
Calderrigg Pl ML6 ..51 E7
Calderside Gr G74 ..76 E3
Calderside Rd G72,G74 ..76 E3
Caldervale High Sch ML6 ..51 F7
Caldervale St ML6 ..51 E4
Calderview ML1 ..79 F7
Calderview Ave ML5 ..50 E4
Calderwood Ave G69 ..48 A3
Calderwood Ct ML2 ..81 B2
Calderwood Dr
Glasgow G69 ..48 A3
Hamilton G72 ..77 D6
Calderwood Gdns
East Kilbride G74 ..76 E3
Glasgow G69 ..48 A3
Calderwood Lodge Prim Sch
G43 ..59 E5
Calderwood Prim Sch
G73 ..61 C6
Calderwood Rd
East Kilbride G74 ..76 B2
Glasgow G43 ..59 D6
Rutherglen G73 ..61 C7
Calderwood Sq 1 G74 ..76 B3
Caldwell Ave G13 ..28 A6
Caldwell Gr Bellshill ML4 ..65 A8
Rutherglen G73 ..61 C2
Caldwell Quadrant ML1 ..79 C5
Caldwell Rd ML8 ..109 B8
Caldwell Terr ML11 ..124 E1
Caledon La G12 ..29 C2
Caledon St G12 ..29 C3
Caledonia Ave
Glasgow G5 ..45 C3
Rutherglen G73 ..61 B8
Caledonia Dr
Glasgow G69 ..48 B3
Motherwell ML1 ..66 E4
Caledonia Gdns ML8 ..95 E3
Caledonia Pl ML10 ..112 E5
Caledonia Prim Sch G69 ..48 A3
Caledonia Rd
Glasgow G69 ..48 A3
Glasgow,Gorbals G5 ..45 C4
Shotts ML7 ..69 E5
Caledonia St G5 ..45 D3
Caledonia Wlk ML3 ..78 E1
Caledonian Ave
Bellshill ML4 ..64 F4
Crawford ML12 ..152 B7
Stonehouse ML9 ..105 E1
Caledonian Cres 5 G12 ..29 E2
Caledonian Ct G75 ..88 E8
Caledonian Gdns ML11 ..137 F6
Caledonian Pk ML2 ..80 D3
Caledonian Pl 7 DG10 ..161 D5
Caledonian Rd
Fauldhouse EH47 ..71 D5
Larkhall ML9 ..93 A3
Wishaw ML2 ..81 A2
Caledonian Terr EH47 ..71 D5
Caley Brae G71 ..63 F6
Calfhill Rd G53 ..43 B2
Calfmuir Rd G66 ..21 A6
Calgary Pk G75 ..88 D8
Calgary Pl 1 G75 ..88 D8
Calgary St G4 ..163 A4
California Pl ML12 ..151 A1
Calla Rd ML11 ..124 F3
Callaghan Wynd G72 ..63 C1
Callander Ct G68 ..11 F4
Callander Rd
Chapelhall ML6 ..51 D1
Cumbernauld G68 ..11 F4
Callander St G20 ..30 A3
Callieburn Ct G64 ..31 A8
Callieburn Rd G64 ..31 A8
Callon St ML6 ..51 A7
Cally Ave G15 ..16 A3
Calton Entry G40 ..163 C1
Calvay Cres G33 ..47 D7
Calvay Pl G33 ..47 E7
Calvay Rd G33 ..47 E7
Cam'nethan St ML9 ..105 F2
Cambourne Rd G69 ..21 F3
Cambridge Ave G81 ..15 B3
Cambridge Rd PA4 ..27 C2
Cambridge St G3 ..162 C3
Camburn St G32 ..46 F5
Cambus Pl G33 ..32 C2
Cambusdoon Rd G33 ..32 C2
Cambuskenneth Gdns
G32 ..47 D5
Cambuskenneth Pl G33 ..32 C2
Cambuslang Ind Est G32 ..62 A8
Cambuslang Investment Pk
G32 ..62 A8
Cambuslang Rd
Cambuslang G32,G72 ..61 F8
Rutherglen G72,G73 ..61 D8
Cambuslang Sta G72 ..61 F6
Cambusnethan Prim Sch
ML2 ..81 D3
Cambusnethan St ML2 ..81 E4
Camden Terr G5 ..45 C4
Camellia Dr ML2 ..80 E1
Camelon Cres G72 ..77 D8
Camelon St G32 ..46 F6
Cameron Cres
Carmunnock G76 ..74 E8
Hamilton ML3 ..78 C3
Cameron Ct
Clydebank G81 ..27 C8
Rutherglen G73 ..61 A7
Cameron Dr
Bearsden G61 ..17 A3
Newton Mearns G77 ..72 E7
Strathaven ML10 ..112 D6
Uddingston G71 ..64 A8
Cameron Path 13 ML9 ..93 C1
Cameron Rd
Carluke ML8 ..109 B8
Wattston ML6 ..24 C2
Cameron Sq G81 ..15 C6
Cameron St
Clydebank G81 ..27 C8
Coatbridge ML5 ..50 B8
Glasgow G52 ..42 F7
Motherwell ML1 ..79 D6
Cameron Way G72 ..77 D8
Cameronian Ct ML11 ..117 C5
Cameronian Dr ML8 ..96 B1
Cameronian Pl ML4 ..64 F3
Cameronian Way 8 ML9 ..93 C1
Camlachie St G31 ..46 B5
Camp Rd Glasgow G69 ..48 B5
Motherwell ML1 ..79 E4
Rutherglen G73 ..45 F2
Symington ML12 ..140 F6
Camp St ML1 ..79 F5
Campbell Cl ML3 ..78 F4
Campbell Cres
Bothwell G71 ..64 A4
Newton Mearns G77 ..72 E6
Campbell Ct G73 ..61 C5
Campbell Dr
Barrhead G78 ..57 C2
Bearsden G61 ..16 D5
Campbell Ho G67 ..11 E2
Campbell La ML3 ..78 E3
Campbell Pl G75 ..88 E7
Campbell St Bellshill ML4 ..65 B5
Glasgow G20 ..29 E7
Campbell St *continued*
Hamilton ML3 ..78 E4
Renfrew PA4 ..27 D5
Wishaw ML2 ..81 C2
Camphill Ave
Glasgow G41 ..59 E8
Kirkintilloch G66 ..20 C8
Camphill Ho G41 ..44 F1
Campion Rd ML1 ..79 E8
Camps Cres PA4 ..27 E1
Camps Rd ML12 ..152 B8
Campsie Ave G78 ..57 C1
Campsie Cres Airdrie ML6 ..50 F8
Kirkintilloch G66 ..20 C6
Campsie Ct
Coatbridge ML5 ..50 C3
Larkhall ML9 ..92 F5
Campsie Dr Bearsden G61 ..16 E7
Paisley PA4 ..42 B8
Campsie Gdns G76 ..73 C7
Campsie Pl G69 ..33 C8
Campsie Rd
East Kilbride G75 ..88 A3
Wishaw ML2 ..80 F3
Campsie St G21 ..31 A5
Campsie View
Cambuslang G72 ..62 E3
Chryston G69 ..33 C8
Coatbridge G69 ..48 F5
Cumbernauld G67 ..12 B3
Hamilton ML3 ..77 F2
Kirkintilloch G66 ..20 A8
Stepps G33 ..32 D4
7 Uddingston G71 ..64 A8
Campsie View Sch G66 ..20 A5
Campston Pl G33 ..32 B1
Camsbusmore Pl G33 ..32 C2
Camsdale Ave ML7 ..53 B2
Camstradden Dr E G61 ..16 D4
Camstradden Dr W G61 ..16 C4
Camus Pl G15 ..15 F4
Canada Ct G1 ..163 A2
Canal Bank G22 ..30 A7
Canal Ct ML5 ..49 F7
Canal St Glasgow G4 ..163 A4
Renfrew PA4 ..27 D4
Canberra Ct G46 ..59 E3
Canberra Dr G75 ..88 D8
Canberra Prim Sch G75 ..88 B8
Cander Ave ML9 ..106 A3
Cander Rigg G64 ..19 A4
Cander St ML9 ..106 B8
Candermill & Marlage Rd
ML9 ..106 E5
Candermill Rd ML9 ..106 B3
Canderside Toll ML9 ..106 B5
Candimilne Ct ML8 ..96 B1
Candleriggs G1 ..163 B2
Candymill Rd ML12 ..133 B4
Caneluk Ave ML8 ..96 B1
Canmore Pl G31 ..46 D4
Canmore St G31 ..46 D4
Cannich Dr PA2 ..42 B1
Cannich Pl ML2 ..81 F6
Canniesburn Rd G61 ..16 D3
Canniesburn Sq G61 ..16 F2
Canniesburn Toll G61 ..16 F3
Canon Ct ML1 ..66 D2
Canonbie Ave G74 ..75 F4
Canonbie La G74 ..75 E4
Canonbie St G34 ..33 D1
Canongate G74 ..76 D4
Canterbury G75 ..88 C7
Canthill Gdns ML7 ..69 A3
Cantieslaw Dr G74 ..76 A3
Canting Way G51 ..44 C7
Canyon Rd ML2 ..80 D2
Capehall Sq ML11 ..114 B2
Capel Ave G77 ..72 F6
Capel Gr G74 ..76 B3
Capelrig Dr
East Kilbride G74 ..76 B3
Newton Mearns G77 ..72 E8
Capelrig La G77 ..72 D6
Capelrig Rd G77 ..72 E6
Capelrig St G46 ..58 F4
Caplaw Pl ML2 ..93 F8
Caplaw Twr ML2 ..93 E7
Caplethill Rd G78 ..57 A6
Cappers Ct EH48 ..41 F4
Caprington Pl G33 ..32 A1
Caprington St G33 ..32 A1
Captain's Wlk ML1 ..67 E1
Cara Dr G51 ..43 E8
Cara Rd ML6 ..51 D5
Caravelle Way 3 PA4 ..27 D1
Carbarns ML2 ..80 E1
Carbarns E ML2 ..80 D1
Carbarns Rd ML2 ..80 D1
Carbarns W ML2 ..80 D1
Carberry Rd G41 ..44 D2
Carbeth St G22 ..30 B4
Carbisdale St G22 ..30 E5
Carbost St 4 G23 ..17 D1
Carbrain Ind Est G67 ..12 B1
Carbrain Prim Sch G67 ..12 B2
Carbrook St G21 ..31 A1
Cardarrach St G21 ..31 A4
Cardean Cres ML11 ..131 B8
Cardean Rd ML4 ..65 E6
Cardell Cres ML6 ..51 D2
Cardinal Newman High Sch
ML4 ..64 F5
Carding St ML12 ..140 F6
Cardon Dr ML12 ..160 C3
Cardonald Coll G52 ..43 D3
Cardonald Ct G52 ..43 A4
Cardonald Dr G52 ..43 A4
Cardonald Gdns G52 ..43 B4
Cardonald Pk G51 ..43 C7
Cardonald Place Rd G52 ..43 B4
Cardonald Prim Sch G52 ..43 B4
Cardonald Sta G52 ..43 D6
Cardow Rd G21 ..31 C4
Cardowan Dr
Cumbernauld G68 ..10 E1
Stepps G33 ..32 E5
Cardowan Pk G71 ..49 B1
Cardowan Rd
Glasgow G32 ..47 A7
Stepps G33 ..32 E5
Cardrona St G33 ..32 B3
Cardross Ct 2 G31 ..45 F7
Cardross Pl G68 ..11 B2
Cardross St G31 ..45 F7
Cardwell St 5 G5 ..45 A4
Cardyke St G21 ..31 A4
Careston Pl G64 ..19 D1
Carey Gdns ML1 ..67 C1
Carfin Dr ML8 ..108 C2
Carfin Ind Est ML1 ..66 A2
Carfin Lourdes Grotto*
ML1 ..66 D2
Carfin Rd Motherwell ML1 ..66 D3
Wishaw ML2 ..80 C4
Carfin St Coatbridge ML5 ..50 B4
Glasgow G42 ..45 B2
Motherwell ML1 ..66 A3
Carfin Sta ML1 ..66 C2
Carfrae St G3 ..44 C8
Cargill Sq G64 ..31 C8
Carham Cres G52 ..43 C5
Carham Dr G52 ..43 C5
Caribou Gn G75 ..88 B8
Carillon Rd G51 ..44 C5
Carisbrooke Cres G64 ..19 B4
Carlaverock Rd G43 ..59 E6
Carleith Quadrant G51 ..43 D7
Carleston St G21 ..30 F4
Carleton Ct G46 ..59 C4
Carleton Dr G46 ..59 C4
Carleton Gate G46 ..59 C4
Carlibar Ave G13 ..27 F7
Carlibar Dr G78 ..57 C3
Carlibar Gdns G78 ..57 C3
Carlibar Prim Sch G78 ..57 C3
Carlibar Rd G78 ..57 C3
Carlin La ML8 ..96 B1
Carlisle La ML6 ..51 C7
Carlisle Rd
Abington ML12 ..145 F2
Airdrie ML6 ..51 C5
Cleland,Omoa ML1 ..67 C4
Cleland,Shawstonfoot ML1 ..67 E1
Crawford ML12 ..152 B7
Hamilton ML3 ..79 B2
Kirkmuirhill ML11 ..113 E6
Kirkmuirhill ML11 ..113 F5
Kirkmuirhill ML11 ..114 B3
Larkhall ML3,ML9 ..92 E7
Lesmahagow,Cairnhouses
ML11 ..138 B8
Lesmahagow,Milton ML11 ..119 E6
Carlisle St G21,G22 ..30 D4
Carlouk La ML8 ..96 B1
Carloway Ct G33 ..47 B8
Carlowrie Ave G72 ..63 C2
Carlton Ct Glasgow G5 ..162 C1
6 Hamilton ML3 ..78 E2
Carlton Pl G5 ..162 C1
Carluke High Sch ML8 ..96 A2
Carluke Prim Sch ML8 ..96 A3
Carluke Sta ML8 ..95 E1
Carlyle Ave Glasgow G52 ..42 F8
Hillington G52 ..43 A8
Carlyle Dr G74 ..76 B2
Carlyle Terr
East Kilbride G74 ..76 B2
Rutherglen G73 ..46 B1
Carmaben Brae EH46 ..126 E2
Carmaben Rd G33 ..47 E8
Carment Dr G41 ..59 D8
Carmichael Ct ML11 ..117 C4
Carmichael Path ML5 ..34 C6
Carmichael Pl G42 ..59 F7
Carmichael Prim Sch
ML12 ..130 E1
Carmichael St
Douglas Water ML11 ..138 F7
Glasgow G51 ..44 C6
Law ML8 ..94 F5
Carmichael Way ML8 ..94 F5
Carmuir ML11 ..122 A1
Carmunnock By-Pass
Carmunnock G45,G76 ..74 C7
Glasgow G45 ..60 C1
Carmunnock La G44 ..60 C5
Carmunnock Prim Sch
G76 ..74 D7
Carmunnock Rd
Clarkston G76 ..74 B6
East Kilbride G76,G74 ..75 B4
Glasgow G45 ..60 C2
Glasgow G45 ..60 D3
Carmyle Ave
Glasgow,Carmyle G32 ..62 B8
Glasgow,Foxley G32 ..47 B2
Carmyle Gdns ML5 ..49 E3
Carmyle Prim Sch G32 ..47 C1
Carmyle Sta G32 ..47 B1
Carna Dr G44 ..60 C5
Carnarvon St G3 ..162 A4
Carnbooth Ct G45 ..60 F2
Carnbroe Prim Sch ML5 ..50 D4
Carnbroe Rd Bellshill ML4 ..65 B8
Coatbridge ML5 ..50 D3

Carnegie Gdns ML11 113 F3
Carnegie Hill G75 88 D8
Carnegie Pl G75 88 D8
Carnegie Rd G52 43 A6
Carnoch St 1 G23 17 D1
Carnock Cres G78 57 B1
Carnock Rd G53 58 C8
Carnoustie Cres
Bishopbriggs G64 19 C1
East Kilbride G75 88 A6
Carnoustie Ct G71 63 F2
Carnoustie Pl
Bellshill ML4 65 A7
Glasgow G5 44 F5
Carnoustie St G5 44 F5
Carnoustie Way G68 11 F6
Carntyne Ind Est G32 46 E6
Carntyne Path G32 46 D7
Carntyne Pl G32 46 D7
Carntyne Prim Sch G33 46 D8
Carntyne Rd
Glasgow,Carntyne G32 46 E7
Glasgow,Lightburn G32 47 A7
Carntyne Sta G32 46 F6
Carntynehall Rd G32 46 F6
Carnwadric Prim Sch
G46 58 F4
Carnwadric Rd G46 58 E4
Carnwath Ave G43 59 F6
Carnwath Rd
Braehead ML11 124 B5
Carluke ML8 96 A1
Carnwath ML11 124 F1
Carstairs Junction ML11 131 C8
Elsrickle ML12 132 F6
Kilncadzow ML8 110 C5
Caroline St G31 46 E5
Carolside Ave G76 73 E7
Carolside Dr G15 16 B3
Carolside Gdns G76 73 E7
Carolside Prim Sch G76 73 E6
Carousel Cres ML2 81 C3
Carr Quadrant ML4 65 D5
Carradale Cres G68 22 F8
Carradale Gdns
Bishopbriggs G64 19 C1
Carluke ML8 109 A8
Carradale St ML5 49 F7
Carranbuie Rd ML8 95 F3
Carrbridge Dr 1 G20 29 D6
Carresbrook Ave G66 21 A6
Carrick Cres Glasgow G46 59 C1
Wishaw ML2 81 A4
Carrick Ct G66 9 A2
Carrick Dr Coatbridge ML5 49 D7
Glasgow G32 47 E4
Rutherglen G73 61 A5
Carrick Gdns Bellshill ML4 65 A8
Carluke ML8 109 A7
Hamilton,Blantyre G72 77 D6
Hamilton,Earnock ML3 77 E2
Carrick Gr G32 47 E4
Carrick Pl Bellshill ML4 65 B7
Coatbridge ML5 49 D7
Glenboig ML5 34 E6
Larkhall ML9 93 B4
Carrick Rd
Bishopbriggs G64 19 C1
Cumbernauld G67 12 A4
East Kilbride G74 75 F3
Rutherglen G73 60 F5
Rutherglen G73 61 A5
Carrick St Glasgow G2 162 B2
7 Larkhall ML9 93 C2
Carrick Vale ML1 67 C1
Carrick View ML5 34 E6
Carrick Way 7 G71 64 A3
Carrickarden Rd G61 16 F3
Carrickstone Rd G68 11 E4
Carrickstone Rdbt G68 11 E5
Carrickstone View G68 11 F5
Carrickvale Ct G68 11 F5
Carrington St G4 29 F2
Carroglen Gdns G32 47 D5
Carroglen Gr G32 47 D5
Carroll Cres ML1 66 D2
Carron Cres Bearsden G61 16 C3
Bishopbriggs G64 19 B1
Glasgow G22 30 D5
Kirkintilloch G66 20 E4
Carron Ct Cambuslang G72 62 D5
Hamilton ML3 78 B1
Carron Pl Coatbridge ML5 34 D1
East Kilbride G75 88 F5
Glasgow G22 30 E5
Carron St Glasgow G22 30 E5
Wishaw ML2 81 B1
Carron Valley Forest Walks*
FK6 2 E4
Carron Way
Motherwell ML1 66 C4
Paisley PA3 42 A7
Carrour Gdns G64 18 F2
Carsaig Dr G52 43 E5
Carsaig Loan ML5 34 C6
Carscallan Rd ML3 91 E5
Carse View Dr G61 17 A6
Carstairs Junction Prim Sch
ML11 131 B8
Carstairs Prim Sch
ML11 130 F8
Carstairs Rd ML11 131 A8
Carstairs St G40 46 A2
Carstairs Sta ML11 131 B8
Carswell Gdns G41 44 E2
Carswell Rd G77 72 B5
Cart St G81 27 B8
Cartbank Gdns G44 60 A4
Cartbank Gr G44 59 F4
Cartbank Rd G44 60 A4
Cartcraigs Rd G43 59 B6
Cartha Cres PA2 42 B3
Cartha St G41 59 E7
Cartland Ave ML8 108 F8
Cartland Rd ML11 116 D8
Cartland View ML11 116 F5
Cartsbridge Rd G76 73 F6
Cartside Dr G76 74 A6
Cartside Pl G76 73 F5
Cartside Quadrant G42 60 A7
Cartside Rd G76 73 F5
Cartside St G42 59 F7
Cartvale Rd G42 59 F7
Cartvale Sch
Glasgow,Govan G51 44 B7
Glasgow,Langside G42 59 F7
Cartview Ct G76 73 F6
Carvale Ave ML7 53 B2
Carwath Prim Sch ML11 124 E1
Carwood Rd ML12 160 D5
Caskie Dr G72 63 E1
Cassels Gr ML1 65 C1
Cassels St Carluke ML8 95 F1
Motherwell ML1 79 E8
Cassiltoun Gdns G45 60 D2
Cassley Ave PA4 27 F2
Castburn Rd G67 12 F6
Castle Ave Bothwell G71 63 E3
Motherwell ML1 66 B6
Castle Chimmins Ave
G72 62 D4
Castle Chimmins Rd G72 62 D3
Castle Ct Cumbernauld G68 12 F8
Kirkintilloch G66 20 D8
Castle Dr ML1 66 B6
Castle Gate
Newton Mearns G77 73 A3
Uddingston G71 63 E5
Castle Gdns G69 21 F2
Castle Gr G65 6 C2
Castle Pl G71 63 E6
Castle Quadrant ML6 51 D7
Castle Rd Airdrie ML6 51 D7
Newton Mearns G77 72 C4
Castle St Chapelhall ML6 51 D2
Glasgow G4 163 C3
Glasgow,Baillieston G69 48 A3
Glasgow,Kelvinhaugh G11 29 C1
Hamilton ML3 78 F4
Rutherglen G73 61 A8
Strathaven ML10 112 E6
Castle View ML2 82 A6
Castle Way Coatbridge G69 48 F5
Cumbernauld G67 12 C4
Castle Wynd Bothwell G71 64 B2
Quarter ML3 91 F3
Castle Yett ML12 160 C3
Castlebank Ct G13 28 E6
Castlebank Gdns G13 28 E6
Castlebank St
Glasgow G11 29 A1
Glasgow G11 29 B1
Castlebank Villas G13 28 E6
Castlebay Dr G22 18 C1
Castlebay Pl G22 30 C8
Castlebay St G22 30 C8
Castlebrae Gdns G44 60 B6
Castlecary Rd G67,G68 12 D7
Castlecroft Gdns G71 63 F5
Castledyke Rd ML11 130 F8
Castledyke View ML11 130 F8
Castlefern Rd G73 61 B3
Castlefield Ct G33 32 B4
Castlefield Gdns G75 88 B5
Castlefield Prim Sch G75 88 B6
Castlegait ML10 112 F6
Castlegate ML11 117 A4
Castleglen Rd G74 75 A4
Castlehill Cres
Banknock FK4 8 E2
Chapelhall ML6 51 F1
Hamilton ML3 78 F3
Hamilton,Allanton ML3 79 D1
Law ML8 95 A4
Renfrew PA4 27 D4
Castlehill Ct ML12 140 F5
Castlehill Dr G77 72 F3
Castlehill Gdns ML3 78 F2
Castlehill Gn G74 74 F4
Castlehill Ind Est ML8 95 E4
Castlehill La ML12 140 F5
Castlehill Prim Sch
Bearsden G61 16 C6
Wishaw ML2 94 A8
Castlehill Rd
Bearsden G61 16 C6
Carluke ML8 95 E5
Overtown ML2 94 B7
Castlehill View G65 6 C2
Castleknowe Gdns ML8 95 E3
Castlelaw Gdns G32 47 B6
Castlelaw St G32 47 B6
Castlemilk Arc G45 60 D3
Castlemilk Cres G44 60 E5
Castlemilk Dr G45 60 E3
Castlemilk High Sch G45 60 E2
Castlemilk Rd
Glasgow,Croftfoot G44 60 E5
Glasgow,King's Park G44 60 E6
Castlemilk Terr G45 60 E1
Castlemount Ave G77 72 F3
Castleton Ave
Bishopbriggs G64 30 E7
Newton Mearns G77 73 A3
Castleton Cres G77 72 F3
Castleton Ct Glasgow G45 60 F2
Castleton Ct *continued*
Newton Mearns G77 72 F3
Castleton Dr G77 72 F3
Castleton Gr G77 72 F3
Castleton Prim Sch G45 60 D3
Castleview
Cumbernauld G68 12 E8
Larkhall ML9 106 A8
Castleview Rd ML10 112 C6
Castleview Terr FK4 8 F3
Cathay St G22 30 C8
Cathburn Holdings ML2 82 D5
Cathburn Rd ML2 82 C5
Cathcart Cres PA2 42 A3
Cathcart Pl G73 60 F7
Cathcart Rd
Glasgow,Govanhill G42 45 B2
Glasgow,Mount Florida G42 60 B8
Cathcart Sta G44 60 A6
Cathedral Prim Sch ML1 79 E7
Cathedral Sq G4 163 C2
Cathedral St G1,G4 163 B3
Catherine St
Kirkintilloch G66 20 C8
Motherwell ML1 79 E4
Catherine Way ML1 65 F3
Catherine's Wlk G72 77 D6
Cathkin Ave
Cambuslang G72 61 E6
Rutherglen G73 61 C7
Cathkin By-Pass G73 61 D3
Cathkin Cres G68 11 E4
Cathkin Ct G45 60 F2
Cathkin Dr G76 73 C8
Cathkin Gdns G71 48 E1
Cathkin High Sch G72 61 E4
Cathkin Pl G72 61 E6
Cathkin Prim Sch G73 61 D3
Cathkin Rd
Carmunnock G76 74 F8
Glasgow G42 59 F7
Rutherglen G73 61 C2
Uddingston G71 48 E1
Cathkin View G32 62 B8
Cathkinview Pl G42 60 B7
Cathkinview Rd G42 60 B7
Catrine G74 75 D2
Catrine Ave 3 G81 15 D3
Catrine Cres ML1 80 A4
Catrine Ct 8 G53 58 A8
Catrine Gdns 7 G53 58 A8
Catrine Pl G53 58 A8
Catrine Rd G53 58 A8
Catrine St 5 ML9 93 C2
Catriona Way ML1 66 B4
Causeway St 2 DG10 161 D5
Causewayside Cres G32 47 A2
Causewayside St G32 47 A2
Causeystanes 4 G72 77 D7
Cavendish Ct 5 G5 45 B4
Cavendish Dr G77 72 F5
Cavendish Pl G5 45 B4
Cavendish St G5 45 B4
Cavin Dr G45 60 E4
Cavin Rd G45 60 F4
Cawder Ct G68 11 D5
Cawder Pl G68 11 E5
Cawder Rd G68 11 E5
Cawder View G68 11 E5
Cawder Way G68 11 E5
Cawdor Cres ML6 51 E3
Cawdor Way G74 75 D3
Cayton Gdns G69 47 F4
Cayzer Ct PA1 42 E5
Cecil St Clarkston G76 73 E7
Coatbridge ML5 50 A5
Glasgow G12 29 D3
Cedar Ave G71 64 B8
Cedar Cres ML3 78 E1
Cedar Ct Cambuslang G72 62 E4
East Kilbride G75 88 C5
Glasgow G20 30 A2
Cedar Dr East Kilbride G75 88 C5
Kirkintilloch G66 20 C5
Uddingston G71 64 C8
Cedar Gdns Law ML8 94 F6
Motherwell ML1 66 C4
Rutherglen G73 61 C4
Cedar La Airdrie ML6 51 C7
Motherwell ML1 66 B4
Cedar Pl Blantyre G72 63 C1
East Kilbride G75 88 C5
Strathaven ML10 112 D5
Cedar Rd Banknock FK4 8 E2
Bishopbriggs G64 31 B8
Cumbernauld G67 12 D3
Cedar St G20 30 A2
Cedar Wlk
Bishopbriggs G64 31 B8
Motherwell ML1 66 D2
Cedar Wynd ML7 70 B4
Cedars Gr G69 49 A6
Cedarwood ML2 80 D1
Cedarwood Ave G77 72 F5
Cedarwood Rd G77 72 F4
Cedric Pl G13 28 D7
Cedric Rd G13 28 D7
Celtic Pk (Celtic FC)*
G40 46 C5
Celtic St G20 29 C7
Cemetery Rd
Fauldhouse EH47 71 D5
Glasgow G52 43 E4
Hamilton G72 77 C6
Shotts ML7 70 B4
Centenary Ave ML6 50 D7
Centenary Cres ML4 65 B6
Centenary Ct
Barrhead G78 57 B2
Clydebank G81 15 B1
Centenary Gdns
Coatbridge ML5 50 A5
2 Hamilton ML3 78 E2
Centenary Quadrant ML1 66 A5
Central Ave
Cambuslang G72 61 F6
Clydebank G81 15 A2
Glasgow G11 28 F2
Glasgow,North Mount Vernon
G32 47 E3
Hamilton G72 77 E5
Motherwell ML1 66 A2
Motherwell,Holytown ML1 65 F5
Uddingston G71 64 C6
Central College of Commerce
G1,G4 163 B3
Central Cres ML9 106 F8
Central Gr
Cambuslang G72 61 F6
Glasgow G32 47 D4
Central Path G32 47 E3
Central Sta Glasgow G2 162 C2
Hamilton ML3 78 E3
Central Way G67 11 F1
Centre Rdbt The G74 75 F1
Centre St Chapelhall ML6 51 D2
Glasgow G5 162 C1
Glenboig ML5 34 C6
Centre W 1 G74 88 E8
Centre Way G78 57 B3
Centurion Pl ML1 65 B1
Ceres Gdns G64 19 D1
Cessnock Pl G72 62 D5
Cessnock Rd G33 32 B4
Cessnock St G51 44 C6
Cessnock Underground Sta
G51 44 C6
Chalmers Cres G75 88 F7
Chalmers Ct
Glasgow G40 163 C1
Uddingston G71 63 F6
Chalmers Dr G75 88 F7
Chalmers Gate G40 163 C1
Chalmers Pl G40 163 C1
Chalmers St
Clydebank G81 15 B1
Glasgow G40 163 C1
Chamberlain La 1 G13 28 E5
Chamberlain Rd
Glasgow,Anniesland G13 28 E6
Glasgow,Jordanhill G13 28 E5
Chancellor St G11 29 C2
Chantinghall Rd ML3 78 B3
Chantinghall Terr ML3 78 B3
Chapel Cres ML3 91 D6
Chapel Ct G73 60 F8
Chapel Rd Clydebank G81 15 A6
Strathaven ML10 112 E6
Wishaw ML2 82 C2
Chapel St Airdrie ML6 51 A8
Carluke ML8 95 F2
Cleland ML1 67 B1
Glasgow G20 29 E5
Hamilton ML3 78 E3
3 Moffat DG10 161 D5
Rutherglen G73 60 F8
Chapel Street Ind Est
G20 29 E5
Chapelcross Ave ML6 36 A1
Chapelgreen Prim Sch
G65 9 E7
Chapelhall Ind Est ML6 51 D4
Chapelhall Prim Sch
ML6 51 D2
Chapelhill Rd PA2 42 A2
Chapelknowe Rd ML1 66 E1
Chapelside Ave ML6 51 A8
Chapelside Prim Sch
ML6 36 A1
Chapelside Rd
East Kilbride G74 76 B5
Nerston G74 76 A6
Chapelton Ave G61 16 F4
Chapelton Gdns G61 16 F4
Chapelton Prim Sch
ML10 103 C5
Chapelton Rd G67 23 D6
Chapelview Gdns DG10 161 C5
Chapland Rd ML11 117 A5
Chaplet Ave G13 28 C8
Chapman Ave ML5 34 C6
Chapman St 4 G42 45 A2
Chappell St G78 57 B3
Charing Cross ML9 93 A3
Charing Cross La G3 162 A3
Charing Cross Sta G2 162 B3
Charles Ave PA4 27 D4
Charles Cres Carluke ML8 96 B1
Kirkintilloch G66 20 D3
Charles Path ML6 51 D1
Charles Quadrant ML1 66 A5
Charles St Glasgow G21 30 F1
Kilsyth G65 6 D1
Shotts ML7 70 B4
Wishaw ML2 80 D4
Charleson Row G65 10 F3
Charlotte Ave G64 19 B8
Charlotte Path ML9 93 A2
Charlotte Pl DG10 161 C5
Charlotte St Glasgow G1 163 B1
Shotts ML7 70 A3
Chassels St ML5 50 A8
Chateau Gr ML3 79 A2
Chatelherault Ave G72 61 E5
Chatelherault Country Pk*
ML3 92 B8
Chatelherault Country Pk
Visitor Ctr* ML3 92 B8
Chatelherault Cres ML3 78 F1
Chatelherault Prim Sch
ML3 78 E1
Chatelherault Wlk ML3 78 E1
Chatham G75 88 C7
Chatton St G23 17 D1
Chatton Wlk ML5 50 D3
Cheapside St
Eaglesham G76 86 F5
Glasgow G3 162 A2
Chelmsford Dr G12 29 B5
Cherry Ave G67 12 E5
Cherry Bank G66 20 B5
Cherry Cres G81 15 A4
Cherry Gr G69 49 B6
Cherry La FK4 8 E2
Cherry Pl
Bishopbriggs G64 31 B8
Motherwell ML1 66 B5
Uddingston G71 64 D7
Cherry Tree Dr ML11 114 A4
Cherry Wlk ML1 79 E3
Cherrybank Rd G43 59 F5
Cherrybank Wlk ML6 50 D8
Cherryhill View ML9 92 F3
Cherryridge Dr G69 49 A6
Cherrytree Cres ML9 93 A5
Cherrytree Dr G72 62 E4
Cherrytree Pl ML10 112 E7
Cherrytree Wynd G75 88 F6
Chester St G32 47 A5
Chesterfield Ave G12 29 B5
Chesters Cres ML1 79 C8
Chesters Pl 3 G73 61 A7
Chesters Rd G61 16 D4
Chestnut Ave G67 12 E5
Chestnut Cres
East Kilbride G75 88 C6
Hamilton ML3 78 F2
Uddingston G71 64 D7
Chestnut Ct G67 12 E5
Chestnut Dr
Clydebank G81 15 A5
Kirkintilloch G66 20 B6
Chestnut Gr Carluke ML8 95 F1
Glenboig G69 34 C6
Hamilton G72 77 C8
Larkhall ML9 93 A5
Motherwell ML1 79 D4
Chestnut Pl G67 12 E5
Chestnut St G22 30 D5
Chestnut Way
Cambuslang G72 62 E4
Quarter ML3 91 F4
Cheviot Ave G78 57 C1
Cheviot Cres
East Kilbride G75 88 B4
Wishaw ML2 80 F4
Cheviot Ct Airdrie ML6 36 B2
Coatbridge ML5 50 C3
Cheviot Dr G77 72 C3
Cheviot Gdns G61 16 D7
Cheviot Rd Glasgow G43 59 C5
Hamilton ML3 78 F2
Larkhall ML9 93 C2
Cheviot St G72 77 C7
Chirmorie Cres G53 43 A1
Chirmorie Pl G53 43 A1
Chirnside Ct G72 77 F5
Chirnside Pl G52 43 B6
Chirnside Rd G52 43 A6
Chirnsyde Prim Sch G22 30 D6
Chisholm Dr G77 72 E6
Chisholm Pl ML1 80 B2
Chisholm St
Coatbridge ML5 50 B8
Glasgow G1 163 B1
Chrighton Gn 3 G71 64 A8
Chriss Ave ML3 91 D7
Christ the King Prim Sch
ML1 66 B6
Christchurch Pl G75 88 B7
Christian St G43 59 C8
Christie Pl G72 62 B5
Christie St ML4 65 D5
Christopher St G21 31 A1
Chryston Bsns Ctr G69 33 C8
Chryston High Sch G69 33 C8
Chryston Prim Sch G69 33 D8
Chryston Rd Chryston G69 33 D8
Kirkintilloch G69,G66 21 C5
Church Ave
Rutherglen G73 61 C5
Stepps G33 32 D6
Wishaw ML2 82 A4
Church Cres ML6 36 E1
Church Ct ML3 78 E4
Church Dr G66 20 C6
Church Gate DG10 161 C5
Church La Carluke ML8 95 F1
Coatbridge ML5 50 A7
8 Kilsyth G65 10 D8
Wiston ML12 140 C2
Church Pl Caldercruix ML6 37 F4
Fauldhouse EH47 71 E6
Moffat DG10 161 C5
Rutherglen G73 61 B8
Church Rd Clarkston G76 73 F6
Glasgow G46 59 D2
Muirhead G69 33 C7
Wishaw ML2 82 D6

Church Sq ML11 119 E4
Church St
Chapelton ML10 103 D6
Clydebank G81 15 A3
Coatbridge ML5 50 A7
Glasgow,Kelvingrove G11 29 C2
Glasgow,Muirhead G69 48 C4
Hamilton ML3 78 E4
Hamilton,Blantyre G72 77 E7
Harthill ML7 55 C5
Kilsyth G65 10 D8
Larkhall ML9 93 A2
Moffat DG10 161 C5
Motherwell ML1 66 F4
Uddingston G71 63 F5
Wanlockhead ML12 154 C8
Church View
Caldercruix ML6 37 F3
Cambuslang G72 62 A7
Coatbridge ML5 50 A7
Church View Gdns ML4 65 A5
Churchill Ave G74,G75 75 F1
Churchill Cres G71 64 B3
Churchill Dr G11 29 A4
Churchyard Ct ML7 69 E4
Circus Dr G31 45 F7
Circus Pl G31 45 F8
Circus Place La G31 45 F8
Citadel Pl ML1 79 C8
Citizen La G1 163 A2
Citrus Cres G71 64 C8
Cityford Cres G73 60 F7
Cityford Dr G73 60 F6
Civic Sq 4 ML1 79 F5
Civic St G4 30 B2
Civic Way G66 20 C7
Clachan Dr 4 G51 43 E8
Clachan The ML2 81 B3
Clachan Way ML5 49 E5
Claddens Holdings G66 21 A4
Claddens Pl G66 20 E4
Claddens Quadrant G22 30 C6
Claddens St G22 30 B6
Cladence Gr G75 88 F5
Clair Rd G64 19 D1
Claire St ML2 82 A5
Clairinsh Gdns 1 PA4 27 C1
Clairmont Gdns G3 162 A4
Clamp Rd ML2 80 C4
Clamps Gr G74 89 A8
Clamps Terr G74 89 B8
Clamps Wood G74 89 A8
Clanrye Dr ML5 50 A4
Clapperhow Rd ML1 66 B1
Clare St G21 31 A2
Claremont Ave G66 20 B8
Claremont High Sch G74 89 C8
Claremont Pas G3 162 A4
Claremont Pl G3 162 A4
Claremont St G3 44 E8
Claremont Terr G3 162 A4
Claremont Terrace La
G3 162 A4
Claremount Ave G46 59 C2
Claremount View ML5 50 C3
Clarence Dr Glasgow G12 29 A3
Paisley PA1 42 A4
Clarence Gdns G11 29 A3
Clarence La G12 29 B3
Clarence St
Clydebank G81 15 C3
Paisley PA1 42 A5
Clarendon Pl
9 Glasgow G20 30 A2
Stepps G33 32 D5
Clarendon Rd ML2 80 E1
Clarendon St G20 30 A2
Clarinda Ct G66 9 A2
Clarinda Pl ML1 66 C3
Clarion Cres G13 28 A8
Clarion Rd G13 28 B7
Clark Pl
Newton Mearns G77 72 B4
Torrance G64 19 C8
Clark St Airdrie ML6 51 B7
Renfrew PA4 27 B3
Wishaw ML2 81 F5
Clark Terr ML11 124 E1
Clark Way ML4 64 F7
Clarkin Ave G75 88 A4
Clarkston & Stamperland Sta
G76 73 E7
Clarkston Ave G44 59 F4
Clarkston Dr ML6 51 D7
Clarkston Prim Sch ML6 51 D8
Clarkston Rd
Clarkston G76 73 E8
Glasgow G44,G76 59 F3
Clarkswalls ML11 124 A8
Clarkwell Rd ML3 77 E3
Clarkwell Terr ML3 77 F3
Clathic Ave G61 17 A4
Claud Rd PA3 42 A6
Claude Ave G72 62 E4
Claude St ML9 93 A3
Clavens Rd G52 42 E6
Claverhouse Pl PA2 42 B3
Claverhouse Rd G52 42 F7
Clay Cres ML4 65 C7
Clay Ct ML1 79 E4
Clay Rd ML4 65 C7
Clayhouse Rd G33 32 E5
Claypotts Pl G33 32 A1
Claypotts Rd G33 32 A1
Clayslaps Rd G3 29 D1
Claythorn Ave G40 163 C1
Claythorn Cir G40 163 C1
Claythorn Ct G40 163 C1
Claythorn Pk G40 45 E5
Claythorn St G40 163 C1
Claythorn Terr G40 163 C1
Clayton Path ML4 65 B7
Clayton Terr 5 G31 45 F7
Clearfield Ave ML3 78 B4
Cleddans Cres G81 15 C5
Cleddans Rd G81 15 C5
Cleddans View
Clydebank G81 15 C4
Glenmavis ML6 35 E4
Cleddens Ct Airdrie ML6 50 D8
Bishopbriggs G64 19 A1
Cleeves Quadrant G53 58 B5
Cleeves Rd G53 58 A5
Cleghorn Ave ML11 117 B5
Cleghorn Dr ML11 117 A5
Cleghorn Rd ML11 117 A5
Cleghorn St G22 30 B3
Cleghorn Terr ML11 130 D8
Cleish Ave G61 16 C8
Cleland Hospl ML1 67 C1
Cleland La G5 45 C5
Cleland Pl G74 76 A3
Cleland Prim Sch ML1 67 C1
Cleland Rd Cleland ML1 67 A2
Wishaw ML2 81 A3
Cleland St G5 45 C5
Cleland Sta ML1 67 C1
Clelland Ave G64 31 A8
Clem Attlee Gdns ML9 93 B2
Clerwood St G32 46 D6
Cleuch Gdns G76 73 D8
Cleughearn Rd G75 88 D1
Cleveden Cres G12 29 B5
Cleveden Crescent La
G12 29 B5
Cleveden Dr Glasgow G12 29 C4
Rutherglen G73 61 C6
Cleveden Drive La G12 29 C4
Cleveden Gdns G12 29 C5
Cleveden Ho G12 29 C4
Cleveden La G12 29 B6
Cleveden Pl G12 29 B6
Cleveden Rd G12 29 B5
Cleveden Sec Sch G12 29 C5
Cleveland La G3 162 A3
Cleveland St G3 162 A3
Cliff Rd G3 162 A4
Clifford Gdns G51 44 B5
Clifford La G51 44 D5
Clifford Pl 3 G51 44 D5
Clifford St G51 44 C5
Clifton Ho 9 G3 29 E1
Clifton Pl Coatbridge ML5 50 C6
1 Glasgow G3 44 E8
Clifton Rd G46 59 B3
Clifton St G3 29 E1
Clifton Terr G72 61 E3
Cliftonville Ct ML5 50 C6
Climpy Rd ML11 85 D3
Clincart Rd G42 60 B8
Clincarthill Rd G73 61 A7
Clive St ML7 69 E5
Cloan Ave G15 16 B2
Cloan Cres G64 19 B3
Cloberhill Rd G13 16 D1
Cloch St G33 47 A8
Clockenhill Pl ML1 66 E4
Cloglands ML11 98 F7
Cloister Ave ML6 51 C4
Clonbeith St G33 32 E2
Closeburn St G22 30 C5
Cloth St G78 57 C2
Clouden Rd G67 12 B2
Cloudhowe Terr G72 63 C1
Clouston Ct 1 G20 29 E4
Clouston La G20 29 E4
Clouston St G20 29 E4
Clova Pl G71 63 F6
Clova St G46 58 F4
Clove Mill Wynd ML9 92 E2
Cloverbank Gdns G21 31 A1
Cloverbank St G21 31 A1
Clovergate G64 18 E1
Cloverhill Gdns ML10 112 E8
Cloverhill Pl G69 33 C8
Cloverhill Terr G74 75 E1
Cloverhill View G74 75 D1
Cluanie Ave ML7 69 E6
Clunie Pl Coatbridge ML5 50 B3
Wishaw ML2 81 F6
Clunie Rd G52 43 E4
Cluny Ave G61 17 A2
Cluny Dr Bearsden G61 17 A2
Newton Mearns G77 72 B5
Paisley PA3 42 A6
Cluny Gdns
Glasgow,Baillieston G69 48 A4
Glasgow,Jordanhill G14 28 E4
Cluny Villas G14 28 E4
Clutha Pl G75 88 A7
Clutha St G51 44 D6
Clyde Ave Barrhead G78 57 D1
Bothwell G71 63 F1
Hamilton ML3 79 C1
Torrance G64 19 B8
Clyde Cres ML11 117 B5
Clyde Ct Carluke ML8 95 E2
Coatbridge ML5 50 C6
Thankerton ML12 131 D1
Clyde Dr Bellshill ML4 65 D4
Shotts ML7 70 B4
Clyde Ho ML3 78 E5
Clyde La ML1 66 A4
Clyde Pl Cambuslang G72 62 D4
Glasgow G5 162 C1
Motherwell ML1 66 A4
Clyde Rd
18 Douglas ML11 138 B1
Paisley PA3 42 B7
Clyde Sh Ctr G81 15 B2
Clyde Sq 2 G67 11 F1
Clyde St Carluke ML8 95 E2
Clydebank G81 27 C8
Coatbridge ML5 50 C7
Glasgow G1 163 A1
Renfrew PA4 27 D5
Clyde Terr Bothwell G71 64 A1
Motherwell ML1 80 C2
Clyde Twr
East Kilbride G74 89 B7
8 Motherwell ML1 79 E5
Clyde Valley Ave ML1 79 E4
Clyde Valley Ctry Est*
ML8 108 B1
Clyde Valley High Sch
ML2 94 B7
Clyde View Ashgill ML9 107 A8
Hamilton ML3 78 B1
Paisley PA2 42 B2
Clyde Way
3 Cumbernauld G67 11 F1
Paisley PA3 42 B7
Clyde Wlk
1 Cumbernauld G67 11 F1
Wishaw ML2 82 A6
Clyde Workshops G32 46 F1
Clydebank Bsns Pk G81 15 B2
Clydebank Coll G81 15 B3
Clydebank High Sch G81 15 A4
Clydebank Mus* G81 15 B1
Clydebank Sta G81 15 B1
Clydebrae Dr G71 78 B8
Clydebrae St G51 44 B8
Clydebuilt Mus* G51 28 A3
Clydeford Dr Glasgow G32 46 E3
Uddingston G71 63 E7
Clydeford Rd G32,G72 62 A7
Clydeholm Rd G14 28 D2
Clydeholm Terr G81 27 D7
Clydeneuk Dr G71 63 D7
Clydesdale Ave
Hamilton ML3 91 D6
Paisley PA3 27 A1
Wishaw ML2 80 D1
Clydesdale Cl ML12 160 D4
Clydesdale Pl ML3 91 D6
Clydesdale Rd ML4 65 D4
Clydesdale St
Hamilton ML3 78 C4
Larkhall ML9 93 A4
Motherwell ML1 65 F4
Clydesholm Ct ML11 116 D4
Clydeside Expressway
G3 44 E7
Clydeside Ind Est G14 28 E1
Clydeside Rd G73 45 F2
Clydesmill Dr G32 62 A7
Clydesmill Gr G32 62 A7
Clydesmill Pl G32 62 A8
Clydesmill Rd G32 62 A8
Clydevale G71 64 B1
Clydeview G71 64 C1
Clydeview Sch ML1 79 B8
Clydeview Sh Ctr G72 77 E7
Clydeview Terr G32 62 C8
Clydeway Ind Est 8 G3 44 E8
Clynder St G51 44 B6
Clyth Dr G46 59 D2
Coach Cl G65 11 A8
Coach Pl G65 10 E7
Coach Rd G65 10 F7
Coalburn Rd Bothwell G71 64 B5
Coalburn ML11 137 F7
Coalburn St ML6 24 F2
Coalhall Ave ML1 66 A1
Coalhill St G31 46 B5
Coatbank St ML5 50 B6
Coatbank Way ML5 50 B6
Coatbridge Bsns Ctr ML5 50 C6
Coatbridge Central Sta
ML5 49 F7
Coatbridge Coll ML5 50 B7
Coatbridge High Sch
ML5 50 A7
Coatbridge Rd
Coatbridge G69 49 A6
Gartcosh G69 34 A3
Glasgow G69 48 E5
Glenboig ML5 34 F5
Glenmavis ML6 35 D3
Coatbridge Sunnyside Sta
ML5 50 A8
Coatbridge Workshops
ML5 50 B6
Coatdyke Sta ML5 50 D7
Coathill Hospl ML5 50 A4
Coathill St ML5 50 B4
Coats Cres G69 48 A5
Coats St ML5 50 B6
Coatshill Ave G72 63 C1
Cobbett Rd ML1 79 B5
Cobblerigg Way G71 63 E6
Cobbleton Rd ML1 65 F2
Cobington Pl G33 32 B1
Cobinshaw St G32 47 A6
Coburg St 3 G5 45 B5
Cochno Rd
Clydebank,Duntocher G81 15 B8
Clydebank,Faifley G81 15 E8
Cochno St G81 15 C1
Cochrane Ct G62 17 C8
Cochrane St Barrhead G78 57 B2
Bellshill ML4 64 F5
Glasgow G1 163 A2
Strathaven ML10 112 E6
Cockburn Pl ML5 49 F4
Cockels Loan PA4 27 D1
Cockenzie St G32 47 A6
Cockhill Way ML4 64 D6
Cockmuir St G21 31 A4
Cockridge Rd ML11 124 A3
Coddington Cres ML1 65 F7
Cogan Pl G78 57 B2
Cogan Rd G43 59 C6
Cogan St Barrhead G78 57 B2
Glasgow G43 59 C7
Coire Loan ML7 70 B3
Colbert St G40 45 F4
Colbreggan Ct G81 15 C6
Colbreggan Gdns G81 15 C6
Colbreggan Pl G81 15 C6
Colchester Dr G12 29 B6
Coldingham Ave G14 27 E6
Coldstream Cres ML2 81 C5
Coldstream Dr
Rutherglen G73 61 D6
Strathaven ML10 112 E8
Coldstream Pl G21 30 C3
Coldstream Rd G81 15 B1
Coldstream St G72 77 D7
Cole Rd G64 19 D6
Colebrooke Pl G12 29 E3
Colebrooke St
Cambuslang G72 62 A6
9 Glasgow G12 29 E3
Colebrooke Terr
Abington ML12 145 F2
Glasgow G12 29 E3
Coleridge G75 88 A7
Coleridge Ave G71 64 B3
Colfin St G34 33 C1
Colgrain Ave G20 30 A6
Colgrain Terr G20 30 A6
Colgrave Cres G32 46 F3
Colinbar Circ G78 57 B1
Colinhill Rd ML10 112 C5
Colinshiel Ct EH48 41 F6
Colinshiel View EH48 41 F7
Colinslie Rd G53 58 D8
Colinton Pl G32 47 B7
Colintraive Ave G33 31 F4
Colintraive Cres G33 31 E4
Coll G74 89 C7
Coll Ave PA4 27 D1
Coll Dr ML5 49 E4
Coll Lea ML3 77 F1
Coll Pl Airdrie ML6 51 C5
Glasgow G21 31 B2
Coll St Glasgow G21 31 B2
Wishaw ML2 81 F6
Colla Gdns G64 19 D2
College Gate G61 16 C6
College La G1 163 B2
College St G1 163 B2
Collessie Dr G33 32 C2
Colliehall Rd ML12 160 E4
Colliers La EH48 41 E5
Colliertree Rd ML6 51 D8
Collina St G20 29 C6
Collins St Clydebank G81 15 C6
Glasgow G4 163 C2
Collree Gdns G34 48 C7
Collylinn Rd G61 16 E4
Colmonell Ave G13 27 F7
Colonel's Entry 23 ML11 138 B1
Colonsay G74 89 C7
Colonsay Ave PA4 27 C1
Colonsay Cres ML5 49 D4
Colonsay Dr G77 72 B5
Colonsay Rd G52 43 E5
Colquhoun Ave G52 43 A7
Colquhoun Ct G41 44 C3
Colquhoun Dr G61 16 E5
Colquhoun Park Prim Sch
G61 16 D3
Colquhoun Pk G52 43 B7
Colson Pl ML4 65 C3
Colston Ave G64 30 F7
Colston Dr G64 30 F7
Colston Gdns G64 30 E7
Colston Gr G64 30 F7
Colston Path G64 30 E7
Colston Pl 2 Airdrie ML6 51 C7
1 Bishopbriggs G64 30 E7
Colston Rd Airdrie ML6 51 C7
Bishopbriggs G64 30 F7
Colston Row 3 ML6 51 C7
Colston Terr 4 ML6 51 C7
Colt Ave ML5 34 E1
Colt Pl ML5 50 A8
Colt Terr ML5 50 A8
Coltmuir Cres G64 30 E8
Coltmuir Dr G64 30 E8
Coltmuir Gdns G64 30 E8
Coltmuir St G22 30 B6
Coltness Ave ML7 82 F8
Coltness Dr ML4 65 B4
Coltness High Sch ML2 81 D4
Coltness La G33 47 D7
Coltness Prim Sch ML2 81 C6
Coltness Rd ML2 81 C6
Coltness St G33 47 C8
Coltpark Ave G64 30 E7
Coltpark La G64 30 F8
Coltsfoot Dr G53 58 B3
Coltswood Ct 1 ML5 50 A8
Coltswood Rd ML5 50 A8
Columba G81 15 D2
Columba Cres ML1 65 D2
Columba Ct G71 64 C7
Columba High Sch ML5 50 A4
Columba Path G72 77 C8
Columba St G51 44 B7
Columbia Pl G75 88 B8
Columbia Way G75 88 B8
Columbine Way ML8 108 F8
Colvend Dr G73 61 B3
Colvend La G40 45 F3
Colvend St G40 45 F3
Colville Ct ML1 66 C1
Colville Dr G73 61 D6
Colvilles Pl G75 89 B6
Colvilles Rd G75 89 A6
Colwood Ave G53 58 A3
Colwood Gdns G53 58 A3
Colwood Path G53 58 A4
Colwood Pl G53 58 A3
Colwood Sq G53 58 A3
Colwyn Ct ML6 36 A1
Colzium Ho* G65 6 F2
Colzium View G65 10 E8
Combe Quadrant ML4 64 E3
Comedie Rd G33 32 E4
Comely Bank ML3 77 F3
Comelypark Pl G31 46 A6
Comelypark St G31 46 A6
Commerce St G5 162 C1
Commercial Ct G5 45 D5
Commercial Rd
Barrhead G78 57 C4
Glasgow G5 45 D5
Strathaven ML10 112 E6
Common Gn Hamilton ML3 78 E4
Strathaven ML10 112 E6
Commonhead Ave ML6 35 F1
Commonhead La ML6 35 F1
Commonhead Rd G34,
G69 48 E8
Commonhead Sch G34 48 D8
Commonhead St ML6 35 F1
Commonside St ML6 35 F1
Commore Ave G78 57 D1
Commore Dr G13 28 A7
Community Ave ML4 65 A2
Community Pl ML4 65 B3
Community Rd ML4 65 A2
Comrie Cres ML3 77 E3
Comrie Rd G33 32 C5
Comrie St G32 47 B3
Cona St G46 58 E4
Conan Ct G72 62 D5
Condor Glen ML1 65 E7
Condorrat Intc G67 23 C8
Condorrat Prim Sch G67 23 B7
Condorrat Rd
Cumbernauld G67,ML6 23 B3
Glenmavis ML6 35 D6
Condorrat Ring Rd
Cumbernauld,Condorrat
G67 23 A6
Cumbernauld,Dalshannon
G67 23 C7
Coneypark Cres FK4 8 C3
Coneypark Pl FK4 8 C3
Congress Rd G3 44 D7
Congress Way G3 44 E7
Conifer Pl G66 20 B6
Conisborough Cl G34 33 A1
Conisborough Path G34 32 F1
Conisborough Rd G34 33 A1
Coniston G75 87 F5
Coniston Cres ML3 91 C6
Coniston Dr ML4 65 B3
Conistone Cres G69 47 F4
Connal St G40 46 B3
Conniston St G32 46 E7
Connor Rd G78 57 B3
Connor St ML6 36 E1
Conon Ave G61 16 D3
Conservation Pl ML2 81 C1
Consett La G33 47 C8
Consett St G33 47 C8
Constantine Way ML1 65 C1
Constarry Rd G65 10 F4
Consul Way ML1 65 C1
Contin Pl G20 29 D5
Convair Way PA4 27 D1
Coo La G76 86 E5
Cook St G5 45 A5
Coolgardie Gn 2 G75 88 C7
Coolgardie Pl 1 G75 88 C7
Cooper Ave ML8 95 E3
Cooper Ct ML11 124 D1
Cooper's Well St G11 29 C1
Cooperage Ct G14 27 D6
Cooperage Pl G3 44 C8
Copeland Prim Sch G51 44 B7
Copenhagen Ave G75 88 E6
Copland Pl G51 44 B6
Copland Quadrant G51 44 B6
Copland Rd G51 44 B6
Coplaw Ct G42 45 A3
Coplaw St G42 45 A3
Copperfield La G71 64 A7
Coralmount Gdns G66 20 E7
Corbett Ct G32 46 F3
Corbett St G32 47 A3
Corbiston Way G67 12 B2
Cordiner Ct ML11 119 E4
Cordiner La G44 60 D2
Cordiner Rd ML11 119 E4
Cordiner St G44 60 B7
Corehouse Dr ML11 121 E7
Corkerhill Gdns G52 43 E4
Corkerhill Pl G52 43 E2
Corkerhill Rd G52 43 D3
Corkerhill Sta G52 43 D2

Corlaich Ave G42 .60 E7
Corlaich Dr G42 .60 E7
Corless Ct G71 .64 A6
Cormiston Rd ML12 .141 B7
Corn St G4 .30 B2
Cornaig Rd G53 .58 B8
Cornalee Gdns G53 .58 B8
Cornalee Pl G53 .58 B8
Cornalee Rd G53 .58 B8
Cornelia St ML1 .65 B1
Cornelian Terr ML4 .65 A4
Cornfield Ct G72 .62 E6
Cornhill Dr ML5 .49 F8
Cornhill Rd ML12 .141 C6
Cornhill St G21 .31 A5
Cornish Ct ML5 .49 F8
Cornishall Terr ML11 .130 E8
Cornmill Ct G81 .15 A6
Cornock Cres G81 .15 B3
Cornock St G81 .15 B3
Cornsilloch Brae ML9 .94 A3
Cornwall Ave G73 .61 D5
Cornwall St
East Kilbride G74 .75 E1
Glasgow G41 .44 D5
Cornwall St S G41 .44 D5
Cornwall Way 18 G74 .75 F1
Coronation Ave ML9 .106 A8
Coronation Cres ML9 .106 A8
Coronation Ct ML1 .65 F4
Coronation Dr ML12 .152 B7
Coronation Pl
Larkhall ML9 .106 B8
Mount Ellen G69 .33 E7
Coronation Rd ML1 .65 F4
Coronation Rd E ML1 .65 F3
Coronation Road Ind Est ML1 .65 F4
Coronation St
Carstairs Junction ML11 .131 B8
Wishaw ML2 .81 D3
Coronation Way G61 .17 A2
Corpach Pl G34 .33 D1
Corpus Christi RC Prim Sch
Airdrie ML6 .51 B3
Glasgow G13 .28 C6
Corra Hill Rd ML8 .115 A8
Corra Linn ML3 .78 A3
Corran Ave G77 .72 C6
Corran St G33 .46 F8
Correen Gdns G61 .16 B7
Corrie Brae G65 .6 C1
Corrie Ct ML3 .77 F2
Corrie Dr Motherwell ML1 .79 B7
Paisley PA1 .42 E4
Corrie Gdns G75 .88 B4
Corrie Gr G44 .59 F4
Corrie Pl G66 .20 E8
Corrie Rd G65 .6 C1
Corrie View G68 .22 F8
Corrie View Cotts G65 .9 E4
Corrie Way ML9 .93 B2
Corrour Rd Glasgow G43 .59 E7
Newton Mearns G77 .72 C6
Corse Rd G52 .42 E6
Corsehill Path G34 .48 C8
Corsehill Pl G34 .48 C8
Corsehill St G34 .48 C8
Corselet Rd Glasgow G53 .58 A3
Glasgow G78,G53 .58 A1
Corsewall Ave G32 .47 E3
Corsewall St ML5 .49 F8
Corsford Dr G53 .58 C6
Corsock Ave ML3 .77 E2
Corsock St G31 .46 C7
Corston St G33 .46 D7
Cortachy Pl G64 .19 D1
Coruisk Dr G76 .73 D8
Corunna Ct ML8 .96 B1
Corunna St 5 G3 .44 E8
Coshneuk Rd G33 .32 B4
Cosy Neuk ML9 .93 C1
Cottar St G20 .29 E7
Cotton St G40 .46 A2
Cotton Street Ent Pk G40 .46 A2
Cotton Vale ML1 .66 E1
Coulin Gdns G22 .30 D4
Coulter Ave
Coatbridge ML5 .49 E8
Wishaw ML2 .81 C7
Coulter Motte Hill* ML12 .141 B7
Coulter Prim Sch ML12 .141 C4
Coulter Rd ML12 .160 C3
Countess Way G69 .49 A5
County Ave G72 .61 E7
County Dr ML11 .117 C3
Couper Pl G4 .163 B4
Couper St G4 .163 B4
Coursington Cres ML1 .80 A7
Coursington Gdns ML1 .79 F7
Coursington Pl ML1 .79 F7
Coursington Rd ML1 .80 A7
Coursington Twr ML1 .79 F7
Courthill G61 .16 D6
Courthill Ave G44 .60 B5
Courthill Cres G65 .10 E8
Coustonholm Rd G43 .59 D8
Couthally Gdns ML11 .124 E1
Couthally Terr ML11 .124 E1
Couther Quadrant ML6 .36 A2
Covanburn Ave ML3 .78 F1
Cove Cres ML7 .69 E6
Covenant Cres ML9 .93 B2
Covenant Pl ML2 .80 C2
Covenanter Rd ML7 .55 D4
Covenanters Way
24 Douglas ML11 .138 B1
Overtown ML2 .94 C6
Coventry Dr G31 .46 B8
Covington Oval ML11 .124 C1
Covington Rd ML12 .131 D3
Cowal Cres G66 .9 B1
Cowal Rd Glasgow G20 .29 C7
Glasgow G20 .29 C7
Cowal St G20 .29 C7
Cowan Cres G78 .57 D3
Cowan La G12 .29 E2
Cowan Rd G68 .11 C2
Cowan St G12 .29 E2
Cowan Wilson Ave
Blantyre G72 .63 D1
Hamilton G72 .77 D8
Cowan Wynd
Overtown ML2 .94 C7
Uddingston G71 .64 A8
Cowcaddens Rd G2,G3, G4 .162 C4
Cowcaddens Underground Sta G4 .162 C4
Cowden Dr G64 .19 A3
Cowden St G51 .43 D7
Cowdenhill Circ G13 .28 D8
Cowdenhill Pl G13 .28 D8
Cowdenhill Rd G13 .28 D8
Cowdray Cres PA4 .27 D3
Cowgate G66 .20 C8
Cowglen Hospl G53 .58 D7
Cowglen Rd G53 .58 C7
Cowlairs Ind Est G22 .30 D5
Cowlairs Rd 5 G21 .30 E4
Coxdale Ave G66 .20 B8
Coxhill St G21 .30 D3
Coxton Pl G33 .32 D1
Coylton Cres ML3 .77 E1
Coylton Rd G43 .59 F5
Crabb Quadrant ML1 .65 C1
Crabtree St ML11 .138 B2
Cragdale G74 .75 C3
Craggan Dr G14 .28 A5
Crags Ave PA2 .42 A1
Cragwell Pk G76 .74 E7
Craig Ave EH47 .56 F6
Craig Cres G66 .21 B7
Craig Gdns G77 .72 C5
Craig Hill G75 .88 C7
Craig Pl G77 .72 B5
Craig Rd G44 .60 A5
Craig St Airdrie ML6 .50 F7
Blackridge EH48 .40 E3
Coatbridge ML5 .49 F4
Hamilton G72 .77 E7
Craigallian Ave G72 .62 D4
Craiganour La G43 .59 C6
Craigard Pl G73 .61 D3
Craigbank Cres G76 .86 E6
Craigbank Dr G53 .58 A6
Craigbank Gr G76 .86 E6
Craigbank Prim Sch ML9 .106 A8
Craigbank Rd ML9 .106 A8
Craigbank St ML9 .93 A1
Craigbanzo St G81 .15 D8
Craigbarnet Ave G64 .19 A8
Craigbarnet Cres G33 .32 B4
Craigbo Ave 14 G23 .17 D1
Craigbo Ct G23 .29 D8
Craigbo Dr 13 G23 .17 D1
Craigbo Pl G23 .29 D8
Craigbo Rd G23 .17 D1
Craigbo St G23 .17 D1
Craigburn Ct ML9 .93 F1
Craigburn St ML3 .91 D8
Craigdhu Ave ML6 .51 E7
Craigdhu Prim Sch G62 .16 F8
Craigdhu Rd G61 .16 E8
Craigellan Rd G43 .59 D6
Craigelvan Ave G67 .22 F6
Craigelvan Ct G67 .22 F6
Craigelvan Dr G67 .22 F6
Craigelvan Gdns G67 .22 F6
Craigelvan Gr G67 .22 F6
Craigelvan Pl G67 .22 F6
Craigelvan View G67 .22 F6
Craigenbay Cres G66 .20 E5
Craigenbay Rd G66 .20 E5
Craigenbay St G21 .31 B4
Craigend Dr ML5 .49 C4
Craigend Pl G13 .28 E6
Craigend Rd
Cumbernauld G67 .22 F5
East Kilbride G75 .87 F1
Craigend St G13 .28 E6
Craigend View G67 .22 F5
Craigendmuir Pk G33 .32 E4
Craigendmuir Rd G33 .32 E4
Craigendmuir St G33 .31 D2
Craigends Ct G65 .10 E8
Craigenhill Rd ML8 .110 A5
Craigens Rd ML1,ML6 .52 C3
Craigfell Ct ML3 .77 E2
Craigflower Gdns G53 .58 A4
Craigflower Rd G53 .58 B3
Craighalbert Rd G68 .11 D3
Craighalbert Rdbt G68 .11 C4
Craighalbert Way G68 .11 C4
Craighall Rd G4 .30 B2
Craighaw St G81 .15 D8
Craighead Ave G33 .31 D3
Craighead La ML11 .119 F5
Craighead Rd ML12 .145 D2
Craighead Sch ML3 .78 B7
Craighead St Airdrie ML6 .51 E8
Barrhead G78 .57 B2
Craighead Way G78 .57 B2
Craighill Dr G76 .73 D6
Craighill Gr G76 .73 D6
Craighill View EH48 .40 E3
Craighirst Dr G81 .15 A7
Craighlaw Ave G76 .73 D2
Craighlaw Dr G76 .73 D2
Craigholme Sch G41 .44 D3
Craighouse St G33 .32 A1
Craigie Dr G77 .72 E3
Craigie La 9 ML9 .93 B4
Craigie Pk G66 .20 E5
Craigie Pl ML5 .49 E5
Craigie St G42 .45 A2
Craigieburn Gdns G20 .29 B8
Craigieburn Rd G67 .11 F1
Craigiehall Pl G51 .44 D6
Craigiehall St G51 .44 E6
Craigielea Ct PA4 .27 C4
Craigielea Pk PA4 .27 C3
Craigielea Rd
Clydebank G81 .15 A7
Renfrew PA4 .27 C3
Craigielea St G31 .46 A8
Craigievar Pl Airdrie ML6 .51 E6
Newton Mearns G77 .72 B5
Craigievar St G33 .32 E2
Craiginn Ct EH48 .40 D3
Craiginn Terr EH48 .40 D3
Craiglea Ct EH48 .40 D3
Craiglea Pl ML6 .51 C8
Craiglea St ML11 .138 F6
Craiglea Terr ML6 .36 F3
Craiglee G75 .88 E5
Craigleith St G32 .46 E6
Craiglinn G68 .11 A2
Craiglinn Park Rd G68 .11 A1
Craiglinn Rdbt G68 .11 A1
Craiglockhart St G33 .32 D1
Craigmaddie Gdns G64 .19 A8
Craigmaddie Rd G62 .18 A8
Craigmaddie Terrace La 7 G3 .29 E1
Craigmarloch Ave G64 .19 B8
Craigmarloch Rdbt G68 .11 C3
Craigmillar Rd G42 .60 A7
Craigmochan Ave ML6 .35 F2
Craigmont Dr G20 .29 E6
Craigmont St G20 .29 E6
Craigmore Pl ML5 .49 E3
Craigmore Rd G61 .16 B7
Craigmore St G31 .46 C6
Craigmore Wynd 12 ML9 .93 B4
Craigmount St G66 .20 D7
Craigmuir Cres G52 .42 F6
Craigmuir Gdns G72 .77 B6
Craigmuir Pl G52 .42 E6
Craigmuir Rd
Glasgow G52 .42 E6
Hamilton G72 .77 B6
Craigneil St G33 .32 E2
Craigneith Ct G74 .76 E4
Craignethan Castle* ML9 .107 F1
Craignethan Cres ML9 .107 D4
Craignethan Rd
Carluke ML8 .95 E3
Rutherglen G46 .73 B7
Craignethan View ML11 .114 A3
Craigneuk Ave ML6 .51 C6
Craigneuk Rd ML1 .66 C1
Craigneuk St ML2 .80 C5
Craignure Cres 4 ML6 .51 E7
Craignure Rd G73 .61 B3
Craigpark G31 .46 A7
Craigpark Dr G31 .46 A7
Craigpark St G81 .15 D7
Craigpark Way G71 .64 A7
Craigs Ave G81 .15 C6
Craigsheen Ave G76 .74 D7
Craigside Ct G68 .22 F7
Craigside Rd G68 .22 F7
Craigson Pl ML6 .51 F6
Craigstone View G65 .10 F8
Craigthornhill Rd ML3, ML10 .105 A6
Craigton Ave G78 .57 E1
Craigton Cres G77 .72 B5
Craigton Dr Barrhead G78 .57 E1
Glasgow G51 .43 F6
Newton Mearns G77 .72 C6
Craigton Ind Est G52 .43 E5
Craigton Pl Blantyre G72 .63 D1
Glasgow G51 .43 E6
Craigton Prim Sch G52 .43 E5
Craigton Rd
Glasgow,Drumoyne G51 .43 F6
Glasgow,West Drumoyne G51 .43 F7
Craigton St G81 .15 D8
Craigvale Cres ML6 .51 E7
Craigvicar Gdns G32 .47 D4
Craigview Rd ML1 .79 F8
Craigwell Ave G73 .61 D6
Crail Cl G72 .77 D3
Crail St G31 .46 D5
Crammond Ave ML5 .49 C4
Cramond Ave PA4 .27 E2
Cramond St G5 .45 E2
Cramond Terr G32 .47 B5
Cranborne Rd G12 .29 A5
Cranbrooke Dr G20 .29 D7
Cranston St G3 .162 A2
Cranworth La G12 .29 D3
Cranworth St G12 .29 D3
Crarae Ave G61 .16 E2
Crarae Pl G77 .72 B5
Crathes Ct Glasgow G44 .59 E4
Crathes Ct *continued*
Wishaw ML2 .81 B3
Crathie Ct Carluke ML8 .95 E3
Glasgow G11 .29 A2
Crathie Dr Glasgow G11 .29 A2
Glenmavis ML6 .35 F4
Crathie Pl G77 .73 B4
Crathie Quadrant ML2 .81 B5
Crawford Ave G66 .20 E3
Crawford Cres
Blantyre G72 .63 D1
Uddingston G71 .63 E7
Crawford Dr
Clydebank G15 .16 A1
East Kilbride G74 .76 B2
Crawford Hill G74 .76 B2
Crawford La G11 .29 A2
Crawford Path G11 .29 A2
Crawford Prim Sch ML12 .152 B7
Crawford St Glasgow G11 .29 A2
Hamilton ML3 .78 A5
Motherwell ML1 .79 D6
Strathaven ML10 .112 D6
Crawforddyke Prim Sch ML8 .109 A8
Crawfordjohn Heritage Venture* ML12 .145 A2
Crawfordjohn Prim Sch ML12 .145 A2
Crawfurd Ave G73 .61 B5
Crawfurd Gdns G73 .61 C4
Crawfurd Rd G73 .61 B4
Crawriggs Ave G66 .20 D6
Craws Knowe ML11 .122 A1
Creamery Rd ML2 .81 D1
Crebar Dr G78 .57 C1
Crebar St G46 .58 E4
Credon Dr ML6 .51 A4
Credon Gdns G73 .61 C4
Cree Ave G64 .19 D1
Cree Gdns G32 .46 F5
Cree Pl G75 .75 B1
Creighton Gr G74 .75 E1
Creran Ct ML3 .78 A1
Creran Dr PA4 .27 B4
Creran Path 12 ML2 .81 F6
Crescent Rd G13 .28 B5
Crescent The
Clarkston G76 .74 A5
Lesmahagow ML11 .119 E6
Longriggend ML6 .25 D2
Milngavie G62 .17 A8
Cressdale Ave G45 .60 C1
Cressdale Ct G45 .60 D2
Cressdale Dr G45 .60 D2
Cresswell Gr G77 .72 D3
Cresswell La G12 .29 D3
Cresswell Pl G77 .72 E2
Cresswell St 5 G12 .29 D3
Cressy St G51 .43 E8
Crest Ave G13 .28 B8
Creswell Terr G71 .63 E6
Crichton Ct G45 .60 F2
Crichton Pl G21 .30 E4
Crichton St
Coatbridge ML5 .50 A7
Glasgow G21 .30 E4
Crieff Ave ML6 .51 D1
Criffel Pl ML1 .66 C3
Criffell Gdns G32 .47 D3
Criffell Rd G32 .47 D3
Crighton Wynd ML4 .64 D5
Crimea St G2 .162 B2
Crimond Pl G65 .6 B1
Crinan Cres ML5 .34 D1
Crinan Gdns G64 .19 C1
Crinan Pl Bellshill ML4 .65 B4
Coatbridge ML5 .34 D1
Crinan Rd G64 .19 C1
Crinan St G31 .46 B8
Crindledyke Cres ML2 .82 B5
Cripps Ave G81 .15 D1
Croft ML9 .92 F2
Croft Pl ML9 .92 F3
Croft Rd Balmore G64 .18 E8
Cambuslang G72 .62 B5
East Kilbride G75 .88 E7
Larkhall ML9 .92 F3
Croft Way PA4 .27 E1
Croft Wynd G71 .64 A6
Croftbank Ave G71 .64 B1
Croftbank Cres
Bothwell G71 .64 B1
Uddingston G71 .63 F6
Croftbank Gate G71 .64 B1
Croftbank St 2 G21 .30 F4
Croftburn Dr G44 .60 D4
Croftcot Ave ML4 .64 F3
Croftcroighn Rd G33 .32 B1
Croftcroighn Sch G33 .32 E1
Croftend Ave G44 .60 E6
Croftend La G44 .60 F5
Croftfoot Cres G45 .61 A4
Croftfoot Dr
Fauldhouse EH47 .122 A7
Glasgow G45 .60 F4
Croftfoot Pl G69 .34 A6
Croftfoot Prim Sch G44 .60 E5
Croftfoot Quadrant G45 .60 E4
Croftfoot Rd G45 .60 E4
Croftfoot St G45 .61 A4
Croftfoot Sta G44 .60 E6
Croftfoot Terr
Biggar ML12 .160 C4
Glasgow G45 .60 F4
Crofthead Cres ML4 .64 F3
Crofthead Pl Bellshill ML4 .64 F3
Crofthead Pl *continued*
Newton Mearns G77 .72 F3
Crofthead St
Strathaven ML10 .112 D5
Uddingston G71 .63 F6
Crofthill Ave G71 .63 F6
Crofthill Ct ML9 .105 E2
Crofthill Rd G44 .60 E5
Crofthouse Dr G44 .60 E4
Croftmont Ave G44 .60 E4
Croftmoraig Ave G69 .22 A4
Crofton Ave G44 .60 D4
Croftpark Ave G44 .60 D5
Croftpark Cres G72 .77 E6
Croftpark Rd G81 .15 B7
Croftpark St ML4 .65 A6
Croftside Ave G44 .60 E4
Croftspar Ave G32 .47 C6
Croftspar Ct G32 .47 D6
Croftspar Dr G32 .47 C6
Croftspar Gate G32 .47 D6
Croftspar Gr G32 .47 D6
Croftspar Pl G32 .47 C6
Croftwood G64 .19 A4
Croftwood Ave G44 .60 D4
Croftwood Rd ML3 .78 D1
Crogal Cres ML6 .51 D2
Cromalt Ave G75 .88 B4
Cromalt Cres G61 .16 D8
Cromarty Ave
Bishopbriggs G64 .19 D2
Glasgow G43 .59 F6
Cromarty Cres G61 .16 F7
Cromarty Gdns G76 .60 A1
Cromarty Pl Chryston G69 .21 D1
East Kilbride G74 .76 C3
Cromarty Rd ML6 .50 F5
Crombie Gdns G69 .48 A3
Cromdale St G51 .43 E7
Cromdale Way ML1 .66 A2
Cromer Gdns G20 .29 F5
Crompton Ave G44 .60 B5
Cromwell La 5 G20 .30 A2
Cromwell St G20 .30 A2
Crona Dr ML3 .77 E4
Cronberry Quadrant G53 .42 F3
Cronberry Terr G53 .42 F3
Cronin Pl ML4 .65 B7
Cronulla Pl G65 .10 F8
Crookedshields Rd G72, G74 .76 B7
Crookfur Cottage Homes G77 .72 D5
Crookfur Prim Sch G77 .72 D7
Crookfur Rd G77 .72 D5
Crookfur Rdbt G77 .72 C6
Crookston Ave G52 .43 A4
Crookston Castle* G53 .43 B2
Crookston Ct 7 G52 .43 A4
Crookston Dr
3 Glasgow G52 .43 A4
Paisley PA1,G52 .42 F4
Crookston Gdns G52 .42 F4
Crookston Gr 6 G52 .43 A4
Crookston Path G52 .42 F4
Crookston Pl G52 .42 F4
Crookston Quadrant 1 G52 .43 A4
Crookston Rd
Glasgow,Crookston G52 .43 A4
Glasgow,Pollok G53 .43 A1
Crookston Sta G52 .42 F4
Crookston Terr 2 G52 .43 A4
Crookstonhill Path G52 .42 F4
Crosbie La G20 .29 C8
Crosbie St G20 .29 C8
Cross Arthurlie Sch G78 .57 B4
Cross Arthurlie St G78 .57 B3
Cross Ct G64 .18 F1
Cross Gates ML4 .65 A4
Cross Key's Cl ML11 .117 A4
Cross Orchard Way ML4 .65 A5
Cross Rd Biggar ML12 .160 E5
Crawfordjohn ML12 .145 A2
Cross St G32 .47 C1
Cross Stone Pl ML1 .79 F6
Cross The Glasgow G1 .163 B1
Stonehouse ML9 .105 F2
Strathaven ML10 .112 E5
Crossbank Ave G42 .45 E1
Crossbank Dr G42 .45 D1
Crossbank Rd G42 .45 D1
Crossbank Terr G42 .45 D1
Crossclyde View ML8 .108 C2
Crossdykes G66 .21 A7
Crossen La ML8 .96 B1
Crossflat Cres PA1 .42 A5
Crossford Dr 8 G23 .17 E1
Crossford Hawk Ctr* ML8 .108 B1
Crossgates St ML9 .92 F4
Crosshill Ave
Glasgow G42 .45 B1
Kirkintilloch G66 .20 D6
Strathaven ML10 .112 D5
Crosshill Cres ML10 .112 D5
Crosshill Dr Cleland ML1 .67 B3
Rutherglen G73 .61 B6
Crosshill Rd
Bishopbriggs G64,G66 .19 E5
Strathaven ML10 .112 D5
Crosshill St Airdrie ML6 .50 F7
Coatbridge ML5 .49 B4
Motherwell ML1 .79 F6
Crosshill Sta G42 .45 B1

Crosshouse Prim Sch G75 88 A5
Crosshouse Rd G75 88 A5
Crossing La ML9 107 B4
Crosskirk Cres ML10 112 F8
Crosslaw Ave ML11 117 C3
Crosslaw Burn DG10 161 E4
Crosslaw Gdns ML11 117 C3
Crosslee St G52 43 D5
Crosslees Ct G46 59 A4
Crosslees Dr Glasgow G46 58 F3
Thornliebank G46 59 A4
Crosslees Pk G46 58 F3
Crosslees Rd G46 58 F2
Crossloan Rd G51 43 F7
Crossloan Terr G51 44 A7
Crossmill Ave G78 57 D4
Crossmount Ct ML8 95 E1
Crossmyloof Gdns G41 44 D1
Crossmyloof Sta G41 44 E1
Crosspoint Dr 7 G23 17 E1
Crosstobs Rd G53 43 A1
Crossview Ave G69 48 D5
Crossview Pl G69 48 D5
Crosswood Terr EH55 123 C2
Crovie Rd G53 58 A7
Crow Ave ML1 66 B5
Crow La G13 28 F5
Crow Rd
Glasgow,Anniesland G13 28 F5
Glasgow,Hyndland G11 29 A2
Glasgow,Kelvindale G13 28 F7
Stonehouse ML9 105 E2
Crow Wood Cres ML6 51 B2
Crow Wood Rd G69 33 B7
Crow Wood Terr G69 33 B7
Crowflat View G71 49 D1
Crowflats Rd G71 63 E6
Crowhall Dr G33 47 E6
Crowhill Cres ML6 35 F2
Crowhill Rd G64 30 F8
Crowhill St G22 30 D6
Crowlin Cres G33 47 B7
Crown Ave G81 15 B3
Crown Cir 7 G12 29 C3
Crown Gdns G12 29 C3
Crown Rd N G12 29 C3
Crown Rd S G12 29 C3
Crown Rig ML12 160 D4
Crown St Calderbank ML6 51 B3
Coatbridge ML5 50 C7
Glasgow G5 45 B4
Glasgow G5 45 C4
Glasgow,Gorbals G5 45 C5
Glasgow,North Mount Vernon G69 47 F3
Crown Terr G12 29 C3
Crownhall Pl G32 47 C5
Crownhall Rd G32 47 C5
Crownhill Ct ML6 35 E3
Crownpoint Rd G40 45 F5
Crowwood Dr ML6 51 D7
Crowwood Rd ML6 51 B2
Croy G74 75 D3
Croy Ave G77 73 A5
Croy Hill Roman Fort* G68 11 A5
Croy Pl G21 31 C5
Croy Rd Coatbridge ML5 49 F4
Glasgow G21 31 C5
Croy Sta G68 10 F3
Cruachan Ave PA4 27 C1
Cruachan Dr
Barrhead G78 57 C1
Newton Mearns G77 72 F3
Cruachan Rd
Bearsden G61 16 B7
Rutherglen G73 61 D3
Cruachan St Glasgow G46 58 F4
Thornliebank G46 59 A4
Cruachan Way G78 57 C1
Cruden St G51 43 F6
Crum Ave G46 59 A3
Crusader Ave G13 16 D1
Cubie St G40 45 F5
Cuckoo Way ML1 66 B5
Cuilhill Rd G69 49 A7
Cuillin Pl Chapelhall ML6 51 F1
Larkhall ML9 93 C2
Cuillin Way G78 57 C2
Cuillins Rd G73 61 D3
Cuillins The
Moodiesburn G69 22 A4
Uddingston G71 48 E1
Cuilmuir Terr G65 10 F4
Cuilmuir View G65 10 F5
Culbin Dr G13 28 A8
Cullen La 1 G75 88 E7
Cullen Pl G71 64 A8
Cullen Rd
East Kilbride G75 88 D7
Motherwell ML1 79 C5
Cullen St G32 47 A4
Cullin Park Gr ML10 112 D6
Cullion Way ML1 67 A5
Culloch Rd G61 16 C8
Cullochrig Rd ML6 23 F1
Culloden Ave ML4 65 D4
Culloden St G31 46 B8
Culrain Gdns G32 47 A5
Culrain St G32 47 A4
Culross Hill G74 75 D1
Culross Pl Coatbridge ML5 49 F7
East Kilbride G74 75 D1
Culross St G32 47 C4
Culross Way G69 22 A3
Cult Rd G66 20 E4
Culterfell Path ML1 67 C2
Cults St G51 43 F6
Cultsykefoot EH47 56 E5
Culvain Ave G61 16 B7
Culzean ML6 35 F5
Culzean Ave ML5 49 E4
Culzean Cres
Glasgow G69 48 A4
Newton Mearns G77 73 A4
Culzean Ct ML5 49 E5
Culzean Dr
East Kilbride G74 75 D3
Glasgow G32 47 D4
Motherwell ML1 66 C3
Culzean Pl G74 75 D3
Cumberland Pl
Coatbridge ML5 49 D4
9 Glasgow G5 45 C4
Cumberland St
Glasgow G5 45 B5
Glasgow G5 45 C4
Cumbernauld Airport G68 12 B7
Cumbernauld Coll G67 11 F1
Cumbernauld Coll (Kirkintilloch Ctr) G66 20 C8
Cumbernauld High Sch G67 12 C1
Cumbernauld Prim Sch
Cumbernauld G67 12 B4
Cumbernauld,Carrickstone G68 11 D5
Cumbernauld Rd
Banknock FK4 8 F2
Chryston G69 33 C7
Cumbernauld G67 22 D4
Glasgow,Dennistoun G31 46 B7
Glasgow,Dennistoun G31, G33 46 C7
Glasgow,Riddrie G33 31 E1
Moodiesburn G68,G69 22 B3
Muirhead G69 33 C7
Stepps G33 32 D5
Cumbernauld Sta G67 24 A8
Cumbrae G74 76 C1
Cumbrae Cres ML5 50 E5
Cumbrae Ct G81 15 B2
Cumbrae Dr ML1 79 C8
Cumbrae Pl ML5 50 E4
Cumbrae Rd PA4 27 D1
Cumbrae St G33 47 A8
Cumlodden Dr G20 29 D7
Cumming Ave ML8 109 C8
Cumming Dr G42 60 B8
Cumnock Dr Airdrie ML6 51 A4
Barrhead G78 57 D1
Hamilton ML3 77 D1
Cumnock Rd G33 31 E6
Cunard Ct G81 27 B8
Cunard St G81 27 B8
Cunningair Dr ML1 79 E4
Cunningham Dr
Glasgow G46 59 E3
Harthill ML7 55 D5
Cunningham Rd G52 42 F8
Cunningham St ML1 79 D6
Cunninghame Rd
East Kilbride G74 75 E1
Rutherglen G73 61 C8
Cuparhead Ave ML5 49 E4
Curfew Pl ML12 151 A2
Curfew Rd G13 16 D1
Curle St Glasgow G14 28 D2
Glasgow G14 28 E2
Curling Cres G44 60 C7
Curlinghaugh Cres ML2 81 C3
Curlingmire G75 88 E7
Curran Ave ML2 80 E1
Currie Pl G20 29 F6
Currie St G20 29 E6
Currie's Cl 19 ML11 138 B1
Currieside Ave ML7 69 E4
Currieside Pl ML7 69 D4
Curtis Ave G44 60 D7
Curzon St G20 29 F6
Cut The G71 63 F5
Cuthbert St G71 64 B7
Cuthbertson Prim Sch G42 45 A3
Cuthbertson St G42 45 A2
Cuthelton Dr G31 46 E4
Cuthelton St G31 46 D4
Cuthelton Terr G31 46 D4
Cypress Ave Blantyre G72 63 C1
Uddingston G71 64 B8
Cypress Cres G75 88 C5
Cypress Ct
East Kilbride G75 88 C5
Hamilton ML3 78 E2
Kirkintilloch G66 20 B6
Cypress Gr G69 49 B6
Cypress Pl G75 88 C5
Cypress St G22 30 D5
Cypress Way G72 62 F4
Cyril St PA1 42 A4

D

Daer Ave PA4 27 E1
Daer Way ML3 78 A3
Daffodil Way ML1 79 E8
Dairsie Ct G44 59 F4
Dairsie Gdns G64 31 D8
Dairsie House Sch G43 59 E6
Dairsie St G44 59 F4
Daisy St G42 45 B2
Dakala Ct ML2 81 A2
Dakota Way PA4 27 D1
Dalbeattie Braes ML6 51 E1
Dalbeth Pl G32 46 F2
Dalbeth Rd G32 46 F2
Dalcharn Pl G34 48 A8
Dalcraig Cres G72 63 C2
Dalcross St G11 29 C2
Dalcruin Gdns G69 22 A4
Daldowie Ave G32 47 D3
Daldowie Doocot* G69 47 F2
Daldowie Rd G71 48 A2
Daldowie St ML5 49 E3
Dale Ave G75 88 D6
Dale Ct ML2 80 C2
Dale Dr ML1 66 A4
Dale Path G40 45 F4
Dale St Douglas ML11 138 C1
Glasgow G40 45 F4
Glasgow G40 46 A4
Dale Way G73 61 B4
Daleview Ave G12 29 B6
Daleview Dr G76 73 D6
Daleview Gr G76 73 D6
Dalfoil Ct PA1 42 F4
Dalgarroch Ave G81 27 E8
Dalhousie Gdns G64 19 A2
Dalhousie La G3 162 B4
Dalhousie St G3 162 C4
Dalilea Dr G34 33 D1
Dalilea Pl G34 33 D1
Dalintober St G5 162 B1
Dalkeith Ave
Bishopbriggs G64 19 B4
Glasgow G41 44 B4
Dalkeith Rd G64 19 B4
Dalmacoulter Rd ML6 36 B3
Dalmahoy St G32 46 E7
Dalmally St G20 29 F3
Dalmarnock Ct G40 46 B3
Dalmarnock Prim Sch G40 46 A4
Dalmarnock Rd G40 46 A3
Dalmarnock Road Trad Est G73 46 B1
Dalmarnock Sta G40 46 A3
Dalmary Dr PA1 42 B5
Dalmellington Ct
East Kilbride G74 75 D2
Hamilton ML3 77 D1
Dalmellington Dr
East Kilbride G74 75 D2
9 Glasgow G53 58 A8
Dalmellington Rd
Glasgow G53 43 A1
Glasgow G53 58 A8
Dalmeny Ave G46 59 C3
Dalmeny Dr G78 57 A2
Dalmeny Rd ML3 78 D2
Dalmeny St G5 45 E2
Dalmore Dr ML6 51 A6
Dalnair St G3 29 D1
Dalness St G32 47 A4
Dalreoch Ave G69 48 C6
Dalreoch Path G69 48 C5
Dalriada G2 162 B2
Dalriada Cres ML1 65 D1
Dalriada Dr G64 19 C8
Dalriada St G40 46 C4
Dalry Gdns ML3 77 D2
Dalry Pl ML6 66 D8
Dalry Rd G71 64 B7
Dalry St G32 47 B4
Dalrymple Ct G66 20 D7
Dalrymple Dr
Coatbridge ML5 49 F5
East Kilbride G74 75 E3
Newton Mearns G77 73 A4
Dalserf Cres G46 59 B1
Dalserf Ct G31 46 B5
Dalserf Gdns G31 46 B5
Dalserf Path 18 ML9 93 C1
Dalserf Prim Sch ML9 106 F8
Dalserf St G31 46 B5
Dalsetter Ave G15 16 A2
Dalsetter Bsns Ctr G15 16 A2
Dalsetter Pl G15 16 A2
Dalshannon Pl G67 23 A7
Dalshannon Rd G67 23 B7
Dalshannon View G67 23 B7
Dalshannon Way G67 23 A7
Dalsholm Ave G20 29 B7
Dalsholm Rd G20 29 B8
Dalswinton Path G34 48 D8
Dalswinton St G34 48 C8
Dalton Ave G81 15 E1
Dalton Hill ML3 77 E2
Dalton St G31 46 E5
Dalveen Ct G78 57 C1
Dalveen Dr G71 63 F8
Dalveen Quadrant ML5 50 D5
Dalveen St G32 46 F5
Dalveen Way G73 61 C3
Dalwhinnie Ave G72 63 C2
Daly Gdns G72 63 E1
Dalzell Ave ML1 80 A4
Dalzell Dr ML1 80 A4
Dalzell Pk* ML1 79 F3
Dalziel Ct ML3 78 A3
Dalziel Dr Glasgow G41 44 C3
Glasgow G41 44 D3
Dalziel High Sch ML1 79 D6
Dalziel Quadrant G41 44 C3
Dalziel Rd G52 42 F8
Dalziel St Hamilton ML3 78 B5
Motherwell ML1 79 F7
Dalziel Twr ML1 80 B3
Damshot Cres G53 43 D1
Damshot Rd G53 58 D8
Danby Rd G69 47 F4
Danes Ave 1 G14 28 C4
Danes Cres G14 28 B5
Danes Dr G14 28 C4
Danes La N 3 G14 28 C4
Danes La S G14 28 C4
Dargarvel Ave G41 44 B4
Dark Brig Rd ML8 108 B2
Darleith St G32 46 F5
Darley Pl ML3 91 B8
Darley Rd G68 11 E5
Darmeid Pl ML7 83 B8
Darnaway Ave G33 32 D2
Darnaway Dr G33 32 D2
Darnaway St G33 32 D2
Darngaber Gdns ML3 91 E3
Darngaber Rd ML3 91 E3
Darngavel Ct ML6 50 D8
Darngavil Rd ML6 36 E6
Darnick St G21 31 B2
Darnley Cres G64 18 F3
Darnley Gdns G41 44 E2
Darnley Ind Est G53 58 B5
Darnley Mains Rd G53 58 C3
Darnley Path G46 58 E5
Darnley Pl G41 44 E2
Darnley Prim Sch G53 58 C3
Darnley Rd Barrhead G78 57 E3
Glasgow G41 44 E2
Darnley St G41 44 F3
Darragh Gn ML2 82 A6
Darroch Way G67 12 A3
Dartford St G22 30 B3
Darvel Cres PA1 42 E4
Darvel Dr G77 73 A5
Darwin Rd G75 88 C8
Davaar G74 76 C1
Davaar Dr Coatbridge ML5 49 D7
Motherwell ML1 65 C2
Davaar Pl G77 72 C6
Davaar Rd PA4 27 D2
Davaar St G40 46 B4
Davan Loan 10 ML2 81 F6
Dave Barrie Ave ML9 92 F5
Daventry Dr G12 29 A5
David Gray Dr G66 9 A1
David Livingstone Ctr* G72 63 E2
David Livingstone Meml Prim Sch G72 63 D1
David Pl Glasgow G69 47 F4
Paisley PA3 42 B7
David St Coatbridge ML5 50 C7
Glasgow G40 46 A5
Salsburgh ML7 53 B2
David Way PA3 42 B7
Davidson Cres G65 9 F3
Davidson Gdns
Glasgow G14 28 E4
Stonehouse ML9 105 E1
Davidson La ML8 96 B1
Davidson Pl G32 47 C6
Davidson St Airdrie ML6 50 F8
Clydebank G81 27 E8
Coatbridge ML5 50 B4
Glasgow G40 46 A2
Davidston Pl G66 20 F4
Davie's Acre G74 74 F4
Davieland Rd G46 59 A1
Davies Quadrant ML1 65 D2
Davington Dr ML3 77 D1
Daviot St 2 G51 43 D6
Dawsholm Ind Est G20 29 B7
Dawson Ave G75 75 B1
Dawson Pl G4 30 B3
Dawson Rd G4 30 B3
Deacons Rd G65 10 E8
Deaconsbank Ave G46 58 E1
Deaconsbank Cres G46 58 D1
Deaconsbank Gdns G46 58 E1
Deaconsbank Gr G46 58 D1
Deaconsbank Pl G46 58 D1
Dealston Rd G78 57 B4
Dean Cres Chryston G69 21 D1
Hamilton ML3 78 C1
Dean Park Ave G71 64 A2
Dean Park Dr G72 62 D4
Dean Park Rd PA4 27 E2
Dean St Bellshill ML4 65 B5
Clydebank G81 15 C1
Deanbrae ML11 124 A8
Deanbrae St G71 63 F6
Deanfield Quadrant G52 42 F6
Deans Ave G72 62 D3
Deanside Rd G52 43 A8
Deanston Ave G78 57 B1
Deanston Dr G41 59 E8
Deanston Gdns G78 57 B1
Deanston Gr ML5 49 E3
Deanston Pk G78 57 B1
Deanstone Pl ML5 50 D3
Deanstone Wlk ML5 50 D2
Deansyke ML11 124 A8
Deanwood Ave G44 59 F3
Deanwood Rd G44 59 F3
Deas Rd ML7 69 C5
Dechmont G75 88 D5
Dechmont Ave
Cambuslang G72 62 D3
Motherwell ML1 79 C7
Dechmont Cotts G72 62 F3
Dechmont Gdns
Blantyre G72 63 C1
Uddingston G71 48 E1
Dechmont Pl G72 62 D3
Dechmont Rd G71 48 E1
Dechmont St
Glasgow G31 46 C4
Hamilton ML3 78 C2
Dechmont View
Bellshill ML4 64 F3
Uddingston G71 64 A7
Dee Ave PA4 27 E3
Dee Path Larkhall ML9 106 A8
Motherwell ML1 66 B5
Dee Pl G75 87 E6
Dee St Coatbridge ML5 34 D2
Glasgow G33 46 D8
Shotts ML7 69 D5
Dee Terr ML3 91 B8
Deedes St ML6 50 D6
Deep Dale G74 75 C3
Deepdene Rd
Bearsden G61 16 D2
Moodiesburn G69 21 F2
Deer Park Ct ML3 91 D7
Deer Park Pl ML3 91 E7
Deer Path ML7 55 E5
Deerdykes Ct N G68 22 E6
Deerdykes Ct S G68 22 E5
Deerdykes Pl G68 22 E6
Deerdykes Rd G67,G68 22 E5
Deerdykes Rdbt G68 22 C5
Deerdykes View G68 22 D6
Deeside Dr ML8 96 A3
Deeside Pl ML5 50 D4
Dell Ave EH48 41 E6
Dell The Bellshill ML4 65 D3
Newton Mearns G77 73 B5
Dellburn St ML1 80 A5
Dellburn Trad Pk ML1 80 A5
Delny Pl G33 47 E7
Delves Ct ML11 117 A4
Delves Pk ML11 117 A4
Delves Rd ML11 117 A3
Delvin Rd G44 60 A6
Dempsey Rd ML4 64 F3
Den Bak Ave ML3 78 A2
Den La ML7 69 D6
Denbeck St G32 46 F5
Denbrae St G32 46 F5
Dene Pk ML12 160 E4
Dene Wlk G64 31 C8
Denham St G22 30 B3
Denholm Cres G75 88 E8
Denholm Dr Glasgow G46 59 C1
Wishaw ML2 81 C6
Denholm Gdns ML3 91 E3
Denholm Gn 3 G75 88 F8
Denholm Gr EH48 41 E7
Denholm Terr ML3 77 E3
Denmark St Glasgow G22 30 C4
Glasgow G22 30 C5
Denmilne Gdns G34 48 C7
Denmilne Path G34 48 C7
Denmilne Rd G34 48 D7
Denmilne St G34 48 C7
Denniston Pl ML11 117 C5
Dennistoun St ML4 65 B5
Dentdale G74 75 C3
Deramore Ave G46 73 A7
Derby St G3 29 E1
Derby Terrace La 4 G3 44 E8
Derby Wynd 1 ML1 66 B1
Dervaig Gdns ML6 25 D3
Derwent Dr ML5 34 D2
Derwent St G22 30 B4
Derwentwater G75 87 F6
Despard Ave G32 47 E4
Despard Gdns G32 47 E4
Deveron Ave G46 59 D2
Deveron Cres ML3 77 E4
Deveron Rd Bearsden G61 16 D2
East Kilbride G74 76 B1
Motherwell ML1 66 B5
Deveron St
Coatbridge ML5 34 D1
Glasgow G33 31 D1
Devine Ct ML2 81 B3
Devine Gr ML2 82 A7
Devlin Gr G72 77 E7
Devol Cres G53 58 B8
Devon Gdns
Bishopbriggs G64 18 F3
Carluke ML8 95 E2
Devon Pl G41 45 B4
Devon St G5 45 B4
Devon Way ML1 79 B6
Devon Wlk G68 22 E8
Devonburn Rd ML11 120 B3
Devondale Ave G72 63 D1
Devonhill Ave ML3 91 D7
Devonport Pk G75 88 A7
Devonshire Gardens La 2 G12 29 B4
Devonshire Gdns 1 G12 29 B4
Devonshire Terr G12 29 B4
Devonshire Terrace La G12 29 B4
Devonside Rd ML12 130 D2
Devonview Pl ML6 50 F6
Devonview St ML6 50 F6
Dewar Cl G71 49 A1
Dewar Dr G15 16 A3
Dewar Gate G15 16 A3
Dewar Wlk ML8 108 B1
Dewshill Cotts ML7 54 B4
Diamond St ML4 65 A4
Diana Ave G13 28 B8
Diana Quadrant ML1 66 A5
Dick Ct ML9 105 E2
Dick Gdns EH47 56 F6
Dick St G20 29 F3
Dickens Ave G81 15 A4

Dickens Gr ML1 66 D2
Dicks Pk G75 88 D8
Dickson Path ML4 64 F2
Dickson Sq ML1 67 B1
Dickson St Larkhall ML9 93 C1
[1] Moffat DG10 161 D5
Differ Ave G65 9 F2
Differick Dr ML11 119 F2
Dillarburn Rd ML11 120 A7
Dillarsview ML11 119 C7
Dilwara Ave G14 28 E2
Dimsdale Cres ML2 81 C1
Dimsdale Rd ML2 81 C1
Dinard Dr G46 59 C4
Dinart St G33 31 D1
Dinduff St G34 33 C1
Dinmont Cres ML1 65 D2
Dinmont Pl [1] G41 44 E1
Dinmont Rd G41 44 D1
Dinnet Way [11] ML2 81 F6
Dinwiddie St G21 31 C2
Dinyra Pl ML5 34 C6
Dipple Pl G15 16 B2
Dirleton Dr G41 59 F8
Dirleton Gate G61 16 D2
Dirleton Pl G41 59 E8
Discover Carmichael Visitor Ctr* ML12 131 A1
Divernia Way G78 57 C1
Dixon Ave G42 45 B1
Dixon Pl G74 75 B3
Dixon Rd G42 45 C1
Dixon St Coatbridge ML5 50 B4
Glasgow G1 162 C1
Hamilton ML3 78 D3
Paisley PA1 42 A4
Dixon Terr EH47 56 F5
Dixons Blazes Ind Est G42,G5 45 C3
Dobbie's Loan G4 163 A4
Dobbie's Loan Pl G4 163 B3
Dobbies Ct ML8 95 A6
Dochart Ave PA4 27 E1
Dochart Dr ML5 34 D2
Dochart St G33 31 E2
Dock St G81 27 D7
Doctor's Cl [14] ML11 138 B1
Dodhill Pl G13 28 B6
Dodside Gdns G32 47 C4
Dodside Pl G32 47 C4
Dodside Rd G77 72 A5
Dodside St G32 47 C4
Dolan St G69 48 B5
Dollar Pk ML1 80 B3
Dollar Terr G20 29 C8
Dolphin Rd G41 44 D2
Dominica Gn [4] G75 75 A1
Don Ave PA4 27 E2
Don Ct ML3 91 A8
Don Path ML9 106 A8
Don St G33 31 D1
Donald Terr ML3 78 C1
Donald Way G71 64 A7
Donaldson Ave G65 10 E7
Donaldson Cres G66 20 C7
Donaldson Dr PA4 27 D3
Donaldson Gn G71 64 B8
Donaldson Pl G66 20 D7
Donaldson Rd ML9 93 C1
Donaldson St
Hamilton ML3 78 A5
Kirkintilloch G66 20 C7
Doncaster St G20 30 A3
Donnelly Way ML2 80 C4
Donohoe Ct G64 19 A1
Doon Cres G61 16 D3
Doon Rd G66 9 A2
Doon Side G67 12 B2
Doon St Clydebank G81 15 D3
Larkhall ML9 93 C2
Motherwell ML1 80 A4
Doon Way G66 9 A1
Doonfoot Ct G74 75 D2
Doonfoot Gdns G74 75 D2
Doonfoot Rd G43 59 D6
Doonside Twr ML1 80 B3
Dora St G40 45 F3
Dorain Rd ML1 66 D3
Dorchester Ave G12 29 A6
Dorchester Ct G12 29 A6
Dorchester Pl G12 29 A5
Dorian Dr G76 73 C8
Dorlin Rd G33 32 F5
Dormanside Ct G53 43 B3
Dormanside Gate G53 43 B3
Dormanside Gr G53 43 B3
Dormanside Pl G53 43 C2
Dormanside Rd G53 43 C3
Dormiston Pl ML11 114 A3
Dormiston Rd ML11 114 A3
Dornal Ave G13 27 E7
Dornford Ave G32 47 D3
Dornford Rd G32 47 D2
Dornie Dr G32 62 B8
Dornie Path [9] ML2 81 F6
Dornie Wynd ML7 70 B3
Dornoch Ave G46 59 C1
Dornoch Ct ML4 65 A5
Dornoch Dr G72 77 D4
Dornoch Pl
Bishopbriggs G64 19 D2
Chryston G69 21 D1
East Kilbride G74 75 C2
Dornoch Rd Bearsden G61 16 D2
Motherwell ML1 66 B5
Dornoch St G40 45 F5
Dornoch Way Airdrie ML6 50 F5
Cumbernauld G68 12 A5
Dornoch Way *continued*
Hamilton G72 77 D4
Dorset Sq G3 162 A3
Dorset St G3 162 A3
Dosk Ave G13 27 F8
Dosk Pl G13 27 F8
Double Row ML11 116 F2
Dougalston Rd G23 17 E1
Dougans Sq EH48 41 F6
Douglas Ave Glasgow G46 59 C1
Glasgow,Carmyle G32 47 B1
Kirkintilloch G66 20 D5
Lesmahagow ML11 119 D6
Rutherglen G73 61 C5
Douglas Cres Airdrie ML6 51 A6
Hamilton ML3 91 D6
Uddingston G71 64 B8
Douglas Ct G66 20 D5
Douglas Dr Ashgill ML9 106 F8
Bellshill ML4 65 D4
Bothwell G71 64 A1
Cambuslang G72 61 F5
Clydebank G15 15 F1
East Kilbride G75 87 E7
Glasgow G69 47 F5
Newton Mearns G77 72 E6
Douglas Drive La G45 60 D3
Douglas Gate G72 61 F5
Douglas Gdns
Bearsden G61 16 F4
Glasgow G46 59 C1
Kirkintilloch G66 20 D5
Uddingston G71 63 F5
Douglas Heritage Mus* ML11 138 B1
Douglas Ind Est ML11 138 C1
Douglas La G2 162 B3
Douglas Muir Rd G81 15 D7
Douglas Park Cres G61 17 A6
Douglas Park La ML3 78 C5
Douglas Pl
[1] Bearsden G61 16 E5
Coatbridge ML5 49 F6
Hamilton ML3 91 D6
Kirkintilloch G66 20 D5
Douglas Prim Sch ML11 138 B1
Douglas Rd PA4 42 A8
Douglas St Airdrie ML6 51 A6
Carluke ML8 95 E2
Glasgow G2 162 B3
Hamilton ML3 78 C5
Hamilton,High Blantyre G72 77 C6
Larkhall ML9 93 A4
Motherwell ML1 79 D6
Overtown ML2 94 D7
Strathaven ML10 112 F4
Uddingston G71 64 B7
Douglas Twr G71 63 D4
Douglas View ML5 49 F3
Douglasdale G74 75 D2
Douglasdale St ML11 139 A6
Dougray Pl G78 57 C2
Dougrie Dr G45 60 D3
Dougrie Gdns G45 60 D2
Dougrie Pl G45 60 E3
Dougrie Rd G45 60 D3
Dougrie St G45 60 E3
Dougrie Terr G45 60 D3
Doune Cres
Bishopbriggs G64 19 B4
Chapelhall ML6 51 D1
Newton Mearns G77 72 F5
Doune Gardens La G20 29 E3
Doune Gdns G20 29 E3
Doune Park Way ML5 49 F4
Doune Quadrant [4] G20 29 E3
Doune Terr ML5 49 E8
Dove Pl G75 87 F6
Dove St G53 58 A5
Dove Wynd ML4 64 F8
Dovecastle Dr ML10 112 E5
Dovecot G43 59 C8
Dovecot La ML11 117 A4
Dovecote View G66 20 F7
Dovecothall Rdbt G78 57 D3
Dovecothall St G78 57 D3
Dovecotwood G65 6 D1
Dover St Coatbridge ML5 34 D2
Glasgow G3 162 A3
Dowan Rd G62 17 E8
Dowanfield Rd G67 11 E1
Dowanhill Prim Sch G11 29 C2
Dowanhill St G12 29 C2
Dowanside La [1] G12 29 C3
Dowanside Rd G12 29 C3
Downcraig Dr G45 60 D2
Downcraig Gr G45 60 C2
Downcraig Rd G45 60 C2
Downcraig Terr G45 60 D2
Downfield Dr ML3 91 B7
Downfield Gdns G71 63 F2
Downfield St G32 46 E3
Downhill St G12 29 C3
Downie Cl G71 64 B8
Downie St ML3 78 D1
Downiebrae Rd G73 46 B2
Downs St G21 30 F5
Dowrie Cres G53 43 B1
Draffan Rd
Kirkmuirhill ML11 113 F6
Netherburn ML9 107 B2
Draffen Ct ML1 79 F7
Draffen St ML1 79 F7
Draffen Twr ML1 79 F7
Drake St G40 45 E5
Drakemire Ave G45 60 C4
Drakemire Dr G45 60 C3
Dreghorn St G31 46 C7
Drimnin Rd G33 32 F5
Drive Rd G51 43 E8
Driverholm Terr ML11 143 E7
Drochil St G34 33 A1
Dromore St G66 20 D7
Drove Hill G68 11 B3
Drove Rd EH48 41 F7
Druid St ML10 104 F3
Drum Mains Pk G68 22 D8
Drumbathie Rd ML6 51 C8
Drumbathie Terr ML6 51 C8
Drumbeg Dr G53 58 A6
Drumbeg Path G72 77 C3
Drumbeg Pl G53 58 A6
Drumbottie Rd G21 31 A5
Drumbowie View G68 11 C3
Drumby Cres G76 73 D8
Drumby Dr G76 73 D8
Drumcavel Rd
Mount Ellen G69 33 F7
Muirhead G69 33 F7
Drumchapel Gdns G15 16 A2
Drumchapel High Sch G15 16 A4
Drumchapel Hospl G15 16 B2
Drumchapel Pl G15 16 B2
Drumchapel Rd G15 16 B2
Drumchapel Sh Ctr G15 15 F3
Drumchapel Sta G15 16 A1
Drumclair Pl ML6 51 D7
Drumclog Gdns G33 31 F6
Drumcross Pl G53 43 C1
Drumcross Rd G53 43 C1
Drumduff G75 88 D5
Drumfin Ave ML6 38 A4
Drumgelloch St ML6 51 D8
Drumgelloch Sta ML6 51 D7
Drumglass Steadings G65 10 E3
Drumglass View G65 10 F4
Drumgray Gdns ML6 24 D1
Drumgray La ML6 24 D1
Drumgrew Rdbt G68 10 B1
Drumhead Pl G32 46 F1
Drumhead Rd G32 46 F1
Drumhill G66 9 B2
Drumilaw Cres G73 61 A5
Drumilaw Rd G73 61 A5
Drumilaw Way G73 61 A5
Drumlaken Ave G23 17 C1
Drumlaken Ct [7] G23 17 D1
Drumlaken Path [11] G23 17 D1
Drumlaken Pl [9] G23 17 D1
Drumlaken St G23 17 C1
Drumlanrig Ave G34 48 D8
Drumlanrig Pl G34 33 D1
Drumlin Dr G62 17 A8
Drumloch Gdns G75 88 E5
Drumlochy Rd G33 32 B1
Drummond Ave G73 60 F8
Drummond Dr
Paisley PA1 42 D4
Wishaw ML2 81 B2
Drummond Hill G74 76 B3
Drummond Ho G67 12 A3
Drummond Pl
Blackridge EH48 40 C3
[3] East Kilbride G74 76 B3
Drummond Way G77 72 A5
Drummore Ave ML5 50 D3
Drummore Rd G15 16 B4
Drummore Sch G15 16 C4
Drumnessie Ct G68 22 F8
Drumnessie Rd G68 22 F8
Drumnessie View G68 22 F8
Drumore Ave ML6 51 D1
Drumover Dr G31 46 E4
Drumoyne Ave G51 43 E7
Drumoyne Cir G51 43 E6
Drumoyne Dr G51 43 E7
Drumoyne Pl G51 43 E6
Drumoyne Prim Sch G51 43 E6
Drumoyne Quadrant G51 43 E6
Drumoyne Rd
Glasgow,Drumoyne G51 43 E6
Glasgow,West Drumoyne G51 43 E7
Drumoyne Sq G51 43 E7
Drumpark Sch G69 49 B6
Drumpark St
Coatbridge ML5 49 C4
Glasgow G46 58 F4
Drumpellier Ave
Coatbridge ML5 49 D6
Cumbernauld G67 23 C7
Glasgow G69 48 B3
Drumpellier Country Pk* ML5 34 C1
Drumpellier Country Pk Visitor Ctr* ML5 34 B1
Drumpellier Cres ML5 49 D6
Drumpellier Ct G67 23 C7
Drumpellier Ctry Pk* ML5 49 D8
Drumpellier Gdns G67 23 C7
Drumpellier Gr G67 23 C7
Drumpellier Pl
Cumbernauld G67 23 C7
Glasgow G69 48 B4
Drumpellier Rd G69 48 A4
Drumpellier St G33 31 D2
Drumreoch Dr G42 60 E8
Drumreoch Pl G42 60 E8
Drumriggend Rd FK1 26 D4
Drumry Pl G15 15 E2
Drumry Prim Sch G15 15 E3
Drumry Rd G81 15 C3
Drumry Rd E G15 15 E2
Drumry Sta G81 15 D2
Drums Rd G53 43 A3
Drumsack Ave G69 33 C8
Drumsargard Rd G73 61 D5
Drumshangie Pl ML6 36 A2
Drumshangie St ML6 36 A2
Drumshaw Dr G32 62 C8
Drumtrocher St G65 10 D8
Drumvale Dr G69 21 E2
Drury Lane Ct G74 76 C4
Drury St G2 162 C2
Dryad St G46 58 E5
Dryburgh Ave G73 61 B7
Dryburgh Gdns G20 29 F3
Dryburgh Hill G74 75 D1
Dryburgh La G74 75 D1
Dryburgh Pl
Coatbridge ML5 49 F7
Kirkintilloch G66 20 F8
Dryburgh Rd
Bearsden G61 16 C6
Wishaw ML2 81 B4
Dryburgh St ML3 78 B6
Dryburgh Way [1] G72 77 D7
Dryburgh Wlk G69 22 A3
Dryburn Ave G52 43 B5
Dryden St ML3 78 B6
Drygate G4 163 C2
Drygate St ML9 93 B4
Drygrange Rd G33 32 C2
Drymen Pl G66 20 D3
Drymen Rd G61 16 E5
Drymen St G52 43 E5
Drymen Wynd G61 16 F3
Drynoch Pl G22 30 B7
Drysdale St G14 27 F5
Duart Dr East Kilbride G74 75 D3
Newton Mearns G77 73 A5
Duart St G20 29 C8
Dubs Rd G78 57 E3
Dubton St G34 33 B1
Duchall Pl G14 28 B4
Duchess Ct ML3 79 A2
Duchess Pl G73 61 C8
Duchess Rd G73 46 C1
Duchess Way G69 48 F5
Duchray Dr PA1 42 F4
Duchray La G33 31 D1
Duchray St G33 31 D1
Dudhope St G33 32 D2
Dudley Dr Coatbridge ML5 34 C2
Glasgow G12 29 A3
Dudley La G12 29 A3
Duffus Pl G32 62 C8
Duffus St G34 33 A1
Duffus Terr G32 62 C8
Duich Gdns G23 17 E1
Duisdale Rd G32 62 C8
Duke St Glasgow G4 163 C2
Glasgow,Barrowfield G31 46 D5
Glasgow,Dennistoun G31 46 B6
Hamilton ML3 78 E3
Larkhall ML9 93 A4
Motherwell ML1 79 E8
Wishaw ML2 81 F6
Duke Street Sta G31 46 B7
Duke's Ct ML9 93 A4
Duke's Rd G72,G73 61 D6
Dukes Ct G72 61 E7
Dukes Gate G71 63 E4
Dukes Pl ML3 91 D6
Dukes Rd G69 48 F5
Dukes Wlk ML11 114 B3
Dullatur Rd G68 11 D6
Dullatur Rdbt G68 11 F5
Dulnain St G72 62 E5
Dulsie Rd G21 31 C6
Dumbarton Rd
Clydebank G81 15 A1
Clydebank,Duntocher G81 15 A6
Glasgow G11 28 F2
Glasgow G14 27 E6
Glasgow,Partick G11 29 B2
Dumbreck Ave G41 44 A4
Dumbreck Ct G41 44 A3
Dumbreck Marsh Nature Reserve* G65 10 B7
Dumbreck Pl
Glasgow G41 44 A3
Kirkintilloch G66 20 E4
Dumbreck Rd G41 44 B3
Dumbreck Sq G41 44 A4
Dumbreck Sta G41 44 C4
Dumbreck Terr G65 9 F8
Dumfries Cres ML6 50 F5
Dumfries Rd ML12 152 B4
Dumgoyne Dr G61 16 D7
Dumgoyne Pl G76 73 C7
Dun Pk G66 20 E8
Dunagoil Gdns G45 60 E2
Dunagoil Pl G45 60 E1
Dunagoil Rd G45 60 D2
Dunagoil St G45 60 E1
Dunalastair Dr G33 32 B5
Dunalastair Rd ML12 152 B7
Dunan Pl G33 47 E7
Dunard Ct ML8 95 F3
Dunard Prim Sch G20 29 F4
Dunard Rd G73 61 B7
Dunard St G20 29 F4
Dunaskin St G11 29 C1
Dunavon Cres ML10 112 D5
Dunavon Pk ML10 112 F6
Dunavon Pl ML5 50 D4
Dunbar Ave
Coatbridge ML5 49 D4
Rutherglen G73 61 C7
Dunbar Dr ML1 80 A4
Dunbar Hill G74 75 C1
Dunbar La ML1 66 A2
Dunbar Pl G74 75 C1
Dunbar St ML3 78 B5
Dunbeath Ave G77 72 F5
Dunbeath Gr G72 77 C3
Dunbeith Pl [4] G20 29 D5
Dunbeth Ave ML5 50 B7
Dunbeth Ct ML5 50 B7
Dunbeth Rd ML5 50 B7
Dunblane Dr G74 75 F2
Dunblane Pl
Coatbridge ML5 49 F4
East Kilbride G74 75 F2
Dunblane St G4 162 C4
Dunbrach Rd G68 11 C2
Dunbreck Ave ML6 38 A5
Duncan Ave G14 28 C4
Duncan Ct ML1 65 D1
Duncan Graham St ML9 93 B4
Duncan La G14 28 C3
Duncan La N [7] G14 28 C4
Duncan La S [13] G14 28 C4
Duncan McIntosh Rd G68 12 C7
Duncan St G81 15 B3
Duncan's Cl ML11 117 A4
Duncanrig Sec Sch G75 75 B1
Duncansby Dr G72 77 C3
Duncansby Rd G33 47 D6
Dunchattan Pl G31 45 F7
Dunchattan St G31 45 F7
Dunchurch Rd PA1 42 D5
Dunclutha Dr G71 64 A1
Dunclutha St G40 46 B2
Duncombe Ave G81 15 B7
Duncombe St G20 29 D7
Duncombe View [6] G81 15 D3
Duncrub Dr G64 18 E1
Duncruin St G20 29 D7
Duncruin Terr G20 29 D7
Duncryne Ave G32 47 E4
Duncryne Gdns G32 47 E4
Duncryne Pl G64 30 E8
Dundaff Hill G68 11 C2
Dundanion Rd DG10 161 D5
Dundas Ave G64 19 B8
Dundas Ct G74 75 E2
Dundas La G1 163 A3
Dundas Pl G74 75 E2
Dundas St G1 163 A3
Dundashill G4 30 B2
Dundasvale Ct G4 162 C4
Dundee Dr G52 43 B3
Dundee Path G52 43 C3
Dundonald Cres
Coatbridge ML5 49 F4
Newton Mearns G77 73 A4
Dundonald Dr ML3 91 D7
Dundonald Rd
Glasgow G12 29 C3
Paisley PA3 42 A7
Dundonald St G72 77 C8
Dundrennan Dr ML6 51 E2
Dundrennan Rd G42 59 F7
Dundyvan Gate ML5 50 A5
Dundyvan Gdns ML5 50 A5
Dundyvan Ind Est ML5 49 F5
Dundyvan La ML2 81 A2
Dundyvan Rd ML5 49 F5
Dundyvan St ML2 81 A2
Dundyvan Way ML5 49 F5
Dunearn Pl PA2 42 A3
Dunearn St G4 29 F2
Duneaton Wynd ML9 93 B1
Dunedin Ct G75 88 A8
Dunedin Dr G75 88 A8
Dunedin Rd ML9 93 B1
Dunedin Terr G81 27 C8
Dunellan Ave G69 22 A2
Dunellan Cres G69 22 A2
Dunellan Ct G69 22 A2
Dunellan Dr G81 15 B7
Dunellan Gdns G69 22 A2
Dunellan Gr G69 21 F2
Dunellan Pl G69 22 A2
Dunellan St G52 43 E5
Dunellan Way G69 22 A2
Dungavel Gdns ML3 91 E8
Dungavel La ML8 96 B1
Dungeonhill Rd G34 48 D8
Dunglass Ave
East Kilbride G74 75 F3
Glasgow G14 28 C4
Dunglass La [8] G14 28 C4
Dunglass La N [5] G14 28 C4
Dunglass La S [11] G14 28 C4
Dunglass Pl G77 72 A5
Dunglass Sq G74 75 F3
Dungoil Ave G68 11 B3
Dungoil Rd G66 20 E4
Dungoyne St G20 29 C8
Dunira St G32 46 F3
Dunivaig Rd G33 47 E8
Dunkeld Ave G73 61 B7
Dunkeld Dr G61 17 B4
Dunkeld Gdns G64 19 B2
Dunkeld La G69 22 A2
Dunkeld Pl
Coatbridge ML5 49 F4
Hamilton ML3 77 E3
Newton Mearns G77 73 B4
Dunkeld St G31 46 C4
Dunkenny Rd G15 15 F3
Dunkenny Sq G15 15 F3

Dunkirk St ML6 38 A5
Dunlin East Kilbride G74 75 E4
Glasgow G12 29 A6
Dunlin Ct ML4 64 E8
Dunlop Cres Bothwell G71 64 B1
Renfrew PA4 27 D4
Dunlop Ct Hamilton ML3 91 E7
Strathaven ML10 112 E5
Dunlop Gr G71 49 A1
Dunlop Pl Ashgill ML9 107 A8
Strathaven ML10 112 E5
Dunlop St Cambuslang G72 62 E6
Glasgow G1 163 A1
Renfrew PA4 27 D4
Strathaven ML10 112 E5
Dunlop Twr G75 88 E8
Dunmore Dr G62 17 D8
Dunmore St G81 27 C8
Dunn Cres ML11 137 F5
Dunn St Glasgow G40 46 A4
Paisley PA1 42 A4
Dunn Terr ML7 55 F6
Dunnachie Dr ML5 49 B4
Dunnachie Pl ML5 49 C4
Dunnet Ave ML6 35 F5
Dunnichen Gdns G64 19 D1
Dunnikier Wlk G68 10 E1
Dunning Dr G68 12 A5
Dunnotar Wlk 16 ML2 81 F6
Dunnottar Cres G74 75 D3
Dunnottar Ct G74 75 C3
Dunnottar St
Bishopbriggs G64 19 D2
Glasgow G33 32 B2
Dunns Wood Rd G67 12 D6
Dunolly Dr G77 72 F5
Dunolly St G21 31 A1
Dunottar Ave ML5 50 B2
Dunottar Pl ML5 50 B3
Dunphail Dr G34 33 D1
Dunphail Rd G34 48 D8
Dunragit St G31 46 C7
Dunrobin Cres G74 75 D3
Dunrobin Ct
Clydebank G81 15 A2
East Kilbride G74 75 D3
Dunrobin Dr G74 75 D3
Dunrobin Gdns ML6 51 E6
Dunrobin Pl ML5 49 F7
Dunrobin Prim Sch ML6 51 E7
Dunrobin Rd ML6 51 E7
Dunrobin St G31 46 B6
Dunrod Hill G74 75 F3
Dunrod St G32 47 B4
Duns Cres ML2 81 C7
Duns Path ML5 50 D3
Dunscore Brae ML3 77 E2
Dunside Dr G53 58 A6
Dunsiston Rd ML6 52 B4
Dunskaith Pl G34 48 D7
Dunskaith St G34 48 D7
Dunsmuir St G51 44 B7
Dunster Gdns G64 19 B4
Dunsyre Pl G23 17 E1
Dunsyre Rd ML11 125 B1
Dunsyre St G33 46 E8
Duntarvie Ave G34 48 C8
Duntarvie Cl G34 48 C8
Duntarvie Cres G34 48 C8
Duntarvie Dr G34 48 B8
Duntarvie Gdns G34 48 C8
Duntarvie Gr G34 48 C8
Duntarvie Pl G34 48 B8
Duntarvie Rd G34 48 B8
Dunterlie Ave G13 28 B6
Dunterlie Ct G78 57 C3
Duntiblae G66 21 A7
Duntiblae Rd G66 21 A7
Duntiglennan Rd G81 15 A6
Duntilland Ave ML7 53 B2
Duntilland Rd Airdrie ML6 52 E8
Salsburgh ML7 53 C5
Duntocher Rd
Bearsden G61 16 B6
Clydebank G81 15 A4
Clydebank,Parkhall G81 15 A5
Duntreath Ave
Clydebank G15 15 F1
Glasgow G13 27 E8
Duntreath Dr G15 15 F1
Duntreath Gdns G15 15 F2
Duntreath Gr G15 15 F1
Duntreath Terr G65 10 D8
Duntroon Pl ML4 65 B3
Duntroon St G31 46 B8
Dunure Dr Hamilton ML3 77 D2
Newton Mearns G77 73 A5
Rutherglen G73 60 F5
Dunure Pl Coatbridge ML5 49 E3
Newton Mearns G77 73 A4
Dunure St Coatbridge ML5 49 E3
Glasgow G20 29 D7
Dunvegan ML6 35 F4
Dunvegan Ave ML5 34 D1
Dunvegan Dr
Bishopbriggs G64 19 A4
Newton Mearns G77 73 A5
Dunvegan Pl
East Kilbride G74 75 D3
Uddingston G71 63 D8
Dunvegan Quadrant PA4 27 B4
Dunwan Ave G13 27 F7
Dunwan Pl G13 27 F7
Dura Rd ML2,ML7 83 C5
Durban Ave G75 88 B4
Durham St G41 44 D5
Durisdeer Dr ML3 77 E1
Durness Ave G61 17 B4
Duror St G32 47 A6
Durris Gdns G32 47 D3
Durward G74 76 E4
Durward Ave G41 44 D1
Durward Ct Glasgow G41 44 D1
Motherwell ML1 65 D1
Duthie Park Gdns 2
G13 28 D6
Duthie Park Pl 1 G13 28 D6
Dyce Ave ML6 50 E4
Dyce La G11 29 A2
Dyer's La G1 163 B1
Dyfrig St Hamilton G72 77 C8
Shotts ML7 69 E5
Dyke Brow ML7 56 A6
Dyke Ct ML7 56 A6
Dyke Rd Glasgow G13,G14 28 A7
Harthill ML7 56 A6
Dyke St Coatbridge ML5 49 B4
Glasgow G69 48 C5
Dykebar Ave G13 28 B6
Dykebar Cres PA2 42 B2
Dykebar Hospl PA2 57 B8
Dykehead Cres ML6 35 F2
Dykehead La G33 47 D7
Dykehead Prim Sch ML7 69 E5
Dykehead Rd Airdrie ML6 36 B3
Coatbridge G69 49 A5
Dullatur G68 11 C6
Queenzieburn G65 9 E8
Stonehouse ML9 129 F6
Dykehead Sq ML3 77 F2
Dykehead St G33 47 D7
Dykemuir Pl G21 31 B4
Dykemuir Quadrant G21 31 A4
Dykemuir St G21 31 A4
Dysart Ct G68 10 E1
Dysart Dr G72 77 D3
Dysart Way ML6 52 A6

E

Eagle Cres G61 16 B5
Eagle St G4 30 C2
Eaglesfield Cres ML10 112 C5
Eaglesham Ct 1 G51 44 E6
Eaglesham Path ML5 34 C6
Eaglesham Pl 2 G51 44 E6
Eaglesham Prim Sch G76 86 F4
Eaglesham Rd
Clarkston G76 73 E5
East Kilbride G75 87 C7
Newton Mearns G77 72 D3
Eamont Lodge 10 G12 29 C3
Earl Ave ML6 38 A5
Earl Haig Rd Glasgow G52 42 F7
Glasgow G52 43 A8
Earl La G14 28 C3
Earl Pl G14 28 C4
Earl St G14 28 B4
Earl View ML1 66 A3
Earl's Gate G71 63 E3
Earl's Hill G68 11 B3
Earlbank Ave G14 28 C4
Earlbank La N
16 Glasgow G14 28 C4
9 Glasgow G14 28 C4
Earlbank La S G14 28 C4
Earls Pl EH47 71 E6
Earlsburn Rd G66 20 E4
Earlscourt G69 21 F1
Earlspark Ave G43 59 F6
Earlston Cres ML5 50 D3
Earlston Pl G21 163 C4
Earlston St ML2 81 C6
Earlybraes Dr G33 47 E6
Earlybraes Gdns G33 47 D6
Earn Ave Bearsden G61 17 B3
Bellshill ML4 64 E6
Renfrew PA4 27 E2
Earn Cres ML2 81 B1
Earn Dr ML11 114 A4
Earn Gdns ML9 106 A8
Earn La ML1 66 A5
Earn Rd G77 72 D7
Earn St G33 31 E1
Earn Terr ML7 69 E6
Earnock Ave ML1 79 C6
Earnock Gdns ML3 78 A2
Earnock High Sch ML3 78 A2
Earnock Rd ML3 77 E2
Earnock St Glasgow G33 31 D4
Hamilton ML3 78 A4
Earnside St G32 47 B5
Easdale G74 89 B7
Easdale Dr G32 47 A4
Easdale Path
Coatbridge ML5 50 D4
Glenboig ML5 34 C6
Easdale Pl G77 72 B5
Easdale Rise ML3 77 E3
East Academy St ML2 81 B2
East Ave Carluke ML8 95 D2
Hamilton G72 77 E5
Motherwell ML1 66 A2
Plains ML6 37 A3
Renfrew PA4 27 D3
Uddingston G71 64 C6
East Barns St G81 27 D7
East Bath La G1 163 A3
East Burnside St 2 G65 10 D8
East Campbell St G1 163 C1
East Dean St ML4 65 B5
East End Terr ML11 131 A8
East Faulds Rd ML11 117 E5
East Forth Rd ML11 124 A8
East Gate Glenboig ML5 34 D7
Wishaw ML2 81 D3
East George St ML5 50 B8
East Glebe Terr ML3 78 D2
East Greenlees Ave G72 62 C3
East Greenlees Cres G72 62 B3
East Greenlees Dr G72 62 C3
East Greenlees Gr G72 61 F3
East Greenlees Rd G72 62 B3
East Hallhill Rd G69 47 F6
East Hamilton St ML2 81 B2
East High St ML6 51 A8
East Ho ML11 117 C4
East Kilbride Rd
Carmunnock G74,G76 74 D4
Clarkston G76 73 F6
Rutherglen G73 61 E4
East Kilbride Sh Ctr G74 75 E1
East Kilbride Sta G74 75 E2
East La PA1 42 B4
East Machan St ML9 93 B1
East Main St
Armadale EH48 41 F6
Harthill ML7 55 F5
East Mains Rd G74 75 E3
East Milton Gr G75 75 B1
East Milton Prim Sch
G75 75 C1
East Rd ML1 66 A4
East Scott Terr ML3 78 D1
East Shawhead Ind Est
ML5 50 B2
East Springfield Terr
G64 31 B8
East Station Ind Est ML9 93 B4
East Stewart Gdns ML5 50 C7
East Stewart Pl ML5 50 C7
East Stewart St ML5 50 C6
East Thomson St G81 15 B3
East Thornlie St ML2 81 B2
East Wellbrae Cres ML3 78 B1
East Wellington St G31 46 D5
Eastbank Acad G32 47 B4
Eastbank Dr G32 47 C5
Eastbank Pl G32 47 C5
Eastbank Prim Sch G32 47 C5
Eastbank Rise G32 47 C5
Eastburn Cres G21 31 B6
Eastburn Pl G21 31 B6
Eastburn Rd G21 31 B6
Eastcote Ave G14 28 E4
Eastcroft G73 61 B8
Eastcroft Terr G21 31 A4
Eastend Ave ML1 66 B1
Easter Craigs G31 46 B8
Easter Cres ML2 81 E4
Easter Garngaber Rd
G66 20 E5
Easter Mews G71 63 E5
Easter Queenslie Rd G33 47 E8
Easter Rd Clarkston G76 74 A6
Shotts ML7 69 D5
Easter Wood Cres G71 49 D1
Easterbrae ML1 79 D4
Eastergreens Ave G66 20 C7
Easterhill Pl G32 46 F3
Easterhill St G32 47 A2
Easterhouse Pl G34 48 C8
Easterhouse Quadrant
G34 48 C7
Easterhouse Rd G69 48 C7
Easterhouse Sta G69 48 C6
Eastermains G66 9 B2
Easterton Ave G76 74 A5
Eastertoun Gdns EH48 41 E6
Eastertoun Prim Sch
EH48 41 E6
Eastertown Rd ML11 121 F1
Eastfield Ave G72 61 E6
Eastfield Prim Sch G68 11 B1
Eastfield Rd
Caldercruix ML6 38 B5
Carluke ML8 109 A8
Cumbernauld G68 11 D4
Fauldhouse EH47 71 F7
Glasgow G21 30 E4
Eastfield Terr ML4 65 D4
Eastfield View EH47 71 F7
Eastgate Gartcosh G69 34 A5
Moffat DG10 161 D5
Easthall Pl G33 47 F7
Easthall Prim Sch G34 47 F7
Eastlea Pl ML6 51 B6
Eastmuir Sch G33 47 D6
Eastmuir St Glasgow G32 47 B5
Wishaw ML2 81 E3
Easton Pl ML5 50 B5
Eastvale Pl G3 44 C8
Eastwood Ave
Giffnock G46 59 D2
Glasgow G41 59 D8
Eastwood Cres G46 58 F4
Eastwood Ct G46 59 A4
Eastwood Dr
Lesmahagow ML11 119 F3
Wishaw ML2 82 A6
Eastwood High Sch G77 72 E7
Eastwood Pk EH47 71 F7
Eastwood Pl ML11 119 F3
Eastwood Rd
Lesmahagow ML11 120 A4
Moodiesburn G69 21 F2
Eastwood Toll G46 59 B1
Eastwood View G72 62 E6
Eastwood Way 2 ML9 93 B4
Eastwoodmains Rd
Clarkston G46 73 D8
Glasgow G46 59 C1
Ebroch Dr G65 10 E8
Ebroch Pk G65 10 E8
Eccles St G22 30 E5
Eck Path ML1 66 A5
Eckford St G32 47 A4
Eday St G22 30 D6
Edderton Pl G34 48 A7
Edderton Way G34 48 A7
Eddington Dr G77 72 C3
Eddleston Pl G72 62 E5
Eddlewood Ct G33 48 A7
Eddlewood Path G33 47 F7
Eddlewood Pl G33 47 F7
Eddlewood Rd G33 47 F7
Eden Dr G75 87 F6
Eden Gdns G75 87 F7
Eden Gr G75 87 F7
Eden La G33 31 D1
Eden Pk G71 63 F2
Eden Pl Cambuslang G72 62 D5
Renfrew PA4 27 E2
Eden St G33 31 D1
Edenhall Ct G77 72 D2
Edenhall Gr G77 72 D2
Edenside G68 12 B7
Edenwood St G31 46 E5
Edgam Dr G52 43 C5
Edgefauld Ave G21 30 F3
Edgefauld Dr G21 30 F3
Edgefauld Pl G21 30 F5
Edgefauld Rd
Glasgow G21 30 F4
Glasgow G21 31 A3
Edgehill La G11 29 A4
Edgehill Rd Bearsden G61 16 E6
Glasgow G11 28 F4
Glasgow G11 29 A4
Edgemont Pk ML3 91 C8
Edgemont St G41 59 E8
Edinbarnet Prim Sch
G81 15 C7
Edinbeg Ave G42 60 E8
Edinbeg Pl G42 60 E8
Edinburgh Rd
Abington ML12 145 F2
Biggar ML12 160 E5
Carnwath ML11 124 F2
Dolphinton EH46 126 E1
Glasgow G33 47 D7
Harthill ML7 55 C5
Moffat DG10 161 C6
Motherwell ML1 66 D7
Edington Gdns G69 21 F3
Edington St G4 30 B2
Edison St G52 42 E8
Edmiston Dr G51 44 A6
Edmonstone Dr G65 10 D7
Edmonton Terr G75 88 C8
Edmund Kean G74 76 C5
Edrom Ct G32 46 F5
Edrom Path G32 46 F5
Edrom St G32 46 F5
Edward Ave PA4 27 E4
Edward St Clydebank G81 27 D7
Coatbridge G69 48 F5
Hamilton ML3 78 D2
Kilsyth G65 6 D1
Motherwell ML1 79 F4
Edwin St G51 44 D5
Edzell Ct G14 28 D2
Edzell Dr G77 72 E4
Edzell Gdns
Bishopbriggs G64 31 C8
Wishaw ML2 81 A2
Edzell Pl G14 28 D3
Edzell St Coatbridge ML5 49 D4
Glasgow G14 28 D2
Egidia Ave G46 59 C2
Egilsay Cres G22 30 C8
Egilsay Pl G22 30 C8
Egilsay St G22 30 C8
Egilsay Terr G22 30 C8
Eglinton Ct G5 45 B5
Eglinton Dr
Eaglesham G76 86 F4
Glasgow G46 59 C2
Eglinton St
Coatbridge ML5 50 B7
Glasgow G5 45 B4
Eglinton Wlk G76 86 F4
Egmont Pk G75 88 A7
Eider G12 29 A7
Eider Ave G75 88 A5
Eider Gr G75 88 A5
Eider Pl G75 88 A4
Eighth St G71 48 E1
Eildon Cres ML6 51 F1
Eildon Dr G78 57 C1
Eildon Rd G66 20 F8
Eileen Gdns G64 19 B2
Eilt Wlk 8 ML2 81 F6
Elcho St G40 45 F6
Elder Cres G72 62 E4
Elder Dr G72 62 E4
Elder Gr G71 64 B8
Elder Grove Ave G51 43 D7
Elder Grove Ct 7 G51 43 D7
Elder Grove Pl 6 G51 43 D7
Elder Park Prim Sch G51 43 E8
Elder St Glasgow G51 43 F7
Glasgow G51 43 F8
Elderbank G61 16 E3
Elderpark Gdns G51 43 F7
Elderpark Gr 1 G51 43 F7
Elderpark St G51 43 F7
Elderpark Workspace
G51 43 F7
Elders Way ML2 81 D3
Elderslea Rd ML8 109 A8
Elderslie Ct G3 162 A3
Elderslie St G3 162 A3
Eldon Ct G11 29 B2
Eldon Gdns G64 18 F1
Eldon St G3 29 E2
Eldrick Ave EH47 71 E5
Eldrick Cres EH47 71 D5
Eldrick La EH47 71 D6
Eldrick View EH47 71 E5
Elgin Ave G74 75 F3
Elgin Gdns G76 73 F8
Elgin Pl Airdrie ML6 50 E5
Coatbridge ML5 50 B3
East Kilbride G74 75 F3
Kilsyth G65 6 D1
Elgin Rd G61 16 F7
Elgin Terr ML3 77 E4
Elgin Way ML4 65 A6
Elgol Path ML7 70 B3
Elibank St G33 32 A1
Elie Ct G68 11 F5
Elie Rd G72 77 D3
Elie St G11 29 C2
Eliot Cres ML3 78 D1
Eliot Terr ML3 78 D2
Elison Ct ML1 80 B4
Elive Ct ML5 50 B3
Elizabeth Cres G46 59 A3
Elizabeth Ct 6 G74 75 F2
Elizabeth Quadrant ML1 65 F5
Elizabeth St G51 44 C6
Elizabeth Wynd ML3 91 D7
Elizabethan Way PA4 27 C1
Ella Gdns ML4 65 C4
Ellangowan Rd G41 59 C8
Ellergreen Rd G61 16 E4
Ellesmere St Glasgow G22 30 B3
Glasgow G22 30 B4
Elliot Ave G46 59 C3
Elliot Cres G74 76 B2
Elliot Ct ML1 65 D1
Elliot Dr G46 59 C3
Elliot Ho G67 12 B2
Elliot Pl Glasgow G3 44 E7
Netherburn ML9 107 B4
Elliot St G3 44 E8
Ellis St ML5 50 A6
Ellis Way 6 ML1 79 F5
Ellisland East Kilbride G74 76 E3
Kirkintilloch G66 9 B2
Ellisland Ave G81 15 C3
Ellisland Cres G73 60 F5
Ellisland Dr Hamilton G72 77 B6
Kirkintilloch G66 9 A2
Ellisland Rd Clarkston G76 73 F5
Cumbernauld G67 12 B2
Glasgow G43 59 D6
Ellisland Sq ML11 114 B2
Ellisland Wynd ML1 66 C3
Ellismuir Farm Rd G69 48 D4
Ellismuir Pl G69 48 C4
Ellismuir Rd G69 48 C4
Ellismuir St ML5 49 E3
Ellismuir Way G71 49 A1
Elliston Ave G53 58 C5
Elliston Cres G53 58 C5
Elliston Dr G53 58 C5
Ellon Way PA3 42 A7
Ellrig G75 88 D5
Elm Ave Kirkintilloch G66 20 C6
Renfrew PA4 27 C4
Elm Bank G64 31 B8
Elm Cres G71 64 D7
Elm Ct 1 Hamilton G72 77 E7
Quarter ML3 91 F4
Elm Dr Cambuslang G72 62 C6
Chapelhall ML6 51 E3
Cumbernauld G67 12 F4
Elm Gdns G61 16 E6
Elm La E 6 G14 28 D3
Elm La W 5 G14 28 D3
Elm Pl G75 88 C6
Elm Quadrant ML6 51 D7
Elm Rd Clydebank G81 15 A5
Motherwell,Carfin ML1 66 A2
Motherwell,Holytown ML1 66 B5
Paisley PA2 42 A2
Rutherglen G73 61 B4
Elm St Clarkston G76 73 F6
Coatbridge ML5 50 C5
Glasgow G14 28 D3
Hamilton G72 77 E7
Motherwell ML1 79 D7
Elm View Ct ML4 65 D4
Elm Way Cambuslang G72 62 E4
Larkhall ML9 93 A5
Elm Wlk G61 16 E6
Elmbank ML11 119 E4
Elmbank Ave G71 64 B7
Elmbank Cres
Glasgow G2 162 B3
Hamilton ML3 78 A4
Elmbank Dr
13 Douglas ML11 138 B1
Larkhall ML9 93 C1
Elmbank St Bellshill ML4 65 A4
Carluke ML8 109 A8
Glasgow G2 162 B3
Elmbank Street La G2 162 B3
Elmfoot St G5 45 D2
Elmhurst ML1 79 D4
Elmira Rd G69 33 D7
Elmore Ave G44 60 B5
Elms The G44 60 B4

Elmslie Ct G69 ... 48 C4
Elmtree Gdns G45 ... 60 F4
Elmvale Prim Sch G22 ... 30 E5
Elmvale Row G21 ... 30 E5
Elmvale St G21 ... 30 E5
Elmwood ML2 ... 80 E1
Elmwood Ave
 Glasgow G11 ... 28 F4
 Newton Mearns G77 ... 72 F6
Elmwood Ct G71 ... 64 A2
Elmwood Gdns G66 ... 20 A5
Elmwood La G11 ... 28 F4
Elmwood Manor G71 ... 64 A2
Elmwood Rd ML7 ... 70 B2
Elphin St G23 ... 17 D1
Elphinstone Cres G75 ... 88 F6
Elphinstone Pl G51 ... 44 C7
Elphinstone Rd G46 ... 73 A7
Elrig Rd G44 ... 60 A5
Elsinore Path G75 ... 88 E6
Elspeth Gdns G64 ... 19 C2
Elswick Dr ML6 ... 38 A4
Eltham St G22 ... 30 B3
Elvan Ct ML1 ... 79 D6
Elvan Pl G75 ... 87 E7
Elvan St Glasgow G32 ... 46 F5
 Motherwell ML1 ... 79 D6
Elvan Twr 4 ML1 ... 79 E5
Elvanfoot Rd ML12 ... 151 A2
Embo Dr G13 ... 28 B6
Emerald Terr ML4 ... 65 A4
Emerson Rd G64 ... 19 A1
Emerson Rd W G64 ... 19 A1
Emily Dr ML1 ... 79 E4
Emma Jay Rd ML4 ... 65 B5
Empire Gate ML7 ... 69 F4
Empire Way ML1 ... 65 C1
Endfield Ave G12 ... 29 B6
Endrick Bank G64 ... 19 A4
Endrick Ct ML5 ... 49 F6
Endrick Dr Bearsden G61 ... 16 F3
 Paisley PA1 ... 42 B6
Endrick St G21 ... 30 D3
English Row ML6 ... 51 C3
English St ML2 ... 80 D3
Ennerdale G75 ... 87 F6
Ennisfree Rd G72 ... 77 D8
Ensay St G22 ... 30 D7
Enterkin St G32 ... 46 F4
Enterprise Ho
 Kirkintilloch G66 ... 20 C7
 Motherwell ML1 ... 79 F7
Entryfoot EH48 ... 39 F2
Eribol Wlk ML1 ... 66 D3
Eriboll Pl G22 ... 30 B7
Eriboll St G22 ... 30 B7
Ericht Pl ML7 ... 69 E6
Ericht Rd G43 ... 59 C5
Eriska Ave G14 ... 28 B5
Eriskay Ave Hamilton ML3 ... 77 F2
 Newton Mearns G77 ... 72 B5
Eriskay Cres G77 ... 72 B5
Ermelo Gdns G75 ... 88 B4
Erradale St G22 ... 30 A7
Errogie St G34 ... 48 B8
Errol Gdns G5 ... 45 C4
Erskine Ave G41 ... 44 B4
Erskine Cres ML6 ... 50 F5
Erskine Gdns ML7 ... 69 D5
Erskine Rd G46 ... 73 B6
Erskine Sq G52 ... 42 F7
Erskine Way ML7 ... 69 E4
Ervie St G34 ... 48 C7
Escart Rd ML8 ... 95 F3
Esdaile Ct ML1 ... 66 A3
Esk Ave PA4 ... 27 E2
Esk Dale G74 ... 75 C3
Esk St G14 ... 27 F5
Eskbank St G32 ... 47 B6
Eskdale G77 ... 73 B5
Eskdale Dr G73 ... 61 D7
Eskdale Rd G61 ... 16 D2
Eskdale St G42 ... 45 B1
Esmond St G3 ... 29 C1
Espieside Cres ML5 ... 49 D8
Essenside Ave G15 ... 16 C2
Essex Dr G14 ... 28 E4
Essex La G14 ... 28 E3
Esslemont Ave G14 ... 28 C5
Estate Quadrant G32 ... 62 C8
Estate Rd G32 ... 62 C8
Etive Ave Bearsden G61 ... 17 B4
 Hamilton ML3 ... 78 A1
Etive Cres
 Bishopbriggs G64 ... 19 B1
 Cumbernauld G67 ... 23 B6
Etive Ct Clydebank G81 ... 15 C5
 Cumbernauld G67 ... 23 B6
Etive Dr Airdrie ML6 ... 51 C5
 Cumbernauld G67 ... 23 B6
 Glasgow G46 ... 59 D1
Etive Pl Cumbernauld G67 ... 23 C6
 Larkhall ML9 ... 92 F5
Etive St Glasgow G32 ... 47 A5
 Wishaw ML2 ... 81 B1
Etive Wlk ML7 ... 70 B3
Etna Ind Est ML2 ... 80 C4
Etna St ML2 ... 80 C4
Eton La 3 G12 ... 29 E2
Etterick Wynd 9 G72 ... 77 C7
Ettrick Ave Hattonrig ML4 ... 65 A7
 Renfrew PA4 ... 27 F2
Ettrick Cres G73 ... 61 C7
Ettrick Ct Cambuslang G72 ... 62 D4
 Coatbridge ML5 ... 50 C3
Ettrick Dr Bearsden G61 ... 16 C7
 Moffat DG10 ... 161 E4
Ettrick Hill 2 G74 ... 76 A3
Ettrick Pl G43 ... 59 D7
Ettrick Rd DG10 ... 161 E5
Ettrick Sq G67 ... 11 F2
Ettrick St ML2 ... 81 A5
Ettrick Way
 9 Cumbernauld G67 ... 11 F1
 Renfrew PA4 ... 27 F2
Ettrick Wlk G67 ... 11 F2
Eurocentral ML4 ... 65 F8
Eurocentral Rail Terminal
 ML1 ... 65 D7
Evan Cres G46 ... 59 D2
Evan Dr G46 ... 59 D2
Evanton Dr G46 ... 58 E3
Evanton Pl G46 ... 58 E3
Everard Ct G21 ... 30 E7
Everard Dr G21 ... 30 E6
Everard Pl 2 G21 ... 30 E7
Everard Quadrant G21 ... 30 E7
Everglades The G69 ... 33 B8
Eversley St G32 ... 47 A3
Everton Rd G53 ... 43 C2
Ewart Cres ML3 ... 78 B1
Ewart Gdns ML3 ... 78 B1
Ewart Terr ML3 ... 78 A2
Ewing Ct ML3 ... 91 C7
Ewing Pl G31 ... 46 C5
Ewing St G73 ... 61 A7
Ewing Wlk G62 ... 17 C8
Excelsior Pk ML2 ... 80 D2
Excelsior St ML!,ML2 ... 80 D3
Exchange Pl G1 ... 163 A2
Exeter Dr G11 ... 29 A2
Exeter La G11 ... 29 A2
Exeter St ML5 ... 50 A5
Exhibition Centre Sta G3 ... 44 E8
Eynort St G22 ... 30 A7
Eyrepoint Ct G33 ... 47 A8

F

Factory Rd ML1 ... 79 E5
Fagan Ct G72 ... 63 E1
Faifley Rd G81 ... 15 C7
Failford Rd ML10 ... 112 F7
Fair Oaks G76 ... 74 E8
Fair View Dr ML11 ... 116 A4
Fairbairn Cres G46 ... 59 A2
Fairbairn Path G40 ... 46 A4
Fairburn St G32 ... 46 F4
Fairfax Ave G44 ... 60 C5
Fairfield Ct G76 ... 73 E5
Fairfield Dr Clarkston G76 ... 73 E5
 Renfrew PA4 ... 27 D1
Fairfield Gdns G51 ... 43 F8
Fairfield Pl Bothwell G71 ... 64 B2
 East Kilbride G74 ... 75 C2
 Glasgow G51 ... 43 F8
 Hamilton ML3 ... 78 E1
Fairfield St G51 ... 43 F8
Fairford Dr G67 ... 23 D7
Fairhaven Ave ML6 ... 51 E6
Fairhaven Rd G23 ... 29 E8
Fairhill Ave Glasgow G53 ... 58 C7
 Hamilton ML3 ... 78 C1
Fairhill Cres ML3 ... 78 C1
Fairhill Pl ML3 ... 91 C7
Fairholm Ave ML3 ... 79 D1
Fairholm St Glasgow G32 ... 46 F4
 Larkhall ML9 ... 92 F4
Fairley St G51 ... 44 B6
Fairlie G74 ... 75 D3
Fairlie Park Dr G11 ... 29 A2
Fairmont Pk EH47 ... 56 F6
Fairway G61 ... 16 C5
Fairways ML9 ... 93 C3
Fairways The G71 ... 64 A2
Fairways View G81 ... 15 D6
Fairweather Pl G77 ... 72 C3
Fairyknowe Ct G71 ... 64 B2
Fairyknowe Gdns G71 ... 64 B2
Falcon Terr G20 ... 29 C8
Falcon Terrace La G20 ... 29 C8
Falconbridge Rd G74 ... 76 C4
Falconer Terr ML3 ... 78 C1
Falfield St 1 G5 ... 45 A4
Falkland Ave G77 ... 73 A5
Falkland Cres G64 ... 31 D8
Falkland Dr G74 ... 75 D1
Falkland La G12 ... 29 B3
Falkland Pk G74 ... 75 D1
Falkland Pl
 Coatbridge ML5 ... 50 B3
 East Kilbride G74 ... 75 D1
Falkland St G12 ... 29 B3
Falla Hill Prim Sch EH47 ... 71 D6
Fallas Pl EH47 ... 71 D5
Falloch Pl ML2 ... 81 F6
Falloch Rd Bearsden G61 ... 16 C2
 Glasgow G42 ... 60 A7
Falls of Clyde* ML11 ... 130 A3
Falls of Clyde (Nature
 Trail)* ML11 ... 121 F7
Falls of Clyde Nature
 Reserve* ML11 ... 130 A4
Fallside Ave G71 ... 64 C6
Fallside Rd G71 ... 64 B4
Fallside Sec Sch G71 ... 64 D6
Falside Rd G32 ... 47 B2
Falstaff G74 ... 76 C5
Fara St G23 ... 29 F8
Faraday Ave ML2 ... 81 C3
Faraday Ret Pk ML5 ... 50 A6
Farie St G73 ... 60 F8
Farm Cres ML1 ... 66 F4
Farm Ct G71 ... 64 B4
Farm Houses The G65 ... 10 E7
Farm La ML4 ... 64 F3
Farm Pk G66 ... 20 D4
Farm Rd Blantyre G72 ... 63 D1
 Clydebank,Duntocher G81 ... 15 A7
 Glasgow G41 ... 44 B5
 Hamilton ML3 ... 77 F4
Farm St ML1 ... 79 D7
Farm Terr ML3 ... 77 F4
Farme Castle Ct G73 ... 46 C1
Farme Castle Est G73 ... 46 C1
Farme Cross G73 ... 46 B1
Farmeloan Rd G73 ... 61 B8
Farmgate Sq ML4 ... 64 F4
Farmington Ave G32 ... 47 D5
Farmington Gate G32 ... 47 D4
Farmington Gdns G32 ... 47 D5
Farmington Gr G32 ... 47 D5
Farndale G74 ... 75 C3
Farne Dr G44 ... 60 C4
Farnell St G4 ... 30 B2
Farquhar Sq EH48 ... 40 C3
Farrier Cres ML10 ... 103 C6
Faskally Ave G64 ... 18 E3
Faskally Wlk 19 ML2 ... 81 F6
Faskin Cres G53 ... 57 F7
Faskin Pl G53 ... 57 F7
Faskin Rd G53 ... 57 F7
Faskine Ave Airdrie ML6 ... 50 F6
 Calderbank ML6 ... 51 B2
Faskine Cres ML6 ... 50 F6
Fasque Pl G15 ... 15 E4
Fastnet St G33 ... 47 A8
Faulas Sq ML11 ... 114 A2
Fauldhouse Bsns Ctr
 EH47 ... 71 E6
Fauldhouse St G5 ... 45 D3
Fauldhouse Sta EH47 ... 71 C5
Faulds G69 ... 48 C5
Faulds Gdns G69 ... 48 C5
Faulds La ML5 ... 49 F3
Faulds St ML5 ... 49 F3
Fauldshead Rd PA4 ... 27 D3
Fauldspark Cres G69 ... 48 C6
Faulkner Gr ML1 ... 80 F8
Fearnach Pl G20 ... 29 B7
Fearnmore Rd G20 ... 29 D7
Felton Pl G13 ... 27 F7
Fence Terr ML11 ... 114 E8
Fendoch St G32 ... 47 A4
Fenella St G32 ... 47 B5
Fennsbank Ave G73 ... 61 D3
Fenwick Dr Barrhead G78 ... 57 D1
 Hamilton ML3 ... 91 E7
Fenwick Pl G46 ... 59 B1
Fenwick Rd G46 ... 59 C3
Ferclay St G81 ... 15 D7
Fereneze Ave
 Barrhead G78 ... 57 B3
 Clarkston G76 ... 73 C8
 Paisley PA4 ... 42 A8
Fereneze Cres
 Glasgow G13 ... 28 A7
 Hamilton ML3 ... 77 F3
Fereneze Gr G78 ... 57 B4
Fergus Ct G20 ... 29 E4
Fergus Dr G20 ... 29 E4
Fergus Gdns ML3 ... 78 F2
Fergus La G20 ... 29 F4
Ferguson Ave PA4 ... 27 D3
Ferguson Dr ML1 ... 79 E3
Ferguson St PA4 ... 27 D3
Ferguson Way ML6 ... 36 B2
Fergusson Pl G74 ... 76 D5
Fergusson Rd G67 ... 11 F2
Ferguston Rd G61 ... 16 F3
Fern Ave Bishopbriggs G64 ... 31 B8
 Kirkintilloch G66 ... 20 C5
Fern Cotts 2 G13 ... 28 F5
Fern Dale ML11 ... 119 F2
Fern Dr G78 ... 57 B4
Fern Gr G69 ... 34 A6
Fern La G13 ... 28 F5
Fern St ML1 ... 80 A4
Fernan St G32 ... 46 F5
Fernbank Ave G72 ... 62 C4
Fernbank St G22 ... 30 E5
Fernbrae Ave G73 ... 61 C3
Fernbrae Way G73 ... 61 B3
Ferncroft Dr G44 ... 60 D5
Ferndale ML9 ... 93 A1
Ferndale Ct G23 ... 29 D8
Ferndale Dr G23 ... 29 D8
Ferndale Gdns G23 ... 29 D8
Ferndale Pl G23 ... 29 D8
Ferness Oval G21 ... 31 C7
Ferness Pl G21 ... 31 C7
Ferness Rd G21 ... 31 C6
Ferngrove Ave G12 ... 29 B6
Fernhill Grange G71 ... 64 A1
Fernhill Rd G73 ... 61 B3
Fernhill Sch G73 ... 61 C3
Fernie Gdns G20 ... 29 E7
Fernieshaw Rd ML1 ... 67 F2
Fernlea G61 ... 16 E3
Fernlea Rd ML10 ... 112 E7
Fernleigh Pl G69 ... 21 F2
Fernleigh Rd G43 ... 59 D5
Fernside Wlk ML3 ... 78 E1
Fernslea Ave G72 ... 77 C8
Ferry Rd Bothwell G71 ... 64 A1
 Glasgow G3 ... 29 B1
 Glasgow G3 ... 29 C1
 Renfrew PA4 ... 27 D5
 Uddingston G71 ... 63 D6
Ferryden Ct G14 ... 28 E2
Ferryden St G14 ... 28 E2
Fersit Ct G43 ... 59 C6
Fersit St G43 ... 59 C6
Fetlar Dr G44 ... 60 C5
Fettercairn Ave G15 ... 15 E4
Fettercairn Gdns G64 ... 19 C1
Fettes St G33 ... 46 F8
Feu Rd ML10 ... 104 E3
Fiddoch Ct ML2 ... 81 F7
Fidra St G33 ... 46 F8
Field Gr G76 ... 73 F5
Field Rd Clarkston G76 ... 73 F5
 Clydebank G81 ... 15 D8
 Larkhall ML9 ... 93 B2
Field St ML3 ... 78 D1
Fielden Pl G40 ... 46 A5
Fielden St G40 ... 46 A5
Fieldhead Dr G43 ... 59 A5
Fieldhead Sq G43 ... 59 A5
Fife Ave Airdrie ML6 ... 51 A5
 Glasgow G52 ... 43 B4
Fife Cres G71 ... 64 A1
Fife Ct G71 ... 64 A1
Fife Dr ML1 ... 65 D2
Fife Way G64 ... 31 D8
Fifth Ave Airdrie ML6 ... 51 C8
 Glasgow G12 ... 28 F5
 Millerston G33 ... 32 B5
 Renfrew PA4 ... 27 C1
Fifth Rd G72 ... 77 E5
Fifty Pitches Pl G51 ... 43 C7
Fifty Pitches Rd G52 ... 43 B7
Finart Dr PA2 ... 42 B1
Finaven Gdns G61 ... 16 B8
Finch Dr G13 ... 28 A8
Finch Way ML4 ... 64 F8
Findhorn Ave PA4 ... 27 E3
Findhorn Ct G75 ... 87 D8
Findhorn Pl G75 ... 87 D8
Findhorn St G33 ... 46 D8
Findlay Ct ML1 ... 79 D8
Findlay St 9 Kilsyth G65 ... 10 D8
 Motherwell ML1 ... 79 F5
Findlay Terr G72 ... 62 D6
Findochty St G33 ... 32 E2
Fingal La G20 ... 29 C7
Fingal St G20 ... 29 D7
Fingask St G32 ... 47 C4
Fingland Ct 12 DG10 ... 161 D5
Finglas Ave PA2 ... 42 B1
Finglen Pl G53 ... 58 B5
Fingleton Ave G78 ... 57 D1
Finhaven St G32 ... 46 E3
Finlarig St G34 ... 48 C7
Finlas St G22 ... 30 D4
Finlay Dr G31 ... 46 A7
Finlay Rise G62 ... 17 C8
Finlayson Dr ML6 ... 51 E7
Finlayson La ML11 ... 125 A2
Finlayson Quadrant 1
 ML6 ... 51 E7
Finlaystone St ML5 ... 49 E7
Finnart Pl ML10 ... 112 D5
Finnart Sq G40 ... 45 F3
Finnart St Glasgow G40 ... 45 F3
 Glasgow G40 ... 45 F4
Finnie Wynd ML1 ... 80 B4
Finnieston Sq 9 G3 ... 44 E8
Finnieston St Glasgow G3 ... 44 E7
 Glasgow G3 ... 44 E8
Finsbay St G51 ... 43 E6
Fintaig La ML2 ... 81 E3
Fintrie Terr ML3 ... 77 E4
Fintry Cres Barrhead G78 ... 57 C1
 Bishopbriggs G64 ... 19 C1
Fintry Ct ML5 ... 50 C3
Fintry Dr G44 ... 60 D7
Fintry Gdns G61 ... 16 C8
Fintry Pl G75 ... 88 B4
Fir Bank Ave ML9 ... 93 B1
Fir Ct G72 ... 62 E4
Fir Dr G75 ... 88 B5
Fir Gr Motherwell ML1 ... 66 A2
 Uddingston G71 ... 64 C8
Fir Park St ML1 ... 79 F4
Fir Pk (Motherwell FC)
 ML1 ... 79 F4
Fir Pl Cambuslang G72 ... 62 C6
 Cleland ML1 ... 67 B1
 Glasgow G69 ... 48 A3
Fir View ML6 ... 51 B2
Firbank Ave G64 ... 19 B8
Firbank Quadrant ML6 ... 51 E3
Firbank Terr G78 ... 57 E1
Firdon Cres G15 ... 16 A1
Firhill Ave ML6 ... 50 F6
Firhill Pk (Partick Thistle FC)
 G20 ... 30 A4
Firhill Rd Glasgow G20 ... 30 A4
 Lesmahagow ML11 ... 119 F2
Firhill St G20 ... 30 A4
Firlee G75 ... 87 F7
Firpark Rd G64 ... 31 B8
Firpark Sch ML1 ... 79 F4
Firpark St G31 ... 45 F8
Firpark Terr G31 ... 45 F7
Firs The G44 ... 60 B4
First Ave Auchinloch G66 ... 20 D1
 Bearsden G61 ... 17 A3
 Glasgow G44 ... 59 F2
 Millerston G33 ... 32 B4
 Renfrew PA4 ... 27 C2
 Uddingston G71 ... 63 F8
First Gdns G41 ... 44 A4
First Rd G72 ... 77 E5
First St G71 ... 63 F8
First Terr G81 ... 15 A3
Firtree Pl ML2 ... 82 B6
Firtree Rd ML2 ... 82 B6
Firwood Cts G77 ... 72 E4
Firwood Dr G44 ... 60 C6
Firwood Rd G77 ... 72 E4
Fisher Ave G65 ... 10 D8
Fisher Cres G81 ... 15 B6
Fisher Ct G31 ... 45 F7
Fisher St ML9 ... 93 B1
Fishers Rd PA4 ... 27 C6
Fishescoates Ave G73 ... 61 C4
Fishescoates Gdns G73 ... 61 D5
Fitzalan Dr PA3 ... 42 A6
Fitzalan Rd PA4 ... 27 A1
Fitzroy La G3 ... 44 E8
Fitzroy Pl 2 G3 ... 44 E8
Five Ways Rd ML9 ... 107 D4
Flakefield G74 ... 75 B2
Flanders St G81 ... 15 C7
Flanigan Gr ML4 ... 65 A5
Flax Mill Rd ML7 ... 55 F5
Flax Rd G71 ... 64 A5
Flaxfield Gr ML1 ... 65 D2
Flaxmill Ave ML2 ... 80 D4
Fleet Ave PA4 ... 27 E1
Fleet St G32 ... 47 B4
Fleming Ave Chryston G69 ... 33 C8
 Clydebank G81 ... 27 D8
Fleming Ct Carluke ML8 ... 95 E1
 Clydebank G81 ... 15 B2
 Hamilton ML3 ... 77 E4
 Motherwell ML1 ... 80 A4
Fleming Gdns ML11 ... 113 F4
Fleming Pl
 Blackridge EH48 ... 40 E3
 East Kilbride G75 ... 88 E8
Fleming Rd Bellshill ML4 ... 65 B7
 Cumbernauld G67 ... 11 F2
Fleming St G31 ... 46 B6
Fleming Way
 Biggar ML12 ... 160 C3
 Hamilton ML3 ... 77 E4
 21 Larkhall ML9 ... 93 C1
Flemington Ave ML10 ... 112 F7
Flemington Ct ML10 ... 112 F7
Flemington Gdns EH47 ... 56 F6
Flemington Ind Est G72 ... 62 E4
Flemington Ind Pk ML1 ... 80 C5
Flemington St G21 ... 30 F3
Flenders Ave G76 ... 73 C6
Flenders Rd G76 ... 73 C6
Fleurs Ave G41 ... 44 B4
Fleurs Rd G41 ... 44 B4
Flinders Pl G75 ... 88 B8
Flloyd St ML5 ... 49 F7
Floors Rd G76 ... 73 C1
Flora Gdns G64 ... 19 C2
Florence Dr G46 ... 59 C2
Florence Gdns G73 ... 61 C4
Florence St G5 ... 45 C5
Florida Ave G42 ... 60 B8
Florida Cres G42 ... 60 B8
Florida Dr G42 ... 60 A8
Florida Gdns G69 ... 48 A5
Florida Sq G42 ... 60 B8
Florida St G42 ... 60 B8
Flowerdale Pl G53 ... 58 B3
Flowerhill Ind Est ML6 ... 51 B8
Flowerhill St ML6 ... 51 B8
Fochabers Dr G52 ... 43 C6
Fogo Pl G20 ... 29 D6
Foinaven Dr G46 ... 59 A5
Foinaven Gdns G46 ... 59 A6
Foinaven Way G46 ... 59 A6
Foinavon Rd ML3 ... 91 E3
Footfield Rd ML4 ... 64 F3
Forbes Dr 1 Glasgow G40 ... 45 F5
 Motherwell ML1 ... 65 C2
Forbes St G40 ... 45 F6
Ford Rd Glasgow G12 ... 29 D4
 Newton Mearns G77 ... 72 D3
Fordneuk St G40 ... 46 A5
Fordoun St G34 ... 48 D8
Fordyce Ct G77 ... 72 D4
Fordyce St G11 ... 29 C2
Fore Row ML3 ... 78 E4
Fore St G14 ... 28 C3
Foreknowe ML12 ... 160 D4
Foremount Terrace La 6
 G12 ... 29 C3
Forest Ave Bellshill ML4 ... 65 D3
 Hamilton ML3 ... 91 D6
Forest Dr G71 ... 64 A3
Forest Gdns G66 ... 20 A4
Forest Kirk ML8 ... 109 B8
Forest La ML3 ... 91 D6
Forest Pk ML2 ... 81 D5
Forest Pl G66 ... 20 A4
Forest Rd
 Cumbernauld,Abronhill G67 ... 12 D2
 Cumbernauld,Wardpark
 G67 ... 12 E6
 Larkhall ML9 ... 93 B3
Forest View G67 ... 12 C3
Forestburn Ct ML6 ... 50 D7
Forestfield Gdns ML6 ... 38 A4
Foresthall Cres G21 ... 31 A3
Foresthall Dr G21 ... 31 A3
Forestlea Rd ML8 ... 109 A8
Forfar Ave G52 ... 43 B4
Forfar Cres G64 ... 31 C8
Forgan Gdns G64 ... 31 D8
Forge Dr ML5 ... 49 F7
Forge Pl G21 ... 31 B2
Forge Rd ML6 ... 51 F6
Forge Row ML6 ... 51 C3
Forge Sh Ctr The G31 ... 46 C5
Forge St G21 ... 31 B2
Forgewood Path ML6 ... 51 F6

Forgewood Rd ML1 65 C2
Forglen St G34 33 B1
Forkens ML11 124 A8
Formby Dr G23 17 D1
Forres Ave G46 59 D3
Forres Cres ML4 65 A6
Forres Gate G46 59 D2
Forres Quadrant ML2 81 B5
Forres St 1 Glasgow G23 17 E1
Hamilton G72 77 C5
Forrest Dr G61 16 B8
Forrest Gate
Hamilton ML3 78 B1
Motherwell G71 49 B1
Forrest La ML11 130 F8
Forrest Pl Crossford ML8 108 B1
Harthill ML7 55 E5
Forrest Rd
Forrestfield ML6 39 A1
Lanark ML11 117 B5
Salsburgh ML6,ML7 54 B6
Forrest St Airdrie ML6 51 D8
Airdrie,Clarkston ML6 51 E8
Glasgow G40 46 A5
Hamilton G72 77 F7
Shotts ML7 69 E5
Forrester Ct 1 G64 30 F8
Forrester Rd EH48 41 F7
Forrestfield Cres G77 72 E5
Forrestfield Gdns G77 72 E5
Forrestfield Rd ML6 38 F7
Forrestfield St G21 31 A1
Forsa Ct G75 88 C4
Forsyth Ct ML11 117 C4
Forsyth St ML6 51 B8
Fort St ML1 79 B8
Forteviot Ave G69 48 C5
Forteviot Pl G69 48 C5
Forth Cres G75 87 E7
Forth Ct G75 87 E7
Forth Gr G75 87 E8
Forth Pl ML9 106 B8
Forth Prim Sch ML11 122 A1
Forth Rd Bearsden G61 16 D2
Torrance G64 19 B8
Forth St Clydebank G81 27 C8
Glasgow G41 44 F3
Forth Terr ML3 91 B8
Forth Wlk 5 G67 11 F1
Forties Cres G46 59 A5
Forties Ct G46 58 F5
Forties Gdns G46 59 A5
Forties Way G46 59 A5
Fortieth Ave G75 88 F5
Fortingall Ave G12 29 C6
Fortingall Pl G12 29 C6
Fortingall Rd G72 77 F5
Fortissat Ave ML7 69 D6
Fortrose Ct G72 77 C3
Fortrose Gdns ML10 112 F8
Fortrose St G11 29 B2
Forum Pl ML1 65 C1
Fossil Gr G66 9 A1
Foswell Dr G15 15 F5
Foswell Pl G15 15 F5
Fotheringay La G41 44 D2
Fotheringay Rd G41 44 E2
Foulburn Rd ML7 68 D2
Foulis La G13 28 F6
Foulis St G13 28 F6
Foulmyres Rd ML9 129 D7
Foulsykes Rd ML2 81 E4
Foundry La G78 57 C2
Foundry Rd Cleland ML1 67 C2
Shotts ML7 69 F4
Fountain Bsns Ctr The
ML5 50 A6
Fountain Craig G12 29 B5
Fountainwell Ave G21 30 D3
Fountainwell Dr G21 30 D2
Fountainwell Pl G21 30 D3
Fountainwell Rd G21 30 D2
Fountainwell Sq G21 30 E2
Fountainwell Terr G21 30 E2
Fourth Ave
Auchinloch G66 20 D1
Millerston G33 32 B5
Renfrew PA4 27 C2
Fourth Gdns G41 44 A4
Fourth St G71 48 F1
Fowlis Dr G77 72 C6
Fox Gr ML1 79 B7
Fox St G1 162 C1
Foxbar Dr G13 28 B6
Foxes Gr G66 20 E5
Foxglove Pl G53 58 B3
Foxhills Pl G23 17 E1
Foxley St G32 47 C1
Foy Gdns ML4 65 A8
Foyers Terr G21 31 A4
Frampton Ho G20 29 E5
Francis St 2 G5 45 A4
Frankfield Rd G33 32 E5
Frankfield St G33 31 E2
Frankfort St G41 44 E1
Franklin Pl G75 75 B1
Franklin St G40 45 F3
Fraser Ave
Newton Mearns G77 72 E6
Rutherglen G73 61 C8
Fraser Cres ML3 78 B2
Fraser Ct ML9 106 A8
Fraser Dr ML11 114 A5
Fraser Gdns G66 20 B8
Fraser River Twr G75 88 D8
Fraser St Cambuslang G72 61 E6
Cleland ML1 67 B2
Fraser Terr ML12 154 C7
Frazer St G40 46 B5
Frederick St ML5 49 E8
Freeland Cres G53 58 B6
Freeland Ct G53 58 C6
Freeland Dr G53 58 B6
Freeland La 7 G75 88 F8
Freeland Pl G66 20 D8
Freeneuk La G72 62 B6
Freeneuk Wynd G72 62 B6
Freesia Ct ML1 79 E5
French St Glasgow G40 45 F3
Renfrew PA4 27 B2
Wishaw ML2 81 B3
Frenchland Dr DG10 161 E5
Freuchie St G34 48 B7
Frew St ML6 51 A8
Friar Ave G64 19 B3
Friar's La ML11 116 F4
Friar's Wynd ML11 116 F4
Friars Croft G66 20 E8
Friars Pk ML11 116 F4
Friars Pl G13 28 D8
Friars Way ML6 51 C4
Friarscourt Ave G13 28 D8
Friarscourt Rd G69 21 B1
Friarsdene ML11 116 F4
Friarsfield Rd ML11 116 F4
Friarton Rd G43 59 F6
Friendship Way PA4 27 D1
Frood St ML1 65 C1
Fruin Ave G77 72 E6
Fruin Dr ML2 81 E3
Fruin Pl G22 30 C4
Fruin Rd G15 15 F1
Fruin Rise ML3 77 F2
Fruin St G22 30 D4
Fulbar Ave PA4 27 C4
Fulbar Ct PA4 27 D4
Fulbar La PA4 27 D4
Fulbar Rd G51 43 C7
Fulbar St PA4 27 D4
Fullarton Ave G32 47 A2
Fullarton Dr G32 47 A1
Fullarton La G32 47 A2
Fullarton Pl ML5 49 E3
Fullarton Rd
Cambuslang G72 61 F8
Cumbernauld G68 11 E5
Glasgow G32 46 F1
Fullarton St ML5 49 E3
Fullers Gate G81 15 C7
Fulmar Ct 4 G64 30 F8
Fulmar Pk G74 75 D3
Fulton St G13 28 E7
Fulwood Ave G13 27 F7
Fulwood Pk Ind Est ML3 78 B4
Fulwood Pl G13 27 F7
Furlongs The ML3 78 E5
Furnace Rd ML3 91 F3
Fyne Ave ML4 64 E6
Fyne Cres ML9 92 F5
Fyne Ct ML3 78 A1
Fyne La ML7 69 E6
Fyne Way ML1 66 A5
Fyneart St ML2 81 E4
Fyvie Ave G43 59 B5
Fyvie Cres ML6 51 F7

G

Gadburn Sch G21 31 C5
Gadie Ave PA4 27 E2
Gadie St G33 46 D8
Gadloch Ave G66 20 D2
Gadloch Gdns G66 20 D3
Gadloch St G22 30 C6
Gadloch View G66 20 D2
Gadsburn Ct G21 31 C6
Gadshill St G21 30 F1
Gailes Pk G71 63 F2
Gailes Rd G68 11 F5
Gailes St G40 46 B4
Gain & Shankburn Rd
G67 23 C2
Gain Rd Annathill ML5 22 F1
Cumbernauld G67,ML5 23 A1
Gainburn Cres G67 22 F6
Gainburn Ct G67 22 F6
Gainburn Gdns G67 22 F5
Gainburn Pl G67 22 F6
Gainburn View G67 23 A6
Gainside Rd ML5 34 C6
Gair Cres Carluke ML8 96 A3
Wishaw ML2 81 B1
Gair Rd ML8 96 B6
Gair Wynd ML7 70 B3
Gairbraid Ave G20 29 D6
Gairbraid Ct G20 29 C6
Gairbraid Pl G20 29 D6
Gairbraid Terr G69 49 A5
Gairloch Gdns G66 9 B1
Gala Ave PA4 27 E2
Gala Cres ML2 81 A5
Gala St G33 31 E2
Galbraith Cres ML8 95 A6
Galbraith Dr Glasgow G51 43 E8
Milngavie G62 16 F8
Galdenoch St G33 32 B2
Gallacher Ct ML1 80 B3
Gallan Ave 3 G23 17 E1
Gallery Gr ML5 50 A6
Gallery of Modern Art*
G1 163 A2
Galloway Ave ML3 91 C7
Galloway Dr G73 61 B3
Galloway Rd Airdrie ML6 50 F4
East Kilbride G74 76 C3
Galloway St G21 30 F6
Gallowflat St G73 61 B8
Gallowgate G1,G40,G31 45 F6
Gallowhall Farm Cotts
ML10 112 F5
Gallowhill ML9 93 A2
Gallowhill Ave G66 20 C6
Gallowhill Gr G66 20 C7
Gallowhill Prim Sch PA3 42 B7
Gallowhill Rd
Carmunnock G76 74 E8
Kirkintilloch G66 20 C6
Lanark ML11 117 A4
Paisley PA3 42 A6
Galston Ave G77 73 A5
Galston Ct ML3 91 E7
Galston St G53 57 F6
Galt Pl G75 88 D7
Gamrie Dr G53 58 A7
Gamrie Gdns G53 58 A7
Gamrie Rd G53 58 A8
Gannochy Dr G64 19 C1
Gantock Cres G33 47 B7
Garden Square Wlk ML6 50 D8
Garden St 137 F5
Gardenhall G75 87 E8
Gardenhall Ct G75 87 E8
Gardenside ML4 65 A4
Gardenside Ave
Glasgow G32 62 B8
Uddingston G71 63 F6
Gardenside Cres G32 62 B8
Gardenside Gr G32 62 B8
Gardenside Pl G32 62 B8
Gardenside Rd ML3 78 D2
Gardenside St G71 63 E6
Gardner Cres EH47 56 F6
Gardner Gr G71 64 A8
Gardner St G11 29 B2
Gardyne St G34 33 A1
Gareloch Ave ML6 35 F2
Garfield Ave ML4 65 C5
Garfield Dr ML4 65 C4
Garfield Pl G33 32 E6
Garfield St G31 46 A6
Garforth Rd G69 47 F4
Gargrave Ave G69 47 F4
Garion Dr G13 28 B5
Garlieston Rd G33 47 F6
Garmouth Ct 3 G51 44 A8
Garmouth Gdns 4 G51 44 A8
Garmouth St G51 43 F8
Garnet St G3 162 B4
Garnetbank Prim Sch
G3 162 B4
Garnethill Convent Sec RC
Sch G3 162 B4
Garnethill St G3 162 B4
Garngaber Ave G66 20 D5
Garngaber Ct G66 20 E5
Garngour Rd ML11 119 D5
Garngrew Rd FK4 8 F3
Garnhall Ditch* G68 8 E1
Garnhall Farm Rd G68 12 E8
Garnkirk La G33 32 E5
Garnock Pk G74 76 B1
Garnock St G21 30 F2
Garrell Ave G65 6 D1
Garrell Gr G65 6 D2
Garrell Pl G65 10 C8
Garrell Rd G65 10 C8
Garrell Way
Cumbernauld G67 11 E2
Kilsyth G65 10 C8
Garrick Ave G77 72 D2
Garrick Ct G77 72 D2
Garrioch Cres 1 G20 29 D5
Garrioch Dr G20 29 D5
Garrioch Gate 8 G20 29 D5
Garrioch Quadrant 2
G20 29 D5
Garrioch Rd G20 29 D5
Garriochmill Rd
Glasgow G20 29 F3
Glasgow G20 29 F3
Garriochmill Way 3 G20 29 F3
Garrion Bsns Pk ML2 94 A8
Garrion Pl ML9 93 F1
Garrion St ML2 94 C6
Garronhill KA18 142 A6
Garrowhill Dr G69 47 F5
Garrowhill Halt G69 47 F6
Garrowhill Prim Sch G69 48 A5
Garry Ave G61 17 B2
Garry St G44 60 A7
Garry Way ML7 69 E6
Garscadden Prim Sch
G13 27 F7
Garscadden Rd G15 16 A2
Garscadden Rd S
Glasgow G13 28 A8
Glasgow G15 27 F8
Garscadden Sta G14 28 A6
Garscadden View 5 G81 15 D3
Garscube Mill G61 17 A2
Garscube Rd G4,G20 30 B2
Gartartan Rd PA1 42 F5
Gartcarron Hill G68 11 C3
Gartcloss Rd ML5 34 C2
Gartconnell Dr G61 16 E6
Gartconnell Gdns G61 16 E6
Gartconnell Rd G61 16 E6
Gartconner Ave G66 21 B8
Gartconner Prim Sch
G66 21 B8
Gartcosh Ind Pk G69 34 B4
Gartcosh Prim Sch G69 33 F4
Gartcosh Rd ML5 34 A1
Gartcosh Sta G69 34 A4
Gartcosh Wlk ML4 64 F5
Gartcraig Pl Glasgow G33 31 F1
Glasgow G33 32 A1
Gartcraig Rd G33 46 E8
Garten Dr ML7 70 B3
Gartferry Ave G69 21 F2
Gartferry Rd
Moodiesburn,Bridgend G69 21 E2
Moodiesburn,Mollinsburn
G68,G69 22 B4
Gartferry St G21 31 A4
Gartfield St ML6 51 B6
Gartgill Rd ML5 34 E2
Garth St G1 163 A2
Garthamlock Rd G33 32 E1
Garthland Dr G31 46 A7
Gartlea Ave ML6 51 B7
Gartlea Gdns 1 ML6 51 B7
Gartlea Rd ML6 51 A7
Gartleahill ML6 51 B6
Gartliston Rd ML5 34 F3
Gartliston Terr G69 49 A5
Gartloch Rd
Glasgow,Gartcosh G33,G69 33 C3
Glasgow,Ruchazie G33 32 A1
Gartly St G44 59 F4
Gartmore Gdns G71 63 E8
Gartmore La G69 22 A2
Gartmore Rd PA1 42 C4
Gartmore Terr G72 61 F3
Gartnavel General Hospl
G12 29 A4
Gartnavel Royal Hospl
G12 29 A4
Gartness Dr ML6 51 E5
Gartness Rd ML6 52 A3
Gartocher Dr G32 47 C5
Gartocher Rd G32 47 C5
Gartocher Terr G32 47 C5
Gartons Rd G21 31 C4
Gartsherrie Ave ML5 34 F5
Gartsherrie Ind Est ML5 34 F1
Gartsherrie Prim Sch
ML5 49 E8
Gartsherrie Rd ML5 49 F8
Gartshore Cres G65 9 F2
Gartshore Gdns G68 10 F1
Garturk St Coatbridge ML5 50 B4
Glasgow G42 45 B2
Garvald Ct G40 46 B3
Garvald St G40 46 B3
Garve Ave G44 60 A5
Garvel Cres G33 47 E6
Garvel Rd G33 47 E6
Garvin Lea ML4 65 A8
Garvock Dr G43 59 B6
Gas Works Rd ML12 160 C4
Gascoyne G75 88 C7
Gask Pl G13 27 F8
Gaskin Path G33 32 E5
Gasworks Rd ML8 95 D3
Gatehouse St G32 47 C4
Gateshaw Wynd ML10 112 E7
Gateside Ave
Cambuslang G72 62 D5
Kilsyth G65 10 B8
Gateside Cres Airdrie ML6 51 A8
Barrhead G78 57 A1
Gateside Ind Est ML11 119 F2
Gateside Pk G65 10 B8
Gateside Rd Barrhead G78 57 A3
Crawfordjohn ML12 145 A3
3 Douglas ML11 138 B1
Whitburn EH47 56 F6
Wishaw ML2 80 E4
Gateside St Glasgow G31 46 B6
Hamilton ML3 78 E3
Gateside Wlk ML11 119 F2
Gateway The G74 76 A4
Gaughan Quadrant ML1 79 D5
Gauldry Ave G52 43 C3
Gavell Rd Kilsyth G65 10 A7
Queenzieburn G65 9 F7
Gavin St ML1 79 F5
Gavins Rd G81 15 B5
Gavinton St G44 59 F5
Gayne Dr ML5 34 C6
Gean Ct G67 12 F4
Gear Terr G40 46 B2
Geary St 3 G23 17 D1
Geddes Hill G74 76 B4
Geddes Rd G21 31 C7
Gelston St G32 47 B4
Gemini Gr ML1 66 B5
Gemmel Pl G77 72 C4
Gemmell Way ML9 105 E2
General Roy Way ML8 109 C8
Generals Gate G71 63 E6
George Allan Pl ML10 112 D7
George Ave G81 15 C3
George Cres G81 15 C3
George Ct ML3 78 A5
George Gray St G73 61 C8
George Mann Terr G73 61 A4
George Paul Rd ML11 124 E1
George Reith Ave G12 28 F5
George Sq G1 163 A2
George St Airdrie ML6 50 F7
Armadale EH48 41 F6
Barrhead G78 57 B3
Carstairs Junction ML11 131 B7
Chapelhall ML6 51 D3
Glasgow G1 163 B2
Glasgow,Baillieston G69 48 B4
George St *continued*
Hamilton ML3 78 A5
Motherwell ML1 79 F4
Motherwell,New Stevenston
ML1 66 B4
George View ML2 80 F2
George Way 10 ML9 93 B4
Georges Cl ML3 78 A5
Gerard Pl ML4 65 B7
Germiston Cres G75 88 A4
Germiston Ct G75 88 A4
Gertrude Pl G78 57 A2
Ghillies La ML1 65 C1
Gibb Ct ML9 105 E2
Gibb St Chapelhall ML6 51 D2
Cleland ML1 67 B1
Gibbon Cres G74 76 C3
Gibbshill Pl ML7 55 D5
Gibson Hts G4 163 C2
Gibson Quadrant ML1 65 C1
Gibson Rd PA4 27 B1
Gibson St Glasgow G4 163 C1
Glasgow,Kelvingrove G12 29 E2
Salsburgh ML7 53 B2
Giffen Pl ML10 112 C6
Giffnock Park Ave G46 59 C4
Giffnock Prim Sch G46 59 C2
Giffnock Sta G46 59 C3
Gifford Dr G52 43 A5
Gifford Pl ML5 49 E3
Gigha Gdns ML8 109 A8
Gigha Quadrant ML2 80 E1
Gilbert Dr ML11 119 D6
Gilbert Rae Ct ML12 160 D4
Gilbert St G3 44 C8
Gilbertfield Path G33 32 B2
Gilbertfield Pl G33 32 B2
Gilbertfield Rd G72 62 E3
Gilbertfield St G33 32 B2
Gilburn Pl ML7 69 F4
Gilchrist Loan ML11 119 D6
Gilchrist St ML5 50 B8
Gilchrist Way ML2 81 B1
Gilderdale G74 75 C2
Gilfillan Pl ML2 94 C7
Gilhill St G20 29 D7
Gill Rd ML2 94 C7
Gillbank Ave ML8 95 D2
Gillbank La 6 ML9 93 C2
Gillburn St ML2 94 C6
Gillespie Pl EH48 41 F4
Gillies Cres G74 76 D5
Gillies La G69 48 C4
Gilmerton St G32 47 A4
Gilmour Ave
Clydebank G81 15 B5
Thorntonhall G74 74 B2
Gilmour Cres
Eaglesham G76 86 E5
Rutherglen G73 60 F8
Gilmour Dr ML3 77 F2
Gilmour Pl Bellshill ML4 64 F5
Coatbridge ML5 49 F8
7 Glasgow G5 45 C4
Gilmour St Clydebank G81 15 C4
Eaglesham G76 86 E5
Gilmourton Cres G77 72 D3
Gilmourton Prim Sch
ML10 128 B3
Gilroy Cl ML11 117 C5
Gilshochill Sta G23 29 E7
Gimmerscroft Cres 1
ML6 51 F6
Girdons Way G71 63 E6
Girthon St G32 47 C4
Girvan Cres ML6 51 D1
Girvan St G33 46 D8
Glade The ML9 93 B2
Gladney Ave G13 27 E8
Gladsmuir ML11 122 A1
Gladsmuir Rd G52 43 A6
Gladstone Ave G78 57 B2
Gladstone Court Mus*
ML12 160 D4
Gladstone Ct ML3 78 A5
Gladstone St Bellshill ML4 65 B5
11 Glasgow G4 30 A2
Glaive Rd G13 16 D1
Glamis Ave Carluke ML8 95 F2
Newton Mearns G77 72 F5
Glamis Ct ML1 66 C2
Glamis Dr G74 75 F3
Glamis Gdns G64 19 B4
Glamis Rd G31 46 D4
Glanderston Ave
Barrhead G78 57 E2
Newton Mearns G77 72 B6
Glanderston Ct G13 28 A7
Glanderston Dr G13 28 A7
Glanderston Gate G77 72 C6
Glasgow & Edinburgh Rd
Calderbank ML1 51 A1
Coatbridge ML5 49 D3
Glasgow G69 48 D5
Motherwell,Newhouse ML1 66 E7
Motherwell,Newhouse ML1 67 B8
Glasgow Acad The G12 29 F3
Glasgow Bot Gdns* G12 29 D4
Glasgow Caledonian Univ
G4 163 A4
Glasgow Cath (St Mungo)*
G4 163 C3
Glasgow Coll of Nautical
Studies G5 45 C5
Glasgow Dental Hospl
G2 162 B3
Glasgow Fort G34 32 E1

Glasgow Gaelic Prim Sch G3 162 A4
Glasgow Homeopathic Hospl G12 29 A4
Glasgow Metropolitan Coll
Glasgow G1 163 A3
Glasgow G1,G4 163 B3
Glasgow,Gallowgate G40 45 F5
Glasgow,Gorbals G5 45 C5
Glasgow Mus Resource Ctr* G53 57 F5
Glasgow Rd Barrhead G78 57 D4
Cambuslang,Silverbank G72 61 F6
Cambuslang,Whitlawburn G72,G73 61 F1
Chapelton ML10 103 C5
Clydebank G81 27 C7
Clydebank,Hardgate G81 15 C6
Coatbridge ML5 49 D5
Cumbernauld G67 23 D8
Cumbernauld,Kildrum G67 12 B4
Eaglesham G76 86 E7
Glasgow G71 48 A4
Hamilton G72 77 E7
Kilsyth G65 10 B8
Kirkintilloch G66 20 A8
Lanark ML11 116 E4
Milngavie G62 17 B8
Nerston G72 76 A8
Nerston G74 76 A7
Paisley PA1 42 C4
Renfrew PA4 27 F2
Rutherglen G73 45 F1
Strathaven ML10 112 D7
Uddingston G71 63 E7
Wishaw ML2 80 E3
Glasgow Royal Concert Hall* G1 163 A3
Glasgow Sch of Art G3 162 B3
Glasgow Sch of Art (Annexe) The G3 162 C4
Glasgow Sch of Art The G3 162 B4
Glasgow Science Ctr* G3 44 D7
Glasgow St G12 29 E2
Glasgow Steiner Sch G3 29 D1
Glasgow Univ (Annexe) G13 28 F7
Glasgow Zoo* G71 48 C2
Glassel Rd G34 33 D1
Glasserton Pl G43 59 F5
Glasserton Rd G43 59 F5
Glassford Prim Sch ML10 104 F2
Glassford Rd
Stonehouse ML3,ML9 105 D5
Strathaven ML10 112 F6
Glassford St Glasgow G1 163 A2
Motherwell ML1 80 A4
Glassford Twr ML1 80 B3
Glaudhall Ave G69 33 E7
Glebe Ave Bothwell G71 64 B2
Carmunnock G76 74 D7
Coatbridge ML5 49 D4
Douglas ML11 138 B1
Glebe Cres Airdrie ML6 51 D8
2 Douglas ML11 138 B1
East Kilbride G74 75 F1
Hamilton ML3 78 C2
Glebe Ct East Kilbride G74 76 D5
Fauldhouse EH47 71 D6
Glasgow G4 163 B3
Lanark ML11 117 A4
Glebe Dr ML11 117 A4
Glebe Gdns ML11 119 E4
Glebe Hollow G71 64 B2
Glebe Ind Est The ML11 138 C1
Glebe La G77 72 D4
Glebe Pl Cambuslang G72 62 B5
Rutherglen G73 60 F8
Glebe Rd G77 72 D4
Glebe St Bellshill ML4 64 F5
East Kilbride G74 75 F1
Glasgow G4 163 B4
Glasgow G4 163 C3
Hamilton ML3 78 D2
Renfrew PA4 27 D3
Glebe The Bothwell G71 64 B2
Lanark ML11 116 F4
Moffat DG10 161 C4
Glebe Wynd G71 64 B2
Gleddoch Rd G52 42 F6
Glen Affric G74 76 B1
Glen Affric Ave G53 58 D4
Glen Affric Way ML6 51 D1
Glen Alby Pl G53 58 C4
Glen Almond G74 76 D2
Glen Arroch G74 76 B1
Glen Ave Glasgow G32 47 B6
Larkhall ML9 92 F1
Moodiesburn G69 21 F2
Glen Avon Dr ML6 51 D1
Glen Bervie G74 76 B2
Glen Cally G74 76 B2
Glen Cannich G74 76 B1
Glen Carron G74 76 B1
Glen Clova G74 76 B2
Glen Clova Dr G68 11 C4
Glen Clunie G74 76 D2
Glen Clunie Dr G53 58 C4
Glen Clunie Pl G53 58 C4
Glen Cona Dr G53 58 C5
Glen Cres G13 27 E7
Glen Ct Coatbridge ML5 49 D5
Motherwell ML1 80 B4
Glen Dene Way G53 58 C4
Glen Derry G74 76 D3
Glen Dessary G74 89 B8
Glen Devon G74 76 D1
Glen Dewar Pl G53 58 C4
Glen Dochart Dr G68 11 C5
Glen Doll G74 76 B2
Glen Douglas Dr G68 11 C4
Glen Dr ML1 66 B5
Glen Dye G74 76 B2
Glen Eagles G74 76 C1
Glen Esk G74 76 C2
Glen Esk Dr G53 58 C4
Glen Etive Pl G73 61 E2
Glen Falloch G74 76 C1
Glen Falloch Way G68 11 C5
Glen Farg G74 76 D1
Glen Farrar G74 76 B1
Glen Feshie G74 89 B8
Glen Fruin Dr 9 ML9 93 C1
Glen Fruin Pl ML6 51 D1
Glen Fyne Rd G68 11 B4
Glen Gairn G74 76 D2
Glen Garrell Pl G65 6 C1
Glen Garry G74 89 B8
Glen Gavin Way PA2 42 B1
Glen Gr East Kilbride G75 88 D7
Kilsyth G65 6 D2
Glen Isla G74 76 C2
Glen Isla Quadrant ML1 81 B8
Glen Kyle Dr G53 58 C4
Glen Lednock Dr G68 11 B4
Glen Lee G74 76 C2
Glen Lethnot G74 76 C2
Glen Livet Pl G53 58 C4
Glen Lochay Gdns G68 11 B4
Glen Loy Pl G53 58 C4
Glen Luss Gdns G68 11 B4
Glen Luss Pl
Coatbridge ML5 50 D5
Glasgow G53 58 C4
Glen Lyon G74 76 C1
Glen Lyon Ct G68 11 B4
Glen Mallie G74 76 C1
Glen Mark G74 76 C2
Glen More G74 76 A1
Glen Moriston G74 76 B1
Glen Moriston Rd
Cumbernauld G68 11 B4
Glasgow G53 58 C4
Glen Moy G74 76 C1
Glen Nevis G74 89 B8
Glen Nevis Pl G73 61 C2
Glen Noble ML1 81 B8
Glen Ochil Rd ML6 51 D1
Glen Ogilvie G74 76 C2
Glen Ogle St G32 47 D4
Glen Orchard Rd G64 18 E8
Glen Orchy Ct G68 11 B5
Glen Orchy Dr
Cumbernauld G68 11 B4
Glasgow G53 58 D4
Glen Orchy Gr G53 58 D4
Glen Orchy Pl
Chapelhall ML6 51 D1
Cumbernauld G68 11 B4
Glasgow G53 58 D4
Glen Orchy Rd ML1 81 A7
Glen Ord Rd ML1 66 B2
Glen Pl G76 73 D7
Glen Prosen G74 76 C2
Glen Quoich G74 76 D3
Glen Rannoch Dr ML6 51 D1
Glen Rd Airdrie ML6 51 E6
Armadale EH48 41 F6
Caldercruix ML6 37 F4
East Kilbride G74 74 F5
East Kilbride G74 75 A4
Glasgow G32 47 B7
Motherwell ML1 66 D7
Shotts ML7 69 F4
Wishaw ML2 81 A4
Glen Rosa Gdns G68 11 B4
Glen Sannox Dr G68 11 C4
Glen Sannox Gr G68 11 C4
Glen Sannox Loan G68 11 C4
Glen Sannox View G68 11 B4
Glen Sannox Way G68 11 C4
Glen Sannox Wynd G68 11 C4
Glen Sax Dr PA4 27 E1
Glen Shee G74 76 C2
Glen Shee Cres ML6 51 D1
Glen Shirva Rd G65 9 F4
Glen St Barrhead G78 57 C3
Cambuslang G72 62 D4
Motherwell ML1 65 E1
Motherwell,Whittagreen ML1 66 D4
Glen Tanner G74 76 D2
Glen Tennet G74 76 C2
Glen Terr ML6 37 F4
Glen Turret G74 76 D2
Glen Twr ML1 80 B3
Glen Urquhart G74 76 B1
Glen View
Cumbernauld G67 12 C3
Hamilton ML3 91 D7
12 Stonehouse ML9 129 E8
Glenacre Cres G71 63 E8
Glenacre Dr Airdrie ML6 51 D6
Glasgow G45 60 D3
Glenacre Gr G45 60 E4
Glenacre Rd G67 23 F8
Glenacre St G45 60 D3
Glenacre Terr G45 60 D3
Glenafeoch Rd ML8 96 A1
Glenafton Gr ML5 49 F5
Glenafton View ML3 91 B8
Glenallan Terr ML1 65 D1
Glenalmond Rd G73 61 D3
Glenalmond St G32 47 A4
Glenalva Ct G65 6 D1
Glenapp Ave PA2 42 B1
Glenapp Pl G69 21 F3
Glenapp Rd PA2 42 B1
Glenapp St G41 44 F3
Glenarklet Cres PA2 57 A8
Glenarklet Dr PA2 42 A1
Glenartney Rd G69 21 C1
Glenashdale Way PA2 42 A1
Glenavon Ct ML3 78 B1
Glenavon Rd G20 29 D7
Glenavon St ML10 112 E4
Glenbank Ave G66 20 D4
Glenbank Ct G46 58 F2
Glenbank Dr G46 58 F2
Glenbank Rd G66 20 D4
Glenbarr St G21 30 F1
Glenbervie Cres G68 11 F5
Glenbervie Pl
15 Glasgow G23 17 D1
Newton Mearns G77 72 A5
Glenboig Farm Rd ML5 34 E6
Glenboig New Rd ML5 34 F6
Glenboig Prim Sch ML5 34 F5
Glenboig Rd Glenboig G69 34 B7
Glenboig ML5 34 C6
Glenbrittle Dr PA2 42 A1
Glenbrittle Way PA2 42 A1
Glenbuck Ave G33 31 F6
Glenbuck Dr G33 31 F6
Glenburn Ave
Cambuslang G72 61 E5
Glasgow G69 48 C5
Moodiesburn G69 21 F2
Motherwell ML1 66 C4
16 Stonehouse ML9 129 E8
Symington ML12 140 F6
Glenburn Cres G71 64 C8
Glenburn Ct
East Kilbride G74 75 A3
3 Kirkintilloch G66 20 D8
Glenburn Gdns
Bishopbriggs G64 18 F2
Glenboig ML5 34 C6
Glenburn La G20 29 E7
Glenburn Rd
Bearsden G61 16 E5
East Kilbride G74 75 A3
Glasgow G46 59 B1
Hamilton ML3 78 B3
Glenburn St G20 29 E7
Glenburn Terr
Carluke ML8 108 E8
Motherwell ML1 66 C1
Glenburn Way G74 74 F3
Glenburn Wlk G69 48 C5
Glenburn Wynd 3 ML9 93 B4
Glenburnie Pl G34 47 F7
Glencairn Ave ML2 80 D4
Glencairn Dr
Coatbridge ML5 49 E5
Glasgow G41 44 E2
Moodiesburn G69 21 E2
Rutherglen G73 60 F8
Glencairn Gdns
Cambuslang G72 62 D5
Glasgow G41 44 E2
Glencairn La G41 44 F2
Glencairn Prim Sch ML1 79 F5
Glencairn Rd
Cumbernauld G67 12 C2
Paisley PA3 42 A7
Glencairn St
Kirkintilloch G66 20 D7
Motherwell ML1 79 F5
Glencairn Twr 1 ML1 79 F5
Glencalder Cres ML4 65 C3
Glencally Ave PA2 42 B1
Glencleland Rd ML2 80 D4
Glenclora Dr PA2 42 A1
Glencloy St G20 29 C7
Glencoe Dr ML1 66 A5
Glencoe Pl Glasgow G13 28 F7
Hamilton ML3 91 B8
Glencoe Rd Carluke ML8 109 A8
Rutherglen G73 61 D3
Glencoe St G13 28 F7
Glenconner Way G66 9 A1
Glencorse St G32 46 E7
Glencraig St ML6 50 E7
Glencroft Ave G71 63 E8
Glencroft Rd G44 60 D5
Glencryan Rd G67 12 B1
Glencryan Sch G67 23 E7
Glendale Ave ML6 51 D6
Glendale Cres G64 31 C8
Glendale Dr G64 31 C8
Glendale Gr ML5 49 E3
Glendale Pl
Bishopbriggs G64 31 C7
Glasgow G31 46 B6
Glendale Prim Sch G41 44 F4
Glendale St G31 46 B6
Glendaruel Ave G61 17 B4
Glendaruel Rd G73 61 E2
Glendarvel Gdns G22 30 D4
Glendee Gdns PA4 27 D2
Glendee Rd PA4 27 D2
Glendermott Ct ML8 95 F3
Glendeveron Way ML1 66 B2
Glendevon Pl ML3 91 B8
Glendevon Sq G33 32 B2
Glendinning Pl G76 86 D4
Glendinning Rd G13 16 E1
Glendoick Pl G77 72 A5
Glendorch Ave ML2 81 C7
Glendore St G14 28 E2
Glendoune Rd G76 73 E5
Glenduffhill Rd G69 47 F5
Gleneagles Ave G68 12 A5
Gleneagles Dr
Bishopbriggs G64 19 A3
Newton Mearns G77 73 B4
Gleneagles Gate G77 73 B4
Gleneagles Gdns G64 19 A3
Gleneagles La N G14 28 C4
Gleneagles La S G14 28 C3
Gleneagles Pk G71 63 F2
Glenelg Cres G66 9 A1
Glenelg Path ML5 34 C6
Glenelg Quadrant G34 33 D1
Glenelm Pl ML4 65 A6
Glenesk Cres G53 58 C4
Glenesk Pl G53 58 C4
Glenfarg Cres G61 17 B4
Glenfarg Ct ML3 91 B8
Glenfarg Rd G73 61 B4
Glenfarg St 12 G20 30 A2
Glenfarm Rd ML1 66 E4
Glenfield Rd G75 89 A6
Glenfinnan Dr
Bearsden G61 17 C3
Glasgow G20 29 D6
Glenfinnan Gr ML4 65 D4
Glenfinnan Pl 4 G20 29 D6
Glenfinnan Rd G20 29 D6
Glenfruin Cres PA2 42 B1
Glenfruin Rd G72 77 C8
Glengarriff Rd ML4 65 B8
Glengarry Dr G52 43 C5
Glengavel Cres G33 31 F6
Glengavel Gdns ML2 81 C7
Glengonnar Cres ML12 145 F2
Glengonnar Halt* ML12 154 D8
Glengonnar St ML9 106 A8
Glengowan Ct ML9 93 A3
Glengowan Prim Sch
Caldercruix ML6 38 A4
Larkhall ML9 93 A3
Glengowan Rd ML6 38 A4
Glengyre St G34 33 C1
Glenhead Cres
Clydebank G81 15 A7
Glasgow G22 30 C6
Glenhead Dr ML1 79 E4
Glenhead Rd
Clydebank G81 15 A5
Kirkintilloch G66 20 D4
Glenhead St G22 30 D6
Glenhove Rd G67 12 B2
Gleniffer Ave G13 28 A6
Gleniffer Dr G78 57 B5
Gleniffer Rd Paisley PA4 42 B8
Renfrew PA4 27 B1
Gleniffer View 4 G81 15 D3
Glenisla Ave G69 22 A4
Glenisla St G31 46 D3
Glenkirk Dr G15 16 B2
Glenlee Prim Sch ML3 78 A5
Glenlee St ML3 77 F5
Glenlora Dr G53 58 A7
Glenlora Terr G53 58 B7
Glenluce Dr G32 47 D4
Glenluce Gdns G69 22 A3
Glenluce Terr G74 75 C2
Glenluggie Rd G66 21 A7
Glenlui Ave G73 61 B5
Glenlyon Ct ML3 91 B8
Glenlyon Pl G73 61 C3
Glenmanor Ave G69 21 E2
Glenmanor Prim Sch G69 21 E2
Glenmanor Rd G69 21 E2
Glenmare Ave G66 21 A7
Glenmavis Cres ML8 96 A1
Glenmavis Ct ML8 96 A1
Glenmavis Rd ML6 35 E2
Glenmavis St G4 162 C4
Glenmore Ave
Bellshill ML4 65 B3
Glasgow G42 60 E8
Glenmore Rd ML1 66 C3
Glenmuir Dr G53 58 B5
Glenochar Heritage Trail* ML12 155 D8
Glenoran La 1 ML9 93 B4
Glenpark ML6 51 E6
Glenpark Ave G46 59 A2
Glenpark Gdns G72 61 E7
Glenpark Ind Est G31 46 B6
Glenpark St Glasgow G31 46 B6
Wishaw ML2 81 A4
Glenpark Terr G72 61 E7
Glenraith Path G33 32 B3
Glenraith Rd G33 32 B2
Glenraith Sq G33 32 B3
Glenraith Wlk G33 32 B3
Glenshee Ct G31 46 D3
Glenshee Gdns G31 46 E4
Glenshee St G31 46 D4
Glenshee Terr ML3 91 B8
Glenshiel Ave PA2 42 A1
Glenshira Ave PA2 42 A1
Glenside Ave G53 43 B2
Glenside Ct EH48 41 E6
Glenside Dr G73 61 E6
Glenside Gdns EH48 41 E6
Glenspean Pl ML5 50 D5
Glenspean St G43 59 D6
Glentanar Ct PA1 42 A4
Glentanar Dr G69 22 A2
Glentanar Pl G22 30 B8
Glentanar Rd G22 30 B7
Glentarbert Rd G73 61 D3
Glentore Quadrant ML6 36 A2
Glentrool Gdns
Glasgow G22 30 D4
Moodiesburn G69 22 A3
Glenturret St G32 47 A4
Glentyan Dr G53 58 A6
Glentynan Pl G53 58 A7
Glenview Airdrie ML6 51 D6
Larkhall ML9 92 F4
Glenview Ave Banknock FK4 8 F3
Caldercruix ML6 38 A4
Glenview Cres G69 22 A4
Glenview Pl G72 63 D1
Glenview St ML6 35 E4
Glenview Terr EH48 41 E6
Glenville Ave G46 59 B3
Glenville Gate G76 74 A5
Glenville Terr G76 74 A5
Glenwell St ML6 35 E3
Glenwood Ave ML6 51 C4
Glenwood Bsns Ctr G45 60 F3
Glenwood Ct G66 20 A5
Glenwood Dr
Armadale EH48 41 D6
Glasgow G46 58 F2
Glenwood Gdns G66 20 A5
Glenwood Path G45 60 E3
Glenwood Pl Glasgow G45 60 E3
Kirkintilloch G66 20 A5
Glenwood Rd G66 20 A5
Glidden Ct ML2 94 C7
Gloucester Ave
Clarkston G76 73 D7
Rutherglen G73 61 D5
Gloucester St G5 45 A5
Goddard Pl ML2 82 B5
Gogar Pl G33 46 E8
Gogar St G33 46 E8
Goil Ave ML4 64 D6
Goil Way ML1 66 A5
Goldberry Ave G14 28 B5
Goldcrest Ct ML1 80 F1
Goldenacre Pl ML6 36 F3
Goldenhill Ct G81 15 B6
Goldenhill Prim Sch G81 15 B6
Goldie Rd G71 64 A4
Goldscaur Row ML12 154 C8
Golf Ave ML4 65 A3
Golf Course Rd G64 18 E8
Golf Ct Carstairs ML11 111 F1
Glasgow G44 59 E2
Golf Dr Clydebank G15 15 F1
Clydebank G15 16 A1
Paisley PA1 42 C4
Golf Gdns ML9 93 C2
Golf Pl ML4 65 B3
Golf Rd Clarkston G76 73 D8
Rutherglen G73 61 B4
Golf View ML10 112 F8
Golfhill Dr Glasgow G31 46 A8
Moffat DG10 161 C4
Golfhill Nursing Home G31 45 F8
Golfhill Prim Sch
Airdrie ML6 35 E2
Glasgow G31 45 F8
Golfhill Quadrant ML6 36 A2
Golfhill Rd ML2 80 E4
Golfview G61 16 C5
Golfview Dr ML5 49 D7
Golfview Pl ML5 49 D6
Golspie Ave ML6 50 E4
Golspie St G51 44 A8
Golspie Way G72 77 C3
Good Bush Hill ML10 112 E5
Goodsburn Rd ML10 112 E5
Goodview Gdns ML9 93 C2
Goosedubbs G1 163 A1
Gopher Ave G71 64 B8
Gorbals Cross
Glasgow G5 45 C5
Larkhall ML9 93 A3
Gorbals St G5 45 C5
Gordon Ave
Glasgow,Garrowhill G69 47 F5
Glasgow,Netherlee G44 59 E2
Hillington G52 42 E7
Gordon Cres G77 72 E6
Gordon Ct ML6 51 E8
Gordon Dr
East Kilbride G74 76 B3
Glasgow G44 59 E3
Gordon La G1 162 C2
Gordon Pl ML4 64 F2
Gordon Rd Glasgow G44 59 E2
Hamilton ML3 77 F4
Gordon St G1 162 C2
Gordon Terr Blantyre G72 63 C1
Hamilton ML3 77 F3
Gorebridge St G32 46 E7
Goremire Rd ML8 109 B8
Gorget Ave G13 16 C1
Gorget Pl G13 16 C1
Gorget Quadrant G13 16 B1
Gorse Dr G78 57 B4
Gorse Pl G71 64 B8
Gorsehall St ML1 67 B2
Gorsewood G64 18 E1
Gorstan Pl G20 29 C5
Gorstan St G23 29 D8
Gosford La G14 28 A4
Gough St G33 46 D8
Gourlay G74 76 D5
Gourlay Dr ML2 94 C6
Gourlay St Glasgow G21 30 D3

Gourlay St *continued*
1 Glasgow,Springburn G21 .30 E4
Gourock St G5 .45 A4
Govan Cross Sh Ctr G51 .44 A8
Govan High Sch G51 .43 E7
Govan Rd Glasgow G51 .43 E8
Glasgow,Plantation G51 .44 C6
Govan Underground Sta G51 .44 A8
Govanhill St Glasgow G42 .45 B2
Glasgow G42 .45 C2
Gowan Brae ML6 .38 B5
Gowanbank ML12 .151 A2
Gowanbank Prim Sch G53 .58 A5
Gowanbrae
Fauldhouse EH47 .71 E5
Kirkintilloch G66 .20 C6
Gowanlea Ave G15 .16 A1
Gowanlea Dr G46 .59 D4
Gowanlea Terr G71 .64 B7
Gowanside Pl ML8 .95 D2
Gower St G51 .44 C4
Gower Terr G41 .44 C5
Gowkhall Ave ML1 .66 F3
Goyle Ave G15 .16 C3
Grace Ave G69 .48 F5
Grace St G3 .162 A2
Grace Wynd ML3 .78 E3
Graeme Ct ML1 .65 D2
Graffham Ave G46 .59 E3
Grafton Pl G1 .163 A3
Graham Ave
Cambuslang G72 .62 D5
Clydebank G81 .15 B3
East Kilbride G74 .75 E2
Hamilton ML3 .91 D8
Graham Ho G67 .11 E2
Graham Pl Ashgill ML9 .93 F1
Kilsyth G65 .6 C2
Graham Rd ML8 .108 B1
Graham Sq G31 .45 F6
Graham St Airdrie ML6 .51 A7
Barrhead G78 .57 B3
Hamilton ML3 .78 E3
Motherwell ML1 .66 A5
Wishaw ML2 .81 B2
Graham Terr G64 .31 B7
Grahamshill Ave ML6 .51 D8
Grahamshill St ML6 .51 C8
Grahamston Cres PA2 .57 C8
Grahamston Ct PA2 .57 C8
Grahamston Pk G78 .57 B5
Grahamston Pl PA2 .57 C8
Grahamston Rd G78 .57 C6
Graignestock Pl 2 G40 .45 E5
Graignestock St G40 .45 E5
Graigside Pl G68 .22 F7
Grainger Rd G64 .19 D1
Grammar School Sq ML3 .78 E4
Grampian Cres
Chapelhall ML6 .51 F1
Glasgow G32 .47 B4
Grampian Ct G61 .16 C8
Grampian Dr G75 .88 B4
Grampian Pl G32 .47 B4
Grampian Rd ML2 .80 F4
Grampian St G32 .47 B4
Grampian Way
Barrhead G78 .57 C1
Bearsden G61 .16 C7
Cumbernauld G68 .11 A2
Gran St G81 .27 E8
Granby Ho 8 G12 .29 E3
Granby La G12 .29 D3
Grandtuly Dr G12 .29 C6
Grange Ave ML2 .80 E1
Grange Ct ML11 .116 F5
Grange Gdns G71 .64 B1
Grange Pl DG10 .161 C6
Grange Rd Bearsden G61 .16 F5
Glasgow G42 .60 A8
Moffat DG10 .161 C6
Pettinain ML11 .131 C5
Grange St ML1 .80 A4
Grange Terr ML11 .131 B5
Grange Twr ML1 .80 B2
Grangeneuk Gdns G68 .11 C1
Grannoch Pl ML5 .50 D2
Grant Ct Airdrie ML6 .51 E8
Hamilton ML3 .91 C7
Grant Gr ML4 .65 A4
Grant St G3 .162 A4
Grantholm Ave ML1 .66 B6
Grantlea Gr G32 .47 D4
Grantlea Terr G32 .47 D4
Grantley Gdns G41 .59 D8
Grantley St G41 .59 D8
Grantoften Path G75 .88 E6
Granton St G5 .45 E2
Grantown Ave ML6 .51 E6
Grantown Gdns ML6 .35 F5
Granville St
Clydebank G81 .15 B3
Glasgow G3 .162 A3
Grasmere G75 .87 F5
Grasmere Ct ML3 .91 D6
Grathellen Ct ML1 .80 A8
Gray Dr G61 .16 F3
Gray St Cleland ML1 .67 B1
Glasgow G3 .29 E1
Kirkintilloch G66 .21 B7
Larkhall ML9 .93 A4
Shotts ML7 .70 A4
Gray's Cl ML11 .116 C4
Gray's Rd G71 .64 B5
Grayshill Rd G68 .22 E6
Grayston Manor G69 .21 E1
Graystonelee Rd ML7 .69 D6
Great Dovehill G1,G4 .163 B1
Great George La 6 G12 .29 D3
Great George St
Glasgow G12 .29 D3
Glasgow G12 .29 E2
Great Kelvin La G12 .29 E2
Great Western Rd
Clydebank G81 .15 C4
Glasgow,Dowanhill G4,G12 .29 D3
Glasgow,Knightswood G15 .28 D7
Great Western Terr 13 G12 .29 C4
Great Western Terrace La 12 G12 .29 C4
Green Ave ML11 .131 A8
Green Bank Rd G68 .11 C2
Green Dale ML2 .81 D5
Green Ferns ML11 .114 A4
Green Gdns ML1 .67 C2
Green Loan ML1 .66 A3
Green Pl Bothwell G71 .64 B2
Calderbank ML6 .51 B2
Green Rd G73 .61 A8
Green St Bothwell G71 .64 B2
Clydebank G81 .15 A3
Glasgow G40 .45 E5
Stonehouse ML9 .105 F2
Strathaven ML10 .112 E6
Green The G40 .45 E4
Green's Rd ML11 .125 B1
Greenacres ML1 .79 C5
Greenacres Ct G53 .58 C4
Greenacres Dr G53 .58 C4
Greenacres Rdbt 4 G64 .31 D8
Greenacres View ML1 .79 C5
Greenacres Way G53 .58 C4
Greenan Ave G42 .60 E7
Greenbank 6 G72 .77 D7
Greenbank Ave G46 .73 A7
Greenbank Cres ML10 .104 E2
Greenbank Gdn* G76 .73 C6
Greenbank Rd ML2 .81 C3
Greenbank St 3 G73 .61 A8
Greenbank Terr 4 ML8 .95 F2
Greenburn ML11 .119 E4
Greenburn Rd EH47 .71 E5
Greendyke St G1 .163 B1
Greenend Pl G32 .47 C7
Greenend View ML4 .64 F5
Greenfarm Rd G77 .72 B6
Greenfaulds Cres G67 .24 A8
Greenfaulds High Sch G67 .23 D7
Greenfaulds Rd G67 .23 E7
Greenfaulds Sta G67 .23 F7
Greenfield Ave G32 .47 B7
Greenfield Cres ML2 .81 D4
Greenfield Dr ML2 .81 D4
Greenfield Pl G32 .47 B6
Greenfield Prim Sch G51 .43 F7
Greenfield Quadrant ML1 .66 F4
Greenfield Rd
Carluke ML8 .95 F3
Clarkston G76 .73 E6
Glasgow G32 .47 C6
Hamilton ML3 .78 A5
Greenfield St
Glasgow G51 .43 F7
Wishaw ML2 .81 D4
Greengairs Ave G51 .43 D8
Greengairs Prim Sch ML6 .24 E2
Greengairs Rd ML6 .24 E1
Greenhall Pl G72 .77 C6
Greenhead Rd
Bearsden G61 .16 F4
Wishaw ML2 .81 D2
Greenhead St G40 .45 E4
Greenhill G64 .31 C8
Greenhill Ave
Glasgow G46 .59 C1
Mount Ellen G69 .33 E7
Greenhill Bsns Ctr ML5 .35 A1
Greenhill Covenanters' Ho* ML12 .160 C5
Greenhill Ct
Fauldhouse EH47 .71 E6
Rutherglen G73 .61 A8
Greenhill Ind Est ML5 .35 A1
Greenhill Prim Sch ML5 .50 A8
Greenhill Rd
Blackridge EH48 .40 E3
Cleland ML1 .67 F3
Rutherglen G73 .61 A8
Greenhill St G73 .61 A7
Greenhills Cres G75 .88 B5
Greenhills Prim Sch G75 .88 C5
Greenhills Rd G75 .88 C5
Greenhills Sq G75 .88 B5
Greenhillstairs DG10 .157 B4
Greenholm Ave
Clarkston G76 .73 E7
Uddingston G71 .63 E7
Greenholme Ct G44 .60 B7
Greenholme St G44 .60 B6
Greenknowe Dr ML8 .94 F6
Greenknowe Rd G43 .59 B6
Greenknowe St ML2 .94 B6
Greenlady Wlk ML11 .117 C4
Greenlaw Ave Paisley PA1 .42 A5
Wishaw ML2 .81 C5
Greenlaw Cres PA1 .42 A6
Greenlaw Dr
Newton Mearns G77 .72 D5
Greenlaw Dr *continued*
Paisley PA1 .42 A5
Greenlaw Ho PA1 .42 A5
Greenlaw Rd Glasgow G14 .27 E6
Newton Mearns G77 .72 D5
Greenlea Rd G69 .33 B8
Greenlea St G13 .28 E6
Greenlees Gdns G72 .61 F3
Greenlees Gr ML5 .50 D5
Greenlees Pk G72 .62 A4
Greenlees Rd G72 .62 A4
Greenloan Ave G51 .43 D8
Greenloan View ML9 .93 B1
Greenmoss Pl ML4 .65 C5
Greenmount G22 .30 A7
Greenock Ave G44 .60 B5
Greenock Rd PA4 .27 A5
Greenrig G71 .63 F6
Greenrig Rd ML11 .121 B7
Greenrig St G33 .31 D3
Greenrigg Cotts ML7 .56 A5
Greenrigg Prim Sch ML7 .55 F6
Greenrigg Rd G67 .12 B1
Greenrigg St G71 .63 F6
Greens Ave G66 .20 C7
Greens Cres G66 .20 C7
Greens Rd G67 .23 F6
Greenshields Ct ML11 .119 D6
Greenshields Rd G69 .48 B5
Greenside G76 .74 E8
Greenside Cl ML11 .117 A4
Greenside Cres G33 .31 E3
Greenside La ML11 .117 A4
Greenside Pl G61 .16 C8
Greenside Rd
Clydebank G81 .15 B7
Motherwell ML1 .66 C8
Wishaw ML2 .81 C2
Greenside St
Coatbridge ML5 .50 B8
Glasgow G33 .31 E3
Motherwell ML1 .66 F4
Greentowers Rd ML11 .116 E8
Greentree Dr G69 .47 F3
Greenview Sch G22 .30 D6
Greenview St G43 .59 C8
Greenway La G72 .77 C5
Greenwell St EH47 .71 F6
Greenwood Ave
Cambuslang G72 .62 E6
Moodiesburn G69 .21 F2
Greenwood Cl DG10 .161 D5
Greenwood Cres ML5 .50 D5
Greenwood Ct G76 .73 E6
Greenwood Dr G61 .17 A4
Greenwood Quadrant G81 .15 D1
Greenwood Rd G76 .73 D7
Greenwood St ML7 .69 E5
Greenyards Intc G67 .12 C1
Greer Quadrant G81 .15 B4
Greig Cres EH48 .41 F5
Grenada Pl G75 .75 B1
Grenadier Gdns ML1 .79 D4
Grenadier Pk G72 .62 A4
Grenville Dr G72 .61 F4
Gresham View ML1 .80 B2
Gretna St G40 .46 B4
Greyfriars Ct ML11 .116 F4
Greyfriars Rd G71 .63 C8
Greyfriars St G32 .46 F7
Greystone Ave G73 .61 C6
Greystone Bauks ML11 .116 F4
Greystone Baulks ML11 .116 A4
Greystone Cl ML10 .112 F7
Greystone Gdns
Rutherglen G73 .61 C6
Strathaven ML10 .112 F7
Greystone Pl ML10 .112 F7
Greywood St G13 .28 E7
Grier Path G31 .46 D5
Grier Pl ML9 .92 F2
Grierson La G33 .46 D8
Grierson St G33 .46 D8
Grieve Croft G71 .63 F1
Grieve Rd G67 .12 A3
Griffin Pl ML4 .65 A8
Griffiths Way ML8 .94 F4
Griqua Terr G71 .64 B2
Grogarry Rd G15 .16 A4
Grossart St ML7 .53 A2
Grosvenor Cres 9 G12 .29 D3
Grosvenor Crescent La 11 G12 .29 D3
Grosvenor La G12 .29 D3
Grosvenor Terr 12 G12 .29 D3
Grove Cres ML9 .93 C2
Grove Pk G66 .20 D4
Grove The G46 .73 B8
Grove Way ML4 .64 F4
Grove Wood G71 .49 D1
Grove Wynd ML1 .66 A3
Groveburn Ave G46 .59 A4
Grovepark Ct G20 .30 A2
Grovepark Gdns G20 .30 A2
Grovepark St G20 .30 A3
Groves The G64 .31 C7
Grovewood Bsns Ctr ML4 .64 E8
Grudie St G34 .48 A8
Gryffe St G44 .60 A7
Guildford St G33 .32 C1
Guildie's Loan ML12 .160 E5
Gullane Cres G68 .11 F6
Gullane Ct ML3 .91 B7
Gullane Dr ML5 .49 F2
Gullane St G11 .29 B1
Gunn Mews ML2 .80 F2
Gunn Quadrant ML4 .64 E3
Gushet Ho ML6 .50 E7
Gushet Pl ML11 .116 A3
Guthrie Ct ML1 .79 C6
Guthrie Dr G71 .49 A1
Guthrie Pl G74 .75 F2
Guthrie St Glasgow G20 .29 D6
Hamilton ML3 .78 D4
Gyle Pl ML2 .81 E3

H

Haberlea Ave G53 .58 C3
Haberlea Gdns G53 .58 C2
Haddington Way ML5 .49 E3
Haddow Gr 6 G71 .64 A8
Haddow St ML3 .78 E3
Hadrian Terr ML1 .79 C8
Hagen Dr ML1 .66 E1
Haggs La G41 .44 C2
Haggs Rd G41 .44 C1
Haggswood Ave G41 .44 C2
Haghill Park Prim Sch G31 .46 C8
Haghill Prim Sch G31 .46 B7
Haghill Rd G31 .46 C7
Hagholm Rd ML11 .117 F7
Hagmill Cres ML5 .50 C2
Hagmill Rd ML5 .50 B2
Hagshaw View 7 ML11 .138 B1
Haig Dr G69 .47 F4
Haig St G21 .31 A4
Hailes Ave G32 .47 D5
Hailstonegreen ML11 .124 A8
Hailstones Cres EH48 .41 F6
Haining Rd PA4 .27 D3
Haining The PA4 .27 D2
Hairmyres G75 .74 F1
Hairmyres Dr G75 .87 F8
Hairmyres Hospl G75 .87 F8
Hairmyres La G75 .74 E1
Hairmyres Pk G75 .87 F8
Hairmyres Rdbt G75 .74 F1
Hairmyres St G42 .45 C2
Hairmyres Sta G75 .74 F1
Hairst St PA4 .27 D4
Halbeath Ave G15 .15 F3
Halbert St G41 .44 E1
Haldane La 9 G14 .28 D3
Haldane Pl G75 .88 F7
Haldane St G14 .28 D3
Halfmerk N G74 .76 A2
Halfmerk S G74 .76 A2
Halfmerke Prim Sch G74 .76 A3
Halgreen Ave G15 .15 E3
Halidon Ave G67 .23 F7
Halifax Way 7 PA4 .27 C1
Halkirk Gate G72 .77 C4
Hall Bar Gdns ML8 .108 E4
Hall Pl Lanark ML11 .117 A4
Stepps G33 .32 F5
Hall Rd ML11 .116 B6
Hall St Clydebank G81 .15 B1
Hamilton ML3 .78 D1
Motherwell ML1 .66 A4
Hallbrae St G33 .31 E2
Hallcraig St ML6 .51 A8
Halley Dr G13 .27 E7
Halley Pl G13 .27 E7
Halley Sq G13 .27 F7
Halley St G13 .27 E7
Hallforest St G33 .32 B2
Hallgraig Pl ML8 .95 D2
Hallhill Cres G33 .47 E6
Hallhill Rd
Glasgow,Barlanark G33 .47 E6
Glasgow,Garrowhill G69 .48 A6
Glasgow,Greenfield G32 .47 B5
Halliburton Rd G33 .47 F7
Halliburton Terr G34 .48 A7
Hallidale Cres PA4 .27 F2
Hallinan Gdns ML2 .80 F1
Hallrule Dr G52 .43 C5
Hallside Ave G72 .62 E5
Hallside Bvd G72 .62 F4
Hallside Cres G72 .62 E5
Hallside Dr G72 .62 E5
Hallside Gdns ML2 .81 E4
Hallside Pl G5 .45 C4
Hallside Prim Sch G72 .62 E4
Hallside Rd
Cambuslang G72 .62 E4
Cambuslang G72 .62 F4
Hallydown Dr G13 .28 C5
Halpin Cl ML4 .64 D5
Halton Gdns G69 .47 F4
Haltons Path G71 .64 A6
Hamersley Pl G75 .88 B7
Hamilcomb Rd ML4 .65 A3
Hamill Dr G65 .10 F8
Hamilton Academicals (FC) ML3 .78 C5
Hamilton Ave G41 .44 C3
Hamilton Bsns Pk ML3 .78 D5
Hamilton Coll ML3 .78 D5
Hamilton Cres
Bearsden G61 .16 E7
Cambuslang G72 .62 C4
Coatbridge ML5 .50 A5
Renfrew PA4 .27 D5
Hamilton Dr Airdrie ML6 .36 B1
Bothwell G71 .64 B1
Cambuslang G72 .62 A5
Drumclog ML10 .135 B8
Glasgow G12 .29 E3
Glasgow,Giffnock G46 .59 D2
Hamilton G72 .77 B5
Motherwell ML1 .79 F4
Hamilton Gdns EH48 .41 F4
Hamilton Gram Sch ML3 .78 D3
Hamilton Int Tech Pk G72 .77 C5
Hamilton Mausoleum* ML3 .78 F5
Hamilton Park Ave G12 .29 E3
Hamilton Pk N ML3 .78 D6
Hamilton Pk S ML3 .78 D6
Hamilton Pl
East Kilbride G75 .88 E7
Hamilton ML3 .91 D6
Motherwell ML1 .66 B4
Motherwell,Whittagreen ML1 .66 C4
Hamilton Rd Bellshill ML4 .64 F4
Bothwell G71 .64 B1
Cambuslang G72 .62 C4
East Kilbride G74 .76 C5
Glasgow G32 .47 D2
Hamilton G72 .77 B6
Larkhall ML9 .92 F5
Motherwell ML1 .79 D6
Rutherglen G73 .61 C7
Strathaven ML10 .112 F7
Hamilton Road Ind Est ML10 .112 F7
Hamilton Sch for the Deaf ML3 .78 A2
Hamilton St Carluke ML8 .95 F1
Clydebank G81 .27 D7
Glasgow G42 .45 C1
Larkhall ML9 .93 A4
Hamilton Terr G81 .27 D7
Hamilton Twr G71 .63 D4
Hamilton View G71 .64 A7
Hamilton Way ML9 .105 E2
Hamiltonhill Cres G22 .30 B4
Hamiltonhill Rd G22 .30 B3
Hamlet G74 .76 B5
Hampden Dr G42 .60 B7
Hampden La G42 .60 B8
Hampden Park Visitors Ctr* G42 .60 C7
Hampden Pk (Queen's Park FC)* G42 .60 B7
Hampden Terr G42 .60 B8
Hampden Way 4 PA4 .27 D1
Handax ML11 .122 A1
Handel Pl 3 G5 .45 C4
Hangingshaw Pl G42 .60 C8
Hanover Cl G42 .60 A8
Hanover Ct Glasgow G1 .163 A3
Paisley PA1 .42 A5
Hanover Gdns G64 .19 A1
Hanover St G1 .163 A2
Hanson Pk G31 .45 F8
Hanson St G31 .45 F8
Hapland Ave G53 .43 C2
Hapland Rd G53 .43 C2
Hapton View ML10 .112 E8
Harburn Pl G23 .17 E1
Harbury Pl G14 .27 F6
Harcourt Dr G31 .46 B8
Hardacres ML11 .117 A5
Hardgate Dr G51 .43 C8
Hardgate Gdns G51 .43 C7
Hardgate Pl G51 .43 C8
Hardgate Rd G51 .43 C8
Hardie Ave G73 .61 C8
Hardie St
Hamilton,Blantyre G72 .77 D7
Hamilton,Laighstonehall ML3 .78 B2
Motherwell ML1 .79 E8
Hardridge Ave G52 .43 E2
Hardridge Pl G52 .43 E2
Hardridge Rd G52 .43 E2
Harefield Dr G14 .28 B5
Harelaw Ave
Barrhead G78 .57 D1
Glasgow G44 .59 E4
Hareleeshill Prim Sch ML9 .93 C1
Hareleeshill Rd ML9 .93 C2
Hareshaw Rd ML1 .67 D5
Hareside ML11 .98 F8
Hareslaw Pl ML9 .129 F8
Harestanes Gdns G66 .9 A1
Harestanes Ind Est ML8 .108 F5
Harestanes Prim Sch G66 .9 A1
Harestanes Rd
Armadale EH48 .41 F4
Braidwood ML8 .108 E4
Harestone Cres ML2 .81 C2
Harestone Rd ML2 .81 C2
Harfield Dr G33 .47 E6
Harfield Gdns G33 .47 E6
Harhill St G51 .44 A8
Harkins Ave G72 .77 C7
Harland Cotts G14 .28 C3
Harland St G14 .28 C3
Harlaw Gdns G64 .19 D2
Harley St G51 .44 C6
Harmetray St G22 .30 D6
Harmony Pl G51 .44 A7
Harmony Row 1 G51 .44 A8
Harmony Sq G51 .44 A7
Harmsworth St G11 .28 F2
Harper Cres ML2 .81 E4
Harport St G46 .58 E4
Harriet Pl G43 .59 B6
Harriet St G73 .61 A7
Harrington Rd G74 .75 E1
Harris Cl G77 .72 B6
Harris Pl ML6 .51 C5
Harris Quadrant ML2 .81 E5
Harris Rd G23 .17 E1

Harrison Dr G51 44 B6
Harrow Ct G15 15 F3
Harrow Pl G15 15 F3
Hart St Clydebank G81 15 D7
Glasgow G31 46 E5
Hartfell Cres DG10 161 D6
Hartfield Terr Paisley PA2 42 A2
Shotts ML7 83 B8
Harthill Ind Est ML7 55 D5
Harthill Rd
Blackridge EH48 40 D2
Fauldhouse EH47 71 D6
Harthope Pl DG10 161 C6
Hartlaw Cres G52 43 A6
Hartree Ave G13 27 E8
Hartree Entries Rd
ML12 160 B1
Hartstone Pl G53 58 B7
Hartstone Rd G53 58 B7
Hartstone Terr G53 58 B7
Hartwood Gdns
Hartwood ML7 69 A2
Newton Mearns G77 72 D2
Hartwood Rd
Hartwood ML7 68 F2
Shotts ML7 69 A3
Hartwoodhill Hospl ML7 69 C4
Harvest Dr ML1 79 D4
Harvey St G4 30 C2
Harvey Way ML4 65 C7
Harvie Ave G77 72 D6
Harvie Gdns EH48 41 F4
Harvie St G51 44 D6
Harwood Gdns G69 22 A3
Harwood St G32 46 E7
Hastie St G3 29 D1
Hastings G75 88 B7
Hatfield Dr G12 29 A5
Hathaway Dr G46 59 B2
Hathaway La G20 29 E5
Hathaway St G20 29 E5
Hathersage Ave G69 48 B5
Hathersage Dr G69 48 B5
Hathersage Gdns [2] G69 48 B5
Hatton Gdns G52 43 A4
Hatton Path G52 43 A4
Hatton Pl ML1 66 C2
Hatton Terr ML1 66 C2
Hattonhill ML1 66 C2
Hattonrigg Rd ML4 65 B6
Haugh Pl ML3 78 E1
Haugh Rd Glasgow G3 44 D8
Kilsyth G65 10 C8
Haughburn Pl G53 58 B7
Haughburn Rd G53 58 B7
Haughburn Terr G53 58 C7
Haughton Ave G65 10 E8
Haughview Rd ML1 79 B6
Havelock La G11 29 C2
Havelock Pk [9] G75 75 A1
Havelock St G11 29 C2
Haven Pk G75 87 F6
Hawbank Rd G74 75 B3
Hawbank Rdbt G74 75 B2
Hawick Cres ML9 93 A2
Hawick Dr ML5 50 D3
Hawick St Glasgow G13 27 E7
Wishaw ML2 81 C5
Hawkhead Ave PA2 42 B2
Hawkhead Hospl PA2 42 C2
Hawkhead Rd PA2 42 B3
Hawkhead Sta PA1 42 B4
Hawksland Rd ML11 120 C4
Hawksland Wlk ML3 78 E1
Hawkwood G75 88 D5
Hawkwood Rd ML6 35 F4
Hawkwood Terr
Forth ML11 124 A8
Wilsontown ML11 122 A1
Hawthorn Ave
Bearsden G61 17 A7
Bishopbriggs G64 31 B8
Kirkintilloch G66 20 C5
Wishaw ML2 82 C6
Hawthorn Ct G76 73 E6
Hawthorn Dr Airdrie ML6 51 D6
Banknock FK4 8 E2
Coatbridge ML5 50 D5
Harthill ML7 55 E6
Motherwell ML1 66 B3
Shotts ML7 70 C4
Wishaw ML2 81 C3
Hawthorn Gdns
Bellshill ML4 65 C4
Cambuslang G72 62 E4
Clarkston G76 73 E6
[11] Larkhall ML9 93 C2
Hawthorn Gr ML8 94 F6
Hawthorn Hill ML3 78 E1
Hawthorn Pl
[5] Douglas ML11 138 B1
Shotts ML7 83 A8
Hawthorn Prim Sch
(Keppoch Campus) G22 30 C3
Hawthorn Quadrant G22 30 C5
Hawthorn Rd
Clarkston G76 73 E6
Cumbernauld G67 12 F4
Strathaven ML10 112 D5
Hawthorn St
Clydebank G81 15 A4
Glasgow G22 30 D5
Hawthorn Terr
East Kilbride G75 88 B6
Uddingston G71 64 B7
Hawthorn Way ML3 91 F4
Hawthorn Wlk G72 61 D5
Hawthornden Gdns G23 17 E1
Hawthorndene ML11 114 A2
Hawthorndens ML11 114 B2
Hayburn Cres G11 29 A3
Hayburn Ct G11 29 A1
Hayburn Gate G11 29 B2
Hayburn La Glasgow G11 29 A3
Glasgow G11 29 A4
Hayburn St G11 29 B2
Hayfield Ct G5 45 D4
Hayfield St G5 45 D4
Hayhill Rd G74 87 C7
Hayle Gdns G69 21 F3
Haylynn St G14 28 E2
Haymarket St G32 46 F7
Haystack Pl G66 20 E4
Hayston Cres G22 30 B5
Hayston Rd
Cumbernauld G68 11 E4
Kirkintilloch G66 20 A8
Hayston St G22 30 B5
Hayward Ave ML8 109 C8
Hayward Ct ML8 109 C8
Haywood Rd DG10 161 E6
Haywood St G22 30 C6
Hazel Ave Bearsden G61 17 A7
Glasgow G44 59 F4
Kirkintilloch G66 20 D6
Hazel Dene G64 31 B8
Hazel Gdns ML1 79 E3
Hazel Gr Kirkintilloch G66 20 D6
Law ML8 94 F6
Shotts ML7 70 B4
Hazel Path ML1 67 B1
Hazel Pk ML3 78 E2
Hazel Rd Banknock FK4 8 E2
Cumbernauld G67 12 D3
Hazel Terr G71 64 B7
Hazel Wood ML2 81 D5
Hazelbank Motherwell ML1 66 B5
Plains ML6 36 F3
Hazelbank Braes ML11 115 D6
Hazelbank Wlk ML6 50 D8
Hazeldean Cres ML2 81 C5
Hazeldean Gdns G44 59 E4
Hazelden Pk G44 59 E4
Hazelden Rd G77 72 D1
Hazeldene La [3] ML9 93 C1
Hazelfield Gr ML6 51 E1
Hazelhead G74 76 B2
Hazellea Dr G46 59 E4
Hazelton ML1 79 D5
Hazelwood Ave G77 72 E4
Hazelwood Dr G72 77 C8
Hazelwood Gdns G73 61 C4
Hazelwood Gr G69 49 A6
Hazelwood Rd
Glasgow G41 44 C4
Strathaven ML10 112 C5
Hazlitt Gdns G20 30 A6
Hazlitt Pl G20 30 B6
Hazlitt St G20 30 B6
Headhouse Ct G75 88 D8
Headhouse Gn G75 88 E8
Headlesscross Rd EH47 70 F2
Headsmuir Ave ML8 95 D2
Heath Ave
Bishopbriggs G64 31 B8
Kirkintilloch G66 20 C4
Heath Rd ML9 93 B3
Heathcliffe Ave G72 63 C1
Heathcot Ave G15 15 E2
Heathcot Pl G15 15 E2
Heather Ave
Barrhead G78 57 A5
Bearsden G61 16 E7
Clydebank G81 15 A7
Motherwell ML1 66 A5
Heather Dr G66 20 A4
Heather Gdns G66 20 A4
Heather Gr [3] G75 88 E7
Heather Pl G66 20 A4
Heather Rd ML11 116 B6
Heather Row ML8 95 E4
Heather St ML6 38 A5
Heather Way ML1 66 A4
Heatherbank Wlk ML6 50 D7
Heatherbrae G64 18 E1
Heathery Knowe G75 88 E7
Heathery Knowe Prim Sch
G75 88 E7
Heathery Lea Ave ML5 50 D3
Heathery Rd ML2 80 F3
Heatheryknowe Rd
Coatbridge G69 48 F7
Glasgow G69 48 F7
Heathfield ML2 94 A7
Heathfield Ave G69 22 A2
Heathfield Dr ML11 114 A4
Heathfield St G33 47 C8
Heathland Terr ML11 124 A8
Heathside Rd G46 59 D3
Heathwood Dr G46 59 A3
Hecla Ave G15 15 F3
Hecla Pl G15 15 F3
Hecla Sq G15 15 F3
Hector Rd G41 59 D8
Heights Rd EH48 40 D4
Helen St
Glasgow,Drumoyne G51,
G52 43 F5
Glasgow,Govan G51 44 A7
Helen Wynd ML9 93 A2
Helena Pl G76 73 E8
Helensburgh Dr G13 28 E6
Helenslea G72 62 E4
Helenslea Pl ML4 64 F4
Helenvale Ct G31 46 D5
Helenvale St G31 46 D4
Helmsdale Ave G72 63 C3
Helmsdale Cl G72 77 D4
Helmsdale Ct G72 62 D5
Hemlock St G13 28 F7
Hemmingen Ct ML8 95 E3
Henderland Dr G61 16 E2
Henderland Rd G61 16 E1
Henderson Ave G72 62 E6
Henderson Ct ML1 79 D7
Henderson St Airdrie ML6 51 B8
Clydebank G81 27 E8
Coatbridge ML5 49 F6
Glasgow G20 29 F3
Moffat DG10 161 C5
Henrietta St G14 28 C3
Henry Bell Gn [6] G75 88 F8
Henry St G78 57 B3
Hepburn Hill ML3 91 C8
Hepburn Rd G52 43 B7
Herald Ave G13 16 D1
Herald Gr ML1 79 D4
Herald Way [2] PA4 27 C1
Herbert St G20 29 F3
Herbertson Gr G72 63 C1
Herbertson St
[4] Glasgow G5 45 B5
[2] Hamilton G72 77 E7
Herbison Ct ML9 93 B4
Hercules Way PA4 27 D1
Heriot Cres G64 19 A3
Heriot Rd G66 20 C3
Heritage Ct G77 72 E5
Heritage View ML5 49 F8
Heritage Way ML5 49 F7
Herma St G23 29 F7
Hermes Way ML4 65 F5
Hermiston Ave G32 47 C6
Hermiston Pl
Glasgow G32 47 C6
Motherwell ML1 66 A5
Hermiston Rd G32 47 B6
Hermitage Ave G13 28 C6
Hermitage Cres ML5 50 B3
Herndon Ct G77 73 A6
Heron Ct G81 15 B5
Heron Way PA4 27 C1
Herries Rd G41 44 C1
Herriet St G41 44 F3
Herriot St ML5 49 E8
Herschell St G13 28 F6
Hertford Ave G12 29 B6
Hexham Gdns G41 44 D1
Heys St G78 57 C2
Hickman St G42 45 C2
Hickman Terr G42 45 C2
Hickory Cres G71 64 C8
Hickory St G22 30 E5
Hie Dyke ML11 98 E8
High Academy Gr EH48 41 E5
High Academy St EH48 41 F5
High Avon St ML9 92 F4
High Banton Rd G65 7 D4
High Barrwood Rd G65 10 F8
High Beeches G76 74 E8
High Blantyre Prim Sch
G72 77 B7
High Blantyre Rd ML3 77 F5
High Burnside Ave ML5 49 E5
High Cleughearn Rd
G75 101 D5
High Coats ML5 50 B7
High Common Rd G74 89 B7
High Cotts G64 19 B5
High Craigends G65 10 E8
High Craighall Rd G4 30 B2
High Flender Rd G76 73 D5
High Kype Rd ML10 129 B4
High Mair PA4 27 C2
High Mdw Carluke ML8 109 C8
Carluke ML8 96 C1
High Mill Prim Sch ML8 95 F2
High Mill Rd ML8 96 A2
High Overton St ML9 107 D4
High Parks Cres ML3 91 D6
High Patrick St ML3 78 E3
High Pleasance ML9 93 A3
High Rd ML1 79 E7
High Sch of Glasgow The
G13 28 F5
High Sch of Glasgow The
(Jun Sch) G61 16 D4
High St Airdrie ML6 50 F8
Biggar ML12 160 D4
Carluke ML8 95 F2
Glasgow G1 163 B2
Lanark ML11 117 A4
Moffat DG10 161 C5
Motherwell ML1 66 F4
Renfrew PA4 27 E3
Rutherglen G73 61 A8
Shotts ML7 69 F4
High Street Sta G1 163 B2
High Whitehills Rd G75 88 E5
High Wood Gdns ML4 64 E5
Highburgh Ave ML11 117 B4
Highburgh Ct ML11 117 B4
Highburgh Dr G73 61 C5
Highburgh Rd G12 29 C2
Highcroft Ave G44 60 D5
Highcross Ave ML5 49 D4
Higherness Way ML5 49 E3
Highfield Cres ML1 80 A8
Highfield Dr
Clarkston G76 73 D7
Glasgow G12 29 B6
Rutherglen G73 61 C4
Highfield Pl
East Kilbride G74 75 F3
Highfield Pl *continued*
Glasgow G12 29 B6
Highfield Rd Larkhall ML9 93 B3
Strathaven ML10 112 C5
Highgrove Rd PA4 27 E3
Highland Ave G72 77 C8
Highland Pk G65 6 D1
Highland Pl G65 6 C2
Highstonehall Rd
Hamilton ML3 78 A1
Hamilton ML3 90 E8
Hilary Dr G69 47 F5
Hilda Cres G33 31 E4
Hill Ave G77 72 C4
Hill Cres G76 73 F6
Hill Dr G76 86 E4
Hill Pl Bellshill ML4 64 F3
Motherwell ML1 66 C2
Shotts ML7 69 E5
Hill Rd Cumbernauld G67 11 E2
Harthill ML7 55 D5
Kilsyth G65 6 D2
Netherburn ML9 106 F5
Stonehouse ML9 105 E2
Hill St Caldercruix ML6 37 F5
Chapelhall ML6 51 D2
Douglas ML11 138 B1
Glasgow G3 162 B4
Hamilton ML3 77 F3
Larkhall ML9 93 B2
Wishaw ML2 81 A3
Hill Terr ML1 66 C2
Hill View G75 88 E8
Hill's Trust Prim Sch G51 44 A8
Hillary Ave G73 61 D6
Hillbrae St [4] G51 43 D6
Hillcrest Carmunnock G76 74 D8
Chryston G69 33 D8
Lesmahagow ML11 119 F2
Hillcrest Ave
Clydebank G81 15 A7
Coatbridge ML5 50 C6
Cumbernauld G67 23 F8
Glasgow,Carmyle G32 62 B8
Glasgow,Muirend G44 59 E4
Wishaw ML2 80 E3
Hillcrest Ct G67 11 F1
Hillcrest Dr G77 73 A5
Hillcrest Rd Bearsden G61 16 F4
Glasgow G72 62 C8
Queenzieburn G65 9 E8
Uddingston G71 64 A7
Hillcrest Terr
Bothwell G71 64 B3
Carstairs Junction ML11 124 C1
Hillcrest View ML9 93 B3
Hillcroft Terr [6] G64 30 F8
Hillend Cres
Clarkston G76 73 C6
Clydebank G81 15 A7
Hillend Rd Clarkston G76 73 D6
Glasgow G22 30 A7
Rutherglen G73 61 B5
Hillfoot Ave Bearsden G61 16 F5
Rutherglen G73 61 A7
Wishaw ML2 81 D7
Hillfoot Cres ML2 81 D7
Hillfoot Dr Bearsden G61 16 F5
Coatbridge ML5 49 D6
Wishaw ML2 81 D7
Hillfoot Gdns
Uddingston G71 63 E7
Wishaw ML2 81 D7
Hillfoot Rd ML6 51 B6
Hillfoot St G31 46 A7
Hillfoot Sta G61 17 A5
Hillfoot Terr ML8 96 A1
Hillhead Ave Banknock FK4 8 E3
Carluke ML8 96 A2
Moodiesburn G69 21 F2
Motherwell ML1 66 A2
Rutherglen G73 61 B4
Hillhead Cres
Hamilton ML3 77 F3
Motherwell ML1 66 A2
Hillhead Dr Airdrie ML6 51 B6
Motherwell ML1 66 A1
Hillhead High Sch G12 29 E2
Hillhead Pl G73 61 B4
Hillhead Prim Sch
Glasgow G12 29 D3
Kirkintilloch G66 20 E8
Hillhead Rd G21 31 D7
Hillhead St G12 29 D2
Hillhead Terr ML3 77 E3
Hillhead Underground Sta
G12 29 D3
Hillhouse Bsns Ctr ML3 78 A4
Hillhouse Cres ML3 77 F3
Hillhouse Farm Gate
ML11 116 E5
Hillhouse Farm Rd
ML11 116 E4
Hillhouse Gate ML8 109 C8
Hillhouse Pk Ind Est ML3 77 F3
Hillhouse Rd
Hamilton,High Blantyre G72 77 B5
Hamilton,Hillhouse ML3 77 E4
Hillhouse St G21 31 A5
Hillhouse Terr ML3 77 F3
Hillhouseridge Rd ML7 69 D5
Hillington East Sta G52 43 B6
Hillington Gdns G52 43 C4
Hillington Ind Est
Glasgow G52 42 E8
Glasgow,North Cardonald
G52 43 A7
Hillington Park Cir G52 43 C5
Hillington Prim Sch G52 43 A6
Hillington Quadrant G52 43 A5
Hillington Rd
Glasgow G52 43 A7
Hillington G52 43 A8
Renfrew G52 27 F1
Hillington Rd S G52 43 A5
Hillington Terr G52 43 A5
Hillington West Sta G52 42 F7
Hillkirk Pl G21 30 F4
Hillkirk St G21 30 F4
Hillkirk Street La [3] G21 30 F4
Hillneuk Ave G61 17 A5
Hillneuk Dr G61 17 A5
Hillpark Dr G43 59 C6
Hillpark Sec Sch G43 59 C5
Hillrigg ML6 24 D1
Hillrigg Ave ML6 51 C8
Hills Rd ML10 112 F6
Hillsborough Rd G69 47 F5
Hillside G65 10 F4
Hillside Ave Bearsden G61 16 F5
Clarkston G76 73 D7
Hillside Cotts ML5 34 E6
Hillside Cres
Coatbridge ML5 49 F4
Hamilton ML3 78 D2
Motherwell ML1 66 D4
Hillside Ct G46 58 F3
Hillside Dr Barrhead G78 57 A3
Bearsden G61 17 A5
Bishopbriggs G64 19 A2
Blackridge EH48 40 D3
Hillside Gardens La [3]
G11 29 B3
Hillside Gdns EH46 126 D1
Hillside Gr G78 57 A2
Hillside La ML3 78 C2
Hillside Pk G81 15 B6
Hillside Pl
Blackridge EH48 40 D3
Motherwell ML1 66 D3
Hillside Quadrant G43 59 B5
Hillside Rd Barrhead G78 57 A3
Glasgow G43 59 B5
Paisley PA2 42 A1
Hillside Terr
Hamilton ML3 78 C2
Moffat DG10 161 C7
Hillswick Cres G22 30 B8
Hilltop Ave ML4 65 A7
Hilltop Rd G69 21 F2
Hillview Banton G65 7 D3
Greengairs ML6 24 F2
Hillview Ave G65 10 E7
Hillview Cotts G65 9 F4
Hillview Cres Bellshill ML4 65 A8
Glespin ML11 143 E7
Larkhall ML9 93 B2
Uddingston G71 63 E8
Hillview Dr Blantyre G72 63 D1
Clarkston G76 73 E7
Hillview Gdns G64 31 D7
Hillview Pl Clarkston G76 73 E7
Newton Mearns G77 72 D4
Hillview Rd ML11 116 A3
Hillview St Glasgow G32 46 F5
Symington ML12 141 A5
Hilton Ct Bishopbriggs G64 19 A3
[7] Hamilton ML3 78 E2
Hilton Gdns G13 28 F7
Hilton Pk G64 18 F4
Hilton Rd G64 19 A3
Hilton Terr
Bishopbriggs G64 18 F3
Cambuslang G72 61 E3
Glasgow G13 28 E7
Hiltonbank St ML3 78 B4
Hindsland Rd ML9 93 B1
Hinshaw St G20 30 A3
Hinshelwood Dr G51 44 A5
Hinshelwood Pl G51 44 B5
Hirsel Pl G71 64 B2
Hirst Gdns ML7 69 C5
Hirst Rd ML7 54 D3
Hobart Quadrant ML2 81 E3
Hobart Rd G75 88 C7
Hobart St G22 30 B4
Hobden St G21 31 A3
Hoddam Ave G45 61 A3
Hoddam Terr G45 61 A3
Hoey Dr ML2 94 C7
Hogan Dr ML10 112 E7
Hogan Way ML1 66 E1
Hogarth Ave G32 46 D7
Hogarth Cres G32 46 D7
Hogarth Dr G32 46 D7
Hogarth Gdns G32 46 D7
Hogg Rd ML6 51 D4
Hogg St ML6 51 A7
Hogganfield Ct G33 31 D2
Hogganfield St G33 31 D2
Holeburn La G43 59 C6
Holeburn Rd G43 59 C6
Holehills Dr ML6 36 B2
Holehills Pl ML6 36 B2
Holehouse Dr G13 28 A6
Holehouse Rd G76 86 F6
Holland St G2 162 B3
Hollandbush Ave FK4 8 E3
Hollandbush Cres FK4 8 F3
Hollandbush Gr ML3 91 D8
Hollandhurst Rd ML5 34 F1
Hollinwell Rd G23 17 D1
Hollowglen Rd G32 47 B6

Hollows The G46 .59 B1
Holly Dr G21 .31 A3
Holly Gr Banknock FK4 .8 F2
Bellshill ML4 .65 F5
Holly St Airdrie ML6 .51 C6
Clydebank G81 .15 B4
Hollybank Pl G72 .62 B4
Hollybank St G21 .31 A1
Hollybrook Pl 2 G42 .45 B2
Hollybrook Sch G42 .45 B2
Hollybrook St G42 .45 B2
Hollybush Rd G52 .42 F5
Hollyhill Gr G69 .49 A6
Hollymount G61 .16 F2
Holm Ave G71 .63 E7
Holm Crest ML8 .108 B2
Holm Ct ML8 .108 B2
Holm Gdns ML4 .65 C4
Holm Ind Est DG10 .161 E5
Holm La G74 .75 E1
Holm Pk DG10 .161 E5
Holm Pl ML9 .92 E2
Holm Rd ML8 .108 B2
Holm St Carluke ML8 .95 E2
Glasgow G2 .162 C2
Moffat DG10 .161 D5
Motherwell ML1 .66 A3
Strathaven ML10 .112 E6
Holm The DG10 .161 E5
Holmbank Ave G41 .59 D7
Holmbrae Ave G71 .63 F7
Holmbrae Rd G71 .63 F8
Holmbyre Ct G45 .60 B1
Holmbyre Rd G45 .60 B1
Holmbyre Terr G45 .60 C2
Holmes Ave PA4 .27 C1
Holmes Quadrant ML4 .65 B4
Holmfauld Rd G51 .28 E1
Holmfauldhead Dr G51 .43 E8
Holmfauldhead Pl 3
G51 .43 E8
Holmfield G66 .20 E7
Holmhead Cres G44 .60 A6
Holmhead Pl G44 .60 A6
Holmhead Rd G44 .60 A5
Holmhill Ave G72 .62 A4
Holmhills Dr G72 .61 F3
Holmhills Gdns G72 .61 F4
Holmhills Gr G72 .61 F4
Holmhills Pl G72 .61 F4
Holmhills Rd G72 .61 F4
Holmhills Terr G72 .61 F4
Holmlea Prim Sch G44 .60 A6
Holmlea Rd G44 .60 A7
Holms Pl G69 .33 E7
Holmswood Ave G72 .63 D1
Holmwood Ave G71 .63 F7
Holmwood Gdns G71 .63 F6
Holmwood Gn ML8 .108 A3
Holmwood Ho* G44 .60 B4
Holmwood Pk ML8 .108 A3
Holy Cross High Sch ML3 .78 E4
Holy Cross Prim Sch
Croy G65 .10 F4
Glasgow G42 .45 B2
Holy Family Prim Sch
G66 .20 B6
Holy Family RC Prim Sch
ML4 .65 C5
Holyrood Cres G20 .29 F2
Holyrood Quadrant 2
G20 .29 F2
Holyrood Sec Sch G42 .45 C1
Holyrood St ML3 .78 A5
Holytown Prim Sch ML1 .66 B5
Holytown Rd ML1 .65 E5
Holytown Sta ML1 .66 A3
Holywell St G31 .46 B5
Home Farm Rd ML7 .68 F3
Home St ML11 .117 C3
Homeblair Ho G46 .59 C5
Homeburn Ho G46 .59 C3
Homeglen Ho G46 .59 C2
Homer Pl ML4 .65 E5
Homeshaw Ho G77 .72 F4
Homeston Ave G71 .64 A3
Honeybank Cres ML8 .96 A3
Honeybog Rd G52 .42 E6
Honeycomb Pl ML9 .107 D4
Honeyman Cres ML11 .117 C4
Honeyman Ct EH48 .41 E7
Honeywell Cres ML6 .51 E1
Hood St G81 .15 D2
Hooper Pl ML4 .65 B5
Hope Cres ML9 .93 B3
Hope Rd ML11 .114 B2
Hope St Bellshill ML4 .65 C5
Carluke ML8 .96 A2
Glasgow G2 .162 C3
Hamilton ML3 .78 E3
Lanark ML11 .117 A4
Motherwell ML1 .79 E7
Wishaw ML2 .82 A4
Hopefield Ave G12 .29 C5
Hopehill Gdns G20 .30 A3
Hopehill Rd G20 .30 A3
Hopeman Ave G46 .58 E4
Hopeman Dr G46 .58 E4
Hopeman Path G46 .58 E5
Hopeman Rd G46 .58 E4
Hopeman St G46 .58 E4
Hopetoun Pl Glasgow G23 .17 E1
Leadhills ML12 .151 A2
Hopetoun Terr G21 .31 A3
Horatius St ML1 .65 B1
Hornal Rd G71 .64 A4
Hornbeam Dr G81 .15 A4
Hornbeam Rd
Cumbernauld G67 .12 E5
Uddingston G71 .64 B8
Horndean Ct G64 .19 A4
Horne St G22 .30 E5
Horner's Pl ML12 .151 A1
Hornock Cotts ML5 .49 F8
Hornock Rd ML5 .34 F1
Hornshill Dr ML1 .67 B2
Hornshill Farm Rd G33 .32 E6
Hornshill St G21 .31 A4
Horsburgh Ave G65 .6 D1
Horsburgh St G33 .32 D2
Horse Shoe La G61 .16 F4
Horse Shoe Rd G61 .16 E4
Horslet St ML5 .49 C4
Horslethill Rd G12 .29 C3
Horsley Brae ML2 .94 B4
Hospital Rd Wishaw ML2 .81 C1
Wishaw ML2 .94 B8
Hospital St ML5 .50 A4
Hospitland Dr ML11 .117 C4
Hotspur St G20 .29 E4
Houldsworth Cres ML7 .83 A8
Houldsworth Ct ML2 .81 C2
Houldsworth La 7 G3 .44 E8
Houldsworth St
Douglas Water ML11 .138 F7
Glasgow G3 .162 A3
House O' Muir Rd ML7 .54 B3
Househillmuir Cres G53 .58 C7
Househillmuir La G53 .58 C7
Househillmuir Pl G53 .58 C7
Househillmuir Prim Sch
G53 .58 A5
Househillmuir Rd G53 .58 B6
Househillwood Cres G53 .58 B7
Househillwood Rd G53 .58 B6
Housel Ave G13 .28 B7
Houston Ct PA4 .27 D4
Houston Pl G5 .162 A1
Houston St Glasgow G5 .44 F5
Hamilton ML3 .78 D1
Renfrew PA4 .27 D4
Wishaw ML2 .81 D2
Houston Terr G74 .75 D2
Howacre ML11 .116 F5
Howard Ave G74 .76 A5
Howard Ct G74 .76 A5
Howard St Glasgow G1 .163 A1
Larkhall ML9 .93 C1
Paisley PA1 .42 A4
Howat St G51 .44 A8
Howburn Cres ML7 .55 E6
Howburn Rd ML7 .55 D6
Howden Ave ML1 .66 D8
Howden Pl ML1 .66 A5
Howe Gdns G71 .64 A7
Howe Rd G65 .10 D7
Howes Brae ML12 .133 B2
Howes St ML5 .50 B4
Howes Way ML11 .131 B7
Howford Rd G52 .43 B4
Howford Sch G53 .43 A2
Howgate Ave G15 .15 F3
Howgate Rd Hamilton ML3 .91 C8
Roberton ML12 .145 F7
Howie Bldgs G76 .73 E8
Howie St ML9 .93 B1
Howieshill Ave G72 .62 B5
Howieshill Rd G72 .62 B5
Howlet Pl ML3 .78 E1
Howletnest Rd ML6 .51 D6
Howson Lea ML1 .80 B4
Howson View ML1 .79 B7
Howth Dr G13 .28 F8
Howth Terr G13 .28 F8
Hoylake Pk G71 .63 F2
Hoylake Pl G23 .17 E1
Hozier Cres G71 .63 F8
Hozier Loan 8 ML9 .93 B4
Hozier Pl 9 G71 .64 B3
Hozier St Carluke ML8 .95 F2
Coatbridge ML5 .50 A4
Hudson Terr G75 .88 C8
Hudson Way G75 .88 C8
Hugh Murray Gr G72 .62 C5
Hughenden Ct G12 .29 B4
Hughenden Dr G12 .29 B4
Hughenden Gdns G12 .29 B4
Hughenden La G12 .29 B4
Hughenden Rd G12 .29 B4
Hughenden Terr G12 .29 B4
Hugo St G20 .29 F5
Hulks Rd Greengairs ML6 .24 D4
Greengairs ML6 .25 B4
Humbie Ct G77 .72 F2
Humbie Gate G77 .72 E2
Humbie Gr G77 .72 E3
Humbie Lawns G77 .72 E2
Humbie Rd
Eaglesham G76 .86 C7
Newton Mearns G77 .72 F2
Hume Dr Bothwell G71 .64 A3
Uddingston G71 .63 E7
Hume Pl G75 .88 D8
Hume Rd G67 .12 A3
Hume St G81 .15 B1
Hunt Hill G68 .10 C1
Hunt Hill Rdbt G68 .10 C1
Hunter Dr G77 .72 B3
Hunter Gr EH47 .56 F5
Hunter High Sch G74 .76 C2
Hunter House Mus*
G74 .76 C4
Hunter Pl ML7 .69 E5
Hunter Prim Sch G74 .76 C2
Hunter Rd Hamilton ML3 .78 B6
Rutherglen G73 .46 C1
Hunter St Airdrie ML6 .36 A1
Bellshill ML4 .65 A5
East Kilbride G74 .75 F2
Glasgow G4 .163 C2
Shotts ML7 .69 D5
Hunter's Cl ML11 .117 A4
Hunter's Way ML11 .114 B2
Hunterfield Dr G72 .61 E5
Hunterhill Tutorial Ctr
PA2 .42 A3
Hunterian Mus* G12 .29 D2
Hunterlees Rd ML10 .105 B3
Hunters Cres G74 .76 C3
Hunters Ct ML12 .145 F2
Hunters Gr G74 .76 C3
Hunters Hill Ct G21 .30 F6
Hunters Pl G74 .76 C3
Huntershill Rd G64 .31 A8
Huntershill St G21 .30 E6
Huntershill Village G64 .30 F8
Huntershill Way G64 .30 F7
Hunthill La G72 .77 B6
Hunthill Pl G76 .74 A5
Hunthill Rd G72 .77 B7
Hunting Lodge Gdns
ML3 .79 A2
Huntingdon Rd G21 .30 E2
Huntingdon Sq G21 .30 E2
Huntingtower Rd
Baillieston G69 .47 F4
Glasgow G69 .48 A3
Huntly Ave Bellshill ML4 .65 A6
Glasgow G46 .59 D2
Huntly Ct G64 .31 A8
Huntly Dr Bearsden G61 .16 E7
Cambuslang G72 .62 B4
Coatbridge ML5 .49 D4
Huntly Gdns Glasgow G12 .29 D3
Hamilton G72 .77 D3
Huntly Path G69 .22 A2
Huntly Quadrant ML2 .81 B5
Huntly Rd
Glasgow,Dowanhill G12 .29 C3
Hillington G52 .27 F1
Huntly Terr Paisley PA2 .42 A1
Shotts ML7 .70 B3
Hurlawcrook Rd G75 .88 F2
Hurlet Cotts G53 .57 F6
Hurlet Rd PA2,G53 .57 D7
Hurlethill Ct G53 .57 F7
Hurlford Ave G13 .27 F7
Hurly Hawkin G64 .31 D8
Hutcheson Rd G46 .59 A2
Hutcheson St G1 .163 A2
Hutchesons' Gram Sch
Glasgow G42 .45 A2
Glasgow,Crossmyloof G41 .44 E2
Hutchinson Pl G72 .62 E3
Hutchinson St ML2 .94 D7
Hutchinson Town Ct 8
G5 .45 C4
Hutchison Ct G46 .59 B1
Hutchison Dr G61 .17 A2
Hutchison Pl ML5 .49 F6
Hutchison St ML3 .78 D1
Hutton G12 .29 A6
Hutton Dr
East Kilbride G74 .75 F4
Glasgow G51 .43 E8
Huxley Pl G20 .29 F6
Hyacinth Way ML8 .108 F8
Hydepark Bsns Ctr G21 .30 E3
Hydepark St G3 .162 A2
Hydro Ave DG10 .161 C7
Hyndal Ave G53 .43 C1
Hyndford Cres ML11 .130 D4
Hyndford Grange ML11 .130 D4
Hyndford Pl ML11 .117 A4
Hyndford Rd ML11 .117 D2
Hyndland Ave G11 .29 B2
Hyndland Ct 11 G12 .29 C3
Hyndland Prim Sch G11 .29 B2
Hyndland Rd G12 .29 B3
Hyndland Sec Sch G12 .29 B3
Hyndland St G11 .29 C2
Hyndland Sta G12 .29 A4
Hyndlee Dr G52 .43 C5
Hyndshaw Rd
Carluke ML8 .96 A3
Law ML8 .95 C8
Hyndshaw View ML8 .95 A4
Hyslop Pl G81 .15 A3
Hyslop St ML6 .50 E8

I

Iain Dr G61 .16 C6
Iain Rd G61 .16 C6
Ian Smith Ct G81 .27 D8
Ibrox Ind Est G51 .44 C6
Ibrox Prim Sch G51 .44 B5
Ibrox St G51 .44 C6
Ibrox Stad (Rangers FC)
G51 .44 B6
Ibrox Terr G51 .44 B6
Ibrox Underground Sta
G51 .44 B6
Ibroxholm Ave G51 .44 B5
Ibroxholm Oval G51 .44 B5
Ibroxholm Pl G51 .44 B5
Ida Quadrant ML4 .64 F5
Ilay Ave Bearsden G61 .28 F8
Glasgow G61 .29 A8
Ilay Ct G61 .29 A8
Ilay Rd G61 .29 A8
Imex Bsns Ctr ML5 .50 C6
Imlach Pl ML1 .79 D5
Imperial Dr ML6 .50 F6
Imperial Pl G71 .64 A2
Imperial Way G71 .64 A2
Inch Garve G74 .76 D1
Inch Keith G74 .76 D1
Inch Marnock G74 .76 D1
Inch Murrin G74 .76 D1
Inchbrae Rd G52 .43 C4
Inchcolm Gdns G69 .22 A3
Inchcolm Pl G74 .75 C2
Inchcruin Pl G15 .15 E4
Inchfad Cres G15 .15 E3
Inchfad Dr G15 .15 E3
Inchfad Pl G15 .15 E3
Inchgower Rd G33 .32 E6
Inchholm La G11 .28 E2
Inchholm St G11 .28 E2
Inchinnan Rd Bellshill ML4 .64 F7
Renfrew PA4 .27 C4
Inchkeith Pl G32 .47 B7
Inchlaggan Pl G15 .15 E4
Inchlee St G14 .28 E3
Inchmoan Pl G15 .15 E4
Inchmurrin Ave G66 .21 B8
Inchmurrin Dr G73 .61 D2
Inchmurrin Gdns G73 .61 D2
Inchmurrin Pl G73 .61 D2
Inchneuk Path ML5 .34 D6
Inchneuk Rd ML5 .34 E6
Inchnock Ave G69 .34 A6
Inchoch St G33 .32 E2
Inchrory Pl G15 .15 E4
Inchwood Ct G68 .23 A7
Inchwood Pl G68 .22 F7
Inchwood Rd G68 .22 F7
India St G2 .162 B3
Industry St G66 .20 D7
Inga St G20 .29 E7
Ingerbreck Ave G73 .61 D4
Ingleby Dr Glasgow G31 .46 B7
Rutherglen G31 .46 A7
Inglefield Ct ML6 .51 A7
Inglefield St G42 .45 B2
Ingleneuk Ave G33 .32 B5
Ingleside G66 .20 C6
Inglestone Ave G46 .59 A2
Inglewood Cres G75 .88 A8
Inglis Ct ML9 .105 F3
Inglis Pl G75 .88 F7
Inglis St Glasgow G31 .46 A6
Wishaw ML2 .80 D2
Ingram St G1 .163 A2
Inishail Rd G33 .32 C1
Inkerman Rd G52 .42 F5
Inkwood Way ML1 .66 B2
Innellan Cres ML7 .69 E6
Innellan Gdns G20 .29 B7
Innellan Pl G20 .29 B7
Inner City Trad Est G4 .163 B4
Innerleithen Dr ML2 .81 D6
Innermanse Quadrant
ML1 .66 F5
Innerwick Dr G52 .43 B5
Innes Ct Airdrie ML6 .51 E8
East Kilbride G74 .75 E4
International Ave G72 .77 D4
Inver Rd G33 .47 E7
Inveraray Gdns ML1 .66 C2
Inverary Dr
Bishopbriggs G64 .19 B4
Gartcosh G69 .33 E4
Inveravon Dr ML1 .79 C5
Invercanny Dr G15 .16 A4
Invercanny Pl G15 .16 A4
Invercargill G75 .88 A7
Invercloy Ct G75 .88 B4
Inverclyde Gdns G73 .61 E3
Invercree Wlk ML5 .34 C6
Inveresk Pl ML5 .50 A8
Inveresk Quadrant G32 .47 A6
Inveresk St G32 .47 A6
Inverewe Ave G46 .58 D2
Inverewe Dr G46 .58 D2
Inverewe Gdns G46 .58 D2
Inverewe Pl G46 .58 D3
Inverewe Way G77 .72 B5
Invergarry Ave G46 .58 D1
Invergarry Ct G46 .58 E1
Invergarry Dr G46 .58 E2
Invergarry Gdns G46 .58 D1
Invergarry Gr G46 .58 D2
Invergarry Pl G46 .58 E2
Invergarry Quad G46 .58 E2
Invergarry View G46 .58 E2
Inverglas Ave PA4 .27 F1
Invergordon Ave G43 .59 F7
Invergordon Pl ML6 .51 A6
Invergyle Dr G52 .43 C5
Invergyle La G52 .43 B5
Inverkip Dr ML7 .69 E5
Inverlair Ave G44 .59 F6
Inverleith St G32 .46 E7
Inverlochy St G33 .32 D1
Inverness St G51 .43 D6
Inveroran Dr G61 .17 B4
Invershiel Rd G23 .17 E1
Invershin Dr 6 G20 .29 D5
Inverurie St G21 .30 D3
Invervale Ave 3 ML6 .51 F6
Inzievar Terr G32 .47 B1
Iona ML6 .51 D6
Iona Ave G74 .76 A4
Iona La G69 .22 A2
Iona Path G72 .77 C7
Iona Pl ML5 .34 D1
Iona Quadrant ML2 .81 E5
Iona Rd Renfrew PA4 .27 C1
Rutherglen G73 .61 E3
Wishaw ML2 .81 F6
Iona Ridge ML3 .77 F1
Iona St Glasgow G51 .44 B7
Motherwell ML1 .65 D1
Iona Way Kirkintilloch G66 .21 B8
Stepps G33 .32 E4
Iona Wlk ML5 .49 E4
Ireland Ave EH47 .56 F6
Iris Ave G45 .61 A3
Irongray St G31 .46 C7
Irvine Cres ML5 .50 C7
Irvine Pl G65 .6 B1
Irvine St Glasgow G40 .46 B3
Glenmavis ML6 .35 F4
Irvine Terr ML3 .91 D8
Irving Ave G81 .15 B6
Irving Ct G81 .15 B6
Irving Quadrant G81 .15 B5
Isabella Gdns ML3 .79 C1
Iser La G41 .59 F8
Isla Ave ML2 .81 F6
Island Rd G67 .11 E1
Islay ML6 .51 E6
Islay Ave G73 .61 E3
Islay Ct ML3 .77 F2
Islay Dr G77 .72 B5
Islay Gdns Carluke ML8 .108 F8
Larkhall ML9 .93 B3
Islay Quadrant ML2 .80 E1
Islay Rd G66 .21 A8
Islay Way ML5 .49 D4
Isobel Mair Sch G76 .59 D1
Ivanhoe G74 .76 D4
Ivanhoe Cres ML2 .81 B3
Ivanhoe Ct ML8 .95 D1
Ivanhoe Dr G66 .20 E8
Ivanhoe Pl ML1 .66 B5
Ivanhoe Rd
Cumbernauld G67 .23 F8
Glasgow G13 .28 D8
Ivy Gr ML5 .50 B6
Ivy Pl Hamilton G72 .77 C8
Motherwell ML1 .66 A3
Ivy Rd G71 .64 C8
Ivy Terr ML1 .66 A5
Ivy Way ML6 .51 E3
Ivybank Ave G72 .62 C4

J

Jack St Hamilton ML3 .91 D8
Motherwell ML1 .80 B4
Jack's Rd G71 .64 A5
Jackson Ct ML5 .50 B6
Jackson Dr G33 .33 A5
Jackson Pl ML8 .95 E3
Jackson St
Coatbridge ML5 .50 B7
Glassford ML10 .104 F3
Jackton Bsns Ctr G75 .87 C7
Jackton Rd G75 .87 D5
Jacob's Ladder Way ML2 .94 C6
Jacobite Pl ML4 .65 D4
Jade Terr ML4 .65 A4
Jagger Gdns G69 .47 F4
Jamaica Dr G75 .75 B1
Jamaica St G1 .162 C1
James Aiton Prim Sch
G72 .62 A6
James Dempsey Ct ML5 .49 F6
James Dempsey Gdns
ML5 .49 F6
James Dunlop Gdns G64 .31 B7
James Gray St G41 .59 E8
James Hamilton Dr ML4 .65 B5
James Hamilton Heritage
Pk* G74 .75 D4
James Healy Dr ML3 .91 C7
James Morrison St G1 .163 B1
James Nisbet St G21 .30 F1
James St Armadale EH48 .41 F5
Bellshill ML4 .64 E7
Carluke ML8 .95 F1
Glasgow G40 .45 E4
Motherwell ML1 .79 D7
James View ML1 .65 F3
James Watt Ave G75 .89 A8
James Watt Pl G74 .75 B3
James Watt St G2 .162 B2
James Wilson Pl ML8 .108 B2
Jamieson Ct
Clydebank G81 .15 B7
1 Glasgow G42 .45 B2
Jamieson Dr G74 .76 A2
Jamieson Gdns
Shotts ML7 .69 E5
Uddingston G71 .63 E6
Jamieson St Glasgow G42 .45 B2
Glasgow G42 .45 C2
Jane Ct ML9 .93 A2
Jane Pl G5 .45 C4
Jane Rae Gdns G81 .27 D8
Jane's Brae G67 .23 F8
Jane's Brae Intc G67 .23 F7
Janebank Ave G72 .62 C4
Janefield Pl G72 .77 C6
Janefield St Glasgow G31 .46 B5
Glasgow G31 .46 C4
Janesmith St ML2 .80 C4
Janetta St G81 .15 A4
Jardine St G20 .29 F3
Jardine Terr G69 .33 F5
Jarvie Ave ML6 .37 B2
Jarvie Cres G65 .10 D7

Jasmine Pl G67 ....23 B6
Jasmine Way ML8 ....108 E8
Java St ML1 ....65 C1
Jean Armour Dr G81 ....15 C3
Jean MacLean Pl G64 ....19 B4
Jeanette Ave ML3 ....91 D7
Jeanfield Rd ML11 ....124 E6
Jedburgh Ave G73 ....61 B7
Jedburgh Gdns 1 G20 ....29 F3
Jedburgh Pl
Coatbridge ML5 ....49 F3
East Kilbride G74 ....75 F2
Jedburgh St Hamilton G72 ....77 D7
Wishaw ML2 ....81 C5
Jedworth Ave G15 ....16 B3
Jedworth Ct 3 G61 ....16 E5
Jedworth Rd G15 ....16 C3
Jeffrey Pl G65 ....6 C1
Jennie Lee Dr ML2 ....94 B7
Jenny Lind Ct G46 ....58 E2
Jennys Well Ct PA2 ....42 B2
Jennys Well Rd PA2 ....42 C2
Jervis Terr G75 ....88 B7
Jerviston Ct ML1 ....66 A1
Jerviston Rd Glasgow G33 ....32 C2
Motherwell ML1 ....66 A1
Jerviston St
Motherwell ML1 ....79 F8
Motherwell,New Stevenston ML1 ....66 A3
New Stevenston ML1 ....66 A4
Jerviswood ML1 ....66 A1
Jerviswood Dr ML11 ....117 F7
Jerviswood Rd ML11 ....117 A4
Jessie St G42 ....45 D1
Jessiman Sq PA4 ....27 B1
Jimmy Sneddon Way ML1 ....65 D2
Joanna Terr G72 ....77 D8
Jocelyn Sq G1 ....163 A1
John Bassy Dr FK4 ....8 D3
John Bowman Gdns ML4 ....65 B6
John Brannan Way ML4 ....64 D6
John Brown Pl G69 ....33 C8
John Burnside Dr G81 ....15 D7
John Ewing Gdns ML9 ....93 A4
John Hastie Mus* ML10 ....112 D6
John Hendry Rd G71 ....64 A4
John Hillhouse Ind Est G72 ....61 D8
John Jarvis Sq G65 ....6 D1
John Knox La ML3 ....77 D4
John Knox St
Clydebank G81 ....27 C7
Glasgow G4 ....163 C2
John Mann Gdns ML11 ....124 E1
John Marshall Dr G64 ....30 E8
John McEwan Way G64 ....19 B8
John Murray Ct ML1 ....79 E3
John Ogilvie High Sch ML3 ....77 F4
John Paul Acad G23 ....17 D1
John Pl ML9 ....106 B7
John Smith Ct ML6 ....50 F8
John Smith Gate G78 ....57 C4
John Smith Gdns ML5 ....50 D5
John Smith Way ML7 ....69 D5
John St Barrhead G78 ....57 B3
Bellshill ML4 ....65 A5
Biggar ML12 ....160 D4
Carluke ML8 ....95 F1
Glasgow G1 ....163 A2
Hamilton ML3 ....78 E3
Hamilton,Blantyre G72 ....77 E8
Larkhall ML9 ....93 B2
Wishaw ML2 ....80 C4
John Wheatley Coll G32 ....47 B5
John Wheatley Coll (Easterhouse Campus) G34 ....48 B8
John Wilson Dr G65 ....6 B1
John Wright Sports Ctr The G74 ....76 A2
John's Loan ML12 ....160 D4
Johnsburn Dr G53 ....58 B6
Johnsburn Rd G53 ....58 B6
Johnshaven St G43 ....59 C7
Johnson Dr G72 ....62 B5
Johnston Ave
Clydebank G81 ....27 D8
Kilsyth G65 ....10 D7
Johnston Rd G69 ....34 B6
Johnston St ML6 ....51 B8
Johnstone Ave G52 ....43 B7
Johnstone Dr G73 ....61 A7
Johnstone La ML8 ....96 B1
Johnstone Rd ML3 ....78 E2
Johnstone St ML4 ....65 C5
Johnstone Terr G65 ....9 F2
Jones Wynd ML1 ....66 E1
Jonquil Way ML8 ....108 F8
Joppa St G33 ....46 E8
Jordan St G14 ....28 D2
Jordanhill Cres G13 ....28 D5
Jordanhill Dr G13 ....28 D6
Jordanhill La G13 ....28 E5
Jordanhill Sch G13 ....28 E5
Jordanhill Sta G11 ....28 F4
Jordanvale Ave G14 ....28 D2
Jowitt Ave G81 ....15 D1
Jubilee Bank G66 ....20 C3
Jubilee Ct
Carstairs ML11 ....130 F8
Glasgow G52 ....42 F7
Larkhall ML9 ....93 A4
Jubilee Gdns G61 ....16 F4
Julian Ave G12 ....29 C4
Julian La G12 ....29 C4
Juniper Ave G75 ....88 D6
Juniper Ct G66 ....20 B5
Juniper Gr ML3 ....78 F2
Juniper Pl Glasgow G32 ....47 F4
Uddingston G71 ....64 D8
Juniper Rd G71 ....64 D8
Juniper Terr G32 ....47 E4
Juniper Wynd ML1 ....66 B5
Juno St ML1 ....65 D2
Jupiter St ML1 ....65 D1
Jura G74 ....89 B7
Jura Ave PA4 ....27 D1
Jura Ct G52 ....43 E5
Jura Dr Blantyre G72 ....63 C3
Kirkintilloch G66 ....21 A8
Newton Mearns G77 ....72 B6
Jura Gdns Carluke ML8 ....109 A8
Hamilton ML3 ....78 A2
Larkhall ML9 ....93 C3
Jura Quadrant ML2 ....80 E1
Jura St G52 ....43 F5
Jura Wynd ML5 ....34 C6

K

Kaim Dr G53 ....58 C6
Kairnhill Ct ML11 ....116 E4
Kames Rd ML7 ....69 E6
Kane Pl ML9 ....105 D1
Karadale Gdns ML9 ....93 A2
Katewell Ave G15 ....15 E4
Katewell Pl G15 ....15 E4
Katherine St ML6 ....51 E8
Katrine Ave
Bishopbriggs G64 ....19 B1
Uddingston ML4 ....64 D6
Katrine Cres ML6 ....35 F1
Katrine Dr G77 ....73 B4
Katrine Pl
Cambuslang G72 ....62 A6
Coatbridge ML5 ....34 D1
Katrine Rd ML7 ....69 E6
Katrine Way 5 G71 ....64 A3
Katrine Wynd ML1 ....66 A5
Katriona Path 12 ML9 ....93 C1
Kay Gdns ML1 ....79 B6
Kay St G21 ....30 F4
Kaystone Rd G15 ....16 A1
Keal Ave G15 ....28 B8
Keal Cres G15 ....28 A8
Keal Dr G15 ....28 A8
Keal Pl G15 ....28 A8
Keane Path ML1 ....80 B3
Kearn Ave G15 ....16 B1
Kearn Pl G15 ....16 B1
Keats Pk G71 ....64 B3
Keir Cres ML2 ....81 B4
Keir Dr G64 ....18 F2
Keir Hardie Ave ML1 ....66 B5
Keir Hardie Ct G64 ....19 A1
Keir Hardie Dr
Bellshill ML4 ....64 F4
13 Kilsyth G65 ....10 D8
Keir Hardie Meml Prim Sch ML1 ....66 D3
Keir Hardie Pl ML4 ....64 F4
Keir Hardie Rd ML9 ....93 C1
Keir St G41 ....44 F3
Keir's Wlk G72 ....62 A6
Keith Ave G46 ....59 D3
Keith Ct G11 ....29 C1
Keith Quadrant ML2 ....81 B5
Keith St Bellshill ML4 ....65 A6
Glasgow G11 ....29 C2
Hamilton ML3 ....78 F4
Kelbourne Cres ML4 ....64 F5
Kelbourne Sch G20 ....29 E4
Kelbourne St G20 ....29 E4
Kelburn St G78 ....57 B2
Kelburne Dr PA1 ....42 B5
Kelburne Gdns
Glasgow G69 ....48 A3
Paisley PA1 ....42 A5
Kelburne Oval PA1 ....42 A5
Kelhead Ave G52 ....42 F4
Kelhead Dr G52 ....42 F5
Kelhead Path G52 ....42 F5
Kelhead Pl G52 ....42 F5
Kellie Gr G74 ....75 D3
Kello Hospl ML12 ....160 D4
Kells Pl G15 ....15 E4
Kelly's La ML8 ....96 B1
Kelso Ave
Lesmahagow ML11 ....119 F2
Rutherglen G73 ....61 B7
Kelso Cres ML2 ....81 B6
Kelso Dr Carluke ML8 ....96 C1
East Kilbride G74 ....76 A3
Kelso Gdns G69 ....21 F3
Kelso Pl G14 ....27 E6
Kelso Quadrant ML5 ....49 F8
Kelso St G13 ....27 F7
Kelt Rd FK4 ....8 E4
Kelton St G32 ....47 B4
Kelvin Ave Glasgow G52 ....42 F8
Glasgow G52 ....43 A8
Hillington G52 ....27 F1
Kelvin Cres Bearsden G61 ....16 F2
East Kilbride G75 ....89 A7
Kelvin Ct East Kilbride G75 ....89 A7
Glasgow G12 ....29 A5
Kelvin Dr Airdrie ML6 ....36 B1
Barrhead G78 ....57 D1
Bishopbriggs G64 ....19 A2
East Kilbride G75 ....88 F7
Glasgow G20 ....29 D4
Kelvin Dr *continued*
Kirkintilloch G66 ....20 A8
Moodiesburn G69 ....21 E2
Shotts ML7 ....70 B4
Kelvin Gdns Hamilton ML3 ....77 E4
Kilsyth G65 ....10 D7
Kelvin Hall G3 ....29 C1
Kelvin Pk S G75 ....89 A4
Kelvin Pl G75 ....89 A7
Kelvin Rd Bellshill ML4 ....65 B7
Cumbernauld G67 ....24 A8
East Kilbride G75 ....89 A7
Uddingston G71 ....63 E7
Kelvin Rd N G67 ....24 A8
Kelvin Sch G3 ....29 D1
Kelvin South Bsns Pk G75 ....88 F3
Kelvin St ML5 ....50 C5
Kelvin Terr G65 ....9 F3
Kelvin View Torrance G64 ....19 C8
Twechar G65 ....9 F3
Kelvin Way
1 Bothwell G71 ....64 A3
Glasgow G3,G12 ....29 E1
Kilsyth G65 ....6 C1
Kirkintilloch G66 ....20 A8
Kelvinbridge Rdbt G64 ....19 B8
Kelvinbridge Underground Sta G4 ....29 E2
Kelvindale Gdns G20 ....29 D6
Kelvindale Pl 3 G20 ....29 D6
Kelvindale Prim Sch G12 ....29 A5
Kelvindale Rd G12,G20 ....29 C5
Kelvingrove Mus & Art Gall* G3 ....29 D1
Kelvingrove St G3 ....44 E8
Kelvinhall Underground Sta G11 ....29 C2
Kelvinhaugh Gate G3 ....44 D8
Kelvinhaugh Pl G3 ....44 D8
Kelvinhaugh Prim Sch G3 ....44 C8
Kelvinhaugh St G3 ....44 D8
Kelvinhead G65 ....7 F2
Kelvinhead Rd G65 ....7 E2
Kelvinside Acad G12 ....29 D4
Kelvinside Ave
Glasgow G20 ....29 E4
Glasgow G20 ....29 F4
Kelvinside Cres G65 ....7 E3
Kelvinside Dr G20 ....29 F4
Kelvinside Gardens La 4 G20 ....29 E4
Kelvinside Gdns G20 ....29 E4
Kelvinside Gdns E G20 ....29 F4
Kelvinside Terr S 3 G20 ....29 E3
Kelvinside Terr W 2 G20 ....29 E3
Kelvinview Ave FK4 ....8 E2
Kemp Ave PA3 ....27 A1
Kemp Ct ML3 ....78 E3
Kemp St 7 Glasgow G21 ....30 E4
Hamilton ML3 ....78 E3
Kempock St G40 ....46 C4
Kempsthorn Cres G53 ....43 B1
Kempsthorn Pl G53 ....43 B1
Kempsthorn Rd G53 ....43 A1
Kendal Ave Glasgow G12 ....29 A6
Glasgow,Giffnock G46 ....59 C3
Kendal Dr G12 ....29 A6
Kendal Rd G75 ....87 F6
Kendoon Ave G15 ....15 E3
Kenilburn Ave ML6 ....36 B2
Kenilburn Cres ML6 ....36 B2
Kenilworth G74 ....76 E4
Kenilworth Ave
Glasgow G41 ....59 D8
Wishaw ML2 ....81 B3
Kenilworth Cres
Bearsden G61 ....16 C6
Bellshill ML4 ....65 A6
Hamilton ML3 ....77 F4
Kenilworth Ct
Carluke ML8 ....95 E1
Cumbernauld G67 ....23 E8
Motherwell ML1 ....66 A5
Kenilworth Dr ML6 ....51 D8
Kenilworth Rd
Kirkintilloch G66 ....20 E8
Lanark ML11 ....117 B4
Kenmar Gdns G71 ....63 E8
Kenmar Rd ML3 ....78 B5
Kenmar Terr ML3 ....78 B5
Kenmore Gdns G61 ....17 B5
Kenmore Rd G67 ....12 B2
Kenmore St G32 ....47 A5
Kenmore Way
Carluke ML8 ....95 F3
Coatbridge ML5 ....50 C3
Kenmuir Ave G32 ....47 E3
Kenmuir Rd Glasgow G32 ....47 E2
Glasgow,Carmyle G32 ....62 D8
Kenmuir St ML5 ....49 C4
Kenmuiraid Pl ML4 ....64 F3
Kenmuirhill Gate G32 ....47 D2
Kenmuirhill Gdns G32 ....47 D2
Kenmuirhill Rd G32 ....47 D2
Kenmure Ave G64 ....18 F1
Kenmure Cres G64 ....18 F1
Kenmure Dr G64 ....18 F1
Kenmure Gdns G64 ....18 E1
Kenmure La G64 ....18 F1
Kenmure Rd G46 ....73 B6
Kenmure St G41 ....44 F3
Kenmure Way G73 ....61 B3
Kennedar Dr G51 ....43 E8
Kennedy Ave G65 ....10 A3
Kennedy Ct G46 ....59 C4
Kennedy Dr ML6 ....50 E7
Kennedy Gdns ML2 ....94 B7
Kennedy Path G4 ....163 B3
Kennedy St Glasgow G4 ....163 B3
Wishaw ML2 ....81 C3
Kennelburn Rd ML6 ....51 D2
Kenneth Rd ML1 ....79 C5
Kennihill ML6 ....36 A1
Kennihill Quadrant ML6 ....36 A1
Kennishead Ave G46 ....58 F5
Kennishead Path G46 ....58 E5
Kennishead Pl G46 ....58 E5
Kennishead Rd
Glasgow G43,G46 ....59 A6
Glasgow G53,G46,G43 ....58 D5
Kennishead Sta G46 ....58 E5
Kennisholm Ave G46 ....58 E5
Kennisholm Path G46 ....58 E5
Kennisholm Pl G46 ....58 E5
Kennoway Dr G11 ....28 F2
Kennyhill Sch G31 ....46 C8
Kennyhill Sq G31 ....46 B8
Kenshaw Ave ML9 ....106 A8
Kenshaw Pl ML9 ....106 A8
Kensington Dr G46 ....59 D1
Kensington Gate 1 G12 ....29 C4
Kensington Gate La 2 G12 ....29 C4
Kensington Rd G12 ....29 C4
Kent Dr G73 ....61 D5
Kent Pl G75 ....87 F6
Kent Rd Bellshill ML4 ....64 D6
Glasgow G3 ....162 A3
Glasgow G3 ....44 E8
Kent St G40 ....163 C1
Kentallen Rd G33 ....47 E6
Kentigern Terr G64 ....31 B8
Kentmere Cl G75 ....88 A6
Kentmere Dr G75 ....88 A6
Kentmere Pl G75 ....88 A6
Keppel Dr G44 ....60 E6
Keppoch St G21 ....30 D3
Keppochhill Dr G21 ....30 D3
Keppochhill Rd G22 ....30 D3
Kerfield La G15 ....15 E4
Kerfield Pl G15 ....15 E4
Kerr Cres ML3 ....78 C1
Kerr Dr Glasgow G40 ....45 F5
Motherwell ML1 ....79 C6
Kerr Gdns G71 ....64 A8
Kerr Grieve Ct 5 ML1 ....79 E5
Kerr Pl G40 ....45 F5
Kerr St Barrhead G78 ....57 B2
Glasgow G40 ....45 F5
Hamilton G72 ....77 E8
Kirkintilloch G66 ....20 C8
Kerrera Pl G33 ....47 D6
Kerrera Rd G33 ....47 D6
Kerry Pl G15 ....15 E3
Kerrycroy Ave G42 ....60 D8
Kerrycroy Pl G42 ....60 D8
Kerrycroy St G42 ....60 D8
Kerrydale St G40 ....46 B4
Kerrylamont Ave G42 ....60 E7
Kersewell Ave ML11 ....125 A1
Kersewell Terr ML11 ....125 A2
Kershaw St ML2 ....94 C7
Kersland La 1 G12 ....29 D3
Kersland Sch PA2 ....42 C1
Kersland St G12 ....29 D3
Kessington Dr G61 ....17 A4
Kessington Rd G61 ....17 B3
Kessington Sq G61 ....17 B3
Kessock Dr G22 ....30 B3
Kessock Pl G22 ....30 B3
Kestrel Ct G81 ....15 A5
Kestrel Rd G13 ....28 C6
Kestrel View Bellshill ML4 ....64 E8
Motherwell ML4 ....49 E1
Keswick Dr ML3 ....91 C6
Keswick Rd G75 ....87 F6
Kethers La ML1 ....79 C7
Kethers St ML1 ....79 C6
Kew Gdns G71 ....64 B7
Kew La G12 ....29 D3
Kew Terr G12 ....29 D3
Keynes Sq ML4 ....65 D4
Keystone Ave G62 ....17 B8
Keystone Quadrant G62 ....17 A8
Keystone Rd G62 ....17 B8
Kibblestane Pl ML10 ....112 C6
Kidston Pl 5 G5 ....45 C4
Kidston Terr 4 G5 ....45 C4
Kierhill Rd G68 ....11 C2
Kilbarchan St 2 G5 ....45 B5
Kilbeg Terr G46 ....58 D3
Kilberry St G21 ....31 A1
Kilbirnie Pl G5 ....45 A4
Kilbirnie St G5 ....45 A4
Kilbowie Pl ML6 ....51 D6
Kilbowie Prim Sch G81 ....15 B3
Kilbowie Rd
Clydebank G81 ....15 B3
Clydebank,Hardgate G81 ....15 B5
Cumbernauld G67 ....12 A1
Kilbowie Ret Pk G81 ....15 C2
Kilbreck Gdns G61 ....16 C8
Kilbreck La ML1 ....66 C3
Kilbrennan Dr ML1 ....79 B7
Kilbride St G5 ....45 D2
Kilbride View G71 ....64 A7
Kilburn Gr G72 ....63 D1
Kilburn Pl G13 ....28 B6
Kilchattan Dr G44 ....60 C7
Kilchoan Rd G33 ....32 C2
Kilcloy Ave G15 ....16 A4
Kildale Way G73 ....60 F8
Kildare Dr ML11 ....117 B4
Kildare Pl ML11 ....117 B4
Kildare Rd ML11 ....117 B4
Kildary Ave G44 ....60 A5
Kildary Rd G44 ....60 A5
Kildermorie Path G34 ....48 A8
Kildermorie Rd G34 ....48 A8
Kildonan Ct ML2 ....81 F7
Kildonan Dr G11 ....29 A2
Kildonan Pl ML1 ....79 C7
Kildonan St ML5 ....50 B7
Kildrostan St G41 ....44 F2
Kildrum Prim Sch G67 ....12 B2
Kildrum Rd G67 ....12 C3
Kildrum South Rdbt G67 ....12 B1
Kildrummy Dr G69 ....33 F4
Kildrummy Pl G74 ....75 D3
Kilearn Rd PA3 ....42 B7
Kilearn Sq PA3 ....42 B7
Kilearn Way PA3 ....42 B7
Kilfinan Rd ML7 ....69 D6
Kilfinan St G22 ....30 B7
Kilgarth St ML5 ....49 C4
Kilkerran Ct G77 ....72 B4
Kilkerran Dr G33 ....31 F6
Kilkerran Pk G77 ....72 B4
Kilkerran Way G77 ....72 B4
Killearn Dr PA1 ....42 F4
Killearn St
Glasgow G21,G22 ....30 D4
Glasgow G22 ....30 C4
Killermont Ave G61 ....17 A2
Killermont Ct G61 ....17 B3
Killermont Mdws G71 ....63 E2
Killermont Prim Sch G61 ....17 A4
Killermont Rd G61 ....17 A2
Killermont St G1 ....163 A3
Killermont View G20 ....17 B2
Killiegrew Rd G41 ....44 D2
Killin Ct ML5 ....50 B3
Killin St G32 ....47 B4
Killoch Dr Barrhead G78 ....57 D1
Glasgow G13 ....28 A6
Kilmailing Rd G44 ....60 B6
Kilmair Pl G20 ....29 D5
Kilmaluag Terr G46 ....58 D3
Kilmany Dr G32 ....46 F5
Kilmany Gdns G32 ....46 F5
Kilmardinny Ave G61 ....16 F6
Kilmardinny Cres G61 ....17 A6
Kilmardinny Dr G61 ....16 F6
Kilmardinny Gate G61 ....16 F5
Kilmardinny Gr G61 ....16 F6
Kilmari Gdns G15 ....15 E4
Kilmarnock Rd G43 ....59 D7
Kilmartin La ML8 ....95 F3
Kilmartin Pl Airdrie ML6 ....51 D6
Glasgow G46 ....58 E4
Motherwell G71 ....49 A1
Kilmaurs Dr G46 ....59 E3
Kilmaurs St G51 ....43 F6
Kilmeny Cres ML2 ....81 C5
Kilmichael Ave ML2 ....82 A6
Kilmore Cres G15 ....15 E4
Kilmore Gr ML5 ....49 F4
Kilmorie Dr G73 ....60 F7
Kilmory Ave G71 ....64 A7
Kilmory Ct G75 ....88 C4
Kilmory Dr G77 ....72 E6
Kilmory Gdns ML8 ....96 A3
Kilmory Rd ML8 ....109 B8
Kilmuir Cres G46 ....58 D4
Kilmuir Dr G46 ....58 E3
Kilmuir Rd Glasgow G46 ....58 E3
Uddingston G71 ....48 F1
Kilmun St G20 ....29 D7
Kilnburn Rd ML1 ....79 C7
Kilncadzow Rd ML8 ....109 E8
Kilncroft Terr 11 ML11 ....138 B1
Kilnside Rd PA1 ....42 A4
Kilnwell Quadrant ML1 ....79 D7
Kiloran Gr G77 ....72 A4
Kiloran Pl G77 ....72 A4
Kiloran St G46 ....58 F4
Kilpatrick Dr
Bearsden G61 ....16 C8
East Kilbride G75 ....88 B3
Paisley PA4 ....42 B8
Stepps G33 ....32 F5
Kilpatrick Gdns G76 ....73 C8
Kilpatrick Way 9 G71 ....64 A8
Kilrymont ML11 ....122 A1
Kilsyth Acad G65 ....6 C1
Kilsyth Gdns G75 ....88 A3
Kilsyth Prim Sch G65 ....10 D8
Kilsyth Rd Banknock FK4 ....8 D3
Queenzieburn G65,G66 ....9 E7
Kiltarie Cres ML6 ....51 F6
Kiltearn Rd G33 ....47 F7
Kiltongue Cotts ML6 ....50 D8
Kilvaxter Dr G46 ....58 E3
Kilwinning Cres
Airdrie ML6 ....36 E1
Hamilton ML3 ....77 E1
Kilwynet Way PA3 ....42 A7
Kimberley Gdns G75 ....88 C8
Kimberley St ML2 ....80 D3
Kinalty Rd G44 ....60 A5
Kinarvie Cres G53 ....57 F7
Kinarvie Gdns G53 ....57 F7
Kinarvie Pl G53 ....57 F7
Kinarvie Rd G53 ....57 F7
Kinarvie Terr G53 ....57 F7
Kinbuck St G22 ....30 D4
Kincaid Gdns G72 ....62 A6
Kincardine Dr G64 ....31 C8

Kincardine Pl
Bishopbriggs G64 31 C7
East Kilbride G74 76 C3
Kincardine Sq G33 32 D1
Kincath Ave G73 61 D3
Kinclaven Ave G15 16 B3
Kinclaven Gdns [2] G15 16 B3
Kinclaven Pl [1] G15 16 B3
Kincraig St G51 43 D6
Kinellan Rd G61 16 F1
Kinellar Dr G14 28 A6
Kinfauns Dr
Clydebank G15 16 B3
Newton Mearns G77 72 F5
King Ct ML1 79 D7
King Edward La [1] G13 28 F5
King Edward Rd G13 28 F5
King George Ct PA4 27 E1
King George Gdns PA4 27 E2
King George Park Ave PA4 27 E2
King George Pl PA4 27 E1
King George Way PA4 27 E1
King Pl G69 49 A5
King St Armadale EH48 41 F6
Carstairs Junction ML11 131 B7
Clydebank G81 27 D8
Coatbridge ML5 49 E6
Glasgow G1 163 A1
Hamilton ML3 78 A4
[4] Kilsyth G65 10 D8
Larkhall ML9 93 A3
Newmains ML2 81 B2
Rutherglen G73 61 A8
Shotts ML7 69 E4
Stonehouse ML9 105 E2
Wishaw ML2 81 F5
Wishaw,Newmains ML2 82 A6
King Street La
[3] Kilsyth G65 10 D8
[5] Rutherglen G73 61 A8
King's Cres
Cambuslang G72 62 B5
Carluke ML8 96 A2
King's Dr Cumbernauld G68 11 F6
Glasgow G40 45 E4
Newton Mearns G77 73 A3
King's Gdns G77 73 A3
King's Inch Rd PA4,G51 27 F4
King's Park Ave G44 60 D6
King's Park Prim Sch G44 60 D6
King's Park Rd G44 60 B7
King's Park Sec Sch G44 60 C5
King's Park Sta G44 60 C6
King's Pl G22 30 B6
King's View G68 11 F6
King's Well Gdns ML10 103 C5
Kingarth La G42 45 A2
Kingarth St Glasgow G42 45 A2
Hamilton ML3 91 D8
Kingfisher Dr G13 27 F7
Kingfisher Gdns G13 28 A7
Kinghorn Dr G44 60 C7
Kinghorn La G44 60 C7
Kinglas Rd G61 16 C2
Kings Ave G72 62 B5
Kings Cres G72 62 B5
Kings Dr ML1 65 F3
Kings Inch Dr G51 28 B2
Kings Inch Pl G51 28 A2
Kings Inn Gdns ML11 124 F7
Kings Myre ML11 117 C4
Kings View G73 60 F7
Kings' Inn Terr ML11 124 F7
Kingsacre Rd G44 60 D7
Kingsbarns Dr G44 60 B7
Kingsborough Gate [1] G12 29 B3
Kingsborough Gdns G12 29 B4
Kingsborough La G12 29 B3
Kingsborough La E G12 29 B3
Kingsbrae Ave G44 60 C7
Kingsbridge Cres G44 60 D6
Kingsbridge Dr G44 60 E6
Kingsbridge Park Gdns G44 60 D6
Kingsburgh Dr PA1 42 B6
Kingsburn Dr G73 61 A6
Kingsburn Gr G73 61 A6
Kingscliffe Ave G44 60 D6
Kingscourt Ave G44 60 D6
Kingsdale Ave G44 60 C7
Kingsdyke Ave G44 60 D7
Kingsford Ave G44 59 E4
Kingsford Ct G77 72 C6
Kingsgate Ret Pk G74 76 A6
Kingsheath Ave G73 60 F6
Kingshill Ave G68 10 E1
Kingshill Dr G44 60 C6
Kingshill Rd ML7 83 A8
Kingshill View Forth ML11 98 F8
Law ML8 95 A4
Kingshouse Ave G44 60 C6
Kingshurst Ave G44 60 C6
Kingsknowe Dr G73 60 E6
Kingsland Cres G52 43 B6
Kingsland Dr G52 43 C6
Kingsland La G52 43 C6
Kingsley Ave G42 45 B1
Kingsley Ct G71 64 A7
Kingslynn Dr G44 60 D6
Kingsmuir Dr
Cumbernauld G68 10 F2
Rutherglen G73 60 E6
Kingston Ave
[1] Airdrie ML6 51 C7
Uddingston G71 64 A8
Kingston Flats G65 6 D1
Kingston Ind Est G5 44 F5
Kingston Rd G65 6 D1
Kingston St G5 162 C1
Kingsway East Kilbride G74 76 A3
Glasgow G14 28 B5
Kilsyth G65 6 D1
Kirkintilloch G66 9 B2
Kingsway Ct G14 28 A5
Kingswood Dr G44 60 C7
Kingussie Dr G44 60 C6
Kiniver Dr G15 16 B1
Kinkell Gdns G66 9 B1
Kinloch Ave G72 62 B4
Kinloch Dr ML1 65 D2
Kinloch Rd
Newton Mearns G77 72 D6
Renfrew PA4 27 B1
Kinloch St G40 46 C4
Kinloss Pl G74 75 F2
Kinmount Ave G44 60 B7
Kinmount La G44 60 C7
Kinnaird Ave G77 73 A5
Kinnaird Cres G61 17 B4
Kinnaird Pl G64 31 B7
Kinnear Rd G40 46 B4
Kinneil Ho ML3 78 E5
Kinneil Pl ML3 77 F2
Kinnell Ave G52 43 D3
Kinnell Cres G52 43 C3
Kinnell Path G52 43 C3
Kinnell Pl G52 43 D3
Kinnell Sq G52 43 C3
Kinning Park Ind Est G5 44 F5
Kinning Park Underground Sta G41 44 D5
Kinning St G5 45 A5
Kinnoul Gdns G61 16 D8
Kinnoull Pl G72 77 D7
Kinpurnie Rd PA1 42 D5
Kinross Ave G52 43 B4
Kinross Pk G74 76 D3
Kinsail Dr G52 42 F6
Kinstone Ave G14 28 A5
Kintail Gdns G66 9 B1
Kintessack Pl G64 19 D2
Kintillo Dr G13 28 B5
Kintore Pk ML3 91 B7
Kintore Rd G43 59 F6
Kintore Twr G72 61 E3
Kintra St G51 44 B7
Kintyre Cres
Coatbridge ML5 49 E4
Newton Mearns G77 72 C6
Plains ML6 37 A3
Kintyre Dr ML5 49 E4
Kintyre Gdns G66 9 B1
Kintyre Rd G72 77 C8
Kintyre St G21 31 A1
Kintyre Wynd ML8 95 F3
Kipland Wlk ML5 50 D5
Kippen Dr G76 74 B5
Kippen St Airdrie ML6 50 E7
Glasgow G22 30 D6
Kippford Pl ML6 51 F1
Kippford St G32 47 C4
Kipps Ave ML6 50 E8
Kippsbyre Ct ML6 50 D7
Kircurrin ML11 124 A8
Kirk Bauk ML12 140 F6
Kirk Ct ML9 105 F2
Kirk Gn Forth ML11 124 A8
Muirkirk KA18 142 A6
Kirk La [2] Bearsden G61 16 E5
Glasgow G43 59 C7
Kirk Mews G72 62 A5
Kirk O'shotts Prim Sch ML7 53 D3
Kirk Path ML7 83 A8
Kirk Pl Bearsden G61 16 E5
Cumbernauld G67 23 A7
Symington ML12 140 F6
Uddingston G71 63 E5
Kirk Rd Bearsden G61 16 E5
Carluke ML8 95 E2
Carmunnock G76 74 D7
Dalserf ML9 94 B2
Motherwell ML1 66 D7
Shotts ML7 69 F4
Wishaw ML2 81 C3
Kirk St Carluke ML8 95 E2
Coatbridge ML5 49 F6
Motherwell ML1 79 E7
Stonehouse ML9 105 F2
Strathaven ML10 112 E5
Kirk Wynd G76 86 E4
Kirkaig Ave PA4 27 F2
Kirkandrews Pl ML6 51 F2
Kirkbean Ave G73 61 B4
Kirkburn Ave G72 62 A4
Kirkcaldy Rd G41 44 D2
Kirkconnel Ave
Cumbernauld G68 10 F1
Glasgow G13 27 F6
Kirkconnel Dr G73 60 F5
Kirkcudbright Pl G74 76 D3
Kirkdale Dr G52 43 E4
Kirkdene Ave G77 73 B5
Kirkdene Bank G77 73 B5
Kirkdene Cres G77 73 B5
Kirkdene Gr G77 73 B4
Kirkdene Pl G77 73 B5
Kirkfield Rd Bothwell G71 64 A3
Kirkfieldbank ML11 116 D3
Kirkfieldbank Brae ML11 116 E4
Kirkfieldbank Prim Sch ML11 116 D4
Kirkfieldbank Rd ML11 130 A1
Kirkfieldbank Way ML3 78 A3
Kirkford Rd G69 21 E2
Kirkgate Douglas ML11 138 B2
Wishaw ML2 81 F4
Kirkhall Rd ML1 66 D4
Kirkhill Ave G72 62 A3
Kirkhill Ct EH47 71 E6
Kirkhill Dr G20 29 D5
Kirkhill Gate G77 73 B4
Kirkhill Gdns G72 62 A3
Kirkhill Gr G72 62 A3
Kirkhill Pl [7] Glasgow G20 29 D5
Wishaw ML2 80 C2
Kirkhill Prim Sch G77 73 B6
Kirkhill Rd Gartcosh G69 33 F5
Newton Mearns G77 73 B5
Strathaven ML10 112 C5
Uddingston G71 63 E8
Wishaw ML2 80 C1
Kirkhill St ML2 80 D1
Kirkhill Sta G72 62 A5
Kirkhill Terr G72 62 A3
Kirkhope Dr G15 16 B1
Kirkinner Rd G32 47 D3
Kirkintilloch High Sch G66 21 A7
Kirkintilloch Rd
Bishopbriggs G64 19 C5
Kirkintilloch,Waterside G66 21 C8
Lenzie G66 20 C5
Kirkland Park Ave ML10 112 D6
Kirkland Pk ML10 112 C6
Kirkland St Glasgow G20 29 F3
Motherwell ML1 79 D7
Kirklandneuk Cres PA4 27 A4
Kirklandneuk Prim Sch PA4 27 B3
Kirklandneuk Rd PA4 27 B4
Kirklandpark Prim Sch ML10 112 D6
Kirklands PA4 27 B3
Kirklands Cres
Bothwell G71 64 A3
Kilsyth G65 10 D7
Kirklands Dr G77 72 D2
Kirklands Hospl G71 64 B3
Kirklands Pl G77 72 D2
Kirklands Rd
Lanark ML11 117 B3
Newton Mearns G77 72 D2
Kirkle Dr G77 73 B5
Kirklee Cir G12 29 D4
Kirklee Gardens La G12 29 D4
Kirklee Gate G12 29 D5
Kirklee Gdns G12 29 C5
Kirklee Pl G12 29 D4
Kirklee Quadrant [1] G12 29 D4
Kirklee Quadrant La G12 29 D4
Kirklee Rd Glasgow G12 29 D4
Motherwell ML1,ML4 65 E3
Kirklee Terr G12 29 C4
Kirklee Terrace La G12 29 D4
Kirklee Terrace Rd [21] G12 29 C4
Kirkliston St G32 46 F6
Kirkmichael Ave [3] G11 29 A3
Kirkmichael Gdns [2] G11 29 A3
Kirkmuir Dr G73 61 B3
Kirkness St ML6 51 A8
Kirknethan ML2 80 C1
Kirknewton St G32 47 B6
Kirkoswald G74 76 D3
Kirkoswald Dr G81 15 C3
Kirkoswald Rd
Glasgow G43 59 D6
Motherwell ML1 66 E4
Kirkpatrick St G40 46 A5
Kirkriggs Ave G73 61 B5
Kirkriggs Gdns G73 61 B5
Kirkriggs Prim Sch G45 61 A5
Kirkriggs View G73 61 B5
Kirkriggs Way G73 61 B5
Kirkshaws Ave ML5 49 F3
Kirkshaws Pl ML5 49 F3
Kirkshaws Prim Sch ML5 49 E4
Kirkshaws Rd ML5 49 E3
Kirkstall Gdns G64 19 B4
Kirkstone G77 73 B5
Kirkstone Cl G75 87 F6
Kirkstyle ML12 160 D4
Kirkstyle Ave ML8 95 E1
Kirkstyle Cotts ML5 49 D3
Kirkstyle Cres ML6 35 F2
Kirkstyle Pl
Glassford ML10 104 F3
Glenmavis ML6 35 D4
Kirksyde Ave G66 20 E7
Kirkton Ave Barrhead G78 57 B1
Carluke ML8 95 E1
Glasgow G13 28 A6
Hamilton G72 77 D5
Kirkton Cres
Coatbridge ML5 50 D4
Glasgow G13 28 A6
Kirkton Ct Carluke ML8 95 E1
Eaglesham G76 86 F4
Kirkton Dr G76 86 E5
Kirkton Gate G74 75 E2
Kirkton Moor Rd G76 86 B4
Kirkton Pk G74 75 F2
Kirkton Pl Coatbridge ML5 50 D4
Kirkton Pl *continued*
East Kilbride G74 75 F2
East Kilbride G74 76 A2
Hamilton G72 77 D6
Kirkton Prim Sch ML8 95 E1
Kirkton Rd G72 62 B5
Kirkton St ML8 95 F1
Kirktonholme Cres G74 75 C1
Kirktonholme Prim Sch G74 75 D2
Kirktonholme Rd G74 75 D1
Kirktonside G78 57 B1
Kirkvale Cres G77 73 B5
Kirkvale Ct
Newton Mearns G77 73 B5
Wishaw ML2 81 B3
Kirkvale Dr G77 73 B5
Kirkview G67 23 A6
Kirkview Ave ML7 53 C2
Kirkview Cres G77 72 E3
Kirkview Ct G67 23 A6
Kirkview Gdns G71 63 F8
Kirkville Pl G15 16 B1
Kirkwall G67 12 A5
Kirkwall Ave G72 63 C3
Kirkwell Rd G44 60 B5
Kirkwood Ave
Clydebank G81 15 E1
Stepps G33 33 A5
Kirkwood Pl ML5 49 E5
Kirkwood Quadrant G81 15 D1
Kirkwood Rd G71 63 F8
Kirkwood St
Coatbridge ML5 49 E5
Glasgow G51 44 C5
Rutherglen G73 61 A8
Kirkwood Sta ML5 49 D5
Kirn St G20 29 C8
Kirriemuir G74 76 D5
Kirriemuir Ave G52 43 C4
Kirriemuir Gdns G64 19 C2
Kirriemuir Pl G52 43 C4
Kirriemuir Rd G64 19 C1
Kirtle Dr PA4 27 E2
Kirtle Pl G75 87 E7
Kirtonholme Cres G74 75 D2
Kishorn Pl G33 32 C1
Kitchener St ML2 81 A3
Kittoch Pl [5] G74 75 F2
Kittoch Sch G75 88 D8
Kittoch St G74 75 F2
Kittochside Rd G76 74 F6
Klondike Ct ML1 66 B3
Knapdale St G22 30 A7
Knights Gate G71 63 E5
Knightsbridge St G13 28 D7
Knightscliffe Ave G13 28 E7
Knightswood Ct G13 28 D6
Knightswood Prim Sch G13 28 E7
Knightswood Rd
Glasgow G13 28 D7
Glasgow G13 28 D8
Knightswood Sec Sch G13 28 D6
Knightswood Sec Sch (Annexe) G13 28 D7
Knightswood Terr G72 63 E1
Knivysbridge Pl ML4 64 F3
Knock St ML12 160 C4
Knock Way PA3 42 A7
Knockburn Prim Sch G21 31 C7
Knockburnie Rd G71 64 A4
Knockhall St G33 32 D1
Knockhill Dr G44 60 B7
Knockhill Rd PA4 27 B1
Knocklea ML12 160 C4
Knocklea Pl ML12 160 C4
Knockside ML12 160 C4
Knoll Croft Rd ML7 70 A3
Knollpark Dr G76 73 D6
Knowe Cres ML1 66 D4
Knowe Rd Chryston G69 33 C8
Paisley PA3 42 B7
Knowehead Dr G71 63 E6
Knowehead Gdns
[5] Glasgow G41 44 E3
Uddingston G71 63 E6
Knowehead Rd ML2 81 C2
Knowehead Terr [4] G41 44 E3
Knoweknack Terr ML11 114 B3
Knowenoble St ML1 67 B2
Knowes Ave G77 72 E5
Knowes Rd G77 72 F5
Knowes View G81 15 C7
Knowetap St G20 29 E7
Knowetop Ave ML1 79 F4
Knowetop Prim Sch ML1 79 F4
Knox Pl G77 72 B4
Knox St ML6 51 B8
Kronborg Way G75 88 E5
Kyle Ct G72 62 A6
Kyle Dr G46 59 E3
Kyle Gr ML1 66 A3
Kyle Pl ML5 49 F5
Kyle Quadrant
Motherwell ML1 66 C3
Wishaw ML2 80 E1
Kyle Rd G67 12 B3
Kyle Sq G73 60 F5
Kyle St Glasgow G4 163 A4
Motherwell ML1 79 B7
Kyleaken Dr G72 63 B2
Kyleakin Rd G46 58 D3
Kyleakin Terr G46 58 D3
Kylemore Cres ML1 65 D2
Kylepark Ave G71 63 D6
Kylepark Cres G71 63 D7
Kylepark Dr G71 63 D7
Kylerhea Rd G46 58 D3
Kype View ML10 112 E5
Kypeside Pl ML10 129 B6

L

La Belle Allee [3] G3 29 E1
La Belle Pl [2] G3 29 E1
La Crosse Terr G12 29 E3
Laberge Gdns ML1 66 B3
Laburnum Ave
Cambuslang G72 62 F3
East Kilbride G75 88 C6
Laburnum Cres ML2 81 B5
Laburnum Ct G75 88 C6
Laburnum Gdns G66 20 B5
Laburnum Gr
Coatbridge ML5 50 B6
Kirkintilloch G66 20 B5
Laburnum Lea ML3 78 E2
Laburnum Rd Banknock FK4 8 E2
Cumbernauld G67 12 D2
Glasgow G41 44 C4
Uddingston G71 64 D8
Lacy St PA1 42 A4
Ladder Ct G75 88 B4
Lade Terr G52 43 A4
Ladeside Cl G77 72 C6
Ladeside Dr G65 6 E1
Ladhope Pl G13 27 E8
Lady Ann Cres ML6 51 C6
Lady Anne St G14 27 F6
Lady Home Hospl ML11 138 C1
Lady Isle Cres G71 63 E6
Lady Jane Gate G71 63 E4
Lady Mary Wlk ML3 78 E1
Lady Watson Gdns ML3 78 A2
Lady Well ML11 116 B6
Lady Wilson St ML6 51 B7
Ladyacre Rd ML11 117 B3
Ladybank G68 11 F6
Ladybank Ct G74 75 E2
Ladybank Dr G52 43 E4
Ladybank Gdns G74 75 F2
Ladybank Pl [2] G74 75 F2
Ladyburn St PA1 42 A4
Ladyhill Dr G69 48 A4
Ladykirk Cres
Glasgow G52 43 B6
Paisley PA2 42 A2
Ladykirk Dr G52 43 C6
Ladykirk Way G74 75 F4
Ladyknowe [10] DG10 161 D5
Ladyknowe Ct [9] DG10 161 D5
Ladyloan Ave G15 15 F4
Ladyloan Ct G15 15 E4
Ladyloan Gdns G15 15 F4
Ladyloan Gr G15 15 F4
Ladyloan Pl G15 15 E4
Ladymuir Cres G53 43 C2
Ladysmith Dr G75 88 A4
Ladysmith St ML2 80 D4
Ladywell Prim Sch ML1 79 D7
Ladywell Rd ML1 79 C7
Ladywell St G4 163 C2
Lagan Rd ML8 96 A1
Laggan Ave ML7 70 B3
Laggan Path ML7 69 E6
Laggan Quadrant ML6 35 F1
Laggan Rd Airdrie ML6 35 F1
Bishopbriggs G64 19 B1
Glasgow G43 59 E5
Newton Mearns G77 72 D7
Laggan Terr PA4 27 B4
Laggan Way ML2 81 F7
Laidlaw Ave ML1 65 F3
Laidlaw Gdns G71 48 F1
Laidlaw St Glasgow G5 162 B1
Glasgow G5 45 A5
Laidon Rd ML6 35 F1
Laidon Wlk [3] ML2 81 F6
Laigh Rd G77 73 C5
Laighlands Rd G71 64 B2
Laighmuir St G71 63 F5
Laighstonehall Rd ML3 78 B2
Laightoun Ct G67 23 A6
Laightoun Dr G67 23 A6
Laightoun Gdns G67 23 A6
Lainshaw Dr G45 60 B2
Laird Gr G71 64 A8
Laird Pl G40 45 F4
Laird St ML5 50 B7
Laird's Hill Ct G65 10 B8
Laird's Hill Pl G65 10 A8
Lairds Gate G71 63 D5
Lairds Hill G67 11 E2
Lairdsland Prim Sch G66 20 C8
Lairg Dr G72 63 C2
Lairhills Rd G75 88 F7
Lairs The ML11 114 A5
Lake Ave ML11 117 D2
Lamb St Glasgow G22 30 B6
Hamilton ML3 78 E3
Lamberton Dr G52 43 C5
Lambhill Quadrant [2] G41 44 E5
Lambhill St G41 44 D5
Lambie Cres G77 72 C5
Lamerton Rd G67 12 C2
Lamington Prim Sch ML12 140 D1
Lamington Rd G52 43 B5
Lamlash Cres G33 47 B8
Lamlash Pl
East Kilbride G75 88 B4

Lamlash Pl *continued*
Glasgow G33 47 B8
Motherwell ML1 79 C7
Lamlash Prim Sch G33 47 B8
Lamlash Sq G33 47 C8
Lammer Wynd 7 ML9 93 C1
Lammerknowes Rd G65 7 E3
Lammermoor G74 76 E4
Lammermoor Ave G52 43 C4
Lammermoor Cres G66 20 F8
Lammermoor Dr G67 23 E7
Lammermoor Gdns G66 20 F8
Lammermoor Prim Sch ML2 81 A5
Lammermoor Rd G66 20 F8
Lammermoor Terr ML2 81 B3
Lammermuir Gdns G61 16 C7
Lammermuir Pl ML1 66 A5
Lammermuir Way ML6 51 E1
Lammermuir Wynd ML9 92 F5
Lamont Rd G21 31 B6
Lampits Rd ML11 131 C8
Lanark Ave ML6 51 A4
Lanark Gram Sch ML11 117 A3
Lanark Ind Est ML11 117 E5
Lanark Moor Ctry Pk* ML11 117 E3
Lanark Mus* ML11 116 F4
Lanark Prim Sch ML11 117 B5
Lanark Rd Ashgill ML9 94 A3
Braidwood ML8,ML11 108 F6
Carluke ML8 95 F1
Crossford ML8 108 A2
Hazelbank ML11 115 D6
Kirkfieldbank ML11 116 A4
Kirkmuirhill ML11 114 D4
Lanark ML11 116 D6
Larkhall ML2,ML9 93 D6
Netherburn ML8 107 D7
Ravenstruther ML11 130 E8
Lanark St G1 163 B1
Lanark Sta ML11 117 B4
Lancaster Ave ML1 66 E8
Lancaster Cres G12 29 C4
Lancaster Crescent La G12 29 C4
Lancaster Rd
Auchenheath ML11 114 D4
Bishopbriggs G64 19 B4
Lancaster Terr 11 G12 29 C4
Lancaster Terrace La 10 G12 29 C4
Lancaster Way 4 PA4 27 C1
Lancefield Quay G3 44 E7
Lancefield St G3 162 A2
Landemer Dr G73 61 A6
Landressy Pl G40 45 F4
Landressy St G40 45 F4
Landsdowne Gdns ML3 78 F3
Landsdowne Rd ML9 93 C2
Lane The G68 11 D6
Lanfine Rd PA1 42 C4
Lang Ave PA4 27 D1
Lang Ct ML10 104 F3
Lang St PA1 42 A4
Langa St G20 29 F7
Langbank Holdings G62 17 E8
Langbank St 1 G5 45 B5
Langbar Cres G33 47 E7
Langbar Gdns G33 47 F7
Langbyres Rd ML1 67 D1
Langcroft Dr G72 62 C4
Langcroft Pl G51 43 C7
Langcroft Rd G51 43 D7
Langcroft Terr G51 43 D7
Langdale East Kilbride G74 75 C3
Newton Mearns G77 73 B5
Langdale Ave G33 31 E3
Langdale Rd G69 21 F2
Langdale St G33 31 E3
Langdales Ave G68 11 D2
Langdykeside ML11 119 E4
Langfaulds Cres G81 15 D6
Langfaulds Prim Sch G15 15 F4
Langford Dr G53 58 B3
Langford Pl G53 58 B3
Langhaul Ct G53 42 F1
Langhaul Pl G53 42 F1
Langhaul Rd G53 42 F1
Langhill Dr G68 11 D3
Langholm G75 87 F6
Langholm Cres ML2 81 B6
Langholm Ct G69 22 A2
Langholm Path 1 G72 77 C7
Langlands Ave
East Kilbride G75 88 F4
Glasgow G51 43 D7
Langlands Ct
East Kilbride G75 88 F4
Glasgow G51 43 F8
Langlands Dr
East Kilbride G75 88 F4
Glasgow G51 43 C8
Langlands Gate G75 88 F3
Langlands Moss Nature Reserve* G75 88 F3
Langlands Pl G75 88 F4
Langlands Rd
East Kilbride G75 88 E3
Glasgow G51 43 E8
Glasgow G51 44 A8
Langlands Sch G51 43 E7
Langlands Sq G75 88 F3
Langlands-Seafar Intc G67 23 E8
Langlea Ave G72 61 D4
Langlea Ct G72 61 E4
Langlea Dr G72 61 E5
Langlea Gdns G72 61 E5
Langlea Gr G72 61 E4
Langlea Rd G72,G73 61 E4
Langlea Way G72 61 E5
Langlees Ave G77 73 B5
Langlees Rd ML12 160 B4
Langley Ave G13 28 B8
Langloan Cres ML5 49 E6
Langloan Pl ML5 49 E6
Langloan Prim Sch ML5 49 E6
Langloan St ML5 49 E6
Langlook Pl G53 57 F8
Langlook Rd G53 42 F1
Langmuir Rd
Coatbridge G69 49 A5
Kirkintilloch G66 9 B1
Langmuir Way G69 49 A5
Langmuirhead Rd G66 20 D1
Langness Rd G33 47 B8
Langoreth Ave ML3 77 F2
Langrig Rd Glasgow G21 31 A4
Newton Mearns G77 72 D3
Langs Gr G20 29 E7
Langshaw Cres ML8 95 F2
Langshot St 4 G51 44 D5
Langside Ave
Glasgow G41 59 F8
Uddingston G71 64 C6
Langside Coll G42 60 A7
Langside Coll (Annexe) G45 60 E3
Langside Coll Annexe G73 61 B6
Langside Ct G71 64 B1
Langside Dr
Blackridge EH48 40 B3
Glasgow G43 59 E5
Langside Gdns G42 60 A7
Langside La G42 45 A1
Langside Pl G41 59 F8
Langside Prim Sch G41 59 E8
Langside Rd Bothwell G71 64 B1
Glasgow,Crosshill G42 60 A8
Glasgow,Govanhill G42 45 A2
Langside St G81 15 E6
Langside Sta G43 59 E6
Langstile Pl G52 42 F5
Langstile Rd G52 42 F5
Langton Cres
Barrhead G78 57 D1
Glasgow G53 43 C1
Langton Gate G77 72 C5
Langton Gdns G69 47 F4
Langton Pl G77 72 C5
Langton Rd G53 43 C1
Langtree Ave G46 59 A1
Langvout Ct ML12 160 E4
Langvout Gate ML12 160 E4
Langvout Sq ML12 160 E4
Langwhang Ct ML11 124 E1
Lanrig Pl G69 33 C8
Lanrig Rd G69 33 C8
Lanrigg Ave EH47 71 E7
Lanrigg Ct EH47 71 F7
Lanrigg Rd EH47 71 E7
Lanrigg View ML9 129 F8
Lansbury Terr ML9 93 C1
Lansdowne Cres
Glasgow G20 29 F2
Shotts ML7 70 B3
Lansdowne Crescent La G20 29 F2
Lansdowne Dr G68 11 F4
Lantana Gr ML1 79 D8
Lanton Dr G52 43 B5
Lanton Rd G43 59 E5
Lappin St G81 27 D8
Larbert St G4 162 C4
Larch Ave
Bishopbriggs G64 31 B8
Kirkintilloch G66 20 C6
Larch Cl G72 62 E3
Larch Cres G66 20 C6
Larch Ct Cumbernauld G67 12 E4
East Kilbride G75 88 B5
Hamilton G72 77 C8
Larch Dr Banknock FK4 8 E2
East Kilbride G75 88 B5
Larch Gr Cumbernauld G67 12 E4
Hamilton ML3 78 F2
Motherwell ML1 66 A5
Larch Pl Cambuslang G72 62 E3
Cumbernauld G67 12 D4
East Kilbride G75 88 B5
Uddingston G71 64 D8
Larch Rd Cumbernauld G67 12 E4
Glasgow G41 44 B4
Larch Sq G72 62 E3
Larch Way ML3 91 F4
Larches The G69 22 A4
Larchfield Ave
Glasgow G14 28 B4
Newton Mearns G77 72 E5
Wishaw ML2 81 D6
Larchfield Cres ML2 81 C6
Larchfield Ct G77 72 D4
Larchfield Dr G73 61 C4
Larchfield Gdns ML2 81 D6
Larchfield Gr ML2 81 D7
Larchfield Path ML7 70 B2
Larchfield Pl Glasgow G14 28 B4
Wishaw ML2 81 D6
Larchfield Rd G61 16 F1
Larchgrove Ave G32 47 C6
Larchgrove Pl G32 47 C7
Larchgrove Rd G32 47 C7
Largie Rd G43 59 F5
Largo La G72 77 D3
Largo Pl G51 43 E7
Lark Way ML4 64 F8
Larkfield Ct G72 77 C6
Larkfield Dr G72 77 D6
Larkfield Rd G66 20 E6
Larkfield St 2 G42 45 B3
Larkhall Acad ML9 92 F1
Larkhall Rd ML10 104 F3
Larkhill Ind Est ML9 106 B8
Larkin Way ML4 64 F7
Larksfield Dr ML8 109 A8
Larkspur Dr G74 75 C4
Larkspur Way ML8 108 F8
Larnark Rd ML9 94 A3
Lashley Gr ML2 94 C7
Lasswade St G14 27 E6
Latherton Dr 5 G20 29 D5
Latimer Gdns G52 43 A4
Latimer Path 8 G52 43 A4
Lauchlin Pl G66 21 B7
Lauchope Rd ML6 66 D7
Lauchope St ML6 51 E2
Lauder Cres ML2 81 B6
Lauder Dr G73 61 D6
Lauder Gdns Blantyre G72 63 C2
Coatbridge ML5 50 D3
Lauder Gn G74 76 B4
Lauder La ML3 77 E3
Lauder St 4 G5 45 A4
Lauderdale Dr G77 72 C3
Lauderdale Gdns G12 29 B3
Lauderdale La G12 29 B3
Laughland Dr ML1 66 D3
Laundry La G33 32 C5
Lauranne Pl ML4 64 E5
Laurel Ave G66 20 D6
Laurel Bank ML3 91 C8
Laurel Ct Cambuslang G72 62 E4
East Kilbride G75 88 D5
Laurel Dr East Kilbride G75 88 D5
Larkhall ML9 93 D2
Wishaw ML2 80 E3
Laurel Gait G72 62 E3
Laurel Gdns
Chapelhall ML6 51 E2
Uddingston G71 63 F8
Laurel Gr ML6 24 F2
Laurel La Cambuslang G72 62 E3
5 Larkhall ML9 93 C1
Laurel Park Cl G13 28 C5
Laurel Park Gdns G13 28 C5
Laurel Pl East Kilbride G75 88 D5
Glasgow G11 29 A2
Laurel Sq FK4 8 E2
Laurel St G11 29 A2
Laurel Way G78 57 B3
Laurel Wlk G73 61 C3
Laurel Wynd G72 62 F3
Laurelbank ML5 50 A8
Laurelbank Rd
Glasgow G32 62 C8
Muirhead G69 33 B7
Laurels The
6 Motherwell ML1 66 B2
Newton Mearns G77 72 D5
Lauren View ML6 50 F7
Laurence Ct G15 15 E3
Laurence Dr
Bearsden G61 16 D6
Clydebank G15 15 E3
Laurence Gdns G15 15 E3
Laurenstone Terr G74 76 B3
Laurie Ct G71 64 A7
Laurieston Cres ML6 51 D1
Laurieston Rd G5 45 C5
Laurieston Way G73 61 A4
Lauriestone Pl ML5 50 D3
Lauriston Gr G77 72 B5
Lavelle Dr ML5 50 C7
Lavender Dr G75 88 D5
Lavender La ML8 108 E8
Laverock Ave ML3 79 A2
Laverock Rd ML6 36 B3
Laverock Terr G69 21 F1
Laverockhall ML11 117 B5
Laverockhall St G21 30 F3
Law Dr ML1 66 C4
Law Pl G74 75 F5
Law Prim Sch ML8 95 A5
Law Rdbt G74 75 E4
Law St G40 46 B5
Law View ML2 94 C6
Lawers Dr G61 16 C7
Lawers La ML1 66 C3
Lawers Rd Glasgow G43 59 B5
Renfrew PA4 27 C1
Lawfield Ave G77 73 B5
Lawhill Ave G45 60 D4
Lawhill Rd ML8 95 B3
Lawhope Mill Rd ML6 51 F3
Lawmoor Ave G5 45 C2
Lawmoor Pl G5 45 C2
Lawmoor Rd G5 45 C3
Lawmoor St G5 45 C3
Lawmuir Cres G81 15 E7
Lawmuir Pl ML4 65 A2
Lawmuir Prim Sch ML4 65 A3
Lawmuir Rd Bellshill ML4 65 A3
Law ML8 94 F6
Lawrence Ave G46 59 D1
Lawrence St G11 29 C2
Lawrie Pl ML1 66 E1
Lawrie St Glasgow G11 29 B2
Stonehouse ML9 105 E3
Wishaw ML2 81 F5
Lawrie Way 11 ML9 93 C1
Lawson Ave ML1 79 E3
Laxford Ave G44 60 A4
Laxford Pl ML5 50 D5
Laxford Way ML1 66 C4
Laxton Dr G66 20 E4
Le Froy Gdns G75 88 C8
Le Froy La G75 88 C8
Lea Rig ML11 119 F7
Leadburn Rd G21 31 C4
Leadburn St G32,G33 46 E7
Leader St G33 31 D1
Leadhills & Wanlockhead Rly* ML12 151 A1
Leadhills Prim Sch ML12 151 A2
Leadhills Rd
Abington ML12 145 E1
Elvanfoot ML12 152 A4
Leadhills Sta* ML12 151 A1
Leaend Rd ML6 35 E1
Leafield Rd ML12 160 E5
Leander Cres Bellshill ML4 65 E5
Renfrew PA4 27 E2
Learigg Rd ML6 37 B3
Leathem Pl ML2 80 C1
Leckethill Ave G68 22 F7
Leckethill Ct G68 22 F7
Leckethill Pl G68 22 F7
Leckethill View G68 22 F7
Leckie Ct ML3 78 C4
Leckie Dr ML3 78 C4
Leckie St G41 59 C8
Ledaig Pl G31 46 C7
Ledaig St G31 46 C7
Ledard Rd G42 59 F7
Ledcameroch Cres G61 16 E4
Ledcameroch Pk G61 16 D4
Ledcameroch Rd G61 16 E4
Ledgowan Pl G20 29 D8
Ledi Dr G61 16 B7
Ledi Path ML1 66 C3
Ledi Rd G43 59 C5
Ledmore Dr G15 15 F4
Lednock Rd Glasgow G52 43 A5
Stepps G33 32 C5
Ledvinka Cres ML3 78 A6
Lee Ave G33 31 E1
Lee Cres G64 31 A8
Lee Meadow Rd ML8 109 A4
Lee Pk ML11 124 E1
Lee Pl ML4 65 D4
Lee's Ct ML5 50 A5
Leebank Dr G44 59 F2
Leechford ML11 117 B5
Leechlee Rd ML3 78 E3
Leefield Dr G44 59 F2
Leehill Rd G21 30 E7
Leemuir View ML8 109 B8
Leesburn Pl G74 75 F4
Leeside Rd G21 30 E7
Leesland G71 64 A8
Leeward Circ G75 75 A1
Leewood Dr G44 60 A2
Lefroy St ML5 49 E7
Legbrannock Ave ML1 66 D7
Legbrannock Cres ML1 66 D4
Legbrannock Rd ML1 66 E5
Leggatson Dr G53 58 C3
Legion Pl ML9 93 A3
Leglen Wood Cres G33 31 D6
Leglen Wood Dr G21 31 D5
Leglen Wood Rd G21 31 D6
Leicester Ave G12 29 B5
Leighton St Glasgow G20 29 F6
Wishaw ML2 81 B2
Leishman Ct EH48 40 D2
Leith Ave ML9 105 F2
Leith St G33 46 D8
Leithland Ave 2 G53 43 B1
Leithland Prim Sch G53 43 B1
Leithland Rd G53 43 B1
Lembert Dr G76 73 D8
Lendal Pl G75 87 E6
Lendale La G64 19 A4
Lendalfoot Gdns ML3 77 D2
Lendel Pl G51 44 D5
Lenihall Dr G45 60 E2
Lenihall Terr G45 60 E2
Lennox Ave
Coatbridge ML5 49 E7
Glasgow G14 28 D3
Lennox Cres G64 30 F8
Lennox Dr Bearsden G61 16 F6
Clydebank G81 15 C7
Newton Mearns G77 72 E2
Lennox Gdns G14 28 D4
Lennox La E G14 28 D3
Lennox La W Glasgow G14 28 C3
Glasgow G14 28 D4
Lennox Rd G67 11 F2
Lennox St Glasgow G20 29 C7
Wishaw ML2 81 E4
Lennox Terr PA3 42 A8
Lentran St G34 48 D7
Leny St G20 29 F4
Lenzie Acad G66 20 C6
Lenzie Moss Prim Sch G66 20 B5
Lenzie Pl G21 30 F6
Lenzie Prim Sch G66 20 C5
Lenzie Rd Kirkintilloch G66 20 D7
Stepps G33 32 D6
Lenzie St G21 30 F5
Lenzie Sta G66 20 C4
Lenzie Terr G21 30 F5
Lenzie Way G21 30 E6
Lenziemill Rd
Cumbernauld,Greenfaulds G67 23 F7
Lenziemill Rd *continued*
Cumbernauld,Lenziemill G67 24 B8
Leonard Gr ML1 66 E1
Lesley Quadrant ML4 64 F2
Leslie Ave G77 72 E7
Leslie Rd G41 44 E3
Leslie St Glasgow G41 44 F3
Motherwell ML1 79 F7
Lesmahagow High Sch ML11 119 E5
Lesmahagow Ind Est ML11 119 F1
Lesmahagow Priory* ML11 119 E4
Lesmahagow Rd
Kirkfieldbank ML11 116 A4
Lesmahagow ML11 118 E8
Strathaven ML10 112 F5
Lesmuir Dr G14 28 A5
Lesmuir Pl G14 27 F5
Letham Ct G43 59 E5
Letham Dr
Bishopbriggs G64 31 D8
Glasgow G43 59 E5
Letham Grange G68 11 F4
Letham Oval G64 31 D8
Lethame Gdns ML10 112 D6
Lethame Rd ML10 112 D6
Lethamhill Cres G33 31 F1
Lethamhill Pl G33 31 E1
Lethamhill Rd G33 31 F1
Lethbridge Pl 4 G75 88 C8
Letherby Dr G44 60 B7
Letheron Dr ML2 81 B5
Lethington Ave G41 59 E8
Lethington Pl G41 59 F8
Lethington Rd G46 73 A7
Letterfearn Rd G23 17 E1
Letterickhills Cres G72 62 E3
Leven Ave G64 19 B1
Leven Ct G78 57 B5
Leven Dr Bearsden G61 16 F3
Hamilton ML3 91 B8
Leven Path ML1 66 A5
Leven Pl ML7 69 E6
Leven Quadrant ML6 35 F2
Leven Rd ML5 34 D1
Leven Sq PA4 27 B4
Leven St Glasgow G41 44 F3
Motherwell ML1 79 E4
Leven Terr ML1 66 C2
Leven View G81 15 B3
Leven Way
6 Cumbernauld G67 11 F1
East Kilbride G75 87 F6
Levenseat Ind Est EH47 71 F4
Levern Bridge Ct G53 57 F7
Levern Bridge Gr G53 57 F6
Levern Bridge Pl G53 57 F6
Levern Bridge Rd G53 57 F6
Levern Bridge Way G53 57 F6
Levern Cres G78 57 B1
Levern Gdns G78 57 B3
Levern Rd G53 57 E6
Leverndale Ct G53 42 F1
Leverndale Hospl G53 42 F2
Leverndale Rd G53 42 F1
Leverside Ave
Barrhead G78 57 A2
Glasgow G53 58 C8
Leverside Cres G53 58 C8
Leverside Rd G53 58 C8
Lewis Ave Renfrew PA4 27 D1
Wishaw ML2 81 E5
Lewis Gdns G61 16 B6
Lewis Pl Airdrie ML6 51 D6
Newton Mearns G77 72 B6
Lewiston Dr 5 G23 17 D1
Lewiston Pl 6 G23 17 D1
Lewiston Rd G23 17 D1
Leyden Ct G20 29 E5
Leyden Gdns G20 29 F5
Leyden St G20 29 E5
Leyland Ave ML3 91 A8
Leyland Wynd ML3 91 A7
Leys Pk ML3 78 A4
Leys The G64 19 A1
Libberton Prim Sch ML11 131 F4
Libberton Way ML3 78 A3
Liberton St G33 46 E8
Liberty Ave G69 49 A5
Liberty Path 7 G72 77 D7
Liberty Rd Bellshill ML4 65 A3
Caldercruix ML6 38 A5
Libo Ave G53 43 D1
Library Gdns G72 61 F6
Library La G46 58 F3
Library Rd ML2 81 B3
Lickprivick Rd G75 88 B6
Liddel Rd G67 11 E1
Liddell Gr G75 88 D7
Liddell St G32 47 C1
Liddells Ct G64 31 A7
Liddesdale Pass G22 30 C7
Liddesdale Pl G22 30 E7
Liddesdale Rd G22 30 C7
Liddesdale Sq G22 30 E7
Liddesdale Terr G22 30 E7
Liddoch Way G73 60 F8
Liff Gdns G64 31 D8
Liff Pl G34 33 C1
Lightburn Hospl G32 47 B7
Lightburn Pl G32 47 B7
Lightburn Rd G72 62 E3

Lighthouse The* G1 ....162 C2
Lilac Ave G67 ....12 F5
Lilac Cres G71 ....64 C8
Lilac Ct G67 ....12 F5
Lilac Gdns G64 ....31 B8
Lilac Hill Cumbernauld G67 .12 F5
Hamilton ML3 ....78 F2
Lilac Pl G67 ....12 F5
Lilac Way ML1 ....66 B5
Lilac Wynd G72 ....62 F4
Lillyburn Pl G15 ....15 E5
Lily St G40 ....46 B3
Lilybank Ave Airdrie ML6 ..36 B2
Cambuslang G72 ....62 C4
Muirhead G69 ....33 C7
Lilybank Gardens La G12 .29 D2
Lilybank Gdns G12 ....29 D2
Lilybank La G12 ....29 D2
Lilybank St ML3 ....78 C4
Lilybank Terr G12 ....29 D2
Lilybank Terrace La G12 ..29 D2
Lime Cres Airdrie ML6 ....51 C7
Cumbernauld G67 ....12 E3
Lime Gr Blantyre G72 ....63 D1
Kirkintilloch G66 ....20 D5
Motherwell ML1 ....79 E4
Lime La 4 G14 ....28 D3
Lime Loan ML1 ....66 B4
Lime St G14 ....28 D3
Lime Wlk ML11 ....130 F8
Limegrove St ML4 ....65 A7
Limekilnburn Rd ML3 ....91 D3
Limekilns Rd G67 ....23 F5
Limekilns St G81 ....15 D7
Limelands Quadrant ML6 .37 F4
Limes The G44 ....60 B4
Limeside Ave G73 ....61 C7
Limeside Gdns G73 ....61 C7
Limetree Ave G71 ....64 C8
Limetree Cres G77 ....72 D4
Limetree Ct ML3 ....78 A5
Limetree Dr G81 ....15 A4
Limetree Quadrant G71 ..64 C7
Limewood Pl G69 ....49 A6
Limpetlaw ML11 ....117 B5
Linacre Dr G32 ....47 C5
Linacre Gdns G32 ....47 D5
Linburn Pl G52 ....43 A6
Linburn Rd G52 ....42 F7
Linburn Sch G52 ....42 F6
Lincluden Path 3 G41 ..44 F4
Lincoln Ave Glasgow G13 .28 C6
Uddingston G71 ....48 F1
Lincoln Ct 4 ML5 ....50 A8
Lincuan Ave G46 ....73 C8
Lindams G71 ....63 F5
Linden Ave ML2 ....81 C6
Linden Ct G81 ....15 A6
Linden Dr Banknock FK4 ....8 E2
Clydebank G81 ....15 A6
Linden Lea ML3 ....78 B4
Linden Pl G13 ....28 F7
Linden St G13 ....28 F7
Linden Way G13 ....28 F7
Linden Wlk ML10 ....112 C5
Lindens The G71 ....64 A1
Lindores Ave G73 ....61 C7
Lindores Dr G74 ....75 C1
Lindores Pl G74 ....75 C1
Lindores St G42 ....60 B8
Lindrick Dr 4 G23 ....17 E1
Lindsay Dr G12 ....29 B6
Lindsay Gr G74 ....75 F2
Lindsay Loan ML11 ....117 C5
Lindsay Pl
East Kilbride G74 ....76 A1
Glasgow G12 ....29 B6
Kirkintilloch G66 ....20 D3
Lindsay Rd G74 ....75 F1
Lindsay Sq ML12 ....152 B7
Lindsaybeg Ct G69 ....33 C8
Lindsaybeg Rd
Chryston G66 ....21 B2
Lenzie G66 ....20 E4
Lindsayfield Ave G75 ....88 C4
Lindsayfield Rd G75 ....88 B4
Lindsaylands Ind Est
ML12 ....160 C4
Lindsaylands Rd ML12 .160 B3
Lindsey Rd ML11 ....114 B3
Lindum Cres ML1 ....79 B8
Lindum St ML1 ....79 B8
Linfern Rd G12 ....29 C3
Linghope Pl ML2 ....93 E7
Lingley Ave ML6 ....51 A6
Linhead Dr G53 ....58 C6
Linhope Pl G75 ....87 E7
Links Rd Glasgow G44 ....60 C4
Glasgow,Mount Vernon G32 .47 D3
Links The G68 ....12 B6
Links View ML9 ....93 C2
Linksview Rd ML1 ....66 B1
Linkwood Ave G15 ....15 F3
Linkwood Cres G15 ....16 A3
Linkwood Dr G15 ....16 A3
Linkwood Gdns G15 ....16 B3
Linkwood Gr 4 G15 ....16 B3
Linkwood Pl G15 ....15 F3
Linlithgow Gdns G32 ....47 D5
Linn Cres ML11 ....116 A4
Linn Dr G44 ....59 F3
Linn Gdns G68 ....11 A2
Linn Park Ind Est G45 ...60 B2
Linn Park Nature Trail*
G44 ....59 F3
Linn Valley View G45 ....60 D3
Linnet Pl G13 ....27 F7
Linnet Rd ML4 ....65 B4
Linnet Way ML4 ....64 F8
Linnhe Ave
Bishopbriggs G64 ....19 B1
Glasgow G44 ....60 A4
Hamilton ML3 ....78 A1
Linnhe Cres ML2 ....81 B1
Linnhe Ct ML9 ....92 F5
Linnhe Dr G78 ....57 B5
Linnhe Pl G72 ....63 C2
Linnhead Dr G53 ....58 C5
Linnhead Pl G14 ....28 A8
Linnpark Ave G44 ....59 F2
Linnpark Ct Glasgow G44 ..59 D2
Netherlee G44 ....59 F2
Linnvale Prim Sch G81 ...15 D1
Linnvale Way G68 ....11 C6
Linrigg Rd ML1 ....67 D7
Linside Ave PA1 ....42 B4
Lint Butts 8 G72 ....77 C7
Lintfield Loan G71 ....64 A5
Linthaugh Gdns ML9 ....105 E1
Linthaugh Rd G53 ....43 A3
Linthaugh Terr G53 ....43 D1
Linthill ML11 ....117 B6
Linthouse Bldgs 1 G51 ..43 E8
Linthouse Rd G51 ....28 E1
Lintie Rd ML1 ....66 C4
Lintlaw G72 ....63 D2
Lintlaw Dr G52 ....43 B6
Linton Pl ML5 ....49 E3
Linton St G33 ....46 E8
Linwood Ave
Clarkston G76 ....73 F7
East Kilbride G74 ....75 A2
Linwood Ct G44 ....60 A5
Linwood Terr ML3 ....78 B4
Lismore G74 ....89 C8
Lismore Ave
Motherwell ML1 ....79 B8
Renfrew PA4 ....27 D1
Lismore Dr ML5 ....49 E4
Lismore Hill ML3 ....77 D3
Lismore Pl Airdrie ML6 ....51 C5
Moodiesburn G69 ....22 A3
Newton Mearns G77 ....72 B6
Lismore Rd G12 ....29 B5
Lister Gdns G76 ....74 A5
Lister Hts G4 ....163 C2
Lister Pl G52 ....43 A7
Lister Rd G52 ....43 A7
Lister St G4 ....163 B4
Lister Twr G75 ....88 F8
Lister Wlk ML4 ....65 C7
Lithgow Ave G66 ....20 E7
Lithgow Cres PA2 ....42 A2
Lithgow Dr ML1 ....67 B1
Lithgow Pl G74 ....75 B2
Little Dovehill G1 ....163 B1
Little John Gdns ML2 ....81 F4
Little St G3 ....162 A2
Littlehill Prim Sch G33 ...31 D3
Littlehill St G21 ....31 A4
Littlemill Ave G68 ....10 E1
Littlemill Cres G53 ....58 A8
Littlemill Dr G53 ....58 A8
Littlemill Gdns 10 G53 ....58 A8
Littlemill Way ML1 ....66 B1
Littleton Dr 8 G23 ....17 D1
Littleton St G23 ....17 D1
Lively Pl 4 G72 ....77 C7
Livingston Dr ML6 ....37 A3
Livingstone Ave G52 ....43 A8
Livingstone Bvd G72 ....77 D4
Livingstone Cres
Blantyre G72 ....63 D1
East Kilbride G75 ....88 D7
Livingstone Dr G75 ....88 E7
Livingstone Gdns ML9 ....93 B3
Livingstone La
3 Bothwell G71 ....64 A3
Cambuslang G72 ....62 A3
Livingstone Pk G65 ....6 C2
Livingstone Pl ML6 ....51 B7
Livingstone Quadrant
ML7 ....55 D4
Livingstone St
Clydebank G81 ....15 D1
Hamilton ML3 ....77 F4
Lloyd Ave G32 ....47 A2
Lloyd Dr ML1 ....66 A1
Lloyd St Glasgow G31 ....46 A8
Motherwell ML1 ....66 A1
Rutherglen G73 ....46 B1
Lloyds St ML5 ....50 A4
Llynallan Rd ML7 ....54 F4
Loan Lea Cres ML9 ....93 B1
Loan Pl ML7 ....55 E6
Loanbank Pl G51 ....44 A7
Loanbank Quadrant G51 .44 A7
Loancroft Ave G69 ....48 C4
Loancroft Gate G71 ....63 E5
Loancroft Gdns G71 ....63 F5
Loancroft Pl G69 ....48 B3
Loanend Cotts G72 ....62 F1
Loanfoot Ave G13 ....28 B7
Loanfoot Gdns ML8 ....108 F4
Loanfoot Rd G72 ....77 D5
Loanhead Ave
Motherwell ML1 ....66 D3
Renfrew PA4 ....27 D3
Loanhead Cres ML1 ....66 D3
Loanhead Rd ML1 ....66 C3
Loanhead St
Coatbridge ML5 ....49 E3
Glasgow G32 ....46 F7
Loaning 1 ML9 ....93 C2
Loaning The
4 Bearsden G61 ....16 E5
Crawfordjohn ML12 ....144 F2
20 Douglas ML11 ....138 B1
Kirkintilloch G66 ....20 C7
Motherwell ML1 ....79 C7
Rutherglen G46 ....73 A7
Lobnitz Ave PA4 ....27 D3
Loch Achray Gdns G32 ...47 C4
Loch Achray St G32 ....47 C4
Loch Assynt G74 ....89 B8
Loch Ave ML8 ....108 F4
Loch Awe G74 ....89 A8
Loch Awe Pl ML5 ....49 F6
Loch Brora Cres ML5 ....49 E6
Loch Goil G74 ....76 A1
Loch Laidon St G32 ....47 D4
Loch Laxford G74 ....89 B8
Loch Long G74 ....89 A8
Loch Loyal G74 ....89 B8
Loch Maree G74 ....89 B8
Loch Meadie G74 ....89 B8
Loch Naver G74 ....89 B8
Loch Park Ave ML8 ....108 F8
Loch Pk ML2 ....81 C3
Loch Prim Sch G73 ....61 D4
Loch Rd
Carstairs Junction ML11 ...124 B2
Chapelhall ML6 ....51 D2
Kirkintilloch G66 ....20 E7
Stepps G33 ....32 D4
Loch Shin G74 ....89 B8
Loch St ML6 ....51 B2
Loch Striven G74 ....76 A1
Loch Torridon G74 ....89 B8
Loch View Calderbank ML6 .51 B2
Caldercruix ML6 ....38 A5
Loch Voil St G32 ....47 D4
Lochaber Cres ML7 ....70 B3
Lochaber Dr G73 ....61 D4
Lochaber Path 8 G72 ....77 D7
Lochaber Pl G74 ....75 F3
Lochaber Rd
Bearsden G61 ....17 B2
Strathaven ML10 ....112 C5
Lochaline Dr G44 ....60 A4
Lochalsh Pl Airdrie ML6 ...51 C5
Blantyre G72 ....63 B2
Lochanbank Dr ML11 ....114 B3
Lochar Cres G53 ....43 D2
Lochar Pl G75 ....87 E7
Lochay St G32 ....47 C4
Lochbrae Dr G73 ....61 D4
Lochbridge Rd G34 ....48 A7
Lochbroom Ct G77 ....72 F6
Lochbroom Dr G77 ....72 F6
Lochbuie La ML6 ....35 E4
Lochburn Cres G20 ....29 E7
Lochburn Gr G20 ....29 E7
Lochburn Pas G20 ....29 E7
Lochburn Rd G20 ....29 E7
Lochdochart Path G34 ...48 D7
Lochdochart Rd G34 ....48 D8
Lochearn Cres ML6 ....35 F2
Lochearnhead Rd G33 ...32 C5
Lochend Ave G69 ....33 E7
Lochend Com High Sch
G34 ....48 C8
Lochend Cres G61 ....16 D3
Lochend Dr G61 ....16 E3
Lochend Rd Bearsden G61 .16 E3
Gartcosh G69 ....33 F6
Glasgow G69 ....33 D1
Gartcosh G69 ....33 F5
Lochend St ML1 ....79 F6
Locher Pl ML5 ....50 D3
Locher Wlk ML5 ....50 C3
Lochfauld Rd G23 ....18 B2
Lochfield Dr PA2 ....42 A1
Lochfield Rd PA2 ....42 A1
Lochgarry Way ML5 ....49 E4
Lochgilp St G20 ....29 C7
Lochgoin Ave G15 ....15 F4
Lochgoin Gdns G15 ....15 E4
Lochgoin Prim Sch G15 ..15 F4
Lochgreen Pl
Coatbridge ML5 ....34 C2
Hamilton ML3 ....91 B8
Lochgreen St G33 ....31 D3
Lochiel Ct ML6 ....50 D7
Lochiel La G73 ....61 D4
Lochiel Rd G46 ....58 F4
Lochinch Pl G77 ....72 A5
Lochinvar Rd G67 ....23 E7
Lochinver Cres G72 ....77 C3
Lochinver Dr G44 ....60 A5
Lochinver Gr G72 ....62 B5
Lochknowe St ML8 ....108 F5
Lochlea East Kilbride G74 ..76 D4
Kirkmuirhill ML11 ....114 A4
Lochlea Ave G81 ....15 C3
Lochlea Dr ML11 ....114 B2
Lochlea Rd Clarkston G76 ..73 E5
Cumbernauld G67 ....12 C3
Glasgow G43 ....59 D6
Rutherglen G73 ....60 F5
Lochlea Way ML1 ....66 E4
Lochlee Loan 4 ML9 ....93 C2
Lochleven La G42 ....60 A7
Lochleven Rd G42 ....60 A7
Lochlibo Ave G13 ....27 F7
Lochlibo Cres G78 ....57 A1
Lochlibo Rd G78 ....57 A1
Lochlibo Terr G78 ....57 A1
Lochmaben Rd
Gartcosh G69 ....33 F4
Glasgow G52 ....42 F4
Lochmaddy Ave G44 ....60 A4
Lochmill Holdings G66 ....9 A5
Lochnagar Dr G61 ....16 B7
Lochnagar Way 20 ML9 ...93 C1
Lochore Ave PA3 ....42 A7
Lochpark Pl ML9 ....93 A1
Lochranza Ct 2 ML1 ....66 B2
Lochranza Dr G75 ....88 B4
Lochranza La G75 ....88 C4
Lochside Bearsden G61 ....16 F3
Gartcosh G69 ....33 F6
Lochside St 2 G41 ....44 E1
Lochview Cres G33 ....31 F3
Lochview Dr G33 ....31 F4
Lochview Gdns G33 ....31 F3
Lochview Pl G33 ....31 F3
Lochview Quadrant ML4 ..64 F3
Lochview Rd
Bearsden G61 ....16 E3
Coatbridge ML5 ....34 C1
Lochview Terr G69 ....33 F5
Lochwood Loan G69 ....22 A3
Lochwood St G33 ....31 E2
Lochy Ave PA4 ....27 F1
Lochy Gdns G64 ....19 B1
Lochy St ML2 ....81 A1
Locke Gr ML1 ....66 F1
Lockerbie Ave G43 ....59 F6
Locket Yett View ML4 ....64 E5
Lockhart Ave G72 ....62 D6
Lockhart Ct G77 ....72 D2
Lockhart Dr
Cambuslang G72 ....62 D6
Lanark ML11 ....116 E5
Newton Mearns G77 ....72 D2
Lockhart Hospl ML11 ...117 C3
Lockhart Pl
Carnwath ML11 ....124 E1
Stonehouse ML9 ....105 F3
Wishaw ML2 ....81 E4
Lockhart St Carluke ML8 ...95 F2
Glasgow G21 ....31 B2
Hamilton ML3 ....91 C6
Stonehouse ML9 ....106 A3
Lockhart Terr G74 ....76 B2
Locks St ML5 ....50 D6
Locksley Ave
Cumbernauld G67 ....23 E7
Glasgow G13 ....28 C8
Locksley Cres G67 ....23 E6
Locksley Ct G67 ....23 E6
Locksley Pl G67 ....23 E6
Locksley Rd G67 ....23 E6
Lodge Pk ML12 ....160 C3
Lodge Twr ML1 ....80 B3
Logan Ave G77 ....72 C6
Logan Dr G68 ....11 D3
Logan Gdns ML1 ....81 B8
Logan St Glasgow G5 ....45 D3
Hamilton G72 ....77 E7
Logan Twr G72 ....62 E4
Logandale Ave ML2 ....81 F6
Loganlea Dr ML1 ....66 A1
Logans Prim Sch ML1 ....79 B7
Logans Rd ML1 ....79 C8
Loganswell Dr G46 ....58 E2
Loganswell Gdns G46 ....58 E2
Loganswell Pl G46 ....58 E2
Loganswell Rd G46 ....58 E2
Logie Pk G74 ....76 A3
Logie Sq G74 ....76 A3
Lomax St G33 ....46 D8
Lomond G75 ....88 E5
Lomond Ave PA4 ....27 B1
Lomond Cres G67 ....23 C7
Lomond Ct Barrhead G78 ..57 C2
Coatbridge ML5 ....50 D7
Cumbernauld G67 ....23 C7
Lomond Dr Airdrie ML6 ....35 F2
Barrhead G78 ....57 B4
Bishopbriggs G64 ....19 A3
Bothwell G71 ....64 B3
Cumbernauld G67 ....23 B7
Newton Mearns G77 ....72 D7
Wishaw ML2 ....81 B1
Lomond Gr G67 ....23 C7
Lomond Pl Coatbridge ML5 .34 E1
Cumbernauld G67 ....23 B7
Stepps G33 ....32 E4
Lomond Rd Bearsden G61 ..16 F2
Coatbridge ML5 ....34 D2
Kirkintilloch G66 ....20 D5
Shotts ML7 ....69 E6
Uddingston G71 ....48 F1
Lomond St G22 ....30 B5
Lomond View
Cambuslang G72 ....62 A1
Cumbernauld G67 ....23 C7
Hamilton ML3 ....77 F2
Lomond Way ML1 ....66 A5
Lomond Wlk
7 Larkhall ML9 ....93 B4
Motherwell ML1 ....66 C4
Lomondside Ave G76 ....73 C7
London Dr G32 ....47 E2
London Rd G31 ....46 D4
London St Larkhall ML9 ....93 A4
Renfrew PA4 ....27 D5
Long Calderwood Prim Sch
G74 ....76 C4
Long Row Glasgow G69 ....48 C6
Kirkintilloch G66 ....21 B7
Lanark ML11 ....116 F2
Wanlockhead ML12 ....154 C8
Longay Pl G22 ....30 C8
Longay St G22 ....30 C8
Longcroft Dr PA4 ....27 C4
Longdales ML11 ....98 F7
Longden St G81 ....27 D8
Longford ML11 ....122 A1
Longford St G33 ....46 D8
Longlee G69 ....48 B4
Longmorn Pl 1 ML1 ....66 B2
Longriggend Rd ML6 ....26 C2
Longstone Rd G33 ....47 B8
Longwill Terr G67 ....12 B4
Lonsdale Ave G46 ....59 D3
Lora Dr G52 ....43 E4
Lord Way G69 ....48 F5
Loretto Pl G33 ....46 F8
Loretto St G33 ....46 F8
Lorimer Cres G75 ....88 D7
Lorn Ave G69 ....33 D8
Lorn Pl G66 ....9 C1
Lorne Cres G64 ....19 D2
Lorne Dr ML1 ....65 D2
Lorne Gdns ML7 ....53 A2
Lorne Pl ML5 ....50 D5
Lorne Rd G52 ....42 F8
Lorne St Glasgow G51 ....44 D6
Hamilton ML3 ....78 C4
Lorne Street Prim Sch
G51 ....44 D6
Lorne Terr G72 ....61 F3
Lorraine Gardens La 5
G12 ....29 C4
Lorraine Gdns 4 G12 ....29 C4
Lorraine Rd 3 G12 ....29 C4
Loskin Dr G22 ....30 B7
Lossie Cres PA4 ....27 F2
Lossie St G33 ....31 D1
Lothian Dr G76 ....73 D8
Lothian Gdns 1 G20 ....29 E3
Lothian St Glasgow G52 ...42 E8
Glasgow G52 ....42 F8
Lothian Way G74 ....76 D3
Louburn EH48 ....40 D3
Louden Hill Dr G33 ....31 E6
Louden Hill Pl G33 ....31 E6
Louden Hill Rd G33 ....31 E6
Louden Hill Way G33 ....31 E6
Louden St ML6 ....51 A7
Loudon G75 ....88 E5
Loudon Rd G33 ....32 B4
Loudon St
Strathaven ML10 ....112 E6
Wishaw ML2 ....81 B6
Loudon Terr
Bearsden G61 ....16 D7
Glasgow G12 ....29 D3
Loudonhill Ave ML3 ....91 E8
Louise Gdns ML1 ....65 F5
Louisville Ave ML2 ....81 D5
Lounsdale Pl G14 ....28 B4
Lourdes Ave G52 ....43 D4
Lourdes Ct G52 ....43 D4
Lourdes Prim Sch G52 ...43 C5
Lourdes Sec Sch G52 ...43 D4
Louvain Gdns EH48 ....41 F4
Lovat Ave G61 ....16 F7
Lovat Dr G66 ....20 B8
Lovat Path 2 ML9 ....93 C2
Lovat Pl Glasgow G52 ....42 E7
Rutherglen G73 ....61 D4
Love Dr ML4 ....65 B6
Low Craigends G65 ....10 E8
Low Cres G81 ....27 E8
Low Flender Rd G76 ....73 D5
Low Moss Ind Est G64 ....19 B4
Low Parks Mus* ML3 ....78 E4
Low Patrick St ML3 ....78 F3
Low Pleasance ML9 ....93 B3
Low Quarry Gdns ML3 ....78 D2
Low Waters Rd ML3 ....78 D1
Lower Auchingramont Rd
ML3 ....78 E4
Lower Bathville EH48 ....41 F4
Lower Bourtree Dr G73 ..61 C4
Lower Mill Rd G76 ....73 F6
Lower Millgate G71 ....63 F6
Lowmoss Rdbt G64 ....19 C5
Lowndes St G78 ....57 C2
Lowrie Pl ML10 ....103 C5
Lowther Ave G61 ....16 C7
Lowther Cres 15 ML9 ....129 E8
Lowther Terr 15 G12 ....29 C4
Lowther View
Carnwath ML11 ....124 E1
Leadhills ML12 ....151 A1
Loyal Gdns G61 ....16 B8
Loyne Dr PA4 ....27 F2
Luath St G51 ....44 A8
Lubas Ave G42 ....60 D7
Lubas Pl G42 ....60 D7
Lubnaig Gdns G61 ....16 C7
Lubnaig Pl ML6 ....35 E2
Lubnaig Rd G43 ....59 E6
Lubnaig Wlk ML1 ....66 A5
Luckenhill Dr ML6 ....25 D3
Lucy Brae G71 ....63 E8
Luffness Gdns G32 ....47 B2
Lugar Dr G52 ....43 E4
Lugar Pl G44 ....60 F5
Lugar St ML5 ....50 B8
Luggie Gr G66 ....21 A7
Luggie Rd ML8 ....95 E3
Luggie View G67 ....23 A6
Luggiebank Pl G69 ....49 A4
Luggiebank Rd G66 ....20 D8
Luing ML6 ....51 E6
Luing Rd G52 ....43 E5
Luma Gdns G51 ....43 C7
Lumloch St G21 ....31 A4
Lumsden La G3 ....29 D1
Lumsden St G3 ....29 D1
Lunan Dr G64 ....31 C8

Lunan Pl G51 43 E7
Lunar Path ML6 51 D1
Luncarty Pl G32 47 A3
Luncarty St G32 47 A3
Lunderston Cl G53 58 B6
Lunderston Dr G53 58 A7
Lunderston Gdns G53 58 B6
Lundie Gdns G64 31 D8
Lundie St G32 46 E3
Luss Brae ML3 77 F2
Luss Rd G51 43 F7
Lusshill Terr G71 48 B2
Lybster Cres G73 61 D3
Lybster Way G72 77 C3
Lye Brae G67 12 B2
Lyell Gr G74 75 E3
Lyell Pl G74 75 E3
Lyle Rd ML6 51 F8
Lyman Dr ML2 81 C7
Lymburn St G3 44 D8
Lymekilns Rd G74 75 D3
Lyndale Pl G20 29 D8
Lyndale Rd G20 29 D8
Lyndhurst Gardens La G20 29 F3
Lyndhurst Gdns G20 29 F3
Lyne Croft G64 19 A4
Lyne St ML2 81 A5
Lynebank Gr G77 72 D2
Lynebank Pl G77 72 D2
Lynedoch Cres G3 162 A4
Lynedoch Pl G3 162 A4
Lynedoch St G3 162 A4
Lynedoch Terr G3 162 A4
Lynn Ct ML9 93 A2
Lynn Dr G76 86 E6
Lynn Wlk G71 64 A5
Lynnburn Ave ML4 65 A6
Lynne Dr G23 17 E1
Lynnhurst G71 63 F7
Lynnwood Rd ML2 82 C6
Lynton Ave G46 59 A1
Lyoncross Ave G78 57 D3
Lyoncross Cres G78 57 D3
Lyoncross Rd G53 43 B2
Lyons Quadrant ML2 80 D4
Lysa Vale Pl ML4 64 E5
Lysander Way 2 PA4 27 D1
Lytham Dr G23 17 E1
Lytham Mdws G71 63 E2
Lythgow Way ML11 117 C5
Lyttleton G75 88 B7

M

Mabel St ML1 79 E5
MacAdam Gdns ML4 65 A6
MacAdam Pl G75 88 E8
MacAllan Mews ML1 66 B2
MacArthur Ave ML6 35 D3
MacArthur Cres G74 75 C4
MacArthur Ct G74 75 C3
MacArthur Dr G74 75 C3
MacArthur Gdns G74 75 C3
MacArthur Wynd G72 62 C5
Macauslan Terr ML11 138 F7
MacBeth G74 76 B5
MacBeth Pl G31 46 D4
MacBeth St G31 46 D4
MacCallum Dr G72 62 C5
MacCrimmon Pk G74 75 B4
MacDairmid Dr ML3 91 B7
MacDiarmid Ct ML12 160 D4
MacDonald Ave
Armadale EH48 41 F6
East Kilbride G74 75 A4
MacDonald Cres G65 9 F3
MacDonald Gr ML4 64 F2
MacDonald St
3 Motherwell ML1 79 F5
1 Rutherglen G73 61 A7
MacDougal Dr G72 62 C5
MacDougal Quadrant ML4 64 F2
MacDougall St G43 59 C7
MacDuff Pl G31 46 D4
MacDuff St G31 46 D4
Mace Rd G13 16 C1
Macedonian Gr ML1 66 C4
MacFarland Rd G61 16 F3
MacFarlane Cres G72 62 C5
MacFarlane Rd G61 17 A3
MacFie Pl G74 75 B4
MacGregor Ct G72 62 C5
Machan Ave ML9 93 A3
Machan Rd ML9 93 B1
Machanhill ML9 93 B2
Machanhill Prim Sch ML9 93 B3
Machanhill View ML9 93 B2
Machrie Dr Glasgow G45 60 F4
Newton Mearns G77 72 E6
Machrie Gn G75 88 B4
Machrie Rd G45 60 F4
Machrie St Glasgow G45 60 F3
Motherwell ML1 79 B7
MacInnes Mews ML1 66 E4
Macintosh Pl G75 88 C7
MacIvor Cres G74 75 A4
Mack St ML6 51 A8
MacKeith St G40 45 F4
MacKenzie Gdns
Dolphinton EH46 126 E1
East Kilbride G74 75 A4
MacKenzie Terr ML4 65 A7
MacKinlay St G5 45 B4
MacKinley Pl G77 72 D4
MacKintosh Ct G72 62 A3
MacLaren Pl G44 59 F2
MacLean Ct G74 75 B4
MacLean Gr G74 75 B4
MacLean Pl G74 75 B4
MacLean Sq G51 44 E6
MacLean St
Clydebank G81 27 E8
Glasgow G51 44 D6
MacLean Terr EH48 40 C3
MacLehose Rd G67 12 C3
MacLellan St G41 44 D5
MacLeod Pl G74 76 B3
MacLeod St G4 163 C2
MacLeod Way G72 62 C5
MacMillan Gdns G71 49 A1
MacMillan St ML9 92 F2
MacNeil St ML9 92 F3
MacNeill Dr G74 75 B4
MacNeill Gdns G74 75 B4
MacNeish Way G74 75 C4
MacNicol Ct G74 75 A4
MacNicol Pk G74 75 A4
MacNicol Pl G74 75 A4
Macpherson Pk G74 75 C3
Macrae Gdns G74 75 C3
Macrimmon Pl G75 88 E8
MacTaggart Rd G67 23 E8
Madison Ave G44 60 B5
Madison Path 9 G72 77 D7
Madras Pl G40 45 F3
Madras St G40 45 F3
Mafeking St Glasgow G51 44 B6
Wishaw ML2 80 D4
Magna St ML1 79 B8
Magnolia Dr G72 62 F3
Magnolia Gdns
Ashgill ML9 93 E1
Motherwell ML1 66 C3
Magnolia Pl G71 64 C8
Magnolia St ML2 81 B5
Magnolia Terr G72 62 F3
Magnus Cres G44 60 B4
Mahon Ct G69 21 F1
Maidenburn Gr ML10 112 E8
Maidens G74 75 D3
Maidens Ave G77 73 A5
Maidland Rd G53 58 C8
Mailerbeg Gdns G69 21 F3
Mailie Wlk ML1 66 C3
Mailing Ave G64 19 C2
Mailings Ct G65 7 E3
Mailings Rd G65 7 E3
Mailings The G65 7 E4
Main Rd
Cumbernauld,Condorrat G67 23 A7
Cumbernauld,Mollinsburn G67 22 E5
Main St Banton G65 7 D3
Barrhead G78 57 C2
Bellshill ML4 64 F5
Bellshill ML4 65 B5
Blackridge EH48 40 C3
Bothwell G71 64 A2
Braehead ML11 124 B5
Calderbank ML6 51 C2
Caldercruix ML6 38 A4
Cambuslang G72 62 A6
Carnwath ML11 124 F1
Chapelhall ML6 51 E3
Chapelton ML10 103 C5
Chryston G69 21 D1
Clarkston G76 73 F6
Cleland ML1 67 C1
Coatbridge ML5 50 A7
Coatbridge,Cliftonville ML5 50 C6
Crawfordjohn ML12 144 F2
Cumbernauld G67 12 B5
Douglas ML11 138 B1
East Kilbride G74 75 F2
Fauldhouse EH47 71 D6
Forth ML11 124 A8
Glasgow,Dalmarnock G40 45 F4
Glasgow,Muirhead G69 48 C4
Glasgow,Thornliebank G46 58 F3
Glenboig ML5 34 E6
Hamilton G72 77 D6
Hamilton G72 77 E5
Kilsyth G65 10 D8
Leadhills ML12 151 A1
Longriggend ML6 26 A1
Milngavie G62 17 A8
Motherwell ML1 66 B6
Newbigging ML11 132 B8
Overtown ML2 94 C6
Plains ML6 37 B2
Rutherglen G73 61 B8
Salsburgh ML7 53 B2
Shotts ML7 70 A3
Strathaven ML10 112 E5
Symington ML12 140 F6
Thornliebank G46 59 A4
Torrance G64 19 B8
Twechar G65 9 F4
Uddingston G71 63 F5
Wilsontown ML11 122 A1
Wishaw ML2 80 F4
Wishaw ML2 81 A3
Wishaw,Newmains ML2 82 A3
Mainhead Terr G67 12 B5
Mainhill Ave G69 48 D5
Mainhill Dr G69 48 C5
Mainhill Pl G69 48 D6
Mainhill Rd G69 48 F5
Mains Ave G46 59 B1
Mains Ct ML11 117 C5
Mains Pl ML4 65 A3
Mains Rd East Kilbride G74 75 F5
Harthill ML7 55 E5
Mainsacre Dr 9 ML9 129 E8
Mair St G51 44 E6
Maitland Bank ML9 93 C3
Maitland Pl PA4 27 B2
Maitland St G4 162 C4
Mal Fleming's Brae G65 10 F7
Malcolm Gdns G74 75 C2
Malcolm St ML1 79 C6
Malin Pl G33 46 F8
Mallaig Pl G51 43 D7
Mallaig Rd G51 43 E7
Mallard Cres G75 88 A5
Mallard La 7 G71 64 B3
Mallard Pl G75 88 A5
Mallard Rd G81 15 B5
Mallard Terr G75 88 A5
Mallard Way ML4 64 F8
Malleable Gdns ML1 65 C2
Malleny Gr G77 72 B3
Malletsheugh Rd G77 72 B3
Malletsheugh Rdbt G77 72 B3
Malloch Pl G74 76 B2
Malloch St G20 29 E5
Mallot's View G77 72 B4
Malov Ct G75 88 E6
Malplaquet Ct ML8 96 B1
Malta Terr G5 45 B4
Maltbarns St G20 30 A3
Malvaig La 3 G72 77 C6
Malvern Ct G31 46 A6
Mambeg Dr G51 43 E8
Mamore Pl G43 59 C6
Mamore St G43 59 C6
Manchester Dr G12 29 B6
Mandora Ct ML8 96 B1
Manitoba Cres G75 75 B1
Mannering G74 76 D4
Mannering Ct G41 59 C8
Mannering Rd G41 59 C8
Mannoch Pl ML5 50 D3
Mannofield G61 16 D4
Manor Dr ML6 50 E8
Manor Gate Bothwell G71 64 B1
Newton Mearns G77 72 F4
Manor Pk ML3 78 D2
Manor Rd Clydebank G15 15 F1
Gartcosh G69 33 F5
Glasgow G14 28 E4
Manor View
Calderbank ML6 51 B2
Larkhall ML9 93 C2
Manor Way G73 61 C4
Manresa Pl 1 G4 30 B2
Manse Ave Armadale EH48 41 E6
Bearsden G61 16 F5
Bothwell G71 64 A2
Coatbridge ML5 49 D4
Manse Brae Ashgill ML9 107 B8
Cambuslang G72 62 F2
Dalserf ML9 94 B1
Glasgow G44 60 B6
Manse Bridge ML8 95 F1
Manse Ct Barrhead G78 57 D3
Kilsyth G65 10 D7
Law ML8 95 A4
Manse Dr ML12 160 E4
Manse Gdns G32 47 D4
Manse La G74 75 F3
Manse Mews ML2 82 A4
Manse Pl ML6 51 A7
Manse Rd Bearsden G61 16 F5
Carmunnock G76 74 D7
Carstairs ML11 124 A1
Crawfordjohn ML12 145 A3
Forth ML11 124 A8
Glasgow,Bargeddie G69 48 E6
Glasgow,Mount Vernon G32 47 D4
Kilsyth G65 10 E7
Lanark ML11 116 F4
Motherwell ML1 79 F4
Muirkirk KA18 142 A6
Salsburgh ML7 53 D1
Shotts ML7 70 A3
Stonehouse ML9 105 C2
Symington ML12 141 A6
Wanlockhead ML12 154 C8
Wilsontown ML11 122 A1
Wishaw ML2 82 A4
Manse Road Gdns G61 16 F5
Manse St Coatbridge ML5 49 F6
Renfrew PA4 27 D4
Manse View
Armadale EH48 41 E5
Coalburn ML11 137 F5
Hamilton G72 77 C6
Motherwell ML1 66 F5
Manse View Terr 8 ML11 138 B1
Mansefield Ave G72 62 A4
Mansefield Cres G76 73 D6
Mansefield Pl ML11 138 F5
Mansefield Rd
Clarkston G76 73 E6
Quarter ML3 91 E6
Mansel St G21 31 A5
Manseview ML9 93 B2
Manseview Terr G76 86 E5
Mansewood Rd G43 59 B5
Mansfield Cres ML10 103 D6
Mansfield Dr G71 64 A6
Mansfield Pl DG10 161 D5
Mansfield Rd Bellshill ML4 64 F4
Glasgow G52 42 F8
Mansfield Sq 5 DG10 161 D5
Mansfield St G11 29 C2
Mansion Ct G72 62 A6
Mansion St
Cambuslang G72 62 A6
Glasgow G22 30 B5
Glasgow G22 30 C5
Mansionhouse Ave G32 62 C8
Mansionhouse Dr G32 47 C6
Mansionhouse Gdns G41 59 E7
Mansionhouse Gr G32 47 E3
Mansionhouse Rd
Glasgow G32 47 E3
Glasgow,Langside G41 59 E7
Paisley PA1 42 A5
Manson Pl G75 89 B5
Manus Duddy Ct
Blantyre G72 63 D1
Hamilton G72 77 D8
Maple Ave G77 72 D4
Maple Bank ML3 78 F2
Maple Cres G72 62 F3
Maple Ct G67 12 F5
Maple Dr Clydebank G81 15 A5
Kirkintilloch G66 20 A5
Larkhall ML9 93 A5
Maple Gr G75 88 B6
Maple Pl Banknock FK4 8 E2
East Kilbride G75 88 B6
Uddingston G71 64 D8
Maple Quadrant ML6 51 D6
Maple Rd
Cumbernauld G67 12 F5
Glasgow G41 44 B4
Motherwell ML1 66 B5
Maple Terr G75 88 B6
Maple Way 7 G72 77 C7
Maplewood ML2 80 D1
Mar Dr G61 16 F7
Mar Gdns G73 61 D4
March St G41 44 F2
Marchbank Gdns PA1 42 D4
Marches The ML11 117 B5
Marchfield G64 18 E3
Marchglen Pl 1 G51 43 D7
Marchmont Gdns
Bishopbriggs G64 18 F2
Strathaven ML10 112 F7
Marchmont Terr 2 G12 29 C3
Mardale G74 75 C3
Maree Dr
Cumbernauld G67 23 B7
Glasgow G52 43 E4
Maree Gdns G64 19 B1
Maree Way G72 77 D8
Maree Wlk 7 ML2 81 F6
Marfield St G32 46 F6
Margaret Ave ML7 53 B2
Margaret Dr ML1 80 B3
Margaret Pl ML4 64 E5
Margaret Rd ML3 78 B6
Margaret St ML5 50 A4
Margaret's Pl ML9 93 A3
Margaretta Bldgs G44 60 A6
Margaretvale Dr ML9 93 A2
Marguerite Ave G66 20 C6
Marguerite Dr G66 20 C6
Marguerite Gdns
Bothwell G71 64 B2
Kirkintilloch G66 20 C6
Marguerite Gr G66 20 C6
Marian Dr ML1 66 C2
Maric La ML6 37 A2
Marigold Ave ML1 79 E8
Marigold Way ML8 108 F8
Marina Ct ML4 64 F3
Marine Cres G51 44 E6
Marine Gdns G51 162 A1
Mariner Ct G81 15 A2
Marion St ML4 65 D5
Mariscat Rd G41 44 E2
Marius Cres ML1 65 C1
Marjory Dr PA3 42 B7
Marjory Rd PA4 27 A1
Markdow Ave G53 43 A1
Market Cl 7 G65 10 D8
Market Ct 15 Kilsyth G65 10 D8
Lanark ML11 117 A4
Market End ML11 117 A4
Market Pl Carluke ML8 95 F2
5 Kilsyth G65 10 D8
Uddingston G71 64 C7
Market Rd Biggar ML12 160 D4
2 Carluke ML8 95 F2
Kirkintilloch G66 21 A7
Uddingston G71 64 C7
Market Sq 6 G65 10 D8
Market St Airdrie ML6 51 A7
Kilsyth G65 10 D8
Uddingston G71 64 C7
Markethill Rd
East Kilbride G74 75 E5
East Kilbride,East Mains G74 75 E3
Markethill Rdbt G74 75 E3
Marlach Pl 13 G53 58 A8
Marlborough Ave G11 28 F3
Marlborough La N 1 G11 28 F3
Marlborough La S G11 28 F3
Marlborough Pk G75 88 A7
Marldon La G11 28 F3
Marley Hill Ave 10 ML9 129 E8
Marlfield Gdns ML4 65 A8
Marlow St G41 44 E5
Marlow Terr G41 44 E4
Marmion Cres ML1 65 D1
Marmion Dr G66 20 F8
Marmion Pl G67 23 E7
Marmion Rd G67 23 E7
Marne St G31 46 B8
Marnoch Dr ML5 34 D6
Marnoch Way G69 21 F2
Marnock Terr PA2 42 A2
Marquis Ave ML3 78 B6
Marquis Gate G71 63 E5
Marr's Wynd ML11 117 C5
Marrs Wynd ML11 117 C5
Marrswood Gn ML3 78 A4
Marrwood Ave G66 21 B6
Marshall Gr ML3 78 B3
Marshall La ML2 81 A3
Marshall Rd ML1 66 D7
Marshall St Larkhall ML9 93 A2
Wishaw ML2 80 F2
Wishaw ML2 81 A3
Mart St G1 163 A1
Martha Pl ML9 93 B2
Martha St G1 163 A3
Martin Cres G69 48 C5
Martin Ct ML3 78 C3
Martin Pl ML1 66 C3
Martin St Coatbridge ML5 50 D7
Glasgow G40 45 F3
Martinside G75 88 E5
Martyn St ML6 50 E6
Martyrs Pl G64 31 A8
Marwick St G31 46 B7
Mary Dr ML4 64 E3
Mary Glen ML2 81 D5
Mary Rae Rd ML4 64 E3
Mary Russell Sch The PA2 42 C2
Mary Sq G69 48 F5
Mary St ML3 78 D2
Mary Young Pl G76 73 F6
Maryhill Prim Sch G20 29 D7
Maryhill Rd
Bearsden G61,G20 17 A1
Glasgow G20 30 A2
Glasgow,Maryhill G20 29 D6
Maryhill Sta G20 29 C8
Maryknowe Rd ML1 66 C2
Maryland Dr G52 43 E5
Maryland Gdns G52 43 E5
Maryston St G33 31 D2
Maryville Ave G46 59 C2
Maryville Gdns G46 59 C2
Maryville La G71 63 E8
Maryville View G71 48 D1
Marywell Path G68 10 F2
Marywood Sq G41 44 F2
Mashock Path ML8 108 B1
Mason Ct ML1 79 E6
Mason La ML1 79 E6
Mason St Larkhall ML9 93 C2
Motherwell ML1 79 E6
Masonfield Ave G68 11 D2
Masterton St G21 30 C3
Masterton Way G71 49 B1
Mathers Ave EH47 56 F6
Matherton Ave G77 73 B5
Mathieson Cres G33 32 F5
Mathieson Rd G73 46 C1
Mathieson St PA1 42 B5
Matilda Rd G41 44 E4
Matthew McWhirter Pl ML9 93 B4
Mauchline G74 76 E3
Mauchline Ave G66 9 A2
Mauchline Ct
Hamilton ML3 77 D2
Kirkintilloch G66 9 A2
Mauchline St G5 45 A4
Maukinfauld Ct G32 46 D3
Maukinfauld Gdns G31 46 E4
Maukinfauld Rd G32 46 E3
Mauldslie Dr ML8 95 A6
Mauldslie Pl ML9 106 F8
Mauldslie Rd ML8 95 B2
Mauldslie St Bellshill ML4 65 A4
Coatbridge ML5 50 A5
Glasgow G40 46 B4
Maule Dr G11 29 A2
Mausoleum Dr ML3 78 F5
Mavis Bank
Bishopbriggs G64 30 F8
6 Hamilton G72 77 C7
Mavisbank Gdns
Bellshill ML4 65 A6
Glasgow G51 44 E6
Mavisbank Rd G51 44 D6
Mavisbank Sch ML6 50 F8
Mavisbank St Airdrie ML6 50 E8
Wishaw ML2 82 C5
Mavor Ave G74 76 A4
Mavor Rdbt G74 75 F4
Maxton Ave G78 57 A3
Maxton Cres ML2 81 C6
Maxton Gr G78 57 A3
Maxton Terr G72 61 F3
Maxwell Ave
Bearsden G61 16 E1
Glasgow G69 48 A5
Glasgow,Pollockshields G41 44 F4
Maxwell Cres G72 77 D6
Maxwell Ct ML5 50 A7
Maxwell Dr
East Kilbride G74 76 A2
Glasgow,Garrowhill G69 48 A5
Glasgow,Pollockshields G41 44 C4
Glasgow,Pollokshields G41 44 E4
Maxwell Gdns G41 44 D4
Maxwell Gr G41 44 D4
Maxwell La G41 44 E4
Maxwell Oval 2 G41 44 F4

Maxwell Park Sta G41 ....44 D2
Maxwell Path 10 ML9 .....93 C2
Maxwell Pl Coatbridge ML5 .49 F5
Glasgow G41 ....45 A3
Kilsyth G65 ....6 D1
Uddingston G71 ....64 A6
Maxwell Rd G41 ....44 F4
Maxwell St Glasgow G1 ..163 A1
Glasgow,Garrowhill G69 ....48 B4
Maxwell Terr G41 ....44 F4
Maxwellton Ave G74 ......76 B3
Maxwellton Pl G74 ....76 B3
Maxwellton Prim Sch
G74 ....76 B3
Maxwellton Rd G74 ......76 C4
Maxwelton Rd G33 ....31 D2
May Gdns ML3 ....78 C5
May St ML3 ....78 D5
May Terr Glasgow G46 .....60 B8
Glasgow,Merrylee G46 .....59 C3
May Wynd ML3 ....78 C5
Maybank La G42 ....45 A1
Maybank St G42 ....45 A1
Mayberry Cres G32 ......47 D5
Mayberry Gdns G32 ......47 D5
Mayberry Gr G32 ....47 D5
Mayberry Pl G72 ....77 D8
Maybole Cres G77 ....73 A4
Maybole Dr ML6 ....51 A4
Maybole Gdns ML3 ....77 D2
Maybole Gr G77 ....73 A4
Maybole Pl ML5 ....50 D3
Maybole St G53 ....57 F6
Mayfield ML11 ....119 E4
Mayfield Ave G76 ....73 E7
Mayfield Ct EH48 ....41 F4
Mayfield Dr EH48 ....41 F5
Mayfield Gdns ML8 .....109 A7
Mayfield Pl Carluke ML8 ..109 A7
Coatbridge ML5 ....50 A3
Mayfield Rd ML3 ....77 F4
Mayfield St G20 ....29 F5
McAdam Gdns ML11 ....113 F4
McAffee Gdns EH48 ......41 F3
McAllister Ave ML6 ......51 D8
McAlpine St Glasgow G2 .162 B2
Wishaw ML2 ....81 B2
McArdle Ave ML1 ....79 B7
McArthur Pk G66 ....20 C7
McArthur St G43 ....59 C7
McAslin Ct G4 ....163 B3
McAslin St G4 ....163 C3
McBride Ave G66 ....20 C7
McCallum Ave G73 ....61 B8
McCallum Ct
Armadale EH48 ....41 F7
East Kilbride G74 ....75 B4
McCallum Gdns ML4 .....64 F2
McCallum Gr G74 ....75 B4
McCallum Pl G74 ....75 B4
McCallum Rd ML9 ....93 B1
McCarrison Rd ML2 ......82 A6
McCash Pl G66 ....20 C7
McCloy Gdns G53 ....57 F5
McClue Ave PA4 ....27 B3
McClue Rd PA4 ....27 C4
McClurg Ct 3 ML1 ....79 E5
McCormack Gdns ML1 ...66 E4
McCourt Gdns ML4 ......65 C5
McCracken Ave PA4 .....27 B2
McCracken Dr G71 ....64 C8
McCreery St G81 ....27 D8
McCulloch Ave G71 ......64 D6
McCulloch St G41 ....44 F4
McCulloch Way G33 .....32 F5
McDonald Cres G81 .....27 D8
McDonald Pl ML1 ....66 A5
McEwan Gdns G74 ....75 A4
McEwans Way ML9 .....105 D1
McFarlane St G4 ....163 C1
McGhee St G81 ....15 B4
McGill Prim Sch G53 .....43 C2
McGoldrick Pl G33 ....32 F5
McGowan Pl ML3 ....78 A5
McGregor Ave
Airdrie ML6 ....51 D8
Renfrew PA4 ....27 B2
McGregor Path ML5 ......34 C6
McGregor Rd G67 ....11 E1
McGregor St
Clydebank G81 ....27 D8
Glasgow G51 ....43 F6
Wishaw ML2 ....80 D4
McGurk Way ML4 ....64 D6
McInnes Ct ML2 ....81 B2
McInnes Gr ML9 ....105 E1
McInnes Pl ML2 ....94 B7
McIntosh Ct 1 G31 ....45 F7
McIntosh Quadrant ML4 ..64 F2
McIntosh St G31 ....45 F7
McIntosh Way
Cumbernauld G67 ....11 F1
Motherwell ML1 ....79 C5
McIntyre St G3 ....162 A2
McIntyre Terr G72 ....62 A6
McIver St G72 ....62 E6
McKay Ct G77 ....72 C3
McKay Gr ML4 ....64 F5
McKay Pl East Kilbride G74 .75 A4
Newton Mearns G77 ......72 C4
McKechnie St G51 ....44 A8
McKenna Dr ML6 ....50 E7
McKenzie Ave G81 ....15 B4
McKenzie Gate G72 ......62 E6
McKenzie's Cl ML11 ....117 A4
McKeown Gdns ML4 .....65 D4
McKerrell St PA1 ....42 A5
McKinnon Rd EH47 ....71 F7
McKirdy Ct ML11 ....114 A5
McKirdy Dr ML11 ....119 D6
McLaren Ave PA4 ....27 C1
McLaren Cres G20 ....29 E7
McLaren Ct G46 ....59 B1
McLaren Dr ML4 ....65 D4
McLaren Gdns G20 ....29 E7
McLaren Gr G74 ....75 A4
McLauchlan View ML7 ...55 F6
McLean Ave ML9 ....129 F8
McLean Dr ML4 ....64 F2
McLean Gdns ML9 ......105 E2
McLees La ML1 ....79 B7
McLellan Galleries*
G3 ....162 C3
McLelland Dr ML6 ....37 B2
McLennan St G42 ....60 B8
McMahon Dr ML2 ....82 A6
McMahon Gr ML4 ....65 B6
McMillan Rd ML2 ....80 D2
McMillan Way ML8 ....94 F5
McNair St G32 ....47 A5
McNeil Ave G81 ....15 E1
McNeil Cres EH48 ....41 F6
McNeil Dr ML1 ....66 A8
McNeil Gdns G5 ....45 D4
McNeil Pl ML2 ....94 C7
McNeil St G5 ....45 D4
McNiven Ct ML9 ....105 E1
McPhail Ave ML1 ....66 F5
McPhail St G40 ....45 E4
McPhater St G4 ....162 C4
McPherson Cres ML6 .....51 E1
McPherson Dr G71 ....64 B3
McPherson St
Bellshill ML4 ....65 D5
Glasgow G1 ....163 B1
McShannon Gr ML4 ......65 A3
McSparran Rd G65 ....10 F4
Meadow Ave G72 ....77 D6
Meadow Bank DG10 .....161 E4
Meadow Bank Rise
DG10 ....161 E4
Meadow Cl G75 ....88 A4
Meadow Cres EH47 ......71 E5
Meadow Ct ML8 ....96 C1
Meadow La Bothwell G71 ..64 B2
Renfrew PA4 ....27 D5
Meadow Path ML6 ....51 D1
Meadow Pl DG10 ....161 C6
Meadow Rd Glasgow G11 ..29 A2
Motherwell ML1 ....79 F5
Meadow Rise G77 ....72 C5
Meadow St ML5 ....50 B4
Meadow View
Cumbernauld G67 ....12 C4
Plains ML6 ....37 A3
Meadow Way G77 ....72 D6
Meadow Wlk ML5 ....50 C6
Meadowbank Ave ML10 .112 E7
Meadowbank La G71 .....63 E6
Meadowbank Pl G77 .....72 D5
Meadowburn
Bishopbriggs G64 ....19 A3
Bishopbriggs G64 ....19 A4
Meadowburn Ave
Kirkintilloch G66 ....20 E5
Newton Mearns G77 ......72 D5
Meadowburn Prim Sch
G64 ....19 A3
Meadowburn Rd ML2 ....81 C3
Meadowfield Pl ML2 .....82 C6
Meadowfoot ML12 ......154 B8
Meadowfoot Rd ML10 ..127 F1
Meadowhead Ave G69 ....21 F2
Meadowhead Rd
Plains ML6 ....36 F2
Wishaw ML2 ....80 C4
Meadowhill G77 ....72 D5
Meadowhill St ML9 ......93 B4
Meadowpark St G31 .....46 B7
Meadows Ave ML9 ....93 B3
Meadowside ML3 ....91 D6
Meadowside Gdns ML6 ...51 D7
Meadowside Ind Est PA4 .27 D6
Meadowside Pl ML6 .....51 D7
Meadowside Rd G65 ....9 F8
Meadowside St
Glasgow G11 ....29 A1
Renfrew PA4 ....27 D5
Meadowwell St G32 .....47 B5
Mealkirk St G81 ....15 C7
Mearns Castle High Sch
G77 ....73 A3
Mearns Ct ML3 ....91 E7
Mearns Prim Sch G77 ....72 B3
Mearns Rd
Motherwell ML1 ....79 C8
Newton Mearns,Mearns
G77 ....72 D1
Newton Mearns,Whitecraigs
G77 ....73 B7
Mearns Way G64 ....19 D2
Mearnscroft Gdns G77 ...72 F3
Mearnscroft Rd G77 .....72 F3
Mearnskirk Rd G77 ......72 D2
Mearsdale Dr DG10 .....161 C6
Mearsdale Pk DG10 .....161 C6
Medlar Ct G72 ....62 F3
Medlar Rd G67 ....12 D2
Medrox Gdns G67 ....22 F5
Medwin Ct G75 ....87 E7
Medwin Gdns G75 ....87 E7
Medwin St G72 ....62 E5
Medwin Terr ML11 .....132 B8
Medwyn St Glasgow G14 ..28 D3
Glasgow G14 ....28 E2
Meek Pl G72 ....62 B5
Megan Gate G40 ....45 F4
Megan St G40 ....45 F4
Meigle Rd ML6 ....50 F5
Meikle Ave PA4 ....27 C2
Meikle Cres
Greengairs ML6 ....36 D8
Hamilton ML3 ....91 C7
Meikle Drumgray Rd
ML6 ....36 E8
Meikle Earnock Rd ML3 ..91 B7
Meikle Rd G53 ....58 C8
Meiklerig Cres G53 ......43 C2
Meiklewood Rd G51 .....43 D6
Melbourne Ave G75 .....88 C8
Melbourne Ct G46 ....59 D3
Melbourne Gn 5 G75 ....88 C8
Melbourne St G31 ....45 F6
Meldon Pl G51 ....43 D7
Meldrum Gdns G41 ......44 D2
Meldrum Mains ML6 .....35 E4
Meldrum St G81 ....27 D8
Melford Ave Glasgow G46 .59 D2
Kirkintilloch G66 ....20 B8
Shotts ML7 ....70 B3
Melford Rd ML4 ....64 E7
Melford Way PA3 ....42 B7
Melfort Ave
Clydebank G81 ....15 C3
Glasgow G41 ....44 B4
Melfort Ct G81 ....15 C2
Melfort Gdns G81 ....15 C2
Melfort Path ML2 ....81 F7
Melfort Quadrant ML1 ...66 D3
Melfort Rd ML3 ....77 E2
Mellerstain Dr G14 ......27 F6
Mellerstain Gr G14 ......27 F6
Melness Pl 2 G51 ....43 D7
Melrose Ave
Chapelhall ML6 ....51 D2
Coatbridge G69 ....48 F6
Motherwell ML1 ....66 B6
Rutherglen G73 ....61 B7
Melrose Cres ML2 ....81 A5
Melrose Ct G73 ....61 B7
Melrose Gdns
Glasgow G20 ....29 F3
Twechar G65 ....9 F4
Uddingston G71 ....48 F1
Melrose Pl Blantyre G72 ..63 C1
Coatbridge ML5 ....49 F7
Larkhall ML9 ....93 A1
Melrose Rd G67 ....23 E7
Melrose St 6 Glasgow G4 .30 A2
Hamilton ML3 ....78 B5
Melrose Terr
East Kilbride G74 ....75 F3
Hamilton ML3 ....78 B6
Melvaig Pl G20 ....29 D5
Melvick Pl 3 G51 ....43 D7
Melville Cres ML1 ....79 F6
Melville Ct G1 ....163 A1
Melville Dr ML1 ....79 E6
Melville Gdns G64 ....19 A2
Melville Pk G74 ....76 B3
Melville Pl ML8 ....95 E2
Melville St G41 ....44 F3
Melvinhall Rd ML11 .....117 A5
Memel St G21 ....30 E5
Memorial Way ML1 ......66 C6
Memus Ave G52 ....43 C4
Mendip La G75 ....88 A4
Mennock Ct ML3 ....77 E2
Mennock Dr G64 ....19 A4
Mennock St ML1 ....67 C2
Menock Rd G44 ....60 D6
Menteith Ave G64 ....19 B1
Menteith Ct ML1 ....79 F6
Menteith Dr G73 ....61 D2
Menteith Gdns G61 ......16 C8
Menteith Loan ML1 ......66 A5
Menteith Pl G73 ....61 D2
Menteith Rd ML1 ....79 E7
Menzies Dr G21 ....31 B5
Menzies Pl Glasgow G21 ..31 B5
Leadhills ML12 ....151 A2
Menzies Rd G21 ....31 A5
Mercat Loan ML12 ......160 D4
Merchant La G1 ....163 A1
Merchiston St G32 ....46 F7
Mere Ct G68 ....11 D6
Merkland Ct Glasgow G11 .29 B1
Kirkintilloch G66 ....9 A1
Merkland Dr G66 ....21 A8
Merkland Pl G66 ....9 A1
Merkland Rd ML5 ....34 C2
Merkland St G11 ....29 B2
Merkland Way G75 ......88 C4
Merlewood Ave G71 .....64 B4
Merlin Ave ML4 ....65 A8
Merlin Way PA3 ....42 B7
Merlindale ML11 ....98 F8
Merlinford Ave PA4 ......27 E3
Merlinford Cres PA4 .....27 E3
Merlinford Dr PA4 ....27 E3
Merlinford Way PA4 .....27 E3
Merrick Ct ML6 ....36 A2
Merrick Dr ML9 ....129 F8
Merrick Gdns
Bearsden G61 ....16 C7
Glasgow G51 ....44 B5
Quarter ML3 ....91 E3
Merrick Path G51 ....44 B5
Merrick Terr G71 ....64 B7
Merrick Way G73 ....61 B3
Merry Ct G72 ....77 E6
Merry St ML1 ....79 F7
Merryburn Ave G46 .....59 D4
Merrycrest Ave G46 .....59 D4
Merrycroft Ave G46 .....59 D4
Merryflats G65 ....9 F4
Merryland Pl G51 ....44 C7
Merryland St Glasgow G51 .44 B7
Glasgow G51 ....44 C7
Merrylee Cres G46 ......59 C5
Merrylee Park Ave G46 ...59 D4
Merrylee Park Mews
G46 ....59 C5
Merrylee Prim Sch G44 ..59 F5
Merrylee Rd G44 ....59 E5
Merrylees Rd G72 ....77 C7
Merryston Ct ML5 ....49 E6
Merrystone St ML5 ......49 F7
Merryton Ave
Clydebank G15 ....16 B3
Glasgow,Merrylee G46 ....59 D4
Merryton Gdns 3 G15 ....16 B3
Merryton Rd Larkhall ML9 ..92 F6
Motherwell ML1 ....80 C2
Merryton St ML9 ....92 F5
Merryton Twr ML1 ....80 B2
Merryvale Ave G46 ......59 D4
Merryvale Pl G46 ....59 D5
Merton Dr G52 ....43 A5
Meryon Gdns G32 ....47 D2
Meryon Rd G32 ....47 D3
Methil St G14 ....28 C3
Methlick Ave ML6 ....50 E4
Methuen Rd Paisley PA3 ...42 A8
Renfrew PA3 ....27 A1
Methven Ave G61 ....17 B5
Methven Pl G74 ....75 C2
Methven Rd G46 ....73 A7
Methven St G31 ....46 D4
Methven Terr ML5 ....35 B1
Metropole La G1 ....163 A1
Mey Ct G77 ....72 A4
Mey Pl G77 ....72 A4
Michael McParland Dr
G64 ....19 B8
Michael Terr ML6 ....51 D1
Micklehouse Oval 2 G69 .48 B6
Micklehouse Pl 1 G69 ...48 B6
Micklehouse Rd G69 .....48 B6
Micklehouse Wynd 3
G69 ....48 B6
Mid Barrwood Rd G65 ....10 F8
Mid Carbarns ML2 ....80 D1
Mid Pk G75 ....88 E8
Mid Rd Biggar ML12 .....160 E4
Cumbernauld G67 ....23 F6
Eaglesham G76 ....86 E4
Mid-Loan St ML8 ......108 E4
Mid-Wharf St G4 ....30 C2
Midas Pl ML4 ....65 E5
Midcroft G64 ....18 E3
Midcroft Ave G44 ....60 E5
Midcroft Pl ML10 ....112 D5
Middle Ward St G81 .....15 D7
Middlefield G75 ....88 E5
Middlefield Residential Sch
G11 ....29 B3
Middlehouse Ct ML8 .....95 D2
Middlemuir Ave G66 .....20 D5
Middlemuir Rd
Kirkintilloch G66 ....20 D6
...........................137 F5
Middlerig ML10 ....112 E5
Middlerigg Rd G68 ....11 D2
Middlesex Gdns 3 G41 ...44 E6
Middlesex St G41 ....44 E5
Middleton Ave ML9 .....106 B8
Middleton St G51 ....44 C6
Midfaulds Ave PA4 ......27 E2
Midfield Rd 137 F5
Midland St G1 ....162 C2
Midlem Dr G52 ....43 C5
Midlem Oval G52 ....43 C5
Midlock St G51 ....44 C6
Midlothian Dr
Glasgow G41 ....44 D1
Glasgow G41 ....59 D8
Midton St G21 ....30 F3
Migvie Pl G20 ....29 D5
Milford G75 ....88 B7
Milford St G33 ....47 A8
Mill Brae Ct ML5 ....49 D5
Mill Cres G40 ....45 F4
Mill Ct Hamilton ML3 .....78 C2
Rutherglen G73 ....61 A8
Mill Gr ML3 ....78 C2
Mill Loan ML6 ....51 A8
Mill Mdws DG10 ....161 D5
Mill Pk ML3 ....78 C2
Mill Pl Thankerton ML12 ..131 D1
Uddingston G71 ....63 F6
Mill Rd Airdrie ML6 ......36 A1
Armadale EH48 ....41 E6
Banton G65 ....7 D3
Bothwell G71 ....64 A1
Cambuslang G72 ....62 D5
Carluke ML8 ....95 E1
Clydebank G81 ....27 D7
Hamilton ML3 ....78 C1
Harthill ML7 ....55 F5
Hartwood ML7 ....68 F1
Lesmahagow ML11 ......119 E4
Motherwell ML1 ....79 F8
Queenzieburn G65 ....9 E7
Shotts ML7 ....82 F8
Thankerton ML12 ....131 D1
Wattston ML6 ....24 B1
Wishaw ML2 ....82 E5
Mill Rig G75 ....88 D5
Mill Rise G66 ....20 D4
Mill St Caldercruix ML6 .....37 F5
Glasgow G40 ....45 F3
Rutherglen G73 ....61 A6
Mill Street Ind Est ML6 ...51 A8
Mill Vennel PA4 ....27 D3
Mill Way G66 ....21 A7
Millands Ave G72 ....63 C2
Millands Rd ML12 ......131 D1
Millar Gr ML3 ....78 B3
Millar St Glassford ML10 ..104 E2
Stonehouse ML9 ....105 F2
Millar Terr G73 ....46 B1
Millarbank St G21 ....30 E4
Millard Ave ML1 ....66 B2
Millars Pl G66 ....20 D4
Millbank Ave ML4 ....65 C3
Millbank Ct ML5 ....49 F3
Millbank Rd ML2 ....80 F1
Millbeg Cres G33 ....47 F5
Millbeg Pl G33 ....47 F5
Millbrae Ave G69 ....33 D8
Millbrae Cres
Clydebank G81 ....27 D7
Glasgow G42 ....59 F7
Millbrae Ct G42 ....59 F7
Millbrae Gdns G42 ......59 F7
Millbrae Rd G42 ....59 F7
Millbrix Ave G14 ....28 A5
Millbrook G74 ....75 B1
Millburn DG10 ....161 D5
Millburn Ave
Clydebank G81 ....27 E8
Renfrew PA4 ....27 E3
Rutherglen G73 ....61 A6
Millburn Cres EH48 ......41 D6
Millburn Ct
East Kilbride G75 ....87 E7
Symington ML12 ....140 F6
Millburn Dr PA4 ....27 E3
Millburn Gate ML9 ....93 F1
Millburn Gdns G75 ......87 E7
Millburn La ML9 ....93 C2
Millburn Pl ML9 ....106 B8
Millburn Rd Ashgill ML9 ..94 A1
Renfrew PA4 ....27 D3
Millburn St Glasgow G21 ..31 A1
Motherwell ML1 ....79 E7
Millburn Way
East Kilbride G75 ....87 E7
Renfrew PA4 ....27 E3
Millcroft Rd
Cumbernauld G67 ....23 E4
Cumbernauld,Carbrain G67 ..12 B1
Cumbernauld,Luggiebank
G67 ....24 A4
Rutherglen G73 ....45 F2
Milldam Rd G81 ....15 C7
Millennium Ct G34 ......48 C8
Millennium Gdns G34 ....48 C7
Miller Cl G64 ....31 D8
Miller Dr G64 ....31 D8
Miller Gdns G64 ....31 D8
Miller La G81 ....15 B1
Miller Pl ML7 ....55 F6
Miller St Carluke ML8 .....96 A2
Clydebank G81 ....15 B1
Coatbridge ML5 ....50 B5
Glasgow G1 ....163 A2
Glasgow,Muirhead G69 ....48 B4
Hamilton ML3 ....78 F3
Harthill ML7 ....55 E6
Larkhall ML9 ....93 B3
Wishaw ML2 ....81 A3
Miller Wlk G64 ....31 D8
Miller's Pl ML6 ....51 B7
Millerfield Pl
Glasgow G40 ....46 B3
Hamilton ML3 ....78 F3
Millerfield Rd G40 ....46 B3
Millersneuk Ave G66 .....20 D3
Millersneuk Cres G33 ....32 B5
Millersneuk Ct G66 ......20 D4
Millersneuk Dr G66 ......20 D4
Millersneuk Prim Sch
G66 ....20 E4
Millersneuk Rd G66 ......20 D4
Millerston St G31 ....46 B6
Millfield Ave ML1 ....79 F8
Millgate G71 ....63 F8
Millgate Ave G71 ....63 F8
Millgate Ct G71 ....63 F7
Millgate Rd ML3 ....78 C1
Millgate Terr ML3 ....78 C1
Millgreen 11 DG10 ......161 D5
Millhall Rd G76 ....87 C3
Millheugh ML9 ....92 E2
Millheugh Brae ML9 .....92 E2
Millheugh Pl G72 ....77 C6
Millheugh Rd ML3 ......105 E5
Millholm Gdns 5 ML9 ...129 E8
Millholm Rd Glasgow G44 .60 B4
Strathaven ML10 ....112 E5
Millhouse Cres G20 .....29 C7
Millhouse Dr G20 ....29 C7
Millichen Rd G23 ....17 E5
Millport Ave G44 ....60 C7
Millrigg Rd ML12 ....140 B3
Millroad Dr G40 ....163 C1
Millroad Gdns 2 G40 .....45 F6
Millroad St G40 ....45 F6
Millstone Pk ML12 ......160 D3
Millstream Cres ML6 .....38 A4
Millstream Ct PA1 ....42 A4
Millview G78 ....57 D3
Millview Pl G53 ....58 B4
Millwell Rd G75 ....101 D7
Millwood St G41 ....59 E8

Milnbank St G31 .46 A8
Milncroft Pl G33 .32 A1
Milncroft Prim Sch G33 .47 C8
Milncroft Rd G33 .32 A1
Milne Ct ML2 .81 E4
Milne St ML11 .111 F1
Milne Way G71 .64 A6
Milner La 7 G13 .28 E5
Milner Rd G13 .28 E5
Milngavie Rd G61 .17 A6
Milnpark Gdns 1 G41 .44 E5
Milnpark St G41 .44 E5
Milnwood Dr Bellshill ML4 .65 D4
Motherwell ML1 .65 C2
Milovaig Ave G23 .17 D1
Milovaig St G23 .17 D1
Milrig Rd G73 .60 F7
Milroy Gdns ML4 .65 A8
Milton ML11 .119 E5
Milton Ave G72 .61 E5
Milton Cres ML8 .95 F1
Milton Ct ML6 .51 A8
Milton Douglas Rd G81 .15 B5
Milton Dr 1 G64 .30 F7
Milton Gdns G71 .63 E8
Milton Ind Est ML11 .119 D7
Milton Mains Rd G81 .15 A5
Milton Park Sq ML11 .119 E6
Milton Prim Sch ML11 .119 E5
Milton Rd Carluke ML8 .108 D7
East Kilbride G74 .75 A2
Milton Sch G22 .30 E7
Milton St Airdrie ML6 .51 A8
Carluke ML8 .95 E2
Glasgow G4 .163 A4
Hamilton ML3 .78 A4
Motherwell ML1 .79 E8
Milton Terr ML3 .78 A5
Miltonbank Prim Sch
G22 .30 C8
Milverton Ave G61 .16 D6
Milverton Rd Glasgow G46 .59 B1
Rutherglen G46 .73 A8
Minard Rd Glasgow G41 .44 E1
Shotts ML7 .69 D6
Minard Way G71 .64 A7
Minch Way ML6 .51 D5
Mincher Cres ML1 .79 E4
Minella Gdns ML4 .65 A8
Minerva Ct 10 G3 .44 E8
Minerva St G3 .44 E8
Minerva Way G3 .44 E8
Mingarry La G20 .29 E4
Mingarry St G20 .29 E4
Mingulay Cres G22 .30 D8
Mingulay Pl G22 .30 E8
Mingulay St G22 .30 D8
Ministers Pk G74 .74 F4
Minmoir Rd G53 .57 F7
Minster Wlk G69 .48 F5
Minstrel Rd G13 .16 D1
Minthill Pl ML7 .55 D5
Minto Ave G73 .61 D4
Minto Cres G52 .43 F5
Minto Pk ML2 .81 C6
Minto St G52 .43 F5
Mireton St G22 .30 B5
Mirren Dr G81 .15 A7
Mirrlees Dr G12 .29 C4
Mirrlees La G12 .29 C4
Mission Gdns ML2 .81 C5
Mitchell Arc G73 .61 B8
Mitchell Ave
Cambuslang G72 .62 E6
Renfrew PA4 .27 B2
Mitchell Ct G74 .75 C2
Mitchell Dr G73 .61 B6
Mitchell Gr G74 .75 C2
Mitchell Hill Rd G45 .60 F2
Mitchell La G1 .162 C2
Mitchell Rd G67 .12 A3
Mitchell St Airdrie ML6 .50 F8
Coatbridge ML5 .49 C5
Glasgow G1 .162 C2
Mitchison Rd G67 .12 A3
Mitre Ct 2 G11 .28 F4
Mitre Gate 1 G11 .28 F4
Mitre La G14 .28 E4
Mitre La W G14 .28 D4
Mitre Rd Glasgow G11 .28 F4
Glasgow G14 .28 E4
Moat Ave G13 .28 C7
Moat Park Heritage Ctr*
ML12 .160 C4
Mochrum Rd G43 .59 E6
Moffat Acad & Prim Sch
DG10 .161 C6
Moffat Ct East Kilbride G75 .87 E7
Kirkmuirhill ML11 .114 A5
Moffat Gdns G75 .87 E7
Moffat Hospl DG10 .161 E5
Moffat Mus* DG10 .161 D5
Moffat Pl Airdrie ML6 .51 F8
Blantyre G72 .63 D1
Coatbridge ML5 .50 E4
East Kilbride G75 .87 E7
Moffat Rd ML6 .51 F7
Moffat St G5 .45 D4
Moffat View ML6 .37 A3
Moffathill ML6 .51 E5
Moidart Ave PA4 .27 B4
Moidart Cres G52 .43 F5
Moidart Ct G78 .57 B4
Moidart Gdns
Kirkintilloch G66 .9 B1
Newton Mearns G77 .72 E6
Moidart Pl G52 .43 F5
Moidart Rd G52 .43 E5
Moir St G1 .163 B1
Molendinar St G1 .163 B1
Mollins Ct G68 .22 D5
Mollins Rd G68 .22 C7
Mollinsburn Rd
Annathill G67,ML5 .22 F2
Glenboig ML5,ML6 .34 F8
Glenmavis ML6 .35 C6
Mollinsburn St G21 .30 E3
Mollison Ave ML7 .55 E6
Monach Rd G33 .47 C8
Monar Dr G22 .30 B3
Monar Pl G22 .30 B3
Monar St G22 .30 B3
Monar Way 5 ML2 .81 F6
Monart Pl G20 .29 F4
Moncrieff Gdns G66 .20 D5
Moncrieff Ave G66 .20 D5
Moncrieffe Rd ML6 .51 D4
Moncur St G40 .163 C1
Moness Dr G52 .43 E4
Money Gr ML1 .80 B4
Monieburgh Cres G65 .6 E1
Monieburgh Rd G65 .6 E1
Monifieth Ave G52 .43 D3
Monikie Gdns G64 .19 D1
Monkcastle Dr G72 .62 A6
Monkland Ave G66 .20 D6
Monkland St ML6 .51 B7
Monkland Terr ML5 .34 D6
Monkland View
Calderbank ML6 .51 B2
Uddingston G71 .49 A1
Monkland View Cres
G69 .49 A5
Monklands District General
Hospl ML6 .50 D7
Monklands Ind Est ML5 .49 F2
Monks Knowe ML11 .119 F3
Monks La ML8 .108 E4
Monks Rd ML6 .51 C4
Monks Way ML11 .119 F3
Monksbridge Ave G13 .16 D1
Monkscourt Ave ML6 .50 E7
Monkscroft Ave 1 G11 .29 A3
Monkscroft Ct G11 .29 A2
Monkscroft Gdns G11 .29 A2
Monkton Cres ML5 .49 E4
Monkton Dr G15 .16 C2
Monkton Gdns G77 .73 A4
Monmouth Ave G12 .29 A5
Monreith Ave G61 .16 D2
Monreith Rd G43 .59 E6
Monreith Rd E G44 .60 A5
Monroe Dr G71 .48 F1
Monroe Pl G71 .48 F1
Montague La G12 .29 B4
Montague St G4 .29 F2
Montalto Ave ML1 .66 B1
Montego Gn 2 G75 .75 A1
Monteith Dr G76 .74 A8
Monteith Gdns G76 .73 F8
Monteith Pl
3 Glasgow G40 .45 E5
Hamilton G72 .77 E8
Monteith Row G40 .45 E5
Monteith St ML11 .131 B7
Monteith Wlk ML7 .69 E6
Montford Ave G44 .60 E7
Montgarrie St 3 G51 .43 D6
Montgomery Ave
Coatbridge ML5 .49 F7
Paisley PA3 .42 B7
Montgomery Cres ML2 .93 E8
Montgomery Ct
Eaglesham G76 .86 E3
Paisley PA3 .42 B7
Montgomery Dr G46 .59 C1
Montgomery Pl
3 East Kilbride G74 .75 F2
Larkhall ML9 .93 B2
Montgomery Rd PA3 .42 B8
Montgomery Sq G76 .86 E4
Montgomery St
Cambuslang G72 .62 E5
Eaglesham G76 .86 E4
4 East Kilbride G74 .75 F2
Glasgow G40 .46 A4
Larkhall ML9 .93 A4
Montraive St G73 .46 C1
Montrave St G52 .43 D4
Montreal Pk G75 .75 C1
Montrose Ave
Glasgow G52 .42 E8
Glasgow G52 .42 F8
Glasgow,Carmyle G32 .47 C1
Hillington G52 .27 E1
Montrose Cres ML3 .78 D4
Montrose Dr G61 .16 E7
Montrose Gdns
Blantyre G72 .63 C2
Kilsyth G65 .6 C1
Montrose La ML3 .78 C4
Montrose St
Clydebank G81 .15 C2
Glasgow G1 .163 B2
Motherwell ML1 .65 D1
Montrose Terr G64 .31 C7
Monymusk Gdns G64 .19 D2
Monymusk Pl G15 .15 E5
Moodiesburn St G33 .31 E2
Moor Rd
Cartland ML8,ML11 .109 E2
Eaglesham G76 .86 D4
Moorburn Ave G46 .59 B3
Moorcroft Dr ML6 .51 E7
Moorcroft Rd G77 .72 C3
Moore Dr G61 .16 F3
Moore Gdns ML3 .91 E7
Moore St Glasgow G31,G40 .45 F6
Motherwell ML1 .66 A3
Mooreland Gdns EH55 .122 E8
Moorfield Cres ML6 .51 F7
Moorfield Rd G72 .77 C6
Moorfoot G64 .19 C2
Moorfoot Ave G46 .59 A3
Moorfoot Dr ML2 .80 F3
Moorfoot Gdns G75 .88 B3
Moorfoot St G32 .46 E6
Moorfoot Way G61 .16 C8
Moorhill Cres G77 .72 C4
Moorhill Rd G77 .72 C3
Moorhouse Ave G13 .27 F6
Moorhouse St G78 .57 C2
Moorland Dr ML6 .51 E7
Moorlands Wlk G71 .64 A5
Moorpark Ave
3 Airdrie ML6 .51 E7
Glasgow G52 .42 F6
Muirhead G69 .33 C7
Moorpark Ct G51 .44 A7
Moorpark Dr G52 .43 A6
Moorpark Pl G52 .42 F6
Moorpark Prim Sch PA4 .27 B2
Moorpark Sq PA4 .27 B2
Moorside St ML8 .96 A2
Morag Ave G72 .63 C1
Moraine Ave G15 .16 B1
Moraine Cir G15 .16 B1
Moraine Dr Clarkston G76 .73 D8
Clydebank G15 .16 B1
Moraine Pl G15 .16 B1
Morar Ave G81 .15 B4
Morar Cres Airdrie ML6 .35 E2
Bishopbriggs G64 .18 F2
Clydebank G81 .15 B4
Coatbridge ML5 .34 D1
Morar Ct Clydebank G81 .15 B4
Cumbernauld G67 .23 B8
Hamilton ML3 .78 A1
Larkhall ML9 .92 F5
Morar Dr Bearsden G61 .17 B3
Clydebank G81 .15 B4
Cumbernauld G67 .23 B8
Rutherglen G73 .61 B3
Morar Pl Clydebank G81 .15 B4
East Kilbride G74 .75 F3
Newton Mearns G77 .72 D7
Renfrew PA4 .27 B4
Morar Rd Clydebank G81 .15 B4
Glasgow G52 .43 E5
Morar St ML2 .81 A1
Morar Terr
Rutherglen G73 .61 D4
Uddingston G71 .64 B7
Morar Way
Motherwell ML1 .66 C3
Shotts ML7 .70 B3
Moravia Ave G71 .64 A3
Moray Ave ML6 .51 A5
Moray Ct G73 .61 A8
Moray Dr G76 .73 F7
Moray Gate G71 .63 F4
Moray Gdns Clarkston G76 .73 F8
Cumbernauld G68 .11 F5
Uddingston G71 .63 F8
Moray Pl Bishopbriggs G64 .19 C1
Chryston G69 .33 D8
Glasgow G41 .44 F2
Hamilton G72 .77 C6
Kirkintilloch G66 .9 B1
Moray Quadrant ML4 .65 A5
Moray Way ML1 .66 A5
Mordaunt St G40 .46 A3
Moredun Cres G32 .47 C7
Moredun St G32 .47 C7
Morefield Rd 10 G51 .43 D7
Morgan Mews 4 G42 .45 B3
Morgan St Hamilton ML3 .78 D2
Larkhall ML9 .92 F3
Morgan Way
Armadale EH48 .41 F3
Armadale EH48 .41 F4
Morina Gdns G53 .58 C3
Morion Rd G13 .28 D8
Moriston Ct ML2 .81 F6
Morland G74 .76 D4
Morley St G42 .60 A7
Morna La G14 .28 E2
Mornay Way ML7 .69 D5
Morningside Prim Sch
ML2 .82 B4
Morningside Rd ML2 .82 C3
Morningside St G33 .46 E8
Morrin Path G21 .30 E3
Morrin St G21 .30 E4
Morris Cres Hamilton G72 .77 D7
Motherwell ML1 .66 E1
Morris St Hamilton ML3 .78 D1
Larkhall ML9 .93 C1
Morrishall Rd G74 .76 C3
Morrison Gdns G64 .19 C8
Morrison Ho G67 .12 A2
Morrison Quadrant G81 .15 E1
Morrison St
Douglas Water ML11 .138 F7
Glasgow G5 .162 B1
Morriston Cres PA4 .27 F1
Morriston Park Dr G72 .62 A6
Morriston St G72 .62 A6
Morton Ct ML11 .114 A5
Morton Gdns G41 .44 C1
Morton St ML1 .79 E8
Morven Ave
Bishopbriggs G64 .19 C1
Blantyre G72 .63 C1
Morven Dr G76 .73 D8
Morven Gdns G71 .63 F8
Morven La G72 .63 C1
Morven Rd Bearsden G61 .16 E6
Cambuslang G72 .61 F3
Morven St Coatbridge ML5 .50 A8
Glasgow G52 .43 E5
Morven Way
1 Bothwell G71 .64 B3
Kirkintilloch G66 .21 B8
Mosesfield St G21 .30 F5
Mosque Ave G5 .45 C5
Moss Ave ML6 .38 A5
Moss Dr G78 .57 A5
Moss Heights Ave G52 .43 D5
Moss Path G69 .47 F3
Moss Rd Airdrie ML6 .51 A6
Carstairs Junction ML11 .131 B8
Cumbernauld G67 .12 F4
East Kilbride G75 .88 C4
Glasgow G51 .43 D8
Kirkintilloch G66 .21 B7
Kirkintilloch,High Gallowhill
G66 .20 B6
Muirhead G69 .33 C7
Strathaven ML10 .112 E5
Wishaw ML2 .81 E3
Moss Side ML11 .119 F2
Moss Side Ave ML6 .50 E8
Moss Side Cres ML12 .160 B3
Moss Side Rd ML12 .160 B3
Moss View ML10 .103 C5
Moss-Side Ave ML8 .95 D2
Moss-Side Rd G41 .44 E1
Mossacre Rd ML2 .81 C4
Mossband La ML7 .69 E6
Mossbank
East Kilbride G75 .87 F8
Hamilton G72 .77 D6
Mossbank Ave G33 .31 F4
Mossbank Cres ML1 .66 F4
Mossbank Dr G33 .31 F4
Mossbank Rd ML2 .81 C4
Mossbell Rd ML4 .64 E6
Mossblown St ML9 .92 F3
Mossburn Ave ML7 .55 D5
Mossburn Rd ML2 .81 D3
Mossburn St ML2 .81 D1
Mosscastle Rd G33 .32 C2
Mossdale G74 .75 C3
Mossdale Ct ML4 .65 D5
Mossdale Gdns ML3 .77 E2
Mossend La G33 .47 D8
Mossend Prim Sch ML4 .65 C4
Mossend St G33 .47 D8
Mossgiel
Auchenheath ML11 .114 D4
East Kilbride G75 .88 B7
Mossgiel Ave G73 .61 A5
Mossgiel Cres G76 .73 F5
Mossgiel Dr G81 .15 C3
Mossgiel Gdns G71 .63 E8
Mossgiel La 1 ML9 .93 C1
Mossgiel Pl G73 .61 A5
Mossgiel Rd
Cumbernauld G67 .12 B2
Glasgow G43 .59 D6
Glasgow G43 .59 D7
Mossgiel Terr G72 .63 C2
Mossgiel Way ML1 .66 C4
Mosshall Gr ML1 .66 F4
Mosshall Rd ML1 .66 D7
Mosshall St ML1 .66 F3
Mosshat Rd EH55 .122 F2
Mosshead Prim Sch G61 .16 E7
Mosshead Rd G61 .17 A7
Mosshill Rd ML4 .65 B7
Mossknowe G67 .12 C2
Mossknowe Wlk ML10 .104 F3
Mossland Dr ML2 .81 C4
Mossland Rd Glasgow G52 .42 E8
Hillington G52 .27 E1
Mosslingal G75 .88 E5
Mossmulloch G75 .88 E5
Mossneuk Ave G75 .87 E8
Mossneuk Cres ML2 .81 D4
Mossneuk Dr
East Kilbride G75 .87 F7
Wishaw ML2 .81 C4
Mossneuk Pk ML2 .81 D4
Mossneuk Prim Sch G75 .87 F7
Mossneuk Rd G75 .88 A8
Mossneuk St ML5 .49 F3
Mosspark Ave G52 .43 F3
Mosspark Bvd G52 .43 E4
Mosspark Dr G52 .43 E3
Mosspark La G52 .43 E3
Mosspark Oval G52 .43 E3
Mosspark Prim Sch G52 .43 E3
Mosspark Rd ML5 .49 D8
Mosspark Sq G52 .43 E3
Mosspark Sta G52 .43 C3
Mossvale Cres G33 .32 C2
Mossvale Path G33 .32 C3
Mossvale Rd G33 .32 C2
Mossvale Sq G33 .32 B2
Mossvale Terr G69 .22 A3
Mossvale Way G33 .32 C2
Mossvale Wlk G33 .32 C2
Mossview Cres ML6 .51 A5
Mossview La G52 .43 C5
Mossview Quadrant G52 .43 D5
Mossview Rd G33 .32 E5
Mossywood Ct G68 .22 F7
Mossywood Pl G68 .22 F7
Mossywood Rd G68 .22 F7
Mote Hill ML3 .78 E5
Motehill Rd PA3 .42 A7
Motherwell Bsns Ctr ML1 .79 F7
Motherwell Coll ML1 .79 F4
Motherwell Heritage Ctr*
ML1 .79 D7
Motherwell Rd
Bellshill ML4 .65 B4
Hamilton ML3 .79 A4
Motherwell ML1 .67 A6
Motherwell,Carfin ML1 .66 C1
Motherwell St ML6 .51 C8
Motherwell Sta ML1 .79 D7
Moulin Cir G52 .43 A4
Moulin Pl G52 .43 A4
Moulin Rd G52 .43 A4
Moulin Terr G52 .43 A4
Mount Annan Dr G44 .60 B7
Mount Cameron Dr N
G74 .89 A8
Mount Cameron Dr S
G74 .89 B8
Mount Cameron Prim Sch
G74 .89 B7
Mount Florida Prim Sch
G42 .60 B7
Mount Florida Sta G42 .60 A8
Mount Harriet Ave G33 .32 E6
Mount Harriet Dr G33 .32 E6
Mount Lockhart G71 .48 B2
Mount Lockhart Gdns
G71 .48 B2
Mount Lockhart Pl G71 .48 B2
Mount Pleasant EH48 .41 F5
Mount St G20 .29 F3
Mount Stewart St ML8 .95 E2
Mount Stuart St G41 .59 E8
Mount The ML1 .79 D6
Mount Vernon Ave
Coatbridge ML5 .49 E7
Glasgow G32,G69 .47 E3
Mount Vernon Prim Sch
G32 .47 D3
Mount Vernon Sta G32 .47 F2
Mountainblue St G31 .46 B5
Mountgarrie Path 8
G51 .43 D7
Mountgarrie Rd 9 G51 .43 D7
Mountherrick G75 .88 E5
Mounthilly Rd ML10 .103 C5
Mountstuart Ave ML11 .138 F6
Mountstuart Ct ML11 .138 F6
Mountstuart St ML11 .138 F6
Mournian Way ML3 .78 D1
Mouse Valley Rd ML11 .111 F2
Mousebank La ML11 .116 F4
Mousebank Rd ML11 .116 F5
Mousemill Rd ML11 .116 D5
Mowbray G74 .76 C4
Mowbray Ave G69 .33 F5
Moy Path 4 ML2 .81 F6
Moy St G11 .29 C2
Moyne Rd G53 .43 A2
Muckcroft Rd G69 .21 C4
Muir Ct G44 .59 F2
Muir Glen ML11 .117 C3
Muir St Bishopbriggs G64 .19 A1
Coatbridge ML5 .49 E7
Hamilton ML3 .78 E4
Hamilton,High Blantyre G72 .77 D6
Larkhall ML9 .93 A3
Law ML8 .94 F6
Motherwell ML1 .79 D7
Renfrew PA4 .27 D4
Muir Street Prim Sch
ML1 .79 D8
Muir Terr PA3 .42 A7
Muirbank Ave G73 .60 F8
Muirbank Gdns G73 .60 F7
Muirbrae Rd G73 .61 B4
Muirbrae Way G73 .61 B4
Muirburn Ave G44 .59 E4
Muirburn Pl
Coalburn ML11 .137 F6
Glassford ML10 .104 F3
Muirburn Rd ML10 .105 A2
Muircroft Dr ML1 .67 B2
Muirdrum Ave G52 .43 D3
Muirdyke Rd
Coatbridge,Brackenhirst
ML5,ML6 .35 A5
Coatbridge,Drumpellier
ML5 .49 D8
Glenboig ML5 .34 F4
Muirdykes Ave 2 G52 .43 A5
Muirdykes Rd G52 .43 A5
Muiredge & Jersy Rd
Cleland ML1,ML7 .68 B6
Shotts ML7 .69 A8
Muiredge Ct G71 .63 F6
Muiredge Prim Sch G71 .64 A6
Muiredge Terr G69 .48 B4
Muirend Ave G44 .59 F5
Muirend Rd G44 .59 E4
Muirend Sta G44 .59 F4
Muirfield Cres 6 G23 .17 E1
Muirfield Ct G44 .59 F4
Muirfield Mdws G71 .63 E2
Muirfield Rd G68 .12 A5
Muirfoot Rd ML11 .138 F5
Muirfoot Terr ML11 .111 B8
Muirhall Terr ML7 .53 B2
Muirhead ML9 .129 E8
Muirhead Cotts G66 .21 B7
Muirhead Ct G69 .48 C4
Muirhead Dr Law ML8 .95 A6
Motherwell ML1 .66 F4

Muirhead Gate 4 G71 . . .64 A8
Muirhead Gdns
Glasgow G69 . . . . .48 C4
Salsburgh ML7 . . . . .53 B2
Muirhead Gr G69 . . . . .48 C4
Muirhead Pl ML7 . . . . .55 D4
Muirhead Rd G69 . . . . .48 B3
Muirhead Rdbt G67 . . . . . .12 B3
Muirhead St G66 . . . . .20 D7
Muirhead Terr ML1 . . . . . .79 E4
Muirhead Way G64 . . . . . .19 D1
Muirhill Ave G44 . . . . .59 E5
Muirhill Cres G13 . . . . . . .28 A7
Muirhill Ct ML3 . . . . .78 D4
Muirhouse Ave
Motherwell ML1 . . . . .80 B3
Wishaw ML2 . . . . .82 B6
Muirhouse Dr ML1 . . . . . . .80 C2
Muirhouse La
Carstairs ML11 . . . . .111 F7
5 East Kilbride G75 . . . . . . .88 F8
Muirhouse Pk G61 . . . . . . .16 D8
Muirhouse Prim Sch
ML1 . . . . .80 B2
Muirhouse Rd ML1 . . . . . . .80 B2
Muirhouse St 1 G41 . . . . .45 A3
Muirhouse Twr ML1 . . . . . .80 B3
Muirkirk Dr Glasgow G13 . .28 F7
Hamilton ML3 . . . . .77 D2
Muirkirk Rd ML10 . . . . . .112 D5
Muirlaun ML11 . . . . .122 A1
Muirlee Rd ML8 . . . . .96 B1
Muirmadkin Rd ML4 . . . . .65 B5
Muirmaillen Ave ML1 . . . . .67 C1
Muirpark Ave PA4 . . . . . . .27 C2
Muirpark Dr G64 . . . . .31 A8
Muirpark St G11 . . . . .29 B2
Muirpark Terr G64 . . . . . .31 A8
Muirshiel Ave G53 . . . . . .58 C6
Muirshiel Cres G53 . . . . . .58 D6
Muirshiel Ct G53 . . . . . . .58 C5
Muirshot Rd ML9 . . . . .93 B4
Muirside Ave
Glasgow G32 . . . . .47 E3
Kirkintilloch G66 . . . . .21 A8
Muirside Pl 21 ML2 . . . . . .81 F6
Muirside Rd Glasgow G69 .48 B4
Strathaven ML10 . . . . .112 E5
Muirside St G69 . . . . .48 B4
Muirskeith Cres G44 . . . . .60 A6
Muirskeith Pl G43 . . . . . . .59 F6
Muirskeith Rd G43 . . . . . .59 F6
Muirsland Pl ML11 . . . . . .119 C6
Muirton Dr G64 . . . . .18 F3
Muiryfauld Dr G31 . . . . . .46 E5
Muiryhall St
Coatbridge ML5 . . . . .50 A7
Coatbridge,Cliftonville ML5 . .50 B7
Muiryhall St E ML5 . . . . . .50 C7
Mulben Cres G53 . . . . .57 F7
Mulben Pl G53 . . . . .57 F7
Mulben Terr G53 . . . . .57 F8
Mulberry Cres ML6 . . . . . .51 E3
Mulberry Dr G75 . . . . .88 C5
Mulberry Rd Glasgow G43 .59 D5
Motherwell G71 . . . . .49 C1
Mulberry Way G75 . . . . . . .88 C5
Mulberry Wynd G72 . . . . . .62 F3
Muldron Terr ML7 . . . . . . .70 B2
Mull Airdrie ML6 . . . . .51 D5
East Kilbride G74 . . . . .89 C8
Mull Ave PA4 . . . . .27 C1
Mull Ct ML3 . . . . .77 F1
Mull Quadrant ML2 . . . . . .81 E5
Mull St G21 . . . . .31 B2
Mullardoch St 12 G23 . . . .17 D1
Mullen Ct G33 . . . . .32 F5
Mulvey Cres ML6 . . . . .50 E7
Mungo Pk G75 . . . . .88 D8
Mungo Pl G71 . . . . .49 A1
Munlochy Rd G51 . . . . . . .43 D7
Munro La G13 . . . . .28 E5
Munro La E G13 . . . . .28 E5
Munro Pl East Kilbride G74 .76 B3
Glasgow G13 . . . . .28 E6
Munro Rd G13 . . . . .28 E5
Murano St G20 . . . . .29 F4
Murchison G12 . . . . .29 A6
Murchison Dr G75 . . . . . . .88 B7
Murdoch Dr G62 . . . . .17 D8
Murdoch Pl ML1 . . . . .65 F3
Murdoch Rd G75 . . . . .88 E8
Murdoch Sq ML4 . . . . .65 C7
Murdostoun Cres ML7 . . . .55 F6
Murdostoun Gdns ML2 . . .81 B5
Murdostoun Pl ML12 . . . .145 F2
Murdostoun Terr ML1 . . . .67 E1
Murdostoun View ML2 . . . .81 F6
Muriel La G78 . . . . .57 C3
Muriel St G78 . . . . .57 C3
Muriel Street Ind Est
G78 . . . . .57 C4
Murray Ave
Crawford ML12 . . . . .152 B7
Kilsyth G65 . . . . .10 D8
Murray Cres Hamilton G72 .77 E6
Wishaw ML2 . . . . .82 A7
Murray Ct Armadale EH48 . .41 F6
Hamilton ML3 . . . . .78 A3
Murray Dr ML9 . . . . .105 F2
Murray Gr G61 . . . . .16 B8
Murray Path G71 . . . . .63 E6
Murray Pl Barrhead G78 . . .57 D4
Bellshill ML4 . . . . .64 E7
Murray Prim Sch G75 . . . .88 E8
Murray Rd Bothwell G71 . . .64 A3
Law ML8 . . . . .94 F4
Murray Rd The G75 . . . . . .88 E7
Murray Rdbt The G75 . . . .88 F8
Murray Sq The 2 G75 . . . .88 E7
Murray St PA4 . . . . .27 C3
Murray Terr
Carnwath ML11 . . . . .124 E1
Motherwell ML1 . . . . .79 B7
Murray Wlk G72 . . . . .77 E6
Murrayfield G64 . . . . .19 A3
Murrayfield Dr G61 . . . . . .16 E1
Murrayfield St G32 . . . . . .46 E7
Murrayhill G75 . . . . .88 D8
Murraysgate Cres EH47 . . .56 F6
Murraysgate Ind Est
EH47 . . . . .56 F6
Murrayside ML9 . . . . .105 D1
Murrin Ave G64 . . . . .19 D1
Murroes Rd G51 . . . . .43 D7
Museum Bsns Pk G53 . . . .57 F5
Museum of Lead Mining*
ML12 . . . . .154 C7
Museum of Scottish Country Life The G76 . . . . .74 F4
Museum of Transport*
G3 .29 C1
Musgrove Pl G75 . . . . .88 C8
Muslin St G40 . . . . .45 F4
Muttonhole Rd ML3 . . . . . .90 E7
Mybster Pl G51 . . . . .43 D7
Myers Cres G71 . . . . .64 A5
Myers Ct ML4 . . . . .64 D6
Myres Rd G53 . . . . .58 D8
Myreside Pl G32 . . . . .46 D6
Myreside St G32 . . . . .46 E6
Myrie Gdns G64 . . . . .19 B2
Myroch Pl G34 . . . . .33 C1
Myrtle Ave G66 . . . . .20 C5
Myrtle Dr Motherwell ML1 . .66 B5
Wishaw ML2 . . . . .80 D4
Myrtle Hill La G42 . . . . . .60 C8
Myrtle La ML9 . . . . .93 C1
Myrtle Pk G42 . . . . .45 C1
Myrtle Pl G42 . . . . .60 C8
Myrtle Rd G71 . . . . .64 B8
Myrtle Sq G64 . . . . .31 A8
Myrtle St G72 . . . . .63 D1
Myrtle View Rd G42 . . . . .60 C8
Myrtle Wlk G72 . . . . .61 F6
Myvot Ave G67 . . . . .23 B6
Myvot Rd
Cumbernauld,Dalshannon
G67 . . . . .23 B6
Cumbernauld,Mollinsburn
G67 . . . . .22 F4

N

Naburn Gate 6 G5 . . . . . .45 C4
Nagle Gdns ML1 . . . . .80 F8
Nairn Ave Bellshill ML4 . . . .65 A6
Blantyre G72 . . . . .63 C2
Nairn Cres ML6 . . . . .51 A5
Nairn Pl G74 . . . . .76 C3
Nairn Quadrant ML2 . . . . .81 B5
Nairn St Glasgow G3 . . . . .29 D1
Hamilton G72 . . . . .77 C6
Larkhall ML9 . . . . .92 F2
Nairn Way G68 . . . . .12 A5
Nairnside Rd G21 . . . . . . .31 C7
Naismith Ct ML9 . . . . . . .105 E1
Naismith St G32 . . . . .62 C8
Naismith Wlk ML4 . . . . . . .65 C7
Nansen St G20 . . . . .30 A3
Napier Ct G68 . . . . .12 D8
Napier Dr G51 . . . . .44 B8
Napier Gdns ML11 . . . . . .113 F3
Napier Hill G75 . . . . .88 E8
Napier La G75 . . . . .88 E8
Napier Pk G68 . . . . .12 C7
Napier Pl
Cumbernauld G68 . . . . .12 D8
Glasgow G51 . . . . .44 B8
Napier Rd
Cumbernauld G68 . . . . .12 C7
Glasgow,Govan G51 . . . . . . .44 B8
Glasgow,North Cardonald
G52 . . . . .42 F8
Hillington G52 . . . . .27 F1
Napier Sq ML4 . . . . .65 C7
Napier St Clydebank G81 . . .27 D7
Glasgow G51 . . . . .44 B8
Napier Terr G51 . . . . .44 B8
Napier Way G68 . . . . .12 C7
Napiershall La G4 . . . . . . .29 F2
Napiershall Pl 3 G20 . . . .29 F2
Napiershall St G20 . . . . . .29 F2
Naproch Pl G77 . . . . .73 C5
Naseby Ave G11 . . . . .28 F3
Naseby La G11 . . . . .28 F4
Nasmyth Ave
Bearsden G61 . . . . .16 B8
East Kilbride G75 . . . . .89 A7
Nasmyth Pl G75 . . . . .88 F7
Nasmyth Rd G52 . . . . .43 A7
Nasmyth Rd N G52 . . . . . .43 A7
Nasmyth Rd S G52 . . . . . .43 A7
Nassau Pl 1 G75 . . . . .75 A1
National Bank La G1 . . . .162 C2
National Piping Ctr The
G4 . . . . .162 C4
Navar Ct ML7 . . . . .70 A3
Navar Pl PA2 . . . . .42 A2
Naver St G33 . . . . .31 E1
Naylor La ML6 . . . . .51 B8
Naysmyth Bank G75 . . . . .88 F8
Needle Gn ML8 . . . . .95 F2
Neidpath G69 . . . . .48 A3
Neidpath Ave ML5 . . . . . . .50 B3
Neidpath E G74 . . . . .75 D2
Neidpath Pl
Coatbridge ML5 . . . . .50 A3
Strathaven ML10 . . . . .112 F7
Neidpath Rd ML8 . . . . .95 E3
Neidpath Rd E G46 . . . . . .73 A6
Neidpath Rd W G46 . . . . . .73 A7
Neidpath W G74 . . . . .75 D1
Neil St PA4 . . . . .27 D5
Neilsland Dr
Hamilton ML3 . . . . .91 C7
Motherwell ML1 . . . . .79 B6
Neilsland Oval G53 . . . . . .43 D1
Neilsland Prim Sch ML3 . .78 A1
Neilsland Rd ML3 . . . . . . .78 B1
Neilsland Sq Glasgow G53 .43 D1
Hamilton ML3 . . . . .78 C1
Neilsland St ML3 . . . . .78 C1
Neilson Ct ML3 . . . . .78 E2
Neilson St ML4 . . . . .65 A5
Neilston Ave G53 . . . . .58 C5
Neilston Ct G53 . . . . .58 C5
Neilston Pl G65 . . . . .6 B1
Neilston Rd G78 . . . . .57 A1
Neilston Wlk G65 . . . . .6 D1
Neilvaig Dr G73 . . . . .61 C3
Neistpoint Dr G33 . . . . . .47 A7
Nellfield Ct ML8 . . . . . . .109 A4
Nellfield Gdns ML8 . . . . .109 A4
Nellfield La ML8 . . . . . . .109 A4
Nelson Ave ML5 . . . . .49 E4
Nelson Cres ML1 . . . . .80 B4
Nelson Mandela Pl G2 . .163 A3
Nelson Pl G69 . . . . .48 B4
Nelson St Glasgow G5 . . .162 B1
Glasgow,Muirhead G69 . . . .48 B4
Nelson Terr G74 . . . . .89 A8
Nemphlar Moor Rd
Crossford ML8,ML11 . . . . .108 D1
Hazelbank ML11 . . . . .115 F8
Nemphlar ML11 . . . . .116 A7
Nemphlar Rd ML11 . . . . .116 A6
Nemphlat Hill ML11 . . . . .116 F5
Neptune St G51 . . . . .44 B7
Neptune Way ML4 . . . . . . .65 E5
Nerston Rd G74 . . . . .75 E6
Nerston Residential Sch
G74 . . . . .76 A7
Ness Dr Blantyre G72 . . . .63 E1
East Kilbride G74 . . . . .76 B1
Ness Gdns
Bishopbriggs G64 . . . . .19 B1
Larkhall ML9 . . . . .106 A8
Ness Rd PA4 . . . . .27 B4
Ness St Glasgow G33 . . . . .31 E1
Wishaw ML2 . . . . .94 B8
Ness Terr ML3 . . . . .78 A1
Ness Way ML1 . . . . .66 A5
Nethan Ave ML2 . . . . .80 C1
Nethan Gate ML3 . . . . . . .78 C3
Nethan Glen ML8 . . . . . . .108 A2
Nethan Path ML9 . . . . . . .106 A8
Nethan Pl ML3 . . . . .91 D6
Nethan St Glasgow G51 . . .44 A8
Motherwell ML1 . . . . .65 C2
Nethan Vale Terr ML11 . .119 E6
Nethan View
Crossford ML8 . . . . .108 A2
Kirkmuirhill ML11 . . . . . . .114 A5
Nethanfoot Brig Rd
ML8 . . . . .108 B2
Nether Auldhouse Rd
G43 . . . . .59 C6
Netherbank Rd ML2 . . . . . .80 D2
Netherburn Ave G44 . . . . .59 F2
Netherburn Prim Sch
ML9 . . . . .107 B3
Netherburn Rd ML9 . . . . .107 A7
Netherby Dr G41 . . . . .44 D4
Nethercairn Pl G77 . . . . . .73 C5
Nethercairn Rd G43 . . . . .59 C4
Nethercliffe Ave G44 . . . .59 F2
Nethercroy Rd G65 . . . . . .10 E5
Netherdale G77 . . . . .73 B5
Netherdale Cres ML2 . . . .80 C2
Netherdale Dr PA1 . . . . . . .42 F4
Netherdale Rd ML2 . . . . . .80 E2
Netherfield St G31 . . . . . .46 C6
Nethergreen Cres PA4 . . .27 B3
Nethergreen Wynd PA4 . . .27 B3
Netherhall Rd ML2 . . . . . .80 D2
Netherhill Ave G44 . . . . . .59 F1
Netherhill Cotts PA3 . . . . .42 B7
Netherhill Cres PA3 . . . . .42 A6
Netherhill Rd
Moodiesburn G69 . . . . .21 F2
Paisley PA3 . . . . .42 B7
Netherhill Way PA3 . . . . . .42 B7
Netherhouse Ave
Coatbridge ML5 . . . . .49 F3
Kirkintilloch G66 . . . . .20 E4
Netherhouse Pl G34 . . . . .48 E8
Netherhouse Rd G34,G69 .48 E7
Netherlee Ct G44 . . . . . . .59 F2
Netherlee Pl G44 . . . . . . .60 A4
Netherlee Prim Sch G44 . .59 F2
Netherlee Rd G44 . . . . . . .60 A4
Nethermains Rd G62 . . . . .17 A8
Netherpark Ave G44 . . . . .59 F1
Netherplace Cres
Glasgow G53 . . . . .58 B8
Newton Mearns G77 . . . . . .72 C3
Netherplace Rd
Glasgow G53 . . . . .58 B8
Newton Mearns G77 . . . . . .72 A3
Netherplace Rd *continued*
Newton Mearns G77 . . . . . .72 C4
Netherton Ave G13 . . . . . .28 E8
Netherton Ct Glasgow G45 .60 F2
Newton Mearns G77 . . . . . .73 A7
Netherton Dr G78 . . . . . . .57 E1
Netherton Farm La 1
G61 . . . . .28 F8
Netherton Ind Est ML2 . . .80 E2
Netherton Prim Sch ML2 .80 E1
Netherton Rd
East Kilbride G75 . . . . .88 A4
East Kilbride,The Murray
G75 . . . . .88 C7
Glasgow G13 . . . . .28 F7
Glasgow G13 . . . . .28 F8
Newton Mearns G77 . . . . . .72 F6
Wishaw ML2 . . . . .80 E1
Netherton St Harthill ML7 .55 D5
Wishaw ML2 . . . . .80 F2
Nethervale Ave G44 . . . . . .59 F1
Netherview Rd G44 . . . . . .60 A1
Netherway G44 . . . . .59 F1
Netherwood Ave G68 . . . . .22 F8
Netherwood Ct
Cumbernauld G68 . . . . .23 A8
Motherwell ML1 . . . . .80 B2
Netherwood Gr G68 . . . . .23 A8
Netherwood Pl G68 . . . . . .22 F8
Netherwood Rd
Cumbernauld G68 . . . . .22 F8
Motherwell ML1 . . . . .80 B3
Netherwood Twr ML1 . . . . .80 B2
Netherwood Way G68 . . . .23 A8
Nethy Way PA4 . . . . .27 F1
Neuk Ave G69 . . . . .33 C7
Neuk The Forth ML11 . . . . .98 F8
Stonehouse ML9 . . . . .129 F8
Wishaw ML2 . . . . .80 E3
Neuk Way G72 . . . . .62 C8
Neville G74 . . . . .76 C4
Nevis Ave ML3 . . . . .78 A1
Nevis Ct Barrhead G78 . . . .57 C1
Coatbridge ML5 . . . . .50 C3
Motherwell ML1 . . . . .79 E4
Nevis Pl ML7 . . . . .70 B3
Nevis Rd Bearsden G61 . . . .16 B7
Glasgow G43 . . . . .59 B5
Renfrew PA4 . . . . .27 B1
Nevison St ML9 . . . . .93 B2
New Albion Ind Est G13 . .27 E7
New Ashtree St ML2 . . . . .80 E3
New Bldgs ML11 . . . . . . .117 A2
New Branziet Cotts G22 . .18 B8
New Century Dr ML7 . . . . .69 E4
New City Rd Glasgow G4 . .162 B4
Glasgow G4 . . . . .162 C4
New Cross ML3 . . . . .78 E3
New Edinburgh Rd G71,
ML4 . . . . .64 B6
New Kirk Rd G61 . . . . .16 E5
New La ML6 . . . . .51 B3
New Lairdsland Rd G66 . . .20 D8
New Lanark Heritage Trail*
ML11 . . . . .117 A1
New Lanark Prim Sch
ML11 . . . . .117 A2
New Lanark Rd ML11 . . . .117 A2
New Lanark World Heritage
Village* ML11 . . . . .117 A2
New Luce Dr G32 . . . . . . .47 D3
New Mill Trout & Deer
Farm* ML11 . . . . .130 D8
New Monkland Prim Sch
ML6 . . . . .35 E4
New Park St ML3 . . . . .78 C5
New Plymouth G75 . . . . . .88 A7
New Rd Cambuslang G72 . . .62 E4
Chapelton ML10 . . . . .103 C5
Lesmahagow ML11 . . . . . .119 E4
New St Clydebank G81 . . . .15 A6
Hamilton G72 . . . . .77 C7
Stonehouse ML9 . . . . .105 F2
New Stevenston Prim Sch
ML1 . . . . .65 F4
New Stevenston Rd
Motherwell ML1 . . . . .66 B2
Motherwell ML1 . . . . .66 C2
New Trows Rd ML11 . . . . .119 D3
New View Cres ML4 . . . . . .65 A3
New View Dr ML4 . . . . .65 A3
New View Pl ML4 . . . . .65 A3
New Wynd G1 . . . . .163 A1
Newark Dr Glasgow G41 . . .44 E3
Wishaw ML2 . . . . .81 C6
Newark Gate ML7 . . . . . . .82 F8
Newark Pl ML2 . . . . .81 D6
Newarthill Prim Sch ML1 .66 E3
Newarthill Rd ML1 . . . . . .66 C2
Newbank Ct G31 . . . . .46 E4
Newbank Gdns G31 . . . . . .46 D4
Newbank Rd G31 . . . . .46 E4
Newbarns St ML8 . . . . . . .95 F3
Newbattle Ave ML6 . . . . . .51 B2
Newbattle Ct G32 . . . . . . .47 B2
Newbattle Gdns G32 . . . . .47 B2
Newbattle Pl G32 . . . . . . .47 B2
Newbattle Rd G32 . . . . . . .47 B2
Newbigging Rd ML11 . . . .126 B3
Newbold Ave 2 G21 . . . . .30 F7
Newburgh St G43 . . . . . . .59 D7
Newcastleton Dr 9 G23 . . .17 E1
Newcraigs Dr G76 . . . . . . .74 D7
Newcroft Dr G44 . . . . .60 D5
Newdyke Ave G66 . . . . . . .20 E8
Newdyke Rd G66 . . . . .20 E8
Newfield Cres ML3 . . . . . .78 B4
Newfield Gdns 18 ML9 . . .129 E8
Newfield La 8 G71 . . . . . .64 B3
Newfield Pl Glasgow G46 . .58 F2
Rutherglen G73 . . . . .60 F8
Newfield Prim Sch ML9 . .129 E8
Newfield Rd ML9 . . . . . . .105 E1
Newfield Sq G53 . . . . .58 A6
Newford Gr G76 . . . . .73 E5
Newgrove Gdns G72 . . . . .62 A6
Newhall St G40 . . . . .45 F3
Newhaven Rd G33 . . . . . . .47 B8
Newhaven St G32 . . . . . . .47 A7
Newhills Rd G33 . . . . .47 E7
Newhouse Ct ML11 . . . . .130 F8
Newhouse Ind Est ML1 . . .66 D7
Newhousemill Cotts G74 .89 C7
Newhousemill Rd
East Kilbride G74 . . . . .89 D7
Hamilton G72,ML3 . . . . . . .77 C1
Newhut Rd ML1 . . . . .65 D1
Newington St G32 . . . . . . .46 F6
Newkayes Rd
Auchenheath ML11 . . . . . .114 E3
Hazelbank ML11 . . . . .115 B3
Newlands Dr ML3 . . . . . . .91 D8
Newlands Pl G74 . . . . .75 E1
Newlands Rd
East Kilbride G75 . . . . .87 E5
East Kilbride,Newlandsmuir
G75 . . . . .88 A7
Glasgow G44 . . . . .59 E6
Uddingston G71 . . . . .63 F8
Newlands St
Coatbridge ML5 . . . . .50 A4
Lanark ML11 . . . . .117 C3
Newlands Terr ML8 . . . . . .95 F2
Newlandsfield Rd G43 . . . .59 D7
Newlandsmuir Rd G75 . . .88 A6
Newmains Home Farm
ML1 . . . . .138 C2
Newmains Prim Sch
Renfrew PA4 . . . . .27 C1
Wishaw ML2 . . . . .82 A4
Newmains Rd PA4 . . . . . . .27 C1
Newmill & Canthill Rd
ML7 . . . . .69 B6
Newmill Gdns ML7 . . . . . . .68 F3
Newmill Rd G21 . . . . .31 C5
Newmilns St G53 . . . . .57 F6
Newnham Rd PA1 . . . . . . .42 E4
Newpark Cres G72 . . . . . .62 A7
Newrose Ave ML4 . . . . . . .65 C7
Newstead Gdns G23 . . . . .17 E1
Newton Ave Barrhead G78 .57 C1
Cambuslang G72 . . . . .62 D7
Newton Brae G72 . . . . .62 F6
Newton Ct
Cambuslang G72 . . . . .62 D6
Newton Mearns G77 . . . . . .72 D3
Strathaven ML10 . . . . .112 E5
Newton Dr
Uddingston G71 . . . . .64 A7
Wishaw ML2 . . . . .82 A5
Newton Farm Rd G72 . . . .63 A6
Newton Gr G77 . . . . .72 D3
Newton Pl Glasgow G3 . . .162 A4
Newton Mearns G77 . . . . . .72 E3
Newton Rd
Kirkintilloch G66 . . . . .20 E4
Strathaven ML10 . . . . .112 E5
Newton St G2,G3 . . . . . . .162 B3
Newton Sta G72 . . . . .62 E5
Newton Station Rd G72 . . .62 E5
Newton Terr G3 . . . . .162 A3
Newton Terrace La G3 . . .162 A3
Newton Way PA3 . . . . .42 B7
Newtongrange Ave G32 . . .47 B2
Newtongrange Gdns G32 .47 B3
Newtonhead Rd ML11 . . .138 F6
Newtonlea Ave G77 . . . . . .72 F4
Newtown St G65 . . . . .10 D8
Newtyle Dr G53 . . . . .42 F1
Newtyle Pl
Bishopbriggs G64 . . . . .19 D1
Glasgow G53 . . . . .42 F1
Newtyle Rd PA1 . . . . .42 C4
Nicholas St G1 . . . . .163 B2
Nicklaus Way ML1 . . . . . . .66 E7
Nicol St ML6 . . . . .36 C1
Nicolson Ct G33 . . . . .32 E5
Niddrie Rd G42 . . . . .45 A2
Niddrie Sq 6 G42 . . . . . . .44 F2
Nigel Gdns G41 . . . . .44 D1
Nigel St ML1 . . . . .79 D6
Nigg Pl G34 . . . . .48 A8
Nikitas Ave ML9 . . . . . . .106 B7
Nimmo Dr G51 . . . . .43 F7
Nimmo Pl Carluke ML8 . . . .95 E3
Carnwath ML11 . . . . .124 E1
Wishaw ML2 . . . . .81 C3
Ninian Rd ML6 . . . . .51 C5
Ninian's Rise G66 . . . . . . .20 F7
Nips Rd ML12 . . . . .140 E1
Nisbet St G31 . . . . .46 D5
Nisbet Way ML11 . . . . . . .130 D8
Nisbett Pl ML6 . . . . .51 E2
Nisbett St ML6 . . . . .51 E2
Nissen Pl G53 . . . . .42 F1
Nith Dr Hamilton ML3 . . . . .91 A8
Renfrew PA4 . . . . .27 E2
Nith La 24 ML2 . . . . .81 F6
Nith Path ML1 . . . . .67 C2
Nith Quadrant ML1 . . . . . .66 C3
Nith St G33 . . . . .31 D1
Nithsdale G74 . . . . .76 D3
Nithsdale Cres G61 . . . . . .16 C6
Nithsdale Cross G41 . . . . .44 D3
Nithsdale Dr G41 . . . . . . .44 F2
Nithsdale Pl G41 . . . . .44 F3

Nithsdale Rd G41 44 D3
Nithsdale St Glasgow G41 44 F2
Shotts ML7 69 D5
Nitshill Prim Sch G53 58 A4
Nitshill Rd G53 58 C3
Nitshill Sta G53 58 A5
Niven St G20 29 C6
Noble Prim Sch ML4 65 A7
Noble Rd ML4 65 B5
Nobles Pl ML4 64 F4
Nobles View ML4 64 F4
Noldrum Ave G32 62 C8
Noldrum Gdns G32 62 C8
Norbreck Dr G46 59 C4
Norby Rd G11 28 F3
Nordic Cres G72 77 E7
Nordic Gdns 3 G72 77 E7
Nordic Gr 6 G72 77 E7
Noremac Way ML4 64 F7
Norfield Dr G44 60 B7
Norfolk Cres G64 18 E3
Norfolk Ct G5 45 B5
Norfolk St G5 45 B5
Norham St G41 44 E1
Norman St G40 45 F3
Norse La N G14 28 C4
Norse La S 14 G14 28 C4
Norse Pl G14 28 C4
Norse Rd G14 28 C4
North & South Rd ML2 81 E8
North Ave Cambuslang G72 61 F6
Carluke ML8 95 D2
Clydebank G81 15 A2
Motherwell ML1 66 A2
North Back Rd ML12 160 D4
North Bank Pl G81 27 C7
North Bank St G81 27 C8
North Berwick Ave G68 11 F5
North Berwick Cres G75 88 A6
North Berwick Gdns G68 11 F5
North Biggar Rd ML6 51 B8
North Bridge St 1 ML6 50 F8
North British Rd G71 63 F6
North Bute St ML5 50 B4
North Caldeen Rd ML5 50 C5
North Calder Dr ML6 51 D6
North Calder Gr G71 48 B2
North Calder Pl G71 48 B2
North Calder Rd G71 49 C1
North Canal Bank G4 30 D2
North Canal Bank St G4 30 C2
North Carbrain Rd G67 11 F1
North Claremont St 4 G3 29 E1
North Court La G1 163 A2
North Ct G1 163 A2
North Dean Park Ave G71 64 A2
North Douglas St G81 27 C8
North Dryburgh Rd ML2 81 B6
North Elgin Pl G81 27 C7
North Elgin St G81 27 D8
North Erskine Pk G61 16 D5
North Faulds Rd ML11 117 E5
North Frederick St G1 163 A3
North Gardner St G11 29 B3
North Glasgow Coll G21 30 F3
North Gower St G51 44 C5
North Grange Rd G61 16 E6
North Hanover St G1,G4 163 A3
North Kilmeny Cres ML2 81 C6
North Lodge Ave ML1 79 E4
North Lodge Rd PA4 27 C4
North Moraine La G15 16 C2
North Orchard St ML1 79 D7
North Park Ave
Barrhead G78 57 B3
Glasgow G46 58 F4
North Portland St G1, G4 163 B2
North Rd Bellshill ML4 65 A7
Carnwath ML11 124 E1
Coatbridge ML5 50 A2
Cumbernauld G68 23 A8
Fauldhouse EH47 71 E7
North Sq ML5 49 E8
North St Armadale EH48 41 F6
Glasgow G3 162 A3
Larkhall ML9 93 A4
Motherwell ML1 79 F8
Strathaven ML10 112 F6
North Vennel ML11 117 A4
North View G61 16 D2
North Wallace St G4 163 B4
North Woodside Rd G20 29 F3
Northall Quadrant ML1 66 B1
Northampton Dr G12 29 B6
Northampton La G12 29 B6
Northbank Ave
Cambuslang G72 62 D6
Kirkintilloch G66 20 C8
Northbank Rd G66 20 C8
Northbank St G72 62 D6
Northbrae Pl G13 28 B6
Northburn Ave ML6 36 B1
Northburn Pl ML6 36 B2
Northburn Rd ML5 35 C1
Northburn St ML6 37 B2
Northcroft Rd G69 21 F2
Northcrofts Rd ML12 160 D5
Northfield G75 87 F7
Northfield Ave ML7 70 B2
Northfield Rd G65 6 B1
Northfield St ML1 79 E8
Northflat Pl ML8 109 C8
Northgate Quadrant G21 31 C6
Northgate Rd G21 31 C7
Northinch Ct G14 28 D2
Northinch St G14 28 D2
Northland Ave G14 28 C5
Northland Dr G14 28 C5
Northland Gdns G14 28 C5
Northland La G14 28 C4
Northmuir Dr ML2 81 D4
Northmuir Rd G15 16 B4
Northpark St G20 29 F4
Northumberland St G20 29 E4
Northway G72 63 C1
Northwood Dr ML2 82 A6
Norval St G11 29 A2
Norwich Dr G12 29 B5
Norwood Ave G66 20 B8
Norwood Dr G46 59 A1
Norwood Pk G61 16 F3
Norwood Terr G71 64 A7
Notre Dame High Sch G12 29 C3
Notre Dame Prim Sch G12 29 C3
Nottingham Ave G12 29 B6
Nottingham La G12 29 B6
Novar Dr G12 29 B4
Novar Gdns G64 18 E2
Novar St ML3 78 D2
Nuneaton St G40 46 A4
Nuneaton Street Ind Est G40 46 A4
Nurseries Rd G69 47 F6
Nursery Ave 12 ML11 138 B1
Nursery Bldgs ML11 117 A2
Nursery Ct Carluke ML8 95 E3
Lanark ML11 116 E4
Nursery Dr ML9 107 A8
Nursery La G41 44 F2
Nursery Pk ML8 95 E2
Nursery Pl G72 77 D6
Nursery St G41 45 A3
Nutberry Ct G42 45 B1
Nutberry Pl ML10 112 C6

O

O'Neill Ave G64 31 B8
O'wood Ave ML1 66 B6
Oak Ave Bearsden G61 16 F7
East Kilbride G75 88 B6
Oak Cres G69 48 A4
Oak Dr Cambuslang G72 62 C4
Kirkintilloch G66 20 B5
Oak Fern Dr G74 75 D4
Oak Fern Gr G74 75 D4
Oak Gr ML6 51 E3
Oak Knowe ML11 114 A4
Oak Lea ML3 78 F2
Oak Path ML1 66 B5
Oak Pk Bishopbriggs G64 19 B1
Motherwell ML1 79 D4
Oak Pl Coatbridge ML5 50 C5
East Kilbride G75 88 B6
Uddingston G71 64 C7
Oak Rd Clydebank G81 15 A5
Cumbernauld G67 12 E4
Paisley PA2 42 A1
Oak St G2 162 B2
Oak Wynd G72 62 F3
Oakbank ML11 119 C6
Oakbank Ave ML2 80 E1
Oakbank Dr G78 57 E1
Oakbank Ind Est G20 30 B3
Oakbank St ML6 51 D7
Oakdene Ave Bellshill ML4 65 A7
Uddingston G71 64 B7
Oakdene Cres ML1 66 C3
Oakfield Ave G12 29 E2
Oakfield Dr 2 ML1 79 E6
Oakfield La 2 G12 29 E2
Oakfield Rd ML1 79 E6
Oakfield Twr 1 ML1 79 E5
Oakgrove Prim Sch G4 30 A2
Oakhill Ave G69 47 F3
Oaklands ML10 112 E7
Oaklea Cres G72 77 C8
Oakley Dr G44 59 F3
Oakley Terr 4 G31 45 F7
Oakridge Rd G69 49 B6
Oaks The G44 60 B4
Oakside Pl ML3 91 D7
Oaktree Gdns G45 60 F4
Oakwood Cres G34 33 D1
Oakwood Dr
Coatbridge ML5 49 D5
Glasgow G34 33 D1
Newton Mearns G77 72 F4
Oates Gdns ML1 80 B4
Oatfield St G21 31 B3
Oban Ct 2 G20 29 E4
Oban Dr G20 29 E4
Oban La G20 29 E4
Oban Pl ML6 51 D6
Oban Way ML1 66 B2
Obiston Gdns G32 47 A5
Observatory La 10 G12 29 D3
Observatory Rd G12 29 C3
Ochel Path ML6 51 F1
Ochil Ct G75 88 B4
Ochil Dr G78 57 C1
Ochil La EH47 56 F6
Ochil Pl G32 47 A4
Ochil Rd Bearsden G61 16 B7
Bishopbriggs G64 19 C1
Renfrew PA4 27 B1
Ochil St Glasgow G32 47 A4
Wishaw ML2 80 F4
Ochil View 8 G71 64 A8
Ochiltree Ave G13 28 F7
Ochiltree Cres ML5 49 E5
Ochiltree Dr ML3 77 E1
Ochilview Sq EH48 41 F5
Odense Ct G75 88 E6
Oggscastle Rd ML11 132 E7
Ogilface Cres EH48 40 C2
Ogilvie Pl G31 46 D4
Ogilvie Prim Sch G33 47 F7
Ogilvie St G31 46 D4
Ogilvy Cres EH47 71 F6
Old Aisle Rd G66 20 F7
Old Avon Rd ML3 79 A2
Old Balmore Rd G64 18 E7
Old Biggar Rd ML6 24 B1
Old Bore Rd ML6 51 E8
Old Bothwell Rd
Bothwell G71 64 B1
Hamilton G71 78 B8
Old Brae ML11 119 E4
Old Bridgend ML8 95 F1
Old Carlisle Rd DG10 161 E4
Old Castle Gdns G44 60 B6
Old Castle Rd G44 60 B5
Old Church Gdns G69 49 A5
Old Coach Rd G74 75 F3
Old Creamery The EH46 126 F2
Old Cross 4 Airdrie ML6 51 A8
Hamilton ML3 78 F4
Old Dalmarnock Rd G40 45 F4
Old Drove Rd ML12 133 B2
Old Dullatur Rd G68 11 D6
Old Dumbarton Rd
Glasgow G3 29 C1
Glasgow G3 29 D1
Old Eastfield St ML7 55 D5
Old Edinburgh Rd
Moffat DG10 161 C7
Uddingston,Calderbraes G71 63 D8
Uddingston,Calderbraes G71 63 F8
Uddingston,Viewpark G71 64 C7
Old Farm Rd 2 G61 28 F8
Old Gartloch Rd G69 33 F5
Old Glasgow Rd
Cumbernauld G67 12 A4
Uddingston G71 63 E5
Uddingston,Kylepark G71 63 D7
Old Govan Rd PA4 27 F3
Old Humbie Rd G77 72 E2
Old Inns Intc G67 12 C5
Old Inns Rdbt G68 12 B6
Old Lanark Rd
Braidwood ML8,ML11 109 B4
Carluke ML8 108 F8
Cartland ML11 109 E1
Old Manse Gdns ML5 50 A7
Old Manse Rd
Glasgow G32 47 D5
Wishaw ML2 80 E1
Old Mill Ct G81 15 A5
Old Mill Gate G73 61 A6
Old Mill La G71 63 F7
Old Mill Rd Bothwell G71 64 B1
Cambuslang G72 62 D5
Clydebank G81 15 A6
East Kilbride G74 75 F2
Hartwood ML7 69 B1
Uddingston G71 63 F7
Old Mill View G65 10 F3
Old Monkland Prim Sch ML5 49 C4
Old Monkland Rd ML5 49 E4
Old Playfield Rd G76 74 D8
Old Quarry Rd G68 22 D5
Old Rutherglen Rd G5 45 D4
Old School Ct ML5 50 A4
Old Shettleston Rd G32 47 A5
Old St G81 15 A6
Old Stable Row ML5 50 B7
Old Station Ct G71 64 A2
Old Union St ML6 51 B7
Old Vic Ct G74 76 C4
Old Well Rd DG10 161 D6
Old Wood Rd G69 48 A4
Old Wynd G1 163 A1
Oldbarhills TP Site PA2 57 D8
Oldhall Rd PA1 42 D5
Oldham Cl ML11 114 A4
Olifard Ave G71 64 B3
Oliphant Cres G76 73 E5
Olive Bank G71 49 C1
Olive Ct ML1 66 B5
Olive St G33 31 D4
Olympia Arc 2 G74 88 F8
Olympia Ct G75 88 F8
Olympia St 3 G40 45 F5
Olympia The 1 G74 88 F8
Olympia Way G74 75 F1
Omoa Rd ML1 67 B1
Onich Pl ML7 70 B3
Onslow G75 88 C7
Onslow Dr G31 46 A7
Onslow Rd G81 15 D2
Onslow Sq G31 46 A7
Ontario Pk G75 75 B1
Ontario Pl G75 75 B1
Onyx St ML4 65 A4
Oran Gate G20 29 E5
Oran Gdns G20 29 E5
Oran Pl G20 29 E4
Oran St G20 29 E4
Orbiston Ct ML1 80 A5
Orbiston Dr Bellshill ML4 65 C4
Clydebank G81 15 D7
Orbiston Pl G81 15 D7
Orbiston Rd Bellshill ML4 64 F4
Bellshill ML4 65 B2
Orbiston Sq ML4 64 F3
Orbiston St ML1 79 F5
Orcades Dr G44 60 C4
Orchard Ave G71 64 B1
Orchard Brae
22 Douglas ML11 138 B1
Hamilton ML3 78 D4
Kirkintilloch G66 20 E4
Orchard Ct Glasgow G32 62 B8
Glasgow,Orchard Pk G46 59 A3
Renfrew PA4 27 D4
Orchard Dr Glasgow G46 59 B3
Hamilton G72 77 D8
Rutherglen G73 60 F7
Orchard Field G66 20 E4
Orchard Gate ML9 93 A2
Orchard Gdns ML10 112 E7
Orchard Gn G74 76 B4
Orchard Gr
Coatbridge ML5 50 B6
Glasgow G46 59 B4
Orchard Park Ave G46 59 B3
Orchard Pk G46 59 C3
Orchard Pl Bellshill ML4 64 F3
Hamilton ML3 78 D3
Kirkintilloch G66 21 A7
Orchard St Carluke ML8 95 F1
Glasgow G69 47 F3
Hamilton ML3 78 E3
Motherwell ML1 79 D7
Overtown ML2 94 B6
Renfrew PA4 27 D4
Orchard View Dr ML11 116 A4
Orchardton Rd G68 22 D7
Orchardton Woods Ind Pk G68 22 C8
Orchy Ave Clarkston G76 73 F8
Glasgow G76 59 F1
Orchy Cres Airdrie ML6 51 C4
Bearsden G61 16 D1
Orchy Ct G81 15 C5
Orchy Dr G76 59 F1
Orchy Gdns G76 59 F1
Orchy St G44 60 A6
Orchy Terr G74 76 A1
Orefield Pl G74 75 E3
Oregon Pl G5 45 C4
Orion Pl ML4 65 E5
Orion Way
Cambuslang G72 62 A6
Carluke ML8 95 D2
Orkney Pl G51 44 B7
Orkney Quadrant ML2 81 D4
Orkney St G51 44 B7
Orlando G74 76 C5
Orleans Ave G14 28 E4
Orleans La G14 28 E3
Orlington Ct ML5 49 F8
Ormiston Ave G14 28 C4
Ormiston Dr ML3 91 C8
Ormiston La 10 G14 28 C4
Ormiston La N 6 G14 28 C4
Ormiston La S 12 G14 28 C4
Ormonde Ave G44 59 F3
Ormonde Cres G44 59 F3
Ormonde Ct G44 59 F3
Ormonde Dr G44 59 F3
Ornsay St G22 30 D7
Oronsay Cres G61 17 B3
Oronsay Pl ML2 81 B1
Oronsay Rd ML6 51 D5
Orr St Glasgow G40 45 F5
Glasgow G40 45 F6
Orr Terr ML7 55 C4
Orton Pl G51 44 A6
Osborne Cres G74 74 B3
Osborne Row 8 DG10 161 D5
Osborne St Clydebank G81 15 A3
Glasgow G1 163 A1
Osprey Cres ML2 81 B4
Osprey Dr G71 64 A7
Ossian Ave PA1 42 F5
Ossian Rd G43 59 E6
Oswald Gdns ML8 108 E4
Oswald St G1 162 C2
Oswald Wlk G62 17 C8
Otago La G12 29 E2
Otago La N G12 29 E2
Otago Pk G75 75 A1
Otago St G12 29 E2
Othello G74 76 B5
Otterburn Dr G46 59 C1
Otterswick Pl G33 32 C2
Oudenarde Ct ML8 96 B1
Our Holy Redeemer's RC Prim Sch G81 27 D7
Our Lady & St Francis RC Prim Sch ML1 66 C2
Our Lady & St Joseph's Prim Sch ML5 34 C7
Our Lady of Lourdes Prim Sch G75 88 D8
Our Lady of the Annunciation G43 59 E5
Our Lady of the Assumption Prim Sch G20 30 A6
Our Lady of the Missions Prim Sch G46 59 A2
Our Lady of the Rosary Prim Sch G52 43 D4
Our Lady's High Sch
Cumbernauld G67 11 D1
Motherwell ML1 80 A2
Oval The Glasgow G76 59 F1
Glenboig ML5 34 C6
Overbrae Gdns G15 15 F5
Overbrae Pl G15 15 F5
Overcroy Rd G65 10 F4
Overdale Ave G42 59 F8
Overdale Gdns G42 59 F8
Overdale Pl ML2 94 C6
Overdale St G42 59 F8
Overjohnstone Dr ML2 80 D4
Overlea Ave G73 61 D6
Overlee Ho G76 73 F7
Overlee Rd G76 73 F7
Overnewton Pl G3 44 D8
Overnewton Sq G3 29 D1
Overnewton St G3 29 D1
Overton Ave ML10 112 E8
Overton Pk ML10 112 F7
Overton Pl G31 46 A5
Overton Rd
Cambuslang G72 62 D4
Netherburn ML9 107 C5
Strathaven ML10 112 E7
Overton St G72 62 D4
Overtoun Dr G73 61 A7
Overtown Ave G53 58 B6
Overtown Prim Sch ML2 94 C7
Overtown Rd ML2 81 F2
Overtown St G31 46 A5
Overwood Dr G44 60 C6
Owen Ave G75 88 C7
Owen Pk G75 88 D7
Owen St ML1 79 E8
Owendale Ave ML4 65 B7
Oxford La Glasgow G5 45 B5
Renfrew PA4 27 C3
Oxford Rd PA4 27 C3
Oxford St Coatbridge ML5 49 F6
Glasgow G5 162 C1
Kirkintilloch G66 20 C8
Oxgang Holdings G66 20 F7
Oxgang Pl G66 20 E7
Oxgang Prim Sch G66 20 F8
Oxgang Rdbt G66 20 F7
Oxton Dr G52 43 B5

P

Paddock St ML5 50 D4
Paddock The
Clarkston G76 74 A5
Hamilton ML3 78 D6
Lanark ML11 116 D7
Paidmyre Cres G77 72 D3
Paidmyre Gdns G77 72 D3
Paidmyre Rd G77 72 D3
Paisley Gram Sch PA1 42 A5
Paisley Rd Barrhead G78 57 B4
Glasgow G5 162 B1
Renfrew PA4 27 C2
Paisley Rd W
Glasgow G51,G52 43 D4
Glasgow,Ibrox G51 44 A5
Palace Grounds Rd ML3 78 F4
Palace of Art* G41 43 F5
Palacecraig St ML5 50 A3
Palacerigg Country Pk* G67 24 F7
Paladin Ave G13 28 B8
Palermo St 2 G21 30 E4
Palladium Pl G14 28 D3
Palm Pl G71 49 C1
Palmer Ave G13 16 D1
Palmer Cres ML10 112 E7
Palmerston G75 88 A7
Palmerston Pl G3 44 D8
Pandora Way G71 64 A7
Pankhurst Pl G74 75 F2
Panmure Path G68 10 F2
Panmure Pl G22 30 B5
Panmure St G20 30 A5
Park Ave Barrhead G78 57 B1
Biggar ML12 141 C4
Bishopbriggs G64 19 B3
Carluke ML8 95 F3
Carstairs Junction ML11 131 B8
Glasgow G3 29 F2
Kirkintilloch G66 20 C8
Motherwell ML1 66 A5
Twechar G65 9 F4
Park Burn Ct ML3 78 A6
Park Burn Ind Est ML3 78 A6
Park Cir Carluke ML8 95 F3
Glasgow G3 162 A4
Park Circ DG10 161 D5
Park Circus La G3 162 A4
Park Circus Pl G3 162 A4
Park Cres Airdrie ML6 50 E8
Bearsden G61 16 C5
Bishopbriggs G64 19 A2
Eaglesham G76 86 E5
Hamilton G72 77 C6
Strathaven ML10 112 E7
Park Ct Bishopbriggs G64 19 B3
Glasgow G46 59 B3
Shotts ML7 69 F4
Park Dr Bellshill ML4 65 A4
Glasgow G3 162 A4
Hamilton ML3 79 C1
Lanark ML11 116 F4
Rutherglen G73 61 A7
Thorntonhall G74 74 C3
Wishaw ML2 82 A5
Park Gardens La G3 29 E1
Park Gate G3 29 E1
Park Gate Pl ML4 64 F5
Park Gdns G3 29 E1
Park La Carluke ML8 95 E1
Glasgow G40 45 F5

Park La *continued*
Hamilton G72 .77 D8
Kilsyth G65 .10 D8
Park Lea ML6 .38 A4
Park Par EH47 .71 E6
Park Pl Bellshill ML4 .64 E3
Biggar ML12 .160 C4
Carnwath ML11 .124 E1
Coatbridge ML5 .50 D4
Lanark ML11 .116 F4
Thorntonhall G74 .74 C3
Park Quadrant
Glasgow G3 .162 A4
Wishaw ML2 .80 E1
Park Rd Bellshill ML4 .65 A4
Bishopbriggs G64 .19 B2
Blackridge EH48 .40 E3
Calderbank ML6 .51 B3
Carnwath ML11 .124 E1
Chryston G69 .33 C8
Coatbridge G69 .49 A5
Glasgow G4 .29 E2
Glasgow,Carmyle G32 .62 C8
Glasgow,Giffnock G46 .59 C2
Hamilton ML3 .78 D3
Harthill ML7 .56 A6
Motherwell ML1 .66 B2
Shotts ML7 .69 D5
Park St Airdrie ML6 .50 E8
Carluke ML8 .95 F1
Cleland ML1 .67 B3
Coatbridge ML5 .50 B8
Kirkintilloch G66 .21 B7
Kirkmuirhill ML11 .114 B2
Motherwell ML1 .79 F6
Motherwell,New Stevenston ML1 .66 A3
.137 F5
Park St S G3 .29 E1
Park Terr East Kilbride G74 .75 E1
Glasgow G3 .29 E1
Park Terrace East La G3 .162 A4
Park Terrace La [1] G3 .29 E1
Park View Caldercruix ML6 .38 A5
Fauldhouse EH47 .71 E7
Larkhall ML9 .93 B2
Strathaven ML10 .112 E6
Park Way G67 .12 B4
Parkandarroch Cres ML8 .96 A1
Parkbrae Ave G20 .30 A6
Parkbrae Dr G20 .30 A6
Parkbrae Gate G20 .30 A6
Parkbrae Gdns G20 .30 A6
Parkbrae La G20 .30 A6
Parkbrae Pl G20 .30 A6
Parkburn Ave G66 .20 C7
Parkburn Rd G65 .6 D1
Parker Pl [12] Kilsyth G65 .10 D8
Larkhall ML9 .93 B4
Parkfield G75 .88 E5
Parkfoot St G65 .6 D1
Parkgrove Ave G46 .59 D4
Parkgrove Terr G3 .29 E1
Parkgrove Terrace La [6] G3 .29 E1
Parkhall Rd G81 .15 A4
Parkhall St G74 .75 F2
Parkhall Terr G81 .15 A5
Parkhead Cross G31 .46 D5
Parkhead Hospl G31 .46 D5
Parkhead La [3] ML6 .51 A8
Parkhead St Airdrie ML6 .51 A8
Motherwell ML1 .79 F5
Parkhill Dr G73 .61 A7
Parkhill Rd G43 .59 D8
Parkholm La G5 .162 A1
Parkhouse Rd G53 .58 A4
Parklands Oval G53 .42 F2
Parklands Rd G44 .59 F3
Parklands View G53 .42 F2
Parklea G64 .18 E3
Parklee Dr G76 .74 E7
Parkneuk Rd Glasgow G43 .59 C4
Hamilton G72 .77 B1
Parkneuk St ML1 .79 E8
Parknook Way [6] ML9 .93 B4
Parks View ML3 .91 D6
Parkside Gdns G20 .30 A6
Parkside Pl G20 .30 A6
Parkside Rd
Motherwell ML1 .79 B6
Shotts ML7 .69 D4
Parkview Ave G66 .20 D6
Parkview Cres ML2 .82 A4
Parkview Ct G66 .20 D7
Parkview Dr
Coatbridge ML5 .49 E7
Stepps G33 .32 E6
Parkview Prim Sch G23 .29 D8
Parkville Dr Hamilton G72 .77 E6
Hamilton G72 .77 F6
Parkville Rd ML4 .65 C7
Parkway G72 .62 C8
Parkway Ct
Coatbridge ML5 .49 E6
Glasgow G69 .48 B7
Parkway Pl ML5 .49 E5
Parliament Rd G66 .20 D7
Parnell St ML6 .50 F5
Parnie St G1 .163 A1
Parry Terr G75 .75 B1
Parson St G4 .163 C3
Parsonage Row G1 .163 B2
Parsonage Sq G4 .163 B2
Partick Bridge St G11 .29 C1
Partick St ML5 .50 C5
Partick Sta (Underground) G11 .29 B1
Partickhill Ave G11 .29 B3
Partickhill Ct G11 .29 B3
Partickhill Rd G11 .29 B2
Patchy Pk ML9 .106 A8
Paterson Pl Bearsden G61 .16 C8
Stonehouse ML9 .129 F8
Paterson St Glasgow G5 .162 B1
Motherwell ML1 .79 E8
Paterson Terr G75 .88 D7
Paterson's Laun G64 .18 E7
Pather St ML2 .81 B2
Pathfoot Smithy ML11 .119 F5
Pathhead ML11 .138 B1
Pathhead Gdns G33 .31 F6
Pathhead Rd G76 .74 D7
Patna Ct ML3 .77 E1
Patna St G40 .46 B3
Paton Ct ML2 .80 D1
Paton St G31 .46 B7
Patrickholm Ave ML9 .129 F8
Patterson Dr ML8 .95 A6
Patterton Dr G78 .57 D1
Patterton Sta G77 .72 D8
Paxstone Cres ML7 .55 E5
Paxstone Dr ML7 .55 E5
Paxton Cres G74 .75 F4
Paxton Ct G74 .75 F4
Payne St G4 .30 C2
Peacock Cross ML3 .78 C4
Peacock Cross Ind Est ML3 .78 C4
Peacock Dr ML3 .78 C4
Peacock Loan ML8 .95 F3
Pearce La G51 .44 A8
Pearce St G51 .44 A8
Pearl St ML4 .65 B3
Pearson Dr PA4 .27 D3
Peat Pl G53 .58 A5
Peat Rd G53 .58 B6
Peathill Ave G69 .21 B1
Peathill St G21 .30 C3
Pebble Dr ML9 .105 D1
Peden St ML7 .55 C5
Pedmyre La G76 .74 D7
Peebles Dr G73 .61 D7
Peebles Path ML5 .50 D3
Peel Ave ML1 .79 E4
Peel Ct G72 .62 A6
Peel Glen Gdns G15 .16 A5
Peel Glen Rd G15,G61 .16 A5
Peel La G11 .29 B2
Peel Park Pl G74 .74 F2
Peel Pl Bothwell G71 .64 A3
Coatbridge ML5 .49 D5
Peel Rd G74 .74 B2
Peel St G11 .29 B2
Peel View [2] G81 .15 D3
Pegasus Ave ML8 .95 E2
Pegasus Rd ML4 .65 E5
Peggies Knowe EH46 .126 D2
Peiter Pl [5] G72 .77 C7
Pembroke G74 .76 D4
Pembroke St G3 .162 A3
Penbury Cres ML3 .90 F7
Pencaitland Dr G32 .47 A3
Pencaitland Gr G32 .47 A3
Pencaitland Pl G23 .17 E1
Pendale Rise G45 .60 D3
Pendeen Cres G33 .47 E5
Pendeen Pl G33 .47 F6
Pendeen Rd G33 .47 F5
Pendicle Cres G61 .16 D3
Pendicle Rd G61 .16 E3
Pendle Ct G69 .33 F6
Penfold Cres G75 .88 D8
Penicuik St G32 .46 D6
Penilee Rd G52 .42 E6
Penilee Terr G52 .42 E6
Peninver Dr G51 .43 E8
Penman Ave G73 .60 F8
Pennan Pl G14 .28 A5
Penneld Rd G52 .42 F5
Pennine Gr ML6 .51 F1
Pennyroyal Ct G74 .75 D4
Penrioch Dr G75 .88 C4
Penrith Ave G46 .59 C2
Penrith Dr G12 .29 A6
Penrith Pl G75 .87 F6
Penryn Gdns G32 .47 D3
Penston Rd G33 .47 D8
Pentland Cres ML9 .92 E5
Pentland Ct Airdrie ML6 .36 B2
Barrhead G78 .57 C1
Coatbridge ML5 .50 C3
Pentland Dr Barrhead G78 .57 C1
Bishopbriggs G64 .19 D2
Paisley PA4 .42 B8
Pentland Gdns ML9 .92 F5
Pentland Pl G61 .16 B7
Pentland Rd Chryston G69 .33 D8
East Kilbride G75 .88 A3
Glasgow G43 .59 C5
Wishaw ML2 .80 E4
Pentland Sch ML5 .34 C1
Pentland Way ML3 .91 A7
Penzance Way G69 .21 F2
People's Palace (Mus)* G40 .45 E5
Peploe Dr G74 .76 D5
Perchy View ML2 .81 C1
Percy Dr G46 .59 C1
Percy Rd PA4 .27 A1
Percy St Glasgow G51 .44 D5
Larkhall ML9 .93 A4
Perran Gdns G69 .21 E2
Perryflatts Rd ML12 .131 C1
Perth Ave ML6 .51 A4
Perth St G3 .162 A2
Peter McEachran Ho G31 .46 C8
Petersburn Pl ML6 .51 D6
Petersburn Prim Sch ML6 .51 C6
Petersburn Rd ML6 .51 D6
Petershill Ct G21 .31 C3
Petershill Dr G21 .31 C3
Petershill Pl G21 .31 B4
Petershill Rd G21 .31 A3
Peterson Dr G13 .27 E8
Peterson Gdns G13 .27 E8
Petition Pl G71 .64 A5
Pettigrew St G32 .47 A5
Pettinain Rd ML11 .131 B7
Peveril Ave Glasgow G41 .44 D1
Rutherglen G73 .61 C5
Peveril Ct G73 .61 C5
Pharonhill St G31 .46 D5
Philip Ct ML4 .65 A4
Philip Murray Rd ML4 .64 D6
Philipshill Gate G74 .74 E3
Philipshill Ind Est G74 .74 E3
Philipshill Rd G76 .74 E4
Phoenix Cres ML4 .64 F8
Phoenix Ct G74 .76 D5
Phoenix Ho G81 .15 A2
Phoenix Pl ML1 .66 A3
Phoenix Rd ML4 .65 E5
Piccadilly St G3 .162 A2
Pickerstonhill ML1 .66 E4
Picketlaw Dr G76 .74 D7
Picketlaw Farm Rd G76 .74 C7
Pierowall Ct ML10 .112 F8
Piershill St G32 .46 F7
Pikeman Rd G13 .28 C7
Pillans Ct ML3 .78 A6
Pilmuir Ave G44 .59 F4
Pilrig St G32 .46 E7
Pilton Rd G15 .16 A4
Pine Ave G72 .62 F3
Pine Cl G67 .12 E4
Pine Cres
Cumbernauld G67 .12 E4
East Kilbride G75 .88 B5
Hamilton ML3 .91 A7
Pine Ct Cumbernauld G67 .12 E4
East Kilbride G75 .88 C5
Pine Gr Calderbank ML6 .51 B2
Coatbridge G69 .49 A6
Cumbernauld G67 .12 E4
Motherwell ML1 .66 B5
Uddingston G71 .64 B8
Pine Ho G75 .88 B5
Pine Lawn ML2 .81 D5
Pine Mews ML1 .66 D2
Pine Pk ML3 .78 E1
Pine Pl Cumbernauld G67 .12 E4
Glasgow G5 .45 C4
Pine Quadrant ML6 .51 E3
Pine Rd G67 .12 E4
Pine St Airdrie ML6 .51 D7
Paisley PA2 .42 A2
Pinelands G64 .19 A4
Pines Pl ML12 .140 F5
Pines The G44 .60 B4
Pineview Ct G15 .16 B3
Pinewood G61 .16 F3
Pinewood Ave G66 .20 A5
Pinewood Ct G66 .20 A5
Pinewood Pl G66 .20 A5
Pinewood Prim Sch G15 .16 C4
Pinewood Sq G15 .16 B3
Pinewood Wlk ML10 .112 E7
Pinkerton Ave G73 .60 F8
Pinkerton La PA4 .27 D1
Pinkston Dr G21 .30 E2
Pinkston Rd G4,G21 .30 D2
Pinmore Pl G53 .57 F5
Pinmore St G53 .57 F5
Pinwherry Dr G33 .31 F6
Pinwherry Pl G71 .64 A3
Piper Rd ML6 .51 C5
Pirnie Pl G65 .10 D8
Pirnmill Ave
East Kilbride G75 .88 B4
Motherwell ML1 .79 B7
Pit Rd Bellshill ML4 .64 F6
Kirkintilloch G66 .21 C7
Pitcairn Cres G75 .87 F8
Pitcairn Gr G75 .88 A8
Pitcairn Pl G75 .87 F8
Pitcairn St G31 .46 E4
Pitcairn Terr ML3 .78 A4
Pitcaple Dr G43 .59 B6
Pitlochry Dr Glasgow G52 .43 C4
Larkhall ML9 .93 C1
Pitmedden Rd G64 .19 D2
Pitmilly Rd G15 .16 C4
Pitreavie Ct ML3 .91 B8
Pitreavie Pl G33 .32 C1
Pitt St G2 .162 B3
Pittenweem Path G72 .77 D3
Pladda Rd PA4 .27 D1
Pladda St ML1 .79 B7
Plains Prim Sch ML6 .37 A2
Plane Pl G71 .49 C1
Planetree Rd G81 .15 A5
Plant St G31 .46 C6
Plantation Ave ML1 .66 B6
Plantation Park Gdns [5] G51 .44 D5
Plantation Sq G51 .44 E6
Platthorn Dr G74 .75 F1
Platthorn Rd G74 .75 F1
Playfair St G40 .46 A3
Plaza The [2] G74 .88 E8
Pleaknowe Cres G69 .21 F2
Pleamuir Pl G68 .11 C2
Plean St G14 .28 A5
Pleasance Row ML11 .122 A2
Pleasance St G43 .59 D7
Pleasance Way G43 .59 D7
Plotcock Rd ML3 .105 D7
Plover Dr G75 .88 A5
Plusgarten Loan ML2 .81 F7
Pochard Way ML4 .64 F8
Poet's View G66 .20 F7
Pointhouse Rd G3 .44 D8
Polbae Cres G76 .86 E5
Polden Ave G75 .88 A3
Polden Ct G75 .88 A3
Polkemmet Bsns Ctr EH47 .56 F5
Polkemmet Ctry Pk* EH47 .56 C7
Polkemmet Dr ML7 .56 A6
Polkemmet La ML7 .55 F5
Polkemmet Rd
Harthill ML7 .55 F6
Whitburn EH47 .56 E5
Pollock Ave
Eaglesham G76 .86 E5
Hamilton ML3 .78 A4
Pollock Rd Bearsden G61 .17 A3
Newton Mearns G77 .72 C4
Pollock St Bellshill ML4 .65 C5
Motherwell ML1 .79 E7
Pollok Ave G43 .59 B8
Pollok Ctry Pk* G43 .44 B1
Pollok Dr G64 .18 E1
Pollok Ho* G43 .58 F8
Pollok La G74 .76 B3
Pollok Pl [2] G74 .76 B3
Pollokshaws East Sta G43 .59 D7
Pollokshaws Rd
Glasgow,Gorbals G41 .45 B4
Glasgow,Pollokshaws G43 .59 C8
Glasgow,Strathbungo G41 .44 F1
Pollokshaws West Sta G43 .59 B7
Pollokshield Sq G41 .44 E2
Pollokshields East Sta G41 .45 A3
Pollokshields Prim Sch G41 .44 F3
Pollokshields Prim Sch Annexe (Infs) G41 .44 F3
Pollokshields Sq G41 .44 E2
Pollokshields West Sta G41 .44 F2
Polmadie Ave G5 .45 D2
Polmadie Ind Est G5,G73 .45 E2
Polmadie Rd G5 .45 D2
Polmadie St G42 .45 C1
Polnoon Ave G13 .28 A6
Polnoon Dr G76 .86 E5
Polnoon Mews G76 .86 E5
Polnoon St G76 .86 D4
Polquhap Ct [4] G53 .58 A8
Polquhap Gdns [6] G53 .58 A8
Polquhap Pl [5] G53 .58 A8
Polquhap Rd G53 .58 A8
Polwarth La Glasgow G12 .29 B3
Glasgow G12 .29 B4
Polwarth St G12 .29 B3
Pomona Pl ML3 .77 F2
Poplar Ave Glasgow G11 .28 F4
Newton Mearns G77 .72 E4
Poplar Cres ML3 .91 F4
Poplar Dr G66 .20 A5
Poplar Gdns G75 .88 C5
Poplar Pl Blantyre G72 .63 C1
Hamilton G72 .77 C8
Motherwell ML1 .66 B4
Uddingston G71 .64 D8
Poplar St ML6 .51 D7
Poplar Way
Cambuslang G72 .62 F3
Motherwell ML1 .66 D2
Poplars The G61 .16 D8
Poplin St G40 .46 A3
Porchester St G33 .32 D2
Port Dundas Pl G1 .163 A3
Port Dundas Rd G4 .163 A4
Port St G3 .162 A2
Portal Rd G13 .28 C8
Porter St G51 .44 C5
Porterfield Rd PA4 .27 B3
Porters La ML6 .51 D2
Porters Well G71 .63 E5
Portia Pl ML1 .79 E7
Portland Pk ML3 .78 E2
Portland Pl
Fauldhouse EH47 .71 C5
Hamilton ML3 .78 E2
Lanark ML11 .117 B4
Portland Rd
Cumbernauld G68 .11 F5
Paisley PA2 .42 B3
Portland Sq ML3 .78 E2
Portland St ML5 .50 B7
Portland Wynd [4] ML9 .93 B4
Portman St G41 .44 E5
Portmarnock Dr G23 .29 E8
Portreath Rd G69 .21 F3
Portree Ave ML5 .49 E4
Portree Pl G15 .15 E4
Portsoy Ave G13 .27 F8
Portsoy Pl G13 .27 F8
Portugal St G5 .45 B5
Portwell ML3 .78 E4
Possil Cross G22 .30 C3
Possil Rd G4 .30 B3
Possilpark & Parkhouse Sta G22 .30 B6
Postgate ML3 .78 E4
Potassels Rd G69 .33 C7
Potrail Pl ML3 .78 A3
Potter Cl G32 .46 E3
Potter Gr G32 .46 E3
Potter Pl G32 .46 E3
Potter St G32 .46 E3
Potterhill Rd G53 .43 B2
Potters Wynd ML11 .117 C5
Potts Way ML1 .65 C1
Powbrone G75 .88 E5
Powburn Cres G71 .63 D7
Powell St ML11 .138 F7
Powfoot St G31 .46 D5
Powforth Cl ML9 .92 E3
Powmillon Ct ML10 .112 E8
Powrie St G33 .32 C3
Poynter Ct G71 .63 E5
Prentice La [5] G71 .64 A8
Prentice Rd ML1 .79 B5
Preston Pl G42 .45 B2
Preston St G42 .45 B2
Prestonfield G62 .16 E8
Prestwick Ct G68 .11 F4
Prestwick Pl G77 .73 A4
Prestwick St G53 .58 A6
Pretoria Ct G75 .88 B4
Priestfield Ind Est G72 .77 D5
Priestfield St G72 .77 C6
Priesthill & Darnley Sta G53 .58 C5
Priesthill Ave G53 .58 C6
Priesthill Cres G53 .58 C6
Priesthill Rd G53 .58 C6
Priestknowe Rdbt G74 .75 F1
Primrose Ave
Bellshill ML4 .65 A7
Larkhall ML9 .106 A8
Primrose Cres ML1 .79 E5
Primrose Ct [1] G14 .28 D3
Primrose Pl
Cumbernauld G67 .23 B6
Strathaven ML10 .112 E7
Uddingston G71 .64 C8
Primrose St G14 .28 D3
Primrose Way ML8 .108 E8
Prince Albert Rd G12 .29 B3
Prince Edward St [2] G42 .45 A2
Prince Of Wales Gdns G20 .29 C8
Prince Pl ML2 .82 A6
Prince's Gdns G12 .29 B3
Prince's Pl [8] G12 .29 C3
Prince's Terr G12 .29 C3
Prince's Terr La [14] G12 .29 C3
Princes Gardens La [5] G12 .29 B3
Princes Gate
Hamilton ML3 .78 F4
Rutherglen G73 .61 A8
Uddingston G71 .63 E4
Princes Sq G78 .57 D3
Princes Square Shop Ctr G1 .163 A2
Princes St Caldercruix ML6 .38 A5
Motherwell ML1 .79 E8
Rutherglen G73 .61 A8
Princess Anne Quadrant ML1 .65 F5
Princess Cres PA1 .42 B6
Princess Dr G69 .49 A5
Princess Rd ML1 .65 F4
Princess Sq ML2 .81 F5
Pringle Ct [13] DG10 .161 D5
Printers Land G76 .74 A6
Priorwood Ct [7] G13 .28 D6
Priorwood Gate G77 .72 B4
Priorwood Gdns [3] G13 .28 D6
Priorwood Pl G13 .28 D6
Priorwood Rd G77 .72 A4
Priorwood Way G77 .72 A4
Priory Ave
Lesmahagow ML11 .119 F4
Paisley PA3 .42 A7
Priory Dr G71 .63 D7
Priory Gate ML2 .94 B7
Priory Pl Cumbernauld G68 .10 E1
Glasgow G13 .28 D7
Lesmahagow ML11 .119 F3
Priory Rd Glasgow G13 .28 D7
Lesmahagow ML11 .119 F3
Priory St G72 .77 D8
Priory Terr ML2 .80 C2
Professors' Sq G12 .29 D2
Progress Dr ML6 .38 A5
Prosen St G32 .46 F3
Prospect Ave
Cambuslang G72 .61 F5
Uddingston G71 .63 F7
Prospect Ct G72 .77 D5
Prospect Dr ML9 .106 F8
Prospect Rd Dullatur G68 .11 D6
Glasgow G43 .59 D8
Prospecthill Cir G42 .60 D8
Prospecthill Cres G42 .60 E8
Prospecthill Dr G42 .60 C8
Prospecthill Gr G42 .60 A8
Prospecthill Pl G42 .60 E8
Prospecthill Rd G42 .60 D8
Prospecthill Sq G42 .60 D8
Prospecthill Way G42 .60 A8
Provan Hall* G34 .32 F1
Provan Rd G33 .46 D8

Provan Wlk G34 32 E1
Provand Hall Cres G69 48 B3
Provand's Lordship Ho* G4 163 C3
Provanhall Prim Sch G34 33 A1
Provanhill St G21 30 F1
Provanmill Rd G33 31 E2
Provost Driver Ct PA4 27 E2
Provost Gate ML9 93 A3
Purdie G74 76 D5
Purdie St ML3 78 A5
Purdon St G11 29 B2
Pyatshaw Rd ML9 93 B1

Q

Quadrangle The G20 29 E5
Quadrant Rd G43 59 E5
Quadrant Sh Ctr ML5 50 A7
Quadrant The G76 73 F8
Quantock Dr G75 88 A4
Quarry Ave G72 62 E3
Quarry Brae Prim Sch G31 46 D5
Quarry Cotts EH48 40 C3
Quarry Ct ML3 78 E3
Quarry Dr G66 20 F8
Quarry La G76 86 D4
Quarry Pk G75 88 E8
Quarry Pl Cambuslang G72 61 E6
Hamilton ML3 78 E3
Shotts ML7 69 D5
Quarry Rd Airdrie ML6 36 A1
Barrhead G78 57 B4
East Kilbride G75 88 D5
Fauldhouse EH47 71 F6
Larkhall ML9 93 A2
Law ML8 95 A3
Shotts ML7 69 D5
Quarry St Coatbridge ML5 50 D7
Hamilton ML3 78 E3
Larkhall ML9 93 B1
Motherwell ML1 66 A4
Shotts ML7 69 D5
Wishaw ML2 81 A5
Quarrybrae Ave G76 73 D7
Quarrybrae Gdns G71 64 C6
Quarrybrae St G31 46 E5
Quarryknowe
Lanark ML11 117 A4
Rutherglen G73 60 F7
Quarryknowe Pl ML4 64 F3
Quarryknowe St
Clydebank G81 15 E7
Glasgow G31 46 E5
Quarryside St ML6 35 E4
Quarrywood Ave G21 31 C4
Quarrywood Rd G21 31 D4
Quarter Prim Sch ML3 91 F3
Quay (Leisure Complex) The G5 162 A1
Quay Rd Glasgow G73 46 A1
Rutherglen G73 60 F8
Quay Rd N G73 46 A1
Quebec Dr G75 75 C1
Quebec Gn G75 75 C1
Quebec Wynd G32 62 C8
Queen Elizabeth Ave G52 42 F7
Queen Elizabeth Ct
Clydebank G81 15 A3
Motherwell ML1 79 D7
Queen Elizabeth Gdns
Clydebank G81 15 A3
Glasgow G5 45 C4
Queen Margaret Ct 3 G20 29 E4
Queen Margaret Dr G20 29 E4
Queen Margaret Rd G20 29 E4
Queen Mary Ave
Clydebank G81 15 D2
Glasgow G42 45 B1
Queen Mary Gdns G81 15 A3
Queen Mary St G40 46 A4
Queen Mother's Hospl The G3 29 C1
Queen Sq G41 44 F2
Queen St Glasgow G1 163 A2
Hamilton ML3 78 A5
Kirkintilloch G66 20 C8
Motherwell ML1 79 E7
Renfrew PA4 27 D3
Rutherglen G73 61 A8
Stonehouse ML9 105 E2
Wishaw ML2 81 F6
Queen Street Sta G1 163 A3
Queen Victoria Ct G14 28 C4
Queen Victoria Dr G14 28 C4
Queen Victoria Gate G13 28 C5
Queen Victoria St ML6 50 F7
Queen's Ave G72 62 B5
Queen's Cres Carluke ML8 96 A2
Chapelhall ML6 51 D3
Cleland ML1 67 B2
Coatbridge G69 48 F5
7 Glasgow G4 30 A2
Queen's Ct G62 17 B8
Queen's Dr
Cumbernauld G68 11 F6
Glasgow G42 45 A1
Queen's Drive La G42 45 A1
Queen's Gate G76 73 E8
Queen's Gdns G12 29 C3
Queen's Park Ave G42 45 B1
Queen's Park Sta G42 45 A2
Queen's Pl G12 29 C3
Queens Cres Bellshill ML4 64 F4
Queens Cres *continued*
Motherwell ML1 65 F4
Queens Dr ML3 91 D6
Queens Gate La 9 G12 29 C3
Queens Gr G66 20 C4
Queens View G64 19 B8
Queensbank Ave G69 33 E7
Queensberry Ave
Bearsden G61 16 E7
Clarkston G76 73 E7
Queensberry Terr DG10 161 E4
Queensborough Gdns 4 G12 29 B3
Queensby Ave 6 G69 48 B6
Queensby Dr G69 48 A6
Queensby Pl G69 48 C6
Queensby Rd G69 48 C6
Queensdale Ave ML9 106 B8
Queensdale Rd ML9 106 B8
Queensferry St G5 45 E2
Queensland Ct G52 43 C6
Queensland Dr G52 43 C6
Queensland Gdns G51 43 D6
Queensland La E G52 43 C6
Queensland La W G52 43 C6
Queenslie Ind Est G33 47 D8
Queenslie St G33 31 D2
Queensway G75 88 E8
Queenzieburn Ind Est G65 9 F7
Quendale Dr G32 46 F3
Quentin St G41 44 E1
Quinton Gdns G69 48 A5

R

Raasay Cres ML6 51 E6
Raasay Gdns G77 72 B5
Raasay Pl G22 30 C8
Raasay St G22 30 C8
Racecourse View ML3 78 E5
Rachan St G34 33 D1
Radnor St Clydebank G81 15 A3
Clydebank,Kilbowie G81 15 B3
Glasgow G3 29 D1
Rae St DG10 161 C5
Raeberry St G20 29 F3
Raebog Cres ML6 35 F2
Raebog Rd ML6 35 F4
Raeburn Ave
East Kilbride G74 76 B4
Paisley PA1 42 A4
Raeburn Comm ML11 131 B5
Raeburn Cres ML3 77 E3
Raeburn Pl G74 76 B4
Raeburn Wlk ML4 65 A7
Raes Rd ML8 108 B8
Raeside Ave G77 72 D3
Raeswood Dr G53 57 F8
Raeswood Gdns G53 57 F8
Raeswood Pl 3 G53 58 A8
Raeswood Rd G53 57 F8
Raewell Cres ML4 64 F3
Raglan St G4 30 A2
Railway Rd Airdrie ML6 50 D7
137 F5
Railway View ML11 130 F8
Raith Ave G45 60 D4
Raith Dr Bellshill ML4 65 B4
Cumbernauld G68 10 D1
Raithburn Ave G45 60 C3
Raithburn Rd G45 60 C3
Ralston Ave Glasgow G52 42 F4
Glasgow PA1 42 F3
Ralston Ct G52 42 F4
Ralston Dr G52 42 F4
Ralston Path G52 42 F4
Ralston Pl G52 42 F4
Ralston Prim Sch PA1 42 E5
Ralston Rd Barrhead G78 57 C2
Bearsden G61 16 E5
Ralston St Airdrie ML6 50 E7
Paisley PA1 42 A4
Ram St G32 46 F5
Ramage Rd ML8 96 B1
Ramillies Ct Carluke ML8 96 A1
Clydebank G81 15 C2
Ramoth ML11 116 D4
Rampart Ave G13 28 B8
Ramsay Ct G77 72 E3
Ramsay Hill 3 G74 76 A3
Ramsay Pl ML5 49 C5
Ramsay Rd ML12 151 A1
Ramscraig Gdns 4 ML9 129 E8
Ramsey Gdns ML11 113 F4
Ramsey Wynd ML4 65 B7
Ranald Gdns G73 61 D3
Randolph Ave G76 60 A1
Randolph Dr
Clarkston G76 60 A1
Glasgow G76 59 F1
Randolph Gate G11 28 F4
Randolph Gdns G76 59 F1
Randolph La G11 28 F3
Randolph Rd G11 28 F4
Ranfurly Dr G68 11 E4
Ranfurly Rd G52 42 F5
Range Ave ML1 80 C3
Range Pl ML3 78 E1
Range Rd ML1 80 B4
Range Road Ind Est ML2 80 C3
Range St ML1 80 B4
Range View ML11 111 F2
Rangerhouse Rd G75 88 F5
Rankin Cres ML6 24 F2
Rankin Ct G69 33 C7
Rankin Dr G77 72 C6
Rankin Gate Ctr 3 ML8 95 F2
Rankin Rd ML2 81 E4
Rankin St ML8 95 F2
Rankin Way G78 57 E3
Rankine Ave G75 89 A7
Rankine Ho G4 30 C2
Rankine Pl G75 89 A7
Rannoch Ave
Bishopbriggs G64 19 B1
Coatbridge ML5 34 D1
Hamilton ML3 78 A1
Newton Mearns G77 72 D7
Rannoch Ct
Cumbernauld G67 23 B6
Hamilton G72 77 F5
Rannoch Dr Bearsden G61 17 B3
Cumbernauld G67 23 B6
Kirkintilloch G66 9 B1
Renfrew PA4 27 C4
Wishaw ML2 81 B1
Rannoch Gdns G64 19 C2
Rannoch Gn G74 75 F3
Rannoch La G69 22 A2
Rannoch Pl Paisley PA2 42 A3
Shotts ML7 69 E6
Rannoch Rd Airdrie ML6 35 F1
Uddingston G71 48 E1
Rannoch St G44 60 A6
Rannoch Terr ML9 93 C1
Rannoch Way 6 G71 64 A3
Rannoch Wynd G73 61 D2
Raploch Ave G14 28 B4
Raploch Cres G81 15 D7
Raploch La G14 28 B4
Raploch Rd ML9 92 F3
Raploch St ML9 92 F3
Rashiehill ML11 122 A1
Rashiehill Cres EH55 122 C7
Rashiehill Terr EH55 122 C7
Rathlin St G51 44 A8
Rathmor Rd ML12 160 C3
Ratho Dr Cumbernauld G68 11 E5
Glasgow G21 30 E4
Ratho Pk ML3 91 B7
Rattray St G32 46 E3
Ravel Row G31 46 D5
Ravel Wynd G71 64 B8
Ravelston Rd G61 16 E2
Ravelston St G32 46 E6
Raven Wynd ML2 81 B3
Ravens Ct 5 G64 30 F8
Ravenscliffe Dr G46 59 B3
Ravenscourt G74 74 C2
Ravenscraig Ct ML4 65 B5
Ravenscraig Dr G53 58 C6
Ravenscraig Terr G53 58 C5
Ravenshall ML1 81 B8
Ravenshall Rd G41 59 C8
Ravenshill Dr ML1 67 C1
Ravenstone Dr G46 59 C4
Ravenswood ML11 98 F8
Ravenswood Dr G41 44 D1
Ravenswood Prim Sch G67 23 E8
Ravenswood Rd
Glasgow G69 48 C5
Strathaven ML10 112 F7
Rawyards Ave ML6 36 B2
Raymond Pl G75 75 C1
Rayne Pl G15 16 B4
Ream Ave 2 ML6 51 F6
Reay Ave G74 75 B2
Reay Gdns G74 75 B2
Red Bridge Ct 3 ML5 50 A8
Red Deer Rd G75 88 C8
Red Rd G21 31 B4
Red Road Ct G21 31 B3
Redan St 2 G40 45 F5
Redbrae Rd G66 20 E8
Redburn Ave G46 73 B8
Redburn Ct G67 12 F6
Redburn Pl G67 12 F6
Redburn Rd
Blackridge EH48 40 B2
Cumbernauld G67 12 F6
Redburn Sch G67 12 C2
Redcastle Sq G33 32 D1
Redcliffe Dr G75 88 B8
Redding Rd ML10 128 E3
Rederech Cres ML3 77 F2
Redford St G33 46 D8
Redgate Pl G14 28 B4
Redgrave G74 76 D5
Redhaws Rd ML7 70 A3
Redhill Rd G68 11 D3
Redholme ML9 93 B1
Redhouse La ML8 95 F3
Redlands La G12 29 C4
Redlands Rd 22 G12 29 C4
Redlands Terr 14 G12 29 C4
Redlands Terrace La 23 G12 29 C4
Redlawood Pl G72 63 A6
Redlawood Rd G72 63 A6
Redmire Cres ML7 83 B8
Redmoss St G22 30 B5
Rednock St G22 30 C4
Redpath Dr
Cambuslang G72 62 D6
Glasgow G52 43 C5
Redwing Gdns ML2 81 A1
Redwood Ave G74 74 E1
Redwood Cl ML3 91 A7
Redwood Cres
Cambuslang G72 62 F3
East Kilbride G74 74 E2
Hamilton ML3 91 A7
Uddingston G71 64 C8
Redwood Ct G75 87 E8
Redwood Dr
East Kilbride G74 74 E3
Glasgow G21 31 A3
Redwood Gr ML5 50 B6
Redwood La ML3 91 A7
Redwood Pl
East Kilbride G74 74 E2
Kirkintilloch G66 20 B5
Uddingston G71 64 C8
Redwood Rd
Cumbernauld G67 12 D2
Motherwell ML1 66 B5
Redwood Way G72 62 F3
Reed St ML10 112 E7
Reelick Ave G13 27 E8
Reelick Quadrant G13 27 E8
Reema Rd ML4 65 B6
Reen Pl G71 64 B4
Regal Gr ML7 69 E4
Regency Ct ML3 79 A2
Regency Way ML1 65 F4
Regent Ct G12 29 B4
Regent Ctr The 2 G66 20 C8
Regent Dr G73 61 A8
Regent Moray St G3 29 D1
Regent Park Sq G41 44 F2
Regent Sq G66 20 C4
Regent St Kirkintilloch G66 20 C8
Paisley PA1 42 B5
Regent Way ML3 78 F3
Regents Gate G71 63 E4
Register Ave ML4 65 A3
Register Rd G65 10 E8
Regwood St G41 59 D8
Reid Ave G61 17 A6
Reid Ct G73 61 B8
Reid Gr Motherwell ML1 80 B4
Stonehouse ML9 105 F2
Reid Pl G40 45 F4
Reid St Airdrie ML6 36 B1
Coatbridge ML5 50 B8
Forth ML11 124 A8
Glasgow G40 45 F3
Hamilton ML3 77 F5
Moffat DG10 161 C5
Rutherglen G73 61 B8
Salsburgh ML7 53 B2
Reidhouse St G21 30 F4
Reidvale St G31 46 A6
Reith Dr G75 88 D7
Remus Pl ML4 65 E5
Renfield La G2 162 C2
Renfield St Glasgow G2 162 C3
Renfrew PA4 27 D4
Renfrew Ct G2 163 A3
Renfrew High Sch PA4 27 D2
Renfrew La G2 162 C3
Renfrew Pl ML5 49 C4
Renfrew Rd Glasgow G51 28 A1
Glasgow G51 28 C1
Paisley PA3 42 A8
Renfrew St
Coatbridge ML5 49 C4
Glasgow G2 162 C3
Rennie Pl G74 75 A3
Rennie Rd G65 6 B1
Renshaw Dr G52 43 B6
Renshaw Pl ML4 65 F8
Renton St G4 163 A4
Renwick Pl ML11 117 C5
Resipol Rd G33 32 E5
Reston Dr G52 43 B6
Reuther Ave G73 61 B7
Revoch Dr G13 28 A7
Reynolds Ave G75 89 A7
Reynolds Dr G33 32 F5
Reynolds Path ML2 81 D1
Rhannan Rd G44 60 A5
Rhannan Terr G44 60 A5
Rhindhouse Pl G69 48 D5
Rhindhouse Rd G69 48 D5
Rhindmuir Ave G69 48 C5
Rhindmuir Cres G69 48 D6
Rhindmuir Ct G69 48 C6
Rhindmuir Dr G69 48 C6
Rhindmuir Gdns G69 48 C6
Rhindmuir Gr G69 48 D6
Rhindmuir Path G69 48 D6
Rhindmuir Pl G69 48 D6
Rhindmuir Rd G69 48 C6
Rhindmuir View G69 48 D6
Rhindmuir Wynd G69 48 D6
Rhinds St ML5 49 C4
Rhindsdale Cres G69 48 C5
Rhu Quadrant ML2 94 C6
Rhyber Ave ML11 117 B5
Rhymebank ML9 105 C1
Rhymer St G21 30 F1
Rhymie Rd G32 47 D3
Rhynie Dr G51 44 B5
Riach Gdns ML1 65 C1
Ribblesdale G74 75 C3
Riccarton G75 88 B7
Riccarton St G42 45 C2
Rice Way ML1 80 B4
Richard St G2 162 B2
Richmond Ave G76 73 E7
Richmond Ct G73 61 C8
Richmond Dr
Bishopbriggs G64 19 B4
Cambuslang G72 61 E5
Rutherglen G73 61 D7
Richmond Gdns G69 33 B8
Richmond Gr G73 61 C7
Richmond Park Sch G5 45 D3
Richmond Pl G73 61 C8
Richmond Rd G73 61 D7
Richmond St
Clydebank G81 15 C1
Glasgow G1 163 B2
Riddell St Clydebank G81 15 C3
Coatbridge ML5 50 D7
Riddon Ave G13 27 E8
Riddon Pl G13 27 E8
Riddrie Cres G33 46 E8
Riddrie Knowes G33 46 E8
Riddrievale Ct G33 31 E1
Riddrievale St G33 31 E1
Ridgepark Dr ML11 116 F5
Ridgepark Sch ML11 116 F6
Rigby St G32 46 E6
Rigg Pl G33 47 E7
Rigghead Ave G67 12 B5
Riggside Rd G33 32 C2
Righead Ind Est ML4 64 D7
Righead Pl ML10 112 D5
Righead Rdbt G74 75 D1
Riglands Gate PA4 27 C4
Riglands Way PA4 27 C3
Riglaw Pl G13 28 A7
Rigmuir Rd G51 43 C7
Rigside Prim sch ML11 138 F5
Rimmon Cres ML7 69 E6
Rimsdale St G40 46 A5
Ringford St G21 30 F3
Ringsdale Ave ML9 106 A8
Ringsdale Ct ML9 106 A8
Ringwell Gdns 6 ML9 129 E8
Ripon Dr G12 29 A6
Ristol Rd G13 28 B5
Ritchie Pl G77 72 C4
Ritchie St 3 Glasgow G5 45 A4
Wishaw ML2 80 D3
Ritchie's Cl ML11 117 A4
River Ct G76 73 F6
River Rd G32 62 B8
Riverbank Dr ML4 65 D3
Riverbank St G43 59 C7
Riverdale Gdns ML3 78 E1
Riverford Rd Glasgow G43 59 D7
Rutherglen G73 46 C1
Riversdale La G14 28 A4
Riverside Ct
Eaglesham G76 73 E1
Glasgow G44 60 A2
Netherlee G44 59 F2
Riverside Gdns
Clarkston G76 73 F5
Larkhall ML9 106 A8
Riverside Pk G44 60 A1
Riverside Pl G72 62 E6
Riverside Rd Glasgow G43 59 E7
Kirkfieldbank ML11 116 C4
Larkhall ML9 106 A8
Waterfoot G76 86 E8
Riverside Terr G76 73 F6
Riverside Wlk ML1 79 F8
Riverton Dr G75 88 B8
Riverview Dr G5 162 B1
Riverview Gdns G5 162 B1
Riverview Pl G5 162 B1
Roadmeetings Hospl ML8 109 C7
Roadside G67 12 B5
Roadside Pl ML6 36 D8
Robb Terr G66 21 A6
Robert Burns Ave
Clydebank G81 15 C3
Motherwell ML1 66 E4
Robert Burns Quadrant ML4 64 F5
Robert Dr G51 44 A7
Robert Gilson Gdns ML5 50 B5
Robert Owen Meml Prim Sch ML11 117 C4
Robert Smillie Cres ML9 93 A1
Robert Smillie Meml Prim Sch ML9 93 A1
Robert St Glasgow G51 44 A8
Shotts ML7 69 E4
Robert Templeton Dr G72 62 B5
Robert Wilson Gate ML9 106 A8
Robert Wynd ML2 82 A6
Roberton Ave G41 44 C2
Roberton St ML6 51 E3
Roberts Quadrant ML4 65 B3
Roberts St ML2 81 A3
Robertson Ave PA4 27 B3
Robertson Cl
Kirkmuirhill ML11 114 A2
Renfrew PA4 27 C3
Robertson Ct EH48 41 F4
Robertson Dr
Bellshill ML4 65 A4
East Kilbride G74 76 B2
Renfrew PA4 27 B3
Robertson La G2 162 C2
Robertson St Airdrie ML6 50 E8
Barrhead G78 57 B2
Glasgow G1,G2 162 C2
Hamilton ML3 77 F5
Robertson Terr G69 48 C5
Robin Pl ML1 81 B3
Robin Way G72 62 C8
Robinsfield G22 18 A7
Robroyston Ave G33 31 E3
Robroyston Rd
Bishopbriggs G64,G66 19 F1
Glasgow G33 31 E6
Glasgow,Barmulloch G33 31 D4

Robroyston Rd *continued*
Glasgow,Blackhill G33 31 E3
Robshill Ct G77 72 D4
Robslee Cres G46 59 B3
Robslee Dr G46 59 B4
Robslee Prim Sch G46 59 A2
Robslee Rd G46 59 A3
Robson Gr [3] G42 45 B3
Rocep Dr G51 27 F2
Rochsoles Cres ML6 36 A2
Rochsoles Dr ML6 36 A2
Rochsolloch Farm Cotts
ML6 50 E7
Rochsolloch Prim Sch
ML6 50 E6
Rochsolloch Rd ML6 50 D6
Rock Gdns ML9 105 D1
Rock St G4 30 B3
Rockall Dr G44 60 C4
Rockbank Pl
Clydebank G81 15 C6
Glasgow G40 46 A5
Rockbank St G40 46 A5
Rockburn Cres ML4 65 A7
Rockburn Dr G76 73 D8
Rockcliffe Path ML6 51 F1
Rockcliffe St G40 45 F3
Rockfield Pl G21 31 C5
Rockfield Rd G21 31 C5
Rockhampton Ave G75 88 B7
Rockliffe Path ML6 51 E1
Rockmount Ave
Barrhead G78 57 D1
Glasgow G46 59 A3
Rockwood Pl ML6 37 D4
Rodding The ML11 117 B5
Roddinghead Rd G46 73 A6
Rodger Ave G77 72 C5
Rodger Dr G73 61 B6
Rodger Pl G73 61 A6
Rodil Ave G44 60 C4
Rodney St G4 30 B2
Roebank Dr G78 57 C1
Roebank St G31 46 B8
Roffey Park Rd PA1 42 D5
Rogart St G40 45 F5
Rogerfield Prim Sch G34 48 C8
Rogerfield Rd G34,G69 48 C7
Rogerhill Cl ML11 114 A3
Rogerhill Dr ML11 114 A3
Rogerhill Gait ML11 114 A3
Rogers Ct ML9 105 D2
Rokeby Cres ML10 112 C7
Rokeby La G12 29 E3
Roland Cres G77 72 F3
Roman Ave Bearsden G61 16 F5
Clydebank G15 16 A1
Roman Ct Bearsden G61 16 F5
Cleghorn ML11 117 F7
Clydebank G81 15 A6
Roman Dr Bearsden G61 16 F5
Bellshill ML4 65 B4
Roman Gdns G61 16 F5
Roman Hill Rd G81 15 B7
Roman Pl ML4 64 E3
Roman Rd Bearsden G61 16 F5
Clydebank G81 15 A6
Kirkintilloch G66 20 B8
Motherwell ML1 79 E7
Roman Way G71 64 C6
Romney Ave G44 60 C5
Romulus Ct ML1 65 C1
Rona St G21 31 B2
Rona Terr G72 61 F3
Ronald St [2] ML5 50 A8
Ronaldsay Dr G64 19 D2
Ronaldsay Pass G22 30 D7
Ronaldsay Pl G67 23 D8
Ronaldsay St G22 30 D7
Ronay St Glasgow G22 30 D8
Wishaw ML2 81 E5
Ropework La G1 163 A1
Rorison Pl ML9 93 F1
Rosa Burn Ave G75 88 B4
Rose Cres ML3 77 F4
Rose Dale G64 31 B8
Rose Gdns ML5 49 F3
Rose Knowe Rd G42 60 D8
Rose Mount Ct ML6 51 C8
Rose St Cumbernauld G67 23 B6
Glasgow G3 162 C4
Kirkintilloch G66 20 D8
Motherwell ML1 80 A5
Rosebank Ave
Blantyre G72 63 E1
Kirkintilloch G66 20 E8
Rosebank Ct G72 77 E8
Rosebank Dr
Cambuslang G72 62 C4
Uddingston G71 64 C7
Rosebank Gdns
Glasgow G71 48 B2
Strathaven ML10 112 C5
Rosebank La [3] G71 64 B3
Rosebank Pl Dullatur G68 11 C6
Glasgow G71 48 B2
Hamilton ML3 78 A3
Rosebank Rd Bellshill ML4 65 B8
Overtown ML2 94 C6
Rosebank St ML6 51 E8
Rosebank Terr G69 49 A4
Rosebank Twr G72 62 A6
Roseberry Ct [13] G12 29 C3
Roseberry La ML6 51 E3
Roseberry Pl ML3 78 A4
Roseberry Rd ML6 51 E4
Roseberry St G5 45 E2
Roseburn Ct G67 12 F6
Rosedale G74 75 C3
Rosedale Dr G69 48 A4
Rosedale Gdns G20 29 C8
Rosedale St ML11 116 F2
Rosedene Terr ML4 65 A6
Rosefield Gdns G71 63 E7
Rosegreen Cres ML4 65 A8
Rosehall Ave ML5 50 B4
Rosehall High Sch ML5 49 F3
Rosehall Ind Est ML5 50 A3
Rosehall Rd Bellshill ML4 64 F6
Shotts ML7 69 C3
Rosehall Terr ML2 80 E1
Rosehill Dr G67 23 A6
Rosehill Rd G64 19 C8
Roselea ML6 37 F4
Roselea Gdns G13 28 F7
Roselea Pl G72 63 D1
Roselea Rd G71 63 E8
Roselea St ML9 93 B4
Rosemary Cres G74 75 D4
Rosemary Pl G74 75 D4
Rosemount G68 11 F5
Rosemount Ave G77 72 D2
Rosemount Cres ML11 130 F8
Rosemount Ct
Carluke ML8 96 A2
Newton Mearns G77 72 D1
Rosemount La [4] ML9 93 C1
Rosemount Mdws G71 63 F2
Rosemount St G21 30 F1
Rosendale Way G72 77 E7
Roseness Pl G33 47 A8
Rosenheath Gate G74 75 C2
Rosepark Ave G71 64 C6
Rosepark Cotts ML5 49 E3
Rosevale Cres
Bellshill ML4 65 C4
Hamilton ML3 78 B2
Rosevale Rd G61 16 E4
Rosevale Sch G22 30 D7
Rosevale St G11 29 A2
Rosewood ML2 80 D1
Rosewood Ave ML4 65 B7
Rosewood Path ML4 64 E5
Rosewood St G13 28 E7
Roslea Dr G31 46 A7
Roslin Twr G72 61 E3
Roslyn Dr G69 48 F6
Rosneath St G51 44 A8
Ross Ave Kirkintilloch G66 20 F8
Renfrew PA4 27 A1
Ross Cres ML1 79 C5
Ross Ct EH55 122 E8
Ross Dr Airdrie ML6 50 E5
Motherwell,Braedale ML1 79 C5
Motherwell,Tannochside
G71 49 C1
Ross Gdns ML1 79 C5
Ross Pl East Kilbride G74 76 C3
Rutherglen G73 61 D4
Ross St Coatbridge ML5 50 A7
Glasgow G40 163 B1
Paisley PA1 42 A3
Ross Terr ML3 79 C1
Rossendale Ct G43 59 C8
Rossendale Rd G43 59 C8
Rosshall Acad G52 43 A4
Rosshall Ave PA1 42 C4
Rosshall Hospl G52 43 A3
Rosshall Pl PA4 27 D3
Rosshill Ave G52 42 F5
Rosshill Rd G52 42 F5
Rossie Cres G64 31 C8
Rossie Gr G77 72 B5
Rosslea Dr G46 59 C2
Rosslyn Ave
East Kilbride G74 76 A3
Rutherglen G73 61 C7
Rosslyn Ct ML3 78 A4
Rosslyn Ho [12] G12 29 C3
Rosslyn Rd Ashgill ML9 106 F8
Bearsden G61 16 B6
Rosslyn Terr [13] G12 29 C4
Rostan Rd G43 59 C5
Rosyth Rd G5 45 E2
Rosyth St G5 45 E2
Rotherwick Dr PA1 42 E4
Rotherwood Ave G13 16 E1
Rotherwood La G13 16 C2
Rotherwood Pl G13 28 D8
Rothes Dr G23 29 D8
Rothes Pl G23 17 C1
Rothesay Cres ML5 50 B4
Rothesay Pl ML5 50 B4
Rothesay St G75 88 E8
Rottenrow Glasgow G4 163 B3
Glasgow G4 163 C2
Rottenrow E G4 163 B2
Roughcraig St ML6 36 A2
Roughrigg Rd ML6 52 C6
Rouken Glen Pk* G46 58 F1
Rouken Glen Rd G46 59 A1
Roukenburn St G46 58 F4
Roundel The ML2 81 C2
Roundknowe Rd G71 48 C1
Rowallan Gdns G11 29 A3
Rowallan La Clarkston G76 73 E7
Glasgow G11 29 A3
Rowallan La E G11 29 A3
Rowallan Rd G46 58 F2
Rowallan Terr G33 32 B4
Rowan Ave PA4 27 C4
Rowan Cres
Chapelhall ML6 51 E3
Rowan Cres *continued*
Kirkintilloch G66 20 C5
Shotts ML7 70 B4
Rowan Ct Cambuslang G72 62 F3
Wishaw ML2 80 D2
Rowan Dr Banknock FK4 8 E2
Bearsden G61 17 A7
Clydebank G81 15 A4
Rowan Gdns Glasgow G41 44 B4
Larkhall ML9 93 B2
Rowan Gr ML3 91 F3
Rowan La ML1 66 A2
Rowan Pl Cambuslang G72 62 C6
Coatbridge ML5 49 E4
Hamilton G72 77 D8
Rowan Rd
Cumbernauld G67 12 D3
Glasgow G41 44 B4
Rowan Rise ML3 78 E2
Rowan St Paisley PA2 42 A1
Wishaw ML2 81 B5
Rowan Wlk ML10 112 C5
Rowanbank Pl ML6 50 D8
Rowand Ave G46 59 C3
Rowandale Ave G69 48 A4
Rowanden Ave ML4 65 A6
Rowanlea ML6 36 F3
Rowanlea Dr G46 59 D4
Rowanpark Dr G78 57 A5
Rowans Gdns G71 64 B4
Rowans The G64 18 F2
Rowantree Ave
Motherwell ML1 66 D7
Rutherglen G73 61 B5
Uddingston G71 64 C7
Rowantree Gdns G73 61 B5
Rowantree Pl ML9 93 D2
Rowantree Terr ML1 66 B5
Rowanwood Cres ML5 49 D5
Rowchester St G40 46 A5
Rowena Ave G13 16 D1
Rowhead Ct ML12 160 C5
Rowhead Terr ML12 160 C4
Roxburgh Dr
Bearsden G61 16 E7
Coatbridge ML5 50 D4
Roxburgh Pk G74 75 F1
Roxburgh Pl [5] G72 77 D7
Roxburgh St G12 29 D3
Roy St G21 30 D3
Royal Bank Pl G1 163 A2
Royal Cres G3 44 E8
Royal Dr ML3 79 A2
Royal Exchange Ct G1 163 A2
Royal Exchange Sq G1 163 A2
Royal Gdns G71 63 E2
Royal Highland Fusiliers
Regimental Mus* G2 162 B4
Royal Hospl (For Sick
Children) G3 29 C1
Royal Inch Cres PA4 27 D5
Royal Infmy Hospl G4 163 C3
Royal Scottish Acad of Music
& Drama G2 162 C3
Royal Terr Glasgow G3 29 E1
Wishaw ML2 81 C7
Royal Terrace La G3 29 E1
Royellen Ave ML3 77 F2
Royston Prim Sch G21 30 F1
Royston Rd G21,G33 31 C3
Royston Sq G21 163 C4
Roystonhill G21 30 F1
Roystonhill Pl G21 30 F1
Rozelle Ave Clydebank G15 16 B3
Newton Mearns G77 72 B4
Rozelle Dr G77 72 B4
Rozelle Pl G77 72 B4
Rubislaw Dr G61 16 E3
Ruby St G40 46 A4
Ruby Terr ML4 65 A4
Ruchazie Pl G32,G33 46 F8
Ruchazie Rd G33 46 F7
Ruchill Pl G20 29 F5
Ruchill Prim Sch G20 29 F6
Ruchill St G20 29 F5
Ruel St G44 60 A7
Rufflees Ave G78 57 D4
Rugby Ave G13 28 B8
Rullion Pl G33 46 F8
Rumford St G40 45 F3
Runciman Pl G74 76 B4
Rupert St G4 29 F2
Rushyhill St G21 31 A4
Ruskin La G12 29 E3
Ruskin Pl Glasgow G12 29 E3
Kilsyth G65 10 D8
Ruskin Sq G64 19 A1
Ruskin Terr Glasgow G12 29 E3
Rutherglen G73 46 B1
Russell Ave EH48 41 F7
Russell Colt St ML5 50 A8
Russell Dr G61 16 F6
Russell Gdns
Newton Mearns G77 72 C4
[10] Uddingston G71 64 A8
Russell La ML2 81 A2
Russell Pl Clarkston G76 74 A5
East Kilbride G75 88 C7
Russell Rd ML11 117 B5
Russell St Bellshill ML4 65 D5
Chapelhall ML6 51 E2
Hamilton ML3 77 F5
Wishaw ML2 81 B2
Rutherford Ave
Bearsden G61 16 B8
Kirkintilloch G66 21 B6
Rutherford Ct G81 15 A2
Rutherford Grange G66 20 C6
Rutherford La G75 88 F8
Rutherford Sq G75 88 F8
Rutherglen Ind Est G73 46 A1
Rutherglen Rd G5,G73 45 E2
Rutherglen Sta G73 61 B8
Ruthven Ave G46 59 D1
Ruthven La
[7] Glasgow G12 29 D3
Glenboig ML5 34 C6
Ruthven Pl G64 31 C8
Ruthven St G12 29 D3
Rutland Cres G51 44 E6
Rutland Ct G51 44 E6
Rutland Pl G51 44 E6
Ryan Rd G64 19 B1
Ryan Way G73 61 C3
Ryat Dr G77 72 C6
Ryat Gn G77 72 C5
Rydal Gr G75 87 F6
Rydal Pl G75 87 F6
Ryde Rd ML2 81 C4
Ryden Mains Rd ML6 35 D4
Rye Cres G21 31 B5
Rye Rd G21 31 C5
Ryebank Rd G21 31 C5
Ryecroft Dr G69 48 B5
Ryedale Pl G15 16 B4
Ryefield Ave ML5 49 D7
Ryefield Rd G21 31 B5
Ryeflat Rd ML11 124 A2
Ryehill Pl G21 31 C5
Ryehill Rd G21 31 C4
Ryeland St ML10 112 D5
Ryemount Rd G21 31 C5
Ryeside Rd G21 31 B4
Rylands Dr G32 47 D4
Rylands Gdns G32 47 E4
Rylees Cres G52 42 E6
Rylees Pl G52 42 E6
Rylees Rd G52 42 E6
Rysland Ave G77 72 E5
Rysland Cres G77 72 E5
Ryvra Rd G13 28 D6

S

Sackville Ave G13 28 F5
Sackville La G13 28 F5
Sacred Heart Prim Sch
G40 45 F4
Sacred Heart RC Prim Sch
ML4 65 A3
Saddell Rd G15 16 B4
Saddlers Ct ML10 112 E4
Saddlers Gate ML10 112 E4
Sadler's Wells Ct G74 76 B4
Saffron Cres ML2 80 E1
Saffronhall Cres ML3 78 D4
Saffronhall La ML3 78 D4
St Agatha's Prim Sch
G66 21 B8
St Agnes' Prim Sch G23 29 E8
St Aidan's High Sch ML2 81 B4
St Aidan's Path ML2 81 C6
St Aidan's RC Prim Sch
ML2 81 C5
St Aidan's Sch G32 46 D6
St Albert's Prim Sch G41 44 E4
St Aloysius Coll G3 162 B4
St Aloysius' Prim Sch
G22 30 E5
St Aloysius' RC Prim Sch
ML6 51 E2
St Ambrose High Sch
ML5 49 E8
St Ambrose's Prim Sch
G22 30 E8
St Andrew's Acad PA2 42 C1
St Andrew's Ave G64 18 E2
St Andrew's Cross G41 45 A3
St Andrew's Ct ML8 95 E1
St Andrew's Dr
Armadale EH48 41 F7
Glasgow G41 44 D3
Hamilton ML3 77 D4
St Andrew's Gdns ML6 51 B8
St Andrew's High Sch
Clydebank G81 27 C8
East Kilbride G75 88 D6
St Andrew's La G1 163 B1
St Andrew's Prim Sch
Airdrie ML6 35 E1
Cumbernauld G68 11 D5
St Andrew's RC Cath*
G1 163 A1
St Andrew's RC Prim Sch
G61 16 C6
St Andrew's Rd
Glasgow G41 44 F4
Renfrew PA4 27 C2
St Andrew's Sec Sch G32 47 A7
St Andrew's Sq G1 163 B1
St Andrew's St G1 163 B1
St Andrew's Way ML2 81 C6
St Andrews Ave G71 64 A1
St Andrews Cres G41 44 E4
St Andrews Ct
Bellshill ML4 65 B5
East Kilbride G75 88 C6
Kirkintilloch G66 20 D7
Motherwell ML1 66 A6
St Andrews Dr
Bearsden G61 16 D7
Coatbridge ML5 49 E6
Cumbernauld G68 12 B6
St Andrews Gate ML4 64 F5
St Andrews Path [10] ML9 93 C1
St Andrews Pl G65 6 C1
St Andrews St ML1 66 A5
St Angela's Prim Sch
G53 58 C3
St Ann's Dr G46 59 C2
St Ann's RC Prim Sch
ML3 91 D8
St Anne's Ct ML3 91 D8
St Anne's Prim Sch G40 46 A5
St Annes Well ML10 112 F4
St Anthony's Prim Sch
Armadale EH48 41 F5
Glasgow G51 43 F8
Rutherglen G73 61 D4
St Athanasius' Prim Sch
ML8 95 F1
St Augustine's Prim Sch
Coatbridge ML5 49 F6
Glasgow G22 30 C7
St Barbara's Prim Sch
G69 33 D7
St Bartholomew's Prim Sch
ML5 34 D1
St Benedict's Prim Sch
G34 33 C1
St Bernadette's Prim Sch
ML1 79 B8
St Bernard's Prim Sch
G53 58 A5
St Bernard's RC Prim Sch
ML5 50 B3
St Blane's Dr G73 60 F6
St Blane's Prim Sch
Glasgow G23 17 D1
Hamilton G72 77 C8
St Boswells Dr ML5 50 D4
St Brendan's Prim Sch
G13 27 F7
St Brendan's RC Prim Sch
ML1 80 B2
St Bride's Ave G71 64 C7
St Bride's High Sch G74 76 A1
St Bride's Prim Sch G72 62 A5
St Bride's RC Prim Sch
G71 64 A4
St Bride's Rd G43 59 D6
St Brides Way G71 64 A4
St Bridget's Prim Sch
G69 48 B5
St Brigid's Prim Sch
Glasgow G42 60 E8
Wishaw ML2 82 A5
St Bryde La G74 75 F2
St Bryde St G74 75 F2
St Cadoc's Prim Sch
Cambuslang G72 62 C4
Newton Mearns G77 72 C5
St Catherine's Prim Sch
PA3 42 A6
St Catherine's RC Prim Sch
G21 31 C5
St Catherine's Rd G46 59 C2
St Catherines Cres ML7 69 E6
St Charles Ave ML11 131 B8
St Charles Prim Sch G72 62 F6
St Charles' Prim Sch G20 29 F4
St Clair Ave G46 59 C3
St Clair St G20 29 F2
St Clare's Prim RC Sch
G15 16 A4
St Columba Dr G66 20 E7
St Columba's High Sch
G81 15 C4
St Columba's RC Prim Sch
G71 64 C7
St Columbkille's Prim Sch
G73 61 B7
St Conval's Prim Sch
G43 59 D8
St Cuthbert Way ML3 77 F5
St Cuthbert's Prim Sch
Glasgow G22 30 B4
Hamilton ML3 78 A5
St Cyrus Gdns G64 19 C1
St Cyrus Rd G64 19 C1
St David's Pl ML9 93 A3
St David's RC Prim Sch
ML6 37 A2
St Davids Dr ML6 51 C4
St Denis Way ML5 49 F8
St Denis' Prim Sch G31 46 B7
St Dominic's Prim Sch
G45 60 F2
St Dominic's RC Prim Sch
ML6 51 D6
St Edmund's Prim Sch
G53 43 D1
St Edward's Prim Sch
ML6 51 C7
St Elizabeth Seton Prim Sch
G33 47 C8
St Enoch Ave G71 64 C8
St Enoch Pl G1 162 C2
St Enoch Sh Ctr G1 163 A1
St Enoch Sq G1 162 C1
St Enoch Underground Sta
G1 162 C1
St Eunan's Prim Sch G81 15 C2
St Fillan's Prim Sch G44 60 B6
St Fillans Rd G33 32 C5
St Flanan Rd G65,G66 9 D2
St Francis of Assisi Prim Sch
G68 23 A7
St Francis Xavier Coll
ML5 50 C4
St Francis' of Assisi Prim
Sch G69 47 F3
St Francis' Prim Sch G5 45 D4

St Gabriel's Prim Sch G71 64 D8
St George's Cross [10] G3 30 A2
St George's Pl [8] G3 30 A2
St George's Prim Sch G52 42 F5
St George's RC Prim Sch ML4 65 A7
St George's Rd G3 30 A2
St Germains G61 16 E4
St Gilbert's RC Prim Sch G21 31 C3
St Giles Pk ML3 78 B2
St Giles Way ML3 78 B2
St Gregory's Prim Sch G20 29 D6
St Helen's Pl EH48 41 F5
St Helen's Prim Sch
Bishopbriggs G64 19 C2
Cumbernauld G67 23 B7
St Helena Cres G81 15 C6
St Hilary's Prim Sch G74 89 B8
St Ignatius's RC Prim Sch ML2 81 B3
St Ives Rd G69 21 F3
St James Ct ML5 49 E3
St James Rd G4 163 B3
St James Way ML5 49 E3
St James' Prim Sch
Coatbridge ML5 49 E4
Glasgow G40 45 E5
Renfrew PA4 27 C3
St Jerome's Prim Sch G51 43 E7
St Joachim's Prim Sch G32 47 C1
St Joan of Arc Sch G22 30 B7
St John Ogilvie Prim Sch PA1 42 B4
St John St ML5 50 A7
St John the Baptist Prim Sch
Fauldhouse EH47 71 E6
Uddingston G71 64 A6
St John's Bvd G71 64 A6
St John's Ct G41 44 E4
St John's Prim Sch
Barrhead G78 57 C4
Glasgow G5 45 B5
Hamilton ML3 78 D3
St John's Prim Sch ML11 114 A4
St John's Quadrant [1] G41 44 E4
St John's Rd G41 44 E4
St Johns Way G65 9 F3
St Joseph's Ct G21 30 F1
St Joseph's Pl G21 30 F1
St Joseph's Prim Sch
Clarkston G76 73 E5
Clydebank G81 15 D7
Glasgow G4 30 B2
Hamilton G72 77 D8
St Joseph's Prim Sch G33 32 E5
St Joseph's View G21 30 F1
St Josephs RC Prim Sch EH47 56 F5
St Jude's Prim Sch G33 47 E6
St Kenneth Dr G51 43 E8
St Kenneth's Prim Sch G74 75 E2
St Kentigerns Rd ML11 117 B5
St Kevin's Prim Sch G69 49 A5
St Kevin's Sch G21 30 E2
St Kilda Dr G14 28 E4
St Kilda Way ML2 81 E5
St Lawrence Ave [17] ML9 129 E8
St Lawrence Pk G75 75 C1
St Leonard St ML11 117 B5
St Leonard's Dr G46 59 C3
St Leonard's Prim Sch G74 76 D3
St Leonard's Rd ML11 117 B4
St Leonard's Sq G74 76 C1
St Leonards Rd G74 76 D2
St Leonards Wlk ML5 50 C3
St Louise's Prim Sch
East Kilbride G75 88 E6
Glasgow G46 58 D4
St Lucy's Prim Sch G67 12 E4
St Luke's Ave ML8 108 E8
St Lukes Pl G5 45 C5
St Lukes Terr G5 45 C5
St Margaret Mary's Prim Sch G45 60 C1
St Margaret Mary's Sec Sch G45 60 D2
St Margaret's Ave G65 7 E3
St Margaret's Dr
Armadale EH48 41 E5
Wishaw ML2 80 E1
St Margaret's High Sch ML6 51 B8
St Margaret's Pl G1 163 A1
St Margarets Ct ML4 65 B5
St Mark Gdns G32 46 F5
St Mark St G32 46 E5
St Mark's Ct ML2 81 C6
St Mark's Prim Sch
Barrhead G78 57 C1
Glasgow G31 46 E5
Hamilton ML3 77 F1
Rutherglen G73 61 B5
St Marnock St G40 46 A5
St Marnock's Prim Sch G53 43 C1
St Marnock's Prim Sch Annexe G53 43 C1
St Martha's RC Prim Sch G21 31 B5
St Martin's Prim Sch G45 60 F2
St Martins Gate ML5 50 A4
St Mary's (Maryhill) Sch G20 29 C7
St Mary's Cres G78 57 D2
St Mary's Ct ML2 81 B2
St Mary's La G2 162 C2
St Mary's Prim Sch
Clydebank G81 15 A6
Cumbernauld G67 11 E1
Hamilton ML3 78 D4
Lanark ML11 117 C3
St Mary's Prim Sch ML9 92 F2
St Mary's RC Prim Sch ML6 37 F5
St Mary's RC Prim Sch
Cleland ML1 67 B1
Coatbridge ML5 50 A5
St Mary's Rd Bellshill ML4 64 E5
Bishopbriggs G64 18 E1
St Marys Ct ML11 117 C4
St Marys Gdns G78 57 D2
St Matthew's Prim Sch G64 19 B2
St Matthew's RC Prim Sch ML2 80 E4
St Maurice's Rdbt G68 11 A1
St Maurices High Sch G68 23 A8
St Michael Rd ML2 80 C1
St Michael's Ct G31 46 C5
St Michael's La G31 46 C5
St Michael's Prim Sch
Glasgow G31 46 C5
Moodiesburn G69 22 A2
St Mirin's Prim Sch G44 60 C5
St Mirren's Rd G65 10 E8
St Modan's Prim Sch G33 47 A8
St Monance St G21 30 F5
St Monica's Prim Sch ML5 49 D4
St Monica's Prim Sch G53 43 B1
St Monicas Way ML5 49 D4
St Mungo Ave G4 163 B3
St Mungo Mus of Religious Life & Art* G4 163 C3
St Mungo Pl Glasgow G4 163 B3
Hamilton ML3 77 D4
St Mungo St G64 30 F8
St Mungo's ML11 117 A3
St Mungo's Acad G40 46 A5
St Mungo's Prim Sch G4 163 C3
St Mungo's Rd G67 11 F1
St Mungo's Wlk G67 11 F2
St Mungos Cres [5] ML1 66 B2
St Nicholas Rd ML11 117 B5
St Ninian Terr G5 45 C5
St Ninian's ML11 117 B5
St Ninian's High Sch
Glasgow G46 59 B2
Kirkintilloch G66 20 B8
St Ninian's Pl ML3 77 F3
St Ninian's Prim Sch G13 16 C1
St Ninian's Prim Sch ML3 77 F3
St Ninian's Rd ML3 77 E3
St Ninians Gr ML2 81 D6
St Ninians Pl ML9 105 E1
St Ninians Rd DG10 161 E5
St Oswold's Sch G44 60 A5
St Patrick's Ct ML11 116 F4
St Patrick's High Sch ML5 50 B7
St Patrick's Prim Sch
Glasgow G3 162 A2
Kilsyth G65 10 D8
Motherwell ML1 65 F3
St Patrick's Prim Sch ML10 112 E6
St Patrick's RC Prim Sch
Coatbridge ML5 50 B7
Shotts ML7 69 E3
St Patrick's Rd ML11 116 F4
St Paul's (Whiteinch) Prim Sch G14 28 D3
St Paul's High Sch G53 58 D8
St Paul's Prim Sch
Glasgow,Shettleston G32 47 A3
Hamilton ML3 78 B6
St Peter's La G2 162 B2
St Peter's Path [13] G4 30 A2
St Peter's Prim Sch
Glasgow G11 29 C2
Hamilton ML3 78 B1
St Peter's St G4 30 A2
St Philip's Sch ML6 36 F1
St Philomena's RC Prim Sch G33 31 D3
St Raymond's Sch G45 60 B2
St Robert's Prim Sch G53 58 C5
St Roberts Gdns G53 58 C5
St Roch's RC Prim Sch G21 31 A1
St Roch's Sec Sch G21 163 C4
St Ronan's Dr
Glasgow G41 59 D8
Hamilton ML3 91 C8
St Ronan's Prep Sch G41 44 D3
St Ronans Dr G73 61 C6
St Rose of Lima Prim Sch G33 32 C2
St Rose of Lima Prim Sch Annexe G33 32 B1
St Saviour's Prim Sch G51 44 B7
St Serf's Prim Sch ML6 36 B2
St Stephen's Ave G73 61 D3
St Stephen's Cres G73 61 E3
St Stephen's Prim Sch G21 30 E2
St Stephen's RC Prim Sch ML5 50 D5
St Stephens Ave G73 61 D3
St Teiling ML11 117 B6
St Teresa's Prim Sch (Keppoch Campus) G21 30 C3
St Teresa's RC Prim Sch ML1 66 D3
St Thomas Aquinas RC Sec Sch G14 28 E4
St Thomas' Prim Sch
Glasgow G33 46 D8
Wishaw ML2 81 A2
St Timothy's Prim Sch ML5 49 F4
St Timothy's Prim Sch G32 47 A6
St Vigeans Ave G77 72 C3
St Vigeans Pl G77 72 C3
St Vincent Cres G3 44 E8
St Vincent Crescent La G3 44 E8
St Vincent La G2 162 C2
St Vincent Pl
East Kilbride G75 88 A8
Glasgow G1 163 A2
Lanark ML11 117 B4
Motherwell ML1 79 E7
St Vincent St G2 162 B3
St Vincent Terr G3 162 A3
St Vincent's Prim Sch
East Kilbride G75 88 B5
Glasgow G46 58 E4
St Vincent's Sch for the Blind & Deaf G32 47 A2
St Winifred's Way ML2 81 A4
Salamanca St G31 46 D5
Salasaig Ct G33 47 A7
Salen Loan ML7 70 B3
Salen St G52 43 F5
Saline St ML6 50 D6
Salisbury G74 76 D4
Salisbury Cres ML1 79 B8
Salisbury Pl ML11 138 F7
Salisbury St [2] G5 45 B4
Salkeld St G5 45 B5
Salmona St G22 30 B4
Saltaire Ave G71 64 A5
Salterland Rd G78 57 E4
Saltire Cres ML9 93 C2
Saltmarket G1 163 B1
Saltmarket Pl G1 163 A1
Saltoun La [8] G12 29 D3
Saltoun St G12 29 D3
Salvia St G72 61 F6
Samson Cres ML8 109 C8
Sanda St G20 29 E4
Sandaig Prim Sch G33 47 F6
Sandaig Rd G33 47 E6
Sandale Path [2] G72 77 C6
Sandalwood ML2 80 D1
Sandalwood Ave G74 75 D4
Sandalwood Ct G74 75 D4
Sandbank Ave G20 29 D6
Sandbank Cres G20 29 D6
Sandbank Dr G20 29 D7
Sandbank St G20 29 D7
Sandbank Terr G20 29 D7
Sandend Rd G53 58 A7
Sanderling Pl G75 88 A5
Sanderson Ave G71 64 D6
Sanderson High Sch G74 89 C8
Sandfield St G20 29 E5
Sandford Gdns G69 48 B5
Sandford Prim Sch ML10 129 C6
Sandford Rd ML9 129 D7
Sandgate Ave G32 47 D3
Sandhaven Pl G53 58 A7
Sandhaven Rd G53 58 A7
Sandhead Cres ML6 51 E1
Sandhead Rd ML10 112 C5
Sandhead Terr G72 77 D2
Sandholm Pl G14 27 F5
Sandholm Terr G14 27 F5
Sandiefield Rd [1] G5 45 C4
Sandilands Cres ML1 79 C5
Sandilands St G32 47 C5
Sandmill St G21 31 A1
Sandpiper Cres ML5 50 D3
Sandpiper Dr G75 88 A5
Sandpiper Pl G75 88 A5
Sandpiper Way ML4 64 E8
Sandra Rd G64 19 C2
Sandringham Ave G77 73 A6
Sandringham Ct G77 73 A5
Sandringham La [2] G12 29 D3
Sandvale Pl ML7 70 A3
Sandwood Cres [4] G52 43 A5
Sandwood Path [1] G52 43 A5
Sandwood Prim Sch G52 43 A5
Sandwood Rd G52 43 A5
Sandy La G11 29 A2
Sandy Rd Carluke ML8 95 F2
Glasgow G11 29 A2
Renfrew PA4 27 C2
Sandy's Ford Rd ML12 141 A6
Sandyfaulds St [1] G5 45 D4
Sandyford Ave ML1 66 D7
Sandyford Pl
Glasgow G3 162 A3
Motherwell ML1 66 D7
Sandyford Place La G3 162 A3
Sandyford Rd
Motherwell ML1 66 D7
Paisley PA3 42 A8
Sandyford St G3 44 C8
Sandyhill Ave ML7 70 A3
Sandyhills Cres G32 47 B3
Sandyhills Dr G32 47 B3
Sandyhills Gr G32 47 B2
Sandyhills Pl G32 47 B3
Sandyhills Rd G32 47 C3
Sandyknowes Rd G67 24 A8
Sannox Dr ML1 79 B7
Sannox Gdns G31 46 B8
Sannox Pl G75 88 B4
Sanquhar Dr G53 58 A8
Sanquhar Gdns
Blantyre G72 63 B2
[1] Glasgow G53 58 A8
Sanquhar Pl [2] G53 58 A8
Sanquhar Rd G53 43 A1
Sanson La ML8 109 C8
Sapphire Rd ML4 65 B4
Saracen Head Rd G1 163 C1
Saracen Prim Sch (Keppoch Campus) G22 30 C4
Saracen St Glasgow G22 30 C4
Glasgow G22 30 C5
Sarazen Ct ML1 80 E8
Sardinia La G12 29 D3
Saskatoon Pl G75 75 B1
Sauchiehall La
Glasgow G2 162 B3
Glasgow G2 162 C3
Sauchiehall St
Glasgow G2 162 B3
Glasgow,Cranston Hill G3 44 E8
Sauchiesmoor Rd ML8 109 A8
Saughs Ave G33 31 F6
Saughs Dr G33 31 F6
Saughs Gate G33 31 F6
Saughs Pl G33 31 F6
Saughs Rd G33 31 F6
Saughton St G32 46 E7
Saunders Ct G78 57 B3
Savoy St G40 45 F4
Sawmill Rd G11 28 F2
Sawmillfield St G4 30 B2
Saxon Rd G13 28 D7
Scalloway Rd G69 33 E4
Scalpay G74 76 C1
Scalpay Pass G22 30 D7
Scalpay Pl G22 30 D7
Scalpay St G22 30 D7
Scamadale Rd ML6 25 D3
Scapa St G23 29 F8
Scaraway Dr G22 30 D8
Scaraway Pl G22 30 D8
Scaraway St G22 30 D8
Scaraway Terr G22 30 D8
Scarba Dr G43 59 B6
Scarba Quadrant ML2 80 E1
Scarhill Ave ML6 50 F5
Scarhill La ML6 51 A5
Scarhill St Cleland ML1 67 B2
Coatbridge ML5 49 F3
Scarletmuir ML11 116 F5
Scarrel Dr G45 61 A4
Scarrel Gdns G45 61 A3
Scarrel Rd G45 61 A3
Scarrel Terr G45 61 A4
Scaut Hill ML12 140 F6
Scavaig Cres G15 15 E4
Schaw Ct G61 16 E6
Schaw Dr Bearsden G61 16 E6
Clydebank G81 15 E7
Schaw Rd PA3 42 A6
Scholar's Gate G75 88 D6
School Ave G72 62 B5
School La Bothwell G71 64 B1
Cambuslang G72 62 E4
Carluke ML8 95 E2
Carnwath ML11 124 E1
Moffat DG10 161 D5
Shotts ML7 83 B8
School Quadrant ML6 35 F2
School Rd
Carmichael ML12 130 F1
Carstairs ML11 111 F1
Coalburn ML11 137 F6
Lesmahagow ML11 119 E5
Newton Mearns G77 72 D4
Paisley PA1 42 E5
Salsburgh ML7 53 D3
Sandford ML10 129 C6
Stepps G33 32 E6
Symington ML12 140 F6
Wishaw ML2 82 A4
Wishaw,Morningside ML2 82 B4
School St Chapelhall ML6 51 D2
Coatbridge ML5 50 A4
Hamilton ML3 78 D1
Shotts ML7 69 F4
School View ML1 79 E5
Schoolhouse Ave 137 F5
Schoolhouse La G72 77 C6
Schoolhouse Rd ML12 141 A5
Scioncroft Ave G73 61 C7
Scone Pl East Kilbride G74 75 D3
Newton Mearns G77 73 B4
Scone St G21 30 C3
Scone Wlk G69 48 A3
Sconser St G23 17 E1
Scorton Gdns G69 47 F4
Scotia Cres ML9 93 A1
Scotia Gdns ML3 91 C7
Scotia St ML1 79 C7
Scotland St G5 44 F5
Scotland St W G41 44 D5
Scotland Street School Mus* G5 44 F5
Scotland Theme Pk* ML1 64 E1
Scotsblair Ave G66 20 C7
Scotsburn Rd G21 31 C4
Scotstoun Prim Sch G14 28 C4
Scotstoun St G14 28 C3
Scotstoun Way ML5 50 C5
Scotstounhill Sta G13 28 B5
Scott Cres G67 23 D7
Scott Dr Bearsden G61 16 C6
Cumbernauld G67 23 D7
Scott Gr ML3 78 D2
Scott Hill [1] G74 76 A3
Scott Ho G67 12 A3
Scott Pl Bellshill ML4 65 B7
Fauldhouse EH47 71 F6
Scott Rd G52 42 F8
Scott St Glasgow G69 48 B4
Glasgow,Garnethill G3 162 B4
Hamilton ML3 78 D1
Kirkmuirhill ML11 114 A2
Larkhall ML9 93 B2
Motherwell ML9 79 E7
Scott's Pl ML6 51 B8
Scott's Rd PA2 42 D3
Scottish Exhibition & Conference Ctr G3 44 D7
Scotus Coll G61 16 D4
Seafar Rd G67 11 F2
Seafar Rdbt G67 23 E8
Seafield Ave G61 16 F7
Seafield Cres G68 10 E1
Seafield Dr G73 61 D3
Seaforth Cres G78 57 B4
Seaforth La G69 22 A2
Seaforth Pl ML4 64 F3
Seaforth Rd
Clydebank G81 15 B2
Glasgow G52 43 A7
Seaforth Rd N G52 43 A7
Seaforth Rd S G52 43 A7
Seagrove St G32 46 D6
Seamill Gdns G74 75 D2
Seamill Path G53 57 F5
Seamill St G53 57 F5
Seamore St [4] G20 29 F2
Seath Ave ML6 50 E7
Seath Rd G73 46 A1
Seath St G42 45 C2
Seaton Terr ML3 78 A4
Seaward La G41,G5 44 E6
Seaward Pl G41 44 F5
Seaward St
[3] Glasgow G41 44 E5
Glasgow G41 44 F5
Secaurin Ave [7] ML9 129 E8
Second Ave
Auchinloch G66 20 D1
Bearsden G61 17 A3
Clydebank G81 15 A3
Glasgow G44 60 B6
Millerston G33 32 B4
Renfrew PA4 27 C2
Uddingston G71 48 E1
Second Ave La G44 60 B7
Second Gdns G41 44 A4
Second Rd G72 77 E5
Second St G71 63 F8
Seedhill Rd PA1 42 A4
Seggielea La G13 28 D6
Seggielea Rd G13 28 D6
Seil Dr G44 60 C4
Selborne Pl [5] G13 28 E5
Selborne Place La [4] G13 28 E5
Selborne Rd G13 28 E5
Selby Gdns G32 47 D5
Selby Pl ML5 34 D2
Selby St ML5 34 D2
Selkirk Ave G52 43 C4
Selkirk Dr G73 61 C7
Selkirk Pl
East Kilbride G74 76 D3
Hamilton ML3 78 E2
Selkirk St
Hamilton,Blantyre G72 77 D7
Hamilton,Silvertonhill ML3 78 E2
Wishaw ML2 81 C5
Selkirk Way Bellshill ML4 65 B7
Coatbridge ML5 50 E3
Sella Rd G64 19 D2
Selvieland Rd G52 42 F5
Semphill Gdns G74 76 B2
Sempie St ML3 77 F4
Senate Pl ML1 65 C1
Senga Cres ML4 65 A7
Seres Rd G76 73 D8
Seton Terr [3] G31 45 F7
Settle Gdns G69 47 F4
Seven Sisters G66 20 E5
Seventh Ave G71 63 F8
Seventh Rd G72 77 E5
Severn Rd G75 87 F7
Seymour Gn G75 88 B7
Seyton Ave G46 59 C1
Seyton Ct G46 59 C1
Seyton La G74 75 E3

Shaftesbury Ct G74 .....76 C5
Shaftesbury St G3 .....162 A3
Shafton Pl G13 .....28 E8
Shafton Rd G13 .....28 E8
Shaftsbury Cres ML1 .....66 D3
Shakespeare Ave G81 .....15 A3
Shakespeare St G20 .....29 E5
Shamrock St
Glasgow G4 .....162 B4
Kirkintilloch G66 .....20 D8
Shand La ML8 .....95 F3
Shand St ML2 .....81 B3
Shandon Cres ML4 .....65 A8
Shandon Terr ML3 .....77 F3
Shandwick St G34 .....48 A8
Shanks Ave G78 .....57 C2
Shanks Ind Pk G78 .....57 C4
Shanks St Airdrie ML6 .....36 A1
Glasgow G20 .....29 E5
Shanks Way G78 .....57 C5
Shannon St G20 .....29 F5
Shapinsay St G22 .....30 D8
Sharnothshield Small Holdings ML2 .....82 E6
Sharp Ave ML5 .....49 C4
Sharp St ML1 .....79 B7
Shaw Ave EH48 .....41 F6
Shaw Cres ML2 .....80 D1
Shaw Ct G77 .....72 F4
Shaw Pl EH48 .....41 F6
Shaw Rd Milngavie G62 .....17 A8
Newton Mearns G77 .....72 E4
Shaw St Glasgow G51 .....44 A8
Larkhall ML9 .....106 B8
Shawbridge Arc G43 .....59 C8
Shawbridge Ind Est G43 .....59 B7
Shawbridge St G43 .....59 C7
Shawburn Cres ML3 .....78 B4
Shawburn St ML3 .....78 B4
Shawfield Cres ML8 .....94 F6
Shawfield Dr G73 .....45 F2
Shawfield Ind Est G73 .....45 F2
Shawfield Rd G73 .....45 F2
Shawgill Ct ML8 .....94 F4
Shawhead Ave ML5 .....50 B4
Shawhead Cotts ML5 .....50 B3
Shawhead Prim Sch ML5 .....50 B3
Shawhill Cres G77 .....72 E3
Shawhill Rd G43 .....59 D8
Shawhill Terr ML12 .....141 C4
Shawholm Cres G43 .....59 C7
Shawlands Acad G41 .....44 E1
Shawlands Arc G41 .....59 D8
Shawlands Cross 5 G41 .....44 E1
Shawlands Prim Sch G41 .....59 D8
Shawlands Sta G41 .....59 D8
Shawmoss Rd G41 .....44 D1
Shawpark St G20 .....29 E6
Shawrigg Rd ML9 .....93 C2
Shaws Rd ML9 .....106 C8
Shawsgate ML9 .....93 E1
Shawstonfoot Rd ML1 .....68 A1
Shawton Rd ML10 .....103 C6
Shawwood Cres G77 .....72 E3
Shearer Dr ML3 .....91 C7
Shearers La PA4 .....27 C3
Sheepburn Rd G71 .....63 E7
Sheephousehill EH47 .....71 F6
Sheila St G33 .....31 E4
Sheildhill 3 G75 .....88 F7
Sheiling Hill ML3 .....78 E4
Shelley Ct G12 .....29 A5
Shelley Dr Bothwell G71 .....64 B2
Clydebank G81 .....15 A4
Shelley Rd G12 .....29 A5
Sherbrooke Ave G41 .....44 C3
Sherbrooke Dr G41 .....44 C4
Sherbrooke Gdns G41 .....44 C3
Sherbrooke Pl G75 .....75 C1
Sherburn Gdns G69 .....47 F3
Sherdale Ave ML6 .....51 D2
Sheriff Park Ave G73 .....61 A7
Sherifflats Rd ML12 .....140 D8
Sherry Ave ML1 .....66 A5
Sherry Dr ML3 .....78 A1
Sherry Hts G72 .....62 A6
Sherwood Ave
Paisley PA1 .....42 A5
Uddingston G71 .....64 A5
Sherwood Dr G46 .....59 A3
Sherwood Pl G15 .....16 B4
Shetland Dr G44 .....60 C4
Shettleston Rd G32 .....47 B5
Shettleston Sheddings G32 .....46 E5
Shettleston Sta G32 .....47 B5
Shiel Ave G74 .....75 F3
Shiel Ct G78 .....57 B5
Shiel Dr ML9 .....92 F5
Shiel Gdns ML7 .....70 A3
Shiel Pl Coatbridge ML5 .....50 D5
East Kilbride G74 .....75 F3
Shiel Rd G64 .....19 B1
Shiel Terr ML2 .....81 F6
Shielbridge Gdns G23 .....17 E1
Shieldaig Dr G73 .....61 B4
Shieldaig Rd G22 .....30 B8
Shieldburn Rd G51 .....43 D7
Shieldhall Gdns G51 .....43 C7
Shieldhall Rd
Glasgow,Shieldhall G51 .....43 C7
Glasgow,West Drumoyne G51 .....43 E6
Shieldhill Rd
Biggar ML12 .....132 B3
Carluke ML8 .....108 E8
Quothquan ML12 .....131 F2
Shieldmuir St ML2 .....80 C4
Shieldmuir Sta ML2 .....80 C3
Shields Ct ML1 .....80 B3
Shields Dr ML1 .....80 B3
Shields Loan ML11 .....116 F5
Shields Rd
East Kilbride G75 .....88 B3
Glasgow G41 .....44 E2
Glasgow G41 .....44 F3
Glasgow G41 .....44 F4
Motherwell ML1 .....80 B3
Shields Road Underground Sta G5 .....44 F5
Shields Twr ML1 .....80 B3
Shilford Ave G13 .....28 A7
Shillay St G22 .....30 E8
Shilton Dr G53 .....58 C5
Shinwell Ave G81 .....15 D1
Shipbank La G1 .....163 A1
Shira Terr G74 .....76 B1
Shirley Quadrant ML1 .....79 D4
Shirley's Cl ML11 .....117 A4
Shirrel Ave ML4 .....65 A7
Shirrel Rd ML1 .....66 B4
Shirva Lea G65 .....9 F4
Shiskine Dr G20 .....29 C8
Shiskine Pl G20 .....29 C8
Shiskine St G20 .....29 C7
Sholto Cres ML4 .....64 D7
Shore St G40 .....46 A2
Shortridge St G20 .....29 E5
Shotts Rd
Fauldhouse EH47 .....71 C4
Harthill ML7 .....54 E2
Shotts St G33 .....47 D8
Shotts Sta ML7 .....69 E4
Shottsburn Rd ML7 .....54 A3
Shottskirk Rd ML7 .....69 C6
Shoulderigg Pl ML11 .....137 F6
Shoulderigg Rd ML11 .....137 F6
Shuna Gdns G20 .....29 F5
Shuna Pl Glasgow G20 .....29 E5
Newton Mearns G77 .....72 B6
Shuna St G20 .....29 E5
Shuttle St Glasgow G1 .....163 B2
Kilsyth G65 .....10 D8
Sidehead Holdings ML9 .....129 F8
Sidehead Rd Harthill ML7 .....55 E5
Stonehouse ML9 .....105 E1
Sidland Rd G21 .....31 C5
Sidlaw Ave Barrhead G78 .....57 C1
Hamilton ML3 .....77 F2
Sidlaw Ct ML5 .....50 C3
Sidlaw Dr ML2 .....80 F3
Sidlaw Rd G61 .....16 B7
Sidlaw Way
Chapelhall ML6 .....51 F1
Larkhall ML9 .....92 F5
Sidmount Ave DG10 .....161 D6
Sielga Pl G34 .....48 A8
Siemens Pl G21 .....31 B1
Siemens St G21 .....31 B1
Sievewright St G73 .....46 C1
Sighthill Loan 5 ML9 .....93 B4
Sighthill Prim Sch G21 .....30 D3
Sighthill Terr ML7 .....53 B2
Sikeside Pl ML5 .....50 D5
Sikeside Prim Sch ML5 .....50 D5
Sikeside St ML5 .....50 D5
Silkin Ave G81 .....15 D1
Sillerknowe Ct ML12 .....160 D4
Sillerknowe La ML12 .....160 D4
Silvan Pl G76 .....74 A5
Silver Birch Dr 4 G51 .....43 D7
Silver Birch Gdns 5 G51 .....43 D7
Silver Firs ML1 .....66 C3
Silver Glade G52 .....43 B4
Silverbirch Gdns ML3 .....91 F3
Silverbirch Gr ML3 .....91 F3
Silverburn Cres ML1 .....66 D3
Silverburn St G33 .....46 E8
Silverdale G74 .....75 C3
Silverdale Cres ML11 .....116 F4
Silverdale Ct ML11 .....116 F4
Silverdale St G31 .....46 C4
Silverdale Terr ML6 .....36 F3
Silverfir St G5 .....45 D3
Silvergrove St G40 .....45 E5
Silvermuir Ave ML11 .....117 F7
Silvermuir Rd ML11 .....130 D8
Silvertonhill Ave ML3 .....78 E1
Silvertonhill Pl ML3 .....91 D7
Silverwells G71 .....64 B1
Silverwells Cres G71 .....64 A1
Silverwood Ct G71 .....64 B1
Simons Cres PA4 .....27 D5
Simpson Ct Clydebank G81 .....15 A2
Uddingston G71 .....63 F6
Simpson Dr G75 .....88 D7
Simpson Gdns G78 .....57 B2
Simpson Hts G4 .....163 C2
Simpson Pl G75 .....88 D7
Simpson St G20 .....29 F3
Simpson Way ML4 .....65 C7
Simshill Prim Sch G44 .....60 B4
Simshill Rd G44 .....60 C4
Sinclair Ave G61 .....16 E6
Sinclair Dr
Coatbridge ML5 .....49 D7
Glasgow G42 .....59 F7
Glasgow G42 .....60 A8
Sinclair Gdns G64 .....31 B8
Sinclair Gr ML4 .....64 F2
Sinclair Pk 4 G75 .....88 F8
Sinclair Pl G75 .....88 F8
Sinclair St G81 .....27 D8
Singer Rd Clydebank G81 .....15 A3
East Kilbride G75 .....88 F6
Singer St G81 .....15 B3
Singer Sta G81 .....15 B2
Sir John Maxwell Prim Sch G43 .....59 C7
Sixth Ave PA4 .....27 C1
Sixth St G71 .....48 E1
Skaethorn Rd G20 .....29 B7
Skara Wlk ML2 .....81 F7
Skaterigg Dr G13 .....28 F5
Skaterigg Gdns G13 .....28 F5
Skaterigg La G13 .....28 E5
Skelbo Path G34 .....33 D1
Skelbo Pl G34 .....33 D1
Skellyton Cres ML9 .....93 B2
Skene Rd G51 .....44 B5
Skerne Gr G75 .....87 F6
Skerray Quadrant G22 .....30 C8
Skerray St G22 .....30 C8
Skerryvore Pl G33 .....47 B8
Skerryvore Rd G33 .....47 B8
Skibo La G46 .....58 E3
Skipness Ave ML8 .....109 A8
Skipness Dr G51 .....43 E8
Skirsa Ct G23 .....30 A8
Skirsa Pl G23 .....29 F7
Skirsa Sq G23 .....30 A7
Skirsa St G23 .....29 F8
Skirving St G41 .....59 E8
Skovlunde Way G75 .....88 E6
Skye G74 .....76 C1
Skye Ave PA4 .....27 C1
Skye Ct G67 .....23 D8
Skye Dr G67 .....23 D8
Skye Gdns G61 .....16 B6
Skye Pl Airdrie ML6 .....51 D6
Cumbernauld G67 .....23 D8
Skye Quadrant ML2 .....81 E5
Skye Rd Cumbernauld G67 .....23 D8
Rutherglen G73 .....61 D3
Skye Wynd ML3 .....77 F1
Skylands Gr ML3 .....91 A8
Skylands Pl ML3 .....91 A7
Skylands Rise ML3 .....91 A8
Skylaw Terr Forth ML11 .....124 A8
Wilsontown ML11 .....122 A1
Slakiewood Ave G69 .....33 E7
Slatefield Ct G31 .....46 A6
Slatefield St G31 .....46 A6
Sleaford Ave ML1 .....79 D4
Slenavon Ave G73 .....61 D3
Slessor Dr G75 .....88 F7
Slioch Sq ML1 .....66 C4
Sloy St Glasgow G22 .....30 D4
Wishaw ML2 .....81 A1
Small Cres G72 .....77 D7
Smeaton Ave G64 .....19 B8
Smeaton Dr G64 .....19 A4
Smeaton Gr G20 .....29 F6
Smeaton St G20 .....29 F6
Smiddy Ct ML11 .....117 A4
Smiddy Loan ML10 .....103 C6
Smith Ave ML2 .....94 A8
Smith Cl G64 .....31 D8
Smith Cres G81 .....15 B5
Smith Gdns G64 .....31 D8
Smith Quadrant ML5 .....50 C7
Smith St G14 .....28 E2
Smith Terr G73 .....46 B1
Smith Way G64 .....31 D8
Smithstone Cres G65 .....10 F5
Smithstone Rd G68 .....10 F2
Smithview ML2 .....94 C7
Smithycroft ML3 .....79 A3
Smithycroft Rd G33 .....31 E1
Smithycroft Sec Sch G33 .....31 E1
Smithyends G67 .....12 B5
Smugglers Brig Rd ML8 .....108 B2
Smyllum Ho ML11 .....117 C4
Smyllum Pk ML11 .....117 C4
Smyllum Rd ML11 .....117 C4
Snaefell Ave G73 .....61 C4
Snaefell Cres G73 .....61 C5
Snead View ML1 .....66 E1
Sneddon Ave ML2 .....81 C1
Sneddon St ML3 .....78 A6
Sneddon Terr ML3 .....77 F6
Snowdon Pl 2 G5 .....45 D4
Snowdon St 3 G5 .....45 D4
Snuff Mill Rd G44 .....60 A5
Society St G31 .....46 B5
Solar Ct ML9 .....106 B8
Sollas Pl G13 .....27 E8
Solsgirth Gdns G66 .....9 B1
Solway Ct ML3 .....91 B8
Solway Pl G69 .....21 D1
Solway Rd G64 .....19 D2
Solway St G73 .....45 F2
Somerford Rd G61 .....16 F1
Somerled Ave PA3 .....27 A1
Somerset Ave ML3 .....78 B4
Somerset Pl G3 .....162 A4
Somerset Place Mews G3 .....162 A4
Somervell St G72 .....61 F6
Somerville Dr
Carnwath ML11 .....124 E1
East Kilbride G75 .....88 F7
Glasgow G42 .....60 B8
Somerville La 2 G75 .....88 F7
Somerville Pl ML11 .....131 B8
Somerville Terr 1 G75 .....88 F7
Sorbie Dr ML9 .....105 E1
Sorby St G31 .....46 D5
Sorley St G11 .....28 F2
Sorn St G40 .....46 B3
Souterhouse Path ML5 .....49 F5
Souterhouse Rd ML5 .....49 F5
South Annandale St G42 .....45 B2
South Ave Carluke ML8 .....95 E2
Clydebank G81 .....15 A2
Hamilton G72 .....77 E5
Paisley PA2 .....57 A8
Renfrew PA4 .....27 D3
South Back Rd ML12 .....160 D4
South Bank St G81 .....27 C7
South Barrwood Rd G65 .....10 E7
South Biggar Rd ML6 .....51 B7
South Bridge St ML6 .....51 A8
South Burn Rd ML6 .....50 D7
South Caldeen Rd ML5 .....50 B5
South Calder ML1 .....79 F8
South Carbrain Rd G67 .....12 B1
South Cathkin Cotts G73 .....75 C8
South Chester St G32 .....47 A5
South Circular Rd ML5 .....50 A6
South Commonhead Ave ML6 .....36 A1
South Croft Rd ML12 .....160 D4
South Crosshill Rd G64 .....19 A1
South Dean Park Ave G71 .....64 A2
South Douglas St G81 .....27 C8
South Dumbreck Rd G65 .....10 B8
South Elgin Pl G81 .....27 C7
South Elgin St G81 .....27 C7
South Erskine Pk G61 .....16 D5
South Exchange Ct G1 .....163 A2
South Frederick St G1 .....163 A2
South Hirst Rd ML7 .....54 D3
South Lanarkshire Coll (Allers Campus) G74 .....76 D4
South Lanarkshire Coll (Cambuslang Campus) G72 .....62 B5
South Lanarkshire Coll (Village Campus) G74 .....75 F2
South Loan G69 .....33 D8
South Medrox St ML5 .....34 C7
South Moraine La G15 .....16 C2
South Muirhead Ct G67 .....12 A2
South Muirhead Rd G67 .....12 A2
South Nimmo St 2 ML6 .....51 B7
South Park Ave G78 .....57 C3
South Park Ct ML12 .....160 C3
South Park Gr ML3 .....78 D3
South Park Prim Sch G75 .....88 C6
South Park Rd ML3 .....78 D2
South Pk EH48 .....41 F4
South Pl ML4 .....64 F4
South Portland St 5 G5 .....45 B5
South Rd Clarkston G76 .....74 A5
Fauldhouse EH47 .....71 E7
South Robertson Pl ML6 .....50 E7
South Scott St G69 .....48 B4
South St Armadale EH48 .....41 F5
Carnwath ML11 .....124 E1
Glasgow G14 .....28 C3
South Vennel ML11 .....117 A4
South Vesalius St G32 .....47 A5
South View Bellshill ML4 .....64 E4
Blantyre G72 .....63 C1
South Woodside Rd
Glasgow G4 .....29 E2
Glasgow G4 .....29 F3
Southampton Dr G12 .....29 B6
Southampton La G12 .....29 B6
Southbank Bsns Pk G66 .....20 C7
Southbank Dr G66 .....20 C7
Southbank Rd G66 .....20 C8
Southbank St G31 .....46 D5
Southbar Ave G13 .....28 A7
Southbrae Dr G13 .....28 D4
Southbrae La 8 G13 .....28 E5
Southcroft Rd G73 .....45 F1
Southcroft St G51 .....44 B7
Southcroft Way ML12 .....160 D4
Southdeen Ave G15 .....16 B3
Southdeen Gr 5 G15 .....16 B3
Southdeen Rd G15 .....16 A3
Southend Ct ML10 .....112 F5
Southend Dr ML10 .....112 F5
Southend Gr ML10 .....112 F5
Southend Pl ML4 .....64 F4
Southend Rd G81 .....15 B5
Southern Ave G73 .....61 B5
Southern General Hospl G51 .....43 D8
Southerness Dr G68 .....12 A5
Southesk Ave G64 .....18 F2
Southesk Gdns G64 .....18 F3
Southfield Ave ML7 .....70 B4
Southfield Cl ML11 .....114 B3
Southfield Cres
Coatbridge ML5 .....50 D5
Glasgow G53 .....58 C8
Shotts ML7 .....70 B4
Strathaven ML10 .....112 D5
Southfield Rd
Cumbernauld G68 .....11 C1
Kirkmuirhill ML11 .....114 C8
Shotts ML7 .....70 B4
Southgate Mall 3 G74 .....88 E8
Southhill Ave G73 .....61 C5
Southinch Ave G14 .....27 E6
Southinch La G14 .....27 E6
Southlea Ave G46 .....59 A3
Southloch Gdns 1 G21 .....30 F3
Southloch St G21 .....30 F3
Southmuir Pl G20 .....29 D5
Southpark Ave G12 .....29 E2
Southpark La 1 G12 .....29 E2
Southpark Terr G12 .....29 E2
Southside Cres 2 G5 .....45 C4
Southview Bearsden G61 .....16 C5
Lesmahagow ML11 .....119 F4
Southview Ave G76 .....73 F5
Southview Ct 3 G64 .....30 F7
Southview Pl G69 .....33 E6
Southview Terr G64 .....30 F7
Southwold Rd PA1 .....42 E5
Southwood Ct G77 .....72 D1
Southwood Dr G44 .....60 C6
Southwood Pl G77 .....72 D2
Soutra Pl G33 .....47 B8
Spairdrum Rd ML6 .....23 F4
Spalehall Dr ML1 .....66 F3
Spean Ave G74 .....76 B1
Spean St G44 .....60 A6
Spectrum Ho G81 .....15 B2
Speirs Rd G61 .....17 B3
Speirs Wharf G4 .....30 B2
Speirshall Cl G14 .....27 F5
Speirshall Terr G14 .....27 F6
Spence St G20 .....29 C8
Spencer St Clydebank G81 .....15 A3
Glasgow G13 .....28 F7
Spencerfield Gdns ML3 .....78 F3
Spey Ct Airdrie ML6 .....51 C5
22 Wishaw ML2 .....81 F6
Spey Dr Coatbridge ML5 .....49 E4
Renfrew PA4 .....27 E2
Spey Gdns ML3 .....91 B8
Spey Gr G75 .....87 F7
Spey Rd G61 .....16 C2
Spey St G33 .....46 F8
Spey Terr G75 .....87 F7
Spey Wlk
8 Cumbernauld G67 .....11 F1
Motherwell ML1 .....66 B5
Spey Wynd ML9 .....106 A8
Speyburn Pl G33 .....32 E6
Spiers Gr G46 .....58 F3
Spiersbridge Ave G46 .....58 E2
Spiersbridge Bsns Pk G46 .....58 E3
Spiersbridge La G46 .....58 E3
Spiersbridge Rd G46 .....58 F3
Spiersbridge Rdbt G46 .....58 F2
Spiersbridge Terr G46 .....58 E3
Spindlehowe Rd
Uddingston G71 .....63 F5
Uddingston,Tannochside G71 .....64 A7
Spindleside Rd ML1 .....67 D1
Spinners Ct G81 .....15 B7
Spinners La G81 .....15 B7
Spinningdale ML9 .....105 D1
Spire View ML11 .....114 B2
Spital Rd ML9 .....113 B6
Spittal Prim Sch G73 .....60 F5
Spittal Rd G73 .....60 F5
Spoutmouth G1 .....163 B1
Sprig Way ML7 .....55 E5
Spring La ML6 .....37 F4
Spring Wlk ML11 .....119 C6
Spring Wynd G5 .....45 C4
Springbank ML11 .....119 C6
Springbank Cres
Hamilton ML3 .....91 A7
Motherwell ML1 .....66 A2
Springbank Rd ML7 .....69 D6
Springbank St G20 .....30 A4
Springbank Terr ML6 .....36 F3
Springbank View ML6 .....36 F3
Springboig Ave G32 .....47 C6
Springboig Rd G32 .....47 C6
Springboig St John's Sch G33 .....47 D7
Springburn Acad G21 .....30 F5
Springburn Mus* G21 .....30 F4
Springburn Pl G74 .....75 A3
Springburn Rd G21 .....30 E4
Springburn Sh Ctr 4 G21 .....30 F4
Springburn Sta G21 .....30 F4
Springburn Way
3 Glasgow G21 .....30 E4
Glasgow G21 .....30 F4
Springcroft Ave G69 .....48 B6
Springcroft Cres G69 .....48 B6
Springcroft Dr G69 .....48 A6
Springcroft Gdns G69 .....48 C6
Springcroft Gr G69 .....48 B6
Springcroft Rd G69 .....48 C6
Springcroft Wynd G69 .....48 B6
Springdale Dr ML12 .....160 E5
Springfield Ave
Bishopbriggs G64 .....31 A7
Paisley PA1 .....42 B4
Uddingston G71 .....63 F5
Springfield Cres
Bishopbriggs G64 .....31 A8
Carluke ML8 .....108 F8
Hamilton G72 .....77 C7
Uddingston G71 .....63 F5
Springfield Ct
Bishopbriggs G64 .....19 B1
Glasgow G1 .....163 A2
Springfield Dr G78 .....57 E1
Springfield Gdns
Lanark ML11 .....116 F5
Uddingston G71 .....63 F5
Springfield Park Rd G73 .....61 C6
Springfield Pl ML10 .....112 F6
Springfield Quay G5 .....162 A1
Springfield Rd
Airdrie ML6 .....51 E8
Barrhead G78 .....57 E1
Bishopbriggs G64 .....19 A1

Springfield Rd *continued*
Cumbernauld G67 12 A4
Glasgow G40 46 B4
Salsburgh ML7 53 A1
Springfield Sq G64 31 A8
Springfield Works G64 19 A1
Springhall Ct G73 61 D3
Springhead Rd ML7 83 A8
Springhill & Leadloch Rd ML7,EH47 70 E2
Springhill Ave Airdrie ML6 51 B8
Coatbridge ML5 49 C4
6 Douglas ML11 138 B1
Springhill Cres 1 ML11 138 B1
Springhill Dr S G69 48 A6
Springhill Farm Gr 3 G69 48 A6
Springhill Farm Pl 1 G69 48 A6
Springhill Farm Rd G69 48 A6
Springhill Farm Way 2 G69 48 A6
Springhill Gdns G41 44 E1
Springhill Parkway G69 48 A7
Springhill Pl ML5 49 C4
Springhill Prim Sch G78 57 B1
Springhill Rd
Barrhead G78 57 B1
Clarkston G76 73 F7
Douglas ML11 138 B1
Glasgow G69 48 A5
Shotts ML7 70 B3
Springhill St ML11 138 B1
Springhill View
4 Douglas ML11 138 B1
Shotts ML7 70 B3
Springholm Dr ML6 35 F2
Springkell Ave G41 44 C2
Springkell Dr G41 44 B2
Springkell Gate G41 44 D2
Springkell Gdns G41 44 D2
Springside Gdns G15 16 A5
Springside Pl G15 16 A4
Springvale Terr 8 G21 30 E4
Springwell Cres G72 77 F7
Springwells Ave ML6 51 C8
Springwells Cres ML6 51 C8
Spruce Ave
Hamilton,Silvertonhill ML3 78 F2
Hamilton,Wheatlands G72 77 C8
Spruce Ct ML3 78 E1
Spruce Dr Cambuslang G72 62 F4
Kirkintilloch G66 20 A5
Spruce Rd
Cumbernauld G67 12 D4
Motherwell G71 49 C1
Spruce St G22 30 D5
Spruce Way
Cambuslang G72 62 F4
Motherwell ML1 66 B4
Spynie Gdns ML10 112 F8
Spynie Pl G64 19 D2
Spynie Way 1 ML2 81 F6
Squire St G14 28 E2
Sraehouse Wynd ML8 96 B1
Stable Rd ML7 70 A4
Stables The G52 43 A3
Stablestone Prim Sch ML11 143 E7
Staffa G74 89 C8
Staffa Ave PA4 27 C1
Staffa Dr Airdrie ML6 51 F7
Kirkintilloch G66 21 B8
Staffa Rd G72 61 F3
Staffa St G31 46 B8
Staffin Dr G23 17 D1
Staffin Path G23 17 E1
Staffin St G23 17 E1
Stafford St Bellshill ML4 64 F4
Glasgow G4 163 B4
Stag Ct G71 64 C6
Stag St G51 44 B7
Staig Wynd ML1 80 A4
Staikhill ML11 116 F5
Staineybraes Pl ML6 35 F2
Stalker St ML2 80 C4
Stamford Rd G31 46 B5
Stamford St G31 46 B5
Stamperland Ave G76 73 F8
Stamperland Cres G76 73 E8
Stamperland Dr G76 73 F8
Stamperland Gdns G76 73 F8
Stamperland Hill
Clarkston G76 59 F1
Clarkston G76 73 E8
Stanalane St G46 58 F4
Standburn Rd
Glasgow G21 31 D6
Glasgow G21 31 D7
Standford Hall G72 62 A6
Stane Gr ML7 70 A3
Stane Prim Sch ML7 70 A4
Stane Rd ML7 70 A2
Staneacre Pk ML3 78 F3
Stanecraigs Pl 20 ML2 81 F6
Stanefield Dr ML1 66 E4
Stanehead Pk ML12 160 E4
Staneholm Rd ML10 112 F7
Stanemuir Rd ML11 124 F1
Stanford St G81 15 C1
Stanhope Dr G73 61 D5
Stanhope Pl ML2 94 A7
Stanistone Rd ML8 96 A2
Stanley Bvd G72 77 D4
Stanley Dr Bellshill ML4 65 A6
Bishopbriggs G64 19 B2
Harthill ML7 56 A6
Stanley Pk ML6 51 B8
Stanley Pl G72 63 D1
Stanley Rd ML7 56 A6
Stanley St Glasgow G41 44 E5
Hamilton ML3 77 F4
Stanley Street La G41 44 E5
Stanmore Ave ML11 117 B5
Stanmore Cres ML11 117 C5
Stanmore Gdns ML11 117 D6
Stanmore House Sch ML11 117 D6
Stanmore Rd
Cleghorn ML11 111 A2
Glasgow G42 60 B8
Lanark ML11 117 D6
Stanrigg St ML6 37 A2
Star St 4 DG10 161 D5
Starling Way ML4 64 E8
Starryshaw Rd ML7 69 E6
Startpoint St G33 47 A8
State Hospl The ML11 131 C8
Station Cres PA4 27 D4
Station Ct Bellshill ML4 64 F5
Netherburn ML9 107 C4
Station Gate G72 77 E8
Station Pk G69 48 C4
Station Pl ML8 95 A6
Station Rd
Abington ML12 145 F2
Airdrie ML6 51 E8
Armadale EH48 41 F3
Bardowie G62 18 B7
Bearsden G61 16 D4
Biggar ML12 160 C3
Blackridge EH48 40 D2
Blantyre G72 63 E1
Bothwell G71 64 A2
Caldercruix ML6 38 A4
Carluke ML8 95 E1
Carstairs Junction ML11 131 B8
Clarkston G46 74 A5
Cleland ML1 67 B1
Douglas ML11 138 A1
Elvanfoot ML12 152 B4
Glasgow G69 48 C4
Glasgow,Giffnock G46 59 C3
Glasgow,Maryhill G20 29 C8
Glassford ML10 104 E3
Hamilton ML3 78 E3
Kilsyth G65 6 D1
Kirkintilloch G66 20 C4
Larkhall ML9 93 B4
Law ML8 95 A6
Leadhills ML12 151 A1
Lesmahagow ML11 119 E5
Millerston G33 32 A5
Motherwell ML1 66 B3
Muirhead G69 33 C6
Netherburn ML9 107 C4
Plains ML6 37 B2
Renfrew PA4 27 E4
Shotts ML7 69 E4
Stepps G33 32 D5
Strathaven ML10 112 E5
Thankerton ML12 131 D1
Uddingston G71 63 E6
Wishaw ML2 81 A2
Station Row ML8 95 A6
Station Way G71 63 E5
Staybrae Dr G53 42 F1
Staybrae Gr G53 42 F1
Steading The ML2 81 B5
Steel Pl ML2 80 F2
Steel St Glasgow G1 163 B1
Wishaw ML2 81 B2
Steel Way ML11 119 D6
Stemac La ML6 37 A2
Stenhouse Ave G69 33 C7
Stenton Cres ML2 80 D1
Stenton Pl ML2 80 D1
Stenton St G32 46 E7
Stenzel Pl G33 32 F5
Stepends Rd Airdrie ML6 52 C8
Plains ML6 37 D2
Stepford Pl G33 47 F7
Stepford Rd G33 48 A7
Stephen Ave ML12 160 E4
Stephen Cres G69 47 F5
Stephens Ave ML6 37 F4
Stephenson Pl 3 G75 88 D8
Stephenson Sq 4 G75 88 D8
Stephenson St G52 42 E8
Stephenson Terr G75 88 D8
Stepps Prim Sch G33 32 E6
Stepps Rd Glasgow G33 47 C8
Kirkintilloch G66 20 E2
Stepps Sta G33 32 E5
Stevens La ML1 66 A3
Stevenson Pl ML4 65 B7
Stevenson St Carluke ML8 95 E2
Glasgow G40 163 C1
Glasgow G40 45 E5
Glasgow G40 45 E5
Stevenston Ct ML1 66 A4
Stevenston St ML1 66 A4
Stewart Ave
Hamilton,Blantyre G72 77 C7
Hamilton,Meikle Earnock ML3 91 A7
Newton Mearns G77 72 E6
Renfrew PA4 27 B1
Stewart Cres
Barrhead G78 57 D4
Wishaw ML2 82 A5
Stewart Ct Barrhead G78 57 C4
Coatbridge ML5 50 C6
Rutherglen G73 61 C7
Stewart Dr Clarkston G76 73 E8
Clydebank G81 15 B6
Stewart Dr *continued*
Coatbridge G69 49 B6
Whitburn EH47 56 F6
Stewart Gr ML7 55 F5
Stewart Pl Barrhead G78 57 D4
1 Carluke ML8 95 F2
Stewart Quadrant ML1 66 B6
Stewart St Barrhead G78 57 D4
Bellshill ML4 65 D5
Carluke ML8 95 E2
Coatbridge ML5 50 A8
Glasgow G4 162 C4
Hamilton ML3 78 A5
Stewartfield Cres G74 75 D3
Stewartfield Dr G74 75 D4
Stewartfield Rd G74 75 C3
Stewartfield Way
East Kilbride,Philipshill G74 74 F4
East Kilbride,Stewartfield G74 75 D4
Stewartgill Pl ML9 93 F1
Stewarton Dr G72 61 F5
Stewarton Rd
Glasgow G46 58 E1
Newton Mearns G77 72 C7
Stewarton St ML2 81 C2
Stewarton Terr ML2 81 C2
Stewarts La ML2 81 C3
Stewartville St G11 29 B2
Stirling Ave G61 16 E2
Stirling Dr Bearsden G61 16 D6
Bishopbriggs G64 18 E3
East Kilbride G74 76 A3
Hamilton ML3 77 E4
Rutherglen G73 61 B5
Stirling Gdns G64 18 E3
Stirling Ind Est ML6 36 B3
Stirling Rd Airdrie ML6 36 B5
Carluke ML8 95 E4
Chapelhall ML6 51 D3
Cumbernauld G67 24 A6
Glasgow G4 163 B3
Kilsyth G65 6 F1
Wattston G67 24 A3
Stirling St Airdrie ML6 51 A7
Coatbridge ML5 49 D4
Cumbernauld G67 12 B4
Motherwell ML1 80 B4
Stirling Way Glasgow G69 48 A4
1 Renfrew PA4 27 D1
Stirlingfauld Pl 7 G5 45 B5
Stirrat St G20 29 C6
Stobcross Bsns Pk 6 G3 44 E8
Stobcross Rd G3 44 D8
Stobcross St
Coatbridge ML5 50 A6
Glasgow G3 44 E7
Stobcross Wynd G3 44 D8
Stobhill Cotts G21 31 A7
Stobhill Hospl G21 31 A6
Stobhill Rd G21 30 F7
Stobo G74 76 C4
Stobo Ct G74 76 C4
Stobo St ML2 81 C5
Stobs Dr G78 57 B4
Stobs Pl G34 33 C1
Stobwood Dyke Rd ML11 124 C8
Stockiemuir Ave G61 16 E7
Stockiemuir Ct G61 16 E7
Stockiemuir Rd G61 16 D7
Stocks Rd Cleland ML1 67 F1
Wishaw ML2 82 A8
Stockwell Pl G1 163 A1
Stockwell St G1 163 A1
Stonebank Gr G45 60 D3
Stonebyres Ct ML3 78 A3
Stonebyres Holdings ML11 115 D4
Stonecraig Rd ML2 81 C2
Stonedyke Cres ML8 96 A3
Stonedyke Gr G15 16 B2
Stonedyke Prim Sch G15 16 B2
Stonedyke Rd ML8 96 B3
Stonefield Ave G12 29 C6
Stonefield Cres
Clarkston G76 73 C8
Hamilton G72 77 C7
Stonefield Gdns ML8 95 F3
Stonefield Park Gdns G72 77 E8
Stonefield Pl G72 77 C6
Stonefield Rd G72 77 C7
Stonefield St ML6 36 B1
Stonehall Ave ML3 78 B2
Stonehaven Cres ML6 50 E5
Stonehill Rd ML12 139 C8
Stonehouse Hospl ML9 105 D1
Stonehouse Prim Sch ML9 105 E1
Stonehouse Rd
Sandford ML10 129 B6
Strathaven ML10 112 F6
Stonelaw Ct G73 61 B7
Stonelaw Dr G73 61 B6
Stonelaw High Sch G73 61 D6
Stonelaw High Sch Annexe G73 61 B8
Stonelaw Rd G73 61 B6
Stonelaw Twrs G73 61 C6
Stoneleigh G12 29 B5
Stoneside Dr G43 59 B6
Stoneside Sq G43 59 A6
Stoneyetts Rd G69 21 F2
Stoneyhill Wynd ML10 103 C6
Stoneymeadow Rd G74 76 D5
Stonyhurst St
Glasgow G22 30 C4
Stonyhurst St *continued*
Glasgow,Firhill G22 30 B4
Stonylee Rd G67 12 A1
Store Row ML3 91 F3
Stormyland Way G78 57 C2
Stornoway Cres ML2 81 E5
Stornoway St G22 30 C8
Stow Coll G3 162 B4
Stow Coll (West Campus) G20 29 E4
Strachan Pl G72 77 D3
Strachan St ML4 65 A4
Strachur St G22 30 A7
Strain Cres ML6 51 B6
Strait Cl ML10 112 E5
Straiton Dr ML3 77 D2
Straiton Pl G72 77 D8
Straiton St G32,G33 46 E7
Stranraer Dr G15 16 C2
Stratford G74 76 D5
Stratford St G20 29 E5
Strath Carron ML8 95 A5
Strath Dearn ML8 95 A5
Strath Elgin ML8 95 A5
Strath Halladale ML8 95 A5
Strath Nairn ML8 95 A5
Strath Naver ML8 95 A5
Strath Peffer ML8 94 F5
Strathallan Ave G75 88 A8
Strathallan Cres ML6 36 A3
Strathallan Gate 11 G75 75 A1
Strathallan Gdns 4 G66 20 D8
Strathallan Wynd G75 74 F1
Strathallon Pl G73 61 D3
Strathaven Acad ML10 112 D5
Strathaven Castle* ML10 112 E5
Strathaven Rd
Eaglesham G76 86 F4
East Kilbride G74,G75 89 B7
Hamilton ML3 91 C5
Kirkmuirhill ML11 113 E1
Lesmahagow ML11 119 D7
Sandford ML10 129 B6
Stonehouse ML9 129 E8
Strathavon Cres ML6 36 A2
Strathblane Cres ML6 36 A3
Strathblane Dr G75 87 E8
Strathblane Gdns G13 28 F8
Strathbran St G31 46 D4
Strathcairn Cres ML6 36 A3
Strathcarron Cres PA2 57 B8
Strathcarron Dr PA2 42 B1
Strathcarron Pl
7 Glasgow G20 29 D6
Paisley PA2 57 B8
Strathcarron Rd PA2 57 B8
Strathcarron Way PA2 42 B1
Strathclyde Arts Ctr G3 162 B2
Strathclyde Bsns Ctr
Cambuslang G72 62 E3
Motherwell ML1 65 F4
Strathclyde Bsns Pk ML4 64 E8
Strathclyde CP Visitor Ctr* ML1 64 D1
Strathclyde Ctry Pk*
Hamilton ML1,ML3 78 E8
Motherwell ML1 64 F1
Strathclyde Dr G73 61 A6
Strathclyde Hospl ML1 79 D5
Strathclyde Path G71 63 E6
Strathclyde Rd ML1 79 B6
Strathclyde St G40 46 A2
Strathclyde View G71 64 B1
Strathclyde Way ML4 65 C7
Strathcona Dr G13 29 A7
Strathcona Gdns G13 29 A7
Strathcona Ho G75 88 E7
Strathcona La 4 G75 88 E7
Strathcona Pl
East Kilbride G75 88 E7
Rutherglen G73 61 D4
Strathcona St G13 28 F6
Strathconon Gdns 1 G75 87 E8
Strathdearn Gr G75 87 E8
Strathdee Ave G81 15 B5
Strathdee Rd G44 59 E2
Strathdon Ave G44 59 F2
Strathdon Dr G44 59 F2
Strathdon Pl 3 G75 87 E8
Strathearn Gr G66 9 B1
Strathearn Rd G76 73 E6
Strathendrick Dr G44 59 E4
Strathfillan Rd G74 75 D2
Strathgoil Cres ML6 36 A3
Strathhalladale Ct 9 G75 87 E8
Strathisla Way 3 ML1 66 B2
Strathkelvin Ave 4 G64 30 F7
Strathkelvin La 8 G75 87 E8
Strathkelvin Ret Pk G64 19 C5
Strathlachlan Ave ML8 96 A1
Strathmiglo Ct 7 G75 87 E8
Strathmore Ave
Blantyre G72 63 C1
Paisley PA1 42 D4
Strathmore Cres ML6 36 A2
Strathmore Ct G14 28 F4
Strathmore Gdns G73 61 D4
Strathmore Gr G75 87 E8
Strathmore Pl ML5 50 D5
Strathmore Rd
Glasgow G22 30 B7
Hamilton ML3 78 E3
Strathmore Wlk ML5 50 D5
Strathmungo Cres ML6 35 F2
Strathnairn Ave G75 87 E8
Strathnairn Ct 4 G75 87 E8
Strathnairn Dr G75 87 E8
Strathnairn Way 5 G75 87 E8
Strathnaver Cres ML6 36 A3
Strathnaver Gdns 6 G75 87 E8
Strathord Pl G69 22 A4
Strathord St G32 47 A3
Strathpeffer Cres ML6 36 A2
Strathpeffer Dr 2 G75 87 E8
Strathrannoch Way G75 87 E8
Strathspey Ave G75 87 E8
Strathspey Cres ML6 36 A3
Strathtay Ave
East Kilbride G75 74 F1
East Kilbride G75 87 E8
Glasgow G44 59 E2
Strathtummel Cres ML6 36 A3
Strathview Gr G44 59 E2
Strathview Pk G44 59 E2
Strathview Rd ML4 64 F3
Strathvithie Gr 10 G75 87 E8
Strathy Pl 5 G20 29 D6
Strathyre Ct 11 G75 87 E8
Strathyre Gdns
Bearsden G61 17 B5
East Kilbride G75 87 E8
Glenmavis ML6 35 F5
Moodiesburn G69 22 A3
Strathyre Rd G72 77 F6
Strathyre St G41 59 E8
Stratton Dr G46 59 B2
Strauss Ave G81 15 E1
Stravanan Ct G45 60 E2
Stravanan Gdns G45 60 C1
Stravanan Pl G45 60 D2
Stravanan Rd G45 60 D2
Stravanan St G45 60 D2
Stravanan Terr G45 60 D2
Stravenhouse Rd ML8 94 F4
Strawfrank Holdings ML11 131 B7
Strawfrank Rd ML11 131 B8
Strawhill Ct G76 73 F7
Strawhill Rd G76 73 F7
Streamfield Gate G33 31 D7
Streamfield Gdns G33 31 E7
Streamfield Lea G33 31 E8
Streamfield Pl G33 31 E7
Strenabey Ave G73 61 D4
Striven Cres ML2 81 A1
Striven Ct ML5 50 B3
Striven Gdns G20 29 F3
Striven Terr ML3 78 A1
Stroma St G21 31 B2
Stromness St G5 45 A4
Strone Gdns G65 10 B8
Strone Path ML5 34 C6
Strone Pl ML6 51 C5
Strone Rd G33 47 B7
Stronend St G22 30 B5
Stronsay Pl G64 19 D2
Stronsay St G21 31 B2
Stronvar Dr G14 28 B4
Stroud Rd G75 88 D6
Strowan Cres G32 47 B4
Strowan St G32 47 C4
Struan Ave G46 59 C3
Struan Gdns G44 60 A5
Struan Rd G44 60 A5
Struie St G34 48 A8
Struma Dr G76 73 C8
Struther & Swinhill Rd ML9 106 D6
Struther St ML9 106 B8
Strutherhill ML9 106 B8
Strutherhill Ind Est ML9 106 C8
Struthers Cres G74 76 B4
Stuart Ave G73 61 B5
Stuart Dr Bishopbriggs G64 30 E8
Lanark ML11 117 B5
Larkhall ML9 93 C1
Stuart Ho G67 12 B3
Stuart Quadrant ML2 80 E1
Stuart Rd G76 74 D8
Stuart St G74 75 F2
Stuart Terr ML11 139 A6
Stuarton Pk G74 75 E2
Succoth St G13 28 F7
Sudbury Cres 2 G75 75 B1
Suffolk St G40 163 B1
Sugworth Ave G69 48 B5
Sumburgh St G33 47 A7
Summer St G40 45 F5
Summerfield Cotts G14 28 E2
Summerfield Rd G67 23 A6
Summerfield St G40 46 B3
Summerhill & Garngibbock Rd G67 23 D4
Summerhill Ave ML9 93 A2
Summerhill Dr G15 16 B4
Summerhill Gdns G15 16 B4
Summerhill Pl
Clydebank G15 16 B4
Shotts ML7 82 F8
Summerhill Prim Sch G15 16 B4
Summerhill Rd
Clarkston G76 73 F7
Clydebank G15 16 B4
Summerhill Way ML4 64 F4
Summerlea Rd G46 58 F4
Summerlee Cotts ML5 49 F7
Summerlee Heritage Mus* ML5 49 F8

Summerlee Rd
Larkhall ML9 .... 92 F5
Wishaw ML2 .... 80 C4
Summerlee St
Coatbridge ML5 .... 49 F7
Glasgow G33 .... 47 C7
Summerston Sta G20 .... 29 D8
Summertown Rd G51 .... 44 B7
Suna Path ML7 .... 70 B3
Sunart Ave PA4 .... 27 B4
Sunart Ct ML3 .... 78 A1
Sunart Gdns G64 .... 19 C1
Sunart Rd
Bishopbriggs G64 .... 19 C1
Glasgow G52 .... 43 F5
Sunart St ML2 .... 81 A1
Sunbury Ave G76 .... 73 C7
Sundale Ave G76 .... 73 D6
Sunflower Gdns ML1 .... 79 D8
Sunningdale Ave G77 .... 72 F6
Sunningdale Rd G23 .... 29 E8
Sunningdale Wynd G71 .. 63 E3
Sunnybank ML7 .... 69 F5
Sunnybank Dr G76 .... 73 D7
Sunnybank Gr G76 .... 73 D6
Sunnybank St G40 .... 46 B3
Sunnybrae ML11 .... 122 A1
Sunnydale Dr EH48 .... 40 E3
Sunnydale Rd EH48 .... 40 E3
Sunnyhill G65 .... 9 F3
Sunnylaw St G22 .... 30 B4
Sunnyside Ave
Motherwell ML1 .... 66 B5
Uddingston G71 .... 63 F5
Sunnyside Cres ML1 .... 66 A5
Sunnyside Dr
Clarkston G76 .... 73 D8
Clydebank G15 .... 16 A1
Coatbridge G69 .... 49 A5
Sunnyside Gate ML1 .... 66 A5
Sunnyside Pl
Barrhead G78 .... 57 B2
Clydebank G15 .... 16 A1
Motherwell ML1 .... 66 A5
Sunnyside Prim Sch G33 . 32 C3
Sunnyside Rd Cleland ML1 . 81 B8
Coatbridge ML5 .... 50 A8
Kirkfieldbank ML11 .... 116 D5
Larkhall ML3,ML9 .... 92 C3
Sunnyside St ML9 .... 92 F4
Sunnyside Terr ML1 .... 66 B5
Surrey La 1 G5 .... 45 B4
Surrey St 3 G5 .... 45 B4
Sussex St G41 .... 44 E5
Sutcliffe Ct G13 .... 28 E7
Sutcliffe Rd G13 .... 28 F7
Sutherland Ave
Bearsden G61 .... 16 E7
Glasgow G41 .... 44 C3
14 Stonehouse ML9 .... 129 E8
Sutherland Cres ML3 .... 78 A4
Sutherland Ct G41 .... 44 E4
Sutherland Dr Airdrie ML6 . 50 F5
Glasgow G46 .... 59 D1
Sutherland La G12 .... 29 D2
Sutherland Pl ML4 .... 64 F2
Sutherland Rd G81 .... 15 B2
Sutherland St G72 .... 77 C5
Sutherland Way G74 .... 76 C3
Sutherness Dr G33 .... 47 A8
Swaledale G74 .... 75 C3
Swallow Gdns G13 .... 27 F7
Swallow Rd
Clydebank G81 .... 15 D7
Wishaw ML2 .... 81 B3
Swan St Glasgow G4 .... 163 A4
Kirkmuirhill ML11 .... 114 A2
Swan Way ML8 .... 94 F4
Swanston St G40 .... 46 A2
Sween Ave G44 .... 60 A4
Sween Dr ML3 .... 78 A1
Sween Path ML4 .... 65 C3
Sweethill Terr ML5 .... 50 D3
Sweethill Wlk ML4 .... 65 C7
Sweethope Gdns G71 .... 64 B2
Sweethope Pl G71 .... 64 A3
Swift Bank ML3 .... 77 E1
Swift Cl ML2 .... 81 B3
Swift Cres G13 .... 27 F8
Swift Pl G75 .... 87 F6
Swinburne Ave G72 .... 77 B7
Swinhill Rd ML9 .... 106 C6
Swinstie Rd ML1 .... 81 D8
Swinstie View ML1 .... 67 C1
Swinton Ave G69 .... 48 D5
Swinton Cres
Coatbridge ML5 .... 49 B4
Glasgow G69 .... 48 D5
Swinton Dr G52 .... 43 B5
Swinton Gdns G69 .... 48 D5
Swinton Path G69 .... 48 D5
Swinton Pl Coatbridge ML5 . 49 B4
Glasgow G52 .... 43 B5
Swinton Prim Sch G69 .... 48 C6
Swinton Rd G69 .... 48 C5
Swinton View G69 .... 48 C5
Swisscot Ave ML3 .... 91 B8
Swisscot Wlk ML3 .... 91 B8
Switchback Rd G61 .... 16 F1
Sword St Airdrie ML6 .... 50 F7
Glasgow G31 .... 45 F6
Swordale Pl G34 .... 48 A8
Sycamore Ave
Kirkintilloch G66 .... 20 D5
Uddingston G71 .... 64 C8
Sycamore Cres
Airdrie ML6 .... 51 D6
East Kilbride G75 .... 88 D6
Sycamore Ct G75 .... 88 D6
Sycamore Dr Airdrie ML6 .. 51 D6
Clydebank G81 .... 15 A4
Hamilton ML3 .... 78 F2
Sycamore Gdns ML11 .... 114 A5
Sycamore Gr G72 .... 77 C8
Sycamore Pl
East Kilbride G75 .... 88 D6
Motherwell ML1 .... 66 C3
Sycamore Way
Cambuslang G72 .... 62 F4
Carmunnock G76 .... 74 D7
Sydenham Ct G12 .... 29 B4
Sydenham La G12 .... 29 C3
Sydenham Rd G12 .... 29 C3
Sydes Brae G72 .... 77 B4
Sydney Dr G75 .... 88 C8
Sydney Pl 6 G75 .... 88 C8
Sydney St G31 .... 163 C1
Sykehead Ave ML4 .... 65 B5
Sykehead Dr ML12 .... 160 E4
Sykeside Rd ML6 .... 50 F4
Sylvania Way G81 .... 15 B2
Sylvania Way S G81 .... 15 B1
Syme St DG10 .... 161 C5
Symington Dr G81 .... 15 B2
Symington Sq 9 G75 .... 88 F8
Symington St ML12 .... 151 A2
Syriam Pl 1 G21 .... 30 F4
Syriam St G21 .... 30 F5

T

Tabard Pl G13 .... 28 C8
Tabard Rd G13 .... 28 C8
Tabernacle La G72 .... 62 A5
Tabernacle St G72 .... 62 A5
Taggart Rd G65 .... 10 F3
Taig Rd G66 .... 21 B7
Tain Terr G72 .... 77 C3
Tait Ave G78 .... 57 D3
Tait Wlk ML8 .... 108 B1
Tak-Ma-Doon Rd G65 .... 6 F3
Takmadoon Rd
Carron Bridge FK6 .... 3 B2
Banton G65,FK6 .... 7 A7
Talbot G74 .... 76 C4
Talbot Cres ML5 .... 49 E4
Talbot Ct G13 .... 28 B5
Talbot Dr G13 .... 28 B5
Talbot Pl G13 .... 28 B5
Talbot Terr Glasgow G13 .. 28 B5
Uddingston G71 .... 63 E8
Talisman G81 .... 15 D2
Talisman Cres ML1 .... 65 D2
Talisman Rd G13 .... 28 C6
Tall Ship The* G3 .... 44 C8
Talla Rd G52 .... 43 B5
Tallant Rd G15 .... 16 B3
Tallant Terr G15 .... 16 C3
Tamar Dr G75 .... 87 F6
Tamarack Cres G71 .... 64 C8
Tambowie St G13 .... 28 E8
Tamshill St G20 .... 29 F5
Tanar Ave PA4 .... 27 F1
Tanar Way PA4 .... 27 E1
Tanera Ave G44 .... 60 C4
Tanfield Pl G32 .... 47 C7
Tanfield St G32 .... 47 C7
Tanhill Rd ML11 .... 113 E6
Tankerland Rd G44 .... 60 A6
Tanna Dr G52 .... 43 F3
Tannadice Ave G52 .... 43 C4
Tannadice Path G52 .... 43 C4
Tannahill Dr G74 .... 76 C3
Tannahill Rd G43 .... 59 F6
Tannoch Dr G67 .... 23 F7
Tannoch Pl G67 .... 23 F7
Tannochside Dr G71 .... 49 B1
Tannochside Pk
Motherwell G71 .... 49 B1
Uddingston G71 .... 64 B8
Tannochside Prim Sch
G71 .... 64 B8
Tannock St G22 .... 30 B4
Tantallon Ct ML8 .... 95 E3
Tantallon Dr ML5 .... 34 C2
Tantallon Pk G74 .... 75 D2
Tantallon Rd
2 Bothwell G71 .... 64 B3
Glasgow,Baillieston G69 .... 48 A3
Glasgow,Langside G41 .... 59 E8
Tanzieknowe Ave G72 .... 62 B3
Tanzieknowe Dr G72 .... 62 B3
Tanzieknowe Pl G72 .... 62 A3
Tanzieknowe Rd G72 .... 62 B3
Taransay Ct G22 .... 30 E7
Taransay St G51 .... 44 A8
Tarbert Ave Blantyre G72 .. 63 C2
Wishaw ML2 .... 81 A1
Tarbert Ct ML3 .... 78 A1
Tarbert Pl ML8 .... 96 A1
Tarbert Way ML5 .... 49 E4
Tarbolton G74 .... 76 D3
Tarbolton Cres ML6 .... 51 D1
Tarbolton Dr G81 .... 15 C3
Tarbolton Path ML9 .... 92 F3
Tarbolton Rd
Cumbernauld G67 .... 12 B2
Glasgow G43 .... 59 D6
Tarbolton Sq G81 .... 15 C3
Tarbrax Path ML7 .... 70 A3
Tarbrax Rd EH55 .... 123 C1
Tarbrax Way ML3 .... 78 A3
Tarff Ave G76 .... 86 E5
Tarfside Ave G52 .... 43 C4
Tarfside Gdns G52 .... 43 D4
Tarfside Oval G52 .... 43 D4
Target Rd ML6 .... 51 B6
Tarland St G51 .... 43 F6
Tarn Gr G33 .... 31 E8
Tarquin Pl ML1 .... 79 C8
Tarras Dr PA4 .... 27 E1
Tarras Pl G72 .... 62 D5
Tashieburn Rd ML11 .... 122 C1
Tasman Dr G75 .... 88 B8
Tasmania Quadrant ML2 .. 81 E3
Tassie Pl G74 .... 76 A2
Tassie St G41 .... 59 D8
Tattershall Rd G33 .... 32 C1
Tavistock Dr G43 .... 59 D5
Tay Ave PA4 .... 27 E3
Tay Cres Bishopbriggs G64 .. 19 B1
Glasgow G33 .... 31 E1
Tay Ct G75 .... 87 E7
Tay Gdns ML3 .... 91 B8
Tay Gr G75 .... 87 E7
Tay La ML2 .... 82 A5
Tay Loan ML1 .... 66 A5
Tay Pl East Kilbride G75 .... 87 E7
Larkhall ML9 .... 106 A8
Shotts ML7 .... 69 E6
Tay Rd Bearsden G61 .... 16 D2
Bishopbriggs G64 .... 19 B1
Tay St ML5 .... 34 C1
Tay Terr G75 .... 87 E7
Tay Wlk 10 G67 .... 11 F1
Tayinloan Dr ML8 .... 109 B8
Taylor Ave ML1 .... 66 D2
Taylor High Sch ML1 .... 66 A3
Taylor Pl G4 .... 163 B3
Taylor Rd EH47 .... 56 F6
Taylor St Clydebank G81 ... 27 C8
Glasgow G4 .... 163 B3
Taymouth St G32 .... 47 B3
Taynish Dr G44 .... 60 B5
Tayside ML6 .... 35 F1
Teak Pl G71 .... 49 D1
Teal Cres G75 .... 87 F5
Teal Ct ML4 .... 64 E8
Teal Dr G13 .... 28 A7
Tealing Ave G52 .... 43 C4
Tealing Cres G52 .... 43 C4
Teasel Ave G53 .... 58 B3
Teawell Rd G77 .... 72 D5
Technology Ave G72 .... 77 C4
Teesdale G74 .... 75 C3
Teiglum Rd ML11 .... 119 D7
Teign Gr G75 .... 87 F6
Teith Ave PA4 .... 27 F2
Teith Dr G61 .... 16 D3
Teith Pl G72 .... 62 D5
Teith St G33 .... 31 E1
Telegraph Rd ML6 .... 38 B7
Telephone La G12 .... 29 C2
Telford Ave ML9 .... 106 C8
Telford Ct G81 .... 15 A2
Telford Pl G67 .... 24 A8
Telford Rd
Cumbernauld G67 .... 24 A8
East Kilbride G75 .... 88 E8
Telford St ML4 .... 65 A6
Telford Terr 8 G75 .... 88 F8
Teme Pl G75 .... 87 F7
Templar Ave G13 .... 16 D1
Temple Cotts G67 .... 23 B7
Temple Gdns G13 .... 28 F7
Temple Locks Ct 1 G13 .... 28 F7
Temple Locks Pl 2 G13 .... 28 F7
Temple Prim Sch G13 .... 28 F7
Temple Rd G13 .... 29 A7
Templeland Rd G53 .... 43 C2
Templeton Bsns Ctr G40 .. 45 E5
Templeton St G40 .... 45 E5
Tennant Ave G74 .... 75 A1
Tennant Complex The
G74 .... 75 A1
Tennant St PA4 .... 27 D4
Tennant Wynd ML4 .... 65 A8
Tennent St ML5 .... 50 B5
Tennyson Dr G31 .... 46 E4
Tennyson Gdns G72 .... 77 D7
Terregles Ave G41 .... 44 D2
Terregles Cres G41 .... 44 C2
Terregles Dr G41 .... 44 C2
Teviot Ave G64 .... 19 A4
Teviot Cres G61 .... 16 D2
Teviot Pl G72 .... 62 E5
Teviot Sq G67 .... 11 F2
Teviot St Coatbridge ML5 .. 34 D2
Glasgow G3 .... 44 C8
Teviot Way 2 G72 .... 77 C7
Teviot Wlk G67 .... 11 F2
Teviotdale
East Kilbride G74 .... 75 D2
Newton Mearns G77 .... 73 B5
Tewkesbury Rd G74 .... 76 D4
Thane Rd G13 .... 28 C6
Thanes Gate G71 .... 63 E5
Thankerton Ave ML1 .... 65 F5
Thankerton Rd ML9 .... 93 B1
Tharsis St G21 .... 30 F1
Theatre Royal* G2 .... 162 C3
Third Ave Auchinloch G66 .. 20 D1
Glasgow G44 .... 60 B7
Millerston G33 .... 32 C5
Renfrew PA4 .... 27 C2
Third Ave La G44 .... 60 B7
Third Gdns G41 .... 44 A4
Third Rd G72 .... 77 E5
Third St G71 .... 63 F8
Thirdpart Cres G13 .... 27 E7
Thirlmere G75 .... 87 F5
Thistle Bank G66 .... 20 D4
Thistle Cres ML9 .... 93 B1
Thistle Gdns ML1 .... 66 A5
Thistle Pl G74 .... 75 D3
Thistle Quadrant ML6 .... 36 B1
Thistle Rd ML1 .... 66 A3
Thistle St Airdrie ML6 .... 36 B1
Cleland ML1 .... 67 C1
Glasgow G5 .... 45 C5
Kirkintilloch G66 .... 20 D7
Thistle Terr G5 .... 45 C4
Thistlebank Gdns ML5 .... 49 E3
Thistledown Gr ML5 .... 50 C6
Thomas Muir Ave G64 .... 31 A8
Thomas Muir High Sch
G64 .... 19 D2
Thompson Pl G81 .... 15 C6
Thomson Ave
Kirkintilloch G66 .... 20 E8
Wishaw ML2 .... 80 D1
Thomson Ct ML9 .... 105 F3
Thomson Dr Airdrie ML6 ... 50 F6
Bearsden G61 .... 16 F6
Bellshill ML4 .... 64 D5
Motherwell ML1 .... 79 D5
Thomson Gr G72 .... 62 A7
Thomson St Carluke ML8 .. 95 F2
Glasgow G31 .... 46 A6
Renfrew PA4 .... 27 C2
Strathaven ML10 .... 112 E5
Thomson Terr ML7 .... 69 D6
Thomson's Cl ML11 .... 117 A4
Thorn Ave G74 .... 74 C3
Thorn Dr Bearsden G61 .... 16 D5
Rutherglen G73 .... 61 C4
Thorn Rd Bearsden G61 .... 16 D5
Bellshill ML4 .... 65 B5
Thornbank St G3 .... 44 C8
Thornbridge Ave
1 Glasgow G12 .... 29 C5
1 Glasgow,Garrowhill G69 . 48 B5
Thornbridge Gdns 3
G69 .... 48 A5
Thornbridge Rd G69 .... 48 A5
Thorncliffe Gdns G41 .... 44 E2
Thorncroft Dr G44 .... 60 D4
Thorndean Ave ML4 .... 65 B4
Thorndean Cres ML4 .... 65 B4
Thornden La G14 .... 28 A4
Thorndene Ave ML1 .... 66 C2
Thorndyke G74 .... 76 C5
Thornhill Ave
Blantyre G72 .... 63 D1
Hamilton G72 .... 77 D8
Thornhill Gdns G77 .... 72 D2
Thornhill La 4 G71 .... 64 B3
Thornhill Path G31 .... 46 D5
Thornhill Rd ML3 .... 77 E4
Thornhill Way ML5 .... 50 D3
Thorniecroft Dr G67 .... 23 C6
Thorniecroft Pl G67 .... 23 C6
Thornielee G74 .... 76 B2
Thorniewood Gdns G71 .. 64 A7
Thorniewood Rd G71 .... 63 F8
Thornkip Pl ML5 .... 50 D5
Thornlea Dr G46 .... 59 D4
Thornlea Pl ML11 .... 117 F7
Thornlea St ML8 .... 109 A8
Thornley Ave G13 .... 28 B6
Thornlie Gill ML2 .... 81 B2
Thornlie Prim Sch ML2 .. 81 A1
Thornliebank Ind Est
G46 .... 58 E3
Thornliebank Prim Sch
G46 .... 59 A4
Thornliebank Rd G46 .... 59 B5
Thornliebank Sta G46 .... 59 A4
Thornly Park Ave PA2 .... 57 A8
Thornton Dr ML11 .... 114 A3
Thornton La G20 .... 29 E7
Thornton Pl
Fauldhouse EH47 .... 71 D5
Hamilton ML3 .... 91 D6
Thornton Rd
Kirkmuirhill ML11 .... 114 A3
Thorntonhall G74 .... 74 C2
Thornton St
Coatbridge ML5 .... 34 D2
Glasgow G20 .... 29 E7
Thorntonhall Sta G74 .... 74 B3
Thorntree Ave ML3 .... 77 F5
Thorntree Dr ML5 .... 49 F5
Thorntree Prim Sch G32 . 47 A6
Thorntree Way G71 .... 64 B3
Thornwood Ave
Glasgow G11 .... 29 A2
Kirkintilloch G66 .... 20 B5
Thornwood Cres G11 .... 28 F3
Thornwood Dr
Glasgow G11 .... 28 F2
4 Glasgow G11 .... 29 A3
Thornwood Gdns G11 .... 29 A2
Thornwood Pl G11 .... 29 A3
Thornwood Prim Sch
G11 .... 28 F2
Thornwood Quadrant
G11 .... 28 F3
Thornwood Rd
Glasgow G11 .... 28 F2
Strathaven ML10 .... 112 C5
Thornwood Terr G11 .... 28 F2
Thornyburn Dr G69 .... 48 D4
Thornyburn Pl G69 .... 48 C4
Thrashbush Ave ML2 .... 81 D4
Thrashbush Cres ML2 .... 81 D4
Thrashbush La ML6 .... 36 B2
Thrashbush Quadrant
ML6 .... 36 A2
Thrashbush Rd
Airdrie ML6 .... 36 B2
Wishaw ML2 .... 81 D4
Threave Ct ML8 .... 95 E3
Threave Pl Gartcosh G69 .. 33 E4
Newton Mearns G77 .... 72 B5
Three Rivers Wlk G75 .... 88 B8
Threestanes Rd ML10 .... 112 D6
Threestonehill Ave G32 .. 47 C6
Threshold G74 .... 76 A2
Threshold Pk G74 .... 76 A2
Thrums G74 .... 76 D5
Thrums Ave G64 .... 19 C1
Thrums Gdns G64 .... 19 C1
Thurso St G11 .... 29 C1
Thurston Rd G52 .... 43 B5
Thyme Sq ML1 .... 79 E8
Tibbermore Rd 6 G11 .... 29 A3
Tiber Ave ML1 .... 65 C1
Tie Road No 2 ML11 .... 131 C6
Tighnasheen Way G72 .... 63 D1
Till St ML2 .... 81 B6
Tillanburn Rd ML1 .... 66 F3
Tillie St G20 .... 29 F3
Tillycairn Ave G33 .... 32 D2
Tillycairn Dr G33 .... 32 D2
Tillycairn Pl G33 .... 32 E2
Tillycairn Rd G33 .... 32 E2
Tillycairn St G33 .... 32 E2
Tilt Rd ML2 .... 81 F6
Tilt St G33 .... 31 E2
Time Capsule* ML5 .... 49 F6
Timmons Gr ML4 .... 65 D5
Timmons Terr ML6 .... 51 D1
Tinker's La ML1 .... 79 C5
Tintagel Gdns G69 .... 21 F3
Tinto Cres ML2 .... 81 D2
Tinto Ct ML5 .... 50 C3
Tinto Dr Barrhead G78 .... 57 C1
Carstairs Junction ML11 .. 124 C1
Cumbernauld G68 .... 11 D2
Tinto Gr G69 .... 49 B6
Tinto Prim Sch
Glasgow G43 .... 59 C6
Symington ML12 .... 140 F6
Tinto Rd Airdrie ML6 .... 51 B6
Bearsden G61 .... 16 C6
Bishopbriggs G64 .... 19 D1
Glasgow G43 .... 59 C5
Tinto St ML2 .... 81 C2
Tinto Terr ML11 .... 124 E1
Tinto View Forth ML11 ... 124 A8
Hamilton ML3 .... 91 E8
Tinto Way Cleland ML1 .... 67 C2
East Kilbride G75 .... 88 B5
Tintock Pl G68 .... 11 D6
Tintock Rd G66 .... 9 B2
Tinwald Path G52 .... 43 A5
Tiree G74 .... 89 C7
Tiree Ave PA4 .... 27 C1
Tiree Cres ML2 .... 81 F6
Tiree Ct G67 .... 23 D8
Tiree Dr G67 .... 23 D8
Tiree Gdns Bearsden G61 .. 16 B6
Glenmavis ML6 .... 35 F5
Tiree Grange ML3 .... 77 F1
Tiree Pl Coatbridge ML5 .... 49 D4
Newton Mearns G77 .... 72 B5
Tiree Rd G67 .... 23 D8
Tiree St G21 .... 31 C2
Tirry Ave PA4 .... 27 F2
Tirry Way PA4 .... 27 F2
Titwood Rd Glasgow G41 .. 44 D1
Glasgow G41 .... 44 E1
Newton Mearns G77 .... 72 D1
Newton Mearns G77 .... 72 E1
Tiverton Ave G32 .... 47 D3
Tivoli Ct G75 .... 88 E6
Tobago Pl
East Kilbride G75 .... 75 A1
Glasgow G40 .... 45 F5
Tobago St G40 .... 45 E5
Tobermory Rd G73 .... 61 D3
Todd Pl G31 .... 46 C7
Todd St G31 .... 46 C7
Todhills 10 G75 .... 88 F8
Todhills N G75 .... 88 F8
Todhills S G75 .... 88 F8
Todholm Cres PA2 .... 42 B2
Todholm Prim Sch PA2 .. 42 B2
Todholm Rd PA2 .... 42 B2
Todholm Terr PA2 .... 42 B2
Todshill St ML10 .... 112 E5
Todstable Gdns 8 ML9 .... 129 E8
Toftcombs Cres ML9 .... 105 D1
Tofthill Ave G64 .... 18 F2
Tofthill Gdns G64 .... 18 F2
Toll La G51 .... 44 E6
Toll St ML1 .... 79 F5
Toll The G76 .... 73 E8
Toll Wynd ML3 .... 91 C7
Tollbrae Ave ML6 .... 51 B7
Tollbrae Prim Sch ML6 .... 51 B7
Tollcross Park Gdns G32 . 46 E3
Tollcross Park Gr G32 .... 46 F3
Tollcross Park View G32 . 46 F3
Tollcross Rd G31,G32 .... 46 E4
Tollhouse Gdns ML4 .... 65 C3
Tollpark Cres ML2 .... 82 A5
Tollpark Pl G68 .... 12 E8
Tollpark Rd G68 .... 12 E8
Tolsta St 2 G23 .... 17 E1
Tomtain Brae G68 .... 22 F7
Tomtain Ct G68 .... 22 F7
Toner Gdns ML2 .... 94 B7
Tontine La G1 .... 163 B1

Tontine Pl G73 61 E4
Topaz Terr ML4 65 A3
Torbeg Gdns G75 88 B4
Torbothie Rd ML7 70 B4
Torbreck St G52 43 F5
Torbrex Rd G67 12 A1
Torburn Ave G46 59 B4
Tordene Path G68 11 D3
Torgyle St G23 17 D1
Torhill KA18 142 A6
Tormeadow Rd G77 72 D5
Tormore Ct G33 32 E6
Tormore St 1 G51 43 D6
Tormusk Dr G45 61 A4
Tormusk Gdns G45 61 A4
Tormusk Gr G45 61 A4
Tormusk Prim Sch G45 61 A3
Tormusk Rd G45 61 A4
Torness St G11 29 C2
Torogay Pl G22 30 E8
Torogay St G22 30 D7
Torogay Terr G22 30 C8
Toronto Wlk G72 62 C8
Torphin Cres G32 47 A7
Torphin Wlk G32 47 B7
Torr Gdns G22 30 D4
Torr Pl G22 30 D4
Torr Rd G64 19 D1
Torr St G22 30 D4
Torran Rd G33 47 F7
Torrance Ave ML6 51 D7
Torrance Rd
East Kilbride G74 75 E2
Torrance G64 19 C7
Torrance Rdbt
Bishopbriggs G64 19 C6
East Kilbride G75 89 B5
Torrance St G21 30 F4
Torranyard Terr ML3 77 E1
Torriden Ct ML5 49 E5
Torriden Pl ML5 49 E5
Torriden St ML5 49 E5
Torridon Ave
Glasgow G41 44 B4
Motherwell ML1 66 D3
Torridon Gdns
Bearsden G61 16 C7
Newton Mearns G77 73 B4
Torrin Loan ML7 70 B3
Torrin Rd G23 17 D1
Torrington Ave
Giffnock G46 59 A1
Rutherglen G46 73 A8
Torrington Cres G32 47 D3
Torrisdale Pl ML5 49 E7
Torrisdale St
Coatbridge ML5 49 E7
1 Glasgow G42 45 A2
Torryburn Rd G21 31 C4
Torwood Brae ML3 77 F2
Torwood La G69 22 A2
Toryglen Prim Sch G42 60 E8
Toryglen Rd G73 60 F8
Toryglen St G5 45 E2
Tourmaline Terr ML4 65 B3
Tournai Path 10 G72 77 D7
Toward Ct Blantyre G72 63 E1
Hamilton G72 77 E8
Toward Rd G33 47 C8
Tower Ave G78 57 D4
Tower Cres PA4 27 B2
Tower Dr PA4 27 B2
Tower Rd
Cumbernauld G67 24 A6
Torrance G64 19 A8
Tower St G41 44 E5
Towerhill Rd G13 16 C1
Towers Pl ML6 51 F7
Towers Rd ML6 51 F7
Towerside Cres G53 43 A2
Towerside Rd G53 43 A2
Towie Pl 2 Glasgow G20 29 D6
Uddingston G71 63 F6
Townfoot Pl ML11 138 F7
Townhead G66 20 D7
Townhead Ave ML1 65 E8
Townhead Ct ML10 112 E5
Townhead Dr ML1 66 F3
Townhead Pl G71 64 A8
Townhead Prim Sch ML5 34 D2
Townhead Rd
Coatbridge ML5 34 C1
Newton Mearns G77 72 D4
Townhead Rdbt G66 20 D8
Townhead St
Glassford ML10 104 F3
Hamilton ML3 78 F3
Kilsyth G65 10 D8
Stonehouse ML10 105 E2
Strathaven ML10 112 D5
Townhill Prim Sch ML3 77 E2
Townhill Rd ML3 77 E3
Townhill Terr ML3 77 E3
Townmill Rd G31 46 A8
Townsend St G4 30 C2
Traction Bsns Ctr ML1 79 C6
Tradeston Ind Est G5 45 A4
Tradeston St G5 45 A5
Trafalgar Ct G68 11 D6
Trafalgar St G40 45 F3
Trainard Ave G32 46 F4
Tranent Pl Cleland ML1 67 C2
Glasgow G33 46 E8
Traquair Ave ML2 81 C5
Traquair Dr G52 43 B5
Traquair Wynd 10 G72 77 C7
Treeburn Ave G46 59 B3
Treefield Gdns ML11 114 B3
Treefield Pk ML11 114 B3
Treemain Rd G46 73 A8
Treespark Ave G78 57 B4
Trefoil Ave G41 59 D8
Trent Pl G75 87 E6
Trent St ML5 34 D2
Tresta Rd G23 29 F8
Triangle Sh Ctr The G64 19 A1
Tribboch St ML9 92 F3
Trident Way PA4 27 C1
Trinidad Gn 3 G75 75 A1
Trinidad Way G75 75 A1
Trinity Ave G52 43 C4
Trinity Dr G72 62 C3
Trinity High Sch
Renfrew PA4 27 D3
Rutherglen G73 61 E6
Trinity Way 14 ML9 93 C1
Trinley Rd G13 16 D1
Triton Pl ML4 65 F5
Trondra Path G34 47 F8
Trondra Pl G34 47 F7
Trongate Glasgow G1 163 A1
Stonehouse ML9 105 F2
Troon Ave G75 88 A6
Troon Ct G75 88 B6
Troon Gdns G68 11 F6
Troon Pl G77 73 A4
Troon St G40 46 B3
Trossachs Ave ML1 66 A5
Trossachs Ct G20 30 A3
Trossachs Rd G73 61 D2
Trossachs St G20 30 A3
Trows Rd ML2 94 B6
Truce Rd G13 28 B8
Truro Ave G69 21 F3
Tryst Rd Cumbernauld G67 11 F1
Cumbernauld,Carbrain G67 12 A2
Tryst Wlk
Cumbernauld G67 12 A2
Cumbernauld G67 11 F1
Tudor La S G14 28 E3
Tudor Rd G14 28 E3
Tudor St G69 47 F3
Tukalo Ct ML10 112 F8
Tukalo Dr ML10 112 F8
Tulley Wynd ML1 65 D2
Tulliallan Pl G74 89 A8
Tullis Ct G40 45 E4
Tullis St G40 45 F4
Tulloch Gdns ML1 80 B4
Tulloch Rd ML7 70 B3
Tulloch St G44 60 A6
Tullochard Pl G73 61 D3
Tullymet Rd ML3 91 D8
Tummel Dr ML6 35 F2
Tummel Gn G74 75 E3
Tummel St G33 31 E2
Tunnel St G3 44 E7
Tuphall Rd ML3 78 D2
Turfholm Mills Ind Est
ML11 119 E4
Turnberry Ave 2 G11 29 B3
Turnberry Cres
Chapelhall ML6 51 E1
Coatbridge ML5 49 E4
Turnberry Dr
Hamilton ML3 77 D2
Newton Mearns G77 73 A5
Rutherglen G73 60 F5
Turnberry Gdns G68 12 A5
Turnberry Pl
East Kilbride G75 88 B6
Rutherglen G73 60 F4
Turnberry Rd
Glasgow G11 29 A3
Glasgow G11 29 B3
Turnberry Wynd G71 63 E2
Turnbull Ct ML10 112 F7
Turnbull High Sch G64 18 E2
Turnbull St G1 163 B1
Turnbull Way ML10 112 F7
Turner St ML5 49 F6
Turning of the Staff
ML11 130 D5
Turnlaw G75 88 D5
Turnlaw Rd G72 62 A2
Turnlaw St G5 45 D4
Turnpike Rd ML11 114 A4
Turquoise Terr ML4 65 B3
Turret Cres G13 28 D8
Turret Rd G13 28 C8
Turriff St G5 45 B4
Twechar Prim Sch G65 10 A3
Tweed Cres Glasgow G33 31 E1
Renfrew PA4 27 E2
Wishaw ML2 81 C5
Tweed Ct ML6 51 C5
Tweed Dr G61 16 D3
Tweed La ML1 66 B5
Tweed St Coatbridge ML5 50 A3
East Kilbride G75 87 F7
Larkhall ML9 93 A1
Tweed Wlk G67 11 F2
Tweedmuir Pl ML5 50 D3
Tweedsmuir G64 19 C2
Tweedsmuir Cres G61 16 E7
Tweedsmuir Pk ML3 91 C8
Tweedsmuir Rd G52 43 B5
Tweedvale Ave G14 27 E6
Tweedvale Pl G14 27 E6
Twinlaw St G34 33 D1
Tylney Rd PA1 42 D5
Tyndrum Rd G61 17 B5
Tyndrum St G4 163 A4
Tyne Pl G75 87 E6
Tynecastle Cres G32 47 B7
Tynecastle Path G32 47 B7
Tynecastle Pl G32 47 B7
Tynecastle St G32 47 B7
Tynron Ct ML3 77 E1
Tynwald Ave G73 61 D4

U

Uddingston Gram Sch
G71 63 E6
Uddingston Rd G71 64 A3
Uddingston Sta G71 63 E6
Udston Ave 11 ML9 129 E8
Udston Hospl ML3 77 F4
Udston Mill Rd ML9 129 E8
Udston Prim Sch ML3 77 E4
Udston Rd Hamilton ML3 77 F5
Stonehouse ML9 129 E7
Udston Terr ML3 77 F5
Uig Pl G33 47 E5
Uig Way ML7 70 A3
Uist Cres G33 32 E4
Uist Dr G66 21 A8
Uist Pl ML6 51 D6
Uist St G51 43 F7
Uist Way ML2 81 E5
Ullswater G75 87 F5
Ulva St G52 43 F5
Ulverston Terr ML3 91 D6
Underbank Prim Sch
ML8 115 B8
Underwood Dr ML2 82 A7
Underwood Rd G73 61 C6
Underwood St G41 59 E8
Union Pl Glasgow G1 162 C2
Moffat DG10 161 C5
Union St Carluke ML8 95 F1
Glasgow G1 162 C2
Hamilton ML3 78 D3
Kirkintilloch G66 20 C8
Larkhall ML9 93 A3
Motherwell ML1 66 A4
Shotts ML7 69 D5
Stonehouse ML9 105 F2
Unitas Cres ML8 95 E1
Unitas Rd ML4 65 C5
Unity Pk ML7 69 D4
Unity Pl G4 30 A2
Univ of Glasgow G11,G12 29 D2
Univ of Glasgow (Bearsden Campus) G61 16 D7
Univ of Glasgow (Kelvin Campus) G20 17 B1
Univ of Glasgow (St Andrew's Building) G3 29 E2
Univ of Glasgow (Veterinary Medicine) G61 29 A8
Univ of Strathclyde G1,
G4 163 B3
University Ave G12 29 D2
University Gdns G12 29 D2
University Pl G12 29 D2
Unsted Pl PA1 42 A4
Unthank Rd ML4 65 C5
UP La G65 10 D8
UP Rd G65 10 D8
Uphall Pl G33 46 E7
Upland La 2 G14 28 C4
Upland Rd G14 28 C4
Upper Bathville EH48 41 F4
Upper Bourtree Ct G73 61 C4
Upper Bourtree Dr G73 61 C4
Upper Glenburn Rd G61 16 D5
Upper Mill St ML6 51 A8
Upper Mill Street Ind Est
ML6 51 A8
Urquhart Cres PA4 27 C2
Urquhart Dr G74 76 A3
Urquhart Pl G69 33 F4
Urrdale Rd G41 44 B5
Usmore Pl G33 47 E5

V

Vaila Pl G23 30 A7
Vaila St G23 29 F7
Vale Wlk G64 31 C8
Valence Twr G71 63 D4
Valerio Ct G72 77 D8
Valeview Terr G42 60 A8
Vallantine Cres G71 64 A8
Vallay St G22 30 D8
Valley Ct ML3 78 C2
Valley International Pk*
ML8 108 C2
Valley View
Cambuslang G72 62 C6
Motherwell ML1 80 B3
Valleybank G65 7 D3
Valleyfield G75 75 D1
Valleyfield Dr G68 10 E1
Valleyfield St 1 G21 30 E3
Vancouver Ct 1 G75 75 B1
Vancouver Dr G75 75 B1
Vancouver La
15 Glasgow G14 28 C4
Glasgow G14 28 D4
Vancouver Rd G14 28 D4
Vanguard St G81 15 D2
Vanguard Way PA4 27 C1
Vardar Ave G76 73 C8
Vardon Lea ML1 66 E1
Varna La G14 28 E3
Varna Rd G14 28 E4
Varnsdorf Way ML6 51 E6
Vasart Pl G20 29 F4
Veitches Ct G81 15 A6
Vennachar St ML7 69 E6
Vennacher Rd PA4 27 B4
Vennard Gdns G41 44 F2
Vere Rd Kirkmuirhill ML11 114 A3
Kirkmuirhill ML11 114 B1
Lesmahagow ML11 119 B8
Vere Terr ML11 114 A2
Vermont Ave G73 61 A7
Vermont St G41 44 E5
Vernon Bank G74 75 E3
Verona Ave G14 28 C4
Verona Gdns 4 G14 28 C4
Verona La G14 28 C4
Vesalius St G32 47 A5
Viaduct Rd G76 73 F7
Vicarfield St G51 44 B7
Vicarland Pl G72 62 A4
Vicarland Rd G72 62 A5
Vicars Rd ML9 105 E2
Vicars Wlk G72 62 B5
Vickers St ML1 79 B8
Victor St ML6 37 A2
Victoria Ave Barrhead G78 57 B4
Carluke ML8 95 E1
Victoria Buildings Bsns Ctr
PA1 42 A4
Victoria Cir G12 29 C3
Victoria Cres Airdrie ML6 50 F6
Barrhead G78 57 B4
Clarkston G76 73 F7
Kilsyth G65 10 B8
Wishaw ML2 80 D4
Victoria Crescent La G12 29 C3
Victoria Crescent Pl 4
G12 29 C3
Victoria Crescent Rd
G12 29 C3
Victoria Cross G42 45 A2
Victoria Ct Larkhall ML9 93 A4
Newton Mearns G77 72 D2
Victoria Dr G78 57 B4
Victoria Dr E PA4 27 C2
Victoria Dr W PA4 27 B3
Victoria Gdns Airdrie ML6 50 F7
Barrhead G78 57 B4
Victoria Glade G68 11 D6
Victoria Gr G78 57 B4
Victoria Infmy G42 60 A8
Victoria La G77 72 D2
Victoria Meml Cottage Hospl
G65 10 B8
Victoria Park Cnr G14 28 D3
Victoria Park Dr N G14 28 E3
Victoria Park Dr S G14 28 D3
Victoria Park Gdns N
G11 28 F3
Victoria Park Gdns S
G11 28 F3
Victoria Park La N G14 28 D3
Victoria Park La S G14 28 D3
Victoria Park Sch ML8 95 F2
Victoria Park St 7 G14 28 D3
Victoria Pk
Fauldhouse EH47 71 F7
* Glasgow G14 28 E3
Kilsyth G65 10 B8
Victoria Pl Airdrie ML6 50 E6
Barrhead G78 57 C4
Bellshill ML4 64 F4
Kilsyth G65 10 C8
Moffat DG10 161 C5
4 Rutherglen G73 61 A8
Victoria Prim Sch
Airdrie ML6 50 F7
Glasgow G42 45 B2
Victoria Quadrant ML1 65 F5
Victoria Rd Barrhead G78 57 B4
Dullatur G68 11 D6
Fauldhouse EH47 71 F7
Glasgow G42 45 A3
Harthill ML7 55 E5
Kirkintilloch G66 20 C3
Rutherglen G73 61 B6
Stepps G33 32 D5
Victoria Sq G77 72 D2
Victoria St
Hamilton,Blantyre G72 77 D7
Hamilton,Whitehill ML3 78 B6
Harthill ML7 55 E5
Kirkintilloch G66 20 C8
Larkhall ML9 93 A4
Rutherglen G73 61 B8
Wishaw ML2 82 A4
Victoria Terr G68 11 D6
Victory Way G69 48 B4
View Park Rd ML12 160 D4
Viewbank G46 59 A3
Viewbank Ave ML6 51 B2
Viewbank St ML5 34 F5
Viewfield Airdrie ML6 50 E7
Moodiesburn G69 21 E4
Viewfield Ave
Bishopbriggs G64 30 E8
Blantyre G72 63 E1
Glasgow G69 47 F5
Kirkintilloch G66 20 C5
Viewfield Dr
Bishopbriggs G64 30 E8
Glasgow G69 47 F5
Viewfield La G12 29 E2
Viewfield Pl ML7 55 F6
Viewfield Rd Banknock FK4 8 D3
Bellshill ML4 64 F3
Bishopbriggs G64 30 E8
Coatbridge ML5 49 C4
Tarbrax EH55 123 C2
Viewfield St ML7 55 F6
Viewglen Ct G45 60 D1
Viewmount Cres ML10 112 E7
Viewmount Dr G20 29 D7
Viewpark Ave G31 46 B8
Viewpark Ct G73 61 C6
Viewpark Dr G73 61 B6
Viewpark Gdns PA4 27 B2
Viewpark Pl ML1 79 C6
Viewpark Rd ML1 79 C6
Viewpark Sh Ctr G71,ML4 64 D6
Viewpoint Pl G21 30 F6
Viewpoint Rd G21 30 F6
Viking Rd ML6 51 B5
Viking Terr G75 88 E6
Viking Way Glasgow G46 58 F5
Renfrew PA4 27 C1
Villafield Ave G64 19 A3
Villafield Dr G64 19 A3
Villafield Loan G64 19 A3
Village Gdns G72 63 E1
Village Rd G72 62 F5
Vincent Ct ML4 65 A4
Vine St G11 29 B2
Vinicombe La 3 G12 29 D3
Vinicombe St G12 29 D3
Vintner St G4 30 C2
Viola Pl G64 19 C8
Violet Bank ML11 114 A3
Violet Cres ML9 129 E8
Violet Gdns ML8 108 E8
Violet Pl ML1 66 B6
Violet St PA1 42 A4
Virginia Ct G1 163 A2
Virginia Gdns G62 17 C8
Virginia Pl G1 163 A2
Virginia St G1 163 A2
Virtue Well View ML6 35 E3
Viscount Ave PA4 27 C1
Viscount Gate G71 63 E5
Voil Dr G44 60 A4
Vorlich Ct G78 57 C1
Vorlich Gdns G61 16 C7
Vorlich Wynd ML1 66 C4
Vryburg Cl G75 88 A4
Vryburg Cres G75 88 A4
Vulcan St 4 Glasgow G21 30 E4
Motherwell ML1 79 E8

W

Waddell Ave ML6 35 D4
Waddell Ct G5 45 D5
Waddell St Airdrie ML6 36 A1
Glasgow G5 45 D4
Waid Ave G77 72 C6
Waldemar Rd G13 28 C7
Waldo St 3 G13 28 F7
Walker Ct G11 29 B1
Walker Path 2 G71 64 A8
Walker Rd EH47 71 D5
Walker St G11 29 B1
Walkerburn Dr ML2 81 C6
Walkerburn Rd G52 43 B4
Walkinshaw St G40 46 A4
Walkmill La G81 15 B6
Wallace Dr
3 Bishopbriggs G64 31 D8
Larkhall ML9 93 C2
Wallace Gate 2 G64 31 D8
Wallace Ho G67 11 E2
Wallace Pl
1 Bishopbriggs G64 31 D8
Blantyre G72 63 E1
Hamilton ML3 79 A2
Kirkmuirhill ML11 114 A2
Wallace Rd
Motherwell ML1 66 B2
Renfrew PA4 27 A1
Wallace St Clydebank G81 15 B1
Coatbridge ML5 50 A5
Glasgow G5 45 A5
Motherwell ML1 79 D7
Plains ML6 37 A2
Rutherglen G73 61 A7
Wallace Way ML11 117 C4
Wallace Wynd
Cambuslang G72 62 A3
Kirkmuirhill ML11 114 A3
Law ML8 95 A6
Wallacewell Cres G21 31 B5
Wallacewell Pl G21 31 B5
Wallacewell Quadrant
G21 31 C6
Wallacewell Rd G21 31 C6
Wallbrae Rd G67 23 F8
Walls St G1 163 B2
Walmer Cres G51 44 C5
Walnut Cl G75 88 C6
Walnut Cres G22 30 D5
Walnut Dr G66 20 B6
Walnut Gate G72 62 F4
Walnut Gr G75 88 C6
Walnut Pl Glasgow G22 30 D5
Motherwell G71 49 C1
Walnut Rd G22 30 D5
Walston Prim Sch ML11 132 F7
Walter St Glasgow G31 46 C7
Wishaw ML2 81 D3
Walton Ave G77 72 C6
Walton Ct G46 59 C2
Walton St Barrhead G78 57 C3
Glasgow G41 59 E8
Wamba Ave G13 28 E8
Wamphray Pl G75 87 D7
Wandilla Ave G81 15 D2

Wanlock St G51 .... 44 A8
Wanlockhead Beam Engine*
ML12 .... 154 B8
Ward The ML10 .... 112 E6
Warden Rd G13 .... 28 D7
Wardhill Rd G21 .... 31 B5
Wardie Pl G33 .... 47 F7
Wardie Rd G34 .... 48 A7
Wardlaw Ave G73 .... 61 B7
Wardlaw Cres G75 .... 89 A7
Wardlaw Dr G73 .... 61 B8
Wardlaw Rd G61 .... 16 F1
Wardpark Ct G67 .... 12 D6
Wardpark East Ind Est
G68 .... 12 E8
Wardpark North Ind Est
G68 .... 12 D7
Wardpark Pl G67 .... 12 D6
Wardpark Rd G67 .... 12 D6
Wardpark Rdbt G68 .... 12 D7
Wardpark South Ind Est
G67 .... 12 D6
Wardrop Cres EH48 .... 41 E5
Wardrop Pl G74 .... 75 F3
Wardrop St 2 G51 .... 44 A8
Wards Cres ML5 .... 49 E5
Ware Rd G34 .... 48 A7
Warilda Ave G81 .... 15 C2
Warnock Cres ML4 .... 65 B4
Warnock Rd G77 .... 72 C7
Warnock St G31 .... 163 C3
Warren Rd ML3 .... 91 D8
Warren St G42 .... 45 B1
Warriston Cres G33 .... 46 D8
Warriston Ct G33 .... 46 F8
Warriston Pl Glasgow G32 .. 47 B7
Moffat DG10 .... 161 E5
Warriston Rd DG10 .... 161 D5
Warriston St G33 .... 46 E8
Warriston Way G73 .... 61 D4
Warroch St G3 .... 162 A2
Warwick G74 .... 76 C4
Warwick Gr ML3 .... 77 E5
Warwick Villas G81 .... 27 E7
Washington Rd G66 .... 20 B8
Washington St G3 .... 162 B2
Watchmeal Cres G81 .... 15 C7
Water Rd G78 .... 57 C3
Water Row G51 .... 44 A8
Waterbank Rd G76 .... 74 D5
Waterfoot Ave G53 .... 58 C8
Waterfoot Rd
Newton Mearns,Kirkhill G77 .73 B3
Newton Mearns,Mearns
G77 .... 72 F3
Waterfoot Row G76 .... 73 D3
Waterfoot Terr G53 .... 58 C8
Waterford Ct G46 .... 59 B2
Waterford Rd G46 .... 59 B3
Waterhaughs Gdns G33 .... 31 D7
Waterhaughs Gr G33 .... 31 D7
Waterlands Gdns ML8 .... 96 A3
Waterlands Pl ML8 .... 95 A4
Waterlands Rd ML8 .... 95 B6
Waterloo Dr ML11 .... 117 A5
Waterloo La G2 .... 162 C2
Waterloo Rd ML11 .... 117 A5
Waterloo St G2 .... 162 C2
Watermill Ave G66 .... 20 D4
Watersaugh Dr ML1 .... 67 B2
Waterside G76 .... 73 F5
Waterside Ave G77 .... 72 C4
Waterside Ct G76 .... 74 D7
Waterside Dr G77 .... 72 C4
Waterside Gdns
Cambuslang G72 .... 62 E3
Carmunnock G76 .... 74 D7
Hamilton ML3 .... 78 E1
Waterside Pl G5 .... 45 D4
Waterside Rd
Carmunnock G76 .... 74 D6
Carmunnock G76 .... 74 D8
Kirkintilloch G66 .... 20 E7
Waterside St Glasgow G5 .. 45 D4
Sandford ML10 .... 129 B6
Strathaven ML10 .... 112 E6
Wateryett Loan ML10 .... 112 C6
Watling Pl 7 G75 .... 75 A1
Watling St
Crawford ML12 .... 152 B8
Motherwell ML1 .... 65 C1
Uddingston G71 .... 63 E8
Watson Ave
Rutherglen G73 .... 60 F7
Stonehouse ML9 .... 106 A3
Watson Cres G65 .... 10 E8
Watson Pl G72 .... 77 B7
Watson St Glasgow G1 .... 163 B1
Hamilton G72 .... 77 C7
Larkhall ML9 .... 92 F3
Motherwell ML1 .... 79 E5
Uddingston G71 .... 63 F6
Watsonville Pk 3 ML1 .... 79 E6
Watstone Rd ML9 .... 106 A2
Watt Ave G33 .... 32 F5
Watt Cres ML4 .... 65 B7
Watt Ct ML9 .... 105 E1
Watt Low Ave G73 .... 60 F6
Watt Pl G72 .... 77 C4
Watt Rd G52 .... 43 A7
Watt St Airdrie ML6 .... 36 C1
Glasgow G5 .... 162 A1
Waukglen Ave G53 .... 58 B2
Waukglen Cres G53 .... 58 C3
Waukglen Dr G53 .... 58 B3
Waukglen Gdns G53 .... 58 B2
Waukglen Path G53 .... 58 B3
Waukglen Pl G53 .... 58 B3
Waukglen Rd G53 .... 58 B3
Waulking Mill Rd G81 .... 15 C7
Waulkmill Ave G78 .... 57 D4
Waulkmill St G46 .... 58 E4
Waulkmill Way G78 .... 57 D4
Waverley Clydebank G81 .... 15 C2
East Kilbride G74 .... 76 D4
Waverley Cres
Cumbernauld G67 .... 23 D7
Hamilton ML3 .... 77 F4
Kirkintilloch G66 .... 20 D8
Lanark ML11 .... 117 C4
Waverley Ct G71 .... 64 A2
Waverley Dr Airdrie ML6 .... 36 B1
Rutherglen G73 .... 61 C7
Wishaw ML2 .... 81 B4
Waverley Gdns G41 .... 44 E1
Waverley Park Rdbt G66 .... 20 E8
Waverley Pk G66 .... 20 D8
Waverley St
Coatbridge ML5 .... 35 B1
Glasgow G41 .... 44 E1
Hamilton ML3 .... 77 F4
Larkhall ML9 .... 106 A8
Waverley Terr G72 .... 77 D5
Weardale La G33 .... 47 C8
Weardale St G33 .... 47 C8
Weaver Ave G77 .... 72 C7
Weaver Cres ML6 .... 51 A5
Weaver Pl G75 .... 87 F7
Weaver St G4 .... 163 B2
Weaver Terr PA2 .... 42 A3
Weavers Ct
1 East Kilbride G74 .... 75 F2
Glassford ML10 .... 104 F3
3 Hamilton ML3 .... 78 E2
Weavers La ML10 .... 104 F3
Weavers Way ML9 .... 105 E1
Weavers Wlk ML11 .... 117 A3
Webster Groves ML2 .... 81 D5
Webster St Clydebank G81 .. 27 E8
Glasgow G40 .... 46 A3
Wedderlea Dr G52 .... 43 B5
Wee Sunnyside Rd ML9 .... 92 B2
Weensmoor Rd G53 .... 57 F4
Weighhouse Rd ML8 .... 95 E3
Weir Ave G78 .... 57 C2
Weir Pl ML8 .... 94 F4
Weir St ML5 .... 50 A7
Weirs Gate ML10 .... 112 E6
Weirwood Ave G69 .... 48 A5
Weirwood Gdns G69 .... 47 F4
Welbeck Rd G53 .... 58 B4
Weldon Pl G65 .... 10 F3
Welfare Ave G72 .... 62 D4
Well Dr ML11 .... 116 E3
Well Gn G43 .... 59 C8
Well Gn Ct G43 .... 59 C8
Well Rd Lanark ML11 .... 117 B3
Moffat DG10 .... 161 E5
Well St DG10 .... 161 D5
Welland Pl G75 .... 87 E7
Wellbank Pl G71 .... 63 F5
Wellbeck Ho 7 G74 .... 75 F2
Wellbrae Chapelton ML10 .. 103 C5
Larkhall ML9 .... 93 A2
Stonehouse ML9 .... 105 E2
Strathaven ML10 .... 112 E5
Wellbrae Dr ML10 .... 112 E7
Wellbrae Rd ML3 .... 78 B1
Wellbrae Terr G69 .... 21 F2
Wellburn Ave ML11 .... 119 C6
Wellburn La ML11 .... 119 D6
Wellbuttslea Dr ML11 .... 116 E3
Wellcroft Pl G5 .... 45 B4
Wellcroft Rd ML3 .... 77 E3
Wellcroft Terr ML3 .... 77 E3
Welldale La ML11 .... 116 B5
Welldale St ML11 .... 138 B1
Wellesley Cres
Cumbernauld G68 .... 22 E8
East Kilbride G75 .... 87 F7
Wellesley Dr
Cumbernauld G68 .... 22 D8
East Kilbride G75 .... 87 F8
Wellesley Pl G68 .... 10 D1
Wellfield Ave G46 .... 59 B3
Wellfield St G21 .... 30 F4
Wellgate ML11 .... 117 A4
Wellgate Ct ML9 .... 93 A4
Wellgate St ML9 .... 93 A3
Wellgatehead ML11 .... 117 A3
Wellhall Ct ML3 .... 78 B4
Wellhall Rd ML3 .... 78 B3
Wellhead Ct ML11 .... 117 B4
Wellhouse Cres G33 .... 47 F7
Wellhouse Gdns G33 .... 47 F7
Wellhouse Gr G33 .... 47 F7
Wellhouse Prim Sch G33 .. 47 E7
Wellhouse Rd G33 .... 47 F7
Wellington G75 .... 88 B7
Wellington La G2 .... 162 C2
Wellington Path G69 .... 48 B4
Wellington Pl
Coatbridge ML5 .... 49 C5
Wishaw ML2 .... 94 D8
Wellington Rd G64 .... 19 B4
Wellington St Airdrie ML6 .. 36 A1
Glasgow G2 .... 162 C2
Wishaw ML2 .... 80 C5
Wellington Terr ML11 .... 116 F5
Wellington Way 5 PA4 .... 27 C1
Wellknowe Ave G74 .... 74 C2
Wellknowe Pl G74 .... 74 C3
Wellknowe Rd G74 .... 74 C3
Wellmeadow Cl G77 .... 72 D5
Wellmeadow Gn G77 .... 72 D5
Wellmeadow Rd G43 .... 59 B6
Wellmeadow Way G77 .... 72 D6
Wellmeadows Ct ML3 .... 78 A2
Wellmeadows La ML3 .... 78 A2
Wellpark Rd Banknock FK4 .. 8 D2
Motherwell ML1 .... 79 C6
Wellpark St G31 .... 163 C2
Wells Quarry Rd G76,G74 .. 75 C5
Wellshot Dr G72 .... 61 F5
Wellshot Prim Sch G32 .. 46 F4
Wellshot Rd G32 .... 46 F4
Wellside Ave ML6 .... 36 A1
Wellside Dr G72 .... 62 C4
Wellside La ML6 .... 36 B1
Wellside Quadrant ML6 .. 36 A1
Wellview Dr ML1 .... 79 D6
Wellwood Ave ML11 .... 117 B5
Wellwood Rd ML11 .... 119 E5
Wellwynd ML6 .... 50 F8
Wellwynd Gdns 2 ML6 .... 50 F8
Welsh Dr
Hamilton,Blantyre G72 .... 77 D6
Hamilton,Eddlewood ML3 .. 91 C7
Welsh Rd EH47 .... 56 F6
Welsh Row ML6 .... 51 C3
Welsh St ML11 .... 138 F7
Wemyss Ave G77 .... 72 C7
Wemyss Dr G68 .... 10 E1
Wemyss Gdns G69 .... 48 A3
Wenlock Rd PA2 .... 42 A2
Wensleydale G74 .... 75 C3
Wentworth Dr 5 G23 .... 17 E1
Wesley St ML6 .... 50 F7
West Academy St ML2 .... 80 E3
West Ave Carluke ML8 .... 95 E1
Hamilton G72 .... 77 E5
Motherwell ML1 .... 66 A2
Plains ML6 .... 37 A3
Renfrew PA4 .... 27 D3
Stepps G33 .... 32 D5
Uddingston G71 .... 64 C6
West Benhar Rd ML7 .... 55 B3
West Burnside St G65 .... 10 D8
West Campbell St G2 .... 162 C3
West Canal St ML5 .... 49 F7
West Chapelton Ave G61 .. 16 F4
West Chapelton Cres
G61 .... 16 F4
West Chapelton Dr G61 .. 16 F4
West Chapelton La G61 .. 16 F4
West Clyde St ML9 .... 93 B2
West Coats Prim Sch
G72 .... 61 F5
West Coats Rd G72 .... 61 F5
West Cross ML2 .... 81 A3
West Dr ML6 .... 51 E6
West End Dr ML4 .... 64 F4
West End Pl ML4 .... 64 F4
West Fairholm St ML9 .... 92 F5
West Faulds Rd ML11 .... 117 E5
West Gate ML2 .... 81 D3
West George La G2 .... 162 C3
West George St
Coatbridge ML5 .... 50 A8
Glasgow G2 .... 162 C3
West Glebe G76 .... 86 F5
West Glebe Terr ML3 .... 78 C2
West Graham St G3 .... 162 B4
West Greenhill Pl G3 .... 44 E8
West Hamilton St ML1 .... 79 E6
West Harwood Crofts
EH55 .... 123 B7
West Kirk St ML6 .... 50 F8
West Lodge Rd PA4 .... 27 B4
West Main St
Armadale EH48 .... 41 E5
Harthill ML7 .... 55 E5
Whitburn EH47 .... 56 F6
West Mains Rd G74 .... 75 D2
West Nemphlar Rd
ML11 .... 116 C6
West Nile St G1 .... 163 A3
West of Scotland Science Pk
(Todd Campus) G20 .... 17 B1
West Pl ML2 .... 82 A5
West Port ML11 .... 116 F4
West Prince's St
6 Glasgow G4 .... 29 E2
Glasgow G4 .... 29 F2
West Regent La G2 .... 162 C3
West Regent St G2 .... 162 C3
West Row ML12 .... 160 C4
West Scott Terr ML3 .... 78 D1
West St Clydebank G81 .... 27 E8
Glasgow G5 .... 45 A5
West Sta ML3 .... 78 C4
West Stewart St ML3 .... 78 C4
West Street Underground Sta
G5 .... 45 A5
West Thomson St G81 .... 15 B3
West Thornlie St ML2 .... 81 A2
West Wellbrae Cres ML3 .. 91 B8
West Whitby St G31 .... 46 C4
Westacres Rd G77 .... 72 B4
Westbank Ct 7 G12 .... 29 E2
Westbank Holdings
ML11 .... 130 E7
Westbank La G12 .... 29 E2
Westbank Quadrant G12 .. 29 E2
Westbank Terr ML11 .... 130 E7
Westbarns Rd ML10 .... 112 E7
Westbourne Cres G61 .... 16 C5
Westbourne Ctr G78 .... 57 B2
Westbourne Dr G61 .... 16 D5
Westbourne Gardens La 6
G12 .... 29 C4
Westbourne Gdns N 7
G12 .... 29 C4
Westbourne Gdns S G12 .. 29 C4
Westbourne Gdns W 8
G12 .... 29 C4
Westbourne Rd G12 .... 29 B4
Westbourne Terrace La N 9
G12 .... 29 C4
Westbourne Terrace La S 3
G12 .... 29 B4
Westbrae Dr G13,G14 .... 28 E4
Westbrae Rd G77 .... 72 F6
Westburn Ave G72 .... 62 D6
Westburn Cres
Clydebank G81 .... 15 B7
Rutherglen G73 .... 60 F7
Westburn Farm Rd G72 .. 62 B6
Westburn Rd
Cambuslang,Newton G72 .. 63 B5
Cambuslang,Westburn G72 .62 D6
Westburn Terr ML11 .... 114 B2
Westcastle Cres G45 .... 60 D3
Westcastle Ct G45 .... 60 D3
Westcastle Gdns G45 .... 60 D3
Westcastle Gr G45 .... 60 D3
Westclyffe St 3 G41 .... 44 E1
Westcott Pl ML11 .... 117 C5
Westcraigs Pk EH48 .... 40 C3
Westcraigs Rd
Blackridge EH48 .... 40 D2
Harthill ML7 .... 55 F6
Westcross Rdbt G77 .... 72 A5
Westend G61 .... 17 A2
Westend Ct ML8 .... 94 F4
Westend Park St G3 .... 29 F2
Westend Ret Pk G11 .... 29 A2
Wester Boghead G66 .... 19 F4
Wester Cleddens Prim Sch
G64 .... 19 A2
Wester Cleddens Rd G64 .. 19 C2
Wester Cochno Holdings
G81 .... 15 A8
Wester Common Dr G22 .. 30 A4
Wester Common Rd G22 .. 30 A4
Wester Mavisbank Ave
ML6 .... 50 F8
Wester Moffat Ave ML6 .. 51 E7
Wester Moffat Cres 2
ML6 .... 51 E7
Wester Moffat Hospl
ML6 .... 51 F8
Wester Myvot Rd G67 .... 23 A4
Wester Overton Prim Sch
ML10 .... 112 E7
Wester Rd G32 .... 47 D3
Westerburn St G32 .... 46 F6
Westercommon Prim Sch
G22 .... 30 A4
Westercraigs G31 .... 45 F7
Westercrofts ML12 .... 160 C4
Westercrofts Brae
ML12 .... 160 C4
Westercrofts Gdns
ML12 .... 160 C4
Westerdale G74 .... 75 C3
Westerfield Rd G76 .... 74 D4
Westergate Sh Ctr G2 .. 162 C2
Westergill Ave ML6 .... 51 E6
Westergreens Ave G66 .. 20 C6
Westerhill Rd G64 .... 19 D3
Westerhouse Ct ML8 .... 95 D2
Westerhouse Rd
Glasgow G34 .... 47 F8
Glasgow G34 .... 48 B8
Westerkirk Dr G23 .... 17 E1
Westerlands G12 .... 29 A6
Westerlands Dr G77 .... 72 B4
Westerlands Gdns G77 .. 72 B4
Westerlands Gr G77 .... 72 B4
Westerlands Pl G77 .... 72 B5
Westermains EH48 .... 41 E5
Westermains Ave G66 .... 20 B7
Western Ave G73 .... 60 F8
Western Infmy G11 .... 29 C2
Western Rd G72 .... 61 F3
Westerpark Ave G72 .... 77 C3
Westerton Ave
Clarkston G76 .... 74 A5
Glasgow G61 .... 28 F8
Larkhall ML9 .... 93 A1
Westerton Ct G76 .... 74 A5
Westerton La G76 .... 74 A5
Westerton Prim Sch G61 .. 16 E2
Westerton Rd G68 .... 11 D6
Westerton Sta G61 .... 16 E1
Westfarm Cres G72 .... 62 D6
Westfarm Gr G72 .... 62 D7
Westfarm Wynd G72 .... 62 D6
Westfield Ave G73 .... 60 F7
Westfield Cres G61 .... 16 E2
Westfield Dr
Bearsden G61 .... 16 E2
Cumbernauld G68 .... 22 F7
Glasgow G52 .... 43 A5
Westfield Ind Area G68 .. 22 D6
Westfield Pk ML10 .... 112 E8
Westfield Pl G68 .... 22 D6
Westfield Prim Sch G68 .. 22 F7
Westfield Rd
Cumbernauld G68 .... 22 E7
Glasgow G46 .... 59 A3
Kilsyth G65 .... 6 B1
Motherwell ML1 .... 66 C7
Westfields G64 .... 18 E3
Westgarth Pl G74 .... 75 A3
Westgate Way ML4 .... 64 F5
Westhorn Dr G32 .... 47 A1
Westhouse Ave G73 .... 60 E7
Westhouse Gdns G73 .... 60 E7
Westknowe Gdns G73 .... 61 B5
Westland Dr G14 .... 28 D4
Westland Drive La 8
G14 .... 28 D3
Westlea Pl ML6 .... 51 B6
Westminster Terr 3 G3 .. 44 E8
Westmoreland St G42 .... 45 A2
Westmuir Pl G73 .... 60 F8
Westmuir St G31 .... 46 D5
Westpark DG10 .... 161 C5
Westport East Kilbride G75 .75 A1
Lanark ML11 .... 116 E3
Westport St 10 G65 .... 10 D8
Westray Ave G77 .... 72 C7
Westray Cir G22 .... 30 D6
Westray Ct G67 .... 23 E8
Westray Pl
Bishopbriggs G64 .... 19 D2
Glasgow G22 .... 30 D7
Westray Rd G67 .... 23 E8
Westray Sq G22 .... 30 D7
Westray St G22 .... 30 C7
Westray Wynd 2 ML2 .... 81 F6
Westshield Rd ML11 .... 124 A4
Westside Gdns G11 .... 29 C2
Westside Rd ML12 .... 140 E5
Westwood Ave G46 .... 59 B3
Westwood Cres ML3 .... 78 C2
Westwood Dr ML1 .... 67 E1
Westwood Hill G75 .... 88 B7
Westwood Quadrant
G81 .... 15 D1
Westwood Rd
East Kilbride G75 .... 88 B8
Glasgow G43 .... 59 B6
Wishaw ML2 .... 81 F7
Wishaw ML2 .... 82 A5
Westwood Sq G75 .... 88 B8
Weymouth Ct G12 .... 29 B6
Weymouth Dr G12 .... 29 A6
Whamflet Ave G69 .... 48 C7
Whamond Twr ML1 .... 79 E5
Whauphill ML11 .... 98 F8
Whauphill Cres ML11 .... 98 F8
Wheatfield Rd G61 .... 16 D2
Wheatholm Cres ML6 .... 36 B1
Wheatholm St ML6 .... 36 B1
Wheatland Ave G72 .... 77 C8
Wheatland Dr ML11 .... 116 F5
Wheatlandhead Ct G72 .. 77 C8
Wheatlandside ML11 .... 116 F5
Wheatley Cres G65 .... 10 D7
Wheatley Ct G32 .... 47 A5
Wheatley Dr G32 .... 47 A5
Wheatley Loan G64 .... 31 C8
Wheatley Pl G32 .... 47 A5
Wheatpark Rd ML11 .... 116 F4
Whifflet Ct ML5 .... 50 B5
Whifflet St ML5 .... 50 B4
Whifflet Sta ML5 .... 50 B5
Whin Ave G78 .... 57 B4
Whin Hill G74 .... 76 B4
Whin Loan G65,G66 .... 9 D8
Whin Pl G74 .... 76 B5
Whin St G81 .... 15 B4
Whinfell Dr G75 .... 88 A6
Whinfell Gdns G75 .... 88 A6
Whinfield Ave G72 .... 61 E7
Whinfield Rd G53 .... 58 A4
Whinhall Ave ML6 .... 35 F1
Whinhall Rd ML6 .... 35 E1
Whinhill Gdns G53 .... 43 A3
Whinhill Pl G53 .... 43 A3
Whinhill Rd Glasgow G53 .. 43 A3
Paisley PA2 .... 42 B2
Whinknowe ML9 .... 106 F8
Whinney Gr ML2 .... 81 E4
Whinnie Knowe ML9 .... 92 F1
Whinny The ML11 .... 114 A4
Whinpark Ave ML4 .... 64 F3
Whinriggs ML9 .... 105 D1
Whins Rd G41 .... 44 C1
Whins The DG10 .... 161 C6
Whirlies Rdbt The G74 .. 76 A3
Whirlow Gdns G69 .... 48 A5
Whirlow Rd G69 .... 48 B5
Whistleberry Cres ML3 .. 78 B7
Whistleberry Dr ML3 .... 78 B7
Whistleberry Ind Est
ML3 .... 78 A7
Whistleberry Pk ML3 .... 78 A7
Whistleberry Rd ML3 .... 78 A7
Whistleberry Ret Pk G72 .77 F7
Whistlefield Ct G61 .... 16 F3
Whitacres Path G53 .... 58 A4
Whitacres Rd G53 .... 58 A4
Whitburn St G32 .... 46 F7
White St Clydebank G81 .. 27 D7
Glasgow G11 .... 29 C2
White's Neuk ML11 .... 117 C5
White-Cart Twr G74 .... 89 B7
Whiteadder Pl G75 .... 87 D7
Whitecraigs Ct G46 .... 73 A8
Whitecraigs Pl G23 .... 29 E8
Whitecraigs Sta G46 .... 73 A8
Whitecrook Bsns Ctr
G81 .... 15 C1
Whitecrook Prim Sch
G81 .... 15 C1
Whitecrook St G81 .... 15 C1
Whitefield Ave G72 .... 62 A4
Whitefield Rd G51 .... 44 C6
Whiteford Ct ML3 .... 91 C6
Whiteford Rd Paisley PA2 .. 42 A2
Stepps G33 .... 33 A5
Whitegates G66 .... 20 C7
Whitehall St G3 .... 162 A2

Whitehaugh Ave PA1 42 B6
Whitehaugh Cres G53 58 A4
Whitehaugh Dr PA1 42 B5
Whitehaugh Rd G53 58 A4
Whitehill Ave Airdrie ML6 36 A1
Cumbernauld G68 11 D2
Stepps G33 32 D6
Whitehill Cres
Carluke ML8 95 F3
Clydebank G81 15 E7
Lanark ML11 116 F4
Whitehill Ct G31 46 A7
Whitehill Farm Rd G33 32 D6
Whitehill Gdns G31 46 A7
Whitehill Gr G77 72 F2
Whitehill La G61 16 D4
Whitehill Rd
Bearsden G61 16 D4
Hamilton ML3 78 B5
Whitehill Sec Sch G31 46 B7
Whitehill St G31 46 A7
Whitehill Street La G31 46 A7
Whitehill Terr ML11 116 F4
Whitehills Dr G75 88 E7
Whitehills Pl G75 88 E7
Whitehills Terr G75 88 E7
Whitehorse Wlk G75 88 B8
Whitehurst G61 16 C6
Whitehurst Pk G61 16 C6
Whiteinch Bsns Pk G14 28 D2
Whiteinch Prim Sch G14 28 E2
Whitekirk Pl G15 16 A2
Whitelaw Ave ML5 34 F5
Whitelaw Cres ML4 65 D4
Whitelaw Gdns G64 19 A3
Whitelaw St
Blackridge EH48 40 D1
Glasgow G20 29 C7
Whitelaw Terr G65 9 F4
Whitelee G75 88 D5
Whitelee Cres G77 72 B6
Whitelee Gate G77 72 B6
Whitelees Prim Sch G67 12 F5
Whitelees Rd
Cumbernauld G67 12 F6
Lanark ML11 117 C3
Lanark,Carstairs ML11 110 F2
Whitelees Rdbt G67 12 F5
Whiteloans G71 64 B3
Whiteloch Rd ML11 124 C2
Whitemoss Ave
East Kilbride G74 75 F1
Glasgow G44 59 F4
Whitemoss Gr G74 76 A2
Whitemoss Rd G74 76 A1
Whitemoss Rdbt G74 76 A1
Whitepond Ave ML4 64 F3
Whiterigg Ct ML6 50 D8
Whiteshaw Ave ML8 95 D1
Whiteshaw Dr ML8 95 D2
Whiteshaw Rd ML8 95 B3
Whiteshaw View ML10 112 E8
Whiteside St ML11 139 A6
Whitestone Ave G68 11 B2
Whitevale St G31 46 A6
Whithope Rd G53 57 F4
Whithope Terr G53 57 F4
Whithorn Cres G69 21 F3
Whitlawburn Ave G72 61 E4
Whitlawburn Rd G72 61 E4
Whitlawburn Terr G72 61 E4
Whitriggs Rd G53 57 F4
Whitslade St G34 33 A1
Whitsun Dale G74 75 C3
Whittagreen Ave ML1 66 D3
Whittagreen Cres ML1 66 D2
Whittagreen Ct ML1 66 D3
Whittingehame Dr G12 29 A5
Whittingehame Gdns
G12 29 A5
Whittingehame La G13 28 F5
Whittingehame Pk G12 28 F5
Whittington St ML5 50 A6
Whittlemuir Ave G44 59 F4
Whitton Dr G46 59 E3
Whitton St G20 29 C8
Whittret Knowe
Forth ML11 98 E8
Forth ML11 98 F7
Whitworth Dr
Clydebank G81 15 A2
Glasgow G20 30 A6
Whitworth Gate G20 30 A5
Whitworth Gdns G20 30 A6
Whyte Ave G72 61 E6
Whyte St ML7 55 F6
Whyte Wynd ML11 119 E4
Wick Ave ML6 50 E4
Wickets The PA1 42 A3
Wickham Ave G77 72 D6
Wide Cl ML11 117 A4
Wigton Ave G77 72 C7
Wigtoun Pl G67 12 B4
Wildman Rd ML8 95 B7
Wilfred Ave G13 28 D7
Wilkie Cres ML9 93 B2
Wilkie Loan ML4 65 B7
Wilkie Rd G71 64 A5
William Dr ML3 91 D7
William Mann Dr G77 72 C4
William Spiers Pl ML9 93 B1
William St Clydebank G81 15 A6
Coatbridge ML5 50 B4
Glasgow G3 162 A3
Hamilton ML3 78 B5
11 Kilsyth G65 10 D8
William Ure Pl G64 19 B5
William Wilson Ct G65 6 D1
Williamsburgh Prim Sch
PA1 42 A5
Williamsburgh Terr PA1 42 A5
Williamson St
Clydebank G81 15 B4
Glasgow G31 46 C4
Williamwood Dr G44 59 F2
Williamwood High Sch
G76 73 D8
Williamwood Pk G44 59 F2
Williamwood Pk W G44 59 F2
Williamwood Sta G46 59 D1
Willock Pl G20 29 E7
Willoughby Dr G13 28 F6
Willoughby La G13 28 F6
Willow Ave
Bishopbriggs G64 31 A8
Fauldhouse EH47 71 F5
Kirkintilloch G66 20 C5
Motherwell ML1 66 A2
Willow Brae EH47 71 F5
Willow Cres ML5 50 A4
Willow Ct G75 88 B6
Willow Dr Airdrie ML6 51 D7
Banknock FK4 8 E2
Hamilton G72 77 C8
Willow Gr
Fauldhouse EH47 71 F5
Motherwell ML1 66 B5
Willow La G32 47 B2
Willow Pk EH47 71 F6
Willow Pl G71 64 D8
Willow St G13 28 F7
Willow View EH47 71 F5
Willow Way ML3 78 E2
Willowbank ML9 93 A5
Willowbank Cres 1 G3 29 F2
Willowbank Gdns G66 20 D8
Willowbank Prim Sch G3 29 F2
Willowbank Sch ML5 49 E6
Willowbank St G3 162 A4
Willowdale Cres G69 48 B4
Willowdale Gdns G69 48 A4
Willowford Rd G53 58 A4
Willowpark Ct 3 ML6 50 F8
Willows The G76 74 E8
Willwood Dr ML2 81 C7
Willwood Rd ML2 81 C7
Wilmot Rd G13 28 D6
Wilsgait St ML1 67 C2
Wilson Ct Bellshill ML4 64 F5
Forth ML11 98 F7
Hamilton ML3 78 A5
Wilson Pl East Kilbride G74 76 A4
Newton Mearns G77 72 C4
20 Stonehouse ML9 129 E8
Wilson Rd ML7 83 A8
Wilson St Airdrie ML6 50 F8
Coatbridge ML5 50 C7
Glasgow G1 163 A2
Hamilton ML3 78 A5
Larkhall ML9 93 B2
Motherwell ML1 79 F7
Renfrew PA4 27 D4
Wilsons Rd ML1 67 E7
Wilsontown Rd ML11 122 B1
Wilton Crescent La G20 29 F3
Wilton Dr G20 29 F3
Wilton Rd ML8 109 A8
Wilton St Coatbridge ML5 34 D2
Glasgow G20 29 F3
Wiltonburn Rd G53 58 A4
Wilverton Rd G13 28 E8
Winburne Cres ML3 78 B4
Winchester Dr G12 29 B6
Windermere St ML4 64 F4
Windermere G75 87 F5
Windermere Gdns ML3 91 C6
Windhill Cres G43 59 B5
Windhill Pk G76 73 E2
Windhill Pl G43 59 C5
Windhill Rd G43 59 C5
Windlaw Ct G45 60 D2
Windlaw Gdns G44 59 F4
Windlaw Park Gdns G44 59 F4
Windlaw Prim Sch G45 60 E2
Windlaw Rd
Carmunnock G76 74 D8
Glasgow G76 60 D1
Windmill Ct ML1 79 F6
Windmill Gdns ML8 95 F2
Windmill Rd ML3 78 D4
Windmillhill St ML1 79 F5
Windrow Terr ML2 81 C7
Windsor Ave G77 72 F5
Windsor Cres
Clydebank G81 15 A3
Paisley PA1 42 A6
Windsor Crescent La
G81 15 B3
Windsor Ct ML8 95 F2
Windsor Dr ML6 35 F4
Windsor Gdns ML3 78 A5
Windsor Path 8 ML9 93 C2
Windsor Pl ML7 69 E5
Windsor Quadrant ML8 95 F2
Windsor Rd
Motherwell ML1 66 A5
Renfrew PA4 27 C2
Windsor St
Coatbridge ML5 49 E3
Glasgow,Springboig G32 47 C6
4 Glasgow,Woodside G20 30 A2
Shotts ML7 69 E5
Windsor Terr G20 30 A2
Windsor Wlk G71 64 B7
Windward Rd G75 75 A1
Windy Wizen KA17 134 C8
Windy Yetts G65 9 F3
Windyedge Cres G13 28 C5
Windyedge Pl G13 28 C5
Windyedge Rd ML1 67 C3
Windyridge
Auchenheath ML11 114 D4
Hamilton ML3 78 E1
Windyridge Pl 11 G72 77 C7
Wingate Cres G74 76 C4
Wingate Dr G74 76 C4
Wingate Pk G74 76 C4
Wingate St ML2 80 E4
Wingfield Gdns G71 64 B1
Winifred St G33 31 D4
Winning Ct G72 63 E1
Winning Quadrant ML2 80 D3
Winning Row G31 46 D5
Winnipeg Dr G75 88 B8
Wintergreen Ct G74 75 D4
Wintergreen Dr G74 75 D4
Winton Ave
Eaglesham G76 86 F4
Glasgow G46 59 C2
Winton Cres G72 77 D7
Winton Dr G12 29 C5
Winton Gdns G71 63 F7
Winton La G12 29 C5
Winton Pk G75 75 A1
Wirran Pl G13 27 E8
Wishart St G4,G31 163 C3
Wishaw Acad (Prim Sch)
ML2 81 B2
Wishaw Bsns Ctr 1 ML2 81 B2
Wishaw General Hospl
ML2 80 E3
Wishaw High Rd ML1 81 C8
Wishaw Low Rd ML1 81 A7
Wishaw Rd ML2 94 E8
Wishaw Sta ML2 81 A2
Wishawhill St ML2 80 F4
Wisner Ct G46 58 F4
Wisteria La ML8 108 F8
Wiston Lodge* ML12 140 C3
Wiston Prim Sch ML12 140 B3
Wiston St G72 62 E5
Witchwood Ct ML5 34 D2
Witcutt Way ML2 80 E1
Woddrop St G40 46 B2
Wolcott Dr G72 77 D8
Wolfe Ave G77 72 C7
Wolseley St G5 45 D3
Wood Aven Dr G74 75 D4
Wood Cres ML1 65 E1
Wood Dr EH47 56 F6
Wood End Cvn Site ML7 82 F8
Wood Farm Rd G46 59 A2
Wood La G64 31 C8
Wood Quadrant G81 27 E8
Wood St Airdrie ML6 36 C1
Coatbridge ML5 49 E7
Glasgow G31 46 B8
Motherwell ML1 79 F8
Paisley PA2 42 B3
Wood View
Motherwell ML1 66 B5
Shotts ML7 82 F8
Woodbank Cres G76 73 E6
Woodburn Ave
Airdrie ML6 50 F6
Clarkston G76 73 E6
Hamilton G72 77 E8
Woodburn Ct G73 61 B6
Woodburn Gr ML3 78 E3
Woodburn Pk ML3 78 E3
Woodburn Rd
Glasgow G43 59 D5
Motherwell ML1 66 D7
Woodburn St ML1 79 E8
Woodburn Terr 9 ML9 93 C2
Woodburn Way G68 11 C2
Woodcroft Ave G11 28 F4
Wooddale ML1 79 D4
Woodend G72 77 D6
Woodend Ct G32 47 E2
Woodend Dr Airdrie ML6 36 C1
Glasgow G13 28 E5
Paisley PA1 42 D4
Woodend Gdns G32 47 D2
Woodend La 6 G13 28 E5
Woodend Rd Carluke ML8 96 A2
Glasgow G32 47 E2
Rutherglen G73 61 B4
Woodend Wlk EH48 41 E6
Woodfarm High Sch G46 59 A3
Woodfield G71 64 C6
Woodfield Ave G64 31 B8
Woodfoot Pl G53 58 A4
Woodfoot Quadrant G53 58 B4
Woodfoot Rd
Glasgow G53 58 A4
Hamilton ML3 78 A2
Woodford St G41 59 E7
Woodgreen Ave G44 60 C6
Woodgreen Ct ML2 94 A8
Woodhall ML1 66 A8
Woodhall Ave
Calderbank ML6 51 B2
Coatbridge ML5 49 F3
Hamilton ML3 78 B4
Motherwell ML1 65 F5
Woodhall Cottage Rd
ML6 51 C1
Woodhall Mill Rd ML6 51 B1
Woodhall Pl ML5 49 F3
Woodhall Rd
Braidwood ML8 108 D2
Braidwood ML8 108 E3
Calderbank ML6 51 B2
Woodhall Rd *continued*
Wishaw ML2 81 F3
Wishaw ML2 82 A3
Woodhall St
Chapelhall ML6 51 D2
Glasgow G40 46 B2
Woodhead Ave
Bothwell G71 64 B1
Cumbernauld G68 22 F7
Kirkintilloch G66 20 D7
Woodhead Cres
Glenmavis ML6 35 E3
Hamilton ML3 91 A8
Uddingston G71 63 F7
Woodhead Ct G68 22 F7
Woodhead Gdns G71 78 B8
Woodhead Gn ML3 91 B8
Woodhead Gr
Armadale EH48 41 D5
Cumbernauld G68 22 F7
Woodhead Pl G68 22 F7
Woodhead Prim Sch
ML3 91 A8
Woodhead Rd
Cumbernauld G68 22 F7
Garnkirk G69 33 B6
Glasgow G53 58 A5
Woodhead Terr G69 33 B7
Woodhead View G68 22 F7
Woodhill Prim Sch G64 19 C2
Woodhill Rd
Blackridge EH48 40 B3
Glasgow G21 31 B6
Strathaven ML10 112 E7
Woodholm Ave G44 60 C6
Woodhouse Ct G76 74 A5
Woodhouse St G13 28 E7
Woodilee Cotts G66 20 E6
Woodilee Ind Est G66 20 E6
Woodilee Rd
Kirkintilloch G66 20 E6
Motherwell ML1 66 E4
Woodland Ave
Airdrie ML6 51 C4
Kirkintilloch G66 20 B8
Woodland Cres
Cambuslang G72 62 C4
Eaglesham G76 86 D5
Woodland Gdns
Carmunnock G76 74 D7
Hamilton ML3 78 F2
Woodland Terr ML9 93 C1
Woodland Way G67 12 B3
Woodlands G46 58 F3
Woodlands Ave
Bothwell G71 64 A3
Law ML8 95 A6
Mount Ellen G69 33 E6
Woodlands Cres
Bothwell G71 64 A3
Glasgow G46 58 F3
Woodlands Ct
8 Glasgow,Kelvingrove G3 29 E1
Glasgow,Thornliebank G46 58 F2
Woodlands Dr
Coatbridge ML5 49 D7
Glasgow G4 29 F2
Motherwell ML1 65 F5
Woodlands Gate
Glasgow G3 162 A4
Glasgow,Thornliebank G46 58 F3
Woodlands Gdns G71 64 A4
Woodlands Pk G46 58 F3
Woodlands Pl ML5 49 D7
Woodlands Prim Sch
G67 23 E7
Woodlands Rd
Glasgow G3 162 A4
Glasgow,Thornliebank G46 58 F2
Motherwell ML1 79 F4
Motherwell,Holytown ML1 66 D7
Thornliebank G46 59 A2
Woodlands St ML1 79 F4
Woodlands Terr G3 162 A4
Woodlands The ML4 65 D3
Woodlands View ML9 106 A3
Woodlea ML11 114 A4
Woodlea Ave ML6 51 C4
Woodlea Dr Glasgow G46 59 D4
Hamilton ML3 91 D8
Woodlea Pl ML6 36 C1
Woodlinn Ave G44 60 B5
Woodmill Gdns G67 22 F6
Woodmuir Pl EH55 122 C7
Woodmuir Prim Sch
EH55 122 C7
Woodmuir Rd EH55 122 C7
Woodneuk La G69 33 F5
Woodneuk Rd
Gartcosh G69 33 F5
Glasgow G53 58 B5
Woodneuk St ML6 51 D1
Woodneuk Terr G69 33 F5
Woodpark ML11 119 F5
Woodpark Prim Sch
ML11 119 F3
Woodrow ML1 66 B8
Woodrow Ave ML1 66 B2
Woodrow Cir G41 44 D4
Woodrow Pl G41 44 C4
Woodrow Rd G41 44 D4
Woodside ML1 65 E8
Woodside Ave
Carstairs Junction ML11 124 C1
Glasgow G46 59 A3
5 Hamilton ML3 78 E2
Kilsyth G65 10 F8
Kirkintilloch G66 20 D5
Woodside Ave *continued*
Rutherglen G73 61 C7
Woodside Cl ML11 119 E4
Woodside Cres
Barrhead G78 57 D2
Carnwath ML11 124 F1
Glasgow G3 162 A4
Wishaw ML2 82 B6
Woodside Ct
Coatbridge ML5 49 D5
4 Hamilton ML3 78 E2
Woodside Dr
Calderbank ML6 51 B2
Eaglesham G76 73 D2
Woodside Gdns
Carmunnock G76 74 D7
Clarkston G76 73 D7
Coatbridge ML5 49 D4
Woodside Gr G73 61 C7
Woodside Pl Glasgow G3 162 A4
Uddingston G71 64 C8
Woodside Place La G3 162 A4
Woodside Prim Sch ML3 78 E2
Woodside Rd
Carmunnock G76 74 D7
Forrestfield ML6 39 A3
Woodside St
Carstairs Junction ML11 131 B8
Chapelhall ML6 51 D2
Coatbridge ML5 49 D4
Motherwell ML1 80 B4
Motherwell,New Stevenston
ML1 66 A3
Woodside Terr
Glasgow G3 162 A4
Tarbrax EH55 123 C2
Woodside Terrace La
G3 162 A4
Woodside Twr ML1 80 B3
Woodside Wlk
Hamilton ML3 78 E2
Strathaven ML10 112 C5
Woodstock Ave
Glasgow G41 44 D1
Kirkintilloch G66 20 F8
Lanark ML11 117 C4
Woodstock Dr
Lanark ML11 117 B4
Wishaw ML2 81 C4
Woodstock Rd ML11 117 B4
Woodvale Ave
Airdrie ML6 51 D4
Bearsden G61 17 B2
Rutherglen G46 73 B8
Woodview G71 64 D8
Woodview Dr Airdrie ML6 51 A5
Bellshill ML4 65 C7
Woodview La ML6 51 A5
Woodview Rd ML9 106 A8
Woodview Terr ML3 78 B4
Woodville Pk G51 44 B6
Woodville St G51 44 B6
Woodyett Pk G76 73 F5
Woodyett Rd G76 73 F5
Woolfords Cotts EH55 123 A4
Wordsworth Way G71 64 B3
Worsley Cres G77 72 C7
Wotherspoon Cres EH48 41 F5
Wraes Ave G78 57 D4
Wrangholm Cres ML1 66 B3
Wrangholm Dr ML1 66 B3
Wren Ct ML4 64 E8
Wren Pl ML2 81 B3
Wright Ave G78 57 A2
Wright St PA4 27 A1
Wright Way ML1 66 A3
Wye Cres ML5 34 D1
Wykeham Pl G13 28 C6
Wykeham Rd G13 28 C6
Wyler Twr ML3 78 E3
Wylie G74 76 D5
Wylie Ave G77 72 D7
Wylie St ML3 78 D2
Wynd The Biggar ML12 160 C4
Cumbernauld G67 12 B5
Wyndford Dr G20 29 D5
Wyndford Pl 3 G20 29 D5
Wyndford Prim Sch G20 29 D5
Wyndford Rd
Cumbernauld G68 12 D8
Glasgow G20 29 D5
Wyndford Terr G71 64 B7
Wyndham Ct G12 29 D4
Wyndham St G12 29 D4
Wynyard Gn G75 88 B8
Wyper Pl G31 46 A6
Wyvil Ave G13 16 E1
Wyvis Ave Bearsden G61 16 C7
Glasgow G13 27 F8
Wyvis Ct G77 72 D2
Wyvis Pl Glasgow G13 27 F8
Newton Mearns G77 72 C2
Shotts ML7 70 B3
Wyvis Quadrant G13 27 F8

Y

Yair Dr G52 43 A6
Yarrow Cres ML2 81 B4
Yarrow Ct G72 62 E5
Yarrow Gardens La 2
G20 29 F3
Yarrow Gdns G20 29 F3
Yarrow Pk G74 76 A1

Yarrow Rd G64 .... 19 A4
Yarrow Way G72 .... 77 E8
Yate Gr G31 .... 46 B5
Yate Rd G31 .... 46 B5
Yate St G31 .... 46 B5
Yetholm Gdns G74 .... 75 F4
Yetholm St G14 .... 27 E6
Yetholm Terr ML3 .... 77 E3
Yett Rd ML1 .... 66 D3
Yetts Cres G66 .... 20 F8
Yetts Hole Rd ML6 .... 35 B5
Yew Dr G21 .... 31 A3
Yews Cres ML3 .... 78 B5
Yieldshields Rd ML8 .... 97 D3
Yoker Ferry Rd G14 .... 27 E6
Yoker Mill Gdns G13 .... 27 E7
Yoker Mill Rd G13 .... 27 F8
Yoker Prim Sch G14 .... 27 F6
Yoker Sta G81 .... 27 D7
Yokerburn Pl G13 .... 27 E7
Yokerburn Terr G81 .... 27 D7
York Dr G73 .... 61 D5
York Pl Bellshill ML4 .... 65 A5
1 Kirkintilloch G66 .... 20 C8
York Rd ML6 .... 66 D8
York St Clydebank G81 .... 15 D2
Glasgow G2 .... 162 B2
Wishaw ML2 .... 81 B2
York Way PA4 .... 27 C1
Yorkhill Par G3 .... 29 C1
Yorkhill St G3 .... 29 D1
Young Pl East Kilbride G75 .... 89 A5
1 Uddingston G71 .... 64 A8
Young Pl *continued*
Wishaw ML2 .... 82 B5
Young Rd ML11 .... 117 E5
Young St Clydebank G81 .... 15 B4
Strathaven ML10 .... 112 F6
Wishaw ML2 .... 81 B3
Young Terr G21 .... 31 A4
Young Wynd ML4 .... 65 A8
Younger Quadrant G64 .... 19 A1
Yukon Terr G75 .... 88 B8
Yvetot Ave ML11 .... 117 B4
Yvetot Ct ML8 .... 95 E3

Z

Zambesi Dr G72 .... 63 C1
Zena Cres G33 .... 31 D4
Zena Pl G33 .... 31 D4
Zena St G33 .... 31 D4
Zetland Rd G52 .... 42 F8